THE ROUTLEDGE COMPANION TO MANAGEMENT BUYOUTS

Management buyouts (MBOs) first came to prominence in the US during the early 1980s, and have subsequently become a global phenomenon. At its peak, the total value of MBO transactions in Western Europe was about €23 billion. The MBO transaction is therefore a highly significant transaction within the corporate restructuring landscape.

This authoritative volume provides a comprehensive reference book on the diverse aspects of management buyouts. It provides a valuable source of reference to scholars on the current state of research and theory and where further developments are likely to occur. Although much recent attention has focused on private equity (PE) backed buyouts, these are only a subset of the total MBO market. This book takes a much broader definition, incorporating PE- and non-PE-backed buyouts, as well as variations such as management buyins and management-employee buyouts.

This unique "go to" reference goes beyond the purely financial perspective, incorporating related disciplines including strategy, organizational change, and HRM. It will be an invaluable reference source on MBOs for researchers and educators as well as practitioners and policymakers in the broader areas of corporate restructuring and ownership change.

Mike Wright is Professor of Entrepreneurship and Director of the Centre for Management Buy-out Research at Imperial College Business School, UK, a Fellow of the British Academy and of the Strategic Management Society. He has published over 50 books and 400 articles in peer-reviewed journals.

Kevin Amess is Associate Professor of Industrial Economics in the Business School at the University of Nottingham, UK. He is currently Co-Editor of the *International Journal of the Economics of Business*. He has advised government and policy officials on LBOs including the UK Treasury, Financial Services Authority, the US Government Accountability Office and the OECD.

Nick Bacon is Professor of Human Resource Management at Cass Business School, UK. His research explores the impact of HRM practices in a wide variety of settings including small and medium-sized enterprises and leveraged buyouts. He is former editor of the *Industrial Relations Journal*.

Donald Siegel is Professor of Public Policy and Management and Director of the School of Public Affairs at Arizona State University, USA. He is an editor of the *Journal of Management Studies* and the *Journal of Technology Transfer* and a former Dean of the School of Business at the University at Albany, SUNY. In 2016, he was elected a Fellow of the Academy of Management.

ROUTLEDGE COMPANIONS IN BUSINESS, MANAGEMENT AND ACCOUNTING

Routledge Companions in Business, Management and Accounting are prestige reference works providing an overview of a whole subject area or sub-discipline. These books survey the state of the discipline including emerging and cutting edge areas. Providing a comprehensive, up to date, definitive work of reference, Routledge Companions can be cited as an authoritative source on the subject.

A key aspect of these Routledge Companions is their international scope and relevance. Edited by an array of highly regarded scholars, these volumes also benefit from teams of contributors which reflect an international range of perspectives.

Individually, Routledge Companions in Business, Management and Accounting provide an impactful one-stop-shop resource for each theme covered. Collectively, they represent a comprehensive learning and research resource for researchers, postgraduate students and practitioners.

Published titles in this series include:

The Routledge Companion to the Geography of International Business
Edited by Jonathan Beaverstock, Gary Cook, Jennifer Johns, Frank McDonald and Naresh Pandit

The Routledge Companion to Employment Relations
Edited by Adrian Wilkinson, Tony Dundon, Jimmy Donaghey and Alex Colvin

The Routledge Companion to Risk, Crisis and Security in Business
Edited by Kurt J. Engemann

The Routledge Companion to Fair Value in Accounting
Edited by Gilad Livne and Garen Markarian

The Routledge Companion to European Business
Edited by Gabriele Suder, Monica Riviere and Johan Lindeque

The Routledge Companion to Management Buyouts
Edited by Mike Wright, Kevin Amess, Nick Bacon and Donald Siegel

For more information about this series, please visit: https://www.routledge.com/Routledge-Companions-in-Business-Management-and-Accounting/book-series/RCBMA

"The Handbook provides a broad and diverse set of perspectives on the history and impact of private equity and leveraged buyouts. There is useful information here for everyone – academics, practitioners, and policymakers."
Steven N. Kaplan, *Neubauer Family Distinguished Service Professor of Entrepreneurship and Finance, University of Chicago Booth School of Business, USA*

"This book is a fascinating collection of articles on one of the most significant forms of corporate restructuring to have emerged over the last few decades. Edited by members of the influential Centre for Management Buy-out Research, it brings together a group of leading scholars to evaluate the origins, source, funding, consequences, and performance of management buyouts. It will be a major reference on the subject for years to come."
Colin Mayer, *Peter Moores Professor of Management Studies, Said Business School, University of Oxford, UK*

"The editors of this volume have put together a remarkable set of contributions representing the best research on important aspects of buyouts, and an important map for future research on the phenomenon. The managerial lessons from each chapter are particularly useful for practitioners and regulators of the art. This volume is highly recommended for scholars, thought leaders, policymakers, and dealmakers."
Phillip H. Phan, *PhD, Alonzo and Virginia Decker Professor of Strategic Management and Entrepreneurship, Johns Hopkins University, Baltimore, USA*

THE ROUTLEDGE COMPANION TO MANAGEMENT BUYOUTS

Edited by Mike Wright, Kevin Amess, Nick Bacon and Donald Siegel

LONDON AND NEW YORK

First published 2019 by Routledge

2 Park Square, Milton Park, Abingdon, Oxon OX14 4RN
605 Third Avenue, New York, NY 10017

Routledge is an imprint of the Taylor & Francis Group, an informa business

First issued in paperback 2022

Publisher's Note

The publisher has gone to great lengths to ensure the quality of this reprint but points out that some imperfections in the original copies may be apparent.

British Library Cataloguing-in-Publication Data
A catalogue record for this book is available from the British Library

Library of Congress Cataloging-in-Publication Data
Names: Wright, Mike, 1952- editor.
Title: The Routledge companion to management buyouts /
[edited by] Mike Wright [and three others].
Description: Abingdon, Oxon ; New York, NY : Routledge, 2018. | Includes index.
Identifiers: LCCN 2018010409 | ISBN 9781138713840 (hardback)
Subjects: LCSH: Management buyouts.
Classification: LCC HD2746.5 .R6859 2018 | DDC 658.1/6--dc23
LC record available at https://lccn.loc.gov/2018010409

ISBN: 978-1-138-71384-0 (hbk)
ISBN: 978-1-03-233893-4 (pbk)
DOI: 10.4324/9781315230597

Typeset in Times New Roman
by Sunrise Setting Ltd, Brixham, UK

To Bob Willott and Michael Cumming for believing in the entrepreneurial opportunity

CONTENTS

FIGURES AND TABLES

Figures

Tables

CONTRIBUTORS

Oliver Ahlers, PhD, completed his PhD in 2013 at the WHU–Otto Beisheim School of Management, Vallendar, Germany, and is currently working as General Manager of the Family Business Friedrich Ahlers GmbH.

Wasim Ahmad is a Lecturer in Finance at Birmingham Business School, University of Birmingham, UK. His research interests are in the area of corporate finance and include IPOs, private equity, capital structure, and corporate innovation.

Yan Alperovych is an Associate Professor of Corporate Finance at EMLyon Business School, France, which he joined in 2011. His research interests are in areas such as entrepreneurial finance, venture capital, private equity, and government venture capital initiatives. He has published his works in international peer-reviewed journals such as *Journal of Business Venturing* (2017), *Small Business Economics* (2013), *European Journal of Operational Research* (2013), and others.

Kevin Amess is Associate Professor of Industrial Economics at Nottingham University Business School, UK. He is a Fellow of the Centre for Management Buy-out Research. His research focuses on the impact of private equity and leveraged buyouts for portfolio firms. His research evaluating the consequences of leveraged buyouts on innovation, employees, and performance has been published in a range of journals, including: *European Economic Review*, *Entrepreneurship Theory & Practice*, and *Journal of Industrial Economics*. He has also co-authored a report for the OECD and advised the US GAO and UK government agencies.

Eileen Appelbaum is Co-Director of the Center for Economic and Policy Research and Visiting Professor at the University of Leicester, UK. She has held positions as Distinguished Professor and Director of the Center for Women and Work at Rutgers University, USA and as Professor of Economics at Temple University, USA. She earned her PhD at the University of Pennsylvania, USA. Her research focuses on financialization, organizational restructuring, and work-family policies. *Private equity at work* (Russell Sage Foundation

Press), co-authored with Rosemary Batt, was selected by the Academy of Management as one of the four best books of 2014–2015. In addition to books, she has published numerous articles in peer-reviewed journals.

Nick Bacon is Professor of Human Resource Management at Cass Business School and an Associate of CMBOR. His research explores the impact of human resource management practices on organizational performance and employee outcomes in a wide variety of settings including manufacturing firms, unionized workplaces, small and medium-sized enterprises, leveraged buyouts and the public sector. He edited the *Industrial Relations Journal* 2004–2008, and co-edited *The SAGE handbook of human resource management* and *The SAGE handbook of industrial relations*.

Rosemary Batt is the Alice Hanson Cook Professor of Women and Work at the ILR School, Cornell University, USA. She received her BA from Cornell University and her PhD from MIT, USA. Her current research focuses on financialization and globalization and their impact on firm behavior, HR management, and employment relations. She is a Professor in Human Resource Studies and International and Comparative Labor and editor of the *ILR Review*. Her most recent book, with Eileen Appelbaum, is *Private equity at work* (Russell Sage Foundation Press).

Fabio Bertoni is Professor of Corporate Finance and Associate Dean for Research at EMLyon Business School, France. His research focuses on the relationship between financing and firm performance, new listings, sovereign wealth funds, venture capital, and corporate governance. He is author of articles in journals including: *Entrepreneurship Theory and Practice*, *Journal of Banking & Finance*, *Journal of Corporate Finance*, *Research Policy*, *Small Business Economics*, and *Strategic Entrepreneurship Journal*.

Aline Bos is a PhD student at the Utrecht University School of Governance in the Netherlands. Her PhD project focuses on the role of private equity buyouts in public service organizations, such as nursing homes. She also works as a senior consultant for several public organizations in the Netherlands, mainly in healthcare.

Paul Boselie is Professor of Governance and Human Resource Management at the Utrecht University School of Governance (USG), Utrecht University, Netherlands. He is the USG Research Director, Associate Editor of the *International Journal of HRM*, author of *Strategic HRM: A balanced approach* and author of over 100 articles and book chapters on HRM, performance management, private equity, and talent management. Paul earned his PhD at the Erasmus University Rotterdam, Netherlands. His research focuses on employment relationships in health care, education, and government.

Hans Bruining is a former Associate Professor of Strategic Management and Entrepreneurship at the Rotterdam School of Management, Erasmus University, Netherlands. He earned his PhD at the School of Economics, Erasmus University, wrote the first Dutch study on performance improvement after management buyout, and co-authored over 75 articles. He is an affiliate member of the Centre for Management Buy-out Research. His research interests include management buyouts, private equity, strategy renewal, and resource management in buyout firms.

Ian Clark is Professor of Work and Employment at Nottingham Trent University, UK. Professor Clark is currently working on the British Academy Future of the Corporation program and also works with the Director of Labour Market Enforcement and the Gangmasters Labour Abuse Authority on low productivity employers such as hand car washes and small unit garment manufacturing which use informalized business and employment practices. He has previously worked on HRM in US multinational firms and the diffusion of new business models associated with hedge funds and private equity and the effects of these on work and employment. Ian currently edits *Work, Employment and Society* and has published in the *British Journal of Industrial Relations*, the *Human Resource Management Journal*, the *Journal of Management Studies*, and *Economic and Industrial Democracy*. His research has been funded by the ESRC, the Anglo-German foundation, the Ethical Trading Initiative, the Treasury, and the GMB union.

Douglas Cumming is a Professor of Finance and Entrepreneurship and the Ontario Research Chair at the Schulich School of Business, York University, Toronto, Canada. Douglas has published over 140 articles in leading refereed academic journals in finance, management, and law and economics, such as the *Academy of Management Journal*, *Journal of Financial Economics*, *Review of Financial Studies*, *Journal of International Business Studies*, and the *Journal of Empirical Legal Studies*. He is the incoming Editor-in-Chief of the *Journal of Corporate Finance*, effective January 2018. He is the Founding Co-Editor of *Annals of Corporate Governance*, and Co-Editor of *Finance Research Letters*, and *Entrepreneurship Theory and Practice*. He is the co-author of *Venture capital and private equity contracting* (Elsevier Academic Press, 2nd edition, 2013), and *Hedge fund structure, regulation and performance around the world* (Oxford University Press, 2013). He is the Editor of the *Oxford handbook of entrepreneurial finance* (Oxford University Press, 2013), the *Oxford handbook of private equity* (Oxford University Press, 2013), the *Oxford handbook of venture capital* (Oxford University Press, 2013), the *Oxford handbook of sovereign wealth funds* (Oxford University Press, 2017), and the *Oxford handbook of IPOs* (Oxford University Press, forthcoming 2018). Douglas' work has been reviewed in numerous media outlets, including *The Economist*, *The New York Times*, the *Globe and Mail*, *Canadian Business*, the *National Post*, and *The New Yorker*.

Na Dai is an Associate Professor of Finance at the State University of New York at Albany. Her research is primarily focused on corporate finance, financing for entrepreneurship and innovation, venture capital, private equity, and hedge funds. Her scholarly works are published in both finance journals and entrepreneurship journals, such as *Financial Management*, *Journal of Banking and Finance*, *Journal of Corporate Finance*, *Journal of International Business Studies*, *Journal of Business Venturing*, and *Entrepreneurship Theory and Practice*. She is the co-author of the book, *Hedge fund structure, regulation and performance around the world* (Oxford University Press, 2013) and editor of the book *Entrepreneurial finance: managerial and policy implications* (World Scientific Publishers, 2017).

Jun Du is Professor of Economics at Economics, Finance and Entrepreneurship Department at Aston Business School, UK. She obtained her PhD degree at the University of Leicester, UK, and is a Research Fellow at the Advanced Institute of Management. Her main research interest is to understand the driving forces and impediments of productivity enhancement and economic growth, from multi-level dimensions of individuals, firms, industries, regions, governments, and their interplays, in both developed and emerging economic contexts. She has expertise in applied econometric methodologies using micro-data from both developed and developing countries. Jun has published in *International Journal of Industrial Organization, Research Policy, Journal of Productivity Analysis, Entrepreneurship Theory and Practice, Journal of Law and Economics, Journal of Business Venturing*, and *International Journal of Business Studies*. Her research has received external funding from the Economic and Social Research Council (ESRC), Leverhulme Foundation, NESTA foundation, and various UK government agencies including UKTI, DTI, and BIS, local governments and authorities, as well as from the private sector. She led the productivity research projects in the Business Demography Research theme in the UK Enterprise Research Centre (ERC), and is currently the Director of the Lloyds Banking Group Centre for British Prosperity.

Anantha Krishna Divakaruni is the Barclays Research Fellow in Entrepreneurial Finance at Saïd Business School, University of Oxford, UK. His research focuses mainly on private equity, and investigates the structuring and financing of buyouts and the performance outcomes of these transactions. Anantha obtained a Bachelor of Engineering degree in Computer Science from Jawaharlal Nehru Technological University, India; a Masters in Finance from Vlerick Business School, Belgium; and a PhD in Business Economics from Gent University, Belgium. He has been a visiting scholar at the Schulich School of Business, Toronto, Canada, to conduct research on international buyouts.

Dirk Engel is Professor for Economics and International Business at the University of Applied Sciences Stralsund, Germany, and research fellow of RWI Research Network. Before joining the University, Dirk Engel worked at the RWI Leibniz-Institut für Wirtschaftsforschung in Essen, Germany, and was employed at the ZEW GmbH in Mannheim, Germany. He received his PhD from European University Viadrina Frankfurt (Oder), Germany. His main research interests are in the fields of international business, entrepreneurship & SMEs, technological competiveness of regions, and entrepreneurial finance.

Sally Gibson is Of Counsel at law firm Debevoise & Plimpton LLP. She advises sponsors of private investment funds and has extensive experience working with clients to navigate the regulatory issues affecting the private equity and fund management sectors. She has been named by various media outlets as among the top funds' lawyers in the world. These include being named a "2015 Rising Star" by Law360, being named as one of Private Funds Management's "30 Under 40," being included in The Lawyer's annual "Hot 100" list, and being named as one of *Financial News*' "40 Under 40."

John Gilligan has worked in the private equity and venture capital industry for over 25 years. He started his career in 1988 at 3i Group plc as a financial analyst. He was a Corporate Finance partner of Deloitte and latterly BDO for 20 years. He is the Director of the Finance Lab at Oxford Said Business School, UK, and a Non-Executive Director and Investment Committee Member of Big Issue Invest, one of the largest social impact investors in the UK. He is also a Visiting Professor at Imperial College Business School, UK, and has degrees from Southampton University, Nottingham University, and London Business School, all UK.

Alexander Groh is Professor of Finance and Director of the Entrepreneurial Finance Research Centre at EMLyon Business School, France. He has held visiting positions at the University of New South Wales, Sydney, IESE Business School, Barcelona, and INSEAD,

France. His research focuses on entrepreneurial finance topics, and includes performance measurement and socio-economic determinants for the development of vibrant risk capital markets. His papers have been published in the *European Economic Review*, the *Journal of Banking and Finance*, the *Journal of Corporate Finance*, the *Journal of International Money and Finance*, the *European Financial Management Journal*, the *Journal of Alternative Investments*, the *Emerging Markets Review*, and *Venture Capital*, among others. He was involved in management training courses for the Invest Europe (formerly EVCA), and has worked for Quadriga Capital, a Frankfurt based private equity fund, since 1996.

Andreas Hack is the Director of the Institute of Organization and Human Resources Management, University of Bern, Switzerland, and visiting Professor at the Witten Institute for Family Business, University of Witten-Herdecke, Germany. His research interests are incentive systems, leadership, decision-making, and family businesses.

Michelle Haynes is an Associate Professor in Industrial Economics at Nottingham University Business School, UK. She has co-authored papers on corporate divestment in a range of journals including the *Journal of Industrial Economics, International Journal of Industrial Organization*, and the *Journal of Economic Behavior and Organization*. She has also contributed to a number of books and undertaken research on the funding of higher education in the UK commissioned by the Russell Group of Universities.

Kim Hoque is Professor of Human Resource Management at Warwick Business School, UK. His recent research has focused on: new forms of union representation; equal opportunities (particularly with regard to disability); HRM in the SME sector; and agency working in health and social care. He has published in journals including *British Journal of Industrial Relations*, *Human Relations*, *Work Employment and Society*, *Human Resource Management*, and *Public Administration*. He is an Associate Editor of *Human Relations*.

Robert E. Hoskisson is the George R. Brown Emeritus Chair of Strategic Management at the Jones School of Business at Rice University, USA. He received his PhD from the University of California–Irvine, USA. His research focuses on corporate and international diversification strategies, corporate governance, innovation and entrepreneurship, acquisitions and divestitures, business groups and strategies of emerging-economy firms, and co-operative strategy. His research has appeared in over 100 peer-reviewed and he has co-authored over 30 books. He is Fellow of the Strategic Management Society and has served as President of the Society. He has served on the Board of Governors and is also a Fellow of the Academy of Management and a charter member of the Academy Journal's Hall of Fame.

Carole Howorth is Chair in Sustainable and Ethical Entrepreneurship at the University of York, UK. She was previously Associate Dean for Research and Interim Dean at the Bradford University School of Management and Professor of Entrepreneurship and Family Business at Lancaster University Management School, both UK. Carole researches entrepreneurship in family and social contexts and has been Chair of the Global STEP Family Enterprising Project since 2015. She is Academic Advisor to the Institute for Family Business Research Foundation.

Ranko Jelic is Professor of Finance and Head of Finance subject group at University of Sussex Business School, UK. He has published over 30 academic papers and contributions to research monographs and is ranked among the top 10% authors on the Social Sciences Research Network (SSRN). Ranko's research focuses on corporate finance, including management buyouts, IPOs, private equity, and corporate bonds.

Jing Jin is an Assistant Professor of Strategic Management at the School of Business at Renmin University of China. She received her PhD from Rice University, USA. Her research focuses on impression management, corporate governance, acquisitions, and top executive compensation.

Andrew McAlpine is a second year analyst in the Investment Banking Group at Sandler O'Neill & Partners, L.P., USA, a full-service investment banking firm focused on the financial services sector. Since joining in 2016, he has worked on several merger and acquisition and capital raising transactions for clients in the community banking and financial technology industries. He is a summa cum laude graduate from the University at Albany, State University of New York, where he graduated with a BSc in Business Administration, a BSc in Accounting, and a BA in Economics.

Alexandra Michel, PhD, completed her PhD in 2016 at the University of St. Gallen, Center for Family Business and is currently working as Post-Doctoral Researcher at the Institute of Organization and Human Resources Management, University of Bern, Switzerland, as well as a financial advisor of family firms.

Victor Murinde is AXA Professor in Global Finance in the School of Finance & Management at SOAS University of London, UK.

Bach Nguyen is an Assistant Professor at Beijing Normal University–Hongkong Baptist University, United International College. He obtained his PhD degree at Aston University, UK. His research expertise includes small business and entrepreneurship. Before joining academia, he spent several years in the financial industry as a professional analyst.

Luc Renneboog is Professor of Corporate Finance and Head of the Finance Department at Tilburg University, Netherlands. He graduated with a BSc/MSc in Management Engineering and a BA in Philosophy from the University of Leuven, Belgium, with an MBA from the University of Chicago, USA, and with a PhD in Financial Economics from London Business School, UK. His work has been published in the *Journal of Finance*, *Journal of Financial Economics*, *American Economic Review*, *Management Science*, *Strategic Management Journal*, etc. His research interests span: corporate governance, M&A, remuneration contracting, law and economics, shareholder activism, corporate social responsibility, and the economics of art.

Nick Robinson is a third generation family member who opted out of the family business. He is Managing Director of Media Dialogue, a writing and editing company who copyedit and proofread papers and journal articles for academics all over the world. He has authored works of fiction and non-fiction, sometimes with his wife Carole Howorth.

Louise Scholes is Reader in Entrepreneurship at Loughborough University, UK. Her main research interests include family firms and their characteristics, and management buyouts and their consequences. Louise is on the editorial board of the *International Small Business*

Journal. She has published articles in a number of mainstream academic journals including *Entrepreneurship Theory and Practice*, *Human Relations*, *Industrial Relations*, *International Small Business Journal*, *Journal of Business Ethics*, *Small Business Economics*, *Journal of Applied Corporate Finance*, *California Management Review*, and *Thunderbird International Business Review*. She has also published many practitioner-focused articles on private equity and family firms.

Wei Shi is currently an Assistant Professor of Management at Kelley School of Business, Indiana University, USA, and will join University of Miami, USA, as an Associate Professor of Management in June 2018. He obtained his PhD from Rice University, USA. His research takes a behavioral approach to examine how corporate governance and top executives influence firms' corporate strategy. His research has been published in *Academy of Management Journal*, *Strategic Management Journal*, *Global Strategy Journal*, *Journal of Corporate Finance*, and *Academy of Management Perspectives*.

Donald Siegel is Professor of Public Policy and Management and Director of the School of Public Affairs at Arizona State University, USA. He is an editor of the *Journal of Management Studies* and the *Journal of Technology Transfer* and a former Dean of the School of Business at the University at Albany, SUNY, USA. In 2016, he was elected a Fellow of the Academy of Management.

Joel Stiebale is Professor of Empirical Industrial Economics at the Düsseldorf Institute for Competition Economics, Germany. Previously, he was employed as an Assistant Professor at the University of Nottingham, UK, and as a postdoctoral researcher at RWI–Leibniz Institute for Economic Research, Germany. He received his PhD at the University of Bochum, Germany, in 2010. His research interests lie in the areas of empirical industrial organization, international trade and multinational firms, economics of innovation, and corporate finance.

Steve Thompson has taught economics and strategy in universities in the UK, Ireland, the USA, and Africa and published over 100 academic papers. His recent work has been on corporate governance, and on the functioning of electronic markets. He recently concluded his second term as economist on the Doctors' and Dentists' Pay Review Body, the independent body responsible for recommending annual pay/contract adjustments for all NHS doctors and dentists.

Steven Toms is Professor of Accounting at the University of Leeds, UK. He earned his PhD at the University of Nottingham, UK, and is author of over 70 articles in peer-reviewed journals. His research focuses on the role of accounting, accountability, and corporate governance in the development of organizations, particularly from a historical perspective. He is a past editor of the journal *Business History*.

Cara Vansteenkiste is a researcher at Tilburg University, Netherlands. She graduated with a BSc/MSc in Business Economics from the University of Leuven, Netherlands, and attended Harvard University, USA, as a visiting researcher during her PhD in Finance at Tilburg University. Her research interests lie in the area of corporate finance and corporate governance, focusing on the international M&A market. Her research has been published in the *Journal of International Business Studies*.

Nick Wilson is Professor of Finance at Leeds University Business School, UK, Head of the Accounting & Finance Division, and Director of the Credit Management Research Centre. He gained his PhD from the University of Nottingham, UK. His research focuses on corporate performance, governance, financial distress and bankruptcy risk, family business, SME financing, and entrepreneurial finance. He has published in a wide range of academic and practitioner journals.

Simon Witney is a Special Counsel with law firm Debevoise & Plimpton LLP and teaches company law and private equity at London School of Economics. He completed his PhD on corporate governance issues in private equity-backed companies in 2017. A prominent member of the UK and European private equity communities, he has served in senior positions within the British Private Equity and Venture Capital Association and the European industry association, Invest Europe. Private Equity International has named him one of the 30 most influential lawyers in global private equity.

Geoffrey Wood is Dean and Professor of International Business at Essex Business School, UK. Previously he was Professor of International Business at Warwick Business School, UK. He has authored/co-authored/edited 16 books, and over 160 articles in peer-reviewed journals. Previously he was Professor of International Business at Warwick Business School, UK. He holds honorary positions at Griffith and Monash University in Australia, and Witwatersrand and Nelson Mandela Universities in South Africa. Geoff's research interests center on the relationship between institutional setting, corporate governance, firm finance, and firm level work and employment relations. Geoffrey Wood is Editor in Chief of the *British Journal of Management*, the *Official Journal of the British Academy of Management* (BAM), Associate Editor of *Academy of Management Perspectives*, and co-editor of the *Annals of Corporate Governance*. He also serves on the BAM Council. He is also editor of the *Chartered ABS Journal Ranking* list. He has had numerous research grants, including funding councils (e.g., ESRC), government departments (e.g., US Department of Labor; UK Department of Works and Pensions), charities (e.g., Nuffield Foundation, Albert Einstein Foundation), the labor movement (e.g., the ITF), and the European Union.

Mike Wright is Professor of Entrepreneurship and founding Director of the Centre for Management Buy-out Research at Imperial College Business School, UK. He is a Fellow of the British Academy, a Fellow of the Strategic Management Society, and an Academician of the Academy of Social Sciences. He earned his PhD at the University of Nottingham, UK, and is the recipient of honorary doctorates from the Universities of Ghent, Belgium, and Derby, UK. He has authored/co-authored/edited over 50 books and over 400 articles in peer-reviewed journals. His research focuses on entrepreneurial ownership mobility, including management buyouts, returnee entrepreneurs, habitual entrepreneurs, and family firms.

Xiwei Yi is an Assistant Professor at Guanghua School of Management, Peking University, China. She received her PhD from Jesse H. Jones Graduate School of Business, Rice University, USA. Her research focuses on CEO succession, internationalization of emerging market firms, and entrepreneurship.

Simona Zambelli is Associate Professor at University of Bologna, Italy, in the field of Economics of Financial Intermediation. After her PhD, Dr. Zambelli specialized in Finance at Birkbeck College, UK, and on Venture Finance at Harvard University, USA. Afterwards, she worked as a Visiting Professor at Rensselaer Polytechnic Institute, USA, and York University, Toronto, Canada. Her main research interests are related to the field of Financial Intermediation and Alternative Investment Funds. She enjoys using an interdisciplinary approach, with a law and empirical finance perspective. She has won a number of grants and awards for her research activity, including two international awards sponsored by the Government of Canada (Faculty Research Program, FRP). Her main publications are in the fields of venture capital and private equity, leveraged acquisitions, buyout regulation and corporate governance, and impact investing. She has written a number of books on entrepreneurial finance, alternative investment funds, venture philanthropy, and mergers and acquisitions.

PREFACE

The management buyout (MBO) corporate restructuring transaction first came to prominence in the US during the early 1980s. It soon emerged in the UK and has subsequently become a global phenomenon. At its peak in 2007, the total value of MBO transactions in the UK reached about £9 billion, while in Western Europe, it was about €23 billion. Thus, MBOs are a significant transaction within the corporate restructuring landscape.

The Centre for Management Buy-out Research (CMBOR) was created in the momentous year of 1986 when the UK signed the Single European Act, and Big Bang hit the financial services sector. This was also the year in which Michael Jensen published his seminal article in the *American Economic Review* on the "Agency costs of free cash flow, corporate finance, and takeovers," providing an important theoretical foundation for academic understanding of the MBO phenomenon. In that same year, Alex Ferguson became manager of Manchester United, an underperforming soccer club, later to be highly successful on the field following a leveraged buyout.

Many of the chapters in this volume were presented at a conference at Imperial College, London, to celebrate the 30th anniversary of CMBOR. Presciently, the anniversary conference was held on the very day that the UK decided to do a buyout of itself from the European Union! Publication of this volume will also be accompanied this year by a reissuing of the original study of *Management buyouts* by Wright and Coyne.[1]

In addition to the contributors to this volume, we thank all those too numerous to mention who have contributed to the work of CMBOR over the years. Special thanks, though, go to Brian Chiplin, John Coyne, and Ken Robbie, original colleagues at CMBOR, and to the long-standing current team of Rod Ball, Margaret Burdett, Karen Tune, and Dena Rapley for their unstinting efforts in making CMBOR work. Bob Willott, then of Spicer and Pegler, was key to setting up the initial sponsorship, subsequently carried on through Adam Mills and Chris Ward. Equistone Partners, and its variously named precursors, have funded CMBOR from the start, and we very warmly thank them for this unflagging support, especially Michael Cumming, Tom Lamb, Christiian Marriott, Brian Blakemore, and Phil Griesbach. Thanks also to Callum Bell and Shaun Mullin at Investec Bank for their current support for CMBOR, as well as to Zinka MacHale and

Kimberly Romaine. Thanks to Gabby Newton for organizing the conference on which this volume is based.

Note

1 Wright, M., & Coyne, J. 1985. *Management buyouts*. Beckenham, UK: Croom Helm.

1
MANAGEMENT BUYOUTS
An introduction and overview

Mike Wright, Kevin Amess, Nick Bacon, and Donald Siegel

Introduction

Management buyouts (MBOs) are part of a family of related forms of transactions where a firm is transferred to a new set of owners, among which senior managers become significant equity holders. To some extent, MBOs are not new. Buyouts of sleeping partners by mill owners and private placements of listed corporations have been consummated for over a century (Wright et al., 2000; Toms & Wright, 2002). What is relatively new is the growth of the phenomenon and the role of specialist equity and debt providers since the late 1980s. As a result, from being a peripheral intellectual curiosity, private equity (PE) and MBOs have become a major part of the overall market for corporate control.

From the initial emergence of the MBO in the US corporate restructuring landscape, MBOs have been controversial. Iconic early first wave examples of MBOs, such as Safeway and RJR Nabisco, were closely associated with improving firm efficiency through reducing agency costs, restructuring, cost-cutting, divestments, employment reductions, etc. and were often portrayed in the public media and in polemics such as "Barbarians at the Gate" (Burrough & Helyar, 1989) and "Stiffed" (Faludi, 1999). This perspective was carried through into the second wave with deals such as Grohe in Germany and the AA and Birds Eye in the UK paraded variously as locusts, casino capitalists, "strippers and flippers" (i.e., stripping assets and exiting in the short term), and the like (Bacon et al., 2013). Bruner and Paine (1988) noted that critics of MBOs were concerned that such highly leveraged transactions could threaten financial stability in the US, the financial restructuring creates no real economic benefit, and managers involved in an MBO suffer a conflict of interest because of managers' fiduciary duty to shareholders.

While the lurid portrayal of buyouts has provided a convenient caricature to whip up media frenzy by critics of PE and buyouts, it has always been a partial view of the market. Academic evidence suggests that incumbent managers involved in an MBO do not exploit their insider information position (Lee, 1992). In practice, a key issue for managers is to establish "mitigation measures" in order to avoid a breach of fiduciary duties. This involves declaring an interest and ensuring they have no involvement in the decision to sell and negotiate on behalf of owners.

Oftentimes the critical perspective has itself been short termist, and some of the critics' *causes célèbres* have turned out not to be as they have been portrayed (Wood & Wright,

2010). For example, Grohe demonstrated significant growth post buyout. Although Birds Eye had been slated for closure by its parent Unilever before the buyout, performance improved in five consecutive years following the buyout (Leyland, 2012).

Many buyouts, such as Unipart, Istel, and DPCE in the UK (Wright & Coyne, 1985/2018) and Seagate Technology (Loihl & Wright, 2002) and Duracell in the US (Wright et al., 2001), in fact pursued significant entrepreneurial and innovative trajectories. Other examples have seen managers expressing themselves, like those in Freedom Securities which became free at last from the constraints of their parent John Hancock that prevented them from pursuing growth opportunities (Wright et al., 2001).

Concern about MBOs' impact on financial stability has also been intermittently debated over time. For instance, the Bank of England (2013) has expressed concerns about high leverage during times of exuberance. Long-standing and continuing areas of debate surround the returns on investing in PE funds, the drivers of MBO activity, and the real economic consequences of MBOs.

The aim of this book is to bring together a wide range of systematic evidence from a variety of disciplines in order to form an overall assessment of the development and impact of PE and MBOs. In this introductory chapter, we begin by providing an overview of the variety and trends in MBO types or organization. This is followed by an outline of the theoretical perspectives that have been advanced to explain buyouts. Next, we summarize the contributions of each of the chapters comprising this volume before synthesizing the essence of the insights provided by the large body of evidence now available. Finally, we make some general comments regarding the future prospects for MBOs and PE.

Variety

A Leveraged Buyout (LBO) involves the transfer of a whole company or part of a company to new owners using high levels of debt to help finance the transaction secured against the firm's assets and/or future cash flows (Thompson & Wright, 1995; Kaplan & Strömberg, 2009).

The term Management Buyout (MBO) is used to define those buyout transactions where serving managers acquire a significant ownership stake. Management Buy-In (MBI) is the term used to define a transaction where outside managers acquire a significant ownership stake (Thompson & Wright, 1995). Another key distinction is between those transactions with backing from PE firms and those without PE-backing. PE firms may or may not take a majority equity stake in the portfolio company. Where PE firms lead the transaction and become the majority owners, these are termed investor-led buyouts (IBOs).

PE firms establish limited life funds (typically about 10 years in duration) to raise capital for the purpose of acquiring a portfolio of existing firms via an LBO. The PE funds are usually established as limited partnerships and there are two types of fund partners: limited partners (LPs) and general partners (GPs). The LPs provide most of a fund's cash and its investors include: wealthy individuals, pension funds, investment banks, and insurance companies. LPs have little say in how the funds are invested, although they may use covenants outlining some broad conditions under which the cash is invested (e.g.,, the proportion of a fund invested in a single deal). GPs in a PE firm manage funds, which involves selecting firms for a buyout deal, structuring its finances, negotiating the deal, and being a representative on portfolio firms' boards of directors. Returns to investors are generated by improving firm performance, making these companies more valuable, and then achieving a capital gain from selling the portfolio firm (i.e., exiting the investment).

Trends

The years since the 1980s have been marked by two major waves of buyouts. Following initial growth from the late 1970s, the first major growth in the market occurred in the second half of the 1980s with a first peak in 1989 (Figure 1.1).

Following the recession of the early 1990s, which saw a collapse in market value but a growth in buyouts of distressed firms, the market recovered during the rest of that decade (CMBOR, 2018). Fall-out from the bursting of the dot.com bubble meant that the PE market went into reverse for a couple of years around the turn of the millennium before resurging to reach a second, larger peak in 2007.

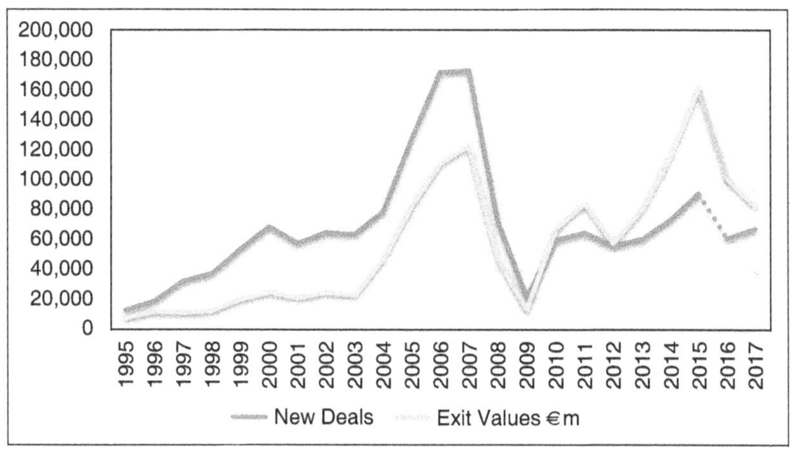

Figure 1.1 Entry and exit values for PE-backed buyouts in Europe
Source: CMBOR/Equistone Partners Europe/Investec Bank.

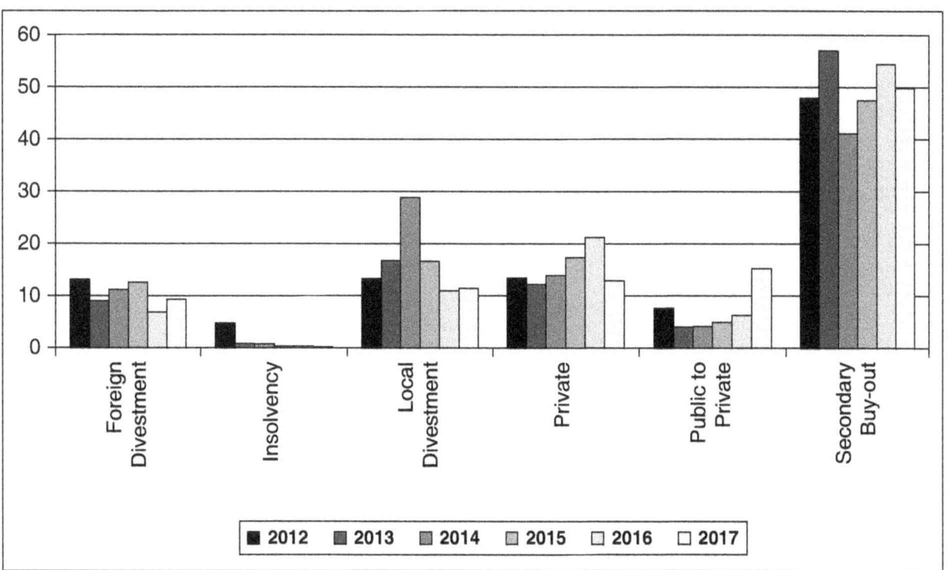

Figure 1.2 Vendor sources of PE-backed buyouts in Europe
Source: CMBOR/Equistone Partners Europe/Investec Bank.

After reaching a nadir in 2009, the market again recovered with PE fund raising continuing at high levels. At the time of writing, market value was heading towards new peaks driven by a relatively small number of larger deals against a backdrop of a sharp decline in deal volume.

The evolution of the market has been marked by a number of shifts in the composition and funding of deals over time. Vendor sources of deals have shifted from a dominance of buyouts of divisions of larger groups in the first wave (CMBOR, 1990) to a more diverse picture in which secondary buyouts (SBOs) are now marginally ahead of primary deals in value terms. Secondary buyouts involve the acquisition of an initial buyout by a new set of PE and management investors, with the initial investors exiting either fully or partially (Figure 1.2).

In the first wave of buyouts, smaller MBOs predominantly of family firms and divisions of larger groups predominated. In the second wave, this picture changed dramatically with much lower volumes of these kinds of deals and a growth in larger MBIs and investor-led buyouts (Figure 1.3).

a. Numbers

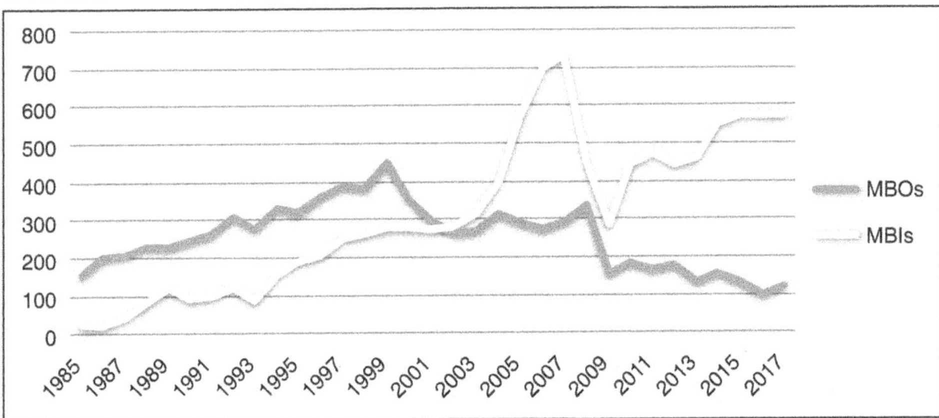

b. Values

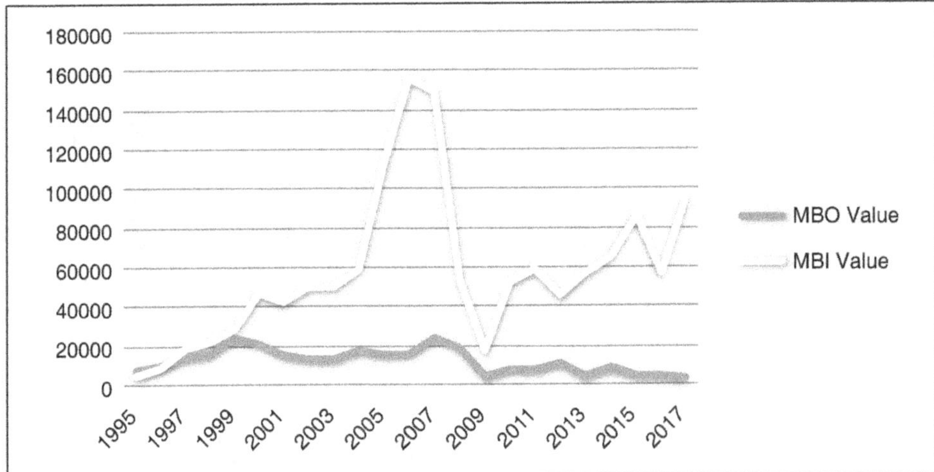

Figure 1.3 From MBOs to MBIs in Europe

Source: CMBOR/Equistone Partners Europe/Investec Bank.

Since the late 1980s, the MBO market has significantly expanded worldwide. In the European context, the overwhelming dominance that the UK had from the 1980s has gradually been eroded as other countries' markets have grown (Figure 1.4). While the UK market remains the largest, the German and French markets are also strong (CMBOR, 2018).

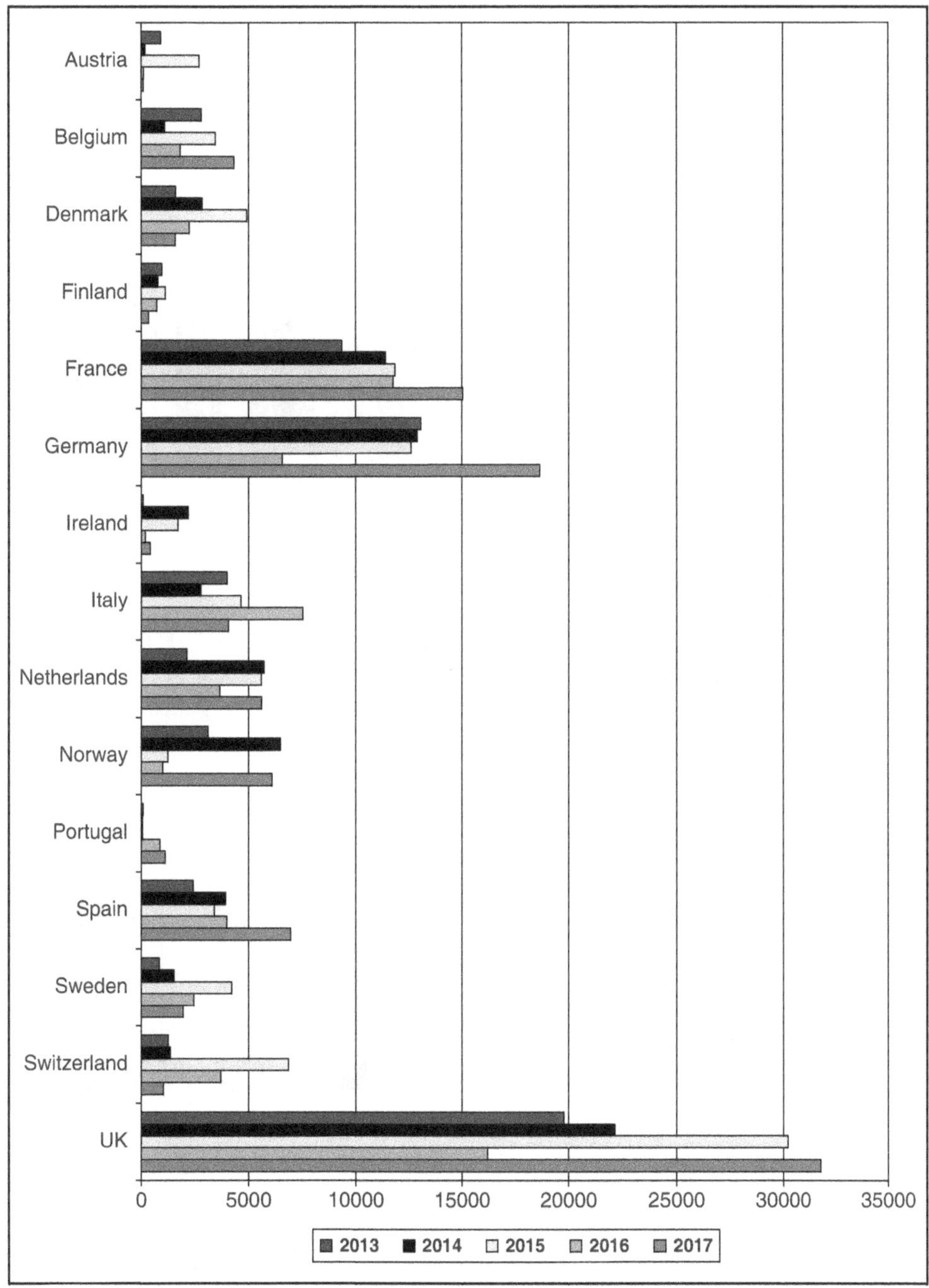

Figure 1.4 European PE-backed buyout markets

Source: CMBOR/Equistone Partners Europe/Investec Bank.

As the market has grown in terms of new deals being completed, so too has the number of existing deals looking for an exit to enable investors to realize their gains. Macroeconomic recovery after the financial recession meant a release of the pent-up demand for realizations, such that for the first time the value of exits has in recent years exceeded the value of new deals (Figure 1.1). The forms of exit have also changed over time, with fewer IPO exits and a marked increase in SBOs as an exit route, such that SBO value has recently exceeded primary buyout value (Figure 1.5).

a. Numbers

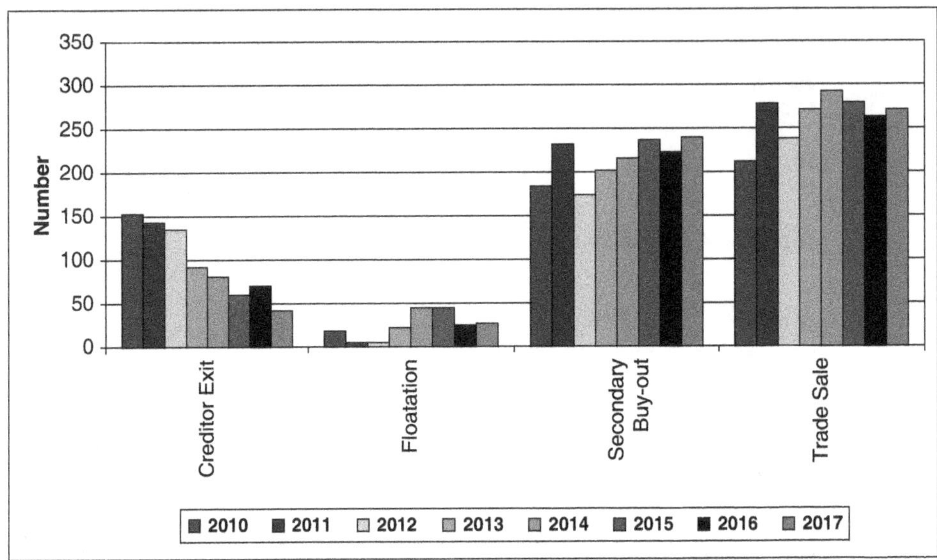

b. Values

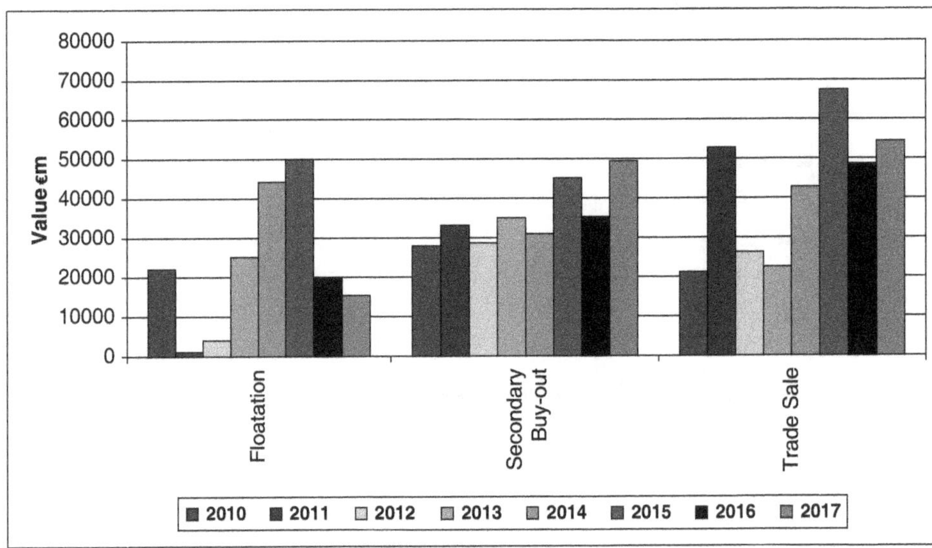

Figure 1.5 Exit routes of European PE-backed buyouts

Source: CMBOR/Equistone Partners Europe/Investec Bank.

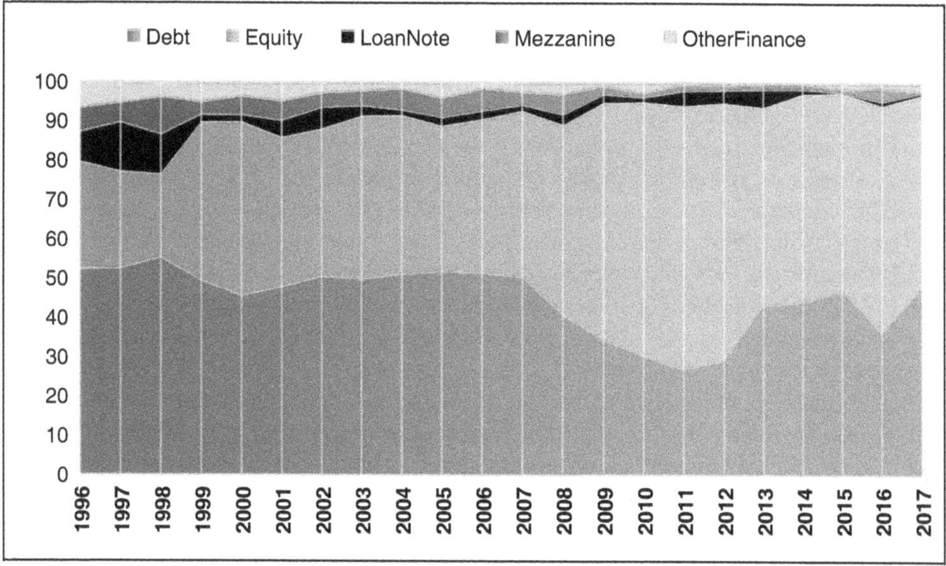

Figure 1.6 Deal financing structures: UK deals above £10 million transaction value
Source: CMBOR/Equistone Partners Europe/Investec Bank.

Financing structures have also changed over time. The average amount of leverage in deals rose through the 1980s during the first buyout wave before falling back during the recession of the early 1990s (CMBOR, 1993). Based on UK data, the impact of the financial crisis that halted the second buyout wave was starkly demonstrated as the average percentage of senior debt in buyouts with a transaction value above £10 million fell from 52% in 2006 to a low of 27% in 2011 (Figure 1.6). Since then there has been something of a recovery but not yet back to pre-financial crisis levels. By the end of 2017, the average senior debt in deals with a transaction value above £10million stood at 48%.

The chapters by Gilligan and Toms in this volume analyze the drivers of these trends in more detail.

Theories

Agency

From an academic perspective MBOs have been largely viewed through three theoretical perspectives: agency theory, behavioral theory, and an entrepreneurial perspective. Historically, agency theory has dominated our theoretical understanding of MBOs. Jensen's (1986) seminal work is pivotal in framing MBOs as a restructuring transaction that improves firms' corporate governance and remedies the agency costs associated with the publicly listed corporation.

Managers are the agents of firms' shareholders and have a fiduciary duty to manage firms' resources in shareholders' best interests, i.e., to maximize firm value. Managers, however, might not always act in shareholders' best interests because they have discretion in the use of firms' resources and so could pursue other objectives for their own private benefit (Jensen & Meckling, 1976). Executive remuneration contracts and the board of directors are internal governance devices seeking to align managers to the objective of maximizing firm value. Doubts remain, however, as to their effectiveness (Bebchuk & Fried, 2006). Jensen (1986) argues that agency costs associated with managers' discretionary behavior are most severe in firms that generate free cash flow, which is cash in excess of that required to fund all a firm's profitable projects. This is because managers will waste cash (e.g.,, on unprofitable capital expenditures) from which they obtain private benefit but destroy shareholder value. These firms underperform and become potential targets for an MBO (Fox & Marcus, 1992).

The MBO governance structure has three features that reduce agency costs (Jensen, 1986; Thompson & Wright, 1995; Kaplan & Strömberg, 2009). First, managers' significant equity stake after a buyout unifies management and ownership roles, creating financial incentives to value-maximize and not waste cash on unprofitable projects. Second, the interest payments on debt require servicing, which encourages managers not to waste cash and motivates managers to generate cash to service the debt. Finally, PE firms have a significant equity stake in their portfolio firms and are therefore financially motivated to be active investors. They normally have board representation and sometimes have a representative as Chair. Theory predicts that improved governance installed after an MBO results in improved performance.

Behavioral

Behavioral approaches to understanding the motivation for MBOs provide competing arguments to those offered by an agency perspective (Fox & Marcus, 1992). Some arguments suggest that an MBO is a response to takeover threat. First, managers in underperforming firms that are targeted for a takeover will likely lose their jobs (Franks & Mayer, 1996). Therefore, incumbent managers might undertake an MBO in order to protect their jobs and to avoid being associated with failure. If underperforming managers are using an MBO to protect their own positions, we would expect to observe continued underperformance after an MBO. Such deals would only be financed if there are imperfections in the capital market with financial backers not conducting sufficient due diligence. Second, managers might want to protect their jobs because they possess human capital that is highly firm-specific and their next best job will pay a lower wage. If a takeover threatens their positions, an MBO becomes a vehicle for managers to protect the incomes they earn from their firm-specific human capital. This motivation for an MBO would suggest performance effects post-MBO similar to those pre-MBO if there are synergies between incumbent management human capital and the corporate assets they control. Third, a takeover bid might undervalue a firm because managers possess inside information that is not easily conveyed to outsiders. Managers might undertake an MBO and be willing to pay a higher price than outsiders if they believe they have superior information about the true value of the firm and the future payoffs of investments (Williamson, 1988). This motivation for an MBO suggests that firms' real economic performance will reveal itself in data in the future.

Behavioral perspectives offer a different analysis of organizational slack compared to agency theory (Fox & Marcus, 1992). Agency theory considers slack to be a cost to shareholders because it reduces the value of the firm. In contrast, the behavioral perspective views slack as a cushion against environmental uncertainty. If the industry or macroeconomic environment becomes more challenging for firms, slack provides a cushion against this. It provides managers with time to either resolve business problems or for economic conditions to become more favorable. Consistent with this view is the notion that there may be financial slack associated with surplus debt capacity. By increasing leverage and exploiting the "tax shield" to its full potential, an MBO is able to extract maximum value from the tax shield. Rappaport (1990) argues that this creates strategic inflexibility. Indeed, unused debt capacity has strategic value if unforeseen investment opportunities arise and debt finance is required to fund them. The strategic value of financial slack is important when firms are competing over investment opportunities.

Typically, scholars who present a behavioral perspective are critical of the motivations for LBOs. Indeed, critics argue that LBOs do not generate economic gains; instead, they transfer wealth from stakeholders to buyout investors (Fox & Marcus, 1992; Kaplan & Strömberg, 2009). First, an MBO would not occur unless it was advantageous for incumbent management. Incumbent managers are willing to pay a premium for control when they are able to exploit inside information with the knowledge that a target firm's true value is higher. Second, firms targeted for an LBO have low levels of debt, so greater value can be obtained from the tax deductibility of debt. Wealth gains are therefore transfers from tax payers. Finally, LBOs occur in firms with the potential to reduce jobs and wages. An LBO represents an opportunity to reduce a firm's wage bill by reducing the size of the workforce and reducing wages. Thus, LBOs are transferring wealth from employees to the new owners (Shleifer & Summers, 1988).

Entrepreneurial

The agency perspective focuses on improvement in governance, which reduces the agency costs associated with managers' discretionary behavior, resulting in cost-cutting. Value creation after an MBO also occurs through the pursuit of profitable growth opportunities. This is attributed to increased entrepreneurial incentives and the freedom to exploit entrepreneurial cognition (Coyne & Wright, 1982; Zahra, 1995; Wright et al., 2000). For senior managers, an MBO substitutes hierarchical incentive systems (e.g., promotion, seniority pay) with market-based incentives. Hierarchical incentives are not always effective in motivating managers to pursue entrepreneurial opportunities and in allocating resources to their best use (Williamson, 1985; Hill, 1988). In addition, for those individuals with an entrepreneurial cognition (i.e., learning and making decisions under conditions of uncertainty), the formal accountability systems of hierarchical systems restricts discretionary decision-making associated with entrepreneurialism (Wright et al., 2000). By contrast, market-based incentives created by an LBO (i.e., senior managers taking a share of the value created) strongly motivate the pursuit of profitable entrepreneurial opportunities. An LBO creates a context where there is discretion to pursue entrepreneurial opportunities and it is rewarded when successful (Wright et al., 2000). Thus, LBOs lead to increased commitment to entrepreneurial activity and this entrepreneurial activity is associated with improved post-LBO performance (Zahra, 1995).

The entrepreneurship perspective also provides a distinctive motivation for firms and divisions of firms targeted for an LBO: those that have growth opportunities and are financially constrained in pursuing them (Boucly et al., 2011). Growth opportunities can arise in the divisions of large corporations due to their failure to properly allocate financial resources to profitable investment opportunities (Williamson, 1985; Hill, 1988). Financially constrained private firms that forego profitable investment opportunities are also potential targets. This can arise when private firms find it difficult to signal their creditworthiness. Thus, the entrepreneurial perspective contends that divisions of large firms and private firms are potential MBO targets. The entrepreneurial perspective also complements the agency perspective by developing a narrative around how the governance structure motivates entrepreneurial behavior. Managers with a significant equity stake have incentives to invest in profitable growth, and there is recognition that PE firms can coach managers to behave more entrepreneurially.

The Centre for Management Buyout Research (CMBOR)

This volume is based on a conference to celebrate and reflect on 30 years of research in CMBOR. Although founded in 1986, the germination of the seed that was to become CMBOR started in 1979 in a conversation between colleagues about divestments between parent corporations. After some initial work (Chiplin & Wright, 1980), with the help of Ron Arnfield then Industrial and Business Liaison Officer for Nottingham University, research funding was sought from 3i (then ICFC). Unfortunately, 3i wasn't interested in this topic but did draw attention to divisions and subsidiaries that were being bought by their managers. They didn't refer to these as MBOs initially. Subsequently, Chiplin and Wright collaborated with ICFC to organize the first conference on MBOs in March 1981 (Arnfield et al., 1981). The emphasis was very much on job saving in a recession, and many of the 120 plus audience wished to remain anonymous for fear that they would be summarily fired if their bosses got wind of their thoughts about doing an MBO.

Subsequently, Mike Wright and John Coyne obtained a modest ESRC (then SSRC) grant to undertake a survey of managerial and industrial relations' changes in MBOs. Paul Brooks, then of ICFC's Nottingham office, was crucial for getting access to portfolio companies to survey since at that time there was publicly available database.

As a follow-up to the 1981 conference, Wright was increasingly contacted by the media, most notably the *Financial Times*, for data on MBO deals, which necessitated ad hoc telephone calls to funders we were aware of who were doing deals. Very basic, but at the time there was no other way to obtain information. Our view was that providing initial coverage in this way would, over time, encourage a greater flow of information. The press coverage we received resulted in our being contacted by the PR agency for Spicer and Pegler accountants about the possibility of funding us to do some work for them on MBOs. Following an initial meeting in February 1984, at which we were asked to provide some suggestions, we proposed three projects, one of which was the idea to establish a monitoring center. Somewhat to our surprise, as this was more ambitious and costly, they said they would like to support the establishment of a monitoring center but would need to find another partner to finance it. Sometime later, what was then Barclays Development Capital agreed to be a co-sponsor alongside Spicer and Pegler and CMBOR was launched on March 1, 1986 with the aim of providing a comprehensive and objective monitoring of the market.

Like many venture-backed start-ups, despite keen practice and policy interest some restructuring and repositioning was needed within the first two years in order to establish the credibility of the database and to enable CMBOR to cope with the level of media interest. The sponsors increased their funding, which meant extra staff could be employed and Brian Chiplin, despite early comments about studying buyouts being a waste of an academic career, joined Mike Wright as a director and made an enormous contribution to establishing the CMBOR database as an authoritative source of data on MBOs and PE.

A major challenge in sustaining both sponsorship and interest over such a long period has been finding something new to say for a press release every quarter. Similarly, there has been the challenge to find new avenues to continue the academic research program. An interesting aspect of the PE and MBO market over time has been the evolution in the size of the market, types and sizes of deals, as well as funding structures. Keying into this changing pattern over time has been crucial to sustaining the academic program as well as press interest. Hence, the research program broadened out from looking at MBOs' drivers and impacts generally to exploring MBIs, buyouts of failed firms, exits and longevity, failure, etc. Similarly, connecting the buyout research agenda to broader debates has also been critical to sustaining CMBOR's longevity. Thus, research was developed to connect to debates about corporate governance, privatization, transition and emerging economies, HRM and employee relations, entrepreneurship and innovation, succession in family firms, etc. Engagement with policy and practice through projects for organizations as varied as the BVCA, EVCA, DVCA, ILO, OECD, NAO, EBRD, ICAEW, to name but a few, provided a symbiotic means to extend the academic research program while at the same time contributing systematic evidence where it was often woefully lacking.

For some 25 years after the founding of CMBOR, it is probably fair to say that there was no particular direct career recognition by the university as a result of the press coverage and impact on practice associated with CMBOR's quarterly reports and analyses. In the context of successive Research Assessment Exercises (RAEs), what mattered was the academic research output stemming from analysis of the database that we were continuing to build in real time. Engaging with practice and policy, not least through making countless (non-fee) presentations at industry conferences and writing articles for trade press, may have seemed an irrational waste of time. However, it helped sustain funding support from sponsors who were focused on the PR coverage, and it also helped in generating ideas for new papers and projects by enabling us to identify emerging themes, challenges, and questions that we would not have formulated from focusing solely on the academic literature. Fortunately, the introduction of impact cases in the UK's 2014 Research Excellence Framework (REF) at last provided an opportunity to demonstrate and have valued the wider contribution of CMBOR's work. Under the vagaries of the REF regulations, although it was possible to transfer the publications to Imperial, the impact case had to be written for Nottingham even though Wright had left some two years earlier. Nevertheless, the impact case was scored in the highest category (Wright, 2013).

The structure and contents of this book

The contributors to this volume draw on a variety of disciplines including business history, law, economics, entrepreneurship and innovation, family business, finance and accounting, HRM and employee relations, and strategy. The volume is divided into five parts as follows.

Part 1: Historical, legal, and regulatory issues

We begin with a practitioner perspective on the development of MBOs and PE. **Gilligan** looks at some of the ups and downs of the industry since the late 1980s. In tracing the various phases of development, he notes that the industry has ridden these waves by metamorphosing from a small niche activity to a vast global industry. Along the way, a number of major changes can be discerned in terms of the nature of both the types of deals and funders. Perhaps most notably, the simple alignment model of backing managers to buy their companies and paying the deal leaders on success has largely disappeared in the emerging financial behemoths that look more like diversified fund managers focused not only on long-term illiquid assets but also with a range of other asset classes. Multiple fees have replaced carried interest as the primary source of the incentives in some large PE firms. Gilligan concludes by commenting that as long as PE funds remain as long-term, ungeared, active investors in unquoted companies, the industry is performing a valuable service to the economy that no other sector has been capable of doing.

In a complementary chapter, **Toms** from an academic perspective examines the history of the MBO, identifying some early examples from the first stages of industrialization. He considers the evolution of the key features of finance, governance, and regulation that coalesced into the first buyout wave of the late 1970s and early 1980s. He then moves on to examine the subsequent trend towards first larger numbers of transactions and then larger value transactions, noting their transformative effects on entire industries and sectors. In doing so, Toms assesses the longer-run significance of the buyout as a vehicle for reviving and institutionalizing important features of entrepreneurship.

Cumming and Zambelli aim to provide policy makers with new insights to better evaluate the current worldwide debate on debt merger acquisitions, as well as shed some light on the perils of stringent financial bans on these types of transactions. As an aftermath of the 2007 financial crisis, a wave of new regulatory proposals and legal reforms of PE and other alternative investment funds (such as hedge funds) was introduced with the purpose of guaranteeing more financial stability and higher investor protection. However, as Cumming and Zambelli emphasize, the growing regulatory attention on PE funds was not due to the fact that they caused the crisis. Rather, the crisis was instead a pretext to regulate PE funds more heavily in the context of substantial confusion about the intrinsic characteristics of LBOs, especially in terms of how they can increase the value of target companies, and how legal reforms may shape investor behavior towards the direction desired by policy makers. Cumming and Zambelli aim to fill this gap by showing the results of recent empirical studies on the impact of corporate governance reforms in the context of PE financing in Italy, a country in which PE transactions were previously prohibited and thereafter legalized. As such, the Italian PE market offers a unique and timely experimental example to better evaluate the efficacy of stringent regulatory restrictions on LBO deals.

Brexit has thrown into sharp relief issues relating to cross-border provision of financial services, and in particular PE. Resulting from the debate about PE associated with the last boom in 2007, effective from 2013, the Alternative Investment Fund Managers Directive (or AIFMD) fundamentally altered the regulatory environment for European PE funds, establishing – for the first time – a set of pan-EU rules for PE and venture capital (VC) funds with assets under management that exceeded certain thresholds. For many fund managers this has entailed considerable change that has permeated most aspects of their business, including additional capital requirements, stricter conduct of business rules, enhanced disclosures to regulators, investors, and the outside world and, for some, has even required amendments to remuneration policies. **Gibson and Witney** review the rules that were included in AIFMD, and note that although the primary aim was to harmonize regulation of private funds at a pan-European level and provide a passport in respect of private funds where none existed before, it also sought to achieve additional objectives related to investor protection, financial stability, and portfolio company governance. They conclude that it is not easy to discern a clear policy objective for many of these changes, and it is therefore hard to assess whether they achieved their aims. Indeed, in relation to many of the new rules, they argue that there is scant evidence that investors wanted them, or that they will benefit from them. They also suggest that it is also unclear how the rules will alleviate systemic risk, particularly insofar as they apply to PE funds. They are skeptical whether the inflexible requirements in the Directive principally aimed at imposing authorization and business conduct requirements for private fund managers, are the best way to achieve protection for investee companies and their stakeholders. They see it as particularly difficult to see why such protection should be triggered by the fact that the relevant fund is subject to the AIFMD.

Part 2: Vendor sources

Thompson and Haynes explore the inter-relationship between divestment and the MBO. They argue that the MBO has been both a contributory cause and a consequence of an ongoing trend towards corporate refocusing as a means to reduce the diversification (or conglomerate) discount. They consider the evolving role of the capital market in facilitating buyouts in general and particularly divestment MBOs. Their review of the empirical literature shows that divestment is consistent with improving the position of underperforming firms, but generally under the stimulus of effective corporate governance and/or some existential threat to top management while the role of accounting performance alone is less clear-cut. They note that while local management is especially well placed to identify opportunities to increase value because of information not available to headquarters, they may choose not to pursue them as this may incur psychic costs that are not adequately incentivized within a conglomerate. The enhanced incentives available through divestment by an MBO may act as a catalyst for change. Divestment MBOs may typically involve peripheral parts of diversified conglomerates, but they may also involve situations where the former division continues to trade with its erstwhile parent. In this latter case, managers in the MBO may be better incentivized to perform than would be possible under the parental norms, and the former parent may benefit in the trading relationship from the asymmetry of dependence between itself and the MBO (Wright, 1986).

Renneboog and Vansteenkiste provide an exhaustive literature review of the motives for public-to-private LBO transactions. First, they develop the theoretical framework for the potential sources of value creation from going private, making a distinction between the reduction in shareholder-related agency costs, stakeholder wealth transfers, tax benefits, transaction costs savings, takeover defense strategies, and corporate undervaluation. Next, they review and summarize whether and how these theories have been empirically verified in the four different strands of literature in LBO research. These strands of literature are categorized by phase of the LBO transaction: Intent (of a buyout), Impact (of the LBO on the various stakeholders), Process (of restructuring after the leveraged buyout), and Duration (of retaining the private status). They show that in the first half of the 2000s, a public-to-private LBO wave re-emerged in the US, UK, and Continental Europe, whose value vastly exceeded that of the 1980s US LBO wave. They conclude with suggestions for further research.

Family firms represent an important segment of the MBO market. Succession is a crucial event in the life cycle of a family business. However, family businesses often fail to solve succession within the family, and thus, increasingly choose an external succession route involving MBOs and PE firms as potential buying sides. Whereas involving a PE firm provides a fruitful option to solve succession while preventing some of the family business characteristics, it, however, also involves some potential conflicts such as differences concerning the future determination of priorities (financial vs. non-financial performance) or strategic orientation (long-term vs. short-term) of the family firm. Recent academic research has increasingly focused on such challenges emerging within the buyout process of a family business to a PE firm. Owing to this, as well as the increasing practical relevance of such buyout transactions, **Ahlers, Michel, and Hack** review the literature on PE and buyouts of family firms, identifying six distinct categories of prior studies as follows. Studies of the family firm buyout market show that they tend to be smaller than other deals on average and involve a significant of market deal volume, but studies do not address different definitions of family firms. With respect to information asymmetries, family firm owners and incumbent management potentially face conflicts of interest, with the high complexity of a buyout requiring long-term planning in order to enable a sound, timely, and collaborative information basis for successful deal-making, with advisors playing a valuable role. Regarding PE perceptions, family firms are perceived by PE investors as different from non-family firm targets and PE investors emphasize the negative side of family influence and in particular the additional risks associated with family firm investments (e.g.,, owner-centricity).With respect to family perceptions sellers assume an active role but might be concerned to whom and how the business is sold rather than simply maximization of the sale price, but reciprocal perceptions of family firms and PE could be a source of conflict, and a positive relationship might be critical in relationships between family firms and PE firms. There is a negative relationship between PE's bargaining power and bidder competition, whereas PE's expertise and the buyout seller's time pressure positively influence PE's bargaining power. Regarding value creation, family firms undergo a greater orientation towards financial goals, but sound empirical evidence remains scarce and may vary between different family configurations.

In a complementary chapter, **Howorth and Robinson** explore the changes involved in the family business aspect of family firms that are bought out. They start by examining what is different about family controlled businesses, reviewing available evidence and exploding some myths in order to establish relevant concepts that help explain approaches and behaviors in family firm MBOs and MBIs. Next, they explain the rationale for family business MBOs and MBIs. They go on to examine the process for MBOs and MBIs of family firms and also provide insights into the variation in negotiation behaviors and implications for outcomes. The authors address the important question of what happens to family firm MBOs and MBIs over time, following the transfer of ownership. They demonstrate that MBOs and MBIs can trigger an increase in firms' professionalization. The authors present evidence suggesting that family firms can be rejuvenated through the influx of non-family talent and expertise.

In times of economic recession the increase in the number of company bankruptcies (insolvencies) is accompanied by a rise in the number of MBOs and MBIs from these failed companies. **Scholes** explores the general characteristics of these buyouts, the role of PE involvement, post-buyout performance, and illustrates the issues by examining three case studies. She observes that these deals, which tend to be buyouts rather than buy-ins, mainly come from viable parts of failed parent companies rather than failed independent businesses. Post-buyout, employment is reduced in only just over a third of cases. Among all of the PE-backed buyout failures, those from already failed companies make up the largest proportion, and this proportion is significantly higher than for non-PE-backed deals. The recent use of pre-pack administration arrangements where management take over an insolvent company, allowing a firm to be sold to a new buyer as a going concern before the traditional administration process takes place, may make subsequent failure less likely. While this speedy process prevents a company from being devalued by news of financial difficulties that could affect customer and supplier loyalty and patronage, it is quite controversial. Proponents argue that by speeding up the process they save jobs, whereas critics suggest that creditors, particularly unsecured creditors, lose out but that the buyers, often the same managers, are able to buy back the more profitable assets at a knock-down price.

Bos and Boselie focus on the role of PE firms in health services, in particular in nursing homes. They start with a conceptual framework that explains why health services are not just another business (the "public value frame"), as distinguished from health services as "just another business" (the "market frame"). They then synthesize two systematic literature reviews on the impact of PE across sectors and for-profit nursing homes. Based on both reviews, they propose that PE owners are mainly successful from a market frame perspective. They seem to enhance financial/organizational performance in health services, but mainly by reduce staffing levels. This comes with no or slightly negative consequences for clients. They suggest that PE owners, especially in nursing homes, should focus on a more strategic balance between organizational/financial performance, employee well-being and client well-being. They recommend two shifts in future research on PE: from its impact on organizational/financial performance to its impact on product and services quality, and from research to what the impact of PE is to case studies that explore how PE creates impact.

MBOs have been used extensively as a mechanism for the privatization of state and local government-owned assets in both developed and emerging economies (Thompson et al., 1990; Robbie & Wright, 2008). In some cases they have been used to sell off peripheral parts of state-owned enterprises as part of the process of preparing the core parent enterprise for stock market flotation, in others entire state-owned enterprises have been sold as buyouts, while in yet other cases state-owned enterprises have been broken up into numerous buyouts (Mulley & Wright, 1986). In emerging economies, buyouts have taken place in various countries either as parts of voucher privatization schemes or through sales (Wright, 1994). **Du and Nguyen** explore MBOs in China, which are distinctive in mainly happening during the era of enterprise reform in the country aimed at helping poorly performing SOEs into modern corporate organizations able to survive in more competitive market conditions. They argue that without a deep understanding of the historical and institutional background in which Chinese MBOs took place, it would be difficult to understand the selection issues that occur in the process of MBOs, and to evaluate MBO performance. There is some doubt about the validity of the management incentive alignment hypothesis as an explanation of MBO performance in the context of China, with the manipulation hypothesis relating to insiders intentionally suppressing the performance of their firms to acquire them at less than fair value having some credence. Despite controversial opinions concerning the source of performance improvements, there is a consensus that Chinese MBO firms are moving towards greater levels of professionalization. They show that the level of ownership concentration in MBOs tends to be less severe than that in firms privatized by other methods. Similarly, the reduction in the importance of the party committee following buyout is more substantial in MBO firms than in the firms privatized through other approaches.

Part 3: Financing, structuring, and private equity firms

Hoskisson, Shi, Yi, and Jin explore the evolution and strategic positioning of PE firms (general partners) themselves (versus previous research focused on buyout portfolio firm implications). Building on resource dependence theory and resource-based theory, they provide a conceptual configuration of PE firms along two dimensions: their financial structure emphasis (the strategic use of debt versus equity among PE portfolio firms) and the diversified scope of their portfolio firms. They use these dimensions to create a typology classifying PE firms into short-term efficiency niche players, niche players with long-term equity positions, diversified players with focused groups of portfolio firms, and short-term diversified efficiency-oriented players.

Returns on investment in PE funds matters not just to wealthy investors, but also to pension funds and other institutional investors. **Appelbaum and Batt** survey empirical evidence of investor returns and provide critical analysis of the methods employed. PE firms often use the internal rate of return (IRR) when reporting fund performance. The concern with this measure is that it is not a good predictor of actual investor returns and is susceptible to manipulation, exaggerating investor returns. An alternative measure used by PE firms is Net Asset Value (NAV), which is realized investments plus PE firms' estimates of the market value of unrealized investments. The estimation process allows PE firms some discretion over valuation. An alternative measure preferred by academics is the public market equivalent (PME), which compares returns in PE funds with returns on listed stock. Typically, US studies make comparisons with the S&P 500. PE funds are more risky investments than the S&P 500, and adjustments for risk reduces estimated returns on PE funds. There is evidence that PE funds have outperformed the S&P 500, but there is a great deal of heterogeneity in fund performance, and recent evidence suggests the PE funds are not providing excess returns. This suggests that PE funds are behaving similar to other asset classes, and their excess returns are competed away.

Divakaruni explores aspects of collaboration and partner selection among participants in PE transactions. Much of the literature looks at collaboration between PE firms and targets and their performance, but this chapter also considers studies on LBOs that examine how PE firms collaborate with banks and raise debt financing for their investments. In particular, these themes concern the role of power differentials among prospective buyout participants notably between banks and PE firms, the extent to which bank syndication networks in the LBO market are an important channel for reducing agency costs during deal formation, and whether differences between home and target countries in legal investor protection exert an asymmetric effect on the cross-border investment preferences of PE firms and banks and hence on the nature of collaboration.

The MBO market has evolved over the period from the 1980s and diffused into new country markets. In particular, there has been a major shift from "traditional" and mature markets in the US and Western Europe towards emerging regions. A major issue for PE firms and limited partner investors in PE funds as these markets emerge is whether to enter early or to wait. These investors have to weigh the benefits of entering early, establishing a network, and gaining experience against the disadvantage caused by lacking local experience and institutional immature investment environments. To help address these concerns, **Groh** develops a composite indicator to assess the attractiveness of countries for PE investment. He suggests that this country attractiveness index can, for example, support allocation decisions by limited partners across a large number of countries. However, he cautions that it cannot determine the best timing when LPs should start allocating capital to emerging markets.

PE buyout funds have become increasingly interested in investing in entrepreneurial firms, which have traditionally been an investment territory of VC funds. There is a dearth of study on how PE firms invest and perform in this space, in comparison to VC firms. The chapter by **Dai and McAlpine** attempts to fill this void. Analyzing a sample of 76,465 investment rounds involving 29,752 US investee companies over the period 1990–2014, the authors show that PEs often prefer expansion and later stage ventures. They are less biased towards California and more likely to invest in non-high-tech companies. Investment size and valuation are significantly larger/higher when PEs participate an investment round. With regard to the exit performance, we find companies with PE participation overall are less likely to exit successfully (measured by both IPOs and M&As); however, they are more likely to exit via IPOs.

There is much debate on the firm-level consequences and performance outcomes of alternative investors, most prominently hedge funds and PE funds. In reviewing this literature, **Cumming and Wood** show that there is much diversity in terms of fund types, and accordingly in the consequences of their activities for investors and other stakeholders. Although some funds perform well on a wide range of fronts, others do much worse, which may reflect agency problems in relations with investors, knowledge imbalances, and in terms of challenges in accurately costing the worth of a target firm's less tangible assets. In the case of hedge funds, they highlight the importance of investor due diligence, and the value of financial regulations that enable transparency and better monitoring. As the fund ecosystem evolves, so will the range of research opportunities for measuring the costs and benefits with delegated asset management under different institutional contexts.

Part 4: Post-MBO firm behavior

In his chapter, **Bertoni** illustrates the main theories and surveys the empirical evidence on the impact of PE LBOs on innovative activity at target companies. Bertoni shows how the theoretical lenses through which LBOs are described have adapted to the changing characteristics of these transactions. He observes that most of the literature has focused on a relatively narrow type of innovation (i.e., technological innovation), and has instead paid less attention to hard-to-measure yet important components of the innovation process (e.g., managerial innovation). He suggests that a major reason for this is that this multidisciplinary literature is highly fragmented, notably between the finance and innovation literatures, and hence in the way innovation is treated.

Engel and Stiebale survey the literature on the effects of PE-financed buyouts on investment of portfolio firms. They show that while the earlier literature has focused on cost-cutting and reduction of over-investment, a newer strand of literature shows that buyouts can accelerate entrepreneurial investment. Although the results of empirical studies are mixed, there is evidence that buyouts can enhance different types of investment and reduce financing constraints. However, the results seem to depend on the characteristics of portfolio firms, investors, and countries analyzed. They also discuss methodological problems of existing studies and provide recommendations for future research.

In light of the considerable debate about whether buyouts are all about efficiency gains and cost-cutting, **Wright** takes a different perspective by setting out to provide a review and synthesis of the theory and systematic empirical evidence relating to entrepreneurship in MBOs. He adopts a Schumpeterian view of entrepreneurial activity which encompasses new product and market development, product and service innovation, and asset and organizational restructuring. He distinguishes between entrepreneurial catch up activities carried out by buyout acquirers with a managerial mindset and more radical entrepreneurial activities by those with a more entrepreneurial mindset. He also shows the importance of the entrepreneurial expertise of the PE investors and boards of directors. Wright reviews the evidence regarding the extent of entrepreneurial activity following a buyout including growth through new product and market development, innovation, and exporting.

The chapter by **Bruining** provides insights into complex resource management decisions and actions that buyouts are required to make. It focuses on resource management in a comprehensive way, including elements of mobilizing strategy; structuring of the resource portfolio; and combining resources to stabilize, enrich, and create capabilities and coordinating actions to support the post-buyout strategy. Case illustrations of divisional-, family firm -, secondary -, and receivership-buyouts offer insights into different scopes of performance improvement and orchestration of value creation. The study contributes to research on resource reconfiguration after a PE-backed MBO, extends the buyout literature on performance improvement, and advances research on the role of PE investors in balancing exploitation and exploration.

Observers of comparative political economy have outlined changes in the nature of capitalism that has occurred since the late 1970s. This literature suggests that full-employment capitalism was replaced by a finance-led capitalism centered on neo-liberalism. Central to these changes are deregulation and privatization which are now embedded in the institutional framework of countries such as the UK. The literature suggests that these changes represent a social revolution from above, designed to restore the power of capital over labor; but these processes are described at an abstracted level where the grounded consequences for work and employment at firm level are less clear. **Clark** develops arguments that the UK state played a key role in facilitating the transition to finance-led capitalism and financialization, and that the financial instruments popularized by PE through LBOs spill over to affect the corporate sector more broadly. The chapter is divided into three parts. Part one provides a theoretical framework which outlines the emergence of finance-led capitalism, the associated diffusion of financialization in the UK economy and its potential effects on labor. Part two outlines the negative implications for work and employment as PE instruments enable and encourage investors to appropriate value from firms. Part three illustrates the arguments with empirical material drawn from two detailed case studies relating to the AA under PE ownership and the collapse of the British Homes Stores pension scheme.

Bacon and Hoque review what is currently known about the impact of buyouts on employees, focusing in particular on the implications for human resource management (HRM) practices. Although critics of buyouts frequently suggest the implications for employees are negative, the chapter offers little support for such claims. Overall, the evidence reviewed suggests that buyouts, in their efforts to improve performance, encourage investments in more sophisticated HRM practices rather than seeking to adopt a cost minimization approach. There is little evidence beyond the conclusions drawn from selective case studies that buyouts have negative overall effects for employees in the areas of employment relations (practices covering training, reward systems, and managing employment change), work relations (the organization of labor to produce or deliver services, such as team-based organization, levels of task discretion, and the management of health and safety), and industrial relations (the role of trade unions and collective bargaining). The chapter also highlights the lack of evidence that outcomes for employees are worse in specific types of buyouts, for example buyouts led by outsiders, PE buyouts, short-hold buyouts, and high-debt buyouts. The implications of buyouts for employees also do not appear especially negative as a result of the investor's country of origin and the national institutional context in which the buyout is located. The authors outline an extensive research agenda on these issues. In doing so, they take note of the significant methodological and data challenges and how these may be overcome, such as how data on HRM practices that are not regularly reported by firms may be uncovered and how the experiences of employees in buyouts may be accessed.

Part 5: Performance and life cycle

Alperovych reviews the extensive evidence on the performance of MBOs and MBIs and concludes that systematic studies corroborate the assumption that improvements in operations and productivity are important drivers of value creation. He shows that these improvements come from various sources, e.g., growth in sales, acquisitions, refocusing firm strategies and operations, cost-cutting mechanisms, divestments of unproductive units, reallocations of labor, etc. Importantly, Alperovych notes that while critics still argue that buyouts harm companies because of excessive use of leverage, short-sightedness of PE firms, and potentially considerably negative social impact (layoffs), the core of the criticisms seems to be case-based while the systematic academic evidence tends to show a quite different picture. Alperovych does note, however, that the underlying mechanisms that generate performance improvements seem to differ over time. Early evidence put an accent on the debt-bonding and cost-cutting strategies while later evidence suggested that value increases have to be also sought in revenue-enhancing strategies and improvements in corporate governance mechanisms. Moreover, as PE firms accumulate experience, they seem to better translate it into the changes operated within portfolio companies.

The impact of buyouts on jobs and wages has been a controversial issue for a number of years, especially those deals that have PE backing. Critics have advanced concerns that investors in buyouts gain at the expense of employees' jobs and wages. **Amess** outlines agency and entrepreneurial perspectives of buyouts and their predictions regarding the impact of buyouts on jobs and wages. He then reviews the evidence on the impact of buyouts on jobs and wages in relation to these theoretical perspectives. Given the extensive use of anecdotal examples by both critics and protagonists, Amess attempts to provide a rigorous assessment by focusing on large-scale studies that use a variety of statistical techniques to analyze data from a variety of countries. Studies examining the average impact on jobs and wages are mixed and the magnitude of the impacts are generally fairly modest. There is some evidence consistent with entrepreneurially motivated buyouts creating jobs. Recent employee-level evidence is most insightful, suggesting low-skilled workers are more likely to suffer job losses and high-skilled workers are more likely to experience wage gains.

Jelic, Wright, Murinde, and Ahmad review the theory and empirical evidence on longevity and post-exit performance (operating and financial (i.e., stock prices)) of MBOs and MBIs based on company-level (i.e., deal-level) rather than PE investor-level (fund) data. They treat PE-backed and non-PE (i.e., pure) buyouts separately, thus highlighting the importance of PE involvement in these transactions beyond changes brought forward by the adoption of buyout structures. They survey studies that examine all types, sources, and buyout exit routes, which covers IPO, strategic/trade sales, SBOs, and liquidations. As the market has evolved considerably over time, they compare early with more recent evidence on longevity and performance of buyouts exiting at the Alternative Investment Market (AIM) and the main London Stock Exchange (LSE).

Wilson examines the empirical evidence on the incidence of financial distress and bankruptcy among PE-backed buyouts and in comparison to buyouts without PE backing and non-buyouts. Studies of PE buyout activity are evaluated over a long time period and cover European economies, the US, and other countries. Financial distress (default on loans or bonds) and legally enforced bankruptcy are the outcomes considered. He shows that the majority of empirical studies find that PE-backed portfolio companies are no more prone to financial distress or bankruptcy than comparable companies. The active involvement of PE owners in strategic management that involves capital and operational investments in PE portfolio companies post-buyout increases their productivity and places portfolio companies on growth trajectories. When PE portfolio companies face stress due to high leverage and/or adverse economic conditions, the PE sponsors are proactive in negotiating resolutions to financial problems with creditors.

Overall assessment of the impact of PE and buyouts

In light of the hundreds of systematic studies reviewed in these chapters we pose a salient research question: What can we conclude about the impact of PE and buyouts? In essence, the key messages from these studies are as follows:

Funds returns

There is considerable debate concerning the conclusions to be drawn from academic studies of the performance of buyout funds. Some US evidence has shown that gross of fees, fund returns exceeded S&P 500 returns but did not when measured net of fees. After correcting for sample bias and overstated accounting values for non-exited investments, average fund performance also changed from slight overperformance to underperformance with respect to S&P 500. Recent studies have questioned the underperformance, but this depends on the use of the appropriate stock market benchmark since buyout funds generally invest in companies that are smaller than the S&P 500. However, there appears to be a declining trend over time as returns have been shown to be higher for buyout funds from the 1980s than those raised in the 1990s and 2000s. Top decile funds rather than top quartile funds had enduring outperformance. As the market matures, PE funds may be behaving in a similar manner to other asset classes and their excess returns are competed away. Major problems in assessing fund performance relate to the use of proprietary databases which may contain biases relating to the performance measures used, whether data have been updated, and whether they cover only part of the market.

Profitability and productivity

Extensive evidence shows improvements in profitability, although performance gains in deals in the second wave appear to be less than in the first wave especially for public-to-private deals. Enhanced profitability is significantly associated with operating gains and the specific expertise of PE firms.

Firm- and establishment-level studies show significant increases in total factor productivity after buyout (Lichtenberg & Siegel, 1990), with UK evidence showing that buyout plants shifted from underperforming their sector pre-buyout to outperforming subsequently (Harris et al., 2005).

Employment and employee relations

The impact of PE on jobs has been a highly contentious issue. Critics claim PE firms seek to cut costs to increase profitability and this cost-cutting involves job losses. In contrast, proponents argue that PE creates value by pursuing profitable growth strategies, which in turn create jobs.

The firm-level evidence is mixed with some studies reporting that PE involvement in the deal has no statistically significant impact on employment. Establishment-level data that accounts for job creation and destruction at establishment levels reveal that PE-backed buyouts are catalysts for a process of creative destruction not captured in firm-level studies.

Types of LBO deals and their source seem to impact employment effects. Employment tends to increase in MBOs (insider-driven deals) and declines in MBIs (outsider-driven deals). Post-IBO employment tends to fall, but these are typically deals involving larger firms, and the drop in employment could reflect subsequent restructuring post-deal. Employment growth tends to be higher in divisional buyouts, private-to-private deals, and SBOs compared to public-to-private buyouts and buyouts of firms in distress.

The impact of PE on jobs depends on the type of job and employee characteristics, with reductions being notable for nonproduction workers and employees performing offshorable job tasks, while production workers and those performing routine and less human capital-specific tasks tend to benefit.

Critics of PE-backed buyouts also argue that they lead to a deterioration of work conditions for employees, but systematic studies find little evidence to support such claims that employee and industrial relations practices such as training, job discretion, consultation, role of trade unions, etc. are negatively affected by buyout (Bacon et al., 2013).

Innovation, investment, entrepreneurship, and growth

Studies have shown that PE backing oftentimes results in an increase in new product development, although evidence on R&D expenditure is mixed. Studies of the impact on innovation tend to show an increase in the effectiveness of patenting activity, investment in information and communication technologies, and generally a release of financing constraints on such activity, although this last aspect seems to vary between countries and samples. These entrepreneurial activities are associated with new venture creation and subsequent growth in PE-backed buyouts.

Life cycle/longevity

While there has been much criticism that PE-backed buyouts essentially involve "stripping and flipping," that is divesting assets and exiting within a short time period, there is little systematic evidence to support this contention. Studies tend to show a heterogeneous time to exit by investors, with some firms remaining with a buyout structure for short periods while others retain the structure for quite long periods. Moreover, the mean time to exit appears to have been increasing since the financial crash. There has been a marked rise in SBOs (as well as third and fourth time buyouts), but the overall conclusion to be drawn from the available studies is that performance is at best mixed.

Critics also argue that PE-backed buyouts are more likely to fail or enter financial distress as a result of the high amounts of leverage taken on at the time of the deal. A number of studies have explored this issue and generally find that PE-backed buyouts are no more likely to enter financial distress or bankruptcy than other comparable companies. In part, this is due to the selection of firms that have strong cash flow to service the debt but also because PE investors are proactive in negotiating the resolution of distress with creditors. Evidence also suggests that the debt recovery rates of PE-backed buyouts that enter bankruptcy proceedings are greater than for non-buyouts.

Buyouts are heterogeneous and there is a need to appreciate that the nature of impact varies across different types.

Concluding comments: furthering the longevity of the research program

Each chapter in this book surveys the main themes relating to MBOs and PE and provides recommendations for further research in these areas. In this section, we provide some general observations regarding the longevity of the buyout and PE research program.

In a seminal article, published at the peak of the first buyout wave, Michael Jensen (1986) famously laid out the role of LBOs in the eclipse of the public corporation. Subsequent articles argued for the longevity of the public corporation (Rappaport, 1990). Jensen's analysis was quite specific about the kinds of corporations that would be appropriate for highly leveraged buyouts as a new long-term organizational form. Evidence subsequently suggested there were broadly two types of LBOs: short-lived shock therapy transactions and long-lived organizational forms (Kaplan, 1991; Wright et al., 1995). Although there has been a decline in the number of listed corporations, most notably in the US, it is hard to see this as solely the result of a paradigm shift towards buyouts and PE. Relatively few buyouts involve listed corporations and this focus has always provided a very partial view of the buyout and PE market.

More recently, at the peak of the second buyout wave, Cheffins and Armour (2008) were predicting the eclipse of PE. They conjectured that this would occur even if conditions were to remain favorable, suggesting that PE would likely be increasingly carried out by broadly based financial groups under the umbrella of public markets, including the importance of IPOs as an exit route. Basel 3, however, means that banks have had to deleverage and reduce their more risky activities. Therefore, universal banks have divested their PE operations. Also, while an IPO might be a useful exit route for large firms, "cold" IPO markets lead to greater use of SBOs and trade sales as exit routes (Jenkinson & Sousa, 2015). Further, many LBOs are of modest size, so the high costs of an IPO relative to other exit routes are likely to deter greater use of IPOs.

Rather than the eclipse of MBOs and PE, as foretold by Cheffins and Armour, the market has shown considerable resilience in its evolution of deal sources and structuring types since the late 1980s. The now substantial body of evidence relating to the impact of MBOs and PE has provided considerable support for agency theoretic explanations. However, evidence of a declining trend, if not elimination, of outperformance by the most recent funds and a dearth of primary deals raises questions about the sustainability of the market. Practitioners face major challenges regarding the future sources of deals and portfolio returns. Concerns regarding the continued generation of efficiency gains from agency cost reductions have seen practitioner searches for alternative means to create returns.

This has been accompanied by the academic development of complementary theoretical perspectives and hypotheses, notably based on entrepreneurship. Indeed, the complementarity of control and entrepreneurship enhancing perspectives was foreshadowed in one of the earliest articles on MBOs (Coyne & Wright, 1982), predating Jensen's approach. We would suggest that it is this complementarity that is enabling the extension of the buyout and PE research program (cf. O'Brien, 1976), rather than a focus only on controlling agency costs.

There remain a number of areas that warrant future attention. As noted earlier, the value of SBOs has recently exceeded primary deals in many markets. SBOs are an increasingly significant exit route and at the same time source of new deals that extends the longevity of the buyout governance structure, albeit with a different set of investors. Major questions remain to be answered regarding the ability of SBOs to sustain the market. SBOs are often motivated by managers under pressure to spend investors' cash and in these circumstances they may destroy value (Arcot et al., 2015; Degeorge et al., 2016). This could be a consequence of a more competitive PE market and/or a reduced number of good quality deals and/or lack of expertise by PE firms. This is not just a problem for investors, it is also a problem for portfolio firms that are subject to a change in ownership and restructuring to enable an initial investor to realize a financial return when there may be no clear economic gain from it. Indeed, it raises questions about the efficacy of these deals in the market for corporate control, because they are not necessarily allocating corporate resources to their best use. SBOs are more likely to create value if there is complementarity between GPs' experience and their portfolio firms. In particular there seem to be some benefits to portfolio firms if PE firms have industry experience (Degeorge et al., 2016) but especially if the human capital on the board of a particular portfolio company has financial and consultancy expertise to assist profitability and growth (Jelic et al., 2018). This suggests that as the industry continues to mature, we are increasingly likely to see PE firms having industry-focused portfolios. An argument advanced is that the new investors introduced in SBOs will have the expertise to enable the firm to grow through penetrating international markets. Although there is an extensive literature on exporting propensity and intensity by entrepreneurial firms (Wright et al., 2007), we lack analysis of such internationalization behavior by PE-backed buyouts and whether PE-backed buyouts differ from other firms in this respect. Many so-called SBOs are also in fact third or fourth time around deals, or more. Research is needed that explores both the characteristics and performance of these multiple times buyouts. For example, to what extent do consecutive deals simply involve a continuation of previous strategies, or efforts to be more entrepreneurial or perhaps turnarounds of struggling firms whose once stable niches are being eroded?

Although recent years have seen significant fund raising by PE firms, downward pressure on returns may in future mean that PE firms face reduced cash investment from certain investors that used PE firms as a third-party service. Pension funds and sovereign wealth funds both use PE as a risky asset in their portfolio of investments. Increasingly, these institutions are making direct investments in their own portfolio firms (Wright & Amess, 2017). For these institutions it has the advantages of avoiding PE firms' management fees, and the institutions can make their own decisions on suitable targets. In some cases they are passive investors, but in other cases they also act as active investors. Where this involves change in management and restructuring, an area is opening up for research to explore changes in portfolio firm performance and other aspects of firm behavior.

Finally, PE firms conduct due diligence on senior executives in a buyout in order to ensure their suitability for managing a portfolio firm and their compatibility for working with GPs. In addition, prior theoretical research has acknowledged the importance of an entrepreneurial mind set. The empirical literature has been slower to address these practical and theoretical issues. Research analyzing the methods PE firms employ in their due diligence of managers involved in buyouts would greatly enhance our understanding of this process, and analysis of their effectiveness would provide novel insights. In addition, assessments of psychological characteristics of managers involved in deals would help us understand better their motivations for being involved in deals and help identify those individual characteristics associated with successful deals.

References

Arcot, S., Fluck, Z., Gaspar, J.-M., & Hege, U. 2015. Fund managers under pressure: Rationale and determinants of secondary buyouts. *Journal of Financial Economics*, 115: 102–135.

Arnfield, R., Chiplin, B., Jarrett, M., & Wright, M. (eds.). 1981. *Management buy-outs: Corporate trend for the '80's? Proceedings of the first national conference on management buy-outs*. University of Nottingham Industrial and Business Liaison Office.

Bacon, N. Wright, M., Ball, R., & Meuleman, M. 2013. Private equity, HRM, and employment. *Academy of Management Perspectives*, 27: 7–21.

Bank of England. 2013. *Quarterly Bulletin*. www.bankofengland.co.uk/publications/Documents/quarterlybulletin/2013/qb130104.ppdf.

Bebchuk, L. A., & Fried, J. M. 2006. Pay without performance: Overview of the issues. *Academy of Management Perspectives*, 20: 5–24.

Boucly, Q., Sraer, D., & Thesmar, D. 2011. Growth LBOs. *Journal of Financial Economics*, 102: 432–453.

Bruner, R. F., & Paine, L. S. 1988. Management buyouts and managerial ethics. *California Management Review*, 30: 89–106.

Burrough, B., & Helyar, J. 1989. *Barbarians at the gate: The fall of RJR Nabisco*. New York: Harper & Row.

Cheffins, B., & Armour, J. 2008. The eclipse of private equity. *Delaware Journal of Corporate Law*, 33: 1–67.

Chiplin, B., & Wright, M. 1980. Divestment and structural change in UK industry. *Nat West Bank Review*, February.

CMBOR. 1990. *UK management buyouts*. CMBOR: Nottingham University Business School.

CMBOR. 1993. *UK management buyouts*. CMBOR: Nottingham University Business School.

CMBOR. 2018. *European buyouts report: Full year 2017*. CMBOR: Imperial College Business School London.

Coyne, J., & Wright, M. 1982. Buyouts and British industry. *Lloyds Bank Review*, 146: 15–31.

Degeorge, F, Martin, J., & Phalippou, L. 2016. On secondary buyouts. *Journal of Financial Economics*, 120: 124–145.

Faludi, S. 1999. *Stiffed: The betrayal of the American man*. New York: Harper Collins.

Fox, I., & Marcus, A. 1992. The causes and consequences of leveraged management buyouts. *Academy of Management Review*, 17: 62–85.

Franks, J., & Mayer, C. 1996. Hostile takeovers and the correction of managerial failure. *Journal of Financial Economics*, 40: 163–181.

Harris, R., Siegel, D. S., & Wright, M. 2005. Assessing the impact of management buyouts on economic efficiency: Plant-level evidence from the United Kingdom. *The Review of Economics and Statistics*, 87(1): 148–153.

Hill, C. W. L., 1988. Internal capital market controls and financial performance in multidivisional firms. *Journal of Industrial Economics*, 37: 67–83.

Jelic, R., Zhou, D., & Wright, M. 2018. Sustaining the buyout governance model: Inside secondary management buyout boards. *British Journal of Management*, forthcoming.

Jenkinson, T., & Sousa, M. 2015. What determines the exit decision for leveraged buyouts? *Journal of Banking & Finance*, 59: 399–408.

Jensen, M. C. 1986. Agency costs of free cash flow, corporate finance and takeover. *American Economic Review*, 76: 323–329.

Jensen, M. C., & Meckling, W. H. 1976. Theory of the firm: managerial behavior, agency costs and ownership structure. *Journal of Financial Economics*, 3: 305–360.

Kaplan, S. 1991. The staying power of leveraged buyouts. *Journal of Financial Economics*, 29: 287–314.

Kaplan, S. N., & Strömberg, P. 2009. Leveraged buyouts and private equity. *Journal of Economic Perspectives*, 23: 121–146.

Lee, D. S. 1992. Management buyout proposals and inside information. *Journal of Finance*, 47: 1061–1080.

Leyland, A. 2012. Glenn to run Birds Eye 'whoever owns us'. *The Grocer*. Available at: www.thegrocer.co.uk/companies/suppliers/glenn-to-run-birds-eye-whoever-owns-us/227865.article#.

Lichtenberg, F., & Siegel, D. 1990. The effect of leveraged buyouts on productivity and related aspects of firm behaviour. *Journal of Financial Economics*, 27(1): 165–194.

Loihl, A., & Wright, M. 2002. *Seagate technology case*. CMBOR, Nottingham University Business School.

Mulley, C., & Wright, M. 1986. Management buyouts and the privatization of National Bus. *Fiscal Studies*, 7: 1–24.

O'Brien, D. 1976. The longevity of Adam Smith's vision: Paradigms, research programmes and falsifiability in the history of economic thought. *Scottish Journal of Political Economy*, 2J: 133–151.

Rappaport, A. 1990. The staying power of the public corporation. *Harvard Business Review*, 68(1): 96–104.

Robbie, K., & Wright, M. 2008. Local authorities, compulsory competitive tendering and buy-outs. *Local Government Studies*, 22: 127–146.
Shleifer, A., & Summers, L. H. 1988. Breach of trust in hostile takeovers. In A. J. Auerbach (Ed.) *Corporate Takeovers: Causes and Consequences*, Chicago, IL: University of Chicago Press.
Thompson, S., & Wright, M. 1995. Corporate governance: The role of restructuring transactions. *Economic Journal*, 105: 690–703.
Thompson, S., Wright, M., & Robbie, K. 1990. Management buy-outs and privatisation: Organisational form and incentive issues. *Fiscal Studies*, 11: 71–88.
Toms, S., & Wright, M. 2002. Corporate governance, strategy and structure in British business history, 1950–2000. *Business History*, 44: 91–124.
Williamson, O. E. 1985. *The economic institutions of capitalism: Firms, markets and relational contracting*. New York: Free Press.
Williamson, O. E. 1988. Corporate finance and corporate governance. *Journal of Finance*, 43: 467–491.
Wood, G., & Wright, M. 2010. Private equity and human resource management: An emerging agenda. *Human Relations*, 63: 1279–1296.
Wright, M. 1986. The make-buy decision and managing markets: The case of management buy-outs. *Journal of Management Studies*, 23: 434–453.
Wright, M. (ed). 1994. *Technical note on management and employee buy-outs in central and eastern Europe*. EBRD/CEEPN, January.
Wright, M. 2013. *The Centre for Management Buyout Research (CMBOR); Providing an evidence-based platform to inform private equity policy and practice*. REF 2014 Impact Case Study.
Wright, M., & Amess, K. 2017. SWF and private equity. In G. Wood, D. Cumming, & I. Filatotchev (Eds.), *Oxford handbook of sovereign wealth funds*, Oxford, UK: Oxford University Press.
Wright, M., Chiplin, B., Robbie, K., & Albrighton, M. 2000. The development of an organisational innovation: Management buy-outs in the UK 1980–1997. *Business History*, 42: 137–184.
Wright, M., & Coyne, J. 1985/2018. *Management buyouts*. Beckenham, UK: Croom Helm.
Wright, M., Hoskisson, R., & Busenitz, L. 2001. Firm rebirth: Buyouts as facilitators of strategic growth and entrepreneurship. *Academy of Management Executive*, 15: 111–125.
Wright, M., Hoskisson, R., Busenitz, L., & Dial, J. 2000. Entrepreneurial growth through privatization: The upside of management buyouts. *Academy of Management Review*, 25: 591–601.
Wright, M., Thompson, S., Robbie, K., & Wong, P. 1995. Management buy-outs in the short and long term. *Journal of Business Finance and Accounting*, 22: 461–482.
Wright, M., Westhead, P., & Ucbasaran, D. 2007. Internationalisation by SMEs: A critique and policy implications. *Regional Studies*, 41: 1013–1030.
Zahra, S. A., 1995. Corporate entrepreneurship and financial performance: The case of management leveraged buyouts. *Journal of Business Venturing*, 10: 225–247.

PART I

Historical, legal, and regulatory issues

2

A BRIEF HISTORY OF PRIVATE EQUITY[1]

John Gilligan

Introduction

This chapter looks at some of the ups and downs of the private equity (PE) industry since the late 1980s. It examines the industry from a practitioner's perspective. Prior to the foundation of CMBOR no comprehensive deal-level databases existed. Today there are competing commercial databases at the transaction, fund, and fund manager levels. This emergence of greater data availability, and the limitations of some of those data sources, explains why the timeline of academic research does not always align with the timeline of an industry practitioner. Those who work within the industry often undertake analysis that is unpublished but significantly pre-dates the peer-reviewed academic equivalents. The author of this chapter, for example, was diligently working through the investment cash flows of all of 3i's portfolio by vintage in 1989, as no doubt many others were elsewhere, long before the data that enabled similar academic work to be undertaken.

While there have always been equity investments made outside the public markets (see Toms, Chapter 3 this volume), PE as we understand the term today, emerged in the 1980s from, broadly, two pre-existing pools of funds: venture capital and development capital. Venture capital provides equity capital to early and emerging businesses. Development capital provides equity capital to expand existing businesses. The term private equity was adopted from the late 1980s. Before then it was more common to hear institutions refer to themselves as venture capitalists in the UK and leveraged buyout firms in the US.

1960s and 1970s asset stripping

In the late 1960s and 1970s corporate raiders sought out companies with undervalued assets (Toms et al., 2016). They scoured the markets for businesses that had saleable assets that were greater in value than it would cost to buy the company. They then bought the businesses, often using debt secured on the assets of the target company. Prior to the transaction the banks would have no security, but immediately on gaining control, the purchaser would give the banks security for the acquisition finance. Having bought the company, they would then close all or part of the business down and sell the assets and any viable businesses at a profit. They repaid the debt and kept the excess. This generated very high returns on equity but also left the unsecured creditors and employees to suffer losses.

1970s ban on financial assistance

In the 1970s in most developed countries it became illegal to use the assets of a target company to offer security to a lender to a bidder for that company. Under the new laws a bidding company could not promise to give security on assets that it did not own; neither could a target company give any other financial assistance to help in the purchase of its own shares. This was specifically designed to stop the asset stripping that had been seen in the late 1960s and 1970s. The idea was to deter corporate raiders by dramatically reducing the availability of debt. You could still buy undervalued companies, but you had to use equity to do so. The financial assistance prohibition effectively made it a criminal offence to asset strip companies in most countries.

1980s relaxing regulation to facilitate the rescue of companies

An unintended consequence of the legislation was that it prevented the rescue of viable companies. In the recession of the 1970s and early 1980s many struggling conglomerates had viable subsidiaries that could be rescued as standalone businesses. However, these subsidiaries could not provide security to a purchaser's bank, even if that bank was happy to lend money to help acquire and rescue a business.

To reverse this unintended prohibition, and to encourage the rescue of viable businesses, a change was made to the law in a number of countries. These changes allowed companies to give financial assistance under certain tightly controlled circumstances. In the UK it was provided in the Companies Act 1981.

The new law on financial assistance broadly required the directors to make a statutory declaration that, as far as they knew at the completion date of the transaction, the company would be solvent for the next 12 months. If they made the declaration knowing it to be untrue, it was a criminal offence.

This created a procedure whereby the company's auditors reviewed the business plan and signed a report confirming broadly that, as far as they could tell at that time, it was reasonable for a director to say that the company looked as if it would be solvent for at least a year.

1980s first buyout boom

This legal change allowed leverage, or gearing, back into the buyout market. Following the change on financial assistance in most jurisdictions, the number of buyouts grew rapidly. Initially growth was seen in the US whereas in Europe the market was overwhelmingly dominated by the UK. By the mid-1980s, 3i, which at that time was jointly owned by the Bank of England and the major clearing banks, had an overwhelmingly strong position in the UK (Toms et al., 2016). Other early UK participants were subsidiaries of banks that had historically focused on development capital and other financial investors with a background in venture capital. These were the so-called "captive" investors.

"Hands-off, eyes-on"

Virtually all early UK funds were generalist investors who had skills in financial engineering and transactions but had little hands-on management input. Investors monitored their investments, but the underlying philosophy was to passively back management to manage. At this stage of the industry it was quite rare for funds to have a formal board position in investee companies. It was more common to have observer rights rather than a formal board seat.

Sources of deals

In the early incarnation of the PE market it was usually the management who sought to "do a buyout." Buyouts were pretty much synonymous with MBOs, where a management team sought support to negotiate to acquire the business they ran. Deals came from three major sources: subsidiaries of larger companies, succession in family companies, and insolvency. There were very few public-to-private transactions ("P2P"s) in Europe in the first wave of buyouts.

In contrast the US saw more P2P activity, especially in larger businesses. This reflected both the amount of available funds in the US vs the rest of the world, and the technical requirements of the London Stock Exchange compared to the New York Stock Exchange. There was more money and it was easier to do P2Ps in the US.

Mid-1980s: new entrants

The returns earned by the early buyout investors, although somewhat opaque, were generally perceived to be very good. For example, a series of studies of 3i's portfolio found that buyouts completed in 1986 had generated a gross IRR of 33.1% by 1992, compared to an overall portfolio IRR over the same period of 19.3%. This led to a growth in the funds committed by existing investors and to the emergence of new funds raised by groups of investors who wished to enter the market. In the UK many of these funds' founder managers were from the relatively small pool of experienced investors; often they were ex-3i executives or accountants. In the US they tended to be from consultancy and investment banking backgrounds.

Taxation and limited liability partnerships

One of the practical issues in raising non-captive PE funds was to find a way to avoid double taxation that didn't create other complex liabilities. Tax is paid by people, companies, and other organizations that have a "tax identity." That is to say they are a discrete taxable thing. If the new funds were established as limited companies, they would have been taxable and then the shareholders would have been taxed again on their distributions.

However, many investors in the funds were exempt from paying some taxes, particularly capital gains tax. Therefore, the industry needed to find a structure that would protect the tax exemption of its investors. If it could not, the returns would be materially lower than directly investing elsewhere.

A solution in the UK was to use an old structure that had been developed to allow temporary partnerships with a limited lifetime, imaginatively known as the "limited life partnership." A limited life partnership is a temporary arrangement and the partners are taxed individually, not collectively. Because of this it is described as being transparent for tax purposes. The tax authorities look straight through the partnership and tax each partner depending on their individual circumstances. One problem that arose with the structure was the fact that the managers and founders of the PE business could be deemed to be earning income, not capital gains. In the 1980s income tax and capital gains tax were taxed at the same rate. There were, however, allowances, called taper reliefs, that both protected individuals from being taxed for inflationary increases in value and also encouraged people to invest in building businesses. To protect those reliefs in both the UK and US it was formally agreed by the tax authorities that carried interest, the share in capital gains that goes to the fund manager, would be taxed as capital gain not income. This later became, and remains, controversial.

In the US and elsewhere similar structural solutions were designed to facilitate creating tax transparent investment vehicles with a limited life. The availability of these structures was a key enabling factor (or impediment in the case of, for example, Australia) in the growth of independent PE funds.

1989: mega deals V1.0

In the US two factors enabled the market to expand rapidly: first, a market for subprime "junk" bonds was created. This enabled investors to issue high yield debt in the public market to fund acquisitions. Second, the early funds generated returns that were widely held to be outperforming the market. This led to ever larger equity funds being raised, capable of doing ever larger deals. The peak of the market was the iconic buyout of RJR Nabisco in 1988 for approximately $23bn.

Due to the relatively smaller size of the European funds, the capacity of the European buyout market was limited and in consequence many transactions were syndicated between equity investors. To put the scale of the industry into context, a large European buyout during this period was generally defined as one in excess of £10m; in the current market it might be defined as perhaps £0.5bn–£1bn or thereabouts. At the end of the 1980s, the largest deal in Europe was the 1989 Isosceles buyout of Gateway Supermarkets for £2.2bn.

Captives versus independents

By the end of the first wave of buyouts in the 1980s, the industry was characterized by a split between so-called "captive funds" that were owned by a large corporate parent and the independent firms that had taken the partnership form that we see as the commonest structure today, plus, in Europe, 3i.

Yield versus capital gain

Captive funds and 3i tended to be longer-term holders of an investment (compared to current structures) without any explicit exit policy. To compensate for this flexibility, they required a higher yield from their investments than the funds with an explicit exit horizon. Independent firms were generally structured as 10-year funds (as we see today) and therefore were more focused on generating capital gains with a defined exit policy and had lower yield requirements. There was therefore something of a trade-off of yield versus exit flexibility. Long-term investors charged higher interest rates on loans and had a need for an ongoing dividend yield. Those focused on exit would forgo the yield in the short term but have either penal rates to encourage sale after five to seven years, or an explicit agreement to pursue a sale before a given date.

Short-term or long-term investors?

Critics say that PE is short term, because closed-end funds have an explicit exit horizon of somewhere between three and seven years. Advocates say that PE investing is long term because the funds are usually at least 10-year commitments and have an option to extend for two more years in most cases. In a sense both are correct. To each individual company,

PE can be (but doesn't have to be) a short-term transition from one ownership to another (evidence on the longevity of PE-backed buyout transactions is presented by Jelic et al. in Chapter 27 this volume). Conversely to the fund managers and investors it is a very long-term commitment to the broad portfolio of illiquid investments.

As long as IRR is used as a measure of investment performance, the pressure to act quickly is intense. IRRs are very sensitive to time, especially when the returns are high.

1990s blow up and buyouts of captive funds

Following the impact of the recession of the early 1990s and high interest rates, many leveraged investments struggled or failed. Appetite to support in-house captive PE declined. This led many of the captive funds to be bought out from their parent companies by their partners. The symbolic importance of PE funds "doing their own buyouts" was a very common refrain heard during this period. In this limited sense the partners of many PE fund managers have taken the risks and earned the rewards of a manager in a buyout.

Virtually all these firms rebranded themselves as PE or buyout firms and abandoned any pretension to venture capital activities (Table 2.1).

Table 2.1 Selected UK PE firms and their predecessors

Name of firm	*Predecessor firm*	*Type of predecessor*
Permira	Schroder Ventures	UK parent captive
Bridgepoint	Nat West Equity Partners	UK parent captive
Equistone	Barclays Private Equity	UK parent captive
Montagu PE	HSBC Private Equity	UK parent captive
August Equity	Kleinwort Benson Development Capital	UK parent captive
Apax Partners	Alan Patricoff Associates (Europe)	US affiliate independent
Graphite Capital	Foreign & Colonial Ventures	UK parent captive
Hg Capital	Mercury Asset Managment	UK parent captive
Duke Street Capital	Hambro European Ventures	UK parent captive
Silverfleet	PPM Ventures	UK parent captive
Livingbridge	Ivory & Sime Development Capital	UK parent captive
Matrix PE	Greater London Enterprise	Public sector pension fund manager
IRRfc	Phildrew Ventures	Swiss parent captive
BC Partners	Baring Capital Partners	UK parent captive
CVC Capital Partners	Citicorp Venture Capital (Europe)	US parent captive
Cinven	Coal Board Investment Managers Venture Capital	Public sector pension fund manager
3i Group	Industrial and Commercial Finance Corporation	Bank and public joint venture
Terra Firma	Nomura Principal Finance Group	Japanese parent captive
Charterhouse Capital	Charterhouse Development Capital	UK parent captive

Source: Gilligan and Wright, 2014.

It is important to understand that the buyouts of PE funds were buyouts of the fund management companies, not purchases of the portfolios of investments. In a typical transaction the parent would retain ownership of the existing portfolio and grant a management contract to the fund managers. The manager would then raise a new fund, often with the assistance of their former parent as a cornerstone investor, creating so-called semi-captives.

Double taxation, interest deductibility, and "loop holes"

There has been a long-running discussion about taxation and interest. It is argued that because interest costs are deductible against corporation tax, then debt is subsidized when compared to equity. The argument then goes on to state that this subsidy can account for the observed performance of highly leveraged firms. The argument is flawed in a number of serious ways.

First, not all interest is deductible in companies' tax accounts. If loans are from connected parties (broadly shareholders) and are not on commercial terms, the interest is simply not deductible. This has been the case since the early 1990s and specifically targeted shareholder loans in PE.

Second, interest deductibility is not a subsidy any more than deducting the costs of stamps or chairs or telephones against tax is a subsidy. Taxation is levied on a company's profits. For a trading company interest is a cost. For a bank it is a revenue. Bank's profits are taxed and these include interest receivable from trading companies. Therefore, banks price the taxation of interest into the price of debt. Interest rates reflect the after tax returns required by banks. So, just as the Royal Mail, IKEA, or British Telecom are taxed on the profits of stamps, chairs, and phones, so banks are taxed on the profits from interest. There is absolutely no difference. If the costs of debt were not allowable, double taxation would result: taxing once in the profits of the borrowing company (by increasing its taxable profit by adding back interest) and then again in the profits of the lending company that receives the interest.

Avoiding double taxation is one of the key drivers of the complex structures that are seen in PE funds and individual deals. Of course there is no sharp distinction between legally minimizing double taxation and legally minimizing taxation generally. But it is important to understand that taxation is far from simple and straightforward, not because of incompetence or conspiracy on anyone's part, but because it necessarily has to be complex to avoid creating loopholes and inequitable double taxation. Tax laws have consistently moved against PE funds since the late 1990s, becoming progressively tighter, not, as the public discourse might lead one to believe, becoming weaker.

Early secondary transactions

The existing portfolio of these businesses was often sold in a separate transaction to a new type of PE investor: a secondary fund. These secondaries involving an entire fund are not to be confused with secondary buyouts involving a particular portfolio company. The early secondary deals often involved selling underperforming assets at a discount. In some cases particular circumstances created large secondary transactions. When RBS successfully bid for Nat West Bank in 2000, the PE management division of Nat West was sold to its management, becoming Bridgepoint, and its portfolio was separately sold to Coller Capital Partners, an independent fund manager with an early focus on these secondary deals.

In recent years, secondary transactions have grown in importance and frequency and they are reshaping the way that the PE market operates.

Hands-on investors and sector specialization

Back in the mainstream deal market, competition for transactions increased and the need to generate value in individual investments increased. This led to a variety of strategies aimed at increasing the success rate and the value of each success to funds. Investors generally became much more active in the management of each individual investment. Many investors began to focus on specific industries and sectors to gain an advantage over the generalist investors. Today most firms have a sector bias and an active investment style.

Deal initiation, proprietary deal flow, and the death of the MBO

As the market became more competitive, funds became increasingly proactive in initiating transactions rather than passively responding to management teams and their advisers. It became common for PE funds (and advisers) to actively seek out management teams where there was a perception that a buyout could occur. The holy grail of PE deal flow became so-called proprietary deal flow: potential transactions the fund owned in some sense and was therefore able to negotiate free from the threat of competition.

This ultimately led to a sharp fall in the number of pure management led MBOs. They were replaced by either institutionally led deals (IBOs) or transactions led by external management (MBIs) or some blend of the two.

Globalization and the growth of global mega-funds

In the late 1990s and after the turn of the century the market began to bifurcate: the largest PE funds became increasingly international in their outlook, while in the mid-market the businesses became more focused on specific sectors or types of business. The trend in globalization led to a huge growth in the number of non-UK investors based in London seeking UK and European transactions.

The largest PE funds, particularly but not exclusively in the US, increasingly diversified away from pure PE. Many opened debt funds, infrastructure funds, and a wide array of other alternative asset funds. They effectively morphed from pure PE into multi-asset managers.

2005–2007: boom

The prolonged period of economic growth with low inflation from the mid-1990s to the 2008 financial crisis was characterized by: ever larger funds, larger deals, greater complexity in structures, greater leverage, and an explosion in the size of PE as a global industry. It was still a poorly understood, little reported industry and operated from a number of unregulated jurisdictions, often for entirely innocuous reasons to do with the availability of easy to use legal structures and confidentiality concerns about the identity of the investors in the fund. As PE funds competed for investment mandates, making public who the investors in a fund were was inviting competitors to approach funders when that commitment was expiring.

The debt markets also metamorphosed, and banks that had previously held loans on their own balance sheets, sold them into the wholesale market. They ceased to earn the majority of their income from net interest payments and became fee-earning businesses that parceled up loans to be sold on to other financial institutions.

Innovation in the debt markets led to the emergence of markets in new forms of derivatives. Most of these instruments were designed to allow risk to be traded. This has always been one of the functions of derivatives, but when they were stripped from their underlying loans, they became tradable assets creating some perverse, unintended incentives.

New businesses emerged that mimicked the use of leverage seen in PE financial structures in individual investments but without certain controls that operate in the traditional fund structures: they created leveraged funds to make leveraged investments, doubling up the risks and apparent rewards. This was at the heart of the so-called Icelandic model that was most widely associated with the highly acquisitive Baugur group.

2007–2008: bust

By 2007 the wholesale debt markets were opaque and poorly understood by most. There was an implicit assumption that there was an available appetite for debt in the global market that was effectively infinite or unlimited. This allowed banking institutions to fund themselves using facilities that were renewed continuously in the highly liquid debt markets. When the default rates on US mortgages turned out to be higher than expected, it was unclear who was holding the associated risk. In the absence of any clear information about who was going to be making losses, banks and institutions started to hold on to all the cash that was available to them and reduced or stopped lending to the wholesale markets. This meant that wholesale credit dried up and banks reliant on renewing facilities were unable to refinance and became insolvent. Initially smaller banks struggled and failed, but as the scale of the confusion spread, the world's largest institutions turned to governments to provide capital and guarantees. In the case of Lehman Brothers, the US government declined to rescue them and the investment bank failed.

The impact on the PE market was abrupt and precipitous. Banks needed to hold cash rather than to generate lending. Deal volumes, which are reliant on leverage, collapsed. The largest deals were the worst affected.

Those who had used debt within their fund structures rapidly faced insolvency as there was a mismatch between the dates they were expecting to realize their investments and the date that their borrowings were repayable.

LP and GP unfunded commitments

If an individual investor in a PE fund cannot fund its commitments to the fund, it faces very harsh penalties. There is therefore a very strong incentive to ensure that commitments are funded. When institutions started to fail, some of their commitments to PE funds were exposed to the risk of being unfunded. HBOS was, for example, a major investor in the UK mid-market PE funds. To avoid crystalizing losses on these exposures there was a flurry of secondary transactions including unfunded commitments. This gave a significant boost to the secondary market for PE funds.

In the case of Candover, one of the largest UK PE funds, it had a particular structure that caused the fund to cease to make new investments. Other funds who had partners that could not fund their commitments had to renegotiate or scale back their funds.

The restructuring of the industry was significant but largely unreported at the time. Importantly it had limited impact on the prospects of the underlying businesses that were in PE portfolios.

2009–2012: hangover

The aftermath of the financial crisis showed both the strengths and weaknesses in the PE model. On the positive side of the balance, the traditional "10+2" (10-year fund with a possible 2-year extension) fund generally did not have any debt and therefore could not become insolvent and did not fail; it was bankrupt remote. Neither could it spread risk through financial markets because the whole risk fell on its partners. This is an important and little publicized fact: PE fund structures in a limited way stopped the creation of systemic risk (Gilligan & Wright, 2014).

However, perverse situations arose between fund managers and their partners. Many funds had raised billions of dollars prior to the crash on the assumption that leverage would be available to support deals. They found themselves charging fees on capital that would be unlikely to be deployed. Investors were understandably unhappy.

The period of extremely low interest rates that followed the crisis prevented the feared collapse of many companies with high levels of borrowings, including buyouts and other PE investments. Had the recession been accompanied by high interest rates, the failure rate would certainly have been materially higher, in all types of business.

2012–2016: recovery

The PE industry adjusts slowly to any crisis. Some funds went into terminal decline, unable to raise new funds and managing out their portfolios motivated by a mix of maintaining fee income and hoping for carried interest to move into positive territories. Others who fared better sought to take advantage of downward pressure on asset prices to buy at the bottom of the cycle, hoping to profit on the upturn.

New organizational models with operating partners and in-house consultancies emerged that embedded active management methodologies into a fund's organization, moving ever further away from the old model of passively backing incumbent management to buy the businesses they run.

Today

As we write a 30th anniversary book of CMBOR, the industry continues to mature, morph, and consolidate. Global PE firms have been created based in both the US and Europe. These started in large buyouts, but global mid-market firms are emerging, in this case mainly led by the US.

If a Martian were to land in the financial markets today, many firms that we know as PE investors would look more like diversified fund managers with a taste for long-term illiquid assets, but with a range of other asset classes in the mix. The simple alignment model of backing managers to buy their companies and paying the deal leaders on success has largely disappeared in these emerging financial behemoths. Multiple fees have replaced carried interest as the primary source of the incentives in some large PE firms.

Returns and the level of analysis

Returns can be calculated at the level of the individual firm invested in, at the fund level, or at the level of the investors and fund managers.

At the firm level, the evidence is extensive and well researched (Kaplan & Schaor, 2005; Wright et al., 2009; Wilson et al., 2012; Harris et al., 2014). There is a wider array of outcomes than in the broad population of companies. PE investment increases the variance of returns, which is unsurprising as gearing or leverage is so-called because it amplifies returns. In addition to increasing the variance, there is also incomplete but strong evidence that PE investment increases the average return. The evidence on risks is not globally available, but in the massive piece of research on the question in the UK undertaken at CMBOR, there was no evidence that failure rates were systematically higher in PE-backed companies (see Wilson, Chapter 28 this volume). So, at the company level, the tentative conclusion is higher returns, more variation in returns, but not higher failures.

At the fund level returns are usually measured as IRRs and multiples of funds invested. This makes perfect sense for a fund that draws down as it needs to and repays when it can. If you calculate fund IRRs and values per dollar invested, you generally find that PE funds perform favorably when compared with public markets (and most other similar measures).

At the investor level there is, however, an issue (Long, 2008). PE funds require their investors to be ready at short notice to provide large amounts of cash. Therefore, if you invest in a PE fund you need to manage your treasury function in a way that ensures you can pay your share when needed (Meads, 2016). PE funds therefore benefit from not having to manage the treasury function themselves. If they drew down all the cash committed by investors and put it in their own treasury function, the IRR received by the investors would be much lower, reflecting the early cash investment and the lower return earned before the funds are invested. In effect, PE funds receive guarantees of funding that not only do they not pay for, but for which they charge fees to the guarantors over the life of the guarantee.

To address this anomaly, a number of methods of varying complexity have been developed to make PE fund performance comparable with other fund types. These adjustments work on a variation of the idea that when assessing a PE fund's contribution to a broader portfolio, a fund manager needs to include the opportunity cost of the capital that is set aside to fund capital draw downs. Once these calculations are made, the clear outperformance of funds disappears. What this suggests is that while PE funds do create significant value, much of that value is appropriated by the fund managers once the whole commitment is considered.

This recognition has led to pressure on fees and carried interest and led to the re-emergence of co-investment.

Co-investment

Co-investment has increased in recent years and is when a fund investor (an LP) invests further monies in a transaction alongside the PE fund on the same terms as the fund. The advantage to the co-investor is that they don't pay fees or carried interest on the portion directly invested outside the fund. This is presented in many different ways in the industry, but the economics are very clear. Co-investing reduces the cost of investing in PE funds. At the extreme, the investors could shrink fund sizes and increase co-investment sizes such that the industry reverts to LPs having on-balance sheet direct investing facilitated by small fund managers rewarded by performance. Alternatively, the so-called Canadian model may prevail. A number of Canadian pension funds have started to direct invest rather than investing in funds.

Conclusions

First we had small groups of people doing deals on behalf of their parent companies paid by bonuses based on capital gains. These grew too big for their parents who sold them off to buyouts. Freed of their parent company's capital constraints, the PE industry grew rapidly propelled by the rumors and glimpses of returns that seemed to outperform other fund types systematically. As more data and research was completed, the question became much more nuanced and larger investors started to assert themselves. PE being full of imaginative people has ridden these waves and metamorphosed from a small niche activity to a vast global industry supporting many thousands both within the industry and within the many thousands of businesses that it invests in.

There are always new structures emerging to tweak the PE model. However, as long as PE funds remain long term, ungeared, active investors in unquoted companies, the industry is performing a valuable service to the economy that no other sector has been capable of doing. Whether the rewards of that service are equitably shared, is an open question.

Note

1 This chapter was adapted by the author with additional material from J Gilligan and M Wright. *Private equity demystified*. ICAEW 2014.

References

Gilligan, J., & Wright, M. 2014. *Private equity demystified*. 3rd edition. London: ICAEW.

Harris, R. S., Jenkinson, T., & Kaplan, S. 2014. Private equity performance: What do we know? *The Journal of Finance*, 69: 1851–1882.

Kaplan, S. N., & Schaor, A. 2005. Private equity performance: Returns, persistence, and capital flows. *The Journal of Finance*, 60: 1791–1823.

Long, A. M. 2008. *The common mathematical foundation of ACG's ICM and AICM and the K&S PME*. Unpublished. Available at: www.j-curve.com/research/files/ACG%20ICM%20vs%20PME%20Jan%202008.pdf.

Meads, C. M. N. 2016. Cash management strategies for private equity investors. *Alternative Investment Analyst Review*, 31–42.

Toms, S., Wilson, N., & Wright, M. 2016. The evolution of private equity: Corporate restructuring in the UK, c.1945–2010. *Business History*, 57: 736–768.

Wilson, N., Wright, M., Siegel, D., & Scholes, L. 2012. Private equity portfolio company performance during the global recession. *Journal of Corporate Finance*, 12: 193–205.

Wright, M., Gilligan, J., & Amess, K. 2009. The economic impact of private equity: What we know and what we would like to know. *Venture Capital*, 11: 1–21.

3

MANAGEMENT BUYOUTS

The history of an organizational innovation

Steven Toms

Introduction

The sources of finance invested in growth sectors have long influenced the character of UK industry and indeed industries that have emerged and developed in many international contexts. Venture capital has a long history in the provision of growth finance and finance for restructuring in the UK (Wright et al., 2000; Toms et al., 2016). Even in such a long-run perspective, the buyout wave of the 1970s that began in the UK and the US and spread rapidly internationally, was nonetheless a revolutionary development. The parallel emergence of private equity (PE) (see Gilligan, Chapter 2 this volume) underpinned new opportunities for entrepreneurial groups of managers to restructure their businesses and enhance performance. That such developments might seem revolutionary, or even surprising, requires some contextual understanding of the evolution of finance for industry up to 1970.

The corporatization of a substantial number of economic sectors, particularly after 1945 and culminating in the wave of corporate takeovers in the 1960s, created a landscape dominated by powerful conglomerates. There were observable negative consequences. There was talk of the demise of the entrepreneur. Stock markets meanwhile attributed discounts to conglomerates, suggesting that they had become unwieldy and over-diversified. All of this developed against a backdrop of intensifying global competition that challenged the dominance of US, UK and European businesses in a number of markets.

In short, conditions were ripe for the emergence of the MBO/PE model by 1975. But when and why had the demise of the entrepreneur occurred, or at least, how was their function apparently subsumed by the corporate model? And what processes led to the over-diversification of the big corporates, and how and why were the smaller businesses that did not become divisions of bigger firms starved of the finance they needed for restructuring and expansion?

The chapter will provide answers to these questions, tracing the character of UK entrepreneurial finance over the long run. In doing so, it considers some early cases of venture capital and buyouts, not hitherto classified as such or considered in the literature. It will identify the reasons for the emergence of a financing gap for growing businesses that was eventually filled by the MBO/PE wave post 1980s. In doing so it will examine differences between the UK and US application of the buyout model. It will then reconsider recent trends in business finance before and after the global financial crisis of 2007 in the context of longer-run patterns in financing. It will conclude with a discussion of the overall contribution of MBOs to economic development and briefly look ahead to consider future challenges.

Entrepreneurial finance, c.1770–1975

The earliest innovators of the industrial revolution were in many ways the most famous. James Watt's modification of Thomas Newcomen's original engine provided steam power with the efficiency and scale necessary for the industrial revolution. Inventors like Watt depended on patent protection, which was not always easy to sustain, as Arkwright's experience with spinning frames demonstrated.

Whereas the evidence on whether intellectual property speeded or slowed the industrial revolution is mixed, there is less doubt about the role of finance. James Watt's partner, Matthew Boulton, was an early example of a venture capitalist, who used wealth from his network of multiple partnerships to support investment in a wide range of industries, from toy manufacture, to mining, and to minting coinage. Boulton's support for Watt's engine ensured its long-run success, providing the finance needed to develop a range of improved engines that could be applied in a wide range of innovative contexts. In similar vein, Arkwright was able to develop commercial scale for his inventions through partnership with established money (Dutton, 1984: 188; Toms & Fleischman, 2015).

A notable feature of the firms of these new industrial firms, however, was their independence from established sources of metropolitan finance. By 1770, London was already an established financial center, based on the wealth of its powerful merchant class. Led by institutions like Rothschilds and Barings, it underwent further dramatic expansion in the nineteenth century (Chapman, 2005). The City of London had its own priorities, driven by the growth of empire and associated infrastructure and commodity investments, and notwithstanding the opportunities that arose from rapid industrialization, remained largely aloof throughout the nineteenth century. Part of the reason was that although industrialization was highly significant as a whole, the financing needs of industrial firms were small relative to, for example, international bond issues for foreign governments (Kynaston, 1995). Frauds, mispricing, and lack of regulation over new stock issues led to disappointment and financial losses for metropolitan investors who did invest in domestic issues, most notably during the railway booms of the 1840s and 1850s (Robb, 2002).

The introduction of joint stock legislation in the 1860s, meanwhile, provided new opportunities for industrialists to raise equity finance. Regional stock markets successfully mobilized local pools of saving and gave rise to new classes of middle and working class investors (Toms, 2001; Thomas, 2013). Through a process of merger, banks developed branch structures that could also service the needs of local industry, albeit restricting such lending to working capital finance.

Notwithstanding the disparate uses of metropolitan and regional finance, London offered some examples of venture capital style finance. Syndicates were created to attract pools of investor finance that could be deployed in risky overseas ventures. For example, the Northumberland Mining Syndicate made serial and portfolio investments in highly risky mining claims in southern Africa during the 1890s (Michie, 1981). The Cycle Industries Trust, formed in 1896[1] at the height of the bicycle and pneumatic tire boom, was a venture fund backed by debentures, with the purpose of purchasing or securing cash flows from patent acquisition; an early example also perhaps of securitization. Horatio Bottomley, who founded the *Financial Times* in 1888, set up the Joint Stock Trust, formed on similar lines, although its scope was not confined to a single industry (Taylor, 2013). Once again, the experience of London investors with these schemes and associated promotion booms was negative, not least because promoters like Bottomley used fraudulent methods and achieved notoriety as a consequence. Citing a 1904 source, Michie (1981) notes that investors in joint stock firms had lost more money than they gained. Financial institutions did not replace individual company promoters until the 1920s (Roberts, 1993: 33), so before then innovative entrepreneurs seeking to exit their investments through initial public offerings faced commensurately higher risk.

If London provided early examples of venture capital provision, smaller regional enterprises offered examples of management buyouts. Indeed such early historical examples are perhaps more common than might be supposed, given that the term only came into general use quite recently and has been applied thus far to describe a post 1980s phenomenon.[2] According to the standard definition, although not described as such by contemporaries, the cotton textile industry was effectively restructured in a buyout wave during the 1890s. Up to around 1896, share prices of publicly quoted cotton mills were depressed by world market conditions. In view of the prolonged depression, many smaller shareholders, including the mill operatives, were keen to sell. An opportunity was thereby created for mill directors to purchase controlling interests in their own companies at low prices. Once control was achieved, the firms increasingly resembled private companies: stock exchange listings were removed, directors' salaries increased, and the publication of accounts was suspended (Toms, 2002). The performance consequences of the buyout wave are difficult to evaluate in the short run. World market conditions recovered quickly after 1896, driven by changed monetary conditions, so the restored profitability of cotton firms does not necessarily reflect the policies of the new owners.

However, the restructuring of the cotton industry along these lines had longer-run consequences that can be traced to the origins of the new buyout wave that impacted the wider UK economy during the 1970s. The British economy of 1900 has been criticized for being dominated by personal capitalists, who failed to innovate (Chandler, 1990). However, this was not exactly true of the managerially controlled cotton mills. The directors used the profits from the mills they already controlled to launch new, more modern mills on a larger scale. These were effectively groups of mills run by syndicates of interlocking directors and investors (Higgins et al., 2015). A series of mill flotation waves expanded the industry, according to some, by too much, so that after the final mill promotion wave of 1920, overcapitalized businesses were in control of too much capacity (Keynes, 1981). Attempts to restructure the industry and to remove these problems were mostly unsuccessful, including a forced amalgamation scheme instigated by the Bank of England in 1929 (Filatotchev & Toms, 2003).

The problems of the textile industry mirrored other staple industrial sectors and hinted at financial problems that were to affect British industry for decades to come. Cotton, like many other industries, utilized bank lending to finance working capital, but lacked access to venture capital and finance for restructuring. The regional stock markets, which had fuelled growth in the nineteenth century, now fell into decline along with the staple industries they mostly served. The long-term financing problem was recognized as early as 1931, referred to by policy makers as the "Macmillan gap."[3] By 2010, the same problem was referred to as the "equity gap" (Green, 2010; Toms et al., 2016).

The gap persisted until the 1970s, so that the buyout wave to some extent filled a vacuum. Earlier attempts to provide long-term capital for industry came from the Bank of England. The Industrial and Commercial Finance Corporation (ICFC), which later became Finance for Industry (FFI) and eventually 3i, had a very limited impact before 1970. ICFC was set up by the clearing banks in 1945. It was criticized for being overcautious in supporting funding applications and was deliberately and consistently under-resourced by the banks.

As a consequence there was limited scrutiny of investee companies compared to the model that developed later under the auspices of PE (Toms et al., 2016). Writing as early as 1950, a commentator in *The Economist* neatly encapsulated the ICFC's present and future impact as "performing a moderately useful function in a moderately cautious way."[4]

A private sector business model that attempted to perform venture capital functions, as characterized by portfolio holdings of high-risk investments requiring expertise and financial support, ended in disaster with the Slater Walker collapse of 1975. Founded and led by entrepreneur Jim Slater, the majority of Slater Walker's transactions were motivated by asset stripping. Valuable assets, particularly property, were sold at good profits, and the maximum cash extracted from the remainder of the assets. Traditional industrial firms acquired by Slater Walker, like Crittall Hope, were effectively destroyed by these practices. In the absence of regulation, the Slater Walker conglomerate also included its own banking division, whose main assets included intercompany loans secured against what proved to be optimistic valuations, once the property boom had turned to bust (Hope, 1976; Raw, 1977; Toms et al., 2016). As a variant of the conglomerate model incorporating some venture capitalist features, Slater Walker revealed serious inadequacies in the provision of entrepreneurial finance via the London Stock Exchange. Many of these weaknesses were subsequently overcome by the emergence of the PE-backed MBO model.

The buyout wave of the 1980s

Although Slater Walker's principal activity had been buying and selling companies, and occasionally investing in those it believed had good prospects, to some extent it typified the conglomerate organization of wider industry. The rise of the managerially controlled corporation and the separation of ownership and control, as recognized by Berle and Means (1991 [1932]) in the 1930s, led Joseph Schumpeter (1976 [1942]) to pronounce the demise of the entrepreneur. In its place came the "techno-structure," a term coined by Galbraith (2015) in 1967 to describe the dominance of production by managerial and technical specialists, backed by government policies that promoted amalgamations. The inauguration of the market for corporate control in the 1960s (Manne, 1965) in the US and the UK meant that the ownership of these large businesses became a matter of managerial competition that tended to subsume other entrepreneurial activities.

The recession of the 1970s posed what proved to be an insuperable challenge to the managerially controlled conglomerate. Ironically, the problems began with the Barber inspired property boom and the subsequent collapse and banking crisis that destroyed Slater Walker (Reid, 1982). The oil crisis added to these problems and firms found themselves overextended. Conglomerates typically traded at higher discounts than their more focused less diversified competitors, not least because they preferred to sit on large cash surpluses, either because they could not be productively reinvested, or due to restrictions on share buybacks, GEC being a leading example (Toms & Wright, 2002).

In the UK, the 1973 crisis had led to the creation of FFI, a successor organization to the ICFC, now expanded with additional funding from the Bank of England. The new organization was more explicitly oriented to venture capital functions. As such, before and after its relaunch as 3i, it was in a good position to support the earliest of the new MBO style transactions (Toms et al., 2016).

Poor macro-economic conditions meanwhile led to rapidly rising unemployment. It was against this backdrop that some of these early buyouts occurred, providing employees with the opportunity to buy their own companies, rather than face redundancy. The new buyout market, which gained momentum in the late 1970s and early 1980s, thus involved recession-related restructurings of failed or distressed companies (Wright et al., 2006). These examples were fairly isolated, and further reform at institutional level was needed to give substantive impetus to the developing wave of buyouts. The introduction of the unlisted securities market provided greater liquidity, and in parallel deregulation promoted the new entrants and greater shareholder activism. Banks, particularly those new to London and unconstrained by the traditional practices of the City, led the way in developing venture capital funds. Citicorp Venture Capital (CVC), a subsidiary of the US commercial banking giant Citicorp developed strong links with Silicon Valley and expanded into Europe in 1974 and subsequently into London in 1980, thereby becoming the first of such organizations to begin operations in the UK. It was quickly followed by similar banking organizations (Lorenz, 1985: 12; Kenney & Florida, 2000).[5]

In the same year, a new *Companies Act* lifted restrictions on capital reduction through share buybacks and financial assistance for the purchase of a company's own shares. These prohibitions had been enshrined in the *Companies Act 1948*, founded on the principles of minority and creditor protection. The provisions had also limited the scope for the use of the assets of target firms as security for debt-financed takeovers. Jim Slater, the Chief Executive of Salter Walker, was convicted for violation of these rules. Pressure to relax these provisions began with the Jenkins Committee in 1962, with an argument that private businesses should be exempt, and the increased perception in the 1970s that the restrictions limited the opportunities to rescue otherwise viable businesses (see Gilligan, Chapter 2 this volume). The *Companies Act 1981*, extended into the *EU Second Directive* and *Companies Act 2006*, relaxed these rules, offering safeguards to minority shareholders and creditors through statutory declarations by directors. These included the private company "whitewash" rules, where firms were allowed to give financial assistance if supported by a special resolution and a directors' statement of solvency (Ferran & Ho, 2014: 232–233).[6]

An important reason for the failure of the conglomerate model had been the exhaustion of scale economies. New technology, developed in the early 1980s in particular promoted flexible specialization, including, for example, those technologies eagerly invested in by CVC in Silicon Valley, based on Computer Numerical Control (CNC) and Computer Aided Design (CAD). These methods now facilitated the exploitation of scope as opposed to scale economies.

These changes explain some of the outstanding features of the earliest MBOs after 1975. Prior to 1981, in part due to the lack of clarity on financial assistance, FFI's legal expertise was an important element of support offered to fledgling buyout transactions. Subsequently, and more commonly, MBOs arose from conglomerate groups' decisions to divest their subsidiaries. The impetus for these sales came from the increasing fragmentation of vertical supply and value chains. MBO companies were characterized by stronger monitoring by investors, notably through direct board representation combined with managerial equity stakes and incentives. Structured debt finance was a significant proportion of the whole package, thereby reducing free cash flow. Taken together, these factors created pressure for further divestment, including pressure to repay debt leading to the divestment of less productive activities. For example, the successful hostile leveraged buyout of Gateway Superstores in 1989 was accompanied by significant divestment of unwanted stores and divisions (Wright et al., 1994).

In such fashion, the MBO model assisted firms that wished to change strategy and refocus their activities. Coats Viyella had made a series of large acquisitions in the 1980s, a strategy predicated on building market share and bargaining power with retail giant Marks & Spencer. Coats had become a £2 billion turnover business by 1990, but had a large number of subsidiaries, many of which were locked into low margin high-risk contract work with retail giant Marks & Spencer (Toms & Zhang, 2016). Financial pressures led to the appointment of a new Chief Executive, and a new focus on becoming a brand-led international services business. As part of this process, the fabrics division was disposed of as an MBO in 1995, illustrating that such transactions also assist the strategy and performance of the divesting organization (Toms & Wright, 2002). In short, the MBO wave assisted the unlocking of the conglomerate discount, often to the benefit of both parties.

In contrast to the earlier forms of entrepreneurial finance, the new waves of MBOs were a significant financial innovation in their own right. Some aspects, such as participating preferred ordinary shares and structured debt finance, were not new, indeed they had been important features of many industrial and other companies floated in the booms of the late nineteenth century. However, the new legal framework allowing redemption and convertibility, allowed sufficient flexibility to establish strong equity-based incentives, underpinned by tailored incentive-adjusted mezzanine finance (another leading feature of the earlier Gateway example) and covenants linked to performance monitoring mechanisms. Where appropriate, these incentives could also be linked to employee share ownership plans.

These structures also promoted product, organizational, and administrative innovation. MBO structures created an increased probability of new product development, improved customer relations, and offered better control systems and cost control. Taken together, all these innovations led to a revival in entrepreneurial opportunity (Wright et al., 2000). As such, it could be said that the disparate functions of entrepreneurs, product development, finance, company promotion, as traditionally carried out by separate individuals, were effectively institutionalized by the development of MBOs.

United Kingdom/United States comparison

The validity of this conclusion can be supported by a comparison with the experience of the US, which developed buyouts in parallel with the UK, but with some strikingly different features. As noted earlier, US venture funds like CVC had made pioneering investments in the new technology firms of Silicon Valley and had exported their model to Europe and the UK. However, the buyout wave that appeared in the US during the 1980s had some important distinguishing features. Most notably, the characteristics of buyouts along with other features of the US market for corporate control, including excessive litigation and arbitrage, led Baumol (1996) to conclude that this was a period of "unproductive" entrepreneurship. Key features of the US model were that whole companies were bought out, most famously RJR Nabisco by Kohlberg, Kravis, Roberts & Co (KKR), the so-called "Barbarians at the Gate" (Burrough & Helyar, 2010). The KKR case also exemplified a second important feature: the use of (sometimes excessive) leverage, which certainly reached levels much higher than in the UK. Transactions in the US were more frequently contested and hostile, and there was a clearer separation between the buyout and venture capital markets than in the UK, where they rapidly integrated. As a consequence, buyouts in the US have been subject to much more scrutiny from lawmakers (Toms & Wright, 2005).

Before and after the global financial crisis, 2007–2008

Figure 3.1 shows the long-run trend in MBOs and MBIs by number and by value. As the figure shows, from small beginnings in the late 1970s, the number of transactions expanded rapidly up to 1990. In value terms the growth was less pronounced before the mid-1990s and finally peaked in 2007, long after the growth cycle in the number of buyouts had reached

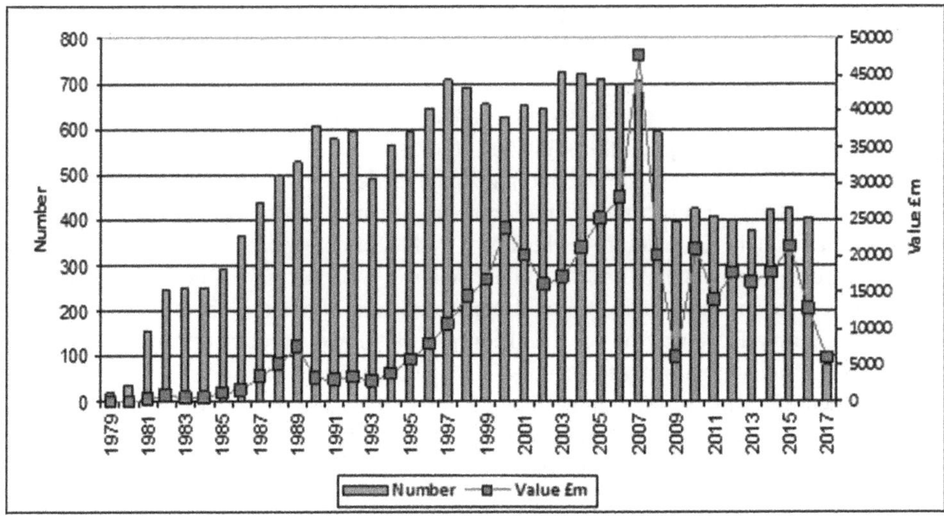

Figure 3.1 United Kingdom buyouts and buyins by number and value (£m)
Source: CMBOR/Equistone Partners Europe/Investec.

its mature phase. The late 1990s and early 2000s were thus characterized by higher value transactions.

A useful illustration of the emergence of the larger-scale MBO during this period is provided by the beer and pub industry. An important initial reason for the involvement of buyout teams was specific regulation against anti-competitive behavior. Following an investigation in 1989, the Monopolies and Mergers Commission concluded that vertically integrated brewing firms controlled too much of the retail (public house) market.[7] The so-called "beer orders" required them to divest significant proportions of their estates. The MBO was an obvious vehicle for this, and as with the earlier buyout waves, both parties stood to gain. For the large vertically integrated brewers, the MBO provided a ready means to comply with the new legislation and refocus on specific areas of the value chain. The bought-out pub estates were now effectively pub-owning companies (Pubcos), and they recognized that higher market share would increase both their bulk buying power and their ability to control the margins of pub managers. A leading example was Enterprise Inns, a venture capital backed MBI which took over an estate divested by Bass Plc in 1991. To achieve this quickly they sought PE backing. They were assisted by Cinven, an international PE firm, led by Morgan Stanley's Princes Gate Investors and Legal & General Ventures, thereby facilitating Enterprise's successful and profitable acquisitions of Unique and Voyager pub groups, whose cash flows were then used to generate securitized loans to finance the Laurel Group's estate of pubs. Their rationale was that pubs could be bundled together and their cash flow securitized, providing access to cheap debt finance. Risk, meanwhile, could effectively be transferred to pub managers through fixed rent and beer charges (Higgins et al., 2016).

The model worked well for the Pubcos, but at some cost to other stakeholders, including entrepreneurs. As a consequence, they have been subject to scrutiny from parliamentary committees of enquiry, amid claims of abuse of tenants and failures to maintain pubs of community value. To limit the possibility of power abuses, there have been attempts to secure appropriate codes of conduct through legislation.[8]

To some extent the criticisms levelled against PE-backed Pubcos are also valid in terms of the effectiveness of entrepreneurial finance. As noted earlier, the great strength of the MBO/PE model was its institutionalization of the hitherto disparate and individual functions of entrepreneurship. In the beer and pub industry, the entrepreneurial function operated precisely at this meso-level, successfully raising substantial financial resources to transform an industry. The problem, however, was the strangulation of micro-level entrepreneurial initiative. Although it was true that pub landlords had some freedom to innovate under Pubco tenancies, their complaint was that any hint of success would be rewarded with an upward rent revision. As a result, lack of incentive structures, exposure to risk, and lack of control over margins and investment, meant that pub licensees were reduced to custodians of a shrinking and impoverished estate, which Pubcos could continue to exploit through asset sales against a backdrop of rising property values (Higgins et al., 2016). The evidence from the beer industry suggests that the MBO/PE model can only be part of the overall provision of entrepreneurial finance. Free of tie pubs, for example, offer greater scope for entrepreneurship at the micro business level.

More generally, however, there is evidence that the supply of finance into smaller businesses via MBOs has reduced since the late 2000s. The trend in Figure 3.1 shows a decline in the number and value of MBOs following the global financial crisis of 2007–2008. In value terms, there was a very substantial fall from the peak achieved immediately before the crisis of 2007. This downward correction was much more significant and persistent than the aftermath of the dot.com crash of 2001.

Following the financial crisis, MBOs appear no longer to address the equity gap as they once did. In the wider economy, particularly after 2007, and notwithstanding the substantial developments of the preceding three decades, there is evidence of the persistence of the equity gap. Firms located in the London and the South East appear to have less of a problem accessing capital, but smaller peripheral firms face substantial barriers (Rowlands, 2009; Amini et al., 2010; Mason & Harrison, 2015).

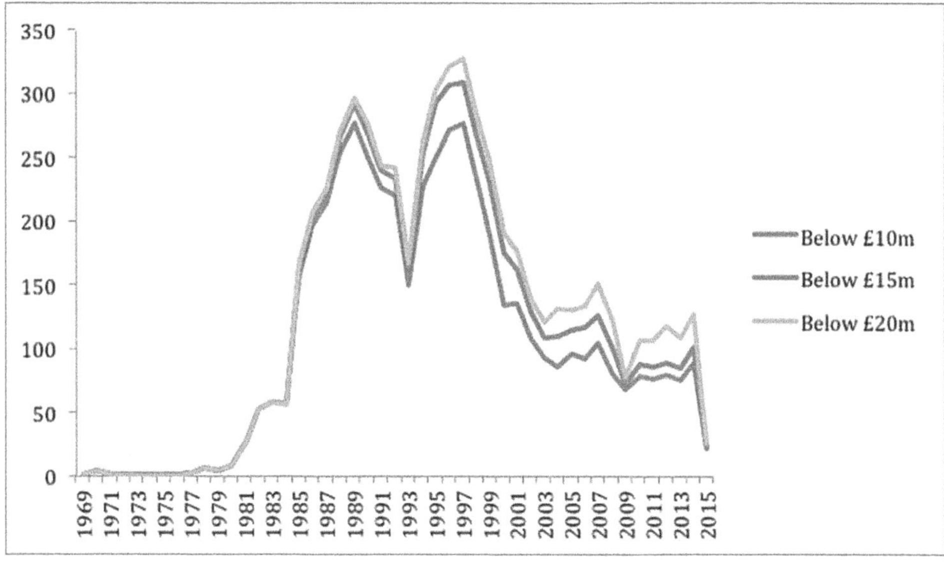

Figure 3.2 Trends in PE-backed smaller buyouts and buyins (numbers)
Source: Wilson and Wright (2017: 23).

Empirical evidence for smaller firms suggest that the buyout surge that rejuvenated much of UK industry has run out of steam and there were signs of this even before the financial crisis (Figure 3.2). Figure 3.2 shows the number of smaller buyouts backed by PE, but the total value of transactions in these size ranges has also generally fallen (Wilson & Wright, 2017). Investors meanwhile, favor larger sizes, thereby avoiding the relatively high transaction cost of smaller opportunities, whose lack of performance track record also accentuates perceived risk (Rowlands, 2009). Taken together, the trends in Figures 3.1 and 3.2 indicate a peak in smaller, entrepreneurial MBOs in the late 1990s, followed by a shift to higher, larger transactions that sustained growth in value terms up to 2007.

Conclusions

Recent trends in buyout activity beg the question of their future role as investment vehicles capable of sustaining economic growth. If history is any guide, it is clear from the discussion in this chapter that structural changes are perhaps more important than cyclical trends. The structural changes in the early 1980s, including company law reform and the deregulation that facilitated the entry of new financial institutions and innovative financing, were of the utmost importance in energizing the wave of buyout activity that followed. That upsurge was strongly characterized by smaller entrepreneurial buyouts, at least until the peak of the dot.com boom at the end of the 1990s. The cyclical downturn that impacted the wider economy had little effect on the level of buyout activity in value terms. In parts of the economy, like the beer and pub industry, the move to larger transactions stifled entrepreneurship at the micro-business level. More generally the number of PE-backed buyouts for small firms declined significantly from the early 2000s. As in the nineteenth century, the preference of investment funds for larger deals with relatively lower risk and transaction costs, has led to a divergence between entrepreneurial opportunity and financial provision.

The significant consequence of all this then appears to be a return to the long-run problem of the equity gap. Further research is needed to assess how this challenge might be met, for example identifying firms and sectors that can be turned around and how the investment needed can be suitably tailored and incentivized. Such research is of clear practical value in terms of assisting the recovery of previously industrialized regions, as in the case of the UK's so-called "Northern Powerhouse." In conducting such research, the lessons of history are valuable. Certainly, the buyout waves of the 1980s and 1990s offered some interruption of the otherwise persistent problem of the equity gap, particularly for smaller, potentially innovative firms, which has now re-emerged in most sectors and regions following the global financial crisis. A final question therefore is whether the underlying features of the buyout model, explored elsewhere in this book, can once again be adapted to respond to the opportunities and threats of new and challenging economic circumstances.

Notes

1 *Times Book of Prospectuses*, The Cycle Industries Corporation, May 13, 1896, 176.
2 Using a standard definition of a management buyout: "an acquisition in which the acquiring group is led by the company's own management and executives" *Financial Times*, http://lexicon.ft.com/Term?term=management-buy_out-(MBO).
3 British Parliamentary Papers, Committee on Finance and Industry (Macmillan Committee): Report of Committee (Cmd. 3897), 1931.
4 "The ICFC in a hesitant economy" *The Economist*, May 20, 1950: 1133.

5 For further examples of these developments, see: "Citicorp opens new European investment unit" *Financial Times*, March 7, 1974: 24; On a slow boat from America, *The Economist*, January 3, 1987: 5.
6 For the arguments discussed in the Jenkins Committee, see: British Parliamentary Papers, Jenkins Committee, *Report of the Company Law Committee* (Cmnd 1749, 1962): 178–179.
7 British Parliamentary Papers, Monopolies and Mergers Commission (MMC). *The Supply of Beer*, Cm. 651 London: HMSO, 1989.
8 See, for example, British Parliamentary Papers, Trade and Industry Committee (2004/2005). *Pub Companies* (Second Report, HC 128-1). London: House of Commons Trade and Industry Committee, 20, London: HMSO; "Statutory code to tackle Pubco abuses" *Financial Times*, January 8, 2013.

References

Amini, S., Keasey, K., & Hudson, R. 2010. The equity funding of smaller growing companies and regional stock exchanges. *International Small Business Journal*, 30: 832–849.

Baumol, W. 1996. Entrepreneurship: Productive, unproductive, and destructive. *Journal of Business Venturing*, 11: 3–22.

Berle, A. A., & Means, G. G. C. 1991 [1932]. *The modern corporation and private property*. London: Transaction Publishers.

Burrough, B., & Helyar, J. 2010. *Barbarians at the gate: The fall of RJR Nabisco*. London: Random House.

Chandler, A. D. 1990. *Scale and scope: The dynamics of industrial competition*. Cambridge, MA: Harvard.

Chapman, S. D. 2005. *The rise of merchant banking*. Abingdon, UK: Taylor & Francis.

Dutton, H. I. 1984. The patent system and inventive activity during the industrial revolution, 1750–1852. Manchester, UK: Manchester University Press.

Ferran, E., & Ho, L. C. 2014. *Principles of corporate finance law*. Oxford, UK: Oxford University Press.

Filatotchev, I., & Toms, S. 2003. Corporate governance, strategy and survival in a declining industry: A study of UK cotton textile companies. *Journal of Management Studies*, 40: 895–920.

Galbraith, J. K. 2015 [1967]. *The new industrial state*. Princeton, NJ: Princeton University Press.

Green, D. 2010. Foreword. In M. Jones (Ed.), *The industrial and commercial finance corporation: Lessons from the past for the future*. London: Civitas, 3–4.

Higgins, D., Toms, S., & Filatotchev, I. 2015. Ownership, financial strategy and performance: The Lancashire cotton textile industry, 1918–1938. *Business History*, 57: 97–121.

Higgins, D., Toms, S., & Uddin, M. 2016. Vertical monopoly power, profit and risk: The British beer industry, c.1970–2004. *Business History*, 58: 667–693.

Hope, M. 1976. On being taken over by Slater Walker. *Journal of Industrial Economics*, 24: 163–179.

Kenney, M., & Florida, R. 2000. Venture capital in Silicon Valley: Fueling new firm formation. In M. Kenney (Ed.), *Understanding Silicon Valley: The anatomy of an entrepreneurial region*. Stanford, CA: Stanford University Press, 98–123.

Keynes, J. M. 1981. *The return to gold and industrial policy II, Collected works*. Cambridge, UK: Cambridge University Press.

Kynaston, D. 1995. *The city of London: Vol. II golden years 1890–1914*. London: Chatto & Windus.

Lorenz, P. 1985. *Venture capital today*. Cambridge, UK: Woodhead Faulkner.

Manne, H. G. 1965. Mergers and the market for corporate control. *The Journal of Political Economy*, 73: 110–120.

Mason, C. M., & Harrison, R. T. 2015. Business angel investment activity in the financial crisis: UK evidence and policy implications. *Environment and Planning C: Government and Policy*, 33: 43–60.

Michie, R. C. 1981. Options, concessions, syndicates, and the provision of venture capital, 1880–1913. *Business History*, 23: 147–164.

Raw, C. 1977. *Slater Walker: An investigation of a financial phenomenon*. London: Andre Deutsch.

Reid, M. 1982. *Secondary banking crisis, 1973–75: Its causes and course*. London: Springer.

Robb, G. 2002. *White-collar crime in modern England: Financial fraud and business morality, 1845–1929*. Cambridge, UK: Cambridge University Press.

Roberts, R. 1993. What's in a name? Merchants, merchant bankers, accepting houses, issuing houses, industrial bankers and investment bankers. *Business History*, 35: 22–38.
Rowlands, C. 2009. *The provision of growth capital to UK small and medium sized enterprises*. Norwich, UK: The Stationery Office.
Schumpeter, J. A. 1976 [1942]. *Socialism, capitalism and democracy*. London: Allen & Unwin.
Taylor, J. 2013. *Boardroom scandal: The criminalization of company fraud in nineteenth-century Britain*. Oxford, UK: Oxford University Press.
Thomas, W. A. 2013. *The provincial stock exchanges*. Abingdon, UK: Routledge.
Toms, J. S. 2001. Information content of earnings in an unregulated market: The co-operative cotton mills of Lancashire, 1880–1900. *Accounting and Business Research*, 31: 175–190.
Toms, J. S. 2002. The rise of modern accounting and the fall of the public company: The Lancashire cotton mills 1870–1914. *Accounting, Organizations and Society*, 27: 61–84.
Toms, S., & Fleischman, R. K. 2015. Accounting fundamentals and accounting change: Boulton & Watt and the Springfield Armory. *Accounting, Organizations and Society*, 41: 1–20.
Toms, S., Wilson, N., & Wright, M. 2016. The evolution of private equity: Corporate restructuring in the UK, c.1945–2010. *Business History*, 57: 736–768.
Toms, S., & Wright, M. 2002. Corporate governance, strategy and structure in British business history, 1950–2000. *Business History*, 44: 91–124.
Toms, S., & Wright, M. 2005. Divergence and convergence within Anglo-American corporate governance systems: Evidence from the US and UK, 1950–2000. *Business History*, 47: 267–295.
Toms, S., & Zhang, Q. 2016. Marks & Spencer and the decline of the British textile Industry, 1950–2000. *Business History Review*, 90: 3–30.
Wilson, N., & Wright, M. 2017. Private equity targets and post investment performance: A study of the corporate sector in the North and regions. Leeds University Business School Working Paper, No.17-02.
Wright, M., Burrows, A., Ball, R., Scholes, L., Burdett, M., & Tune, K. 2006. *Management buy-outs 1986–2006 past achievements, future challenges*. Available at: https://workspace.imperial.ac.uk/entrepreneurship/Public/cmbor20[1].pdf.
Wright, M., Chiplin, B., Robbie, K., & Albrighton, M. 2000. The development of an organizational innovation: UK management buy-outs 1980–1997. *Business History*, 42: 137–142.
Wright, M., Wilson, N., Robbie, K., & Ennew, C. 1994. Restructuring and failure in buy-outs and buy-ins. *Business Strategy Review*, 5: 21–40.

4

INTERPRETING THE M&A BLACK BOX BY THINKING OUTSIDE THE BOX

Douglas Cumming and Simona Zambelli

Introduction

The main purpose of this chapter is to provide policy makers with new insights to better evaluate the current worldwide debate on debt merger acquisitions, as well as shed some light on the perils of stringent financial bans on these types of transactions. Debt merger acquisitions (M&A) represent deals that are financed primarily with debt and are accomplished with a merger between the target and the investee company. These types of deals are very common in the European private equity (PE) industry and play an important role in reinforcing the market for corporate control, as well as in reducing agency costs by reorganizing the ownership structure of target companies and guaranteeing a better alignment of stakeholders' interests.

Debt M&A, also known as leveraged buyouts (LBO), have been at the center of an intensive worldwide debate and criticism since the late 1990s, especially after the 2007 financial crisis. PE funds have been repeatedly criticized for their lack of regulation and insufficient disclosure (see, e.g., Ferran, 2007; Jelic & Wright, 2011). In the US, critics have also asserted that LBOs should be prohibited given their potential detrimental effects on the target's assets due to the high amount of debt involved in the transaction (Stein, 2006). PE investors financing LBOs have even been labeled as "locusts" (Petitt, 2014; *The Wall Street Journal*, 2005) or asset strippers (e.g., *The Guardian*, 2007) who cut jobs and contribute to the weakening of the acquired companies by depriving them of their strategic assets and increasing their risk of bankruptcy.[1] In line with this view, legal scholars (doctrine) and courts (jurisprudence), as well as European policy makers (e.g., Financial Service Authority, 2006) have strongly criticized LBOs emphasizing the need for a more restrictive and harmonized regulatory environment (Cumming & Johan, 2007).[2] The Italian Supreme Court even deemed the LBO scheme illegal and prohibited its adoption within the domestic market (Supreme Court Decision 5503/2000).

The criticism against LBOs intensified after 2007 and an increasing call for more stringent regulations and bans on LBO transactions was repeatedly echoed by the media, unions, and politicians around the world (see, e.g., *The Economist*, 2016). As an aftermath of the crisis, a wave of new regulatory proposals and legal reforms of PE and other alternative investment funds (such as hedge funds) was introduced with the purpose of guaranteeing more financial stability and higher investor protection (Avgouleas, 2009; Davidoff & Zaring,

2009; Ferran, 2011; Claessens & Kodres, 2014; De Fontenay, 2014).[3] It is worth noting that the growing regulatory attention on PE funds was not due to the fact that they caused the crisis (see, e.g., Allen & Carletti, 2010). The crisis was instead a pretext to regulate PE funds more heavily, as ironically commented by *The Economist* (2009) "When a fight breaks out in a bar, you don't hit the man who started it. You clobber the person you don't like instead."[4]

Understanding the new current legal environment regulating M&A, as well as the controversial issues underlying PE transactions and other alternative investments is crucial for PE investors, especially when evaluating the opportunity to carry out cross-border M&A. As shown in the law and finance literature, the legal environment affects investors' behavior (e.g., Lerner & Schoar, 2005; Cumming et al., 2006; Kaplan et al., 2007; Bottazzi et al., 2009; Cumming & Johan, 2013; Cumming & Zambelli, 2017), as well as transactional risk (Cumming & Zambelli, 2010), and fund performance (Cumming & Zambelli, 2013).

Despite the growing literature on the positive impact of PE transactions on investee performance (e.g., Cumming et al., 2007; Nikoskelainen & Wright, 2007; Renneboog, 2007; Cao & Lerner, 2009; Harris et al., 2014, 2015; Liu, 2014; Buchner et al., 2016; Gompers et al., 2016; Hooke et al., 2016),[5] an international concern is whether PE transactions should be more heavily regulated in order to better protect the assets of target firms and their stakeholders. In the economic literature little empirical attention is dedicated to the impact of PE regulatory reforms, and the majority of the available studies on this matter are essentially industry reports or legal reviews (e.g., Enriques, 2002; Giannino, 2006; Enriques & Volpin, 2007; Ferran, 2007, 2011; Heed, 2010; EVCA, 2015; Invest Europe, 2017).

Notwithstanding the ongoing regulatory and media attention devoted to the PE industry, there continues to exist a substantial confusion about the intrinsic characteristics of LBOs, especially in terms of how they can increase the value of target companies (De Fontenay, 2014), and how legal reforms may shape investor behavior towards the direction desired by policy makers. This chapter aims at filling this gap by showing the results of recent empirical studies on the impact of corporate governance reforms in the context of PE financing in Italy, a country in which PE transactions were previously prohibited and thereafter legalized. In this perspective, the Italian PE market offers a unique and timely experimental example to better evaluate the efficacy of stringent regulatory restrictions on LBO deals.

PE investors are characterized by their active involvement in their investee companies (see, e.g., Cumming & Johan, 2013), and such fund involvement is crucial to maximize the value added of their investments, both in terms of fund returns and investee performance (e.g., Jelic & Wright, 2011; Bonini et al., 2012; Borel & Heger, 2014; Gao, 2014). The introduction of extreme regulations or bans may have detrimental effects on target companies as they may reduce the quantity and quality of fund involvement and this, in turn, may negatively affect the entire investment cycle (Cumming & Dai, 2011), the governance of the target companies (Cumming & Zambelli, 2010), as well as the due diligence process (Cumming & Zambelli, 2017), and the potential value-added that PE investors could generate in their portfolio firms (see, e.g., Suchard, 2009; Hamdouni, 2011; Cumming & Zambelli, 2013).

The remainder of this chapter is organized as follows. The next section describes the financial structure of LBOs by discussing the typical LBO investment process and highlighting what is inside the LBO black box. The following section sheds light on the previous and ongoing criticism raised against LBOs ("dark side") and discusses the reasons why LBOs were deemed illegal in Italy. Also, this section has the purpose of better clarifying the legal status of LBOs by describing the new corporate governance reform issued in Italy. Furthermore, the section highlights unresolved issues associated with the legitimacy of LBOs, as well as important challenges and criticism raised by the tax authorities. Understanding the previous and current legal issues surrounding LBOs is crucial for international investors in order to allow them to better evaluate their transaction risk. Thereafter we discuss the economic impact of the new LBO reforms in terms of investor behavior, due diligence, and investee performance. The last section provides concluding remarks.

Financial structure of LBOs: opening the black box

For the purpose of this study, PE financing refers to equity investments in existing and developed companies, and LBOs are the acquisition of a company (called target) by another company (called newco) accomplished with a large amount of debt relative to the asset value of the acquired company (typically the debt represents the 60–70% of target asset value; see, e.g., Axelson et al., 2009a, 2009b; Siegel et al., 2011; Baldi, 2015).

Buyouts have always played a dominant role within the Italian PE market. In 2015, for example, the total amount invested in buyouts in Italy was €3,255 million, representing 70.5% of the entire PE industry (Figure 4.1).

The main criticism surrounding LBO transactions is connected to the interpretation of their financial structure and economic results. The most criticized result of an LBO is the shifting of the financial burdens from the purchaser (newco) to the acquired company (target). In order to better understand the criticism against LBO transactions, in the following sub-section we focus on the steps that are typically followed by PE investors to accomplish LBOs. We also focus on the criticism raised by legal scholars and courts within the Italian PE industry, whose transactions experienced relevant and unique legal changes, from prohibition to legalization.

LBO investment process

The structure of an LBO may be quite complex, and the entire LBO process involves a number of different steps and actors (Baldi, 2015), as summarized below and shown in Figure 4.2.

Phase 1: Establishment of a new company (vehicle). The first step towards accomplishing an LBO is represented by the incorporation of a new company (holding company or

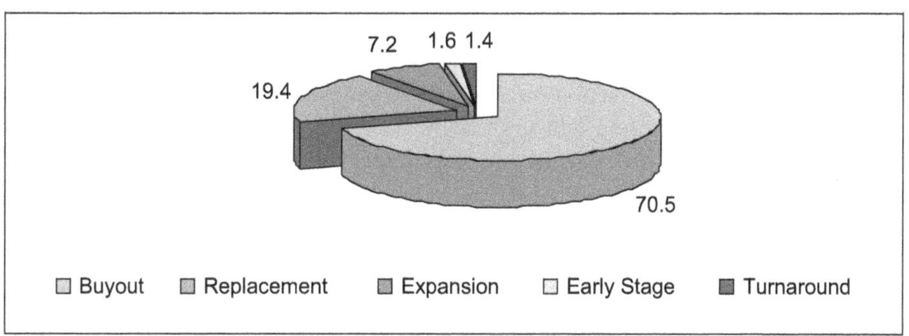

Figure 4.1 Buyouts in 2015

This figure shows the relative proportions of buyouts carried out in Italy in 2015 relative to the total amount invested in the entire PE industry (numbers reflect percentages)

Source: Elaboration from AIFI Statistics Reports (2015).

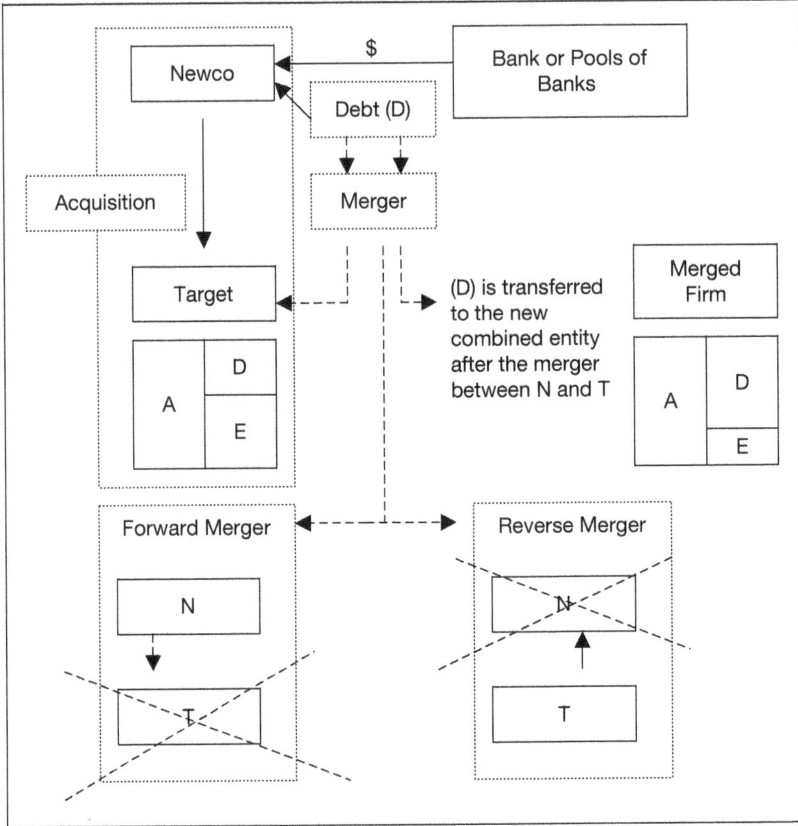

Figure 4.2 Buyout structure: steps, effects, and implications

This figure represents the typical steps involved in the buyout process, from the establishment of the newco to the merger between the newco and the target.

Source: Authors.

newco, which is created with the sole purpose of acquiring a specific target firm. The newco, typically, is not an active producing company, but it serves as a special purpose vehicle (SPV) to accomplish the transaction and generally takes the form of a limited liability company. The equity necessary to establish the newco is often supplied by PE investors, who may co-invest either with the management of the target (MBO) or with an outside management team (MBI).

Phase 2: The acquisition of a loan. One characteristic of LBOs is that these types of transactions occur with the adoption of a relatively high amount of debt (60–70%) with respect to the asset value of the target company. In this phase, the debt acquired by the newco typically takes the form of short-term debt (bridge financing) and it will be renegotiated into a longer-term debt once the buyout has been completed.

Another crucial (and highly criticized) characteristic of LBOs is that the debt is arranged and obtained by the newco under the expectation that it will be secured and repaid by the target company with its future cash flows or the sale of its non-strategic assets. As such, the expected target's cash flows, as well as the quantity and quality of the target's assets, represent a crucial precondition for the accomplishment of LBOs, as they serve as collateral for the debt. Given that in an LBO the target firm bears most of the economic costs related to its acquisition, the success of the entire LBO process depends on the financial and economic conditions of the target, as well as its growth potential. In line with the free cash flow theory applied to buyouts (see, e.g., Jensen, 1986, 1989; Opler & Titman, 1993), an ideal candidate for an LBO acquisition should have a modest level of initial debt, as well as a business plan with sufficiently high expected cash flows in order to prove the feasibility of the entire transaction and the target capacity to effectively repay its debt obligations.

Phase 3: Purchase of the target's share. LBO transactions usually target mature companies with the purpose of completely restructuring them (see, e.g., Cumming & Johan, 2013). In order to minimize the risk of a dispute with minority shareholders, in a typical LBO the newco acquires the totality (or at least a majority stake) of the target's shares. After the acquisition, the target's share will appear on the asset side of the newco balance sheet.

Phase 4: Merger between newco and target. In Italy, the LBO acquisition is typically followed by a merger between the target and the newco. After the merger the bridge financing, originally arranged by the newco, is replaced by a new medium- or long-term debt, secured by the assets of the merged company. The main effect of the merger is the concentration into a new combined entity of all the assets and obligations that previously belonged to the newco and the target.

As a result of the merger, the combined company is left with a higher leverage ratio (debt-to-equity ratio) compared to the one the target company had before the acquisition. In the end, the loan originally obtained by the newco is merged into the target's liabilities ("debt push down"), and any claims by the newco's creditors are therefore transferred to the target's asset.[6]

As summarized in Figure 4.2, two types of mergers exist: forward and reverse. In a forward merger, the target is engulfed into the newco and, as a result, the target legally disappears. As a consequence, the target's shares previously acquired by the newco are cancelled and substituted with the assets of the target. In a reverse merger, the newco is engulfed into the target and, as such, the newco legally disappears and the target is the sole remaining company. In both cases, the new combined company enjoys all the rights and it is subject to all the obligations that the two prior companies had before. As a result of a reverse merger, the equity participation acquired by the newco for the purchase of the target company will be included inside the target's assets.[7]

Industry evolution and related legal changes

Table 4.1 shows the evolution of the Italian buyout market from 1988 to 2015, in terms of frequency, average deal size, and number of investors actively involved in the industry. As discussed in Zambelli (2010), both the volume and the value of buyouts carried out in Italy increased sharply over the 1990s. From 2000 until 2006, however, the evolution of buyouts in Italy followed a puzzling zig-zag trend, alternating periods characterized by strong decreases in the buyout frequency (e.g., from 2000 to 2001) with periods characterized by sharp increases in the number of buyouts (e.g., after 2004). One possible explanation for this puzzling trend may be associated with the drastic legal changes experienced by the Italian PE industry, as summarized in Figure 4.3 and discussed in the following sub-sections.

Table 4.1 Buyout market over the 1988–2015 period

	1998	*1999*	*2000*	*2001*	*2002*	*2003*	*2004*	*2005*	*2006*
Number of PE investors actively involved in the buyout industry	na	na	na	21	36	36	30	44	54
Number of buyouts	38	65	53	30	76	59	48	75	100
Total amount invested (€m)	242	878	1363	1014	1550	2258	916	2401	2444
Percentage of buyouts, relative to other PE transactions (in terms of number)	15%	18%	8%	6%	25%	18%	19%	27%	34%
Percentage of buyouts, relative to other PE transactions (in terms of amount invested)	25%	50%	46%	34%	64%	74%	62%	78%	66%
	2007	*2008*	*2009*	*2010*	*2011*	*2012*	*2013*	*2014*	*2015*
Number of PE investors actively involved in the buyout industry	50	57	42	35	40	38	38	52	57
Number of buyouts	87	113	72	56	63	65	51	91	101
Total amount invested (€m)	3295	2869	1688	1647	2261	2069	2151	2181	3255
Percentage of buyouts, relative to other PE transactions (in terms of number)	29%	30%	25%	19%	19%	19%	14%	29%	30%
Percentage of buyouts, relative to other PE transactions (in terms of amount invested)	79%	53%	65%	67%	63%	64%	63%	62%	70%

Table 4.1 shows the evolution of the Italian buyout market over the 1998–2015 period, in terms of number of deals, amount invested, and number of PE investors.

Source: Elaboration from AIFI statistics reports, various years.

LBO criticism and regulatory changes: causes, implications, and unresolved issues

Over the last decades, an intensive debate has emerged about the legitimacy of LBOs, as well as about the necessity of imposing more regulatory restrictions on LBOs in order to better protect the interests of target companies and their stakeholders.

While in Europe the debate intensified after the global financial crises, in Italy the greatest LBO criticism started in the late 1990s. Over the 1990s, in fact, the legitimacy of LBOs was critically challenged by Italian courts and remained uncertain until the issuance of a new corporate governance reform (Legislative Decree 6/2003, effective as of January 1, 2004). The debate on the LBO legitimacy exacerbated in 2000 when a Supreme Court's

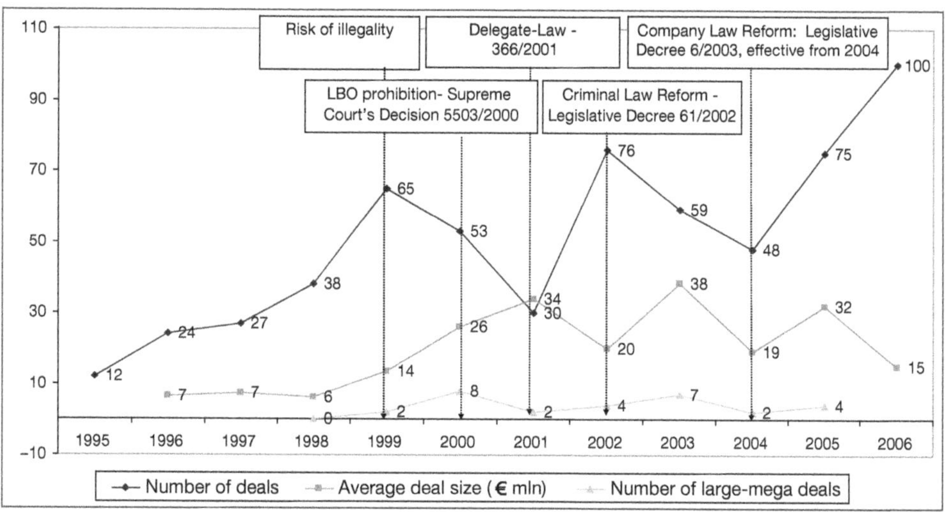

Figure 4.3 LBO market trend and related regulatory changes (1995–2006)

Figure 4.3 shows the puzzling evolution of the Italian buyout market in relation to the most recent changes in the regulatory environment, especially after 1999.

Source: Zambelli (2008: 64).

Decision deemed the LBO scheme illegal and prohibited its adoption within the Italian market (Supreme Court Decision 5503/2000, February 4, 2000).

In the following sub-sections, we will provide more detailed information on the reasons underlying the LBO criticisms and the accusations of illegality raised against these types of transactions.

LBO criticisms and illegality accusations

As mentioned earlier, over the 1990s and until 2004, the legitimacy of LBOs was uncertain and strongly debated. The Italian case law (jurisprudence) and legal scholars (doctrine) provided contrasting and inconsistent interpretations, which contributed to increasing the uncertainty and risk associated with these types of transactions.[8]

LBOs were accused of involving a lack of transparency and contributing to the weakening of the target firms. LBOs were also accused of being examples of indirect financial assistance provided by the target for the acquisition of its own shares. This type of financial support is against the law and, in particular, is a breach of the financial assistance ban set by European Law, according to which a company cannot grant a loan or provide a guarantee for the acquisition of its own shares. Such a ban was originally introduced in Europe by article 23 of the Second Directive on Corporate Law (Directive 77/91/EC, December 13, 1976) and was applied by each member State in a different way. Some countries, such as the UK and Germany, applied the ban to public companies only and allowed private companies to provide financial assistance for the purposes of share repurchases. Other countries, such as Italy, applied the ban to all companies, public and private.[9]

By looking at the Italian court's decisions, the core of the criticism against LBOs was focused on the interpretation of the ultimate economic result of these types of deals, often taken for a fraudulent share buyback transaction. In particular, a few legal provisions of the Civil Code were invoked against the legitimacy of LBOs: article 2357, article 2358, and article 1344. Article 2357 limits the possibility for a company to acquire its own shares. Article 2358 prohibits a company from providing financial assistance or a guarantee for the acquisition of its own shares. This article aims at protecting the integrity of the company's assets, to the benefit of its creditors and stakeholders. Given the fact that the debt underlying the LBO transaction is acquired by the newco under the expectation of being repaid by the target and that the target's assets serve as a guarantee for such debt, LBOs were accused of breaching the financial assistance ban. Article 1344 invalidates any agreement whose ultimate result is to create a situation which is elusive of imperative provisions of the law. Article 1344 was invoked to invalidate the merger agreement between the newco and the target (for more details, see Giannino, 2006; Zambelli, 2008, 2010).

A particular interpretation of the law (hereafter "illegality view") viewed LBOs as share buyback deals, and interpreted them as financial tools fraudulently adopted by the target to elude the law by allowing the latter to implement a share buyback outside the restrictions imposed by the Italian regulation. From this perspective, LBOs allow the target to: (a) acquire its own shares eluding the restrictions set by article 2357 and (b) provide a guarantee for the loan that was arranged to acquire its own shares, in breach of the financial assistance ban set by article 2358. In application of the "illegality view," a number of LBOs were invalidated by Italian courts because they were interpreted as being equivalent to an *indirect share buyback deal* (see Figure 4.4), as well as instances of *indirect financial assistance* fraudulently provided by the target for the repurchase of its own shares (see Figure 4.5). The newco, in turn, was considered merely an intermediary acting on behalf of the target to help the latter elude the law.

The breach of the financial assistance ban appeared more evident in the cases of LBOs carried out without the merger, as well as in the cases of reverse merger LBOs, as visualized in Figure 4.4 (see Zambelli, 2008 for more details).

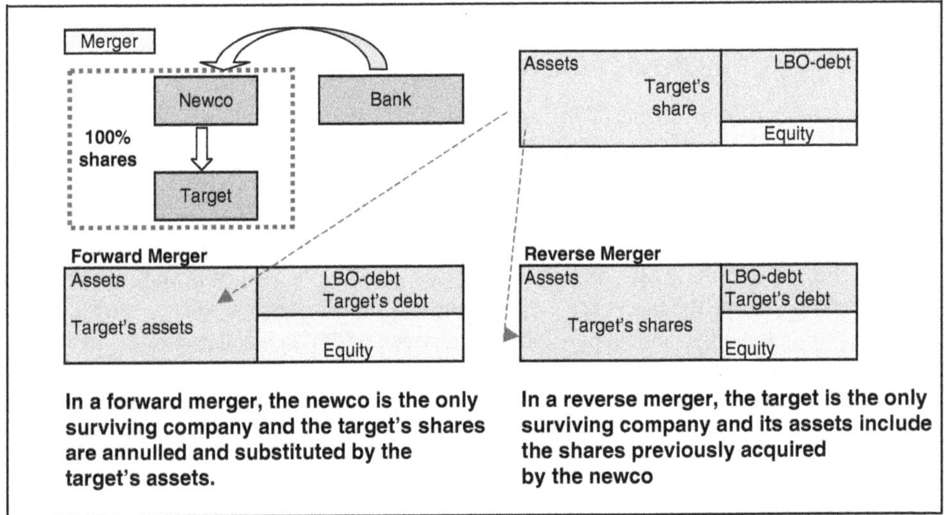

Figure 4.4 LBO scheme, interpreted as an indirect share buyback

This figure summarizes the criticism against the LBO scheme which appears to produce the results of a share buyback implemented by the target with the intermediation of the newco, against the limits set by article 2357 of the Civil Code.

Source: Zambelli (2008: 70).

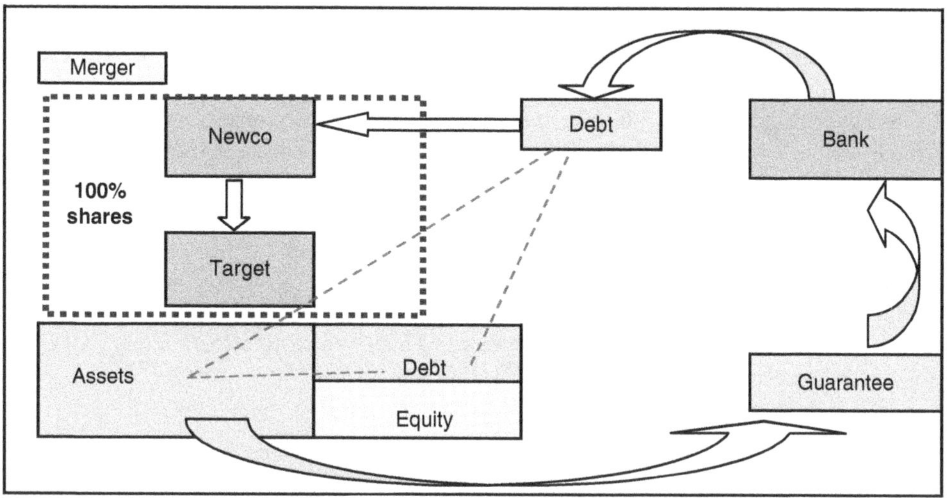

Figure 4.5 LBO scheme, interpreted as a breach of the financial assistance ban

This figure summarizes the criticism against LBOs: as a result of the merger, the target assets serve as a guarantee for the loan previously obtained by the newco. This is against the restrictions imposed by article 2358 of the Civil Code and, as such, the effects of the merger may be invalidated by article of the Civil Code.

Source: Zambelli (2008: 71).

Legal scholars and courts also challenged the validity of the merger agreement between the target and the newco. The court's decisions on this matter, however, were inconsistent and did not offer any clear guidance to investors.[10] Sometimes, the merger was considered a natural way to complete the LBO deal, allowing a concentration of assets between the newco and the target.

Other times, the merger was considered void because it was interpreted as a tool fraudulently adopted to obtain the exact same results that would otherwise be prohibited by the law. Therefore, the merger was invalidated by invoking the content of article 1344 (see Zambelli, 2008 for critical discussions of these draconian interpretations).

Following a different line of reasoning, in 1999 the Court of Milan intervened and suggested a case-by-case assessment approach, according to which LBO transactions should be considered legal if they are supported by sound business reasons aimed at promoting the development of the company with a proper project and a valid industrial plan ("rule of reasons" or "business judgment approach").[11]

Notwithstanding the innovativeness of this approach, the decision of the Court of Milan was criticized, because it left the ultimate assessment of the economic reasons underlying LBOs to the discretionary power of judges and did not provide investors with sufficient guidance, nor examples of business reasons that could be considered sufficient to ensure the legality of LBO transactions. Therefore, the legal uncertainty and the associated risk of receiving an illegality declaration by a Court was still very high, despite the new "business judgment" approach introduced by the Court of Milan.

The debate on LBO legitimacy intensified in 2000 when the Supreme Court intervened and reinforced the illegality view of LBOs. The Supreme Court deemed the LBO scheme illegal, interpreting it as a direct breach of the financial assistance ban, and therefore prohibited its adoption within the Italian context (Supreme Court Decision 5503/2000 regarding the D'Andria case). From a PE perspective, this decision was quite astonishing, especially because the statements of the Supreme Court applied to all LBOs carried out in Italy, and not merely the case that was judged by the Supreme Court. Considering the dominant role that LBOs have always played within the Italian PE market, the Supreme Court's decision was strongly criticized by the PE industry and increased the LBO debate, rather than solving it.

The high legal uncertainty surrounding LBO legitimacy raised strong concerns among PE investors, especially in consideration of the relevant *criminal consequences* that they could receive if a Court were to judge an LBO transaction to be in breach of the financial assistance ban. In fact, in the case of a legal dispute, if an LBO deal was charged with eluding the financial assistance ban, the directors involved in the transaction ran the risk of receiving criminal prosecutions of up to three years in prison (article 2630 of the Civil Code, now abolished by the Legislative Decree 61/2002).

What happened after the Supreme Court's decision?

By looking at the PE industry evolution subsequent to the Supreme Court's Decision, it is puzzling to note that LBOs *did not disappear from the market* despite the prohibition. The Supreme Court's ban only diminished the LBO frequency, but did not exclude them. These types of deals were carried out anyway, especially in the form of *mega deals* (over €150 million). Clearly, investors were only willing to run the transaction risk underlying LBOs for relevant deals, in terms of size and expected returns. Furthermore, in order to minimize the risks of receiving an illegitimacy declaration, several LBOs were also implemented with the adoption of complex *multi-layered* structures, characterized by more than one newco firm, one of which was typically located abroad.[12] As summarized in Zambelli (2010), a first holding company (newco 1) was typically incorporated abroad with the purpose of providing the equity capital to set up a second holding firm, located in Italy (newco 2). Newco 2 was established in Italy with the purpose of acquiring the shares of an Italian target company. From a financing point of view, newco 1 required a first loan to complete the acquisition of newco 2. Thereafter, the loan was indirectly transferred or pushed down to newco 2, either in the form of a high share premium or through a non-interest bearing loan (see Figure 4.6). Following the acquisition, newco 2 and the target would merge. Once the merger procedure was accomplished, the share premium (or the non-interest bearing loan) was paid back to newco 1 through a loan agreement between newco 2 and newco 1.[13] These complex structures were severely criticized by the Italian Tax Authority, which continued to challenge the legality of LBOs until 2016 (see Italian Tax Authority, 2016).

By the end of 2001, the Italian Parliament intervened and issued a Bill of Law (Bill of Law 366, October 2001) announcing its intention to overrule the Supreme Court's decision and legalize LBOs. With this Bill, in fact, Parliament assigned the Government the task of changing the entire corporate law, as well as introducing a safer and more precise legal harbor for LBOs (article 7, letter d).[14] This Bill did not, however, have an immediate efficacy in Italy. It was merely an *enabling act* through which the Parliament assigned the Government the task of issuing one or more legislative decrees aimed at reforming the entire Italian corporate governance law according to a set of guidelines, principles, and conditions. Furthermore, there was no certainty of when and how the new reform would be issued. Despite the uncertainty regarding the timing of the new reform, this Bill provided investors with some hope of a more favorable legal harbor for LBOs. Thereafter, in 2002, a new criminal law became effective and new criminal prosecutions were introduced with a potential

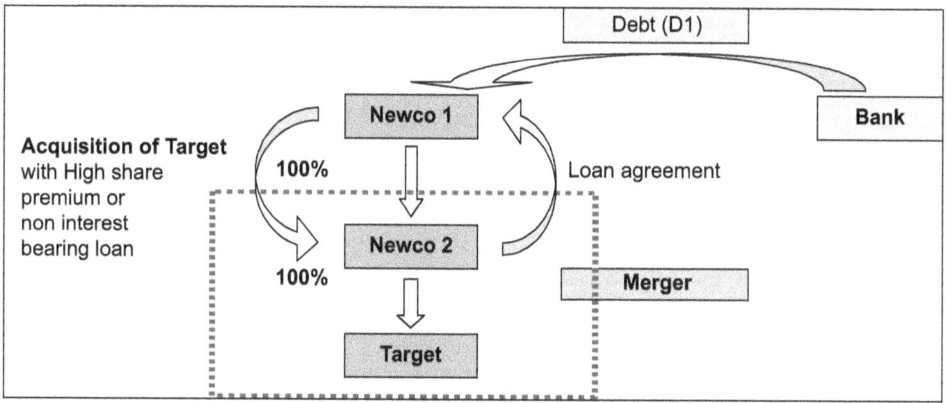

Figure 4.6 LBOs structured as multi-layered deals

This figure shows the typical structure of LBO deals over the period in which their legitimacy was uncertain and challenged by the courts (illegality period). Over the illegality period LBOs were carried out anyway, mainly in the form of *multi-layered deals*, with more than one newco firm, one of which was typically located abroad.

Source: Zambelli (2008: 73).

applicability to LBOs (Legislative Decree 61/2002). This Decree increased the confusion and legal uncertainty among buyout investors (for more details, see Zambelli, 2010).

In 2003, a new corporate governance reform was introduced and LBOs were legalized subject to a number of specific conditions (Legislative Decree number 6/2003). This reform became effective as of January 1, 2004 (hereafter "the 2004 reform"). With this reform, the Italian Government introduced a new provision (article 2501-bis of the Civil Code) aimed at better clarifying the legal status of LBOs, as well as specifying a number of requirements to ensure the legality of LBO transactions (contingent legalization). These requirements focus mainly on information disclosure, fair deal certification, business plan feasibility, and financial plan reasonableness (for more details on the specific requirements set by article 2501-bis, see, e.g., Giannino, 2006; Zambelli, 2008). Contrary to what has occurred in the past, with the 2004 reform the *burden of proof* is now reversed: if the conditions set by the new law are fulfilled, LBOs should be considered legal, unless proven otherwise.

Unresolved issues and tax challenges

The 2004 reform legalizes only LBOs that are accomplished with a merger between the newco and the target (merger LBOs).[15] The legitimacy of LBOs accomplished without a merger continues to remain uncertain, as well as the admissibility of LBOs that do not follow the specific procedure and conditions outlined by article 2501-bis. Reverse merger LBOs may still raise concerns: in these cases, in fact, breaches of the financial assistance ban may appear more evident in the eyes of a judge. The debate remains open also with reference to the legal consequences and sanctions applied to the directors involved in an LBO deal in case of bankruptcy of the target (for details see Zambelli, 2010).

Notwithstanding the 2004 LBO reform, LBOs remained highly criticized from a fiscal point of view. In particular, a decision by the Supreme Court (Tribunal Section, 24930,

November 25, 2011) and a number of Tax Authority interpretations (e.g., Circular 19E/2009) reopened the debate on the legitimacy of LBOs. Since the late 2000s, the Italian Tax Authority has severely challenged LBOs because they are viewed as fraudulent tools implemented by PE investors to elude the fiscal law, as well as to evade taxes.[16] The Italian Tax Authority has viewed all LBO transactions with great skepticism, especially the cross-border buyouts implemented with a multi-layered structure, and repeatedly contested the deductibility of the interest expenses connected to the loan underlying these types of deals. In some cases, the Italian Tax Authority has highlighted a lack of direct pertinence between the debt arranged by the newco and the business activity of the target and, as such, the Authority denied the deductibility of the related interest expenses.[17]

In other cases, the Tax Authority has not contested the lack of pertinence between the debt and the business activity of the target, but challenged the merger between the newco and the target, emphasizing the tax elusion result derived from the merger. In the view of the Tax Authority, in fact, the result of the merger is to transfer the liabilities of the newco onto the target's balance sheet ("debt push down") and, in doing so, the merger helps the newly combined company reduce the taxable income and evade taxes. This line of thought was especially applied in the cases of cross-border multi-layered deals, characterized by more than one controlling company (newco), one of which was located abroad (newco 1) and the other located in Italy (newco 2). In these circumstances, once the merger between newco 2 and the Italian target company was accomplished, the Tax Authority challenged the LBOs by applying the "transfer price rule" (set by article 110 TUIR) and allocated to the new Italian merged entity a higher taxable revenue, proportionately to the amount of debt pushed down to the target. Paradoxically, the Italian Tax Authority applied a tax on a debt (the loan underlying the LBO transaction), by interpreting such loan as a revenue that the newco could receive thanks to the service of financial assistance provided by the target for its own acquisition (Capizzi et al., 2017). This interpretation adopted by the Italian Tax Authority was inconsistent with the OCSE Guide Lines, according to which the financing costs must be allocated to the party that used the debt (see Grimaldi, 2014).

These draconian interpretations of LBOs by the Italian Tax Authority led to a great deal of criticism especially among PE investors who had to bear the costs of higher taxes and sanctions, even if they were following the 2004 LBO reforms. The public pressure by the PE industry forced the Italian Tax Authority to reconsider the essence of LBOs. Recently, the Tax Authority issued a new Circular Letter (6/E, March 30, 2016)[18] providing important clarifications on merger LBOs and admitting the deductibility of the interest payments connected to these types of transactions. The debate on LBO legitimacy is now closed and the Tax Authority has conformed to the 2004 reform.

Despite the unresolved issues highlighted here, the 2004 reform represents an important turning point for the Italian PE industry, as well as a unique example of contingent legalization of LBOs that could guide other policy makers around the world. As it will be explained in the following section, this reform has contributed positively to accelerating the development of both the Italian PE industry and its target firms.

Impact of the LBO legalization and policy implications

This section discusses the economic impact of the 2004 LBO reform on target firms and PE investor behavior.

In the absence of detailed public information on buyout deals, we carried out a three-stage survey of Italian PE funds who invested in Italy during 1999–2006 and exited their target firms between 2000 and 2013. Our data includes the vast majority (84%) of the buyout funds active in Italy.[19] We also performed a number of survey improvements by collecting further information from different public sources (e.g., Datastream by Thomson Corporation, Italian Venture Capital Association, Private Equity Monitor or PEM® database, investment reports, and PE fund websites) in order to double check, eventually correct and integrate the information obtained with the survey procedure, as well as to collect other relevant control variables (e.g., market returns, industry market to book values, capital under management, other fund characteristics, and balance sheets of target companies).

Our ultimate dataset comprises unique and detailed information on 178 target firms and their performance, actual contractual provisions and control rights included in the PE acquisition deal, as well as information on due diligence and screening criteria of target firms (see Cumming & Zambelli, 2017). In particular, our dataset provides information on the entire PE investment cycle, and is summarized as follows:

- Amount invested, investment year, transaction type, and deal structure;
- Selection criteria, due diligence, and methods of valuation of the target;
- Sources of finance used to accomplish the purchase of the target;
- Board rights and other control rights held by investors;
- Investor exit expectations;
- Exit routes and related fund returns;
- Performance of the target firms.

In the following sub-section, we will discuss the main results emerging from our empirical tests with reference to the impact of the 2004 LBO reforms. In particular, in the following section, we will analyze the impact of LBO regulation on the investors' behavior, deal structure, governance of target firms, firm performance, and due diligence. In order to better evaluate the economic impact of the LBO reform, we divided the regulatory changes into three main periods, metaphorically labeled as: Dark period (or period of illegality); Hope period (or period in which the Parliament announced its intention to legalize LBOs); and Sun period (or period of legality). The three sub-periods are also summarized below in Figure 4.7 (for more details, see Cumming and Zambelli, 2010; Zambelli, 2010).

Dark Period	**Hope Period**	**Sun Period**
Period in which the legitimacy of LBOs was uncertain and highly contested. ↓	Period in which the Italian Parliament announced its intention to legalize LBOs. ↓	Period in which LBOs were legalized ↓
Timing: January 1999 – September 2001	Timing: October 2001 – December 2003	Timing: January 2004 – July 2006

Figure 4.7 The three sub-periods of LBO regulation: Dark, Hope, and Sun

Figure 4.7 defines the characteristics of the three sub-periods (Dark, Hope, and Sun) according to the main changes experienced by the Italian regulatory environment.

Source: Cumming and Zambelli (2010).

The impact of the LBO legalization on fund involvement, due diligence, and firm performance

In this section, we discuss the main results underlying the studies of Cumming and Zambelli (2010, 2013, 2017).[20]

In the first of three papers, Cumming and Zambelli (2010) empirically examined the effects of LBO regulations on the structure of LBO transactions. Cumming and Zambelli show that even though LBOs were deemed to be illegal, they were not eliminated from the market. LBOs still existed, albeit they were less common than during periods of legality. LBOs in the period of illegality were more inefficiently structured, since the managerial focus was on evading illegality regulations. Specifically, during the period of illegality, LBOs were characterized with PE fund investors only having a minority of the board seats, fewer control rights, and smaller equity ownership percentages, relative to LBOs in the period of legality. PE fund managers screened target companies for their fit ("agreeableness") with the target firm management, unlike the period of legality when LBOs were more intensively screened for the quality of the deal. The examination of the data leads Cumming and Zambelli (2010) to suggest that uncertainty regarding the legal validity of LBOs impedes efficient governance and distorts decision making.

Cumming and Zambelli (2013) extend their 2010 study by examining the impact of LBO illegality in Italy on PE returns (in terms of IRR) and investee firm performance (in terms of EBITDA/sales). In theory, the effects could go either way. On the one hand, when goods are made illegal and there is still a supply of those goods, then prices tend to be higher. Consider for example the market for illegal drugs and diamonds, or the US experience with alcohol prohibition. As such, we may expect returns to be higher as there are fewer LBO deals in periods of illegality. On the other hand, regulation that lowers the quality of the transactions (the type and extent of due diligence and the involvement of the PE firms in governance and management) could reduce returns. The data examined by Cumming and Zambelli are consistent with the latter view: in the period of illegality, PE returns and investee performance were substantially worse, and the likelihood of PE-backed IPO exits was substantially lower. These performance reductions due to illegality were large: almost as pronounced in magnitude as the impact of the global financial crisis.

Cumming and Zambelli (2017) further extend their analyses by focusing more specifically on the economic value of due diligence. They investigate the relationship between due diligence and investee performance, and control for the reverse possibility that expected performance causes due diligence. The data are strongly consistent with the view that more extensive due diligence is associated with improved investee performance. Also, Cumming and Zambelli (2017) show that due diligence is more effective when it is performed by the PE fund managers themselves, and not by external agents including consultants, lawyers, and accountants.

Policy implications

The Italian 2004 LBO reform offers a unique experimental example in the field of entrepreneurial finance to evaluate the economic impact of restrictive regulations. The Italian changes in LBO regulation help assess whether or not an outright prohibition or a stringent financial ban on LBOs would improve the governance and the performance of target firms and the financing structure of buyouts.

The data underlying Cumming and Zambelli (2010, 2013, 2017) show that a prohibition of LBOs is not an efficient policy measure to protect the interest of target firms (see the

Appendix, Panels A, B, C, for more details on the underlying main findings). Over the period of prohibition, in fact, LBOs were still carried out, mainly with the adoption of multi-layered structures aimed at evading regulatory restrictions and minimizing the transaction risk. The illegality declaration not only inhibited the efficient structure of LBOs but also distorted the decision-making process of PE funds, who seemed more focused on minimizing the risk of a legal dispute rather than adding value to their target firms. The screening process was more focused on maximizing the agreeableness with the management of the target firms, instead of adopting more crucial selection criteria such as the business plan feasibility, market conditions, and growth potential of the target firms. Over the illegality period, investors minimized their involvement in their target firms by retaining just a minority position on the board of directors, having fewer control rights, and lower ownership stakes. This was detrimental for target firms because it negatively impacted their performances.

The LBO legalization, instead, had a positive impact not only on the frequency of buyout transactions but also on the financial structure of LBOs. It produced significant improvements on the governance and performance of target firms. PE funds increased their involvement in their portfolio firms in terms of invested capital, ownership percentage, board control, and other control rights. Furthermore, the legalization of LBOs positively affected the due diligence process, as well as the investor returns and performance of target firms.

The main policy implication from our data is that the interests of target firms and their stakeholders are not efficiently protected by a prohibiting regulation, but rather by other forms of regulation, such as a legalization subject to specific conditions related, for example, to the disclosure of the deal and the business plan feasibility, as was emphasized in Italy with the 2004 corporate governance reform. Other possible forms of regulation could introduce limits on the debt-to-earnings ratio. Future research is needed to assess and empirically investigate the efficacy of different forms of financial regulations.

Conclusions

This chapter highlights the perils of stringent financial bans and regulations in the context of debt merger and acquisitions (i.e., acquisitions that are financed primarily with debt and are completed with a merger between the companies involved). We provide evidence and insights on the inefficiency of excessive regulations by commenting on the empirical evidence related to the Italian PE market, whose transactions were previously prohibited and thereafter legalized. Our empirical analyses are based on a novel proprietary database composed of PE-backed transactions carried out in Italy over the 1999–2006 period and divested over the exit period from 2000 to 2009 (see Panels A, B, C of the Appendix for more details of the main findings of Cumming and Zambelli, 2010, 2013, 2017). Our analyses show the positive impact of the 2004 corporate governance reform that legalized LBOs, subject to a set of specific requirements ("contingent legalization" of LBOs). Our data also show the perils underlying stringent regulations on these types of transactions. Stringent regulations distort the due diligence, the fund involvement, and the allocation of time and attention dedicated to the target companies. These effects are detrimental for the target companies and are against the interests that legislators and policy makers around the world declare to protect.

Since the late 1990s, LBOs have been severely challenged by policy makers, tax authorities, legal scholars, and courts. At the core of the dispute was the interpretation of LBOs as fraudulent tools employed by PE investors in order to evade the law or to deprive target firms of their strategic assets. In 2000, the Italian Supreme Court even prohibited these types of transactions because it considered them a breach of the financial assistance ban. Since the early 2010s, the Italian Tax Authority has repeatedly challenged the legitimacy of LBOs by contesting the deductibility of the interest expenses associated with the debt underlying these types of deals. Only recently did the Italian Tax Authority begin to accept that the deductibility of the interest payments connected to the LBO loan are deductible (see the Circular Letter 6/E, March 30, 2016). The Italian LBO reform represents an innovative example of the prevention of abusive opportunistic behaviors by newco companies to the detriment of their target firms. The empirical studies of Cumming and Zambelli (2010, 2013, 2017) show that LBOs are merely financial tools. Like any other tool, LBOs can be used properly or misused. But when properly adopted, they allow a target firm to access alternative sources of funds (De Fontenay, 2014) and contribute to improving the performance of the acquired firms, as well as the fund involvement in managing them (Cumming and Zambelli, 2013).

In response to the ongoing debate on the need for more stringent regulation and bans on LBOs, legislators and policy makers aiming to better protect target firms and their stakeholders could follow the Italian example provided by the new Italian LBO reform introduced in 2004. Instead of prohibiting LBOs, the studies of Cumming and Zambelli (2010, 2013, 2017) show that the target's interests are better protected when LBOs are legalized under a set of conditions aimed at increasing the disclosure of the deal. Overall, our studies are consistent with the views that the legal environment significantly affects investor behavior and a prohibiting or stringent LBO regulation inhibits the efficient LBO structure and the governance of target firms. It reduces the incentives for PE funds to be actively involved in the management of their portfolio firms and it distorts the PE funds' decision-making process, to the detriment of target firms and their stakeholders.

Notes

1 For an overview of the criticism against LBOs, see, e.g., Yeoh (2007); Zambelli (2008, 2012); Thomsen (2009); Ferran (2011). See also: *The Economist* (2005, 2016); *BBC News* (2007) and *The Guardian* (2008).

2 For an overview of the criticism raised against LBOs by scholars and courts in Italy and Europe, see Ferran (2007); Zambelli (2008); Payne (2011).

3 Examples of new reforms affecting alternative investment funds are: The Dodd-Frank Reform and the Volcker Rule in the US and the Alternative Investment Fund Manager Directive (AIFMD) in Europe. Both reforms are currently under discussion for a revision. For updates on the various reforms and proposals recently introduced worldwide, see Payne (2011); Gibson and Sullivan (2015); Invest Europe (2017).

4 *The Economist*, November 19, 2009.

5 See also Jensen (1989, 1998); Wright et al. (1992, 1996, 2001, 2006, 2009); Holmstrom and Kaplan (2001); Chou et al. (2006); Kaplan and Strömberg (2009).

6 For the efficacy of the merger procedure, the approval of the shareholders' meetings of both merging companies is necessary (article 2501 of the Civil Code). Once approved, the merger becomes effective only after a waiting period of two months has passed; this waiting period has the purpose of allowing the creditors of both companies to oppose the merger (article 2503 of the Civil Code). If creditors oppose it, the merger is suspended and a court must intervene, unless a bank guarantee is granted in favor of the opposing creditors (article 2503 of the Civil Code, III paragraph).

7 For more details on the LBO deal structure, see Baldi (2015).

8 Examples of court decisions against the admissibility of LBOs are: Criminal Tribunal of Milan, June 30, 1992; Ivrea Tribunal, August 12, 1995; Tribunal of Milan, May 4, 1999; Supreme Court, February 4, 2000. Examples of court decisions in favor of LBOs are: Tribunal of Milan, May 14, 1992; Tribunal of Brescia, June 1, 1993; Tribunal of Milan, May 13, 1999.

9 For more details on the European context of LBO regulation, see, e.g., Giannino (2006); Ferran (2007); Zambelli (2012).

10 Article 1344 was typically invoked to invalidate the merger agreements.
11 Decision of Milan Court, May 13, 1999 with reference to the Trenno case.
12 These types of structures were severely contested by the Italian Tax Authority.
13 For more details, see Negri Clementi and Montironi (2002) and Silvestri (2005).
14 Article 7(d) of the Bill of Law 366/2001 states: "The merger of two companies, one of which had received debt financing in order to acquire the control over the other, does not imply a violation of the prohibition to make loans or provide guarantees for the purchase or the subscription of own shares."
15 On September 15, 2008, Italy introduced a new law (Legislative Decree 142/2008), aimed at creating exceptions to the financial assistance ban outlined by article 2358 of the Civil Code, in line with the principles included in the European Directive 2006/68. See Rusconi (2008) for more details.
16 See, e.g., Italian Tax Authority (2009).
17 For more details see: Capizzi et al. (2017). See also Morri and Guarino (2016).
18 The Circular issued by the Italian Tax Authority (2016) is available at: https://dato-images.imgix.net/45/1461337783-Circolaren.6_Edel30marzo2016.pdf?ixlib=rb-1.1.0. For more details and comments on the Circular recently issued by the Italian Tax Authority, see, e.g., Clifford Chance (2016); Deloitte (2016); Ernst & Young (2016); Morri and Guarino (2016); Saltarelli et al. (2016).
19 For recent details on the data collection procedure, see Cumming and Zambelli (2017).
20 In the Appendix (Panels A, B, C) we provide a more detailed overview of the main findings underlying Cumming and Zambelli (2010, 2013, 2017).

References

AIFI. 2015. *Statistics reports*. Milan, Italy: AIFI (Italian Venture Capital Association).

Allen, F., & Carletti, E. 2010. An overview of the crisis: Causes, consequences, and solutions. *International Review of Finance*, 10: 1–26.

Avgouleas, E. 2009. The global financial crisis, behavioural finance, and financial regulation: In search of a new orthodoxy. *Journal of Corporate Law Studies*, 9: 23–59.

Axelson, U., Strömberg, P., & Weisbach, M. 2009a. Why are buyouts levered? The financial structure of private equity firms. *Journal of Finance*, 64: 1549–1582.

Axelson, U., Weisbach, M., & Strömberg, P. 2009b. The financial structure of private equity funds. *Journal of Finance*, 64: 1549–1582.

Baldi, F. 2015. *The economics of leveraged buyouts*. Torino, Italy: Giappichelli.

BBC News. 2007, June 20. *Q&A: Private equity debate*. Available at: http://news.bbc.co.uk/2/hi/business/6221466.stm.

Bonini, S., Alkan, S., & Salvi, A. 2012. The effects of venture capitalists on the governance of firms. *Corporate Governance: An International Review*, 20: 21–45.

Borel, M., & Heger, D. 2014. *Sources of value creation through private equity-backed mergers and acquisitions: The case of buy-and-build strategies*. Working paper presented at the EFMA meeting 2014.

Bottazzi, L., Da Rin, M., & Hellmann, T. 2009. What is the role of legal systems in financial intermediation? Theory and evidence. *Journal of Financial Intermediation*, 18: 559–598.

Buchner, A., Mohamed, A., & Schwienbacher, A. 2016. Does risk explain persistence in private equity performance? *Journal of Corporate Finance*, 39: 18–35.

Cao, J., & Lerner, J. 2009. The performance of reverse leveraged buyouts. *Journal of Financial Economics*, 91: 139–157.

Capizzi, V., Parlamento, P., & Zambelli, S. 2017. Leveraged acquisitions: Technical, financial, fiscal and legal issues. In S. Gatti & S. Caselli (Eds.), *Structured finance*. Berlin: Springer.

Chou, D-W., Gombola, M., & Liu, F-Y. 2006. Earnings management and stock performance of reverse leveraged buyouts. *Journal of Financial and Quantitative*, 41: 407–428.

Claessens, S., & Kodres, L. 2014. *The regulatory responses to the global financial crisis: Some uncomfortable questions*. IMF Working Paper 14/46.

Clifford Chance. 2016. *Italy – Tax authorities finally publish guidelines on LBO transactions. Glass half full*. Available at: www.cliffordchance.com/briefings/2016/04/italy_tax_authoritiesfinallypublis.html and www.cliffordchance.com/content/dam/cliffordchance/Feature_topics/PDFs/tax_and_global_M_and_A.pdf.

Cumming, D., & Dai, N. 2011. Limited attention, fund size and the valuation of venture capital backed companies. *Journal of Empirical Finance*, 18: 2–15.
Cumming, D., Fleming, G., & Schwienbacher, A. 2006. Legality and venture capital exits. *Journal of Corporate Finance*, 12: 214–245.
Cumming, D., & Johan, S. 2007. Regulatory harmonization and the development of private equity markets. *Journal of Banking and Finance*, 31: 3218–3250.
Cumming, D., & Johan, S. 2013. *Venture capital and private equity contracting: An international perspective*. London: Elsevier Academic Press.
Cumming, D., Siegel, D., & Wright, M. 2007. Private equity, leveraged buyouts and governance. *Journal of Corporate Finance*, 13: 439–460.
Cumming, D., & Zambelli, S. 2010. Illegal buyouts. *Journal of Banking and Finance*, 34: 441–456.
Cumming, D., & Zambelli, S. 2013. Private equity performance under extreme regulation. *Journal of Banking and Finance*, 37: 1508–1523.
Cumming, D., & Zambelli, S. 2017. Due diligence and investee performance. *European Financial Management*, 23: 211–253.
Davidoff, S., & Zaring, D. T. 2009. Regulation by deal: The government's response to the financial crisis. *Administrative Law Review*, 61: 463–541.
De Fontenay, E. 2014. Private equity firms as gatekeepers. *Review of Banking & Financial Law*, 33: 115–189.
Deloitte. 2016. *Taxation and investment in Italy 2016*. Available at: www2.deloitte.com/content/dam/Deloitte/global/Documents/Tax/dttl-tax-italyguide-2016.pdf.
The Economist. 2005, May 26. *Locust versus locust*. Available at: www.economist.com/node/4010780.
The Economist. 2009, November 19. *Payback time*. Available at: www.economist.com/node/14921335.
The Economist. 2016, October 22. *Private equity. The barbarian establishment*. Available at: www.economist.com/news/briefing/21709007-private-equity-has-prospered-while-almost-every-other-approach-business-has-stumbled.
Enriques, L. 2002. Do corporate law judges matter? Some evidence From Milan. *European Business Organization Law Review*, 3: 756–821.
Enriques, L., & Volpin, P. F. 2007. Corporate governance reforms in continental Europe. *Journal of Economic Perspectives*, 21: 117–140.
Ernst & Young, 2016. *Italy issues important clarifications on (merger) leveraged buyout transaction*. Ernst & Young Global Limited. Report available at: www.ey.com/Publication/vwLUAssets/Italy_issues_important_clarifications_on_(mergerleveraged_buyout_transactions/$FILE/2016G_00314-161Gbl_Italy%20issues%20important%20clarifications%20on%20(merger)%20leveraged%20buyout%20transactions.pdf.
EVCA. 2015. *Public affairs overview*. Report available at: www.investeurope.eu/media/379999/EVCA-PA-Overview_April-2015.pdf.
Ferran, E. 2007. *Regulation of private equity-backed leveraged buyout activity in Europe*. ECGI Working paper 84/2007.
Ferran, E. 2011. The regulation of hedge funds and private equity in the EU. *European Business Organization Law Review*, 12: 379–414.
Financial Services Authority (FSA). 2006. *Private equity: A discussion of risk and regulatory engagement*. FSA November 6.
Gao, L. 2014. *Value creation in private equity-sponsored leveraged buyouts: Estimating a many-to-many matching game*. Available at SSRN: https://ssrn.com/abstract=2383049.
Giannino, M. 2006. *The regulation of LBOs under English and Italian company laws*. Available at SSRN: https://ssrn.com/abstract=1448719.
Gibson, S., & Sullivan, J. 2015. *Raising your next fund: The rising tide of global regulatory change*. Report available at: www.kwm.com/en/hk/knowledge/insights/raising-your-next-fund-the-rising-tide-of-global-regulatory-change-20150527.
Gompers, P., Kaplan, S., & Mukharlyamov, V. 2016. What do private equity firms say they do? *Journal of Financial Economics*, 121: 449–476.
Grimaldi. A. 2014. *Merger leveraged buy out, ecco perché l'Agenzia delle Entrate li contesta*. Available at: http://www.firstonline.info/News/2014/02/13/merger-leveraged-buy-out-ecco-perche-lagenzia-delle-entrate-li-contesta/ZjQ3ODk2ODAtYzFhOC00NjUwLTlkNjktOTE1MjJmNjk5ZGE0XzIwMTQtMDItMTNfRk9M.
The Guardian. 2007. *Saviours or asset-strippers – The private equity debate*. February, 11.

The Guardian. 2008. *Taming the private equity 'locusts'*. April, 10.
Hamdouni, A. 2011. Venture capitalist's monitoring through board membership and the performance of IPO firms: Empirical evidence from France. *International Research Journal of Finance and Economics*, 65: 124–133.
Harris, R., Jenkinson, T., & Kaplan, S. 2014. Private equity performance: What do we know? *The Journal of Finance*, 69: 1851–1882.
Harris, R., Jenkinson, T., & Kaplan, S. 2015. *How do private equity investments perform compared to public equity?* Darden Business School Working Paper No. 2597259. Available at SSRN: https://ssrn.com/abstract=2597259.
Heed, A. 2010. Regulation of private equity. *Journal of Banking Regulation*, 12: 24–47.
Holmstrom B., & Kaplan S. N. 2001. Corporate governance and merger activity in the United States: Making sense of the 1980s and 1990s. *Journal of Economic Perspectives*, 15: 121–144.
Hooke, J., Yook, K., & Hee, S. 2016. *The performance of mostly liquidated buyout funds, 2000–2007 vintage years*. Available at SSRN: https://ssrn.com/abstract=2718473.
Invest Europe. 2017. *Public affairs overview*. Available online at: www.investeurope.eu.
Italian Tax Authority (Agenzia delle Entrate). 2009. *Circolare n. 19/E del 21/04/2009. Modifiche alla disciplina della deducibilità degli interessi passivi dal reddito di impresa* - Legge 24 dicembre 2007, n. 244 (legge finanziaria per il 2008). Available at: www.agenziaentrate.gov.it/wps/file/nsilib/nsi/documentazione/provvedimenti+circolari+e+risoluzioni/circolari/archivio+circolari/circolari+2009/aprile+2009/circolare+19+del+21+04+2009/circ19Edel21aprile2009.pdf.
Italian Tax Authority (Agenzia delle Entrate). 2016. *Circolare n. 6/E del 30/03/2016. Chiarimenti in merito al trattamento fiscale delle "operazioni di acquisizione con indebitamento" - La deducibilità degli interessi passivi ed il trattamento delle componenti reddituali destinate a soggetti localizzati in paesi esteri*. Available at: https://dato-images.imgix.net/45/1461337783-Circolaren.6_Edel30marzo2016.pdf?ixlib=rb-1.1.0.
Jelic, R., & Wright, M. 2011. Exits, performance, and late stage private equity: The case of UK management buy-outs. *European Financial Management*, 17: 560–593.
Jensen, M. 1986. Agency costs of free cash flow, corporate finance and takeovers. *American Economic Review*, 76: 323–329.
Jensen, M. 1989. The eclipse of the public corporation. *Harvard Business Review*, 67: 61–74.
Jensen, M., 1998. Active investors, LBOs, and the privatization of bankruptcy. *Journal of Applied Corporate Finance*, 2: 235–244.
Kaplan, S., Martel, F., & Strömberg, P. 2007. How do legal differences and experience affect financial contracts? *Journal of Financial Intermediation*, 16: 273–311.
Kaplan, S., & Strömberg, P. 2009. Leveraged buyouts and private equity. *Journal of Economic Perspectives*, 23: 121–146.
Lerner, J., & Schoar, A. 2005. Does legal enforcement affect financial transactions? The contractual channel in private equity. *Quarterly Journal of Economics*, 120: 223–246.
Liu, C. 2014. *Debt structure, private equity reputation, and performance in leveraged buyouts*. Available at SSRN: https://ssrn.com/abstract=2312150.
Morri, S., & Guarino, S. 2016. *Leveraged buy-out and foreign shareholder loans: Issues from the recent approach of the Italian Tax Authority*. Available at: www.mralex.it/mm/LBO%20-%20shareholder%20loans.pdf.
Negri Clementi, A., & Montironi, P. 2002. *Leveraged buy-outs*. Discussion paper available at: www.altassets.com/casefor/countries/2002/nz3432.php.
Nikoskelainen, E., & Wright, M., 2007. The impact of corporate governance mechanisms on value increase in leveraged buyouts. *Journal of Corporate Finance*, 13: 511–537.
Opler, T., & Titman, S., 1993. The determinants of leveraged buyout activity: Free cash flow vs. financial distress costs. *Journal of Finance*, 48: 1985–1999.
Payne, J. 2011. Private equity and its regulation in Europe. *European Business Organization Law Review*, 12: 559–585.
Petitt, B. 2014. *The return of the leveraged buyout 'locusts'*. Financial Times. Available at: www.ft.com/content/6235cb46-882a-11e3-a926-00144feab7de.
Renneboog, L., 2007. Leveraged and management buyouts in Europe. *MCA – Tijdschrift voor Organisaties in Control*, 11: 16–28.
Rusconi, L. 2008. *Italy enacts new regulation on financial assistance*. Available at: www.bakernet.com/NR/rdonlyres/117CF60F-D2EB-4463-B7AB-8F663B2F3610/0/italy_newfinancialassistance_ca_nov08.pdf.

Saltarelli, F., Bosco, L., & Schiavello, S. 2016. *Italy tax alert. Authorities clarify tax treatment of LBO transactions*. Available at: www2.deloitte.com/content/dam/Deloitte/global/Documents/Tax/dttl-tax-alert-italy-6-april-2016.pdf.

Siegel, D. S., Wright, M., & Filatotchev, I. 2011. Private equity, LBOs, and corporate governance: International evidence. *Corporate Governance And International Review*, 19: 185–194.

Silvestri, M. 2005. The new Italian law on merger leveraged buy-outs: A law and economics perspective. *European Business Organization Law Review*, 6: 101–147.

Stein, B. 2006. On buyouts, there ought to be a law. *The New York Times*, September 3. Available at: www.nytimes.com/2006/09/03/business/yourmoney/03every.html?ex=1314936000&en=6679077c5af5c4a6&ei=5088&partner=rssnyt&emc=rss.

Suchard, J. A. 2009. The impact of venture capital backing on the corporate governance of Australian initial public offerings. *Journal of Banking and Finance*, 33: 765–774.

Thomsen, S. 2009. Should private equity be regulated? *European Business Organization Law Review*, 10: 97–114.

The Wall Street Journal. 2005. *German party calls investors 'locusts'*. Available at:www.wsj.com/articles/SB111498371843621593.

Wright, M., Ames, K., Weir, C., & Girma, S. 2009. Private equity and corporate governance: Retrospect and prospect. *Corporate Governance: An International Review*, 17: 353–375.

Wright, M., Hoskisson, R. E., Busenitz, L. W., & Dial, J. 2001. Finance and management buyouts: Agency versus entrepreneurship perspectives. *Venture Capital: An International Journal of Entrepreneurial Finance*, 3: 239–262.

Wright, M., Renneboog, L., Simons, T., & Scholes, L. 2006. Leveraged buyouts in the U.K. and Continental Europe: Retrospect and prospect. *Journal of Applied Corporate Finance*, 18: 38–55.

Wright, M., Thompson, S., & Robbie, K. 1992. Venture capital and management-led leveraged buyouts: A European perspective. *Journal of Business Venturing*, 7: 47–71.

Wright, M., Wilson, N., & Robbie, K. 1996. The longer term effects of management-led buyouts. *Journal of Entrepreneurial and Small Business Finance*, 5: 213–234.

Yeoh, P. 2007. Should private equity funds be further regulated? *Journal of Asset Management*, 8: 215–225.

Zambelli, S. 2008. The dark side of LBOs. Investors be forewarned! *Corporate Ownership and Control*, 5: 59–78.

Zambelli, S. 2010. Private equity and leveraged buyouts in Italy: To prohibit or not to prohibit, that is the question. In D. Cumming (Ed.), *Private equity: Fund types, risks and returns, and regulation*. Kolb Series in Finance. Hoboken, NJ: Wiley.

Zambelli, S. (2012). Private equity governance and financing decisions. In Cumming, D. (Ed) *The Oxford handbook of private equity*. Oxford, UK: Oxford University Press.

Appendix: Overview of the empirical analyses underlying the studies of Cumming and Zambelli (2010, 2013, 2017)

Panel A *Authors*	*Purpose*	*Data source(s)*	*Time period*	*Data coverage*	*Ultimate dataset*	*Main hypotheses and findings*
Cumming and Zambelli (2010)	The paper empirically investigates the efficacy of a restrictive or prohibiting LBO regulation and its impact on the structure of buyouts and the governance of target firms. Furthermore, the paper investigates the impact of buyout regulation on the frequency of LBOs, as well as the motivations underlying these types of transactions.	The data are derived from a survey of 27 PE investors involved in Italy over the 1999–2006 period.	The time period spans from 1999 to July 2006 and it is divided into three sub-periods: a. Dark period (or period of illegality and uncertain LBO legitimacy); b. Hope period (or period of potential legality). This period started with the Parliament announcement of a new safer LBO legal harbor; c. Sun period (or period of legalization).	The data cover 84% of the buyout funds actively involved in Italy over the period from 1999 to 2006.	The database consists of 103 buyout firms, acquired during the 1999–2006 period.	Hypotheses • H1: The LBO legalization in 2004 (Sun period) increases the frequency of buyouts; • H2: The period of illegality (Dark period) decreases the ownership stake retained by investors and their invested capital into the target firms; • H3: The Hope and Sun periods increase the fund involvement and control rights detained by PE funds. Main results The three hypotheses find strong support in the empirical analyses. The data show that with a prohibiting or stringent regulation: • The frequency of buyouts is reduced but LBOs are still carried out with a more inefficient structure; • PE funds invest less, have less cash flow and control rights, and focus their screening process more on the level of agreeableness with the target's management instead of focusing on more crucial factors (such as business plan and market conditions).

(Continued)

Appendix (Continued)

Panel B Authors	*Purpose*	*Data source(s)*	*Time period*	*Data coverage*	*Ultimate dataset*	*Main hypotheses and findings*
Cumming and Zambelli (2013)	The paper empirically investigates the impact of excessive regulation on PE returns (IRR) and firm performance (EBITDA/sales ratio). History shows that extreme regulation reduces the supply of capital and enhances returns (as seen in the case of drug, gun, and diamond trades). However, in a PE context, extreme regulation also reduces the fund involvement. The net impact in the context of PE is therefore doubtful. Furthermore, the paper investigates the impact of excessive regulation on exit outcomes.	The data are derived from a *two-stage survey* of PE investors involved in Italy over the 1999–2006 period. The *first stage* focuses on governance, screening, and deal structure. The *second stage* focuses on exit outcomes and fund returns.	Investment period: from 1999 to July 2006; Divestment period: from 2000 to 2009. The time framework is divided into three sub-periods, in line with the LBO regulatory changes occurring in Italy: a. Dark period (or period of illegality and uncertain LBO legitimacy); b. Hope period (or period of potential legality); c. Sun period (or period of legalization).	The data cover 27 PE funds, representing approximately 85% of the buyout funds actively involved in Italy over the period from 1999 to 2006.	The ultimate database consists of : • 178 PE-backed firms acquired over the investment period 1999–2006; • 125 divestments that occurred over the exit period 2000–2009. (among the 178 investments made over the investment period, 125 exits occurred within December 2009).w	Hypotheses • H1: The periods of illegality and uncertain legality of LBOs are associated with lower PE returns (in terms of IRRs); • H2: The periods of illegality and uncertain legality of LBOs are associated with lower firm performance; • H3: The illegality and uncertain legality of PE sponsored buyouts negatively reduce the probability of IPO exits. Main results The three hypotheses find strong support in the empirical analyses. • The data show that the prohibition of buyouts reduced both the supply of capital and fund returns, unlike other examples of prohibiting regulations, such as drug and gun trades, (where the prohibition was associated with a reduction of supply and an increase of returns). This difference is due to the fact that in a PE context, the illegality reduces the quality of funds' involvement in the target firms and, as such, the ultimate value added is compromised. • Moreover, the data show the negative impact of LBO prohibition on IPO exits.

Panel C Authors	*Purpose*	*Data source(s)*	*Time period*	*Data coverage*	*Ultimate dataset*	*Main hypotheses and findings*
Cumming and Zambelli (2017)	The paper is the first to empirically investigate the economic value of due diligence in the context of PE in relation to firm performance. The firm performances are measured in terms of Return on Assets (ROA) and EBITDA/ sales ratios. The performances are calculated in terms of differences over one, two, and three years after the investment. Furthermore, the paper investigates the impact of different types of due diligence (internal and external) and the role played by external agents in performing such evaluation tasks.	The data are derived from a *three-stage survey* of PE investors involved in Italy over the 1999–2006 period. The *first stage* focuses on PE investment cycle, governance, screening, and deal structure. The *second stage* focuses on PE returns. The *third stage* focuses on divestments and firm performance.	**Investment period:** from 1999 to 2006 (July); Divestment period: from January 2000 to December 2012. The time framework is divided into three sub-periods, in line with the LBO regulatory changes: a. Dark period (or period of illegality and uncertain LBO legitimacy); b. Hope period (or period of potential legality); c. Sun period (or period of legalization).	The data cover 27 PE funds, representing approximately 85% of the buyout funds actively involved in Italy over the period from 1999 to 2006.	The ultimate database consists of : • 178 PE-backed firms acquired over the investment period from 1999 to July 2006; • 150 divestments that occurred over the exit period, from 2000 to December 2012 (among the 178 investments made, 150 exits occurred within December 2012).	Hypotheses • H1: There is a positive and diminishing relationship between the time spent on due diligence and investee performance, due to the improved screening and matching; • H2: When due diligence is primarily performed by the PE fund manager ("internal due diligence"), there is a stronger positive association between the effort spent on due diligence and performance, due to the improved matching of PE funds and target firms. Main results After controlling for endogeneity, the data strongly support the above hypotheses. Based on a unique proprietary dataset, the empirical analyses show that the time spent on due diligence is an important source of value and is associated with improved firm performance. In particular: • The data show a significant link between the time spent on due diligence and the future performance of investee firms, measured in terms of changes in ROA and EBITDA/sales ratios exhibited by target firms over the first three years of the investments; • The data also show that the internal due diligence has a more pronounced impact on firm performance (while no significant impact on performance is associated with external due diligence).

This Appendix shows the main empirical analyses underlying the studies of Cumming and Zambelli (2010) (Panel A); Cumming and Zambelli (2013) (Panel B); Cumming and Zambelli (2013) (Panel C).

5

POLICY, REGULATION, AND PRIVATE EQUITY

A rich research agenda?

Sally Gibson and Simon Witney[1]

Introduction

Until a few years ago, private equity (PE) fund manager regulation in Europe was a matter for national governments, and the EU's "hands-off" approach gave rise to a variety of policy responses. On the one hand, many European countries judged PE to be a relatively low priority for regulators, given its mainly institutional and sophisticated investor base and perceived lack of systemic risk. In a number of EU jurisdictions (including, for example, Germany), that meant virtually no industry-specific regulation at all,[2] while in others (most notably the UK) fund managers were regulated, but in a relatively "light touch" way and mainly on the basis of "principles-based" standards. On the other hand, a few countries (France being the most important example) opted to put prescriptive rules in place, designed mainly to protect investors. Whether these regulatory choices had any significant impact on the development of national PE and venture capital industries is an interesting question in itself, but one that became moot when, following the financial crisis, EU regulators decided that pan-European rules were needed[3] – a decision that culminated, in 2011, in the Alternative Investment Fund Managers Directive[4] (the "AIFMD" or "the Directive"[5]). The Directive mainly regulates hedge fund and larger private equity fund managers, and had an implementation date of 2013, with transitional provisions expiring in 2014.[6]

Some practitioners[7] and academics[8] have argued that the AIFMD represents poor regulation, even if most acknowledge that the final version of the Directive was manageable and not as burdensome or restrictive as it might have been. It is certainly arguable that the Directive is an ill-conceived response that failed properly to identify the problems that it was seeking to address, and suffers from some ambiguous and anomalous drafting. However, with the rules now fully implemented and with the first review of the AIFMD underway at the time of writing,[9] there is an opportunity to take stock and to seek some empirical evidence on the impact of the AIFMD on the industry, both in terms of consequential changes to the operations of fund managers and the funds they manage and the impact of the new regulatory regime on European institutional (or professional) investors. Not only is that an important exercise for the EU regulators, but it will also be of great interest to the Financial Conduct Authority (the "FCA," the relevant UK regulator) as it decides how to regulate the fund management sector in a post-Brexit world.

This chapter will briefly review the main regulatory objectives of the AIFMD, insofar as they are capable of being discerned, and suggest an implied research agenda.

Scope of the Directive and the costs of opting in

The Directive seeks to regulate all alternative investment fund managers (each an AIFM)[10] operating or marketing funds in the EU,[11] but with a registration-only requirement for fund managers with assets under management ("AUM") falling below a certain size threshold. Fund managers with AUM below the threshold are, in fact, exempt from almost all of the Directive's requirements because they are "unlikely to have individually significant consequences for financial stability,"[12] An EU-based AIFM that is above the threshold must be authorized under the Directive (even if it does not wish to benefit from its passporting provisions), and its home state regulator must assess its ability to comply with the Directive's requirements. Its regulator will also assess the suitability of those running the business of the EU-based AIFM and its substantial shareholders. Certain provisions of the Directive (for example, those relating to controlled European portfolio companies and regulatory reporting) also apply to AIFMs established outside the EU if they have actively marketed their fund within the EU under national fund marketing rules.

The thresholds themselves differ according to the characteristics of the funds managed by the fund manager but, unfortunately, because of the uncertainty relating to the definition of "leverage" in the Directive (see further later), it is not always entirely clear which of the thresholds applies. The basic threshold is AUM of €100 million, with a higher value of €500 million set for managers of funds that are "unleveraged" and that offer no redemption rights exercisable for the first five years after initial closing. It seems clear that the higher threshold was intended to cover PE and venture capital funds, but adoption of the concept of leverage as a distinguishing feature of such funds is not entirely satisfactory.

The definition of AUM excludes undrawn commitments from investors, which means that when a fund is first raised it is likely to remain below the threshold and only exceed it as investments are made and/or increase in value. A manager must aggregate the AUM of all of the funds that it manages in order to determine whether it has exceeded the relevant threshold, although some transitional grandfathering provisions allow older funds to be excluded.

However, having excluded smaller fund managers from the scope of the Directive, a decision was also taken to exclude such managers from the EU's single market.[13] It is not entirely clear why the EU's institutions decided that exclusion from the AIFMD on the grounds that smaller fund managers and their funds did not pose risks for financial stability also entailed excluding them from the benefit of the EU-wide passport that was made available to AIFMD authorized fund managers (see later). As a consequence of the implementation of the Directive into the national laws of the EU jurisdictions, the national private placement rules were revisited and redefined and, in a number of jurisdictions, no real consideration was given to the position of EU-based smaller fund managers. The Directive does allow smaller fund managers to opt into the Directive, accepting all of its obligations in return for the passport, and – to the extent that managers feel obliged to do so in order to benefit from the single market's advantages – this would seem to impose *de facto* burdens and costs on fund managers (and ultimately their investors) that were not deemed to be necessary by the regulators. It would be interesting to identify the extent to which smaller fund managers have in fact voluntarily opted in to the Directive in this way and the burdens that it entails.

Prevention of fraud or malpractice: the value of a depositary

Those who framed the AIFMD were clearly concerned by the risk of fraud or malpractice or dissipation of fund assets. Perhaps conscious of some high-profile cases involving hedge funds, including the Madoff fraud and the collapse of Lehman Brothers, various provisions of the AIFMD provide for significant regulatory oversight of fund managers and their operations. The most significant way in which the Directive seeks to achieve these objectives is through the fund manager's obligation to engage a depository for each of its funds. Investors (who negotiate bespoke partnership agreements and insist on a wide range of investor protections) had typically required some outside financial oversight over the fund manager and the fund by an auditor (even if the domestic law did not require that), but had not typically required an outside custodian or a third party with a broader oversight function. However, the Directive imposes an obligatory gatekeeper role on an independent outsider, whose responsibilities extend significantly beyond safekeeping of assets.[14]

A depositary is generally required to be an EEA credit institution, an investment firm authorized under the Markets in Financial Instruments Directive (MiFID) that is subject to the same capital requirements as a credit institution, or a prudentially regulated and supervised institution that is eligible to be a depositary under the Undertakings for Collective Investment in Transferable Securities (UCITS) IV Directive. However, recognizing that such a strict set of eligibility requirements might be unnecessary for funds that do not have redemption rights within their first five years and do not generally invest in assets that require safekeeping (most notably PE funds), it is possible to appoint an alternative depositary, regulated in its own right. Many new entrants have ensured that there is a competitive market for alternative depositary services, and a significant number of PE funds have opted for such a solution.

The depositary is required to monitor fund cash flows, ensure that investor subscriptions and all funds are held in appropriately segregated accounts with an EU credit institution or similar institution, hold certain assets in custody and verify the ownership of "non-custody assets," ensure compliance with certain of the fund's rules, and perform certain other oversight tasks. The depositary has significant potential liability to investors in the event that these obligations are not complied with, although other than in relation to safekeeping of custody assets, liability only arises from intentional or negligent failures.

The requirement to appoint a depositary was one of the Directive's most controversial provisions,[15] particularly for UK-based managers who, unlike many in France and Luxembourg, were not familiar with such a requirement. There was a widespread view that the depositary would add cost and bureaucracy without significant additional protection for investors. A study that sought to measure the costs and benefits of the depositary function for PE fund managers, and the settled reaction of investors (who largely bear the costs) and fund managers, would make a helpful contribution to the evidence base.

Protecting investors: conduct of business rules

Apparently taking the view that investors in PE (and hedge) funds are not capable of negotiating appropriate terms in the bespoke partnership agreements that typically regulate their contract with the fund manager, the AIFMD seeks to regulate, through AIFMD-mandated standards of behaviors and conduct of business rules, certain aspects of the contractual bargain. No evidence was produced during the legislative process preceding the Directive to demonstrate a failure of contracting, and the requirements for optimal contractual bargaining would appear to be present.[16]

The standards of behavior and conduct of business rules included in the AIFMD effectively supplement the content of the fund's limited partnership agreement itself and are presumably intended to offer additional protection to investors.[17] For example, the AIFM must "act honestly, with due skill, care and diligence and fairly in conducting their activities"; ensure that its governing body has appropriate skill and expertise, act in the best interests of the funds or their investors; establish policies and procedures to prevent malpractice; operate due diligence policies and practices; and manage conflicts of interests and treat investors fairly. Investors can only be given preferential treatment if this is fully disclosed, but the Directive goes further and actually prohibits certain terms even if they are contractually agreed: any "preferential treatment" given to one investor must not result in an "overall material disadvantage to other investors"[18] (whatever that may mean). There are requirements to maintain a segregated risk management process;[19] to undertake specified levels of due diligence before investment and to keep certain records;[20] to develop and implement strategies on the exercise of voting rights;[21] and to maintain and apply an appropriate best execution policy.[22]

The AIFMD also regulates the fees that may be earned by the fund manager and, once again, goes beyond establishing a default rule: it expressly prohibits certain practices even if disclosed to and agreed by investors. In particular, fees received from any third party are prohibited unless (among other things) they are "designed to enhance the quality of the … service" provided to the fund.[23]

Remuneration

The AIFMD also includes restrictions on the way in which senior fund management employees[24] can be paid, largely following the content of rules originally drafted for the banking sector and now included in the Capital Requirements Directive.[25] The purpose of the rules is to ensure that remuneration practices "are consistent with and promote sound and effective risk management and do not encourage risk-taking which is inconsistent with the risk profiles, rules or instruments of incorporation of the AIFs they manage";[26] in other words, to align the interests of the senior staff and the fund's investors. There are no restrictions on the level of risk that can be taken by the fund manager in respect of its fund (subject to agreement with, and appropriate disclosure to, investors), so the need for prescriptive rules regulating, for example, the proportion of remuneration that can be paid as a bonus – rules that cannot be varied with investor consent – could restrict the ability of the fund manager and its senior staff to contractually agree appropriate remuneration policies.

In PE funds, it is typical for fund managers to receive a share of the profits of the fund, usually after the investors have received back their investment and an appropriate "preferred" return, which is known as "carried interest." It is clear from the Guidelines issued by the European regulator,[27] ESMA, that carried interest is, for AIFMD purposes, to be treated as "remuneration" and is therefore subject to the rules – although if the carried interest complies with specified criteria it will be deemed to fulfill certain of the requirements that would normally apply to variable remuneration.[28] In addition, the UK's FCA guidance on the application of the remuneration rules allows many fund managers to dis-apply certain rules applicable to variable remuneration on proportionality grounds.[29] Nevertheless, the fact that certain aspects of the remuneration structure are fixed even if the investors and the manager wish to negotiate an alternative arrangement constrains contractual flexibility and could lead to suboptimal outcomes in certain circumstances. In practice, given the provisions relating to carried interest and the flexibility to dis-apply certain requirements on proportionality grounds, it seems unlikely that the rules have heralded any significant changes to practice, although research on the impact of the rules on remuneration practices would be valuable.

Valuation

PE fund managers typically value their portfolio companies periodically and report those values to their investors. Such valuation is clearly not straightforward, given that there may be no readily available market price for the underlying assets, and industry guidelines have been developed to assist valuers.[30] Even though such valuations are rarely used to determine payouts to managers (because carried interest is paid only when profits are realized), the AIFMD adds its own requirements to those that are mandated by contractual agreement with the fund's investors. In particular, the valuation and the portfolio management function must be independent of each other, with appropriate rules to mitigate conflicts of interest, or an external valuer must be used. It seems unlikely that many PE firms would have appointed an external valuer, or that they would have made any significant changes to internal valuation procedures, but it would be useful to see what impact the Directive has had in this regard.

Delegation

The Directive restricts the extent to which an EU-based AIFM is able to delegate its functions to a third party.[31] The rules differ according to whether the manager is delegating one of its two core functions – risk management and portfolio management – or whether it is delegating other, non-core, services such as fund administration. For any delegation, the AIFM remains liable to the fund for adequate performance of the delegated matters and will need to notify its regulator and investors. In addition, the delegation must be objectively justifiable, undertaken after appropriate due diligence and the AIFM must retain oversight of the delegate. Specifically for risk or portfolio management, the EU-based AIFM cannot delegate to a depositary and can generally only delegate to regulated entities within the EU or those outside the EU where the relevant regulators have entered into a co-operation agreement.

General

Overall, whether investors draw additional comfort from these provisions, whether it has any discernible effect on their willingness to invest in PE funds, and whether any additional comfort that they do take is justified by the actual protection provided by the regulation, would be interesting research questions. It is plausible that the regulation encourages certain (less sophisticated) investors, relying on the regulated status of the manager, to invest in the asset class when they otherwise would not have done so and/or to negotiate weaker contractual protections than they otherwise might have done. If that is the case, there is a question as to whether any such reliance on the regulation is justified.

Regulatory capital

The Directive mandates fairly substantial capital requirements for fund managers,[32] with an initial capital requirement of €300,000 for AIFMs of internally managed AIFs and €125,000 for AIFMs of externally managed AIFs. It is not clear why such high levels of capital are required for firms with little exposure on their balance sheet and whose activities are comparable to firms benefiting from lower capital requirements under MiFID (such as the €50,000 requirement for firms that do not hold client money or securities and do not deal on own account or underwrite on a firm commitment basis). If the capital requirement is designed to enable the orderly wind-down of a failed firm, the requirements imposed by the AIFMD would seem to be excessive, given that it is typical for the manager to have a regular income stream from the underlying fund that will generally be sufficient to fund its ongoing operating expenses and enable orderly wind-down should the firm fail. In the UK, before the AIFMD (and still for firms that are outside the scope of the AIFMD),[33] the relevant capital requirement could be as low as £5,000, and the additional amount mandated by the Directive adds a significant cost to operating an authorized manager and could deter new entrants, especially since the requirement is to hold much of the capital in liquid assets. To give some idea of the extent of the ongoing requirement, an AIFMD-authorized manager of externally managed AIFs with assets under management of €1 billion could be required to hold liquid assets (which it could not use for the purposes of its own working capital) of around €325,000.[34]

Protecting the financial system

A desire to protect the financial system is evident in a number of the Directive's provisions. There was a view among the legislators at the time the Directive was being discussed that, although they did not cause the financial crisis, hedge funds had amplified its severity and were a source of systemic risk. On the other hand, while it was clear that such charges could not be leveled at the PE industry, some argued that leverage at the level of a PE-backed portfolio company and a lack of transparency might pose a threat to financial stability in the future.[35] For example, the ECB concluded that: "All in all, while the likelihood of LBO activity posing systemic risks for the banking sector appears remote at the EU level, the survey results underlined the fact that behind recent rapid growth in the market some pockets of vulnerability could be developing."[36]

However, if these concerns about systemic risk did motivate the legislators, it is far from clear how effectively the final version of the Directive addresses them, which perhaps reflects the fact that the concerns were not well supported by evidence, and indeed were strongly disputed by the PE industry.[37]

The Directive does impose a certain level of disclosure (both to regulators[38] and to investors[39]) on fund managers in relation to the amount and type of "leverage" employed by its funds, especially those that employ leverage on a substantial basis,[40] although it does not directly limit the amount of leverage that a fund can take on. Instead, the fund manager must set and declare its own leverage limit,[41] and the supervisors are therefore theoretically able to monitor the build-up of leverage in the system. National regulators are empowered to impose leverage limits when that is deemed necessary, and ESMA is given powers to "advise" national supervisors in that regard.[42]

However, the Directive itself left open the precise definition of leverage,[43] which is dealt with in the Level 2 rules,[44] and the resulting definition seems to disregard leverage taken on by a company owned by the fund, provided that there is no recourse to the fund for that debt.[45] Such a position is entirely logical, because the other assets of the fund are not put at risk by a default on the part of the underlying company, and would appear to acknowledge the industry's argument that the PE leverage model is not a source of systemic risk in itself.

This definition of leverage, and the exclusion of debt incurred by an underlying portfolio company, is important not just because it determines whether additional disclosures are required and the methods of calculating the ratios to be disclosed, but also because, if a fund is "unleveraged," the manager may be able to benefit from the higher AUM thresholds referred to above. Unfortunately, there appear to be a number of other problems with the methods of calculation mandated by the Commission that may confound the apparent intention of the draftsperson. A rigorous analysis of these calculation methodologies and their implications for funds would be useful, and may help regulators to make sense of the information they receive in respect of leveraged funds.

In addition to rules relating to leverage reporting, the Directive also includes requirements for an AIFM to report regularly to national regulators on a range of other matters. In general, the frequency of such reporting depends upon the AUM of the AIFM, but AIFMs that only manage unleveraged funds investing in non-listed companies (intended as a proxy for PE funds) need only report annually. Regulator reporting is quite a burdensome process – the reporting template is quite detailed, including (for example) information on investments made, the strategies of the fund, and the markets on which it trades.

Protecting employees and stakeholders more generally

Legislators expressed some concerns during discussions about the AIFMD that PE-backed companies could have their capital depleted by the PE fund, weakening the company's own long-term prospects,[46] and the lack of disclosure required from these large companies had also given rise to concerns that, in the UK, the industry had addressed this voluntarily through the Walker Guidelines on Disclosure and Transparency in Private Equity.[47] In fact, these concerns, rather than concerns about systemic risk, appear to have been more prevalent in the debates about PE (as opposed to hedge funds) and were taken up by a number of European trade unions and politicians.

As a result, although the Directive does not directly regulate PE-backed companies, it does impose various obligations on an EU-based AIFM in relation to EU-based companies controlled by a fund or funds that it manages (either alone or jointly with another fund).[48] With exclusions for SMEs,[49] the fund manager is required to disclose its stake in an EU-based portfolio company when it reaches certain ownership thresholds, and must make additional disclosures to an unlisted company and its shareholders, and the regulator, when the fund owns more than 50% (or 30% for a listed company).[50] In addition, on the acquisition of control of an EU-based company (listed or unlisted), the AIFM must disclose its policy for preventing and managing conflicts of interest and "the policy for external and internal communication relating to the company in particular as regards employees"; for private companies, the intentions for the business and likely repercussions on employment must also be given. The AIFM is obliged to make efforts to ensure that these communications are passed to employees or their representatives, and (for a private company) is also required to give information on the financing of the acquisition to the AIFM's regulator and the fund investors.

There are also continuing obligations: an affected unlisted company's annual report, or that of the fund manager, must include a fair review of the development of the company's business, details of important events since the end of the financial year, and information relating to share buybacks and the company's likely future development. Again, efforts must be made to make this information available to employees and to the fund's investors.

It might be doubted that these requirements have had any meaningful impact on the relationships among a fund manager, a portfolio company acquired by its fund, and the company's shareholders and employees, or whether they have improved the quality of information relayed to the fund investors, but research on that question would be valuable.

Another impact of the Directive for an EU-based AIFM was the introduction of new rules restricting certain distributions to shareholders of European portfolio companies controlled by one of its funds. Again, the regulation affects the AIFM rather than the underlying company, and mandates the manager to vote against, or otherwise take steps to prevent, certain distributions, capital reductions, share redemptions, or share buybacks for a period of two years after the initial acquisition of control unless (in the case of a distribution) the proposed distribution does not cause net assets to fall below the subscribed capital and is made from net profit. The rules are poorly drafted and include a number of ambiguities that make their application hard to understand in many situations and give rise to potentially perverse effects. However, they appear to aim to prevent a situation that was in any case rather rare and so may not have had any significant effect on behavior.

The passport

As we have seen, the Directive imposes considerable additional regulation on an EU-based AIFM. However, in return, such a fund manager receives a significant benefit: the right to manage and market its funds freely across the EU, without requiring any separate authorization in any other member state.[51] In reality, the passport has proved less seamless than might have been hoped, with a number of member states imposing fees on AIFMs that make use of the marketing passport in their territory. However, the alternative – a patchwork of national regulations that enable AIFs to be marketed to domestic investors to varying degrees – is generally more costly to navigate when a manager wishes to raise money from investors in a variety of EU countries and, consequently, an EU-based AIFM generally is able to market to investors more easily than an out-of-scope fund manager (unless such fund manager opts in or qualifies for a passport under separate regimes applicable to venture capital and social entrepreneurship funds)[52] or one that is based in a non-EU country. Whether this benefit outweighs the costs of the Directive for the fund manager concerned would be an interesting research question, and an analysis of the fund managers that are outside the scope of the Directive but that have chosen to opt in could be a valuable way to analyze it.

As mentioned earlier, it remains unclear why smaller buyout fund managers, whose lack of systemic importance is acknowledged by the Directive, are not able to benefit from access to the single market on a passported basis, but, despite some proposed reforms to the venture capital and social entrepreneurship regulations, there do not seem to be any immediate plans to bring forward a more generalized passport for EU firms that pose no risk to financial stability and that are therefore excluded from pan-European regulation. If the costs of that were better understood, the data could help persuade the EU institutions to alter their current approach.

One important, unresolved issue arising from the AIFMD is the availability of a marketing passport for non-EU-based fund managers (and for EU-based fund managers who wish to market a non-EU AIF). According to the terms of the Directive,[53] such a passport should have been made available under delegated acts following positive advice from ESMA, which was to be delivered by July 2015. In fact, ESMA did provide some advice in accordance with those provisions in relation to six countries, but the Commission opted to defer the passport while ESMA expanded its analysis.[54] In September 2016 ESMA issued revised advice,[55] the substance of which was that there are no significant barriers to an extension of the passport to a number of non-EU countries, including Switzerland and the Channel Islands. However, notwithstanding that advice and the provisions of the Directive, which would appear to require the Commission to draft a delegated act, the third country passport has so far not been made available.[56] There is some speculation that the delay is a reaction to Brexit, on the basis that it would be very difficult to deny the passport to UK-based managers after the UK leaves the EU if it has been made available to fund managers in other non-EU countries. A recent speech by Steven Maijoor, Chairman of ESMA,[57] also suggests that the EU may take a more restrictive stance towards equivalence and be less willing to grant equivalence decisions to third country jurisdictions that enable firms from those jurisdictions to provide services in the EU on a cross-border basis without a license. Although the comments were made in the context of the equivalence regime for central counterparty clearinghouses, they could equally apply to the other equivalence regimes contained in recent financial services legislation.

The impact of the lack of a passport for non-EU fund managers, combined with the difficulties in accessing European investors under the patchwork of national private placement rules that are now in place, may be having a significant impact on the level of access European-based investors have to non-EU fund managers and their funds. While it is clear that some non-EU fund managers might be willing to navigate the domestic rules in some EU countries (especially those that have a relatively high number of prospective investors and relatively straightforward marketing rules, like the UK), it seems plausible that many will simply avoid marketing to European investors in some jurisdictions (or perhaps in most or all jurisdictions) given the costs associated with doing so. On the other hand, the costs of accessing the passport – if it were to be made available – would also be significant, and might be prohibitive for a fund manager raising capital for its fund largely from non-EU investors. Implementing a passport and then closing down national private placement rules, as envisaged by the Directive,[58] could therefore make the position worse for EU investors. Research on the likely impact of the continuing delay in implementing the third country passport could help to shed light on this question, and might also inform the approach that is taken to the arrangements between the EU and the UK in a post-Brexit world.

Conclusions

The Directive sought to achieve multiple, unrelated objectives within a single piece of legislation. Although the primary aim was to harmonize regulation of private funds at a pan-European level and provide a passport in respect of private funds where none existed before, the Directive also sought to achieve additional objectives related to investor protection, financial stability, and portfolio company governance. It is questionable whether such unrelated objectives have been satisfactorily addressed in the Directive or whether it would have been better to confine the Directive to a narrower set of objectives. The EU has developed a sophisticated framework for financial stability, with the European Systemic Risk Board working together with the European Supervisory Authorities to monitor risks to financial stability and adopt measures that are more suitable for addressing financial stability and macro-prudential concerns than the hard-wired requirements in the AIFMD. Corporate governance regulation is also evolving in the EU, and it is far from clear that inflexible requirements in a Directive principally aimed at imposing authorization and business conduct requirements for private fund managers are the best way to achieve protection for investee companies and their stakeholders. It is particularly difficult to see why such protection, if necessary at all, should be triggered by the fact that the relevant fund is subject to the AIFMD.

Notes

1 The authors are grateful to Aatif Ahmad, International Counsel, Debevoise & Plimpton for his assistance in the preparation of this chapter.
2 Although there was an absence of targeted, industry-specific regulation, many activities of PE fund managers were, of course, subject to regulation, and it would perhaps be misleading to say that they were "unregulated" – see Duncan et al. (2011).
3 It was not only EU regulators that came to this conclusion: The Dodd-Frank Act, passed in the US in 2010, also regulates PE fund managers, and because many European PE managers raise significant funds from US investors, some aspects of the US regulations cover some European managers as well as those based in the US.
4 Directive 2011/61/EU of the European Parliament and of the Council of 8 June 2011 on Alternative Investment Fund Managers.
5 The AIFMD is supplemented by Level 2 Regulations (Commission Delegated Regulation (EU) No 231/2013 of 19 December 2012), hereafter "Level 2," and was implemented in the UK by The Alternative Investment Fund Managers Regulations 2013 (SI 2013 / 1773) and the rules and guidance of the FCA (as set out principally in the FUND sourcebook of the FCA *Handbook*).
6 See Article 66 (setting a deadline for transposition by member states of 22 July 2013) and Article 61 (providing for a one-year period after transposition for managers to become authorised).
7 See, for example, Funds flee offshore to evade 'bad' regulation, *Financial Times*, October 16, 2011, available at: www.ft.com/content/60642840-f5b4-11e0-be8c-00144feab49a.
8 See, for example, Payne (2011), who argues (p. 585) that PE was swept into a regulatory agenda which will add costs and put it at a competitive disadvantage, even though "the justifications for the regulation of PE at EU level are much weaker than in relation to hedge funds." For further discussion of the background to and the reasons for regulating the PE and hedge fund industries, as well as a comprehensive analysis of the AIFMD's main provisions, see Ferran (2011). For a review of the legislative process, see James (2014).
9 AIFMD Article 69, which reads: "By 22 July 2017, the Commission shall, on the basis of public consultation and in the light of the discussions with competent authorities, start a review on the application and the scope of this Directive. That review shall analyse the experience acquired in applying this Directive, its impact on investors, AIFs or AIFMs, in the Union and in third countries, and the degree to which the objectives of this Directive have been achieved."
10 Some of the critical definitions in the AIFMD, including that of an "alternative investment fund" (or AIF), are notoriously difficult to apply at the margins. In broad terms, the AIFMD Article 4(1)(a) defines an AIF as a collective investment undertaking that raises capital from a number of investors, invests in accordance with a defined investment policy, and is not regulated under the UCITS Directive (2009/65/EC), and an AIFM is a manager of such a fund.
11 Technically, the territorial scope of the AIFMD is the EEA, which is the EU plus Norway, Iceland, and Lichtenstein. However, the terms of the implementation of the Directive in some EU countries, and the delayed implementation in some EEA states, has made the position rather complicated, and for the purposes of this chapter we have referred to the territorial scope as "the EU."
12 AIFMD Recital 17 and Article 3.
13 Unless the fund manager falls within the regimes applicable to venture capital funds and social entrepreneurship funds; see footnote 53 below.
14 AIFMD Article 21.
15 See Ernst & Young (2012: 22).
16 Various academic analyses of venture capital and PE limited partnerships suggest that sophisticated and bespoke contracting does take place – see, for example, Gompers and Lerner (1996) and Metrick and Yasuda (2010). See, however, Phalippou et al. (2015) for evidence that regulatory intervention has altered the negotiated outcome in relation to fees charged and retained by PE managers.
17 AIFMD Article 12.
18 Level 2 Article 23.
19 AIFMD Article 15.
20 Level 2 Articles 18 and 19.
21 Level 2 Article 37.
22 Level 2 Article 27.

23 Level 2 Article 24.
24 The rules apply to staff of the AIFM whose activities have a material impact on the risk profile of the fund manager and the funds it manages.
25 Directive 2013/36/EU of the European Parliament and of the Council of 26 June 2013.
26 AIFMD Article 13.
27 ESMA, *Guidelines on sound remuneration policies under the AIFMD*, available at: www.esma.europa.eu/sites/default/files/library/2015/11/2013-232_aifmd_guidelines_on_remuneration_-_en.pdf.
28 ESMA, *Guidelines on sound remuneration policies under the AIFMD*, ibid., at paragraph 159 on p. 32.
29 FCA, *General guidance on the AIFM Remuneration Code (SYSC 19B)*, available at www.fca.org.uk/publication/finalised-guidance/fg14-02.pdf.
30 See *International Private Equity and Venture Capital Valuation Guidelines*, December 2015, available at www.privateequityvaluation.com/download/i/mark_dl/u/4012990401/4625734325/151222%20IPEV%20Valuation%20Guidelines%20December%202015%20Final.pdf.
31 AIFMD Article 20.
32 The capital requirements are set out in Article 9 of the AIFMD.
33 The capital requirements for a "small authorised UK AIFM" are set by the Financial Conduct Authority and set out in the relevant rulebook: IPRU-INV 5.4.
34 See Invest Europe's Guide to the AIFMD, *AIFMD Essentials*, published July 2013 and available at: www.investeurope.eu/policy/evca-publications/#i, p. 30. This calculation assumes that one-quarter of fixed overheads would be €225,000 and that the AIFM would choose to hold additional capital instead of maintaining professional indemnity insurance to meet the Directive's requirements.
35 See, for example, the influential report produced by the PSE (Socialist Group in the European Parliament), *Hedge Funds and Private Equity – A Critical Analysis*, available at: www.socialistsanddemocrats.eu/sites/default/files/2239_EN_publication_hedge_funds_1.pdf; *Draft Report of the European Parliament (Committee on Economic and Monetary Affairs) with recommendations to the Commission on hedge funds and private equity (2007/2238(INI))*, April 2008, available at www.europarl.europa.eu/sides/getDoc.do?pubRef=-//EP//NONSGML+COMPARL+PE-404.764+01+DOC+PDF+V0//EN&language=EN, p. 14; Ferran (2011: 382–385) and, more recently, the Bank of England's Quarterly Bulletin 2013 Q, *Private equity and financial stability*, available at www.bankofengland.co.uk/publications/Documents/quarterlybulletin/2013/qb130104.pdf.
36 The European Central Bank, *Large banks and private equity-sponsored leveraged buyouts in the EU*, April 2007, available at: www.ecb.europa.eu/pub/pdf/other/largebanksandprivateequity200704en.pdf.
37 See EVCA, *Private equity and venture capital in the European economy – An industry response to the European Parliament and the European Commission*, February 2009, available at: www.investeurope.eu/uploadedfiles/news1/news_items/evca_submission_to_ec_and_ep_fullpaper.pdf. Many argued that, if there were concerns that banks were over-exposed to the debt of PE-backed companies, that concern should be dealt with by banking regulation and not at the borrower level.
38 AIFMD Article 24.
39 AIFMD Article 23.
40 Level 2 Article 111 stipulates that leverage employed on a substantial basis arises where the exposure of the AIF exceeds three times its net asset value.
41 AIFMD Article 15(4).
42 AIFMD Article 25.
43 AIFMD Article 4(v) defines leverage as "any method by which the AIFM increases the exposure of an AIF it manages whether through borrowing of cash or securities, or leverage embedded in derivative positions or by any other means," and Article 4(3) mandates delegated acts to further specify the methods of calculating leverage, including "any financial and/or legal structures involving third parties controlled by the relevant AIF."
44 Level 2 Section 2.
45 Level 2 Article 6(3) says: "For AIFs whose core investment policy is to acquire control of non-listed companies or issuers, the AIFM shall not include in the calculation of the leverage any exposure that exists at the level of those non-listed companies and issuers provided that the AIF or the AIFM acting on behalf of the AIF does not have to bear potential losses beyond its investment in the

respective company or issuer." ESMA's Q&A on the AIFMD, Section VII: Calculation of leverage, updated in May 2015 (available at www.esma.europa.eu/file/20454/download?token=hLXnqKCi, confirms that interpretation.

46 See, for example, PSE (Socialist Group in the European Parliament), *Hedge Funds and Private Equity – A Critical Analysis*, available at: www.socialistsanddemocrats.eu/sites/default/files/2239_EN_publication_hedge_funds_1.pdf; *Draft Report of the European Parliament (Committee on Economic and Monetary Affairs) with recommendations to the Commission on hedge funds and private equity (2007/2238(INI))*, April 2008, available at www.europarl.europa.eu/sides/getDoc.do?pubRef=-//EP//NONSGML+COMPARL+PE-404.764+01+DOC+PDF+V0//EN&language=EN, p. 14. See also Ferran (2011: 386–387).

47 See http://privateequityreportinggroup.co.uk/.

48 AIFMD Articles 26–30.

49 SMEs are as defined in Article 2(1) of the Annex to Commission Recommendation 2003/361/EC of 6 May 2003 concerning the definition of micro, small and medium-sized enterprises and, broadly, are companies with less than 250 employees and either turnover equal to or less than €50 million or a balance sheet total equal to or less than €43 million.

50 In fact, the threshold for a listed company will vary from country to country, as these are specified by the member state under Article 5(3) of the Takeover Directive (Directive 2004/25/EC). In the UK, the relevant threshold is 30%.

51 AIFMD Articles 32 and 33.

52 Regulation (EU) No 345/2013 of the European Parliament and of the Council of 17 April 2013 on European venture capital funds and Regulation (EU) No 346/2013 of the European Parliament and of the Council of 17 April 2013 on European social entrepreneurship funds.

53 AIFMD Article 67.

54 www.esma.europa.eu/sites/default/files/library/eu_commission_letter_aifmd_passport.pdf.

55 www.esma.europa.eu/press-news/esma-news/esma-advises-extension-funds-passport-12-non-eu-countries. The original advice was issued in July 2016, but updated in September.

56 While the Commission appears to be obliged to adopt the delegated act extending the passport once it receives positive advice, ESMA left the door open for the Commission to delay the delegated act by stating in its advice that the Commission may "wish to consider whether to wait until ESMA has delivered positive advice on a sufficient number of non-EU countries before triggering the legislative procedures [to adopt the delegated act]."

57 See www.esma.europa.eu/press-news/esma-news/steven-maijoors-address-alde-seminar-review-european-supervisory-authorities.

58 AIFMD Article 68.

References

Duncan, A., Curtin, E., & Crosignani, M. 2011. Alternative regulation: The directive on alternative investment fund managers. *Capital Markets Law Journal*, 6: 326–363.

Ernst & Young. 2012. *Game changing regulation? The perceived impact of the AIFM Directive on private equity in Europe*. EYG no. FR0059. EYGM Ltd.

Ferran, E. 2011. After the crisis: The regulation of hedge funds and private equity in the EU. *E.B.O.R.*, 12: 379–414.

Gompers, P. A., & Lerner, J. 1996. The use of covenants: An empirical analysis of venture partnership agreements. *Journal of Law and Economics*, 39: 463–498.

James, S. 2014. *A report on lessons learnt from the negotiation of the alternative investment fund managers' directive*. London: British Private Equity & Venture Capital Association.

Metrick, A., & Yasuda, A. 2010. The economics of private equity funds. *Review of Financial Studies*, 23: 2303–2341.

Payne, J. 2011. Private equity and its regulation in Europe. *European Business Organization Law Review*, 12: 559–585.

Phalippou, L., Rauch, C., & Umber, M. P. 2015. *Private equity portfolio company fees*. Saïd Business School WP 2015-22. Available at SSRN: https://ssrn.com/abstract=2703354.

PART II

Vendor sources

6
MANAGEMENT BUYOUTS AND DIVESTMENT

Steve Thompson and Michelle Haynes

Introduction

The passing of control from ageing or infirm business owners to their senior employees or managers has no doubt always been a part of leadership succession and is probably as old as enterprise itself. However, the management buyout (MBO) – that is the transfer of enterprise ownership to a new, specially created company in which the existing senior managers are significant equity investors – became a recognized business format only in the late 1970s; although it spread rapidly thereafter. From those early beginnings onwards, the MBO was seen as a solution to a variety of problems. As shown in the following chapters in this part of this volume, these included not merely leadership succession, but also the rescue of failing enterprises, and the privatization of (at least the smaller) state-owned businesses. Significantly, MBOs also emerged as a destination for divested subsidiaries or divisions as some multiproduct firms began to rationalize their activities. Over the course of the subsequent years, the MBO has been both a contributory cause and a consequence of an ongoing trend towards corporate refocusing.

This chapter explores the inter-relationship between divestment and the MBO. In so doing it also considers the evolving role of the capital market in facilitating buyouts in general and particularly divestment MBOs. Had the MBO been simply an interesting design for a highly incentivized and decentralized corporate form, it might have been little more than an historical curiosity, perhaps like the employee co-ops that immediately preceded it in the 1970s. Most managers then as now – and certainly from middle management – would lack the funds to buy their companies. MBO deals needed the enabling development of institutions willing to advance senior and subordinated debt to the new company, thereby allowing the management team to hold a substantial proportion of the voting equity in return for a relatively modest investment.

Posing a set of single-product, management-owned businesses as an alternative to the diversified, multiproduct corporation implies a greater role for the external suppliers of capital. Following Williamson (1975), the multidivisional form, as described by Chandler (1962, 1977), was widely seen as a device to finance investment *within* the firm by reallocating funds from profit-rich but growth-poor divisions (the "cash cows" of the Boston Consulting Group fame) to those younger siblings possessing potential. In essence, this internalized the role of the capital market. Divestment required an external market willing and able to back credible management teams.

Not merely did the MBO as a phenomenon develop rapidly after its initial appearances in the late 1970s, but so did academic interest in its form and consequences. Within a decade, journals in management, finance, and economics were carrying articles that explored the incentives inherent in the MBO, the limits if any to its applicability, and the performance consequences of its adoption. The *Harvard Business Review* featured a fierce polemic from leading finance academic Michael Jensen (1989) hailing the buyout's "eclipse" of the public corporation and an equally strong defense and critique of high-leverage buyouts by Rappaport (1990).

To the fore in developing academic interest in MBOs has been the Centre for Management Buy-Out Research (CMBOR), the research centre whose anniversary occasioned this conference volume. CMBOR, founded at Nottingham by Mike Wright and John Coyne in 1986, recognized the MBO phenomenon, documented its growth, and analyzed its consequences. It provided the hub for a growing network of researchers in the field and encouraged both directly, through collaboration and the maintenance of a database, and indirectly via, for example, the export of interest in buyout deals to countries where these were just emerging.

In celebration of the role of CMBOR, this chapter begins by looking at the development of the study of buyouts before going on to consider their consequences. It looks in particular at the role of the MBO in corporate refocusing, thereby exploring both the pull and push factors that have led so many multiproduct firms to roll back diversification and re-concentrate their efforts on core activities.

Management buyouts: emergence and identification

The significance of the MBO phenomenon was first noted, almost at the start of its rise, by three young academics, Mike Wright, Brian Chiplin, and John Coyne, at the University of Nottingham. They were members of the University's Department of Industrial Economics, a uniquely applied economics school whose alumni went in large measure either to jobs in industrial management or to academic positions teaching industrial organization. Research within the Department was then particularly centered on two topics of contemporary interest – the labor-managed firm and the consequences of merger activity. Each of these had obvious associations with the MBO.

Interest in labor-managed or worker co-ops followed the establishment of several such firms by the Wilson-Callaghan governments of the 1970s in response to the failure of conventional for-profit businesses. Interest then tended to wither as these firms themselves failed. The study of merger activity, of course, has proved more durable. Circa 1980, mergers were being studied as the source of both industry and aggregate concentration. Empirical work in Nottingham, as elsewhere, explored the performance effects of M&As. Moreover, powered by the spread of support for the efficient markets hypothesis (Fama et al., 1969), the availability for the first time of machine-readable share-price data and recent access to mainframe computing, "event" studies of merger activity were starting to become a cottage industry.[1]

Chiplin and Wright observed that among corporate deals there was also a growing – if largely unremarked – number of sell-offs. This led them to query the then widely-assumed view that diversification by acquisition was essentially a unidirectional process. In Chiplin and Wright (1980) they showed that alongside the much-documented merger activity there was an increasing flow of break-up transactions. Some of these were merely the fallout from firms acquiring other diversified companies: widget maker A acquires diversified widget maker B and then sells off B's unwanted parts. Others represented the start of the trend, so encouraged by management scholars such as Porter (1980), away from the multiproduct, multidivisional form of organization towards more narrowly focused companies specializing in only those activities in which the firm enjoyed a competitive advantage.

Among the divestment transactions observed by Chiplin and Wright was an increasing trend towards sales to incumbent management teams. The MBO was becoming a viable disposal option for the would-be divesting firm. Wright, together with John Coyne, a colleague with a background in the study of labor-managed firms, began to describe the buyout form (Coyne & Wright, 1982) and to collect data documenting its antecedents and diffusion (Wright et al., 1984; Wright & Coyne, 1985).

In contrast to M&A deals, particularly those involving quoted target companies, data on MBO deals was hard to acquire. The annual reports of firms divesting divisions or subsidiaries rarely provided much information, beyond perhaps noting there had been a disposal. (To the extent that sell-offs often followed disappointing acquisitions and/or a business unit's poor performance, the vendor was particularly unlikely to give the event more than minimal publicity.) Therefore, from the start, the Nottingham researchers, eager to compile a database of done deals, pursued a dual strategy of screening secondary sources (press releases, news reports, etc.) while building relations with the institutions which financed the deals.

Data collection, though laborious, was aided by the initially small number of financing institutions. Most of the early deals were funded by Finance for Industry (FFI), soon to be Investors in Industry (3i), a venture funded by the clearing banks. (FFI was itself the product of a merger of two ventures – the Industrial and Commercial Finance Corporation and Finance Corporation for Industry – which had been established by the post-war Atlee government to try to bridge the so-called "Macmillan gap" of finance for industry, and to permit restructuring of failing enterprises, respectively.) Thus the expertise of buyout financiers, led by 3i, developed symbiotically with the MBO itself. As more institutions entered the deal market, so they co-operated with CMBOR to source information on industry trends and, in so doing, provide the Centre with more deal data.

By building relationships with the funders, the Nottingham researchers were able to compile lists of completed MBO deals which were otherwise unavailable. Subsequent desk work was then necessary to flesh out the details. This work of database construction was formalized in 1986 through the establishment of CMBOR. From the start the Centre has been sponsored by, and has maintained close links, with financial institutions. This has helped build up a unique database of 30,000+ deals.

Chiplin, Wright and others working with them interpreted the MBO as the solution to an incentive problem. Since Berle and Means (1932), economists had concerned themselves with agency issues in large, diversified corporations. If there was a divorce of ownership from control, as Berle and Means suggested, then why shouldn't self-serving managers pursue non-profit objectives, as the managerial theorists (Baumol, 1959; Williamson, 1964; etc.) hypothesized? If so, the MBO could be seen as a return to the old order. The deal restored the ownership status of senior executives, reconnecting their interests and the profit motive.

Furthermore, the incentive effects were not restricted to the direct beneficial interests of senior management. The debt structure necessary to permit high levels of management equity ownership intensified incentives to minimize costs: if debt contracts were not met, the management team stood to lose all. Wright and Coyne (1985) also observed that MBO finance often involved convertible instruments with performance-contingent outcomes allowing managerial voting equity to rise or fall with the venture's performance. This "equity ratchet" further intensified incentives. Finally, the financing institution's role was not limited to the supply of funds. Wright and Coyne (1985) found that institutions supplied expertise, played a monitoring role – often with a seat on the new company's board – and, if necessary, used their position to enforce changes in the buyout firm.

Contemporaneously with the Nottingham researchers, Michael Jensen (1986) used the parallel example of leveraged buyouts (LBOs) in the US in the development of his "free cash flow" theory. He suggested, following Mueller (1969) and others, that managers in enterprises that generate cash flow in excess of their profitable reinvestment opportunities have weak incentives to maximize profits. By substituting debt for equity in the firm's balance sheet, the leveraged transaction put the managers under pressure to make the business perform. Theory and practice appeared in perfect synchronization, as buyout specialists KKR pulled off the then record $25 billion deal to acquire and break up food conglomerate RJR Nabisco in 1989.

Why divest to enterprise management?

Setting aside buyouts from privatization – which though commonplace arguably involve the consideration of more non-commercial factors than conventional private-to-private deals[2] – it is useful to consider the question: why sell to enterprise management? Exploring buyouts on divestment requires a consideration of two inter-related decisions: the "push" factors leading the existing owners to sell as well as the "pull" factors causing local managers to seek to buy – hence own and control – their businesses rather than seeing these go in a trade sale. The decisions are inter-related in that, non-financial motivations aside, any sale to a new company based around existing enterprise management implies this company puts a higher valuation on the enterprise than does the vendor.

Why divest?

The conglomerate firm arguably reached its zenith in the early 1970s and has been in decline ever since. Management thinkers have cautioned against the generalist manager's ability to pick and operate winners as part of a diverse portfolio of products. Instead, following Porter (1980), executives are urged to look to their core businesses ("sticking to the knitting") and to divest peripheral activities. With some exceptions, most obviously GE under Jack Welch and Warren Buffet's Berkshire Hathaway, the stock market has come to view highly diversified firms with distaste.

The diversification discount: A substantial body of empirical evidence (beginning with Lang & Stultz, 1994 and Berger & Ofek, 1995) has suggested that, on average, shares in a diversified firm trade at a substantial discount compared to a portfolio of shares in single-product enterprises whose activity set matches the former's. This discount offers an obvious incentive for breaking up diversified firms (Berger & Ofek, 1996). A considerable literature has tried to determine the precise extent of the discount and its sources. This has concluded that an average conglomerate discount is a significant attribute of stock markets, most obviously in the US and Europe but also elsewhere including South America (Jara-Bertin et al., 2015), although the discount is not apparent in Asia. However, what is contested is the degree to which the discount is a selection artefact rather than a reflection of some underlying weakness of diversified firms. If the latter, how far is the discount a function of the corporate governance and the activity set of the firm?

While allowing that on average diversified firms do trade at a discount compared to their standalone counterparts, it may be argued that reverse causality is involved (Villalonga, 2004). That is poor performers and/or those in the mature phase of their product's life cycle may diversify to escape the growth constraints of their core activities and hence are over-represented in any sample of diversified firms used in a comparison with single-product firms' valuations. This would lead to a spurious conclusion that diversification destroys value. Following Villalonga (2004), sample selection correction – though not an unproblematic exercise – has been generally applied in diversification studies and, as seen later, this typically[3] reduces but does not eliminate the discount.

Does the diversification discount reveal the weakness of the internal capital market?

Williamson (1975) first contrasted the efficiency of the internal allocation of funds with financing via the external capital market. He suggested that the multiproduct multidivisional (M-) form of organization, as described by Chandler (1962, 1977), operated as an internal capital market. Funds generated at the divisional level are remitted to the center. Divisions then compete for their re-investment, with HQ funding projects with a positive net present value (NPV). He suggested that in this process the information available internally is typically greater than that available to an outside financier. Furthermore, while an outsider lending to the firm has little voice unless the loan's conditions are breached, the corporate HQ can monitor progress continuously and, in intervening, choose from a spectrum of rewards and punishments as the project develops. Williamson further suggested that since the bulk of the firm's assets were operated at the divisional level by managers whose remuneration depended on divisional performance, there was a reduced tendency for the M-form to divert resources to less profitable uses, as the managerial theorists, including Williamson (1964) himself, had earlier argued.

Increasing dissatisfaction with conglomerate firm performance, not least as reflected in the diversification discount, led researchers to question the unambiguous support for the internal capital market voiced by Williamson. In the wake of Jensen's (1986) free cash flow theory, a number of studies – e.g., Baltagi and Griffin (1989) and see also Hubbard (1998) for a review – explored cash flow as a determinant of firm-level expenditures on investment and R&D. In the absence of financial constraints, firms should pursue all positive NPV projects, so the finding of a positive coefficient on (lagged) cash flow in investment equations in these studies was interpreted as support for over-investment.

The possibility of bias in the internal allocation of funds has been widely considered in the finance literature. Matsusaka and Nanda (2002), for example, develop a model with an explicit trade-off between the deadweight costs of using the external capital market and the costs of over-investment in preferred projects. The greater flexibility of the internal market offers real option benefits, but reduced control over reallocation of funds, suggesting, in their model, that the internal/external choice is contingent on governance and activity characteristics. In Rajan, Servaes, and Zingales (2000) inter-divisional rivalry is problematic, particularly where there are wide disparities in divisional size and influence. These may be exploited to misallocate funds where suitable governance mechanisms are lacking. Support for this conclusion is offered by Hoechlieb et al. (2012). They use a Heckman two-stage model and find that while sample selection alone cannot account for the discount, the inclusion of corporate governance characteristics shrinks it by up to 37%, according to specification.

The diversification discount is constant across neither firms (see Edorf et al., 2012) nor time periods (Kuppaswamy & Villalonga, 2015). Aggarawal and Zhao (2004) observe that while the discount applies at the mean, some 30–40% of conglomerate firms exhibit a share-price premium. They compare the transaction costs of internal and external markets and conclude that although the internal market is preferred in financing activities where information asymmetry is acute, the external market dominates for more routine businesses. They present valuation comparisons in support and conclude that while the diversified form may be appropriate for new/high-tech products, mature cash-generating activities are better managed as single-product firms under the scrutiny of the external market. Their findings are also consistent with the free cash flow hypothesis (Jensen, 1986) that value-damaging diversification is associated with a combination of slack corporate governance and profitable core activities with limited re-investment opportunities.

Where does refocusing occur and does it work?

Berger and Ofek (1999) reported that US corporations suffering the greatest value losses from diversification displayed the greatest likelihood of sell-offs, as did those with greater cross-subsidization across divisions, while relatedness among activities lowered the likelihood. They noted that to the extent that refocusing represented a reversal of prior corporate strategy, it was unlikely to be a routine activity and they noted it was frequently triggered by some market event such as a takeover approach.

In the UK, Haynes et al. (2000) used count data models to explore both the number and the intensity of divestment across a sample of large firms. They reported that although size and diversification had their predicted positive effects, corporate governance factors played a significant role. Like Berger and Ofek (1999) they found a non-routine trigger to be important – in this case a change of top management. Accounting performance was insignificant, although leverage did have a significant positive effect.

A follow-up study (Haynes et al., 2003) by the same researchers, using an extended sample and time period and a panel design to counter any reverse causality, largely confirmed their cross-sectional results. However, perhaps because the panel model allowed divestment to respond quickly to changes in the firm's circumstances, accounting performance now exercised a significant negative effect on divestment intensity. Interacting performance with corporate governance characteristics reinforced this: firms operating under a "strong" corporate governance regime were more performance-sensitive than those under a "weak" regime. When a "threat of takeover" dummy was created from business reports and inserted into the model. it too exerted a major positive impact on divestment. This reinforced the Berger-Ofek contention that abnormal events play a major part in overcoming inertia with respect to corporate refocusing.

In short, the empirical literature is consistent with divestment being undertaken to improve the position of underperforming firms, but generally under the stimulus of effective corporate governance and/or some existential threat to top management. The role of accounting performance alone is less clear-cut.[4]

Even if diversification does destroy value, it does not necessarily mean that its reversal will recreate it. However, the very strong trend towards divestment, the corporate strategy of refocusing on core activities, exhibited since the 1970s – documented by Toms and Wright (2002) for the UK and Markides (1995) for the US – provides ample scope to test this proposition.

The most comprehensive evidence is provided by Lee and Madhavan (2010) who undertook a meta-analysis of 94 performance studies, using a variety of performance measures.

Their study reports a strong overall positive impact for the divesting firm. The gains vary according to the type of measure employed, with accounting measures showing a substantially greater effect than market-based variables. Similarly, using a variety of moderating variables, they find the impact of divestment is context-specific. (Surprisingly the degree of relatedness does not figure as a significant moderator.) While the Lee-Madhavan work suffers from the potential weaknesses of other meta-studies, not least that of publication bias – here that insignificant performance-divestment results fail to interest the journals – the magnitude of their finding is difficult to dispute.

Why MBOs?

Allowing that a substantial literature on performance broadly supports the negative view of diversified firms, it seems reasonable to ask why divested business units should be sold to an MBO company rather than, say, via a trade sale or other disposal? Assuming the vendor is seeking the highest attainable price, any prospective new owners must envisage greater value creation under their stewardship than the business unit is currently achieving. That is, some combination of asymmetric information and enhanced incentives, making the new company's anticipated performance superior, might be expected to justify the deal.[5]

Local management is particularly well placed to spot ways of improving performance and thereby raising the potential value of the enterprise. That is, with asymmetric information about the potential for performance, a business may be more highly valued by a new buyout company than it is as part of a conglomerate. If local managers can identify existing inefficiencies in resource use but choose not to eliminate these, it might be considered that incentives in the diversified firm are deficient. Removing inefficiencies may require implementing unpopular changes with psychic costs to the managers themselves. These are costs which managers will only incur if incentivized to do so. Hence the buyout deal with the enhanced incentives inherent in equity ownership, reinforced by the bonding effects of debt, may act as a catalyst for change.

There is broad empirical support for this argument. Early research on the consequences of buyouts was often limited by small samples, poor operational data for the new companies, and the risk of selection bias. However, a very large literature – see Gilligan and Wright (2014) and chapters elsewhere in this volume for extensive surveys – now points to positive financial and operational performance effects of MBOs, whether using firm-level or plant-level data. In general, these effects are not attributable to reductions in employment and investment or to wage cuts but are associated with improvements in total factor productivity, especially in the years immediately following the deal (Harris et al., 2005; Amess, 2002, 2003). These gains are also consistent with post-buyout changes in HRM practices leading to greater employee commitment (Bacon et al., 2008; and see Gilligan & Wright, 2014: 183–184).

The extent and immediacy of the post-buyout improvement revealed in studies such as Harris et al. (2005) is supportive of the asymmetric information-plus-enhanced-incentive argument. Managers who have identified new practices to improve efficiency introduce these as quickly as possible while the incentives to do so are at their height. The subsequent tailing off of performance improvements suggests either that the lowest hanging fruit have been picked and/or that the motivational effects of ownership weaken over time.

Conclusions

This chapter has reviewed the emergence of the freestanding buyout form as an alternative to the division/subsidiary located in a diversified multidivisional form firm. It has noted that corporate divestment – essentially the process of disposing of peripheral activities and refocusing on core products – became a dominant strategy in the latter two decades or so of the last century and has remained so. Over the same period, a major destination for divested business units became the MBO. Moreover, divestment appears to have been performance-enhancing for both the vendor and the transferred business units. Shifting control of the enterprise to its newly-incentivized top management appears to boost performance, certainly over the first two or three years.

The previous paragraph is full of generalizations, none of which holds in every case. Clearly some conglomerates work. Some divestments fail. Some MBOs display serious weaknesses, especially when credit market conditions worsen leaving indebted businesses in trouble. Moreover, the longevity of the MBO form – much debated – is beyond our scope here but is tackled elsewhere in this volume in Chapter 27 by Jelic and colleagues.

Nonetheless as this volume marks the 30th anniversary of CMBOR (and almost 40 years since Chiplin and Wright first drew attention to the rise in divestment), it is clear that the Nottingham researchers of the early 1980s showed remarkable foresight. What was then merely a trickle of deals, some of them quite tiny, has grown into a PE-backed phenomenon that has ultimately led to a complete rethink on the superiority of the diversified corporation and the role of the internal capital market.

The role of MBOs in this process continues to offer opportunities for a significant research program. MBOs arising on the divestment of divisions continue but at a reduced level compared to the 1980s and 1990s (CMBOR, 2017), not least because the major restructuring of diversified corporations has long been completed. Studies are required that explore the changing extent, rationale, process, and nature of divestment through MBO over time. For example, to what extent and why has there been a shift from smaller management-led MBOs to larger transactions led by PE firms? What has been the impact on the performance of these divested divisions and how performance changes have been achieved? To what extent has it become more difficult to achieve performance improvements through efficiency gains? How are the effects of these divestments reflected in the performance of the former parent company? Is the choice between divestment through MBO versus divestment through sale to another corporation simply a question of price, or to what extent are other factors influential, such as anti-trust issues?

Further studies might also explore other contextual influences on divestment through MBO, such as the impact of institutional and cultural factors relating to MBO regulations, attitudes to entrepreneurship, and the nature of governance pressures on corporate performance in different countries. These contextual factors might influence divestment to MBO by domestic corporations but also by foreign owned corporations seeking to restructure their overseas activities.

Notes

1 The semi-strong form of the efficient markets hypothesis holds that all publicly available information is impounded into the share price upon release. It follows that if A acquires B, the price response of their respective shares on the merger announcement would give an unbiased estimate of the wealth creating/destroying potential of the event.

2 Privatization to existing managers avoids some of the immediate problems that might follow a trade sale. These include politically unpopular plant closures through rationalization and an increase in industry concentration that would accompany a sale to a competitor (see, e.g., Thompson et al., 1990 for a review).

3 He (2009) revisited the US data and found a discount in the pre-1998 period, but after selection correction, a premium for 1998 onwards, although the premium was *negatively* related to the degree of diversification.

4 Part of the reluctance of management to downsize in the absence of strong pressure may be explained by the persistently high elasticity of managerial remuneration with respect to firm size. If remuneration consultants/committees make comparisons on, say, turnover, a major sell-off could leave executives apparently overpaid. Haynes et al. (2007) explicitly include a divestment variable in an executive pay equation and report that divestment is only rewarded in firms with "strong" corporate governance regimes.
5 A discrepancy in valuation between the vendor and buyer company *could* arise as a result of a difference in business confidence. Following Malmandier and Tate (2005), a number of finance papers have reported that "over-confident" executives make systematically different choices from those of their less-optimistic rivals. However, had divestment buyout been largely motivated by over-confidence, they would have been unlikely to show the success which has sustained the phenomenon.

References

Aggarawal, R., & Zhao, S. 2004. The diversification discount puzzle: Evidence for a transaction cost resolution. *Financial Review*, 44: 113–135.

Amess, K. 2002. Management buyouts and firm-level productivity: Evidence from a panel of UK manufacturing firms. *Scottish Journal of Political Economy*, 49: 304–317.

Amess, K. 2003. The effects of management buyouts and on firm-level technical efficiency: Evidence from a panel of UK machinery and equipment manufacturers. *Journal of Industrial Economics*, 51: 35–44.

Bacon, N., Wright, M., & Demina, N. 2008. The effects of private equity and buyouts on HRM in the UK and the Netherlands. *Human Relations*, 61: 1399–1433.

Baltagi, B., & Griffin, J. 1989. Alternative models of managerial behavior: Empirical tests for the petroleum industry. *Review of Economics and Statistics*, 71: 579–585.

Baumol, W. J. 1959. *Business behavior, value and growth*. New York: Macmillan.

Berger, P., & Ofek, E. 1995. Tobin's q, corporate diversification and firm performance. *Journal of Political Economy*, 102: 1248–1280.

Berger, P., & Ofek, E. 1996. Bust-up takeovers of value destroying diversified firms. *Journal of Finance*, 51: 1175–1200.

Berger, P. G., & Ofek, E. 1999. Causes and effects of corporate diversification programs. *Review of Financial Studies*, 12: 311–345.

Berle, A., & Means, G. 1932. *The modern corporation and private property*. New York: Harcourt Brace.

Chandler, A. D. 1962. *Strategy and structure*. Cambridge, MA: MIT Press.

Chandler, A. D. 1977. *The visible hand*. Boston, MA: Harvard University Press.

Chiplin, B., & Wright, M. 1980. Divestment and structural change in UK industry. *National Westminster Quarterly Review*, 42–51.

CMBOR. 2017. *Management buyouts: Quarterly review from the Centre for Management Buyout Research*. London: Imperial College. Autumn.

Coyne, J., & Wright, M. 1982. Buyouts and British industry. *Lloyds Bank Review*, 15–31.

Edorf, S., Hartmann-Wendels, T., Heinrichs N., & Matz, M. 2012. *Corporate diversification and firm value: A survey of recent literature*. Cologne Graduate School Working Paper, vol. 31.1.

Fama, E., Fisher, M., Jensen, M., & Roll, R. 1969. The adjustment of stock prices to new information. *International Economic Review*, 10: 1–21.

Gilligan, J., & Wright, M. 2014. *Private equity demystified: An explanatory guide*, 3rd edition. London: ICEAW.

Harris, R., Siegel, D., & Wright, M. 2005. Assessing the impact of management buyouts on economic efficiency: Plant-level evidence from the United Kingdom. *The Review of Economics and Statistics*, 87: 148–153.

Haynes, M., Thompson, S., & Wright, M. 2000. The determinants of corporate divestment in the UK. *International Journal of Industrial Organization*, 18: 1201–1222.

Haynes, M., Thompson, S., & Wright, M. 2003. The determinants of corporate divestment: Evidence from a panel of UK firms. *Journal of Economic Behavior and Organization*, 52: 147–166.

Haynes, M., Thompson, S., & Wright, M. 2007. Executive remuneration and corporate divestment: Motivating managers to make unpalatable decisions. *Journal of Business Finance and Accounting*, 34: 792–818.

He, X. 2009. Corporate diversification and firm value: Evidence from post-1997 data. *International Review of Finance*, 9: 359–385.
Hoechlieb, D., Schmid, M., Walter, I., & Yermack, D. 2012. How much of the diversification discount can be explained by poor corporate governance? *Journal of Financial Economics*, 103: 41–60.
Hubbard, G. 1998. Capital market imperfections and investment. *Journal of Economic Literature*, 36: 193–225.
Jara-Bertin, M., Lopez-Iturriaga, F., & Espinosa, C. 2015. Is there a corporate diversification discount or premium? Evidence from Chile. *Academia Revista Latinoamericana de Administracion*, 28: 396–418.
Jensen, M. 1986. Agency costs of free cash flows, corporate finance and takeovers. *American Economic Review*, 76: 323–329.
Jensen, M. 1989. Eclipse of the public corporation. *Harvard Business Review*, 67: 61–74.
Kuppaswamy, V., & Villalonga, B. 2015. Does diversification create value in the presence of external financing constraints? Evidence from the 2007–08 financial crisis. *Management Science*, 62: 905–923.
Lang, L., & Stultz, R. 1994. Tobin's q, corporate diversification and firm performance. *Journal of Political Economy*, 102: 1248–1280.
Lee, D., & Madhavan, R. 2010. Divestiture and firm performance: A meta-analysis. *Journal of Management*, 36: 1345–1361.
Malmandier, U., & Tate, G. 2005. Does overconfidence affect corporate investment? CEO overconfidence measures revisited. *European Financial Management*, 11: 649–659.
Markides, C. 1995. *Diversification, restructuring and economics performance*. Cambridge, MA: MIT Press.
Matsusaka, J., & Nanda, V. 2002. Internal capital markets and corporate refocusing. *Journal of Financial Intermediation*, 11: 176–211.
Mueller, D. C. 1969. A theory of conglomerate mergers. *Quarterly Journal of Economics*, 83: 643–659.
Porter, M. 1980. *Competitive strategy*. New York: Free Press.
Rajan, R., Servaes, H., & Zingales, L. 2000. The cost of diversity: The diversification discount and inefficient investment. *Journal of Finance*, 55: 35–80.
Rappaport, A. 1990. The staying power of the public corporation. *Harvard Business Review*, 68: 953–970.
Thompson, S., Wright, M., & Robbie, K. 1990. Management buy-outs and privatisation: Organisational form and incentive issues. *Fiscal Studies*, 11: 71–88.
Toms, S., & Wright, M. 2002. Corporate governance, strategy and structure in British business history, 1950–2000. *Business History*, 44: 91–124.
Villalonga, B. 2004. Does diversification cause the 'diversification discount'? *Financial Management*, 33: 5–27.
Williamson, O. E. 1964. *The economics of discretionary behavior: Managerial objectives in a theory of the firm*. Englewood Cliffs, NJ: Prentice-Hall.
Williamson, O. E. 1975. *Markets and hierarchies: Analysis and antitrust implications*. New York: Free Press.
Wright, M., & Coyne, J. 1985. *Management buyouts*. Beckenham, UK: Croom Helm.
Wright, M., Coyne, J., & Lockley, H. 1984. Regional aspects of management buyouts: Some evidence. *Regional Studies*, 18: 428–431.

7
PUBLIC-TO-PRIVATE LEVERAGED BUYOUTS

Luc Renneboog and Cara Vansteenkiste

Introduction

The public corporation is often believed to have important advantages over its private counterpart. A stock market listing enables firms to raise funds in public capital markets, increases the share liquidity for investors, allows founders and entrepreneurs to diversify their wealth, and enables the use of options in remuneration packages. Also, the higher degree of visibility and media exposure of public firms can be an effective tool in the marketing of the company. On a personal level, founders and managers of public corporations generally enjoy more prestige. However, a public company with dispersed ownership may suffer from too high a degree of managerial discretion resulting from a lack of monitoring which may lead to "empire building" to the detriment of shareholder value. One way of refocusing management's attention on shareholder value creation is the leveraged buyout (LBO), in which an acquirer takes control of the firm in a transaction financed largely by funds borrowed against the target's assets and/or cash flows.

This type of transaction – labelled "bootstrapping acquisition" (Gilhully, 1999) during its infancy in the 1960s – was aggressively promoted in the 1970s by Wall Street practitioners such as Jerome Kohlberg, Jr. During the 1980s, LBOs grew substantially in the US, and gradually spilled over to the UK. Between 1979 and 1989, the market capitalization of public-to-private (PTP) transactions in the US alone was in excess of $250 billion (Opler & Titman, 1993). This PTP trend was not just limited to the smaller public companies. For instance, in 1989, the LBO-boutique Kohlberg, Kravis and Roberts (KKR) took over and delisted RJR Nabisco in a deal valued at $25 billion. Apparently, executives, financiers, and investors regarded the private firm as a strong alternative to the public corporation such that some even predicted the "eclipse of the public corporation" (Jensen, 1989: 61).

The sources of wealth gains from PTP transactions have been a focal point of academic research. While the critics of going-private transactions have continuously emphasized tax advantages and the expropriation of non-equity stakeholders as the main sources of wealth gains from going private, systematic evidence on PTP transactions is not consistent with this view. Other potential sources of wealth gains are a stronger incentive alignment with a focus on performance and value, the reduction in wasting corporate resources, and improved monitoring capabilities embedded in the governance structure of an LBO. In addition, going private eliminates the costs associated with maintaining a stock market listing, but may also be motivated by a defensive strategy against hostile takeovers. Finally, going private may simply constitute a monetization of an undervalued asset.

The beginning of the 2000s saw a new wave of PTP transactions in the US, UK, and Continental Europe, fueled by cheap debt in the collateralized debt obligation (CDO) markets. Despite vastly exceeding the 1980s LBO wave in value terms, it came to a halt with the demise of the securitized debt markets at the end of 2007. The strong increase in the number of deals and average deal value and the fact that past LBO research was limited in scope (given the focus on the US and on the 1980s) call for further research. To facilitate the development of a new research agenda, we analyze the motives for taking public firms private and provide a structured overview of the empirical research in this area. We examine which types of firms go private as well as the determinants of takeover premiums in LBO transactions. We also investigate whether the post-transaction value creation as well as the duration of private status can be explained by the above-mentioned potential value drivers. We answer the questions whether or not PTP transactions lead to superior organization forms compared to public firms, and whether going private is a shock therapy to restructure firms, which generates both strong short- and long-term returns. Finally, the chapter documents the trends and drivers of global LBO activity in the 1980s, 1990s, and subsequent decades.

The chapter is organized as follows. The next section briefly discusses the different types of LBOs and going-private transactions. The third section discusses the theoretical considerations underlying the sources of wealth gains from going-private deals. The fourth section focuses on the four main strands of the literature (the Intent to do an LBO, the Impact of the LBO measured by changes in the share price returns, the LBO Process or how the firm is restructured post-buyout, and the Duration of being a private firm) and on which of the eight motives are empirically upheld in each strand of the literature. The fifth section explains the drivers behind the observed LBO waves that have emerged since the 1980s while the final section lays out a future research agenda.

Definitions and taxonomy of LBO transactions

When a listed company is acquired by a non-strategic buyer and subsequently delisted, the transaction is referred to as a PTP or a going-private transaction.[1] As virtually all such transactions are financed by borrowing substantially beyond the industry average, they are called LBOs or highly-leveraged transactions (HLTs) – an overview of the different types of LBOs is given in Table 7.1. In fact, LBOs comprise not only PTP transactions but also non-listed firms that undergo a similarly leveraged acquisition. Due to better data availability, recent research is increasingly able to investigate not only PTP LBO transactions, but also these private buyout transactions. However, in line with the scope of this chapter, we will focus on PTP LBO deals and use the terms LBO and PTP transaction interchangeably. We will state explicitly when a cited paper refers to the wider definition of LBOs (going beyond the PTP transactions).

Four categories of LBOs are generally emphasized in the academic literature. To date, management-led transactions comprise the majority of PTP activity. When the incumbent management team takes over the firm (frequently backed by private equity (PE) investors), the LBO is called a management buyout or MBO. When an outside management team acquires the firm and takes it private, the literature refers to this transaction as a management buyin (MBI). The fact that an outside management team does not have the same level of private information as the incumbent managers in MBOs, makes MBIs a completely different

Table 7.1 Summary of definitions of public-to-private terms

Term	*Definition*
LBO	Leveraged buyout. An acquisition whereby a non-strategic bidder acquires a listed or non-listed company, utilizing funds containing a proportion of debt substantially beyond the industry average. In case the acquired company is listed, it is subsequently delisted and remains private for a short to medium period of time
MBO	Management buyout. An LBO in which the target company's existing management bids for control of the firm, often supported by a third-party PE investor
MBI	Management buyin. An LBO in which an outside management team acquires (often backed by a third-party PE investor) a company and replaces the incumbent management team
BIMBO	Buyin management buyout. An LBO in which the bidding team comprises members of the incumbent management team and externally-hired managers, often alongside a third-party PE investor
IBO	Institutional buyin. An LBO in which an institutional investor or PE house acquires a company. Incumbent management can be retained and may be rewarded with equity participations
RLBO	Reverse LBO. A transaction in which a firm that was previously taken private re-obtains public status through a secondary initial public offering

type of deal. An outside management team will generally target firms where the incumbent management cannot or does not want to realize the full potential of corporate value, which entails that MBIs are more frequently hostile transactions (Robbie & Wright, 1995). A deal in which the bidding team comprises members of the incumbent management team and new, externally hired managers is sometimes referred as a buyin-management buyout (BIMBO).

When the new owners of a delisted firm are solely institutional investors or PE firms, one tends to refer to these transactions as institutional buyouts (IBOs), which are sometimes also called Bought Deals or Finance Purchases. In some IBOs, the continuing effort of the incumbent management team is central to the success of the offer, while in other cases the management team is removed. For the typical IBO in which management stays on, it is customary to reward managerial performance with equity stakes in the new private firm via so-called equity ratchets[2] (Wright et al., 1991). In terms of equity ownership, what separates MBOs from IBOs is that in the former the management team has gained its equity interest through being part of the bidding group whereas in the latter it has gained its equity interest via its remuneration package. As the incumbent management in an IBO does not negotiate on behalf of the bidding group, IBOs do not spark the same controversy as MBOs.[3]

After holding their investment for some time, PE investors can opt to exit their investment through a secondary initial public offering (SIPO). Firms that were previously taken private and subsequently re-obtain public status are referred to as reverse LBOs (RLBOs). Other means of exiting their investment are trade sales or secondary buyouts, a detailed discussion of which is beyond the scope of this chapter.

What motivates PTP transactions?

Essentially, there are several sources of wealth gains that may motivate the going-private decision: the reduction in shareholder-related agency costs (due to incentive realignment, control concentration, or free cash flow (FCF) reasons), wealth transfers from bondholders or other stakeholders, tax benefits, transaction costs reduction, takeover defense strategies, and corporate undervaluation. In this section, we review these motives and relate whether these arguments have been sustained in previous research.

Shareholder-related agency costs hypotheses

In this particular case, the central dilemma of the principal-agent model (see Sappington, 1991 for a general discussion of incentive problems in principal-agent models) is how to get the manager (the agent) of a company to act in the best interests of the shareholder of the company (the principal) given that the agent has diverging interests from those of the principal as well as an informational advantage. Agency theory (Jensen & Meckling, 1976) conjectures that the manager of a privately owned company or a listed firm with a major blockholder will be more prone to act in the best interests of the shareholder than the manager of a listed company with a dissipated ownership structure. Three hypotheses underlie this claim: the incentive realignment hypothesis, the FCF hypothesis, and the control hypothesis.

Incentive realignment hypothesis

The insights of Smith (1776) and Berle and Means (1932) into the divergence of interests between managers and stockholders in a joint stock corporation are formalized by Jensen and Meckling (1976). In this model, when the manager sells off a proportion of the residual claims to outsiders, the marginal costs of non-pecuniary[4] benefits decrease as s/he will bear only a fraction of those costs. As a result, the manager increases his/her private benefits (a behavioral pattern called "shirking"), which decreases the firm's value for the principal. PE firms rely on various mechanisms to reward key managers for good performance when they undertake a PTP transaction (for a detailed review, see Fenn et al., 1995). These PE firms (the principal) try to re-align the interests of the managers (the agents) with their interests. Equity ownership is one straightforward way of doing so. For instance, Kaplan (1989a) reports a median increase in equity ownership of 4.41% for the two top officers and of 9.96% for the other managers in MBOs. This is supported in a more recent study on LBOs from 1996 to 2004 which documents a median increase of 5.4% in equity ownership by the CEO and an increase of 16% for the management team taken together (Kaplan & Stromberg, 2009). For the UK, Acharya et al. (2009) similarly report that the median CEO receives 3% of equity, with the management team as a whole receiving 15% of equity.

> The incentive realignment hypothesis states that shareholder wealth gains from going private largely result from an improved system of incentives providing better rewards for managers and ensuring that they act in line with the investors' interests.

The effects of the incentive realignment hypothesis at intermediate levels of managerial ownership are contested because entrenchment effects (Morck et al., 1988; McConnell & Servaes, 1990) may render management – even in the wake of poor performance – immune to board restructuring and may delay corporate restructuring (Franks et al., 2001).

Free cash flow hypothesis

Jensen (1986: 323) defines FCF as "cash flow in excess of that required to fund all projects that have positive net present value (NPV) when discounted at a relevant cost of capital." Based on empirical results on executive remuneration and corporate performance documented by Murphy (1985), Jensen argues that managers have incentives to retain resources and grow the firm beyond its optimal size – so-called "empire building" – which is in direct conflict with the interests of shareholders.[5] By exchanging equity for debt through higher leverage in an LBO, managers credibly "bond their promise" to pay out future cash flows rather than retaining them to invest in negative NPV projects (Jensen, 1986). At the same time, the risk of default attached to the capital restructuring via LBOs increases the downside risk for managers (e.g., losing their jobs) who do not act in the best interests of the principal.

> The free cash flow hypothesis suggests that the shareholder wealth gains from going private are largely the result of debt-induced mechanisms forcing managers to pay out free cash flows.

However, relying on debt to motivate managers may bring about significant agency costs of debt (e.g., an asset-substitution problem (Calcagno & Renneboog, 2007).

Control hypothesis

Easterbrook and Fischel (1983) and Grossman and Hart (1988: 176) explain why individual shareholders in corporations with a dispersed shareholder base may underinvest in monitoring activities (the so-called free-rider problem). After an LBO, the equity ownership of a company is highly concentrated, giving the investors (the principal) stronger incentives and more information to invest in monitoring management (Admati et al., 1994; Maug, 1998). Furthermore, judging from the viability and success of buyout specialists, DeAngelo et al. (1984) argue that these third-party investors may have a comparative advantage in monitoring.[6] Altogether, this means that LBOs may create value by resolving the free-rider problem on the monitoring of management (the agent). Subsequent to the transaction, the control function of the investors may not only be more intensive but also of greater quality.

> The control hypothesis suggests that shareholder wealth gains from going private largely result from an improved monitoring system imposed on the management team.

While agency cost theory predicts these three distinct sources of wealth gains for LBOs, it may be difficult in practice to distinguish between these hypotheses. Lowenstein (1985) best explains this issue with the carrot-and-stick theory: the carrot represents the increased managerial share ownership allowing managers to reap more of the benefits from their efforts (incentive realignment hypothesis). The stick appears when the default risk of high leverage "forces the managers to efficiently run the company to avoid default" (Cotter & Peck, 2001: 102) and pay out FCFs in servicing the debt (FCF hypothesis). The control hypothesis states that PE firms can step in for corrective action at any point in time, also when bankruptcy is not imminent.

Hypotheses related to wealth transfers from bondholders and other stakeholders

Wealth transfers from bondholders

There are three main mechanisms through which a firm can transfer wealth from bondholders to shareholders: by (i) an unexpected increase in the risk of investment projects, (ii) dividend payments, or (iii) an unexpected issue of debt of higher or equal seniority or shorter maturity. All these mechanisms can cause wealth expropriation of specific stakeholders. In a going-private transaction, the third mechanism in particular can lead to substantial bondholder wealth expropriation.[7]

> The bondholder wealth transfer hypothesis suggests that shareholder wealth gains from going private result from the expropriation of pre-transaction bondholders.

Table 7.2 The bondholder wealth effects in public-to-private transactions

Study	*Sample period/ country*	*Obs.*	*Deal Type*	*Event window*	*Loss/ gain to bondholders*	*Benchmark*
Marais et al. (1989)	1974–1985 US	33	ALL	[−69,0] days	0.00%	Dow Jones Bond index
Asquith and Wizmann (1990)	1980–1988 US	199	ALL	[0,1] month	−1.1%**	Shearson-Lehman-Hutton bond index
Cook et al. (1992)	1981–1989 US	62	MBO	[0,1] month	−2.56%**	Shearson-Lehman-Hutton bond index
Travlos & Cornett (1993)	1975–1983 US	10	ALL	[−1,0] days	−1.08%*	CRSP equally weighted index.
Warga & Welch (1993)	1985–1989 US	36	ALL	[−2,2] months	−5.00%**	Rating and maturity weighted Lehman Bond Index
Billett et al. (2008)	1991–2006 US	39 (without covenant protection) 10 (with covenant protection)	ALL	[−1,0] months	−6.76%*** +2.30%	Rating and maturity weighted Lehman Bond Index

This table shows the estimated bondholder losses of the total public debt. Losses are calculated using an event study methodology. The benchmark returns used in the market models are specified. N is the number of different bonds that were used in the analysis (some were issued by the same company). ***, **, * stand for statistically significant at the 1, 5, and 10% level, respectively.

Empirical research provides some evidence of wealth expropriation, mainly for those bondholders who are not protected by covenants (see Table 7.2). Marais et al. (1989), Amihud (1989), and Weinstein (1983) do not find negative abnormal bond returns but document that going-private transactions are followed by "pervasive" debt downgrades by Moody's. Travlos and Cornett (1993) find a statistically significant bondholder loss of 1.08%, while Warga and Welch (1993) confirm significant bondholder wealth losses for successful LBOs in the 1985–1989 periods. Asquith and Wizmann (1990) report significant losses of 1.1% for unprotected corporate bonds around the buyout, whereas bonds protected by covenants against increases in leverage or against reductions in net worth through mergers experience abnormal gains. Correspondingly, Cook et al. (1992) find that bondholder losses are sensitive to the presence of restrictive covenants. Billett et al. (2008) confirm, using a sample of LBOs from 1980 to 2006, that bondholders protected by change-in-control covenants do indeed earn positive returns, but that – although protective covenants have become gradually more widely adopted since the end of the 1980s – unprotected bondholders experience losses. Still, Amihud (1989) explains that the wealth transfer does not represent a loss for bondholders, but is rather a recuperation of the protection which was greater than originally contracted for.[8]

Wealth transfers from other stakeholders

The empirical literature has paid much less attention to wealth transfers other than those related to bondholders. Shleifer and Summers (1988) argue that new investors in hostile takeovers may break the implicit contracts between the firm and stakeholders (in particular the employees, by reducing employment and wages). Nevertheless, Weston et al. (1998) note that such hostility against employees is not observed in PTP transactions, although there is some evidence of falls in employment and wages after adjustment for industry effects in both the US and the UK (Kaplan, 1989a; Smith, 1990; Harris et al., 2005; Davis et al., 2014).

> The wealth transfer hypothesis suggests that shareholder wealth gains from going private result from the expropriation of pre-transaction stakeholders such as employees.

Tax benefit hypothesis

As the vast majority of PTP transactions cause a substantial increase in leverage, the increase in interest-related tax deductions may constitute an important source of wealth gains (Lowenstein, 1985), depending on the fiscal regime and marginal tax rates. Tax deductibility of the interest on the new loans creates a major tax shield increasing the post-transaction (or post-recapitalization) value. For the period 1980 to 1986, Kaplan (1989b) estimates the tax benefits of US PTP transactions to be between 21% and 72% of the premium paid to shareholders to take the company private.[9] Kaplan (1989b: 613) adds that "a public company arguably could obtain many of the tax benefits without going private."

> The tax benefit hypothesis states that shareholder wealth gains from going private result from tax benefits associated with the increase in leverage following the transaction.

Still, in spite of the apparent advantages of high leverage in LBOs, it is questionable whether high leverage constitutes a credible motive for going private; in a competitive market for corporate control, the predictable and obtainable tax benefits will be appropriated by the pre-buyout investors (Kaplan, 1989b), leaving no tax-related incentives for the post-buyout investors to take a company private.[10] Moreover, LBOs in the 1990s and 2000s were less levered than their 1980s counterparts, limiting the wealth gains from tax benefits.

Transaction costs hypothesis

DeAngelo et al. (1984) note that the costs of maintaining a stock exchange listing are very high. From the proxy statements of, for example, Barbara Lynn Stores Inc., they infer that the costs of public ownership, registration, listing, and other stockholder servicing costs, are about $100,000 per annum. Perpetuity-capitalized at a 10% discount rate,[11] this implies a $1 million value increase from going private. Other US estimates of servicing costs mentioned in their paper range from $30,000 to $200,000, excluding management time. For the UK, Benoit (1999) reports that for UK quoted firms, the fees paid to stock-brokers, registrars, lawyers, merchant bankers, and financial PR companies, as well as the stock exchange fee and the auditing, printing, and distribution of accounts, amount to £250,000. Some UK CEOs estimate the City-associated costs to be even higher, i.e., between £400,000 and £1 million.[12] Given the high costs of maintaining a stock exchange listing, the benefits from remaining public may not outweigh the costs. Mehran and Peristiani (2010)'s financial visibility hypothesis proposes that firms choose to go private because they fail to attract recognition from investors or analysts and thus are unable to reap the benefits of a public listing.

> The transaction costs hypothesis suggests that shareholder wealth gains from going private result from the elimination of the direct and indirect costs associated with a listing on the stock exchange.

Takeover defense hypothesis

Lowenstein (1985: 743) reports that some corporations have gone private via an MBO "as a final defensive measure against a hostile shareholder or tender offer," an observation which supports the theoretical arguments set out by Michel and Shaked (1986). Singh (1990) confirms that US MBOs were under significantly greater takeover pressure prior to the MBO than a sample of matched non-MBO firms. Afraid of losing their jobs when the hostile suitor takes control,[13] management may decide to take the company private. Therefore, the takeover defense hypothesis suggests that the premiums in PTPs reflect the fact that the management team may intend to buy out the other shareholders in order to insulate itself from an unsolicited takeover.

> The takeover defense hypothesis suggests that shareholder wealth gains from going private result from the management's willingness to pay a high premium to buy out the other shareholders in order to retain control.

Undervaluation hypothesis

As a firm is a portfolio of projects (Kieschnick, 1987), there may be asymmetric information between the management and outsiders about the maximum value that can be realized with the assets in place (Ross, 1977; Lehn et al., 1990). It is possible that the management, which has superior information, realizes that the share price is undervalued in relation to the true potential of the firm. This problem may be exacerbated when listed corporations, especially smaller ones, find it troublesome to use the equity market to fund expansion, as it may be difficult to attract the interest of institutional shareholders, analysts, and fund managers.

Lowenstein (1985) argues that when the management is the acquiring party, it may employ specific accounting and finance techniques to depress the pre-announcement share price (Schadler & Karns, 1990). By manipulating dividends, manipulating balance sheets through asset revaluation, refusing to meet with security analysts, or even deliberately depressing earnings, managers can use the information asymmetry to their advantage prior to an MBO.

Table 7.3 Overview of hypotheses on wealth gains from public-to-private transactions

Hypothesis	*Description*	*Source of theory underlying the hypothesis*
Incentive realignment	Shareholder wealth gains from going private result from a system of incentives providing higher rewards for managers acting in line with the investors' interests	Smith (1776) Berle & Means (1932) Jensen & Meckling (1976)
Free cash flow	Shareholder wealth gains from going private result from debt-induced mechanisms forcing managers to pay out free cash flows	Jensen & Meckling (1976)
Control	Shareholder wealth gains from going private result from an improved monitoring system imposed on the management team	Grossman & Hart (1988) Easterbrook & Fischel (1983) DeAngelo et al. (1984)
Wealth transfers	Shareholder wealth gains from going private result from the expropriation of pre-transaction bondholders, employees, or other stakeholders	Weinstein (1983) Shleifer & Summers (1988)
Tax benefit	Shareholder wealth gains from going private result from tax benefits brought about by the financial structure underlying the transaction	Lowenstein (1985) Kaplan (1989b)
Transaction costs	Shareholder wealth gains from going private result from the elimination of the direct and indirect costs associated with a listing on the stock exchange	DeAngelo et al. (1984) Mehran & Peristiani (2010)
Takeover defence	Shareholder wealth gains from going private result from the management team's willingness to pay a premium to buy out other shareholders in order to retain control	Michel & Shaked (1986)
Undervaluation	Shareholder wealth gains from going private result from the fact that the assets are undervalued (in the eyes of the acquiring party)	Ross (1977) Kieschnick (1987) Lehn et al. (1990) Fischer & Louis (2008)

Harlow and Howe (1993) and Kaestner and Liu (1996) find that MBOs are preceded by significant abnormal buying of company shares by insiders, whereas outsider-induced buyouts are not, confirming that pre-buyout insider trading is associated with private managerial information. However, managers in MBOs also have a positive earnings management incentive, as this may increase their ability to obtain MBO financing from external parties and obtain that financing at a lower price (Fischer and Louis, 2008; Linck et al., 2013).

An overview of the hypotheses as well as the seminal papers of the theories discussed are presented in Table 7.3.

> The undervaluation hypothesis suggests that shareholder wealth gains from going private result from the undervaluation of assets (in the eyes of the acquiring party)

Four strands in the empirical PTP literature

The literature on PTP transactions and LBOs can be classified into four broad strands. Each strand corresponds to a phase of the buyout process, and requires different econometric methodologies to investigate the sources of wealth creation from LBOs. Figure 7.1 presents this classification and depicts the research methods used to study each phase of the going-private process. The literature related to the phase of *intent* describes the characteristics of firms prior to their decision to go private and compares these characteristics to those of firms that remain publicly quoted. A discriminant analysis or likelihood model is usually employed to measure the probability that a firm will go private. A (tender) offer for the shares outstanding terminates the phase of intent.

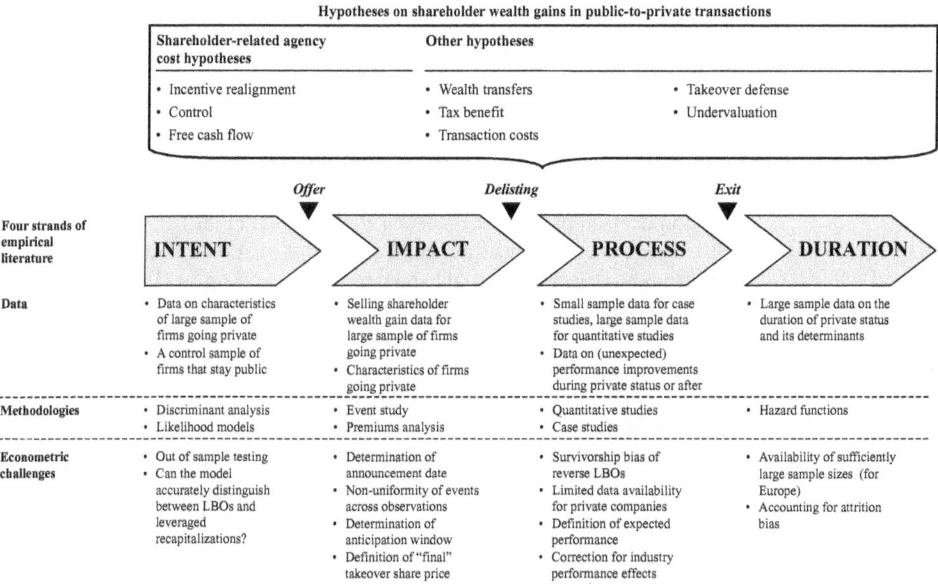

Figure 7.1 The theoretical framework on the public-to-private literature

Source: Authors.

The second strand of the empirical literature measures the *impact* of such an offer and this is estimated by analyzing the immediate stock price reaction (cumulative abnormal return) or the premium paid to pre-transaction shareholders. Once a company is taken private, the literature on the *process* phase investigates the post-buyout process of wealth creation, by means of quantitative or case study methodologies. If and when the investor decides to end the company's private status through an exit (e.g., via a secondary initial public offering or SIPO), hazard or duration analysis can be performed to examine the longevity of private ownership and its determinants. This constitutes the fourth strand of the literature, here referred to as the *duration* literature. We examine which of the eight hypotheses from the earlier section are empirically upheld by each of the four strands of this vast body of literature.

First strand: Intent

Methodological issues

To identify the variables that distinguish best between LBOs and non-LBOs, discriminant analysis (DA) is traditionally the commonly used methodology in this strand of the literature. DA consists of finding a transform, which gives the maximum ratio of the difference between a pair of group multivariate means to the multivariate variance within the two groups. Accordingly, an attempt is made to delineate groups based upon maximizing between-group variance while minimizing within-group variance. To predict group membership (LBO versus no LBO) from a set of predictors, often called the "training set," likelihood models like logit and probit analysis are also frequently used. A difficulty in applying these models is that firms that are good candidates for an LBO are usually also good candidates for financial restructuring through a leveraged recapitalization. To predict membership of various types of LBOs (pure MBOs, PE-backed deals, etc.) versus remaining listed, a multinomial logistic regression can be used which generalizes logit and probit models to problems with multiple classes. Last, Cox's proportional hazard model can be used to determine the probability that a firm will go private over its lifetime, based on its initial firm characteristics and their development over time.

Empirical results

Maupin et al. (1984) examine whether it is possible to separate ex ante those firms that engage in an MBO from those that remain public. First, their discriminant analysis shows that the 63 formerly listed companies they study are systematically associated with high managerial shareholdings prior to the PTP transaction. This is inconsistent with the incentive realignment hypothesis, as one would expect that in firms with stronger managerial ownership the agency costs of equity would be lower and hence that there are smaller gains from going private. Second, formerly quoted firms have a more stable cash flow stream than their counterparts that remain public. Third, a systematically lower price-to-book ratio in the buyout sample suggests that undervaluation may be the prime motivation for going private.

For a sample of 102 MBOs over the period 1981–1985, Kieschnick (1989) also finds strong support for the undervaluation hypothesis, while the data corroborate neither the FCF nor the transaction cost hypotheses. Judging that tax benefits could be retrieved by any potential buyer, he discards taxation as a factor driving MBOs. In contrast, Lehn and

Poulsen (1989) find the opposite results supporting the FCF hypothesis for a sample of going-private transactions over largely the same period (1980–1987). In addition, takeover speculation and the presence of competing bidders are significantly positively related to the likelihood of going private, which may be interpreted as support for the takeover defense hypothesis. Furthermore, as outsiders are not expected to possess the same level of superior information as insiders, the authors interpret this finding as failing to support the undervaluation hypothesis. Kieschnick (1998) re-examines Lehn and Poulsen's (1989) dataset and documents that, accounting for outliers and for misspecified variables, the data fail to support the FCF hypothesis. He claims that potential tax bill reductions and firm size are the significant variables, as is the earlier takeover interest.

Opler and Titman (1993) remark that little attention has been paid to the role of financial distress in the decision to go private. Using a sample of going-private transactions that span the 1980s, they find strong significant evidence that the costs of potential financial distress deter firms from going private in a leveraged transaction; a finding that Weir et al. (2004) do not support for the UK.

Firms that go private can be classified into two different groups based on pre-transaction managerial ownership. Halpern et al. (1999) find that firms with low pre-transaction managerial shareholdings experience more prior takeover interest and exhibit lower leverage than their counterparts that remain public. In contrast, firms with high pre-transaction managerial control concentration have higher levels of leverage and poorer ex ante stock price performance than the matched firms that remain listed. The results show a positive relation between the propensity to go private and the managerial shareholdings for firms with higher levels of director ownership, which is inconsistent with the incentive realignment hypothesis. For either subgroup, they refute the FCF hypothesis as a determinant for going private.

A more recent study over the period 1980–2006 by Billett et al. (2008) compares LBOs in the 1980s wave to those in the 2000s wave. They find that the FCF and the undervaluation hypotheses were better supported in the 1980s compared to more recent LBOs. Moreover, change-in-control covenants protecting bondholders against wealth expropriation have become commonplace relative to the 1980s, but firms that issued bonds lacking this covenant protection are twice as likely to be involved in an LBO. This indicates that bondholder expropriation is an important consideration when choosing LBO targets in the second LBO wave. Mehran and Peristiani (2010) also investigate the second LBO wave using a sample of PTPs from 1990 to 2007. In addition to the FCF hypothesis, they find that an important determinant of the decision to go private in this second LBO wave was the failure to attract market visibility. They report that firms that went private were mainly young firms with declining growth in analyst coverage, declining institutional ownership, and low stock turnover. Related to the transaction cost hypothesis, the benefits of public ownership did not outweigh the high costs. These results are supported by Bharath and Dittmar (2010) who track a sample of 1,377 US firms from IPO to LBO over the period 1980 to 2004, and find that firms are more likely to go private when they have less analyst coverage and lower institutional ownership. In addition, they stress the importance of liquidity and access to capital as a public firm, as firms subject to PTPs are less liquid and less financially constrained than their peers that remain public. Importantly, they find that many of these firm characteristics were already apparent at the time of the IPO. They also find support for the FCF hypothesis, but only in the 1980s LBO wave.

One of the first systematic UK studies on the determinants of going private is made by Weir et al. (2005a). They find support for the incentive realignment and control hypotheses, but refute the takeover defense, the FCF, the accounting underperformance, and the tax savings hypotheses. In a follow-up study, they document that firms going private experience

Table 7.4 Summary of previous empirical results for the first strand of literature: Intent

Study	*Sample period/ country*	*Obs.*	*Transaction type*	*Econometric technique*	*Tax*	*Incentive realignment*	*Control*	*Free cash flow*	*Wealth transfer*	*Transaction costs*	*Takeover defence*	*Under-valuation*
Maupin et al. (1984)	1972–1983 US	63	MBO	Discriminant analysis	–	No	–	No	–	–	–	Yes
Lehn & Poulsen (1989)	1981–1985 US	102	ALL	Logistic regressions	No	–	–	Yes	–	–	Inconcl.	No
Kieschnick (1989)	1980–1987 US	263	MBO	Logistic regressions	No	–	–	No	–	No	–	Yes
Kieschnick (1998)	1980–1987 US	263	ALL	Logistic regressions	Yes	–	–	No	–	–	Yes	No
Ippolito & James (1992)	1980–1987 US	169	ALL	Logistic regressions	–	–	–	Inconcl	Inconcl	–	–	–
Opler & Titman (1993)	1980–1990 US	180	ALL	Logistic regressions	No	–	–	Yes	–	–	–	–
Halpern et al. (1999)	1981–1985 US	126	ALL	Multinomial logistic regr.	Yes	No	–	No	–	–	Yes	–
Kosedag & Lane (2002)	1980–1996 US	21	ALL	Logistic regressions	Yes	–	–	No	–	–	–	–
Weir et al. (2004)	1998–2001 UK	117	ALL	Logistic regressions	–	Inconcl.	No	No	–	–	–	–
Weir et al. (2005a)	1998–2000 UK	95	ALL	Logistic regressions	No	Yes	Yes	No	–	–	No	–
Weir et al. (2005b)	1998–2000 UK	84	ALL	Logistic regressions	No	Yes	Yes	No			No	Yes
Billett et al. (2008)	1980–2006 US	562	ALL	Logistic regression	–	–	–	Yes	Yes	–	–	Yes
Mehran & Peristiani (2010)	1990–2007 US	169	ALL	Hazard model	No	–	–	Yes	Yes	Yes	–	No
Bharath & Dittmar (2010)	1980–2004 US	1,377	ALL	Hazard model	–	–	–	Yes	–	Yes	–	Yes
Fidrmuc et al. (2013)	1997–2003 UK	33	Pure MBOs	Multinomial logit model	No	–	–	Yes	–	No	Yes	Yes
		37	PE MBOs		No	–	–	No	–	No	Yes	Yes

This table shows the studies that refer to strand 1 of PTP research. Yes = supportive, No = unsupportive, Inconcl. = inconclusive.
Transaction type refers to which types of deals were considered in the paper: ALL = all going private deals; MBO = MBO deals only.

falling market values in the year before going private, while the control sample firms have rising market values (Weir et al., 2005b). Controlling for other motivations, this perceived undervaluation is a statistically significant determinant of the decision to go private. It is, however, important to take into account that some buyouts, and MBOs in particular, may be subject to downwards earnings and stock price manipulation (Perry & Williams, 1994; Mao & Renneboog, 2015). Fidrmuc et al. (2013) distinguish between pure UK MBOs and PE-backed UK MBOs. They find that management opts for a pure MBO rather than a PE-backed deal when financing constraints are relatively low, i.e., when the firm is undervalued, has higher cash levels, is less financially visible, and has higher levels of managerial ownership. However, both types of PTPs support the takeover defense hypothesis.

Synthesis: Intent

To conclude, Table 7.4 shows that tax benefits are well documented by the 1990s US literature, but lack support in more recent US-based studies. The fact that firms with greater tax shields are more likely to go private does not necessarily mean that the size of a tax shield is an important determinant, as it is straightforward to predict the tax benefits of an LBO such that the pre-transaction shareholders are able to fully appropriate these benefits (Kaplan, 1989b). It may therefore not be a motive for the parties initiating the LBO or MBO. Moreover, LBOs in the most recent LBO wave were less levered than their 1980s counterparts, casting further doubt on tax benefits as the main incentive for going private. Out of all agency-related hypotheses, the FCF hypothesis receives the most support, especially by more recent studies. However, FCF-based incentives have become less important drivers, as improvements in corporate governance in the 1990s have diminished their importance in the second LBO wave relative to LBOs in the 1980s. The second LBO wave appears driven by the trade-off between transaction costs and financial visibility, and the presence of bond covenants. Going-private decisions in the US in the 1980s were also frequently motivated by takeover defense strategies, but this motive has weakened over time, as more recent evidence appears more mixed. In contrast, the undervaluation hypothesis found mixed support in the 1980s, but support from the second LBO wave is stronger, with undervaluation being especially important in pure MBOs.

Second strand: Impact

If LBOs and MBOs are associated with value creation, then who is the receiver of these benefits? The wealth effects of going-private transactions have been investigated for several groups of stakeholders: a growing strand of literature has focused on the returns generated by PE funds for their investors, but the majority of the empirical literature has focused on those for the pre-buyout (selling) shareholders. As not all PTP buyouts involve PE investors, we limit our overview to the latter group of studies.

Methodological issues

Essentially, there are two ways to measure the shareholder wealth effects in PTP research, namely abnormal return estimation and premiums analysis (see Renneboog et al., 2007 for the methodological discussion). In this section, the econometric issues with both approaches will be discussed, along with the empirical results.

Cumulative abnormal returns (CARs) measure the information effect of an event on the market value of a firm. They compare the expected return, based on the CAPM, to the return observed once the information is released. Table 7.5 presents the results of event studies in going-private research. The typical abnormal return at the announcement of an MBO

Table 7.5 Cumulative average abnormal returns in event studies of public-to-private transactions

Study	*Sample period/ country*	*Type of deal*	*Event window*	*Obs.*	*CAR*
DeAngelo et al. (1984)	1973–1980 US	ALL	−1,0 days	72	22.27%***
			−10,10 days	72	28.05%***
Torabzadeh & Bertin (1987)	1982–1985 US	ALL	−1,0 months	48	18.64%***
			−1,1 months	48	20.57%***
Lehn & Poulsen (1989)	1980–1987 US	ALL	−1,1 days	244	16.30%***
			−10,10 days	244	19.90%***
Amihud (1989)	1983–1986 US	MBO	−20,0 days	15	19.60%***
Kaplan (1989a)	1980–1985 US	MBO	−40,60 days	76	26.00%***
Marais et al. (1989)	1974–1985 US	ALL	0,1 days	80	13.00%***
			−69,1 days	80	22.00%***
Slovin et al. (1991)	1980–1988 US	ALL	−1,0 days	128	17.35%***
			−15,15 days	128	24.86%***
Lee (1992)	1973–1989 US	MBO	−1,0 days	114	14.90%***
			−69,0 days	114	22.40%***
Frankfurter & Gunay (1992)	1979–1984 US	MBO	−50,50 days	110	27.32%***
			−1,0 days	110	17.24%***
Travlos & Cornett (1993)	1975–1983 US	ALL	−1,0 days	56	16.20%***
			−10,10 days	56	19.24%***
Lee et al. (1992)	1983–1989 US	MBO	−1,0 days	50	17.84%***
			−5,0 days	50	20.96%***
Van de Gucht & Moore (1998)	1980–1992 US	ALL	−1,1 days	187	15.60%***
			−10,10 days	187	20.20%***
Goh et al. (2002)	1980–1996 US	ALL	−20,1 days	323	21.31%***
			0,1 days	323	12.68%***
Andres et al. (2003)	1996–2002 EU	ALL	−1,1 days	99 99	15.78%***
			−15,15 days		21.89%***
Renneboog et al. (2007)	1997–2003 UK	ALL	−1,0 days	177	22.68%***
			−5,5 days	177	25.53%***
			−40,40 days	177	29.28%***
Billett et al. (2008)	1980–1990	ALL	−60,3 days	195	28.74%
	1991–2006 US			212	24.13%
Brown et al. (2009)	1980–2001 US	ALL	−1,1 days	352	18.58%***
Officer et al. (2010)	1984–2007 US	ALL (club)	−1,1 days	70	11.45%
		ALL (sole)		128	18.26%
Fidrmuc et al. (2013)	1997–2003 UK	Pure MBO	−1,1 days	33	21.04%
		PE MBO		37	19.30%

This table shows all papers that estimate the shareholder wealth effects using event study analysis.
***, **, * stand for statistically significant at the 1, 5, and 10% level, respectively.
ALL = all going-private deals; MBO = MBO deals only

or LBO is around 20%, with most of the buyout information generally incorporated in the share price from one day before until one day after the event date and with abnormal returns being slightly lower in the second LBO wave. This 20% abnormal return seems to be rather low compared to the 25–30% range for tender offers and mergers.[14]

Renneboog et al. (2007) point out an important measurement problem with abnormal returns: LBO CARs may be cross-sectionally incomparable, due to the non-uniformity of the information release underlying the stock-price reaction. Two subsamples of firms going private can be distinguished: for the first one, investors immediately know that the type of deal is a leveraged PTP of the type MBO, MBI, or IBO. For the second subsample, information reaches the market in two stages: there is an initial notification of a takeover deal[15] (event 1), followed by the announcement disclosing the deal type (LBO, MBO, etc.) (event 2). Some earlier research has taken the second date as the event date, but the results from this approach are strongly biased given that the initial announcement (event 1) has a large effect on the share price and that the information content of event 2 should merely be regarded as a correction to the price effect generated by event 1.

Table 7.6 Premiums paid above market price to take a firm private

Study	*Sample period/ country*	*Type of deal*	*Anticipation window*	*Obs.*	*Mean premium offered*
DeAngelo et al. (1984)	1973–1980 US	ALL	40 days	72	56.3%
Lowenstein (1985)	1979–1984 US	MBO	30 days	28	56.0%
Lehn & Poulsen (1989)	1980–1987 US	ALL	20 days	257	36.1%
Amihud (1989)	1983–1986 US	MBO	20 days	15	42.9%
Kaplan (1989a, 1989b)	1980–1985 US	MBO	2 months	76	42.3%
Asquith & Wizmann (1990)	1980–1988 US	ALL	1 day	47	37.9%
Harlow & Howe (1993)	1980–1989 US	ALL	20 days	121	44.9%
Travlos & Cornett (1993)	1975–1983 US	ALL	1 month	56	41.9%
Easterwood et al. (1994)	1978–1988 US	MBO	20 days	184	32.9%
Weir et al. (2005a)	1998–2000 UK	ALL	1 month	95	44.9%
Renneboog et al. (2007)	1997–2003 UK	ALL	20 days	177	41.00%
Guo et al. (2011)	1990–2006 US	ALL	1 month	192	29.2%
Officer et al. (2010)	1984–2007 US	ALL (club)	250 days	70	24.04%
		ALL (sole)		128	36.11%
Fidrmuc et al. (2013)	1997–2003 UK	Pure MBO	2 months	33	38.68%
		PE MBO		37	39.10%

This table shows all papers that estimate the shareholder wealth effects of going private through premiums analysis. The results are not independent due to partially overlapping samples.
***, **, * stand for statistically significant at the 1, 5, and 10% level, respectively.
ALL = all going-private deals; MBO = MBO deals only.

An alternative methodology to measure the wealth effect is a *premiums analysis*, which calculates the real premium paid in the transaction. Instead of comparing the realized returns to estimated benchmark returns, this methodology measures the premium as the difference in the firm value between the final takeover share price and the pre-announcement price of the firm. Premiums are measured over the full period of the going-private transaction, and therefore incorporate all relevant information (and hence do not suffer from the problems abnormal returns suffer from as described earlier). As Table 7.6 shows, the average premiums are around 45% in the 1980s LBO wave, but they decline in the second LBO wave, varying at around 30%. Renneboog et al. (2007) point out that a premiums analysis is complicated because of two problems: the choice of the right pre-takeover share price, and the definition of the final takeover share price. To allow for the share price run-up in the period preceding the first announcement of takeover interest, an anticipation window of 20 to 250 days prior to the event date is chosen. Kaplan's (1989a) LBO study on the US, and Goergen and Renneboog's (2004) and Martynova and Renneboog's (2008b) studies on European M&As both mention that the anticipation window spans approximately the two months before the initial announcement. In earlier research, both the final price offered in the winning bid and the final share price quoted on the stock exchange before delisting have been used. The former price is preferred as the latter only reflects the true value of the bid if shareholders sell their shares to the acquiring party through the stock exchange. However, if shareholders can accept an offer without involvement of the stock exchange (as in the UK), the last quoted share price may reflect only speculative movements.

As can be observed from Tables 7.5 and 7.6, the short-term wealth effects measured by abnormal returns are very different from those measured by premiums. Several explanations account for this difference. First, the CARs are corrected for the expected return whereas the reported average premiums are not. Second, part of the difference can also be attributed to the fact that abnormal returns which capture the market expectations of the future profits of the buyout, include the probability that a bid fails, while the premium does not. DeAngelo et al. (1984) show that the withdrawal of an offer triggers a two-day abnormal loss of 8.88% (significant at the 1% level), which Marais et al. (1989) confirm.

Empirical results

As the empirical literature in this strand is abundant, we organize the literature along the hypotheses outlined in the previous section. We also discuss the effects of bidder competition and divisional buyouts on the share prices.

Shareholder-related agency cost hypotheses

The first systematic study on the cross-sectional variation of shareholder wealth effects in going-private transactions was performed by DeAngelo et al. (1984). They report that the average CARs around the announcement depend on the managerial equity stake prior to the PTP transaction. In transactions where the pre-buyout management stake is at least 50%, the CARs are 20% higher than in transactions where the management owns smaller stakes. However, they do not find a significant difference in the premiums offered in these two types of transactions. This implies a larger probability of success for firms with strong initial managerial control (more than 50%). Abnormal returns occurring at the announcement of the buyout also depend on the post-transaction equity stake held by the manager: the market reaction to the MBO announcement is higher when the management becomes the sole owner than when control is shared with a third party. Lehn and Poulsen (1989) find that premiums depend on the level of FCF, but when partitioning the sample based on managerial ownership the FCF variable proves insignificant for equity stakes above the median. This is consistent with the FCF hypothesis, as agency costs are higher in firms with low levels of managerial ownership. Kieschnick (1998) revisits the Lehn and Poulsen sample, but finds no support for the FCF hypothesis after accounting for outliers and redefining the variables. With respect to the effects of managerial ownership, Frankfurter and Gunay (1992) find that the level of insider net divestment is a significantly positive determinant of abnormal returns. They note that such deals are driven by insiders' need for liquidity, and fail to find evidence supporting the incentive realignment hypothesis for deals with high levels of pre-buyout managerial ownership. For firms whose managers already own a large equity stake, the reunification of ownership and control is thus not the prime motive for going private. This is confirmed by Halpern et al. (1999), who report a U-shaped relation between managerial equity ownership and buyout premiums for poorly performing firms. Jointly testing the taxation, bondholder wealth transfers, asymmetric information, transaction costs, and agency costs hypotheses in a cross-sectional analysis, Travlos and Cornett (1993) find that the industry-adjusted price-earnings ratio (deemed to be an inverse proxy for agency costs) negatively affects abnormal returns. Consistent with DeAngelo et al. (1984), they find that the stock price reaction to MBO announcements is significantly higher than for third-party transactions (MBIs and IBOs).

Calculating CARs and average premiums for a sample of UK PTP transactions, Renneboog et al. (2007) find support for the incentive realignment hypothesis, whereas the pre-transaction FCF has no impact, as also previously observed by other work on the UK. However, control is a significant determinant of the shareholder wealth effects of going private, an effect that is especially strong in the presence of corporations as monitors.

A number of studies examine the pricing of deals in the recent LBO wave relative to the buyout wave of the 1980s. Both Oxman and Yildirim (2007) and Guo et al. (2011) observe lower premiums and less leverage in the recent LBO wave. However, deals completed towards the end of the wave are priced higher and have riskier capital structures. The premiums are positively related to FCFs and to the current interest on long-term debt in pre-buyout firms, but better performing firms receive lower premiums, whereas high premiums are paid to firms that are not currently profitable but have large growth potential, providing support for the undervaluation hypothesis (Oxman & Yildirim, 2007). Demiroglu and James (2010) find that in the recent LBO wave, the reputation of PE buyers is positively related to buyout leverage (LBO debt divided by the target's pre-LBO EBITDA), and that leverage is positively related to the price of the deal, suggesting that PE reputation reduces the agency costs of LBO debt.

Hypotheses related to wealth transfers

Marais et al. (1989) investigate the relation between pre-buyout debt ratios and abnormal returns, but do not find significant evidence supporting the bondholder wealth transfer hypothesis. Warga and Welch (1993) do however show that in going-private transactions, an increase of one dollar in the firm market value of equity is associated with a five cents decrease in the overall value of debt. Likewise, Asquith and Wizmann (1990) estimate abnormal losses to bondholders of 3.2% of the gains made by shareholders. This evidence confirms that the bondholder wealth transfer hypothesis cannot be rejected, but also that bondholder expropriation cannot be a principal source of wealth gains to shareholders in

PTP transactions. In response to the observed expropriation of bondholder wealth in the 1980s LBO wave, the US introduced change-in-control covenants to protect bondholders. Investigating the effect of such protection on the returns to bondholders in the second LBO wave, Billett et al. (2008) report abnormal returns to bondholders lacking covenant protection of −6.76%, whereas protected bondholders earn +2.30%. They conclude that expropriation of bondholders is an important determinant in LBOs and that bondholder wealth effects depend on the existence of such change-in-control covenants.

Andres et al. (2003) are the first to test for the employee wealth transfer hypothesis, but find no support. Brown et al. (2009) investigate a supplier wealth expropriation effect: suppliers experience significantly negative announcement returns around the announcement of a downstream LBO, with the effect being more negative for suppliers that have made substantial relationship-specific investments. The authors conclude that the increased leverage combined with changes in the organizational form in the LBO increases these firms' bargaining power with their suppliers, as their results do not appear to be induced by decreases in demand for the suppliers' products or services.

Tax benefit hypothesis

Kaplan (1989b) argues that tax benefits constitute an important source of wealth gains in going-private transactions. His models show that 76% of the total tax shield is paid out as a premium to the selling investors, supporting the claim that predictable potential tax benefits are appropriable by pre-transaction investors in a competitive market for corporate control. Tax savings and firm size should thus have a positive impact on the wealth gains in LBOs, a finding that is confirmed by Kieschnick (1998). However, Lehn and Poulsen (1989) and more recently Oxman and Yildirim (2007) find that the potential for tax savings does not significantly affect premiums in US LBOs. For the UK, Renneboog et al. (2007) reject the tax benefit hypothesis, but Dicker (1990), Andres et al. (2003), and Weir et al. (2005a) point out that the tax advantages of financing firms with debt are smaller in Continental Europe and the UK than in the US.

Transaction costs hypothesis

Travlos and Cornett (1993) are the first to test the hypothesis of transaction cost savings by employing annual costs of listing according to NYSE and AMEX fee schedules (scaled by the market value of equity), but conclude that this hypothesis is not upheld, perhaps reflecting the fact that the true costs of a stock market quotation are much higher than just the listing costs. Renneboog et al. (2007) do find some support for the transaction costs hypothesis: the savings realized by the direct and indirect costs of a listing significantly contribute to the shareholder wealth effects from going private. In a study on US PTPs from 1990 to 2007, Mehran and Peristiani (2010) report that failure to attract market visibility combined with the high costs associated with a public listing led many firms to go private in the second LBO wave.

Undervaluation hypothesis

Some support for the undervaluation hypothesis is found by Kaestner and Liu (1996), who find evidence suggesting that insider net buying before an MBO is driven by superior knowledge about the true value of the firm. Harlow and Howe (1993) also find that MBOs are preceded by significant abnormal buying of company shares by insiders, whereas outsider-induced buyouts are not, and that going-private premiums paid by third parties are higher than those paid by management teams. Fidrmuc et al. (2013), however, find no significant difference between premiums paid in pure (management-led) and PE-sponsored UK MBOs, although pure MBOs are more undervalued than PE-backed deals. Goh et al. (2002) report significant upward revisions of earnings forecasts around the PTP announcement for institutional buyins (but less so for MBOs), and show that abnormal revisions of analysts' forecast earnings are positively related to the abnormal returns at the PTP announcement. This suggests that going-private announcements indeed convey favorable information about future earnings. Although Lee (1992) reports that there are no sustained shareholder wealth increases from MBO announcements that are subsequently withdrawn, Andres et al. (2003) and Renneboog et al. (2007) confirm Goh et al.'s (2002) conclusions. They find that the target's past share price performance is a significant determinant of shareholder wealth gains and abnormal returns, both for MBOs and IBOs.

Management may employ specific accounting and finance techniques to depress the pre-announcement share price or understate earnings in MBOs (Lowenstein, 1985), For the US, DeAngelo (1986) finds no evidence of systematic earnings manipulation, but Perry and Williams (1994) and Wu (1997) do document negative earnings manipulation prior to MBOs, decreasing the acquisition price by 19%. Similarly, for the UK, Mao and Renneboog (2015) find that strong negative earnings management occurs prior to MBOs, whereas positive earnings management takes place in IBOs. Consistent with the hypothesis that positive earnings management can be used as a signal about the company's prospects thereby easing its financial constraints (Linck et al., 2013), Fischer and Louis (2008) find that managers in MBOs that rely most on external funding manipulate earnings downward the least.

Bidder competition

PTP transactions with multiple bidders are associated with higher premiums. For instance, Lowenstein (1985) reports that the premiums paid to shareholders in MBO transactions involving three or more competing bidders were on average 19% higher than the premiums paid in cases with a single bidder. Amihud (1989) confirms his findings: 9 out of 15 of the largest LBO transactions over the period 1983–1986 received competing bids and the final premium paid was 52.2% compared to 30.7% for cases without bidder competition. Similarly, Easterwood et al. (1994) demonstrate that the premium in a multiple bidder process is about 17% higher. Consistent with the idea that multiple bidders are associated with higher premiums, Officer et al. (2010) find that "club bidding" by PE investors (a common practice in PE where multiple bidders jointly submit a single bid) reduces competition and hence depresses the value accrued to target shareholders: premiums are 40% lower and target shareholders earn 10% less of the pre-LBO firm value in club deals relative to LBOs with a single buyer. These results are more pronounced in target firms with less institutional ownership, suggesting that institutions can bargain more effectively with clubs, offsetting some of the effects of reduced competition on prices.

The interpretation of these higher premiums in contested LBOs is not straightforward. While the empirical literature usually attributes higher premiums to the mechanics of the competitive process, further nuance is needed. Indeed, Guo et al. (2011) show that post-buyout returns are higher for deals with multiple PE bidders, but they do not find evidence that these returns are related to bidder competition. Deals with multiple PE bidders already generate higher pre-buyout returns, which suggests that deals with better ex ante prospects are more likely to attract multiple bidders. Higher premiums in contested bids may also occur because of PE overpayment resulting from irrationality or "deal fever" (see e.g., Andres et al., 2003). Alternatively, contested LBOs may signal severe undervaluation, in which case a higher premium is justified.

Empirical results on divisional buyouts

Studies on divisional buyouts focus on the effects on parent shareholders. Bae and Jo (2002) and Hite and Vetsuypens (1989) argue that there are considerable differences between divisional and whole-firm buyouts. It is expected that divisional buyouts suffer less from the absence of arm's length bargaining, because the parent company's management negotiates with the divisional buyout team. Therefore, a conflict-prone role of managers in MBOs is likely not to arise. For a sample of 65 MBO divestments over the period 1984–1989, Briston et al. (1992) find significantly negative returns of −1.79% to parent shareholders. Apparently, divisional managers still succeed in negotiating a relatively low price for the assets they buy from the parent company. This contradicts the findings of US divisional MBOs (Muscarella & Vetsuypens, 1990) in which the parent shareholders do not lose on average.

Synthesis: Impact

Table 7.7 summarizes this second strand of the literature. First, we conclude that the undervaluation hypothesis has gained increasing support from US, UK, and Continental European studies, in particular from those on MBO deals, which are best placed to exploit undervaluation due to information asymmetries. Second, bondholder wealth transfers exist, but only play a limited role in the wealth gains of pre-buyout shareholders, and bondholder wealth effects strongly depend on the existence of protective change-in-control covenants. In addition, suppliers to LBO firms also appear to be negatively affected by downstream LBOs. Third, the evidence on the shareholder-related agency costs hypotheses, more specifically the incentive realignment and FCF hypotheses, is mixed. There is evidence that the incentive realignment hypothesis is only valid for firms where pre-transaction managers hold small equity stakes. The control hypothesis has gained more support in recent studies, however. Fourth, the empirical evidence does not seem to support the argument that increased tax shields from going private are an important source of wealth gains. Fifth, it is remarkable that the majority of the evidence from this strand of the literature comes from the US and to a lesser extent the UK. This calls for systematic research on this strand from other parts of the world.

Third strand: Process

So far, we have discussed the empirical results for the determinants of the firm-specific probability of going private, and how much acquirers generally pay in order to obtain the required proportion of shares to delist the company. After these two initial phases, the firm starts a new life away from public scrutiny and usually disappears from the public forum. Fox and Marcus (1992) note that it is imperative that these firms do not vanish from the academic radar. After all, the scientific debate about the real role of leveraged going-private transactions, being either more efficient organizational forms (Jensen, 1989) or simply vehicles to gain tax benefits (e.g., Lowenstein, 1985), cannot possibly be resolved without a detailed study of the post-transaction performance. After the acquiring party has paid a premium to take the company private, the process by which it recovers these out-of-pocket costs and puts

Table 7.7 Summary of the second strand of the literature: Impact

Study	*Sample period/ country*	*Obs.*	*Type of deal*	*Event window*	*CAR*	*Anticipation Window*	*Premium*	*Tax*	*Incentive Realignm.*	*Control*	*FCF*	*Wealth transfer*	*Trans. tost*	*Defen-sive*	*Under-Val.*	*Bidder tomp.*
DeAngelo et al. (1984)	1973–1980 US	72	ALL	−1,0 days −10,10 days	22.27%*** 28.05%***	40 days	56.3%	–	Inconcl.	Inconcl.	–	–	–	–	–	–
Lowenstein (1985)	1979–1984	28	MBO	–	–	30 days	56.0%	–	–	–	–	–	–	–	–	Yes
Torabzadeh & Bertin (1987)	1982–1985 US	48	ALL	−1,0 months −1,1 months	18.64%*** 20.57%***	–	–	–	–	–	–	–	–	–	–	–
Lehn & Poulsen (1989)	1980–1987 US	244	ALL	−1,1 days −10,10 days	16.30%*** 19.90%***	20 days	36.1%	No	–	–	Yes	–	–	–	–	–
Amihud (1989)	1983–1986 US	15	MBO	−20,0 days	19.60%***	20 days	42.9%	–	–	–	–	–	–	–	–	Yes
Kaplan (1989a, 1989b)	1980–1985 US	76	MBO	−40,60 days	26.00%***	40 days	42.3%	Yes	–	–	–	–	–	–	–	–
Marais et al. (1989)	1974–1985 US	80	ALL	0,1 days −69,1 days	13.00%*** 22.00%***	–	–	–	–	–	–	No	–	–	–	–
Asquith & Wizmann (1990)	1980–1988 US	47	ALL	–	–	1 day	37.9%	–	–	–	–	No	–	–	–	–
Lee (1992)	1973–1989 US	114	MBO	−1,0 days −69, 0 days	14.90%*** 22.40%***	–	–	–	–	–	–	–	–	–	No	–
Lee et al. (1992)	1983–1989 US	50	MBO	−1,0 days −5,0 days	17.84%*** 20.96%***	–	–	–	–	–	–	–	–	–	–	Yes
Frankfurter & Gunay (1992)	1979–1984 US	110	MBO	−50,50 days −1,0 days	27.32%*** 17.24%***	–	–	Yes	No	–	Yes	–	–	–	–	–

Travlos & Cornett (1993)	1975–1983 US	56	ALL	−1,0 days −10,10 days	16.20%*** 19.24%***	1 month	41.9%	Inconcl.	Inconcl.	Inconcl	Inconcl.	No	No	–	Yes	–
Harlow & Howe (1993)	1980–1989 US	121	ALL	–	–	20 days	44.9%	–	–	–	–	–	–	–	Yes	–
Easterwood et al. (1994)	1978–1988 US	184	MBO	–	–	20 days	32.9%	–	–	–	–	–	–	–	–	Yes
Halpern et al. (1999)	1981–1985 US	126	ALL	–	–	–	Not mentioned	No	No	–	No	–	–	–	–	Yes
Goh et al. (2002)	1980–1996 US	323	ALL	−20,1 days 0,1 days	21.31%*** 12.68%***	–	–	–	–	–	–	–	–	–	Yes	–
Andres et al. (2003)	1996–2002 EU	99	ALL	−1,1 days −15,15 days	15.78%*** 21.89%***	–	–	No	No	Yes	No	No	–	–	Yes	–
Renneboog et al. (2007)	1997–2003 UK	177	ALL	−1,0 days −5,5 days −40,40 days	22.68%*** 25.53%*** 29.28%***	20 days	41.0%	No	Yes	Yes	No	–	Yes	No	Yes	Yes
Andres et al. (2007)	1997–2005 EU	115	ALL	−30, 30 days	24.20%***	250 days	–	–	No	Yes	No	–	–	–	Yes	–
Oxman & Yildirim (2007)	1986–2005 US	164	ALL	–	–	–	29.2% (small) 33.8% (big)	No	–	–	Yes	–	–	–	Yes	–
Officer et al. (2010)	1984–2007 US	198	ALL	−1,1 days	–	250 days	–	–	–	Yes	–	–	–	–	Yes	Yes

This table shows the most important papers that deal with strand 2 of PTP research. Yes = supportive, No = unsupportive, Inconcl. = inconclusive. All estimated shareholder wealth effects from Table 7.3 and 7.4 are reproduced here. ***, **, * stand for statistically significant at the 1, 5, and 10% level, respectively.
ALL = all going-private deals; MBO = MBO deals only; FCF = Free cash flow hypothesis; Bidder comp. = Bidder competition.

the resources under its control to a more valuable use, can result in interesting insights into the real sources of wealth gains from buyouts.

Methodological issues

The empirical research in this strand is based on two distinct research methods: while most researchers have employed large-sample quantitative studies, some have successfully used case studies and interviews/surveys to detect the sources of wealth creation from going private.

Quantitative studies have employed samples ranging from around 30 (Liebeskind et al., 1992) to 35,752 observations (Harris et al., 2005). Using performance data, the studies deploy a variety of econometric methodologies (univariate and multivariate) to assess the (sources of) changes in performance. The majority of studies compare the pre- and post-LBO performance. In addition, a substantial number of papers focuses on RLBOs (secondary IPOs), and compares the performance during the public, the private, and the renewed public status of the firms. Fox and Marcus (1992) and Wright et al. (1995), however, argue that RLBO performance studies should not be used to make inferences about going private in general, as these studies use samples biased towards those LBOs that return into public hands, which are likely to be the strongest performers.

In general, quantitative studies suffer from three econometric challenges. First, data availability is problematic, as private firms do not have to comply with detailed disclosure of financial information. Furthermore, the available information on private firms induces a size bias because larger private firms still release more information than smaller firms. Second, Smart and Waldfogel (1994) and Palepu (1990) claim that quantitative studies mistakenly compare post-transaction performance to pre-transaction performance: post-transaction performance should be compared to the *expected* performance that would have occurred without a buyout in order to ascertain whether or not performance improvements are attributable to the LBO process. A third econometric problem, mainly prevalent in older studies, is that some papers match LBO firms with non-LBO firms without controlling for industry and time effects.

A small number of studies employ the case study methodology. Yin (1989) argues that case studies can provide more direct answers through their ability to deal with research settings with a large number of variables, or where variables tend to be qualitative. Case studies can therefore better explore the organizational links between going private and performance improvements (Baker & Wruck, 1989).

Empirical results

This section discusses the most important papers from the large body of empirical work on the post-buyout wealth creation process. We categorize the papers according to the research methodology employed. The quantitative studies are subdivided into two types depending on whether their sample is based on (i) firms under private ownership or (ii) RLBOs. Case studies are a third type. Each type is discussed in a different section.

Quantitative studies: firms under private ownership

Based on a sample of 48 MBOs that took place between 1980 and 1986 and after controlling for divestitures, Kaplan (1989a) finds that industry-adjusted operating income increases in the three years post-buyout. Smith (1990) confirms that post-buyout operating performance increases more than the industry median, but finds that this cannot be explained by a reduction of spending on discretionary items or capital expenditures. Smart and Waldfogel (1994) revisit Kaplan's (1989a) sample and compare performance against pre-buyout *expected* performance,[16] but still show similarly strong operating performance improvements. Muscarella and Vetsuypens (1990) look at a sample of PTPs that went public again (RLBOs), as such deals require disclosing financial statements covering several years of operation under private ownership. They find that efficiency improvements after an MBO reflect real operating gains resulting from restructuring activities and cost-cutting, and not from revenue generation. This is confirmed by Liebeskind et al. (1992) and Jones (1992), who find that managers resort to more downsizing of their businesses and to expanding production lines less, and that improved planning techniques that match the organizational context better drive operational efficiency improvements. More recently, Fidrmuc et al. (2013) find that "pure" MBOs (without backing from a PE partner) show improved operating performance, whereas PE-backed deals already outperform their peers before the deal takes place.

Many papers also elaborate on the effects of a PTP transaction on the firm's employees. Their conclusions are summarized in Table 7.8. Despite the popular view being that employees of an LBO are subjected to layoffs and wage reductions, empirical research concludes that employees benefit from the spillover effects of investments in production methods and operations by the new owners (Agrawal & Tambe, 2016). When controlling for reduced employment resulting from post-transaction divestitures, Kaplan (1989a) reports that median employment rises by 0.9%. Muscarella and Vetsuypens (1990) report that going-private transactions do not cause layoffs, results that are confirmed by Smith (1990) who also notes that the number of employees from the year before the MBO until the year after the deal grows, but more slowly than the industry average. Davis et al. (2014) investigate 150,000 target "establishments" (factories, offices, and other physical locations where business takes place) in US PE deals from 1980 to 2005. They find that, although LBO firms' employment declines by 6% (relative to control firms), LBO firms also create more new jobs at new establishments, resulting in net employment declines of less than 1%. Agrawal and Tambe (2016) even find that target workers' employability improves, especially for those whose jobs are transformed by production upgrades by the new owners after an LBO: whereas technological change would have rendered their skills obsolete, workers in LBO firms earn higher long-run wages and their post-LBO employment spells (fraction of time that a worker is employed relative to the total amount of time observed in the work force) are 6 to 9 percentage points longer. For UK LBOs, Amess and Wright (2007) find that, relative to non-LBOs, wage growth is lower for both MBOs and MBIs, and employment growth is higher for MBOs but lower for MBIs. The authors interpret this as evidence that MBIs are more likely to break implicit agreements and transfer wealth from employees to the new owners, while MBOs are more capable of exploiting higher growth opportunities.

In another interesting plant-level study, Lichtenberg and Siegel (1990) document that white-collar workers experience compensation and employment losses, whereas blue-collar workers are not affected. Over the three years following a going-private transaction, total factor productivity growth at the plant level increases by 8.3% above the industry mean, and research spending increases both on an absolute basis and relative to peer firms. Similarly, Harris et al. (2005) report plant-level productivity increases in UK MBOs, probably arising from agency cost reductions and resource relocation. Lerner et al. (2011) also find for a sample of public and private US LBOs backed by PE funds that firms' patent quality increases in the post-buyout years. Amess et al. (2016), however, distinguish between public-to-private and private-to-private PE-backed LBOs in the UK, and find that, although patent stock

Table 7.8 Post-buyout employment effects

Study	*Sample period/ country*	*Type of deal*	*Obs.*	*Operating performance*	*Change in employee base*	*Wages*
Kaplan (1989a)	1980–1986, US	MBO	76	Incr.	Incr. (0.9%)	–
Muscarella & Vetsuypens (1990)	1976–1987, US	LBO	26	Incr.	Decr. (−0.6%)	–
Smith (1990)	1977–1986, US	MBO	58	Incr.	Incr. (+2.0%)	–
Lichtenberg & Siegel (1990)	1983–1986, US	LBO	1,108	Incr.	–	Incr. (+3.6%) if prod. worker Decr. (−5.2%) if nonprod. worker
Amess & Wright (2007)	1999–2004, UK	MBO MBI	1,014 336	Insign. Incr.	Incr. (+0.51%) Decr. (−0.81%)	Decr (−0.31%) Decr (−0.97%)
Amess & Wright (2012)	1993–2004, UK	LBO	533	–	Insign.	–
Davis et al. (2014)	1980–2005, US (incl. private-to-private)	LBO	150,000	Incr.	Decr. (−6.0%)	Decr. (−2.4%)
Agrawal & Tambe (2016)	1995–2010, US	LBO	4,193	–	Incr..	Incr. (+8.9%)

This table shows all papers that consider the effects of going private on the target firms' employees, in terms of wages and layoffs. LBO = all leveraged buyout deals; MBO = management buyout deals only; MBI = management buyin deals only.

increases in the private-to-private transactions, there is some evidence that public-to-private transactions reduce patent activity. Based on interview data, Zahra (1995), however, also documents that innovation and risk-taking is not stifled post-buyout and that performance improvements arise from an increased emphasis on commercialization and R&D alliances, as well as from improved quality of the R&D function and intensified venturing activities.

An important nuance to the positive view sketched in some of these papers is given by Kaplan and Stein (1993). They point out that US PTP transactions made in the latter half of the 1980s were pricier and riskier, which eroded the returns of taking a company private. This is confirmed by Long and Ravenscraft (1993), but they add that performance and efficiency improvements remain substantial. For instance, Opler (1992) calculates that for the 20 largest transactions in the 1985–1990 period, operating profits per dollar of sales rise by 11.6% on an industry-corrected basis. Guo et al. (2011) and Cohn et al. (2014) investigate value creation in the recent LBO wave. In line with the results for the 1980s wave, deals in the latter half of the 2000s wave were priced higher and had riskier capital structures. Operating performance in post-buyout firms appears to be enhanced by increases in leverage and improved corporate governance activities, although there is little evidence of improved performance relative to benchmark firms. In contrast, Boucly et al. (2011) and Bergström et al. (2007) are able to identify operating improvements in French and Swedish LBO targets, respectively. For the UK, Wilson et al. (2012) find that PE-backed buyouts were more productive and more profitable (relative to comparable non-buyout firms) both before and after the 2007 financial crisis.

Although there are case studies on individual going-private firms in trouble (see e.g., Wruck, 1991; Bruner & Eades, 1992) as well as some large sample studies (e.g., Andrade & Kaplan, 1998; Easterwood, 1998), research which directly tests the effects of economic recessions is scarce. Nevertheless, Wright et al. (1996) find that the probability of failure of buyouts and buyins of unquoted companies is reduced by managerial incentive plans and well-timed corporate restructuring. Consistent with Bruner and Eades (1992), they find that excessive leverage is a strong predictor for failure when macro-economic conditions turn sour. For a more recent sample of PE-backed buyouts between 1995 and 2010, however, Wilson and Wright (2013) find that leverage is not a strong predictor of failure, and that PE-backed buyouts are no more prone to financial distress than non-buyouts or other types of MBIs.

Quantitative studies: RLBOs

Some papers focus on RLBOs. Degeorge and Zeckhauser (1993) predict that asymmetric information, debt overhang, and behavioral problems can create a pattern of superior performance before the RLBO (the private stage), and disappointing results afterwards (the public stage). This is confirmed by Holthausen and Larcker (1996) who find that, although leverage and insider equity ownership are reduced in RLBOs, both remain high relative to the industry-adjusted numbers of quoted firms. Thus, they argue that RLBOs are in fact hybrid organizations because they retain some of the characteristics of an LBO after the flotation. In line with the incentive realignment hypothesis, these firms outperform their industry and do not show stock price underperformance for at least four years post-RLBO, but they experience a performance decline afterwards. The authors argue that the lagged effect of performance reduction is due to RLBOs gradually losing their typical LBO characteristics and evolving towards the typical firm of the industry. RLBOs also appear to be rationally priced as they do not suffer from long-term underperformance (Ritter, 1991), which is confirmed by Cao and Lerner (2009) in that RLBOs appear to perform at least as well as other IPOs and the stock market as a whole. They find that, relative to the 1980s wave, RLBOs in the second wave are larger, more leveraged, more profitable, and have more profitable underwriters, but buyout returns appear to decline over time due to increased competition for transactions.

Case studies

Some interesting clinical studies have been published to explore the organizational links between going private and performance improvements. Investigating the MBO of O.M. Scott & Sons Company, Baker and Wruck (1989) confirm the results of large sample studies that high leverage and managerial equity ownership lead to improved incentives and, subsequently, to improved performance. Of equal importance in terms of their contribution to performance, however, are the restrictions imposed by debt covenants, the emphasis on managerial compensation (and the incentives it creates), the decentralization of decision making, and the relations Scott managers had with the third-party buyout team of Clayton & Dubilier partners. Denis (1994) compares a leveraged recapitalization (Kroger Co.) with

Table 7.9 Summary of the third strand of literature: Process

Study	*Sample period/ country*	*N*	*Transaction type*	*Tax*	*Incentive realignment*	*Control*	*Free cash flow*	*Wealth transfer*	*Transaction costs*	*Takeover defence*	*Under-valuation*
Kaplan (1989a)	1980–1985 US	76	MBO	–	Yes	–	–	No	–	–	No
Baker & Wruck (1989)	1986 US	1	MBO	–	Yes	Yes	Yes	No	–	–	No
Smith (1990)	1977–1986 US	58	MBO	–	Yes	–	–	No	–	–	No
Muscarella & Vetsuypens (1990)	1973–1985 US	151	MBO	–	Yes	Yes	–	No	–	–	Yes
Lichtenberg & Siegel (1990)	1981–1986 US	244	ALL	–	–	Yes	–	No	–	–	–
Jones (1992)	1984–1985 US	17	MBO	–	Yes	–	–	–	–	–	–
Opler (1992)	1985–1989 US	45	ALL	Yes	Yes	–	–	–	–	–	Inconcl.
Liebeskind et al. (1992)	1980–1984 US	33	ALL	–	Yes	–	–	–	–	–	–
Green (1992)	1980–1984 UK	8	MBO	–	No	–	–	–	–	–	–
Long & Ravenscraft (1993)	1978–1989 US	48	ALL	Yes	–	–	Yes	–	–	–	–
Denis (1994)	1986 US	2	LBO	–	Yes	Yes	Yes	–	–	–	No
Zahra (1995)	1992 US	47	ALL	–	Inconcl.	Inconcl.	Inconcl.	–	–	–	–
Robbie & Wright (1995)	1987–1989 UK	5	MBI	–	Yes	Yes	–	–	–	–	Yes
Holthausen & Larcker (1996)	1983–1988 US	90	ALL	–	Yes	–	No	–	–	–	–
Bruton et al. (2002)	1980–1988 US	39	ALL	–	Yes	–	–	–	–	–	–
Harris et al. (2005)	1994–1998 UK	35,752 (establishments)	MBO	–	Yes	–	–	–	–	–	–
Guo et al. (2011)	1900–2006 US	192	ALL	Yes	Yes	Yes	Yes	–	–	–	No
Cohn et al. (2014)	1995–2007 US	317	ALL	Yes	–	–	–	–	–	–	Yes

This table shows the most important papers that deal with strand 3 of the PTP research. Yes = supportive, No = unsupportive, Inconcl. = inconclusive. Type of deal ALL refers to all going-private transactions, MBO and MBI stand for management buyout and management buyin transactions, respectively.

an LBO (Safeway Stores Inc.) and similarly finds that, although both firms considerably increase leverage, the improved managerial equity ownership, boardroom change, monitoring by an LBO specialist firm, and executive compensation associated with the LBO are responsible for the more productive cash generation in Safeway Stores. The results from these papers suggest that an LBO is not only about leveraging the business; performance improvements are related to specific value improving characteristics of LBOs, and do not occur just because these improvements were not made before when the firm was still in public hands.

Green (1992) studies the effect of changes in ownership on the motivation of managers in eight case studies of UK divisional MBOs. Although managers in the investigated MBOs seem to work harder and are more entrepreneurial, the prospect of financial rewards does not appear to be the main motivator. Contrary to beliefs commonly held by financial economists, the changed working conditions allow them to do their work more effectively. In fact, this finding casts doubt on the incentive realignment hypothesis, as it means that innovativeness drives ownership concentration, rather than the other way around. Indeed, Bruining and Wright (2002) find that MBOs of non-listed firms occur mostly in firms where entrepreneurial opportunities exist. Clearly, these case studies confirm the claim that MBOs are more than just a vehicle to improve efficiency in a mature-sector company (Wright et al., 2000). However, for MBIs of unquoted UK firms, Robbie and Wright (1995) find that all too often, MBI teams cannot adequately deal with post-transaction problems that were not anticipated in the due diligence examination but substantially impede the execution of a new strategy. Such a lack of accurate information turns out to be a major cause of problems in third-party transactions. In line with the incentive realignment hypothesis and underlining the importance of the improved monitoring function in LBOs, they also find that the success of an MBI depends on the incentive package taking into consideration the context of the transaction, leaving sufficient flexibility on the side of capital suppliers and monitors to respond to emerging problems.

Synthesis: Process

Table 7.9 summarizes the main results discussed in this section. We conclude that the 1980s LBO wave triggered considerable operational improvements. The causes of the performance and efficiency improvements were primarily the organizational structure of the LBO, characterized by high leverage and strong (managerial) ownership concentration. Almost unambiguously, the studies in this strand of the literature support the role of incentive realignment in the post-buyout value creating process, while the employee wealth transfer hypothesis is mostly discarded and the undervaluation hypothesis remains disputed. Evidence from the most recent LBO wave documents only limited performance improvements for US LBOs, although the change in performance seems to depend on the form of the deal: pure MBOs and private-to-private LBOs show performance improvements, whereas PE-backed MBOs were already performing well before the deal and PTP LBOs show no improvements. In contrast to their US counterparts, there is, however, some evidence that Continental European LBOs show significant increases in operating performance post-buyout. A consistent finding in both the first and the second LBO wave is that deals towards the end of the wave show less value creation, as they are generally riskier and higher priced. Despite popular belief, LBOs are associated with growth in employment and wages, although employment growth is slower relative to industry peers and is less likely to occur in LBOs with third-party involvement (e.g., MBIs and IBOs). In addition, LBO firms tend to invest more in long-term innovation.

Fourth strand: Duration

Jensen (1989) argues that LBO firms constitute a superior organizational form to publicly held firms, due to the better incentives they offer to managers and monitors. Management incentives relating pay to performance, decentralization of control, high leverage, and other bonding or pre-commitment agreements, combined with reputational concerns of the LBO sponsors, reduce the agency cost problems inherent in the structure of the public corporation in low-growth industries. Nevertheless, Rappaport (1990: 101) contests Jensen's (1989) proclaimed superiority of the LBO organization to public corporations, arguing that the latter are "vibrant, dynamic institutions – capable of long periods of underperformance, to be sure, but also fully capable of self-correction." Kaplan (1991) refers to Rappaport's (1990) view of "going-private as a shock therapy." After the necessary changes have been brought about under highly leveraged private ownership, the costs of inflexibility, illiquidity, and the need for risk diversification will exceed the benefits of the LBO as an organizational form, with a return to public ownership as an inevitable consequence. Clearly, according to this view, the time horizon associated with the private phase will generally be shorter than the "significant period of time" Jensen (1989) deems necessary. Kaplan (1991) highlights the importance of evidence on LBO-duration in the discussion of the role of PTP transactions, the reasons why they occur, and the sources of wealth gains that motivate going-private transactions. Therefore, this section reviews the empirical work on the duration of private ownership after a PTP transaction.

Methodological issues

To measure the duration of the private status of a firm (from LBO to secondary IPO), hazard functions – designed to measure the "survival time" – are estimated. There are two major reasons why duration analysis of LBOs cannot be carried out by straightforward multiple regression techniques. First, the dependent variable (duration of private status) is most likely not normally distributed (it usually follows an exponential Weibull distribution). Second, there is the problem of censoring. A Cox proportional hazard model is the most general form of the regression models because it is not based on any assumptions concerning the nature and shape of the underlying survival distribution. The model assumes that the underlying hazard *rate* (rather than survival time) is a function of the independent variables (covariates) such that no assumptions are made about the nature or shape of the hazard function. In order to use a hazard model a minimum number of 30 LBO observations is needed, which is difficult to find in some countries. Furthermore, in past Anglo-American studies, the attrition bias is not accounted for in the estimation (some LBO firms go bankrupt after the delisting such that an RLBO is not an option). Therefore, the correct duration of LBOs is based on the probability of a return to public ownership conditional on survival during the phase under private ownership.

Empirical results

Kaplan (1991) is the first to formally address LBO duration and finds that companies that return to public ownership do so after a median time under private status of only 2.63 years. For his sample of 183 large going-private transactions from 1979–1986, he finds an unconditional median life of 6.82 years for whole-firm and divisional LBOs. Using hazard functions, Kaplan (1991) observes constant duration dependence in years 2 through 5, and negative duration dependence beyond this period. This means that the likelihood of returning to public ownership is largest in years 2 to 5, while this likelihood decreases as time under private ownership increases beyond this period. This result leaves room for both the existence of Rappaport's (1990) arguments about the shock therapy of LBOs, as well as for Jensen's (1989) idea that firms that go private will remain private for longer periods of time due to the advantages of incentive realignment. Consistent with Kaplan (1991), Holthausen and Larcker (1996) confirm that LBOs reverting to public ownership retain some of the characteristics they exhibited under private ownership. Using a sample of 343 whole-firm and divisional buyouts from 1980–1992, Van de Gucht and Moore (1998) confirm the results found by Kaplan (1991, 1993) on the median duration of the private status (conditional on the firm reverting back to a public listing). However, when they employ a split population hazard model that does not implicitly assume that all firms that went private eventually return to public ownership (as Kaplan, 1991 does), they document that the likelihood of returning to a listing increases up to the seventh year, but decreases subsequently. Interestingly, the climate of the financial markets significantly influences the reverting moment.

Halpern et al. (1999) reconcile the contradicting claims by Rappaport (1990) ("going-private as a short-run shock therapy") and Jensen (1989) ("LBO firms constitute a superior organizational form") and state that the probability of remaining private is positively related to managerial shareholdings. Poorly performing firms with low managerial shareholdings remain private only for a short time, consistent with Rappaport's claim. After restructuring the operations after the buyout, these firms become publicly listed again. For firms with ex ante high managerial shareholdings, the private status is a more efficient form of organization and hence these firms remain delisted.

Wright et al. (1995) investigate a sample of 182 UK buyouts and buyins between 1983–1986, including PTP transactions as well as buyouts of non-listed firms, and both divisional and whole-firm buyouts and buyins. This study shows that – in line with the US findings – the hazard coefficient increases strongly from approximately three to six years after the buyout, after which a negative duration dependence persists. Survivor analysis estimations show that size is a significantly negative determinant of the duration in buyouts. Quantitative analysis is combined with three case studies in Wright et al. (1994) who investigate the influence of a whole array of management buyout types on the duration of a firm's private status. Their evidence suggests that ownership, financial, and market-related factors are the prime factors explaining the duration of the buyout. Third-party financial institutions are associated with the propensity to exit fairly rapidly after a transaction, as these institutions seek a return within a relatively short pre-established time frame. If the management of the buyout firm owns a relatively small fraction of the equity, it will be not able to extend the private status of the firm for long. Finally, the study documents that environmental dynamism and competitive pressure are important determinants of buyout longevity.

Using a sample of over 21,000 public-to-private and private-to-private global LBOs over the period 1970–2007, Strömberg (2007) reports a median holding period of nine years, supporting Jensen's (1989) claim that the LBO organizational form is an optimal governance structure over the long run. Whereas this holding period is longer than those reported in previous studies, he finds evidence that holding periods increase over time: from six to seven years in the 1980s to more than nine years in the 1990s. Interestingly, he finds that LBO firms going public were more likely to be privately held pre-LBO (private-to-private LBOs), whereas most of the public-to-private LBO firms remain private. Consistent with Wright et al. (1994), he finds that LBOs with more PE involvement have shorter holding periods and are more likely to go public.

Table 7.10 Summary of previous empirical results for the fourth strand of literature: Duration

Study	*Sample period/ country*	*Type of deal*	*Obs.*	*Main result of the study*
Kaplan (1991)	1979–1986 US	ALL	183	After year 5, the conditional probability of returning to public ownership decreases
Van de Gucht & Moore (1998)	1980–1992 US	ALL	343	Until year 7, the conditional probability of returning to public markets increases, while after seven years, it decreases. The timing of reversion is influenced by the financial markets' climate
Wright et al. (1994)	1981–1992 UK	ALL	2,023	Ownership, financial, and market-related factors determine the duration of the private status
Wright et al. (1995)	1983–1986 UK	ALL	140	The conditional probability of reversion increases strongly between year 3 and year 6, and subsequently decreases
Halpern et al. (1999)	1981–1985 US	ALL	126	Longevity of the private status is increasing in managerial equity stake
Strömberg (2007)	1970–2007 Global (includes also private-to-private deals)	ALL	Over 21,000	Longevity of the private status increases over time. Privately held pre-LBO firms are more likely to go public than firms in public-to-private LBO deals. PE-backed LBOs are more likely to exit early than MBOs
Cao & Lerner (2009)	1981–2003 US	ALL	526	Average duration of 3.5 years. Returns decrease for longer holding periods, but quick flips perform even more poorly

Table 7.10 shows the most important papers that deal with strand 4 of PTP research. ALL stands for all going-private transactions (LBOs, MBOs, MBIs, IBOs).

Synthesis: Duration

Table 7.10 gives an overview of the main results of the papers discussed in this section and shows that there is a dichotomy among the firms that go private. Some firms seem to use the organizational form of a going-private transaction as a temporary shock therapy to enable them to restructure efficiently, while others regard the LBO as a sustainable superior organizational form. The decision to organize an RLBO (or a secondary IPO) depends both on firm-specific characteristics and environmental factors. However, privately owned holding periods in the second LBO boom increased relative to the 1980s wave, providing support for the sustainable organization form theory of private ownership. Issues of longevity are discussed further in Chapter 27 in this volume.

International public-to-private trends

An abundant body of empirical literature has documented the drivers of waves in M&A activity (see e.g., Golbe & White, 1993; Andrade et al., 2001; Auster & Sirower, 2002; Martynova & Renneboog, 2008a, 2011b; Maksimovic et al., 2013). Likewise, LBO activity seems to occur in cycles (Smit & Van Den Berg, 2006) and the following two factors seem to be the main determinants. First, the opportunities for value creation from PTP deals vary

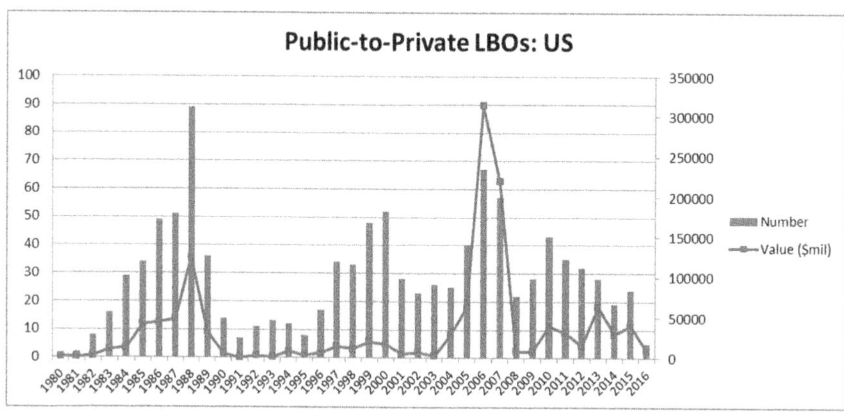

Figure 7.2 US public-to-private activity

This figure shows the number of public-to-private transactions (left-hand scale) and the value in USD millions (right-hand scale).

Source: SDC Global Platinum and own calculations.

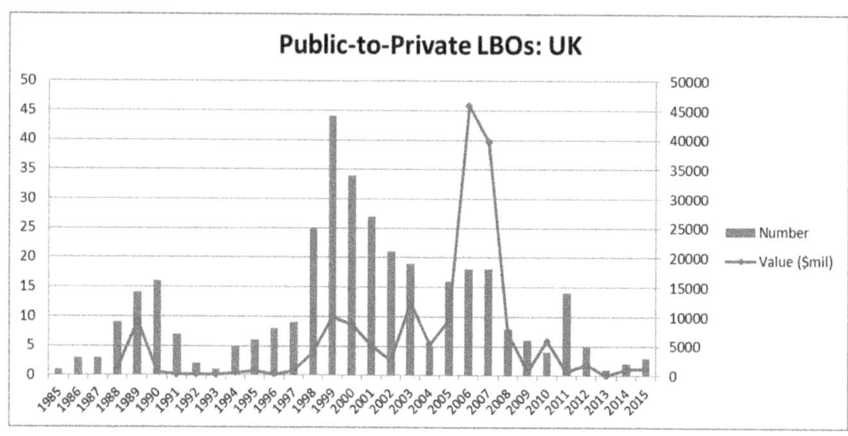

Figure 7.3 UK public-to-private activity

This figure shows the number of public-to-private transactions (left-hand scale) and the value in USD millions (right-hand scale).

Source: SDC Global Platinum and own calculations.

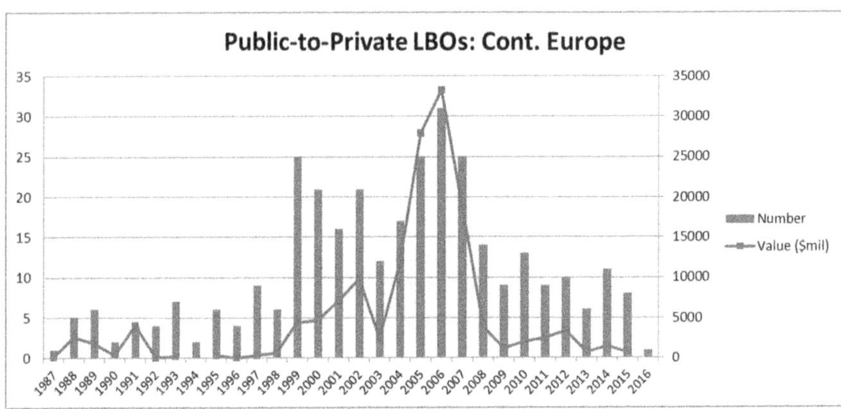

Figure 7.4 Continental European public-to-private activity

This figure shows the number of public-to-private transactions (left-hand scale) and the value in USD millions (right-hand scale).

Source: SDC Global Platinum and own calculations.

over time, which determines the demand for PE capital. Second, the extent to which the supply of PE capital can meet this demand, depends on the economics of the PE model in a given region or market (Fenn et al., 1995). The economics are determined by, e.g., the political economy and the general acceptance of LBOs as financial transactions, the capital market conditions, and the legal/fiscal infrastructure. In this section, the occurrence of the LBO waves in the 1980s and 2000s is explained by the arguments based on the supply and demand for PE capital made above. Figures 7.2, 7.3, and 7.4 show the evolution of PTP volumes and values for the period 1980–2016 for the US, the UK, and Continental Europe.

The LBO wave of the 1980s

The US economy of the 1980s was characterized by a large number of (hostile) corporate takeovers and restructuring. Mitchell and Mulherin (1996) argue that 57% of US quoted firms were takeover targets or were restructured between 1982 and 1989. As some mergers failed and substantial excess capacity was created, the M&A wave also triggered a significant increase in LBO activity. Going-private transactions facilitated the reduction in excess capacity that "complacent corporate America" was unable to solve itself (Jensen, 1991). This alludes to agency cost-related explanations of wealth gains from LBOs.

Shleifer and Vishny (1990) argue that LBOs enabled the deregulation and resulting deconglomeration of the large corporate groups created in the 1960s and 1970s. The development of the high-yield or junk bond market by Drexel Burnham Lambert's Michael Milken improved access to acquisition finance to pursue these going-private transactions (for a review, see Yago, 1990; Kelley et al., 1993; Scott, 2000). In addition, hostile going-private transactions were facilitated by the 1982 Supreme Court reduction of state anti-takeover laws (Jarrell & Poulsen, 1987; Pound, 1987; Jarrell, 1992). As a result, many of these transactions were also motivated by the takeover defense hypothesis as described earlier.

In the first half of the 1980s, LBOs performed their role of catalyzing corporate restructuring so well that Jensen (1989) predicted the eclipse of the public corporation. However, the culmination of the LBO wave in the second half of the 1980s was associated with many bankruptcies (see Jensen, 1991; Kaplan & Stein, 1993) and evoked fierce public and political resistance (Shleifer & Vishny, 1991). The LBO wave of the 1980s dried up as a consequence of the resulting re-enactment of state anti-takeover legislation,[17] the political pressure against high leverage,[18] the crisis in the high yield bond market, and a credit crunch (see Holmstrom & Kaplan, 2001 and Jensen, 1991 for a review).

The phenomenon of PTP transactions quickly traversed the Atlantic, with the first UK MBO (Haden Maclellan Holdings Plc) being undertaken in 1985. Although smaller in scale, the activity in the UK going-private market kept pace with that of the US and the first wave also peaked in 1989. Wealth gains from LBOs in the 1980s in the UK appear similar to those in the US. Public controversy[19] about the increased hostility in going-private transactions induced the Takeover Panel[20] to adopt new rules regulating the behavior and procedures in going-private transactions (Wright et al., 1991). The drop in deals after 1989 made it seem as if the going-private transaction had already outlived its short life. The 1980s LBO wave was primarily a US/UK phenomenon; PTP transactions on the European Continent during the 1980s were virtually nonexistent in that period.

The LBO wave of the 2000s

Anglo-American trends: US and UK

Although favorable conditions (with the exception of the anti-takeover measures) were restored in the US in the early 1990s, going-private activity did not take off. Kaplan (1997) and Holmstrom and Kaplan (2001) argue that the 1980-style deals were not necessary anymore. The reason is that, on the whole, corporations themselves seem to have reduced the agency costs between shareholders and managers by realigning managerial incentives and strengthening shareholder control. The subsequent declined rate of hostility (Holmstrom & Kaplan, 2001) had also reduced the scope of MBOs as a defensive mechanism, and the recession of the early 1990s brought whatever LBO activity that was left to an end, as many deals then defaulted (Guo et al., 2011). The most important sources of wealth gains of US LBOs from the 1980s appeared to be no longer available.

However, going-private activity reached a new peak in the 2000s, raising questions about the mechanisms of value creation during this period. Shivdasani and Wang (2011) find that, from 2004 to 2007, $535 billion in LBOs were completed in the US, vastly exceeding the $227 billion in the first LBO wave in the 1980s. However, whereas transactions in the first buyout wave involved mostly large firms in mature industries, the bulk of buyouts in the second LBO wave was made of mid-cycle private firms in new and growing industries. Nevertheless, going-private transactions still made up 34% of transaction values in the 2000s wave, relative to 9% in the early 1990s (Kaplan & Stromberg, 2009). The second LBO wave was mainly fueled by growth in the securitization markets, providing easier and cheaper access to deal financing. With the collapse of the collateralized debt obligation (CDO) markets, however, LBO volume dropped by 94% in the last quarter of 2007.

Block (2004) surveys 40% of the firms going private over the period 2001 to 2003 and finds that the main reasons for going private are: (i) pressure by the market on top management to increase corporate performance, (ii) lack of analyst coverage and market liquidity, and (iii) the threat of being delisted by Nasdaq. This is supported by Mehran and Peristiani (2010) who find that lack of financial visibility and of interest by analysts and institutional investors was a primary reason for young IPO firms to go private between 1990 and 2007. In addition, the implementation of the Sarbanes-Oxley Act substantially increased the costs of a listing (e.g., Perino, 2003; Ribstein, 2003; Coustan et al., 2004). This additional regulatory burden has a fixed cost component that falls disproportionally on the smaller quoted companies (Holmstrom & Kaplan, 2003; Engel et al., 2007). This rise in the costs of a stock listing and the likely inability to reap the benefits of a public listing appear to be the main reasons for small US companies to go private from the late 1990s onwards (Carney, 2005; Engel et al., 2007; Kamar et al., 2009; Mehran & Peristiani, 2010). This provides strong support for the transaction cost hypothesis of wealth gains for LBOs. Guo et al. (2011) compare the first and second LBO waves and find that, despite being less levered than deals in the 1980s wave, deals in the second wave still face substantial default risk. They are also characterized by more conservative pricing, multiple PE partners, and considerable asset restructuring.

As in the US, financial backers in the UK were unprepared to take any risks at the beginning of the 1990s, which resulted in a dormant PTP market. Nevertheless, Figure 7.3 shows that a new wave of going-private transactions started in 1998. The LBO market from 1998 to 2003 was characterized by many small firms going private, indicated by the high peak in the number of deals, but the relatively small peak in deal value. This suggests that, as shown for the US by Mehran and Peristiani (2010), the first half of the second LBO wave consisted of young IPO firms going private. Although the number of deals did not exceed that in the first half the 2000s, going-private transactions attained unprecedented values from 2003 to 2007: deals in the year 2006 alone reached a total value of $45 billion. As in the US markets, however, the crash of the securitized debt markets at the end of 2007 also meant the end of the second LBO wave in the UK.

Explanations for the second going-private wave at the end of the 1990s generally emphasize the access to cheap debt financing driven by growth in the CDO markets (Shivdasani & Wang, 2011), but also increased confidence of PE and debt financiers on access to key information, due diligence, management support, target shareholder support, and the expectation that 100% of the shares could be acquired (e.g., through squeeze-out provisions)[21] (Ashurst et al., 2002; CMBOR, 2002). Also, innovative techniques such as inducement fees and "hard" exclusivity agreements have facilitated the reduction of risks in going-private transactions (Davis & Day, 1998). Arguably, these changes have improved the economics of the PE model substantially. As to the demand for PE capital, anecdotal evidence suggests that the UK LBO wave of the late 1990s was triggered primarily by (temporary) undervaluation, which led to increased wealth gains in LBOs. Especially small firms turned to PE as institutional investors disregarded such small firms (Weir et al., 2005b: 949). The consolidation in the fund management industry, with bigger funds requiring greater minimum investment and free float, is frequently mentioned as a reason for this institutional disinterest in small companies (*Financial Times*, September 17, 1999; CMBOR, 2002). The lack of liquidity and the need for expansion capital as a consequence of the limited availability of institutional equity finance depressed stock prices and drove small companies into the arms of PE firms to obtain funding (*Financial Times*, June 11, 2003).

The year 2007 was the year of the largest UK PTP deal to date, when Alliance Boots went private through a £11.1 billion LBO. With the start of the financial crisis at the end of 2007, however, going-private activity has dwindled and has virtually disappeared in the UK ever since.

Continental Europe trends

Although the first LBO wave was mainly apparent in the US, Canada, and the UK, the second LBO boom in the mid-2000s also spilled over to Continental Europe. The increase in

LBO activity in Continental Europe at the end of the 1990s and beginning of the 2000s is induced by various institutional and regulatory changes, which we discuss later. Figure 7.4 shows that European LBO activity in the second half of the 2000s follows patterns similar to those in the Anglo-American markets: going-private transactions reached a peak in terms of deal numbers and value in 2006, but substantially decreased with the start of the financial crisis in 2007. Since the demise of the CDO markets in 2007, LBO activity in the US, UK, and Europe has remained at relatively low levels. It is remarkable that, whereas European going-private activity substantially lagged behind that of the US and UK until the beginning of the 2000s, Strömberg (2007) reports that non-US PE activity has since outgrown that in the US, with activity in Continental Europe being particularly strong. However, LBO activity outside of North America and Western Europe remains relatively weak even in the early 2000s, accounting for only 13% of global LBO transactions in numerical terms and 7% in value terms.

What financial, economic, and regulatory changes induced the increase in LBO activity in Continental Europe at the beginning of the 2000s? First, Continental Europe's public capital markets were historically underdeveloped relative to the UK. One consequence is that a larger fraction of economic activity is privately financed, which reduces the number of potential targets and hence the scope of PTP transactions in corporate restructuring. In addition, public bond markets for small and mid-sized companies are virtually absent (Andres et al., 2003; Martynova & Renneboog, 2009), as are (junk) bond markets as a source of finance in LBOs. Sponsors therefore largely rely on banks for financing and experience less financial flexibility when arranging an LBO. However, Boucly et al. (2011) suggest that in countries where capital and credit markets are not as developed as in the US and the UK, LBOs can provide new sources of value creation by helping relax targets' credit constraints and allowing them to grow faster. Their findings that French LBOs lead to large increases in target profitability suggest that the conflicting findings in terms of value creation in the second LBO wave in US studies relative to European studies are due to the potential for Continental European buyouts to improve performance by relaxing targets' credit constraints. In addition, the emergence of new debt instruments in Europe such as second-lien bonds and loans with lower covenant limitations and more attractive rates and maturities further facilitated LBO finance (Wright et al., 2006).

Second, a survey by CMBOR (2002) indicates that some Continental European countries lack the legal provisions to limit the risk of taking a public company private. With greater uncertainty and risk, fewer PE houses are prepared to back PTP transactions. This lack of an LBO infrastructure leads to lower levels of activity. Nevertheless, since 2000, many European countries have introduced changes favorable for LBO activity (Goergen et al., 2005; Martynova & Renneboog, 2011a, 2013). For instance, the transparency, shareholder protection, takeover rules, and development of risk capital as provided for in Italy's 1998 Company Law reform allowed for more flexibility in structuring PE deals and provided more reassurance to Italian going-private transactions (Ulissi, 2000; Lovells, 2003). Similarly, the German Takeover Act provided a set of mandatory rules that govern the time schedule of a going-private bid, guarantee the equal treatment of all shareholders of the same class, limit prolonged resistance by the target managing board, and introduce a squeeze-out rule at 95% of the equity (Goergen et al., 2005).

Third, fiscal regimes in some countries in Continental Europe were deemed "unhelpful" to enable PTP transactions by the CMBOR (2002) survey. For example, in Switzerland, the interest on LBOs cannot be offset against the company's earnings, and tax deductions are not possible in France if the 95% level of tendered shares is not achieved. But other Continental

European countries are looking more favorably at LBOs. The German tax reform eliminated the corporate capital gains tax on the disposal of shares, facilitating the sale of blocks of shares of listed firms to PE investors (Ashurst et al., 2002). The French Minister of the Economy declared that the French usury law does not apply to corporate bonds, high yield issues, or debt instruments (Fried & Frank, 2003). This has eliminated the need for French borrowers in LBO transactions to set up new companies in jurisdictions other than France. In the Netherlands, the Dutch Fiscal Unity law of January 1, 2003, enabled acquisition vehicles of PE investors to allocate the losses of high interest payments from acquisition-related leverage to the operations of the target. In Italy, LBOs were even prohibited until a law reform in 2004 rendered LBOs legal again. The allocation of cash flow and control rights was less efficient during the period of illegality and the returns to PE transactions were then lower (Cumming & Zambelli, 2010, 2013).

Fourth, the "culture" on the European Continent has historically been less favorable to LBOs. Especially in Mediterranean economies, family companies with a stock listing are a great source of pride and their management teams may not even consider going private, even if necessary (CMBOR, 2002).

Conclusions and suggestions for additional research

Overall, although some studies focus on non-Anglo-American countries (e.g., Boucly et al., 2011 for France; Bergström et al., 2007 for Sweden; and Strömberg, 2007 using a global sample), systematic research on the sources of wealth and post-buyout performance in going-private transactions for countries other than the US and the UK is still limited. The findings from these studies, however, do suggest that what is currently known about going-private transactions based on US samples cannot always be generalized to, for example, Continental European LBOs.

There are compelling reasons why extrapolation of US LBO research to UK and Continental European PTP transactions is not straightforward. First, the nature and extent of debt financing in US PTP transactions differ substantially from UK/European deals (Toms & Wright, 2004). Whereas US deals of the 1980s were primarily financed with junk bonds, mezzanine was and still is the standard in the UK and Continental Europe. Since these two sources of funds have different characteristics (in terms of flexibility, interest rates, maturity, and covenants), it is not unlikely that the financing choice will influence the incentive mechanisms in all phases of a going-private transaction. In addition, the debt levels associated with UK transactions are generally lower than those of US deals. Continental Europe's public capital markets were historically less developed than those of the US and the UK, resulting in relatively more private financing, which reduces the financial flexibility when arranging an LBO and hence the scope of potential PTP transactions. In addition, public bond markets as a source of finance in LBOs are virtually absent (Andres et al., 2007; Martynova & Renneboog, 2009), such that investors largely have to rely on bank financing. However, in countries where capital and credit markets are not as developed as in the US and the UK, LBOs can provide new sources of value creation by helping relax targets' credit constraints (Boucly et al., 2011).

Second, tax benefits have been proven to be an important source of wealth gains in US transactions in the 1980s, but they have become less important in the second LBO wave of the 1990s, and their importance has further declined under UK tax law. In Continental Europe, however, favorable fiscal regime changes since 2000 in, for example, Germany, France, the Netherlands, and Italy may have had a considerable effect on the wealth gains in LBOs (but few studies have investigated the effects of these fiscal changes on returns in LBOs).

Third, in the US market for corporate control, more hostile deals occur. The UK going-private wave of the late 1990s exhibits a hostility rate of merely 7.3% (Renneboog et al., 2007). This discrepancy can affect the bidding process for firms going private, and illustrates that the takeover defense hypothesis is not expected to hold for the UK and Continental Europe. Moreover, family-controlled companies in Continental Europe often refuse to go private, as family companies with a public listing may be a source of pride.

Fourth, venture capital and buyout markets in the UK and Continental Europe have traditionally been more closely linked than those in the US. Thus, the UK going-private activity has focused on growth opportunities, whereas US LBOs have occurred more frequently in mature, cash-rich industries.

Finally, the UK and Continental European markets for corporate control are organized and regulated differently than the US ones. Whereas US state regulation has effectively been able to regulate unsolicited takeover activity, the UK system has preferred self-regulation, thereby favoring the unrestricted functioning of market forces (Miller, 2000: 534; McCahery & Renneboog, 2004; Ferrarini & Miller, 2009; Calcagno & Falconieri, 2014).

These differences in regulation influence the sources of wealth creation in going-private transactions. Moreover, the subtle idiosyncrasies in financial practices and culture on either side of the Atlantic further reduce the generalizability of US-based results to the UK/Continental European situation. This implies that there is a strong need for further systematic and multi-country research on the second LBO wave.

We propose some issues that may be addressed in a future research agenda. First, future research should analyze the types of company that go private. Given that the level and volatility of cash flows varies across companies, an analysis of how to structure the capital by type of firm across different types of debt (including convertible debt) and (preferred) equity while balancing the size of tax shield and distress risk is interesting. Most existing research considers only the level of leverage, without taking into consideration the composition of the firm's debt structure and how this may affect post-buyout performance and the risk of financial distress.

Second, future research should estimate and analyze the wealth effects for shareholders and especially for bondholders in PTP transactions and investigate why (if at all) these wealth effects differ across corporate governance regimes. Countries differ substantially in terms of creditor protection and shareholder rights, both of which may affect the distribution of wealth in LBO deals. In addition, other stakeholders such as suppliers and employees may also be affected differently by country-level governance and labor regulations. These factors could play an important role in explaining the conflicting (although limited) findings on the effects of LBOs on firms' employment. Multi-country studies should take into account these cross-country differences when investigating the wealth effects of LBOs for various stakeholder groups.

Third, the process of the realization of wealth creation once the firm has been taken private should also attract research interest, as little is known about that LBO stage in particular, apart from the fact that working capital management can create additional value. With the growing availability of data on private firms, future research should be able to address this issue. The majority of evidence relating to post-buyout performance is based on PE-backed deals, with evidence for other types of buyouts (such as non-PE-backed MBOs) being scarce.

Fourth, future research should address the duration of the private status of formerly public firms and its determinants. Special attention could then be given to international comparisons and the role of going private as a corporate restructuring device in a multi-country setting, as the majority of research has focused on US samples. Moreover, country-specific regulations may considerably affect the duration of LBO firms' private status. Also, the type of firm going private may affect the duration of its private status, as certain types may prefer a longer or shorter period of being private.

Fifth, with exception of Mao and Renneboog (2015), there is little non-US research on earnings manipulation in firms prior to an LBO. The incentives to manipulate earnings may differ between MBOs and IBOs, across firms with various levels of financial constraints, or they may affect the likelihood of the firm becoming publicly listed again. Again, the extent to which earnings or stock valuations are manipulated and the effect on performance may depend on country-specific rules and regulations.

Sixth, most of our knowledge about LBOs is confined to public-to-private transactions. However, the increased data availability on private-to-private deals calls for additional research on this type of LBO transaction. A growing strand of literature focuses on private-to-private transactions, but evidence for public-to-private deals still largely outweighs the evidence for private-to-private deals. Given the large differences in terms of governance, financial, and ownership structure between public and privately held firms, conclusions based on public-to-private LBOs cannot easily be extrapolated to private-to-private LBOs.

Notes

1 The European Private Equity and Venture Capital Association (EVCA) defines public-to-private transactions as follows: "a transaction involving an offer for the entire share capital of a listed target company by a new company – Newco – and the subsequent re-registration of that listed target company as a private company. The shareholders of Newco usually comprise members of the target company's management and PE providers. Additional financing for the offer is normally provided by other debt providers."

2 This is an incentive device that enables management in a post-buyout firm to increase its equity holdings upon meeting specified performance targets.

3 Schadler and Karns (1990) discuss the conflicts of interest of the incumbent managers in an MBO.

4 These non-pecuniary (also called non-marketable perquisites or private) benefits are not transferable and are investor-specific. Possible benefits could be the reputation or symbolic value of being in control (Aghion & Bolton, 1992), salary, and value expropriated from shareholders (Dyck & Zingales, 2004), e.g., through the use of corporate jets (Edgerton, 2012) or acquiring large and costly mansions and estates (Liu & Yermack, 2012).

5 This problem is most severe in cash-generating industries with low growth prospects, as exemplified by the US oil industry in the late 1970s (Jensen, 1986) or the life insurance industry in the 1990s (Wells et al., 1995).

6 For a review of the mechanisms through which control can be exerted, please see Fenn et al. (1995: 33).

7 Weinstein (1983) presents a more formal bond beta model in which the sensitivity of bond returns to the capital structure confirms the conjectured increase in risk for bondholders in case of an unexpected increase in leverage. This is empirically confirmed by Masulis (1980), who documents negative bondholder returns in debt-for-equity exchange offers. The bondholder wealth transfer hypothesis then dictates that this increases risk, leads to debtholder wealth losses, and constitutes a wealth transfer to equity holders.

8 For a detailed overview of this literature on bond wealth effects, see Renneboog and Szilagyi (2008). In a recent paper on the more general context of takeovers, Renneboog et al. (2017) show that bond returns respond to cross-border acquisitions where the target and bidding firms are located in countries with different creditor protection and claims enforcement.

9 These calculations assume that the debt is repaid in eight years, that the buyout company can generate sufficient taxable income, that the marginal tax rate is applied (excluding ESOP tax deductions), and that asset step-ups are effectuated.

10 Renneboog et al. (2007), however, do not find any relation between the premium paid and the expected tax shields.
11 The discount rate is calculated based on the CAPM with the following parameters: a risk-free rate of 5% (current 3-month US T-bill rate from Bloomberg), a long-term market risk premium of 5% (Copeland et al., 2000), and a beta of 1 (beta of the market).
12 All UK numbers are from *The Financial Times* of August 31, 1999.
13 Franks and Mayer (1996) show that over a period of two years subsequent to a takeover in the UK, virtually all board members of the target firm left the merged firm.
14 For an overview of abnormal returns around mergers and acquisitions, see Martynova and Renneboog (2008b).
15 E.g., the UK City Code requires firms to disclose takeover negotiations when there are rumours, speculation, or an untoward price movement in the shares, if it can reasonably be determined to be caused by the bidder's actions. Typically, this type of announcement does not embody more than the notification of a negotiation that "may or may not lead to an offer for the shares of the company."
16 Due to conflicting past evidence on the appropriate measures, Smart and Waldfogel (1994) use two methodologies to calculate expected performance improvements before the announcement of the LBO. In the first, they make forecasts of the sales/income ratio by estimating a dynamic performance regression on the firm's annual performance history up to the year before the transaction. The second measure is the last expected income/sales improvement as predicted by analyst forecasts in Value Line before the LBO announcement.
17 Most influential was the re-enactment of the Delaware Merger Moratorium Law, prohibiting hostile suitors from merging their acquisition vehicle with the target company for at least three years after acquiring a majority stake lower than 85%.
18 For example, the regulator restricted investment by insurance companies and financial institutions in commercial bonds and junk bonds to fund LBOs (Holmstrom & Kaplan, 2001).
19 Part of the controversy came from the £629 million Magnet Plc hostile MBO deal. Institutional investors took the lead in the public protest against the MBO attempt of the Magnet management team, which was accused of depriving shareholders of the chance to invest over the long term.
20 The Panel on Takeovers and Mergers ("the Takeover Panel") is the regulatory body which administers the City Code on Takeovers and Mergers.
21 A squeeze-out is described in section 429 of the UK Companies Act as follows: when 90% of the shares to which the takeover relates are acquired, the rest can be compulsory acquired.

References

Acharya, V. V., Hahn, M., & Kehoe, C. 2009. Corporate governance and value creation: Evidence from private equity. *Review of Financial Studies*, 26: 368–402.
Admati, A. R., Pleiderer, P., & Zechner, J. 1994. Large shareholder activism, risk sharing, and financial market equilibrium. *Journal of Political Economy*, 102: 1097–1130.
Aghion, P., & Bolton, P. 1992. An incomplete contract approach to financial contracting. *Review of Economic Studies*, 59: 473–494.
Agrawal, A., & Tambe, P. 2016. Private equity and workers' career paths: The role of technological change. *Review of Financial Studies*, 9: 2455–2489.
Amess, K., Stiebale, J., & Wright, M. 2016. The impact of private equity on firms' patenting activity. *European Economic Review*, 86: 147–160.
Amess, K., & Wright, M. 2007. The wage and employment effects of leveraged buyouts in the UK. *International Journal of the Economics of Business*, 14: 179–195.
Amess, K., & Wright, M. 2012. Leveraged buyouts, private equity, and jobs. *Small Business Economics*, 38: 419–430.
Amihud, Y. 1989. *Leveraged management buy-outs*. New York: Dow-Jones Irwin.
Andrade, G., & Kaplan, S. N. 1998. How costly is financial (not economic) distress? Evidence from highly leveraged transactions that became distressed. *The Journal of Finance*, 53: 1443–1492.
Andrade, G., Mitchell, M., & Stafford, E. 2001. New evidence and perspectives on mergers. *Journal of Economic Perspectives*, 15: 103–120.

Andres, C., Betzer, A., & Hoffman, M. 2003. *Going private via LBO – Shareholder gains in the European market*. University of Bonn Working Paper.

Andres, C., Betzer, A., & Weir, C. 2007. Shareholder wealth gains through better corporate governance: The case of European LBO-transactions. *Financial Markets and Portfolio Management*, 21: 403–424.

Ashurst, Morris & Crisp. 2002. *Public-to-private takeovers in Germany*. Ashurst, Morris, Crisp Investment Banking Briefing.

Asquith, P., & Wizmann, T. A. 1990. Event risk, covenants and bondholder returns in leveraged buyouts. *Journal of Financial Economics*, 27: 195–213.

Auster, E. R., & Sirower, M. L. 2002. The dynamics of merger and acquisition waves. *Journal of Applied Behavioral Science*, 38: 216–244.

Bae, S. C., & Jo, H. 2002. Consolidating corporate control: Divisional versus whole-company leveraged buyouts. *Journal of Financial Research*, 25: 247–262.

Baker, G., & Wruck, K. 1989. Organizational changes and value creation in leveraged buyouts: The case of the O.M. Scott & Sons company. *Journal of Financial Economics*, 25: 163–190.

Benoit, B. 1999. Companies and Finance: UK: Professional expenses prove a deterrent to maintaining stock market exposure: But costs of public-to-private deals can also be considerable. Bertrand Benoit reports. *The Financial Times*, August 31, p. 18.

Bergström, C., Grubb, M., & Jonsson, S. 2007. The operating impact of buyouts in Sweden: A study of value creation. *Journal of Private Equity*, 11: 22–39.

Berle, A. A. Jr., & Means, G. C. 1932. *The modern corporation and private property*. New York: Macmillan.

Bharath, S. T., & Dittmar, A. K. 2010. Do firms use private equity to opt out of public markets? *Review of Financial Studies*, 23: 1771–1818.

Billett, M. T., Jiang, Z., & Lie, E. 2008. *The role of bondholder wealth expropriation in LBO transactions*. Available at SSRN: https://ssrn.com/abstract=1107448.

Block, S. B. 2004. The latest movement to going private: An empirical study. *Journal of Applied Finance*, 14: 36–44.

Boucly, Q., Sraer, D., & Thesmar, D. 2011. Growth LBOs. *Journal of Financial Economics*, 102: 432–453.

Briston, R. J., Saadouni, B., Mallin, C. A., & Coutts, J. A. 1992. Management buyout announcements and securities returns: A UK study 1984–1989. *Journal of Business Finance and Accounting*, 19: 641–655.

Brown, D. T., Fee, C. E., & Thomas, S. E. 2009. Financial leverage and bargaining power with suppliers: Evidence from leveraged buyouts. *Journal of Corporate Finance*, 15: 196–211.

Bruining, H., & Wright, M. 2002. Entrepreneurial orientation in management buy-outs and the contribution of venture capital. *Venture Capital: An International Journal of Entrepreneurial Finance*, 4: 147–168.

Bruner, R. F., & Eades, K. M. 1992. The crash of the Revco leveraged buyout: The hypothesis of inadequate capital. *Financial Management*, 21: 35–49.

Bruton, G., Keels, J., & Scifres, E. 2002. Corporate restructuring and performance: An agency perspective on the complete buyout cycle. *Journal of Business Research*, 55: 709–724.

Calcagno, R., & Falconieri, S. 2014. Competition and dynamics in takeover contests. *Journal of Corporate Finance*, 26: 36–56.

Calcagno, R., & Renneboog, L. 2007. The incentive to give incentives: On the relative seniority of debt claims and managerial compensation. *Journal of Banking and Finance*, 31: 1795–1815.

Cao, J., & Lerner, J. 2009. The performance of reverse leveraged buyouts. *Journal of Financial Economics*, 91: 139–157.

Carney, W. J. 2005. The costs of being public after Sarbanes-Oxley: The irony of going private. Emory Law and Economics Research Paper.

CMBOR. 2002. Public-to-private buy-outs in the UK and Continental Europe. Section 3 in *UK Quarterly Review Summer 2002*. University of Nottingham: Centre For Management Buy-out Research.

Cohn, J. B., Mills, L. F., & Towery, E. M. 2014. The evolution of capital structure and operating performance after leveraged buyouts: Evidence from US corporate tax returns. *Journal of Financial Economics*, 111: 469–494.

Cook, D. O., Easterwood, J. C., & Martin, J. D. 1992. Bondholder wealth effects of management buyouts. *Financial Management*, 21: 102–113.

Copeland, T., Koller, T., & Murrin, J. 2000. *Valuation: Measuring and managing the value of companies*. New York: John Wiley and Sons, Inc.
Cotter, J., & Peck, S. 2001. The structure of debt and active equity investors: The case of the buyout specialist. *Journal of Financial Economics*, 59: 101–147.
Coustan, H., Leinicke, L. M., Rexford, W. M., & Ostrosky, J. A. 2004. Sarbanes-Oxley: What it means to the market place. *Journal of Accountancy*, 197: 43–47.
Cumming, D., & Zambelli, S. 2010. Illegal buyouts. *Journal of Banking and Finance*, 34: 441–456.
Cumming, D., & Zambelli, S. 2013. Private equity performance under extreme regulation. *Journal of Banking and Finance*, 37: 1508–1523.
Davis, S., & Day, R. 1998. Public-to-private deals: Reducing the risk and removing the uncertainty. *UK Venture Capital Journal*, 5: 1–6.
Davis, S. J., Haltiwanger, J. C., Handley, K., Jarmin, R. S., Lerner, J., & Miranda, J. 2014. Private equity, jobs, and productivity. *American Economic Review*, 104: 3956–3990.
DeAngelo, H., DeAngelo, L., & Rice, E. M. 1984. Going private: Minority freezeouts and stockholder wealth. *Journal of Law and Economics*, 27: 367–401.
DeAngelo, L. 1986. Accounting numbers as market valuation substitutes: A study of management buyouts of public stockholders. *The Accounting Review*, 61: 400–420.
Degeorge, F., & Zeckhauser, R. 1993. The reverse LBO decision and firm performance: Theory and evidence. *The Journal of Finance*, 48: 1323–1348.
Demiroglu, C., & James, C. M. 2010. The role of private equity group reputation in LBO financing. *Journal of Financial Economics*, 96: 306–330.
Denis, D. J. 1994. Organizational form and the consequences of highly leveraged transactions: Kroger's recapitalization and Safeway's LBO. *Journal of Financial Economics*, 36: 193–224.
Dicker, A. 1990. *Corporate restructuring*. London: Euromoney Publications.
Dyck, A., & Zingales, L. 2004., The private benefits of control: An international comparison. *Journal of Finance*, 59: 537–600.
Easterbrook, F. H., & Fischel, D. R. 1983. Voting in corporate law. *Journal of Law and Economics*, 26: 395–428.
Easterwood, J. C. 1998. Divestments and financial distress in leveraged buyouts. *Journal of Banking and Finance*, 22: 129–159.
Easterwood, J. C., Singer, R., Seth, A., & Lang, D. 1994. Controlling the conflict of interest in management buyouts. Review of Economics and Statistics, 76: 512–522.
Edgerton, J. 2012. Agency problems in public firms: Evidence from corporate jets in leveraged buyouts. *Journal of Finance*, 67: 2187–2213.
Engel, E., Hayes, R. M., & Wang, X. 2007. The Sarbanes-Oxley act and firms' going private decisions. *Journal of Accounting and Economics*, 44: 116–145.
Fenn, G. W., Liang, N., & Prowse, S. 1995. *The economics of the private equity market*. Federal Reserve System Staff Paper.
Ferrarini, G., & Miller, G. P. 2009. A simple theory of takeover regulation in the United States and Europe. *Cornell International Law Journal*, 42: 301–334.
Fidrmuc, J. P., Palandri, A., Roosenboom, P., & Van Dijk, D. 2013. When do managers seek private equity backing in public-to-private transactions? *Review of Finance*, 17: 1099–1139.
Fischer, P. E., & Louis, H. 2008. Financial reporting and conflicting managerial incentives: The case of management buyouts. *Management Science*, 54: 1700–1714.
Fox, I., & Marcus, A. 1992. The causes and consequences of leveraged management buyouts. *Academy of Management Review*, 17: 62–85.
Frankfurter, G. M., & Gunay, E. 1992. Management buy-outs: The sources and sharing of wealth between insiders and outside shareholders. *Quarterly Review of Economics and Finance*, 32: 82–95.
Franks, J., & Mayer, C. 1996. Hostile takeovers in the UK and the correction of managerial failure. *Journal of Financial Economics*, 40: 163–181.
Franks, J., Mayer, C., & Renneboog, L. 2001. Who disciplines management of poorly performing companies? *Journal of Financial Intermediation*, 10: 209–248.
Fried and Frank. 2003. *French usury law does not apply to corporate bonds*. Fried, Frank, Harris, Shriver, and Jacobson Client Memorandum.
Gilhully, E. A. 1999. Private equity investors in the new European marketplace. In *US-German Economic Yearbook 1999*. Philadelphia, PA: German-American Chamber of Commerce, Inc.

Goergen, M., Martynova, M., & Renneboog, L. 2005. Corporate governance convergence: Evidence from takeover regulation reforms in Europe. *Oxford Review of Economic Policy*, 21: 243–269.

Goergen, M., & Renneboog, L. 2004. Shareholder wealth effects of European domestic and cross-border takeover bids. *European Financial Management Journal*, 10: 9–45.

Goh, J., Gombola, M., Liu, F. Y., & Chou, D. W. 2002. Going-private restructuring and earnings expectations: A test of the release of favorable information for target firms and industry rivals. Working paper, Singapore Management University.

Golbe, D. L., & White, L. J. 1993. Catch a wave: The time series behaviour of mergers. *Review of Economics and Statistics*, 75: 493–497.

Green, S. 1992. The impact of ownership and capital structure on managerial motivation and strategy in management buy-outs: A cultural analysis. *Journal of Management Studies*, 29: 523–535.

Grossman, S. J., & Hart, O. D. 1988. One-share one-vote and the market for corporate control. *Journal of Financial Economics*, 20: 175–202.

Guo, S., Hotchkiss, E. S., & Song, W. 2011. Do buyouts (still) create value? *Journal of Finance*, 66: 479–517.

Halpern, P., Kieschnick, R., & Rotenberg, W. 1999. On the heterogeneity of leveraged going private transactions. *Review of Financial Studies*, 12: 281–309.

Harlow, W. V., & Howe, J. S. 1993. Leveraged buyouts and insider nontrading. *Financial Management*, 22: 109–118.

Harris, R., Siegel, D., & Wright, M. 2005. Assessing the impact of management buyouts on economic efficiency: Plant-level evidence from the United Kingdom. *Review of Economics and Statistics*, 87: 148–153.

Hite, G. L., & Vetsuypens, M. R. 1989. Management buyouts of divisions and shareholder wealth. *Journal of Finance*, 44: 953–970.

Holmstrom, B., & Kaplan, S. N. 2001. Corporate governance and merger activity in the U.S.: Making sense of the '80s and '90s. *Journal of Economic Perspectives*, 15: 121–144.

Holmstrom, B., & Kaplan, S. N. 2003. The state of US corporate governance: What's right and what's wrong. *Journal of Applied Corporate Finance*, 15: 8–20.

Holthausen, R. W., & Larcker, D. F. 1996. The financial performance of reverse leveraged buyouts. *Journal of Financial Economics*, 42: 293–332.

Ippolito, R. A., & James, W. H. 1992. LBOs, reversions, and implicit contracts. *Journal of Finance*, 47: 139–167.

Jarrell, G. A. 1992. The 1980s takeover boom and government regulation. *Regulation*, 15: 44–53.

Jarrell, G. A., & Poulsen, A. 1987. Shark repellents and stock prices: The effects of antitakeover amendments since 1980. *Journal of Financial Economics*, 19: 127–168.

Jensen, M. C. 1986. Agency costs of free cash flow, corporate finance and takeovers. *American Economic Review*, 76: 323–329.

Jensen, M. C. 1989. The eclipse of the public corporation. *Harvard Business Review*, 67: 61–74.

Jensen, M. C. 1991. Corporate control and the politics of finance. *Journal of Applied Corporate Finance*, 4: 13–33.

Jensen, M. C., & Meckling, W. 1976. Theory of the firm: Managerial behavior, agency costs and ownership structure. *Journal of Financial Economics*, 3: 305–360.

Jones, C. S. 1992. The attitudes of owner-managers towards accounting control systems following management buyout. *Accounting, Organizations and Society*, 17: 151–168.

Kaestner, R., & Liu, F. Y. 1996. Going private restructuring: The role of insider trading. *Journal of Business Finance and Accounting*, 23: 779–806.

Kamar, E., Karaca-Mandic, P., & Talley, E. 2009. Going private decisions and the Sarbanes-Oxley act of 2002: A cross-country analysis. *Journal of Law, Economics, and Organization*, 25: 107–133.

Kaplan, S. N. 1989a. The effects of management buyouts on operating performance and value. *Journal of Financial Economics*, 24: 217–254.

Kaplan, S. N. 1989b. Management buyouts: Evidence on taxes as a source of value. *Journal of Finance*, 44: 611–632.

Kaplan, S. N. 1991. The staying power of leveraged buyouts. *Journal of Financial Economics*, 29: 287–313.

Kaplan, S. N. 1993. The staying power of leveraged buyouts. *Journal of Applied Corporate Finance*, 6: 15–24.

Kaplan, S. N. 1997. The evolution of corporate governance: We are all Henry Kravis now.*Journal of Private Equity* Fall: 7–14.

Kaplan, S. N., & Stein, J. 1993. The evolution of buy-out pricing and financial structure in the 1980s. *Quarterly Journal of Economics*, 108: 313–359.

Kaplan, S. N., & Stromberg, P. 2009. Leveraged buyouts and private equity. Journal of Economic Perspectives, 23: 121–146.

Kelley, D., Scott, J., & Echo, G. 1993, *Reason Magazine*, 24, No. 9, February.

Kieschnick, R. L. 1987. Management buyouts of public corporations: An empirical study. Doctoral dissertation, University of Texas, Austin.

Kieschnick, R. L. 1989. Management buyouts of public corporations: An analysis of prior characteristics. In Y. Amihud (Ed.), *Leveraged management buy-outs*. New York: Dow-Jones Irwin.

Kieschnick, R. L. 1998. Free cash flow and stockholder gains in going private transactions revisited. *Journal of Business Finance and Accounting*, 25: 187–202.

Kosedag, A., & Lane, W. 2002. Is it free cash flow, tax savings or neither? An empirical confirmation of two leading going-private explanations. *Journal of Business Finance and Accounting*, 29: 257–274.

Lee, C. I., Rosenstein, S., Rangan, N., & Davidson, W. N. III 1992. Board composition and shareholder wealth: The case of management buyouts. *Financial Management*, 21: 58–72.

Lee, D. S. 1992. Management buyout proposals and inside information. *Journal of Finance*, 47: 1061–1079.

Lehn, K., Netter, J., & Poulsen, A. 1990. Consolidating corporate control: Dual class recapitalizations versus leveraged buyouts. *Journal of Financial Economics*, 27: 557–580.

Lehn, K., & Poulsen, A. 1989. Free cash flow and stockholder gains in going private transactions. *Journal of Finance*, 44: 771–788.

Lerner, J., Sorensen, M., & Strömberg, P. 2011. Private equity and long-run investment: The case of innovation. *Journal of Finance*, 66: 445–477.

Lichtenberg, F., & Siegel, D. 1990. The effects of leveraged buyouts on productivity and related aspects on firm behavior. *Journal of Financial Economics*, 27: 557–580.

Liebeskind, J., Wiersema, M., & Hansen, G. 1992. LBOs, corporate restructuring, and the incentive-intensity hypothesis. *Financial Management*, 21: 73–88.

Linck, J. S., Netter, J., & Shu, T. 2013. Can managers use discretionary accruals to ease financial constraints? Evidence from discretionary accruals prior to investment? *The Accounting Review*, 88: 2117–2143.

Liu, C., & Yermack, D. 2012. Where are the shareholders' mansions? CEOs' home purchases, stock sales, and subsequent company performance. In S. Boubaker, B. Nguyen, & D. Nguyen (Eds.), *Corporate governance: Recent developments and new trends*. Berlin, Heidelberg: Springer, 3–28.

Long, W. F., & Ravenscraft, D. J. 1993. *The financial performance of whole company LBOs*. US Bureau of Census Discussion Paper CES 93–16.

Lovells 2003. European private equity. *Lovells Newsletter*, March 2003.

Lowenstein, L. 1985. Management buyouts. *Columbia Law Review*, 85: 730–784.

Maksimovic, V., Phillips, G., & Yang, L. 2013. Private and public merger waves. *Journal of Finance*, 68: 2177–2217.

Mao, Y., & Renneboog, L. 2015. Do managers manipulate earnings prior to management buyouts? *Journal of Corporate Finance*, 35: 43–61.

Marais, L., Schipper, K., & Smith, A. 1989. Wealth effects of going private for senior securities. *Journal of Financial Economics*, 23: 155–191.

Martynova, M., & Renneboog, L. 2008a. A century of corporate takeovers: What have we learned and where do we stand? *Journal of Corporate Finance*, 15: 290–315.

Martynova, M., & Renneboog, L. 2008b. Spillover of corporate governance standards in cross-border mergers and acquisitions. *Journal of Corporate Finance*, 14: 200–223.

Martynova, M., & Renneboog, L. 2009. What determines the financing decision in corporate takeovers: Cost of capital, agency problems, or the means of payment? *Journal of Corporate Finance*, 15: 290–315.

Martynova, M., & Renneboog, L. 2011a. Evidence on the international evolution and convergence of corporate governance regulations. *Journal of Corporate Finance*, 17: 1531–1557.

Martynova, M., & Renneboog, L. 2011b. The performance of the European market for corporate control: Evidence from the 5th takeover wave. *European Financial Management*, 17: 208–260.

Martynova, M., & Renneboog, L. 2013. An international corporate governance index. In M. Wright, D. Siegel, K. Keasey, & I. Filatotchev (Eds.), *Handbook of Corporate Governance*. Oxford, UK: Oxford University Press, 97–131.

Masulis, R. 1980. The effects of capital structure on changes on security prices: A study of exchange offers. *Journal of Financial Economics*, 8: 139–178.

Maug, E. 1998. Large shareholders as monitors: Is there a trade-off between liquidity and control? *Journal of Finance*, 53: 65–98.

Maupin, R. J., Bidwell, C. M., & Ortegren, A. K. 1984. An empirical investigation of the characteristics of publicly quoted corporations that change to closely held ownership through management buyouts. *Journal of Business Finance and Accounting*, 11: 435–450.

McCahery, J., & Renneboog, L. 2004. The economics of takeover regulation. In G. Ferrarini, K. Hopt, J. Winter & E. Wymeersch (Eds.), *Reforming company and takeover law in Europe*. Oxford, UK: Oxford University Press.

McConnell, J. J., & Servaes, H. 1990. Additional evidence on equity ownership and corporate value. *Journal of Financial Economics*, 27: 595–612.

Mehran, H., & Peristiani, S. 2010. Financial visibility and the decision to go private. *Review of Financial Studies*, 23: 519–547.

Michel, A., & Shaked, I. 1986. *Takeover madness: Corporate America fights back*. New York: John Wiley and Sons.

Miller, G. P. 2000. Takeovers: English and American. *European Financial Management*, 6: 533–541.

Mitchell, M., & Mulherin, H. 1996. The impact of industry shocks on takeover and restructuring activity. *Journal of Financial Economics*, 41: 193–229.

Morck, R., Shleifer, A., & Vishny, R. W. 1988. Management ownership and market valuation: An empirical analysis. *Journal of Financial Economics*, 20: 293–315.

Murphy, K. J. 1985. Corporate performance and managerial remuneration: An empirical analysis. *Journal of Accounting and Economics*, 7: 11–42.

Muscarella, C. J., & Vetsuypens, M. R. 1990. Efficiency and organizational structure: A study of reverse LBOs. *Journal of Finance*, 45: 1389–1413.

Officer, M. S., Ozbas, O., & Sensoy, B. A. 2010. Club deals in leveraged buyouts. *Journal of Financial Economics*, 98: 214–240.

Opler T. C. 1992. Operating performance in leveraged buyouts: Evidence from 1985–1989. *Financial Management*, 21: 27–34.

Opler, T. C., & Titman, S. 1993. The determinants of leveraged buyout activity, free cash flow versus financial distress costs. *Journal of Finance*, 48: 1985–1999.

Oxman, J., & Yildirim, Y. 2007. *Evidence of competition in the leveraged buyout market*. SSRN working paper. Available at SSRN: http://ssrn.com/abstract=972060.

Palepu, K. G. 1990. Consequences of leveraged buyouts. *Journal of Financial Economics*, 27: 247–262.

Perino, M. A. 2003. American corporate reform abroad: Sarbanes-Oxley and the foreign private issuer. *European Business Organization Law Review*, 4: 213–244.

Perry, S., & Williams, T. 1994. Earnings management preceding management buyout offers. *Journal of Accounting and Economics*, 18: 157–179.

Pound, J. 1987. The effects of antitakeover amendments on takeover activity: Some direct evidence. *Journal of Law and Economics*, 30: 353–367.

Rappaport, A. 1990. The staying power of the public corporation. *Harvard Business Review*, 68: 96–104.

Renneboog, L., Simons, T., & Wright, M. 2007. Why do firms go private in the UK? *Journal of Corporate Finance*, 13: 591–628.

Renneboog, L., & Szilagyi, P. 2008. Corporate restructuring and bondholder wealth. *European Financial Management*, 14: 792–819.

Renneboog, L., Szilagyi, P., & Vansteenkiste, C. 2017. Creditor rights, claims enforcement, and bond performance in mergers and acquisitions. *Journal of International Business Studies*, 48: 174–194.

Ribstein, L. E. 2003. International implications of Sarbanes-Oxley: Raising the rent on US law. *Journal of Corporate Law Studies*, 3: 299–327.

Ritter, J. 1991. The long-run underperformance of initial public offerings. *Journal of Finance*, 46: 3–27.

Robbie, K., & Wright, M. 1995. Managerial and ownership succession and corporate restructuring: The case of management buy-ins. *Journal of Management Studies*, 32: 527–549.

Ross, S. A. 1977. The determination of capital structure: The incentive signaling approach. *Bell Journal of Economics*, 8: 249–259.
Sappington, D. 1991. Incentives in principal agent relationships. *Journal of Economic Perspectives*, 3: 45–66.
Schadler, F. P., & Karns, J. E. 1990. The unethical exploitation of shareholders in management buyout transactions. *Journal of Business Ethics*, 9: 595–602.
Scott, J. 2000. *Drexel Burnham Lambert: A ten-year retrospective.* Working paper presented at the Austrian Scholar's Conference March 23–24.
Shivdasani, A., & Wang, Y. 2011. Did structured credit fuel the LBO boom? *Journal of Finance*, 66: 1291–1328.
Shleifer, A., & Summers, L. H. 1988. Breach of trust in hostile takeovers. In A. J. Auerbach (Ed.), *Corporate takeovers: Causes and consequences*. Chicago, IL: University of Chicago Press.
Shleifer, A., & Vishny, R. W. 1990. The takeover wave of the 1980s. *Science*, 249: 745–749.
Shleifer, A., & Vishny, R. W. 1991. The takeover wave of the 1980s. *Journal of Applied Corporate Finance*, 4: 49–56.
Singh, H. 1990. Management buyouts: Distinguishing characteristics and operating changes prior to public offering. *Strategic Management Journal*, 11: 111–129.
Slovin, M. B., Sushka, M. E., & Bendeck, Y. M. 1991. The intra-industry effects of going-private proposals. *Journal of Finance*, 46: 1537–1550.
Smart, S. B., & Waldfogel, J. 1994. Measuring the effect of restructuring on corporate performance: The case of management buyouts. *Review of Economics and Statistics*, 76: 503–511.
Smit, H. T. J., & Van Den Berg, W. A. 2006. *Private equity waves*. Tinbergen Institute Discussion Paper No. 06–053/2. Available at SSRN: https://ssrn.com/abstract=909169.
Smith, A. 1776. *The wealth of nations*. Glasgow, UK (ed. 1976).
Smith, A. 1990. Corporate ownership structure and performance: The case of management buyouts. *Journal of Financial Economics*, 27: 704–739.
Strömberg, P. 2007. *The new demography of private equity*. SIFR working paper.
Toms, S., & Wright, M. 2004. Divergence and convergence within Anglo-American corporate governance systems: Evidence from the US and UK 1950–2000. *Business History*, 47: 267–295.
Torabzadeh, K. M., & Bertin, W. J. 1987. Leveraged buyouts and shareholder wealth. *Journal of Financial Research*, 10: 313–319.
Travlos, N. G., & Cornett, M. M. 1993. Going private buyouts and determinants of shareholders' returns. *Journal of Accounting, Auditing and Finance*, 8: 1–25.
Ulissi, R. 2000. Company law reform in Italy: An overview of current initiatives. In *Company law review in OECD countries: A comparative outlook of current trends*. OECD publication.
Van de Gucht, L. M., & Moore, W. T. 1998. Predicting the duration and reversal probability of leveraged buyouts. *Journal of Empirical Finance*, 5: 299–315.
Warga, A., & Welch, I. 1993. Bondholder losses in leveraged buyouts. *The Review of Financial Studies*, 6: 959–982.
Weinstein, M. 1983. Bond systematic risk and the option pricing model. *Journal of Finance*, 38: 1415–1430.
Weir, C., Laing, D., & Wright, M. 2005a. Incentive effects, monitoring mechanisms and the threat from the market for corporate control: An analysis of the factors affecting public to private transactions in the UK. *Journal of Business Finance and Accounting*, 32: 909–943.
Weir, C., Laing, D., & Wright, M. 2005b. Undervaluation, private information, agency costs and the decision to go private. *Applied Financial Economics*, 15: 947–961.
Weir, C., Laing, D., Wright, M., & Burrows, A. 2004. Financial distress costs, incentive realignment, private equity and the decision to go private: Public to private activity in the UK. Working Paper, University of Nottingham.
Wells, B. P., Cox, L. A., & Gaver, K. M. 1995. Free cash flows in the life insurance industry. *Journal of Risk and Insurance*, 62: 50–66.
Weston, J. F., Chung, K. S., & Siu, J. A. 1998. *Takeovers, restructuring and corporate governance, second edition*. New York: Prentice-Hall.
Wilson, N., & Wright, M. 2013. Private equity, buy-outs, and insolvency risk. *Journal of Business, Finance, & Accounting*, 40: 949–990.
Wilson, N., Wright, M., Siegel, D. S., & Scholes, L. 2012. Private equity portfolio company performance during the global recession. *Journal of Corporate Finance*, 18: 193–205.

Wright, M., Hoskissen, R. E., Busenitz, L. W., & Dial, J. 2000. Entrepreneurial growth through privatization: The upside of management buyouts. *The Academy of Management Journal*, 25: 591–601.

Wright, M., Renneboog, L., Scholes, L., & Simons, T. 2006. Leveraged buyouts in the UK and Continental Europe. *Journal of Applied Corporate Finance*, 18: 38–55.

Wright, M., Robbie, K., Thompson, S., & Starkey, K. 1994. Longevity and the life-cycle of management buy-outs. *Strategic Management Journal*, 15: 215–227.

Wright, M., Thompson, S., Chiplin, B., & Robbie, K. 1991. *Buy-ins and buy-outs: New strategies in corporate management*. London: Graham & Trotman Ltd.

Wright, M., Thompson, S., Robbie, K., & Wong P. 1995. Management buy-outs in the short and long term. *Journal of Business Finance and Accounting*, 22: 461–483.

Wright, M., Wilson, N., Robbie, K., & Ennew, C. 1996. An analysis of management buy-out failure. *Managerial and Decision Economics*, 17: 57–70.

Wruck, K. H. 1991. What really went wrong at Revco? *Journal of Applied Corporate Finance*, 4: 79–92.

Wu, Y. U. 1997. Management buyouts and earnings management. *Journal of Accounting and Finance*, 12: 373–389.

Yago, G. 1990. *Junk bonds: How high-yield securities restructured corporate America*. Oxford, UK: Oxford University Press.

Yin, R. K. 1989. *Case study research: Design and methods*. London: Sage.

Zahra, S. A. 1995. Corporate entrepreneurship and financial performance: The case of management leveraged buyouts. *Journal of Business Venturing*, 10: 225–247.

8

"MY CHILDREN DO NOT WANT THE FIRM"

Private equity as a succession option in family businesses
A review and future directions

Oliver Ahlers, Alexandra Michel, and Andreas Hack

Introduction

Family firms are of particular significance for the global economy (Klein, 2000; Anderson & Reeb, 2003; Astrachan & Shanker, 2003; Morck & Yeung, 2003). Prior research acknowledges that family firms are considerably different from non-family firms and the source of distinction clearly is the "family" (Sharma, 2004). Previous literature has defined family firms as those firms with at least 50% of ownership concentrated among family owners, and which have member(s) of the family active in the business, whether it be in management or governance roles (e.g., Eddleston & Kellermanns, 2007; Kellermanns et al., 2012). Although family firms are a heterogeneous group with varying degrees of family influence, differences in size, industry, and geography (Tsang, 2002; Chrisman et al., 2012; Chua et al., 2012), they all face the same challenge sooner or later, i.e to ensure succession and the survival of the firm as a family-owned entity (Cabrera-Suárez et al., 2001).

Succession is a highly difficult issue for family businesses. When family owners have to secure family succession, it is a decision overshadowed by emotions (Miller et al., 2003; Sharma et al., 2003). This is not surprising as a key driver for many family firms is to secure trans-generational control over the business (Zellweger et al., 2012). Emotional attachment is what most family entrepreneurs feel when it comes to the question of how their "lifetime achievement" will continue once they leave the business (Zellweger & Astrachan, 2008; Memili et al., 2013). There are a number of reasons why family succession might fail. Most commonly, the incumbent family CEO is unwilling to let go or there is simply no willing and/or qualified family successor available (Kets Vries de, 1993; Sharma et al., 2001; Sharma & Irving, 2005).

What opportunities do family firms have to ensure succession if no family successor is available? It is possible to take a succession route outside of the family. "External" family succession is when a non-family member takes over a business. Prior family business research has been primarily concerned with how to secure intra-family succession and has neglected the external succession route (Howorth et al., 2004; Niedermeyer et al., 2010). There are multiple options to ensure ownership transition in the external succession route, such as trade sale, initial public offering (IPO), and management buyout (MBO) (Goossens et al., 2008; Scholes et al., 2008). Trade sale involves the sale to another company, which might even be a competitor (Scholes et al., 2007). Inevitably, in a trade sale the identity and culture of the former family firm can be put at risk (Scholes et al., 2007). An IPO, the floating of shares on the stock market, is a complex and costly process, and thus, only an option for large family firms (Scholes et al., 2008). MBOs which usually involve private equity (PE) firms are another option. In general, a buyout is when PE firms together with the incumbent and/or external management take over the business (Meuleman et al., 2009).

PE firms usually acquire the majority stakes in corporations and focus their investments on established companies which are usually characterized by stable cash flow streams. Investment in more developed companies ("later stage") rather than investments in companies that are just emerging or newly found ("early stage") is what distinguishes PE from venture capital (VC) as an investment class (Cumming & Johan, 2009). Businesses which are acquired by PE firms are usually referred to as "portfolio firms" or "PE-backed firms."

Buyouts by PE firms can have some advantages over IPOs and trade sales. First, in a buyout the former family business could ensure independent ownership and maintain (at least part of) the family culture, as PE firms usually treat their portfolio firms on a standalone basis, i.e., they remain independently run companies (Jensen, 1989; Scholes et al., 2007). Second, members of the family could stay associated with the business if they prefer to do so (Scholes et al., 2008; Niedermeyer et al., 2010). Third, the majority of the management team could remain in place if the MBO is structured accordingly (Scholes et al., 2007).

Today, family firms constitute an important deal source for PE firms (Scholes et al., 2009). However, according to existing research, there is considerable potential for conflict because family firms and PE firms may follow very different business "philosophies" (Poech et al., 2005; Achleitner et al., 2010; Dawson, 2011). Family firms are known to have a long-term perspective on the business and often pursue non-financial goals (Berrone et al., 2012) whereas PE firms buy businesses in order to resell them at a profit (Braun et al., 2011; Tappeiner et al., 2012). Furthermore, PE firms have been widely criticized for unsustainable performance effects in portfolio firms (Wright et al., 2009).

PE firms increasingly face competition from peers and have to specify their value proposition as well as build up capabilities to succeed in a difficult market environment (Cressy et al., 2007; Wilson et al., 2012). Specifically, PE firms need to source deals and have to successfully increase the economic value of their portfolio companies (Kaplan & Strömberg, 2009). However, PE firms are not always able to successfully create value in former family firms (Wulf et al., 2010) and the general perception PE firms have of family firms tends to be negative (Granata & Chirico, 2010; Dawson, 2011). In order for PE firms to successfully buy a family business, they may need to build up their knowledge on how to target and deal with family firms over the life cycle of an MBO (Tappeiner et al., 2012).

In the remainder of this chapter, first, we aim to provide an overview of the current literature on PE and family firms. Thereby, we structure our analysis of the prior literature along six distinct categories. Second, we discuss gaps in the existing literature and future research opportunities focusing on methods and theories used in studies on PE in family firms, gaps within the current categories, as well as possible new categories.

Method

A clear methodology is required to conduct a literature review. The "systematic" literature review procedure (Tranfield et al., 2003) was broken down into five steps which are (1) identification of search terms, (2) selection criteria, (3) selection of databases, (4) literature identification, and (5) analysis strategy. In the following, each step is briefly explained to maximize transparency, objectivity, replicability, and reliability of the literature review (Tranfield et al., 2003).

Literature review process

(1) Identification of search terms. This literature review deals with the research interface of (a) PE and (b) family firms. Comprehensive literature reviews for each singular research topic and multiple sub-issues are already available for family firms (Handler, 1994; Sharma et al., 1997; Casillas & Acedo, 2007; Debicki et al., 2009) and PE (Wright Robbie, 1998; Cumming et al., 2007; Wood & Wright, 2009). Thus, this review is specifically focused on the interface of PE and family firms which usually takes place when PE firms invest in family firm buyout targets. Research which goes beyond or has no particular implications for the research interface is of minor interest for this review. Accordingly, the identification of search terms began with keywords related to each side of the interface – (a) PE and (b) family firms. The initial list of keywords relate to the author's prior experience and is complemented by three interviews conducted with two experienced academics in the field of family business research and one practitioner from the PE industry. For part (a) PE, 13 keywords were identified.[1] For part (b) family firm, 4 keywords were identified.[2] Part (a) and part (b) keywords were combined and resulted in the creation of 52 search strings (13*4).

(2) Selection criteria. Selection criteria were used to specify the scope of the literature review, i.e., to make it manageable. First, the review only included peer-reviewed journals and peer-reviewed conference contributions to ensure academic quality of reviewed works. Working papers were only added if they seemed to provide the very latest research insights. Second, only research published after 1995 was utilized in order for the research to be current. Third, all industries and all countries in which research was undertaken relating to this subject were considered. Fourth, research on PE minority investments (i.e., deals involving no majority control of PE firms) was included. Inclusion of PE minority investments' research was needed because it could reveal insights about the relationship between family firms and PE and because minority investments can trigger buyouts at a later stage (Tappeiner et al., 2012). Fifth, only academic work was considered, be it conceptual or empirical, and hence, work dedicated primarily to practitioners was excluded. Sixth, works focusing on the technical specifics of deal-making only relevant for specialists such as legal, tax, or accounting issues were not included. Seventh, academic work focused on early stage investments (i.e., VC) was excluded. However, since the use of the terms "venture capital" and "private equity" is sometimes confusingly similar, papers dealing with VC when the definition was apparently referring to PE were also included. Eighth, academic work which did not devote a significant proportion of its content to the interface of PE and family firms, or did not have significant implications, was eliminated. For example, some papers on entrepreneurial exit that did not focus particularly on family firms or on the PE/buyout route were removed (DeTienne, 2010; DeTienne & Cardon, 2012). However, papers on "emotional value" were included because they could have significant implications for valuation

in buyout deals, a key part of deal-making (Granata & Chirico, 2010). It is acknowledged that some form of academic "judgment" is needed for this criterion. Ninth, papers dealing with small business firms, PE, and negotiations in combination were included because small business firms are in practice often privately held by a family, and we considered this an important area when dealing with PE buyouts. Finally, only papers written in either English or German were considered for the review.

(3) Selection of databases. For the literature search, two prominent databases for management research were used, these being "EBSCO host" (Business Source Premier) and "ScienceDirect." Coverage of research outlets within the aforementioned databases is subject to change and was complemented by "manual search" for which "Google Scholar" was employed. The search strings generated in step (1) were used in the respective databases. Furthermore, search in the databases was narrowed to include only the title, abstract, and author-provided keywords to make the number of search results manageable.

(4) Literature identification. For the database "EBSCO host," a total of 380 unique search results was identified, i.e., duplicative results due to similar search strings were eliminated. "ScienceDirect" yielded 159 unique search results. The 539 papers were reviewed and used to refine the selection criteria described in step (2). Using the selection criteria, 14 papers were selected from "EBSCO host," along with 4 papers from "ScienceDirect" (after removing duplicates with "EBSCO host"), and 10 were selected from "manual search." Thus, a total of 28 papers were identified and selected for the literature review.

(5) Reviewing strategy. To review all 28 papers in a consistent and systematic manner, each work was summarized and classified in terms of (a) "specific research topic," (b) "research question," (c) "research perspective," (d) "theories applied," (e) "characteristics of the sample," (f) "geographic scope," and (g) "key findings." Six (largely) distinct categories can be distilled from the findings of this prior research. The categories are (A) "market," (B) "information asymmetry," (C) "PE firms' perception and decision-making," (D) "family firms' perception and decision-making," (E) "bargaining power in buyout negotiations," and (F) "value creation in family firm buyouts." An overview of each work and composition of each category is given in Table 8.1. Table 8.1 describes the sample of selected studies in terms of publication date, research approach, key research, and theories applied. Findings of the literature review are discussed in the next section.

Discussion of key findings

In the remainder of this chapter, the key findings of the literature review are presented according to the six content categories into which the selected works have been grouped and which are illustrated in Figure 8.1. Subsequently, the key overall findings of each content category are summarized and evaluated.

(A) Market. There is very limited information available on the market size and quantitative characteristics of family firm buyouts. Only one of the studies comprises a detailed review of market information on family firm buyouts (Scholes et al., 2009). Unfortunately, information is only given until 2007 and no follow-up studies are available. Although buyout markets have undergone changes since 2007, including contraction during the financial market crises (Wilson et al., 2012), the information available does shed some light on specific characteristics of family firm buyouts.

Three aspects can be concluded from the market-related research study. First, family buyouts are usually smaller in size. It is important to recognize the size of family buyout deals because smaller firms (SMEs) might have distinct characteristics in deal-making due to size

Table 8.1 Literature review: overview of selected works

Authors/year of publication	*Topics*	*Research question*	*Perspective*	*Type of research*	*Theory*	*Sample*	*Country/ region*	*Key message*
(A) Market								
Scholes et al. (2009)	Market overview Strategic changes	What is the market size for family firm (FF) buyouts in Europe? How do former FFs change strategically in the post-buyout period?	Neutral; management for 2nd research question	Empirical	N/a	Database with ~30,000 buyout deals; sample with 104 managers in FFs which underwent a buyout	Europe	• ~29% of all buyouts in Europe between 1998 and 2007 are classified as FF buyouts; in 2007 this corresponds to 559 family deals and an average deal size of ~€45m • Strategic changes related to efficiency improvements and company growth are higher when a founder leads the family business pre-buyout and the TMT is run and controlled by family members
(B) Information asymmetry								
Howorth et al. (2004)	Level of information asymmetries Inhibitors of information asymmetries Deal satisfaction	How do information asymmetries impact the buyout process when FFs are concerned?	Buyer/ vendor	Empirical	Agency, trust, negotiation	8 case studies	UK	• Buyouts comprise a high degree of information asymmetries between vendor and buyer especially in MBI deals • Information asymmetries are lower if the buyout is part of the FF's long-term plan, mutual involvement of vendor/seller sides, and positive relationships (trust, friendship, understanding) • Deal satisfaction is higher with low information asymmetries, positive relationships, trust, mutual involvement, and co-operative negotiation behavior • Continuous involvement post-buyout of the former family owner mitigates information asymmetries
Scholes et al. (2007)	Information sharing Price agreement	How are FF's ownership and governance structures associated with balanced information sharing and a mutually agreed sale price?	Buyer	Empirical	Agency, game theory	114 respondents each representing a buyout	Europe	• Information-sharing: founder-run FFs and those with a priority for financial objectives are associated with equal information sharing; explanation: founders prefer to stay involved post-buyout and financial objectives suggest a de-prioritization of family goals • Mutually agreed price: FFs without a family successor, a priority for financial goals, and early involvement of investors increase a mutually agreed sale price

(*Continued*)

Table 8.1 (Continued)

Authors/year of publication	*Topics*	*Research question*	*Perspective*	*Type of research*	*Theory*	*Sample*	*Country/ region*	*Key message*
Scholes et al. (2008)	Information sharing Price agreement	How are FF's ownership and governance structures associated with balanced information sharing and a mutually agreed sale price?	Buyer	Empirical	Agency	114 respondents each representing a buyout	Europe	• Information-sharing: mutual involvement of FF owners and management in succession planning leads to lower information asymmetries • Agreed price: mutual involvement in succession planning and information-sharing increases the probability for a mutually agreed sale price • PE firm involvement negatively affects a mutually agreed sale price because it could more effectively challenge the vendor
Dehlen et al. (2014)	Succession paths	How do information asymmetries on potential external successors affect the probability for internal (family) succession vs. external succession via buyout?	Successors	Empirical	Information asymmetry theory, SEW	613 respondents	Germany, Switzerland	• Information asymmetries between owners and potential external entrants as successors lead to a higher likelihood for intra-family succession • External succession through MBI/MBO can become more likely if owners increase screening efforts (inverted U-shape relationship) and potential external successors signal suitability (e.g., experience, education) • Above-mentioned relationships are weakened with increasing firm age as a driver of emotional attachment
(C) PE perceptions and decision-making								
Upton and Petty (2000)	Investment criteria	What perceptions and criteria of investors regarding FFs are important for succession financing?	Buyer/ vendor	Empirical	N/a	53 PE investors, 85 family owners	US	• Financing of family succession is of high relevance for FFs, but owners prefer to use family capital, the firm's cash flow, or bank loans • PE firms are willing to participate in succession financing and are compensated for by debt, shares, and warrants or conversion rights • PE firm's evaluation of transition investments considers successor qualification, future business strategy, and family harmony
Silva (2006)	Perceptions Investment criteria	Is investing in FFs any different for PE managers?	Buyer	Empirical	N/a	7 interviews	Finland	• FFs are considered an important source of deal flow but in comparison to non-FFs, they are more complex and riskier • The same investment criteria are used for family and non-FFs, but deal structuring could differ because PE firms recognize families' need for control

Granata (2010)	Perceptions	How do PE managers perceive FFs?	Buyer	Empirical	N/a	154 respondents	Western Europe	• Differences between family and non-FFs are recognized, but do not necessarily trigger different evaluations • PE managers that perceive FFs differently associate higher investment risks and less professional management structures with FFs
Granata and Chirico (2010)	Evaluation	How do buyers value the family business?	Buyer	Empirical	RBV, stewardship	73 matched pairs of family and non-FFs	Western Europe	• FFs are acquired at a discount of ~16% • Investors do not recognize FFs' true value because FFs are perceived as rather unprofessional and inefficient
Dawson (2011)	Investment criteria	Which investment criteria are used by PE managers for FF targets?	Buyer	Empirical	Agency, RBV	41 respondents, 1312 observations in conjoint analysis	Italy	• Aspects specific to FFs are used to make investment decisions • Professionalized FFs (with family members who possess outside work experience and non-family managers) and future reduction of family involvement after deal closure are considered positive by PE managers
Ahlers et al. (2014)	Family firm valuation outcomes in PE buyouts	How does the family factor influence the family firm valuation?	Company	Conceptual	Real options perspective	3 case studies to illustrate conceptual findings	Europe	• The family factor can lead to all three outcomes: a valuation premium, a valuation parity, and a valuation discount • Family exit after the sale triggers a loss of family dependent attributes, which may subsequently reduce economic value
(D) Family perceptions and decision-making								
Poutziouris (2001)[3]	Capital preferences Family concerns	Do family and non-FFs have different rationales and perceptions for dealing with PE investors?	Buyer	Empirical	Pecking order theory	240 companies, 150 non-family and 90 FFs	UK	• FFs prefer to rely on internal capital to ensure growth and survival • Families' greatest concern is to share control and displacement of family managers
Poech et al. (2005)	Psychological barriers Intermediaries	What psychological barriers inhibit deal closure?	Buyer	Empirical	Sender-receiver model	21 interviews	Germany	• Different mindsets, stereotypes, and selective information processing between family owners and PE firms inhibit collaboration • Intermediaries are suggested as mitigating relationship difficulties

(*Continued*)

Table 8.1 (Continued)

Authors/year of publication	*Topics*	*Research question*	*Perspective*	*Type of research*	*Theory*	*Sample*	*Country/ region*	*Key message*
Astrachan and Jaskiewicz (2008)	Valuation	How do family sellers value their business?	Buyer	Conceptual	Utility theory	–	US	• Sellers value their business based on emotional returns and costs • Depending on whether emotional returns or costs weigh more, the family business is perceived as worth more or less compared to non-family firms
Zellweger and Astrachan (2008)	Evaluation	How do family sellers value their business?	Buyer	Conceptual	Endowment, possession attachment	–	Europe/ U.S.	• "Emotional value" is the residual between the financial value of the firm and the sellers' WTA driven by emotional returns and costs • Emotional value unrelated to the financial value of the firm inhibits transfer of ownership • Multiple factors such as the owner's demographics or marketability of the firm influence effects of emotional costs and returns on WTA
Niedermeyer et al. (2010)	Drivers of deal satisfaction	What drives family sellers' satisfaction when selling the family business?	Vendor	Conceptual (empirical)	Utility theory	1 exemplary case study	Germany	• Family sellers' initial sale satisfaction is affected by the level of perceived fairness during interactions, the level of control, flexibility to select buyers, goal alignment, and realization of adequate sale price • Family sellers' retrospective satisfaction is affected by ongoing association with the business, information exchange with new owners, and the pursuit of new entrepreneurial activities
Graebner and Eisenhardt (2004)	Selection criteria	What is important for owners in privately owned businesses when selling the business?	Vendor	Empirical	N/A	12 cases; 80 interviews	US	• Entrepreneurial sellers adopt an active and influential role in the sale process, which centers around a long-term and sustainable perspective for the business • Sellers' decision-making comprises multiple factors which go beyond price maximization and self-interest • Sellers feel more inclined to sell the business to investors who offer potential for synergies and to whom they feel connected (organizational rapport)

Salvato et al. (2010)	Role of family heritage	What psychologically affects family sellers when selling the business?	Vendor	Empirical	Strategic change, commitment	1 case study	Italy	• Selling the business or parts of it can be a source of strategic renewal for the FF • Family has to identify a suitable pathway that ensures preservation of institutional identity and anchoring in the founders' heritage when selling parts of the business
Zellweger et al. (2011)	Evaluation	How do family sellers value their business?	Vendor	Empirical	Socio emotional wealth (SEW), Prospect theory	83 respondents in Swiss sample and 148 in German sample	Germany, Switzer-land	• Family sellers require SEW which increases with the need for transgenerational control • Due to SEW, family sellers would sell the business for a lower price to family members
Tappeiner et al. (2012)	Selection criteria for minority financing	What shapes FFs' demand for PE minority investments?	Buyer / vendor/ management	Empirical	Agency	21 case studies	Germany	• FFs' demand and likelihood for PE investment are driven by three factors: (1) financing need, (2) PE firms' non-financial resource contribution, (3) costs for ceding control rights • Incompleteness of pecking-order hypothesis for FFs because factors of family influence are ignored • PE firms are granted increased control rights if family conflicts are solved, PE firm's neutrality is assumed, and relational trust exists
Ahlers et al. (2016)	Behavior of family sellers in buyouts	How does the seller's affective commitment influence buyout deal-making?	Buyer	Empirical	Affective commitment	Responses from 174 PE firms	Germany, Italy, France, UK, Spain	• FF differ from non-FF as sellers in buyout transactions • Increased importance of relational and non-financial factors in PE buyouts • The factors trust and goal congruence positively affect perceived deal commitment
(E) Bargaining power in buyout negotiations								
Ahlers et al. (2016)	PE's bargaining power in negotiations	How do PE firms perform in negotiations with firm sellers and does specialization play a role?	Buyer	Empirical	Bargaining power	176 PE professionals	Europe	• Power in negotiations is key factor that determines who is able to claim more value from an agreement • Bidder competition, expertise, and time pressure as negotiation power sources (for the buying side) • Different forms of PE firm specialization provide competitive advantage in negotiations

(Continued)

Table 8.1 (Continued)

Authors/year of publication	*Topics*	*Research question*	*Perspective*	*Type of research*	*Theory*	*Sample*	*Country/ region*	*Key message*
Amatucci and Swartz (2011)	Gender-related negotiation styles in PE investment processes	(1) Are women's negotiation styles problematic? (2) What strategies have been effective for women entrepreneurs? (3) What are some of the major challenges for women entrepreneurs?	Vendor	Mixed method	Gender	12 women entrepreneurs who participated in PE negotiations	US	• Women utilize multi-faceted approaches and responses to the challenge posed by raising PE • Personal and professional networks appear to have been the most valuable source of unearthing potential investors • The qualitative data support the proposition that behavior among these female CEOs spans a gamut of multi-faceted responses to the challenge of negotiating access to PE
(F) Value creation in family firm buyouts								
Goossens et al. (2008)	Growth and efficiency	How does the new ownership post-buyout influence growth and efficiency in the former FF?	N/A	Empirical	Agency	167 buyouts, 43 FFs	Belgium	• Family- and non-FF buyouts with and without PE involvement are compared • If strategic change is measured as "growth" in total assets, sales, and employees – no significant differences occur between family and non-family buyouts; PE involvement is associated only with employee growth • If strategic change is measured as "efficiency" improvements, neither previous family ownership nor involvement of PE have a significant differentiating effect
Klöckner (2009)	Value creation	What are the changes associated with FF buyouts for corporate governance, managerial control instruments, and finance?	Buyer/ vendor	Empirical	Agency, Stewardship	32 case studies	Germany	• Buyouts create value in FFs through "professionalization" and "economization" while potentially creating higher agency costs when FFs change from stewardship to agency governance • "Professionalization" refers to the enhancement of corporate governance and organizational processes – PE firms enable strategies of internationalization and M&A, hire more professional managers, increase monetary incentives, introduce ambitious targets, establish supervisory boards to tighten control, and improve planning, accounting, and performance management practices • "Economization" refers to new corporate goals that prioritize financial over non-financial goals

Scholes et al. (2010)	Growth and efficiency Effects of family configurations	How do family characteristics pre-buyout affect growth and efficiency changes post-buyout?	Management	Empirical	Agency, Stewardship	104 buyouts	Europe	• Univariate analysis: strategic change measured as efficiency gains and strategic growth are higher in PE-backed buyouts if the founder was present, no NED, and no non-family management existed before deal closure; involvement of PE firms or internal management pre-buyout also triggered these changes • Multivariate analysis: only non-family management without equity shares pre-buyout is confirmed to induce strategic change (efficiency, growth) post-buyout
Achleitner et al. (2010)	Governance/ value creation	Do FFs offer potential for value creation based on governance engineering?	Buyer / vendor/ management	Empirical	Agency	1 case study	Germany	• Value creation through governance engineering by PE firms does not originate in ownership concentration, but changes in strategy, operations, and incentives through PE firms' board representation • Buyouts can be a force to reinforce family entrepreneurship
Wulf et al. (2010)	Performance enhancing activities of PE	What is the effect of PE firms' involvement in former FFs?	Company	Empirical	RBV	118	Europe	• Many support activities (e.g., financial management, operational, strategic) of PE firms do not add performance to the former family business except if PE fosters co-operation and networking with other portfolio firms • For a sub-group of underperforming FFs pre-buyout, PE firms support activities related to professionalization of organizational structures and systems are positively related to performance – the impact can be negative if PE firms get involved in operational activities
Braun et al. (2011)	Differences in governance structures	How do governance structures between FFs and LBOs differ and what are its performance implications?	Company	Conceptual	Agency, stewardship	–	US	• FFs' governance structures are characterized by long-term business orientation and both financial and non-financial objectives • LBOs' governance structures reflect short-termism and shareholder value maximization • FFs' governance structures have performance advantages during times of economic stagnation whereas LBO structures outperform in economic growth cycles

(*Continued*)

Table 8.1 (Continued)

Authors/year of publication	*Topics*	*Research question*	*Perspective*	*Type of research*	*Theory*	*Sample*	*Country/ region*	*Key message*
Grundström, et al. (2012)	Innovation Succession paths	How is innovative behavior affected when comparing internal (family) succession to external succession (e.g., buyouts)?	Buyer/ vendor	Empirical	Organizational culture; family firm succession	5 internal succession cases, 5 external succession cases (mainly buyouts)	Sweden	• New owners in external succession exhibit higher orientation towards innovating behavior • Family successors tend to focus on incremental innovation and diversify businesses so that resource shedding can be avoided • Intermediating factors such as customer involvement or acquirers' motives need to be considered
Chrisman et al. (2012)	Governance/ value creation	How do agency costs develop post-buyout?	Company	Conceptual	Agency	–	US/ Europe	• Value creation in MBOs is conceived as a reduction in agency costs • Agency cost reduction is dependent on pre-buyout agency costs associated with different family configurations (e.g., solely owned vs. dispersed ownership), minimization of agency costs between upper and lower level management, and balancing the relationship of agency control costs and residual losses

Source: Author.

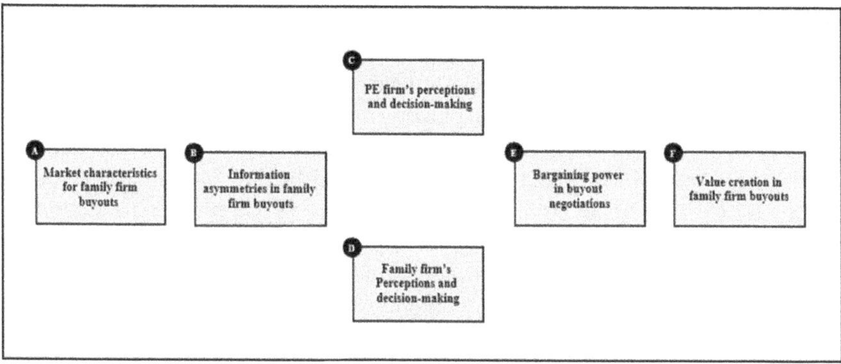

Figure 8.1 Identified categories of literature review

Source: Authors.

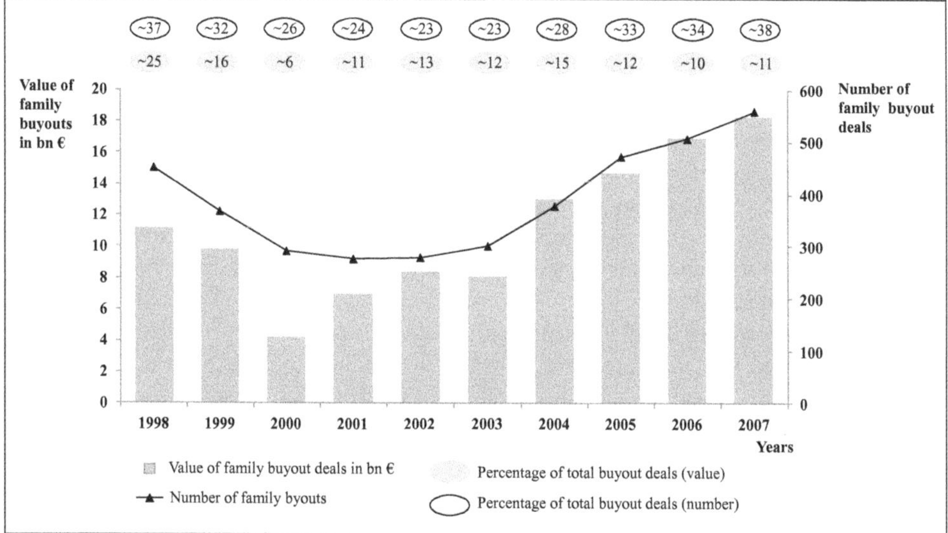

Figure 8.2 Buyout market for family firms

Source: Modified, based on Scholes et al. (2009).

and not due to family influence. Thus, one needs to be cautious when attributing phenomena to family influence when it could occur because of the firm size. For example, smaller firms might face expertise disadvantages when dealing with PE firms because they possess insufficient resources and capabilities (Barney, 1986; Barney, 1991; Peteraf, 1993). Second, family firms constitute a key source of deals for PE firms and thus represent a large share of the buyout market. Third, one needs to be cautious when interpreting the information on family buyout markets. It has already been acknowledged that definitions of family firms differ and the reviewed work only employs one of many definitions (Klein, 2000; Astrachan et al., 2002; Klein et al., 2005; Chua et al., 2012). Thus, other definitions of family firms might yield considerably different results.[4] Figure 8.2 displays all data from 1998 until 2007.

(B) Information asymmetries and decision-making. Four studies dealing with aspects of information asymmetry could be identified. In particular, one study highlights the role of information asymmetries in selecting a succession route (Dehlen et al., 2014) and three studies deal with information asymmetries in buyouts (Howorth et al., 2004; Scholes et al., 2007, 2008). Howorth et al. (2004) emphasize the role of positive relationships and relational factors such as trust and mutual involvement between the deal parties when planning for the buyout which facilitates the flow of information. The work of Scholes et al. (2007) illustrates how family firm characteristics such as the involvement of the founder and professionalized management structures can contribute to improved information-sharing. Scholes et al. (2008) show that mutual involvement of the management team and the selling family firm owner when planning the succession is beneficial, in that it limits information asymmetries and helps address conflicts of interest in family firm buyouts.

A mutually agreed sale price is more likely to result when no family successor is available or financial objectives are of the family firms' priority (Scholes et al., 2007). However, the role of PE firms in achieving a mutually agreed sale price remains unclear – Scholes et al. (2007) show that a mutually agreed sale price is more likely when the PE firms are involved in buyout planning whereas in the subsequent study of Scholes et al. (2008) PE firms' involvement leads to a mutually agreed sale price being less likely.

The study of Dehlen et al. (2014) underlines the role of information asymmetries one step earlier, i.e., when the decision for a succession path is made by (family) owners. It illustrates that family firms are generally biased towards intra-family succession paths (Dehlen et al., 2014). However, if family owners undertake efforts to reduce information asymmetries, such as screening, the external succession through a buyout can become more likely (Dehlen et al., 2014). Socioemotional wealth (SEW), measured by age of firm, can limit screening activities, and the authors conclude that emotional attachment makes family succession more likely and leads to increased difficulties for family departure from business activities (Dehlen et al., 2014).

The prominent role of information asymmetries is unsurprising given adjacent literature. Most family firms are often privately held (Klein, 2000; Wang, 2006; Praet, 2013). The quality and quantity of information available about private firms is usually lower compared to information about public firms (Capron & Shen, 2007). Limited information availability on privately held companies is due to a weaker market for corporate control (analysts, investment banks, etc.) and less stringent regulations on information disclosure (Shen & Reuer, 2005; Ragozzino & Reuer, 2010). The market for corporate control has an important function in providing information and supporting asset evaluation (Capron & Shen, 2007). In addition, information availability could be further constrained by family firms' high degree of tacitness and a lower willingness to share information with those outside the family (Nonaka & Takeuchi, 1995; Cabrera-Suárez et al., 2001; Lee et al., 2003). In particular, management buyin (MBI) deals might suffer from information asymmetries because the existing management is not part of the buying coalition (Howorth et al., 2004).

A few preliminary conclusions can be drawn from the selected literature on information asymmetries. First, family firm owners and the incumbent management team potentially face conflicts of interest, especially in MBI deals, in which case the buying and selling side should be wary (Howorth et al., 2004). Second, the high complexity of a buyout route requires long-term planning in order to prepare and to achieve a sound information basis for successful deal-making. The collaboration of management and family owners appears to be beneficial in this process (Scholes et al., 2008). Families' needs for SEW potentially lead to a "biased" or "postponed" succession process (Dehlen et al., 2014). Third, the actual relationship between buyer and seller in buyout deals can play a key role in facilitating information flows and co-operative bargaining solutions (Howorth et al., 2004). Last, advisors might play a valuable role in facilitating the buyout process and in brokering deals (Scholes et al., 2009).

(C) PE firms' perceptions and decision-making. Another category of papers examines if and how family firms are perceived by PE investors, compared to non-family firms. There are six identifiable papers in this category (Upton & Petty, 2000; Silva, 2006; Granata, 2010; Granata & Chirico, 2010; Dawson, 2011; Ahlers et al., 2014). Family firms are often perceived differently by potential acquirers, compared to non-family buyout targets – which is highlighted in several studies (Silva, 2006; Granata, 2010; Dawson, 2011). In particular, family firms are considered riskier investment targets because of the higher complexity resulting from the intertwinement of family and business systems (Silva, 2006; Granata, 2010). Additionally, family firms are associated with less professional management that could favor particular family interests and by doing so emphasize non-financial goals over financial ones (Granata, 2010), leading to lower company valuations (Granata & Chirico, 2010). Dawson (2011) argues that family firm investment targets could be perceived more positively by PE investors if selling owners exit the business soon after the buyout and if management structures are already professionalized. If PE investors participate in succession financing (usually minority investments), the qualifications of the successor, the business strategy, and the degree of harmony in family relationships are considered by PE firms (Upton & Petty, 2000).

Two main findings can be concluded from this review category. First, family firms are indeed perceived by PE investors as being different from non-family firm targets (Ahlers et al., 2014). Second, the difference in perception is rather negative, i.e., PE investors emphasize the negative side of family influence and in particular the additional risks associated with family firm investments (e.g., owner-centricity). However, these findings contrast with research on family firms highlighting performance advantages of family firms (Anderson & Reeb, 2003; Villalonga & Amit, 2006) and prior research that argues family firms can be both a source of performance advantage, but also disadvantage (Sirmon & Hitt, 2003; Miller & Le Breton-Miller, 2006).

(D) Family firms' perceptions and decision-making. The perception of PE firms represents only one perspective of the relationship between family firms and PE (deals). It is not surprising that another strand of studies examines the family or vendors' perspective. A total of 10 works fall into this category (Poutziouris, 2001; Graebner & Eisenhardt, 2004; Poech et al., 2005; Astrachan & Jaskiewicz, 2008; Zellweger & Astrachan, 2008; Niedermeyer et al., 2010; Salvato et al., 2010; Zellweger et al., 2011; Tappeiner et al., 2012; Ahlers et al., 2016). Poutziouris (2001) shows how family firms are hesitant to use external sources of financing and in particular sources that would require them to give up ownership control, which applies to PE financing – indicating that the pecking-order hypothesis could apply to family firms. The pecking-order hypothesis proposes the preference of internal funds over debt, and, once debt capacities are maximized, external equity is used (Myers, 1984). However, Tappeiner et al. (2012) argue the pecking-order hypothesis needs modification and refinement where family firms are concerned. In particular, the authors illustrate that family firms' demands and the likelihood of utilizing PE (minority) investment are driven not only by financing needs but also by how well PE firms are equipped to provide non-financial resources, the costs associated with ceding control rights, and how relational factors play out (Tappeiner et al., 2012). Furthermore, it is important to consider family influence such as the need for SEW to understand financing decisions of family firms (Tappeiner et al., 2012). For example, family owners would be willing to cede control rights if family conflicts can be resolved due to PE firm involvement, the PE firm is able to provide complementary expertise, and if the PE firm is regarded as trustworthy (Tappeiner et al., 2012).

SEW seems to play a bigger role when families exit the business. Family firm owners struggle to sell their businesses and have difficulties letting go of their businesses due to emotional attachment which is driven by the emotional costs and benefits that have occurred over time (Astrachan & Jaskiewicz, 2008; Zellweger & Astrachan, 2008). In particular, it can be a feeling of responsibility to carry on the family's heritage that makes it difficult to make decisions as to how to shed resources (Salvato et al., 2010). Zellweger and Astrachan (2008) emphasize how family business owners' emotional attachment is a key dimension of SEW that can develop over time and may distort family business owners' value perception, i.e., family sellers attach a higher value to the firm that cannot be explained by the financial value of business performance, but rather by "emotions." This might make it difficult to transfer the business to a PE firm in a buyout, as "emotions" cannot help justify to the market what might be an acceptable price for the family firm (Zellweger & Astrachan, 2008). In a similar vein, it was confirmed that a positive relationship exists between trust and goal congruence influencing the family business seller's affective deal commitment (Ahlers et al., 2016). However, emotional value can also lower the market price when family CEOs sell to family members – as shown by Zellweger and colleagues (2011). Moreover, it is not only the type of buyer but also the quality of the buyer-seller relationship (with factors such as organizational rapport, relational trust, cultural fit and a long-term interest shown by the buyer in the prosperity of the business) that plays an important role (Graebner & Eisenhardt, 2004; Ahlers et al., 2014). Unsurprisingly, Niedermeyer et al. (2010) hypothesize how families' deal satisfaction can be driven not just by an adequate sales price but also by factors of procedural fairness, goal alignment, opportunities to select among different buyers, and an ongoing post-sale connection with the former family business (Romano et al., 2001; Niedermeyer et al., 2010).

Psychological "barriers" might exist when family firms are dealing with PE firms. The study of Poech et al. (2005) illuminates how family sellers often feel confronted with a different "mindset" which does not match family firm philosophy when dealing with PE firms (Poech et al., 2005). Family perceptions, however, might be biased according to stereotypes and a lack of prior experience/knowledge when dealing with PE, and accentuated by selective information processing (Poech et al., 2005).

From the literature on family business sellers' perceptions and decision-making, three conclusions can be made. First, sellers assume an active role when selling the business. Second, family firm sellers might be concerned to whom and how the business is sold while the maximization of the sale price is only one of many sale objectives. Third, reciprocal perceptions of family firms and PE could be a source of conflict and a positive relationship might be critical in relationships between family firms and PE firms.

(E) Bargaining power in buyout negotiations. We identified two papers dealing with "negotiations and bargaining power"; moreover, several further papers that we assigned to the information asymmetry category also touched on the topic of price negotiations. Based on negotiation theory, which explores what makes people work together towards an agreed goal or price, the authors of one of these papers investigate two areas of concern. First, that information in the negotiation process is not equally distributed and second, that some negotiation parties aim to achieve a maximization of their goals rather than a mutual agreement. Especially in sales negotiations, vendors who aim to maximize the price may not disclose all information. Generally, vendors are less reluctant to share information and thus more willing to engage in fruitful negotiations if the vendor is the original business founder, who primarily focuses on strategic objectives and long-term success of the firm. Moreover, it is also the case if no clear successor is present and if the buyer is already involved in succession planning before the actual negotiation process starts (Scholes et al., 2007).

A recent study on small business firms in general, which can also be applied to family businesses, has investigated the perceived bargaining power between PE firms and (family) business owners selling their business. Thereby, the three factors *competition*, *expertise*, and *time pressure* determine the perceived bargaining power of PE firms. A negative relationship between PE's bargaining power and bidder competition exists, whereas PE's expertise and the buyout seller's time pressure positively influence PE's bargaining power (Ahlers et al., 2016). A further area of interest are the attributes of the vendor such as first or later generation (Scholes et al., 2007) or their gender as Amatucci and Swartz (2011) showed that women vendors negotiate differently than male vendors.

(F) Value creation in family firm buyouts. Eight papers can be identified as falling into the "value creation" category (Goossens et al., 2008; Klöckner, 2009; Achleitner et al., 2010; Scholes et al., 2010; Wulf et al., 2010; Braun et al., 2011; Grundström et al., 2012; Chrisman et al., 2012). Klöckner (2009) subsumes the effects PE buyouts can have on the former family firm broadly under "economization" and "professionalization" – the former referring to all activities, be they strategic (e.g., M&A) or operational (e.g., planning) and the latter comprises a general shift from partially non-financial goals to purely financial ones (Klöckner, 2009). Thus, "economization" and "professionalization" stimulate the creation of economic value in family firm buyouts (Klöckner, 2009). "Professionalization" is also emphasized in the work of Braun et al. (2011) who argue that governance structures of family firms and buyout vehicles represent two different "business philosophies." While family firms are generally regarded as having a long-term orientation (Carney et al., 2015) and show co-existence of financial and non-financial objectives, buyout structures especially in the form of LBOs are reckoned to be characterized by short-termism and purely financial goals (Braun et al., 2011). Furthermore, the authors argue that LBOs are more successful in economic growth cycles, whereas family firms have performance advantages in economic downward cycles (Braun et al., 2011; Bertoni et al., 2011). In another work related to innovative behavior, the case study's evidence suggests that family successors show cautious innovation behavior whereas external succession through buyouts is associated with a higher degree of strong innovation behavior (Grundström et al., 2012).

Achleitner et al. (2010) agree with prior research that changes in corporate governance ("governance engineering") can stimulate value creation in buyouts, but "how" it occurs in family business buyouts is distinctively different from non-family buyouts. While value creation in non-family buyouts, in particular those involving publicly held companies, originates in creating more concentrated ownership structures with lower agency costs (Jensen, 1989), this line of argument could not be applied to family firm buyouts that most commonly already have concentrated ownership (Achleitner et al., 2010). Thus, according to Achleitner et al. (2010), value creation in family buyouts originates from strategic and operational improvements achieved by the representation of PE managers in supervisory boards as well as higher incentivization of the top management in portfolio firms. Similarly, the work of Chrisman et al. (2012) highlights how different family firm governance configurations (ownership, management) create different levels of agency costs pre-buyout, which leads to greater unpredictability of agency cost reduction in the post-buyout period. This is in line with related literature on family firm governance, which argues that family influence can be both beneficial and detrimental to the firm's financial structure (Koropp et al., 2014) and performance – the potential agency cost advantage might be lost due to owner-manager or owner-owner agency problems leading to asymmetric altruism, managerial entrenchment, and hold-up (Schulze et al., 2001, 2003a, 2003b; Villalonga & Amit, 2006). Furthermore, Chrisman et al. (2012) hypothesize agency cost reductions in family firm buyouts could occur on other levels than previously thought, i.e., not between owners and managers, but between upper and lower management. Former asymmetric altruism (e.g., favoring family members) with detrimental effects on agency costs (Schulze et al., 2001) can be reduced in the post-buyout phase. Last, it is also emphasized that buyouts in family firms will shift the composition of agency costs from residual losses (due to opportunism) to newly created agency control costs, as former family firms rely less on formal control mechanisms (Chrisman et al., 2012).

Empirical studies that use a quantitative approach do not entirely confirm that value creation in family firm buyouts is any different from non-family buyouts. Goosens et al. (2008) could not find differences in post-buyout performance where changes in efficiency and company growth are concerned. On the contrary, Scholes et al. (2010) could confirm for family configurations with no "non-family management with equity stakes" (who would have no incentive to perform higher because they have no equity stake) in the former family firm are associated with higher growth and efficiency. Wulf et al. (2010) only found positive effects of PE involvement on performance for formerly underperforming family firms when it comes to professionalization of organizational structures and systems. The impact of PE firms could turn negative if PE firms' involvement becomes operational (cost-saving) in nature (Wulf et al., 2010).

Three conclusions can be drawn from the literature on value creation. First, family firms might undergo strategic changes after a buyout. These changes stem from a greater orientation towards financial goals in the post-buyout period. Second, strategic changes and financial value creation are not certain and sound empirical evidence remains scarce. Third, different family configurations might need investigating to determine whether and under what circumstances value creation occurs.

Literature gaps and future research

After having reviewed the works dealing with the interface of family firms and PE, literature gaps become evident. Literature gaps are structured according to (1) opportunities for methodological or theoretical improvement which is needed in future research, (2) research issues within current research categories not yet covered, and (3) new research categories requiring consideration in the future.

(1) Methodology and theory. High-quality research requires both a strong theoretical basis and an appropriate as well as reliable methodology (Bird et al., 2002). Concerning the papers in this literature review, the methodologies used offer opportunities for improvement and future research.

Future research might rely more on quantitative empirical research. The majority of reviewed studies are either conceptual or, if empirical, rely heavily on case study evidence.[5] Case study research is especially appropriate in early stages of research development to provide inductively a foundation upon which quantitative research methods can be built deductively (Miles & Huberman, 1985; Eisenhardt & Graebner, 2007). Thus, the key objective of case study research is to identify and recognize key elements, structures, and relationships of a "field situation" (Barzelay, 2007; Eisenhardt & Graebner, 2007). Given the comparably low number of publications on family firms and PE, case study research can be considered as being a suitable means to prepare the ground work for further quantitative research.

Existing quantitative empirical research in existing literature would have benefitted from greater methodological rigor, such as the application of more sophisticated statistical techniques, including multiple regression, moderation and mediation analysis, structural equation modeling, and the use of statistical constructs confirmed by factor analysis (Baron & Kenny, 1986; Hair, 1987; Kline, 2005). For example, Scholes et al. (2007) acknowledge that their use of logistic regression analysis for cross-sectional data would benefit from techniques of structural equation modeling to establish causality and interactions between variables. Furthermore, Scholes et al. (2007) or Wulf et al. (2010) use single-item variables which could suffer from measurement error compared to statistical constructs (Scholes et al., 2007). In the work of Scholes et al. (2008), bivariate non-parametric statistical tests (such as Mann-Whitney "U" test, Chi-square test) were used to analyze whether statistically significant differences between respondent groups exist. However, these kinds of statistical tests require the complementary use of statistical techniques such as moderation or mediation analysis in multiple regression so that control variables can be included (Hair, 1987). Scholes et al. (2010) use of univariate analysis and when testing also multivariate analysis have to relativize their results. There are notable exceptions in this literature review whose authors exhibit great methodological rigor such as the works of Dehlen et al. (2014) and Zellweger et al. (2011). Also, relatively new statistical approaches – such as conjoint analysis in the study of Dawson (2011) who examines trade-offs in decision-making – can be considered a promising route for future research (Lohrke et al., 2009). Future empirical research might try to validate current research findings by using robust and state-of-the-art statistical techniques.

The treatment of family firms also needs more sophistication in current work on family firms and PE. It was previously mentioned that family firms exhibit great heterogeneity, so simple dichotomous differentiations might be misleading (Tsang, 2002; Hack, 2009; Chrisman et al., 2012; Chua et al., 2012). In the prominent study of Villalonga and Amit (2006), it was shown how a change from defining family based solely on ownership rights leads to different forms of family involvement and thus changes family firm performance from being positive to negative (Hack, 2009). Therefore, it may be necessary to test various forms and configurations of family firms to appropriately differentiate between varying degrees of family influence and its consequences. If family influence is not investigated comprehensively, research might fall victim to unjustified generalizations (Melin & Nordqvist, 2007). Moderation and mediation analysis might be appropriate means to ensure more sophisticated treatment of family firm configurations in statistical analysis, but researchers also need to capture different characteristics of family influence (e.g., ownership, management) in surveys as a precondition.

Multiple respondent studies and larger sample sizes could also contribute to higher statistical reliability. Most quantitative empirical studies rely on the key informant approach (Kumar et al., 1993) and studies often either take the perspective of the buyer or seller (Niedermeyer et al., 2010; Dawson, 2011). New insights and more representativeness might be achieved if multiple respondents from both the buying and selling side are investigated simultaneously to capture a less biased perspective (Eddleston & Kellermanns, 2007). Additionally, most studies rely on comparably low sample sizes (Granata & Chirico, 2010; Dawson, 2011) compared to other fields of management research. This is likely due to the difficulty in gaining access to data, given the confidentiality that surrounds buyout deals.

The use of novel theories could inspire new research insights. Established theories such as agency theory, stewardship theory, and the resource based view (RBV) dominate works in this literature review. However, management theory is not limited to the aforementioned theories, but offers a broader spectrum of theories. More diverse theoretical approaches could point out interesting insights. A number of prominent theories such as upper-echelon (Hambrick & Mason, 1984), institutional theory (Meyer & Rowan, 1977; DiMaggio & Powell, 1983), commitment-trust theory (Allen & Meyer, 1990; Meyer & Allen, 1991) or insights from the field of behavioral finance (Thaler, 1993; Ackert & Deaves, 2010) might provide promising paths for future research.

(2) Research gaps within current categories. The literature review followed the different research categories that had been identified. Within the *market* category, there is a need to provide more recent information on the dimension and characteristics of family firm buyouts. Furthermore, it might be necessary to distinguish between different definitions of family firms that could yield different results for the market characteristics of family firm buyouts and PE activity. Additionally, it would be beneficial to have more detailed insights into the contractual terms of family deals vs. non-family deals (e.g., covenants, degree of control) and potential antecedents.

Within the *information asymmetries* category, it would be complementary to existing research if long-term consequences of information asymmetries for buyout deals were investigated, i.e., the consequences for financial success and deal satisfaction of the involved parties. In particular, for the buying side, it could be insightful to evaluate whether specific strategies in the due diligence process of PE firms focused on family aspects reduce information asymmetries (Puranam et al., 2006).

Research within the category *PE perceptions and decision-making* has not yet assessed how perceptions on family firms might lead to cognitive biases in the investment decision-making of PE firms (e.g., overconfidence) (Thaler, 1993; Kahneman et al., 1999; Ackert & Deaves, 2010). For example, PE firms might not recognize company strengths in family firms because family firms are cognitively associated with certain weaknesses. Furthermore, PE managers might refrain from investments in family firms as they try to avoid higher perceived risk due to family involvement or use certain strategies to mitigate risks. For example, PE firms might negotiate specific investment contracts (e.g., earn out) or use certain monitoring arrangements.

Within the category *Family firm perceptions and decision-making*, literature gaps become apparent when specific selection criteria of family sellers are concerned. While there is a strong indication that the relationship side matters to family sellers (Graebner & Eisenhardt, 2004; Poech et al., 2005; Niedermeyer et al., 2010; Tappeiner et al., 2012), the specific elements of the relationship that matter the most are yet to be fully discovered. Conjoint analysis could be a methodological instrument to investigate decision trade-offs of family owners (Dawson, 2011). Specifically, it needs to be evaluated how financial and non-financial objectives are weighted relative to each other, given that family firms have a preference for non-financial goals (Corbetta & Salvato, 2004; Chrisman et al., 2007; Gómez-Mejía et al., 2007). For example, how does a characteristic of the relationship, such as trust, have an effect on sellers' financial objectives during the sale? Additionally, there is a need to understand whether and how negative perceptions of family sellers on PE firms might change once family sellers interact with PE firms (Poech et al., 2005).

For *Bargaining power in buyout negotiations*, literature has so far mostly neglected the negotiation phase of deal-making; however, this phase is considered as highly important in many transactions due to the complexity of deals and the lack of market transparency (Birley, 1984; Tyebjee & Bruno, 1984; Cumming & Johan, 2009). Multiple aspects of negotiations could be important, such as bargaining power or bargaining tactics (Kim et al., 2005), and how they affect the outcome of the firm transferring process. Moreover, attributes of the vendor such as gender (Amatucci & Swartz, 2011) are also so far understudied.

The *Value creation in family business buyouts* literature needs to close the gap on whether value creation strategies for family firms need to be different and how. In particular, it could be beneficial to identify whether forms of family influence post-buyout are successful given adjacent literature claiming that family influence can be both a source of high performance and low performance (Sirmon & Hitt, 2003). Combined influence of former family business owners and PE management could create value, as complementary expertise could be combined to achieve competitive advantage. All these facets need to be investigated over longer time periods to effectively differentiate between short-term and long-term effects.

(3) Future research categories. The reviewed literature does not touch some areas that can have importance in family firm buyout deals. First, there are literature gaps regarding the increasing importance of the role of advisors and intermediaries (Strike, 2012). For example, we do not know if family sellers employ advisors to support them in deal-making (Michel & Kammerlander, 2015) and the selection of PE partners as well as how family sellers select such advisors. Second, literature gaps exist when it comes to the initiation of buyout deals. It might be particularly interesting to find out how family sellers and PE firms get into contact with each. Third, the whole planning process family firms undergo to prepare a buyout and how this affects the success of the deal could be of great research interest. Fourth, future literature might resolve contradictory issues arising from different research categories – such as the valuation of family targets (Ahlers et al., 2014) given findings related to lower valuations in the marketplace (Granata, 2010; Granata & Chirico, 2010), but higher valuations by family sellers (Zellweger & Astrachan, 2008; Zellweger et al., 2011).

Conclusions

From this literature review, some key messages can be distilled. Information asymmetries might be characteristic for buyout deals when family firms and PE firms are involved. It is also evident that two different management philosophies could "clash" when PE firms interact with family firms in buyout deals. Reciprocal perceptions might not be entirely positive, and decision-making criteria and deal objectives might place different emphases on financial and non-financial objectives. More research is needed to fill the outlined research gaps within the existing and entirely new categories. Future research might also be concerned with more quantitative empirical research and the methodological rigor needed to address the complexity of buyout deals as well as the breadth and diversity among family firms. More diverse theories should be able to stimulate new insights.

Notes

1 The keywords are: acquisition, business transfer, business exit, buyout, divestment, divesture, emotional value, financial investor, LBO, MBI, MBO, private equity, and takeover.
2 The keywords are: family business, family firm, family ownership, privately-owned business.
3 Poutziouris subsumes under venture capital what is usually referred to as PE/buyout investments.
4 Scholes et al. (2009) have defined family firms as where a single family group has >50% ownership of a firm.
5 See Table 8.1.

References

Achleitner, A. K., Herman, K., Lerner, J., & Lutz, E. 2010. Family business and private equity: Conflict or collaboration? The case of Messer Griesheim. *The Journal of Private Equity*, 13: 7–20.

Ackert, L. F., & Deaves, R. 2010. *Behavioral finance: Psychology, decision-making, and markets*. Mason, OH: South-Western Cengage Learning.
Ahlers, O., Hack, A., & Kellermanns, F. W. 2014. "Stepping into the buyers' shoes": Looking at the value of family firms through the eyes of private equity investors. *Journal of Family Business Strategy*, 5: 384–396.
Ahlers, O., Hack, A., Kellermanns, F., & Wright, M. 2016. Opening the black box: Power in buyout negotiations and the moderating role of private equity specialization. *Journal of Small Business Management*, 54: 1171–1192.
Ahlers, O., Hack, A., Madison, K., Wright, M., & Kellermanns, F. W. 2016. Is it all about money? Affective commitment and the difference between family and non-family sellers in buyouts. *British Journal of Management*, 28: 159–179.
Allen, N. J., & Meyer, J. P. 1990. The measurement and antecedents of affective, continuance and normative commitment to the organization. *Journal of Occupational Psychology*, 63: 1–18.
Amatucci, F. M., & Swartz, E. 2011. Through a fractured lens: Women entrepreneurs and the private equity negotiation process. *Journal of Developmental Entrepreneurship*, 16: 333–350.
Anderson, R. C., & Reeb, D. M. 2003. Founding-family ownership and firm performance: Evidence from the S&P 500. *Journal of Finance*, 58: 1301–1328.
Astrachan, J. H., & Jaskiewicz, P. 2008. Emotional returns and emotional costs in privately held family businesses: Advancing traditional business valuation. *Family Business Review*, 21: 139–149.
Astrachan, J. H., Klein, S. B., & Smyrnios, K. X. 2002. The F-PEC scale of family influence: A proposal for solving the family business definition problem. *Family Business Review*, 15: 45–58.
Astrachan, J. H., & Shanker, M. C. 2003. Family businesses' contribution to the US economy: A closer look. *Family Business Review*, 16: 211–219.
Barney, J. 1991. Firm resources and sustained competitive advantage. *Journal of Management*, 17: 99–120.
Barney, J. B. 1986. Strategic factor markets: Expectations, luck, and business strategy. *Management Science*, 32: 1231–1241.
Baron, R. M., & Kenny, D. A. 1986. The moderator–mediator variable distinction in social psychological research: Conceptual, strategic, and statistical considerations. *Journal of Personality and Social Psychology*, 51: 1173–1182.
Barzelay, M. 2007. Learning from second-hand experience: Methodology for extrapolation-oriented case research. *Governance*, 20: 521–543.
Berrone, P., Cruz, C., & Gomez-Mejia, L. R. 2012. Socioemotional wealth in family firms theoretical dimensions, assessment approaches, and agenda for future research. *Family Business Review*, 25: 258–279.
Bertoni, F., Ferrer, M. A., & Martí, J. 2011. The different roles played by venture capital and private equity investors on the investment activity of their portfolio firms. *Small Business Economics*, 40: 607–633.
Bird, B., Welsch, H., Astrachan, J. H., & Pistrui, D. 2002. Family business research: The evolution of an academic field. *Family Business Review*, 15: 337–350.
Birley, S. 1984. Success and failure in management buyouts. *Long Range Planning*, 17: 32–40.
Braun, M., Zacharias, L., & Latham, S. 2011. Family firms versus leveraged buyouts: A conceptual comparison of distinctive governance structures. *Journal of Family Business Management*, 1: 89–106.
Cabrera-Suárez, K., De Saá-Pérez, P., & García-Almeida, D. 2001. The succession process from a resource-and knowledge-based view of the family firm. *Family Business Review*, 14: 37–46.
Capron, L., & Shen, J.-C. 2007. Acquisitions of private vs. public firms: Private information, target selection, and acquirer returns. *Strategic Management Journal*, 28: 891–911.
Carney, M., Van Essen, M., Gedajlovic, E. R., & Heugens, P. P. 2015. What do we know about private family firms? A meta-analytical review. *Entrepreneurship Theory and Practice*, 39: 513–544.
Casillas, J., & Acedo, F. 2007. Evolution of the intellectual structure of family business literature: A bibliometric study of FBR. *Family Business Review*, 20: 141–162.
Chrisman, J. J., Chua, J. H., Kellermanns, F. W., & Chang, E. P. C. 2007. Are family managers agents or stewards? An exploratory study in privately held family firms: Family Influences on Firms. *Journal of Business Research*, 60: 1030–1038.
Chrisman, J. J., Chua, J. H., Pearson, A. W., & Barnett, T. 2012. Family involvement, family influence, and family-centered non-economic goals in small firms. *Entrepreneurship Theory and Practice*, 36: 267–293.

Chrisman, J. J., Chua, J. H., Steier, L. P., Wright, M., & McKee, D. N. 2012. An agency theoretic analysis of value creation through management buy-outs of family firms. *Journal of Family Business Strategy*, 3: 197–206.

Chua, J. H., Chrisman, J. J., Steier, L. P., & Rau, S. B. 2012. Sources of heterogeneity in family firms: An introduction. *Entrepreneurship Theory and Practice*, 36: 1103–1113.

Corbetta, G., & Salvato, C. 2004. Self-serving or self-actualizing? Models of man and agency costs in different types of family firms: A commentary on "Comparing the agency costs of family and non-family firms: Conceptual issues and exploratory evidence." *Entrepreneurship Theory and Practice*, 28: 355–362.

Cressy, R., Munari, F., & Malipiero, A. 2007. Playing to their strengths? Evidence that specialization in the private equity industry confers competitive advantage. *Journal of Corporate Finance*, 13: 647–669.

Cumming, D., & Johan, S. A. 2009. *Venture capital and private equity contracting: An international perspective*. Malden, MA: Academic Press.

Cumming, D., Siegel, D. S., & Wright, M. 2007. Private equity, leveraged buyouts and governance. *Journal of Corporate Finance*, 13: 439–460.

Dawson, A. 2011. Private equity investment decisions in family firms: The role of human resources and agency costs. *Journal of Business Venturing*, 26: 189–199.

Debicki, B. J., Matherne, C. F., Kellermanns, F. W., & Chrisman, J. J. 2009. Family business research in the new millennium an overview of the who, the where, the what, and the why. *Family Business Review*, 22: 151–166.

Dehlen, T., Zellweger, T. M., Kammerlander, N., & Halter, F. 2014. The role of information asymmetry in the choice of entrepreneurial exit routes. *Journal of Business Venturing*, 29: 193–209.

DeTienne, D. R. 2010. Entrepreneurial exit as a critical component of the entrepreneurial process: Theoretical development. *Journal of Business Venturing*, 25: 203–215.

DeTienne, D. R., & Cardon, M. 2012. Impact of founder experience on exit intentions. *Small Business Economics*, 38: 351–374.

DiMaggio, P. J., & Powell, W. W. 1983. The iron cage revisited: Institutional isomorphism and collective rationality in organizational fields. *American Sociological Review*, 48: 147–160.

Eddleston, K. A., & Kellermanns, F. W. 2007. Destructive and productive family relationships: A stewardship theory perspective. *Journal of Business Venturing*, 22: 545–565.

Eisenhardt, K. M., & Graebner, M. E. 2007. Theory building from cases: Opportunities and challenges. *Academy of Management Journal*, 50: 25–32.

Gómez-Mejía, L. R., Haynes, K. T., Nuñez-Nickel, M., Jacobson, K. J. L., & Moyano-Fuentes, J. 2007. Socioemotional wealth and business risks in family-controlled firms: Evidence from Spanish olive oil mills. *Administrative Science Quarterly*, 52: 106–137.

Goossens, L., Manigart, S., & Meuleman, M. 2008. The change in ownership after a buyout: Impact on performance. *The Journal of Private Equity*, 12: 31.

Graebner, M. E., & Eisenhardt, K. M. 2004. The seller's side of the story: Acquisition as courtship and governance as syndicate in entrepreneurial firms. *Administrative Science Quarterly*, 49: 366–403.

Granata, D. 2010. Sale: An alternative succession route for family firms. Valuation issues and acquirers' perception. PhD thesis, University of Lugano, Switzerland.

Granata, D., & Chirico, F. 2010. Measures of value in acquisitions: Family versus nonfamily firms. *Family Business Review*, 23: 341–354.

Grundström, C., Öberg, C., & Öhrwall Rönnbäck, A. 2012. Family-owned manufacturing SMEs and innovativeness: A comparison between within-family successions and external takeovers: Culture and values: Understanding the long-term perspectives of family businesses. *Journal of Family Business Strategy*, 3: 162–173.

Hack, A. 2009. Sind Familienunternehmen anders? Eine kritische Bestandsaufnahme des aktuellen Forschungsstands. *Zeitschrift für Betriebswirtschaftslehre*, 79(2/Special Issue): 1–29.

Hair, J. F. 1987. *Multivariate data analysis (3rd ed.)*. Upper Saddle River, NJ: Macmillan Publishing Company.

Hambrick, D. C., & Mason, P. A. 1984. Upper echelons: The organization as a reflection of its top managers. *The Academy of Management Review*, 9: 193–206.

Handler, W. C. 1994. Succession in family business: A review of the research. *Family Business Review*, 7: 133–157.

Howorth, C., Westhead, P., & Wright, M. 2004. Buyouts, information asymmetry and the family management dyad. *Journal of Business Venturing*, 19: 509–534.

Jensen, M. C. 1989. Eclipse of the public corporation. *Harvard Business Review*, 67: 61–74.
Kahneman, D., Slovic, P., & Tversky, A. 1999. *Judgement under uncertainty: Heuristics and biases* (Reprint.). Cambridge, UK: Cambridge University Press.
Kaplan, S. N., & Strömberg, P. 2009. Leveraged buyouts and private equity. *The Journal of Economic Perspectives*, 23: 121–146.
Kellermanns, F. W., Eddleston, K. A., & Zellweger, T. M. 2012. Extending the socioemotional wealth perspective: A look at the dark side. *Entrepreneurship Theory and Practice*, 36: 1175–1182.
Kets Vries de, M. F. R. 1993. The dynamics of family controlled firms: The good and the bad news. *Organizational Dynamics*, 21: 59–71.
Kim, P. H., Pinkley, R. L., & Fragale, A. R. 2005. Power dynamics in negotiation. *Academy of Management Review*, 30: 799–822.
Klein, S. B. 2000. Family businesses in Germany: Significance and structure. *Family Business Review*, 13: 157–181.
Klein, S. B., Astrachan, J. H., & Smyrnios, K. X. 2005. The F-PEC scale of family influence: Construction, validation, and further implication for theory. *Entrepreneurship Theory & Practice*, 29: 321–339.
Kline, R. B. 2005. *Principles and practice of structural equation modeling*, 2nd edition. New York: Guilford Press.
Klöckner, O. 2009. *Buy-outs in family businesses: Changes in corporate governance, instruments of managerial control, and financial practices*. Wiesbaden, Germany: Gabler.
Koropp, C., Kellermanns, F. W., Grichnik, D., & Stanley, L. 2014. Financial decision making in family firms: An adaptation of the theory of planned behavior. *Family Business Review*, 27: 307–327.
Kumar, N., Stern, L. W., & Anderson, J. C. 1993. Conducting interorganizational research using key informants. *The Academy of Management Journal*, 36: 1633–1651.
Lee, K. S., Lim, G. H., & Lim, W. S. 2003. Family business succession: Appropriation risk and choice of successor. *Academy of Management Review*, 28: 657–666.
Lohrke, F. T., Holloway, B. B., & Woolley, T. W. 2009. Conjoint analysis in entrepreneurship research: A review and research agenda. *Organizational Research Methods*, 13: 16–30.
Melin, L., & Nordqvist, M. 2007. The reflexive dynamics of institutionalization: The case of the family business. *Strategic Organization*, 5: 321–333.
Memili, E., Zellweger, T. M., & Fang, H. C. 2013. The determinants of family owner-managers' affective organizational commitment. *Family Relations*, 62: 443–456.
Meuleman, M., Amess, K., Wright, M., & Scholes, L. 2009. Agency, strategic entrepreneurship, and the performance of private equity-backed buyouts. *Entrepreneurship Theory and Practice*, 33: 213–239.
Meyer, J. P., & Allen, N. J. 1991. A three-component conceptualization of organizational commitment. *Human Resource Management Review*, 1: 61–89.
Meyer, J. W., & Rowan, B. 1977. Institutionalized organizations: Formal structure as myth and ceremony. *American Journal of Sociology*, 83: 340–363.
Michel, A., & Kammerlander, N. 2015. Trusted advisors in a family business's succession-planning process: An agency perspective. *Journal of Family Business Strategy*, 6: 45–57.
Miles, M. B., & Huberman, A. M. 1985. *Qualitative data analysis*. Thousand Oaks, CA: Sage.
Miller, D., & Le Breton-Miller, I. 2006. Family governance and firm performance: Agency, stewardship, and capabilities. *Family Business Review*, 14: 73–87.
Miller, D., Steier, L., & Le Breton-Miller, I. 2003. Lost in time: Intergenerational succession, change, and failure in family business. *Journal of Business Venturing*, 18: 513–531.
Morck, R., & Yeung, B. 2003. Agency problems in large family business groups. *Entrepreneurship Theory and Practice*, 27: 367–382.
Myers, S. C. 1984. Capital structure puzzle. *Journal of Finance*, 39: 575–592.
Niedermeyer, C., Jaskiewicz, P., & Klein, S. B. 2010. 'Can't get no satisfaction?' Evaluating the sale of the family business from the family's perspective and deriving implications for new venture activities. *Entrepreneurship and Regional Development*, 22: 293–320.
Nonaka, I., & Takeuchi, H. 1995. *The knowledge-creating company: How Japanese companies create the dynamics of information*. New York: Oxford University Press.
Peteraf, M. A. 1993. The cornerstones of competitive advantage: A resource-based view. *Strategic Management Journal*, 14: 179–191.
Poech, A., Achleitner, A. K., & Burger-Calderon, M. 2005. Private equity in familienunternehmen: Eine empirische untersuchung zu psychologischen aspekten der transaktionsentscheidung. *Finanz Betrieb*, 7: 289–295.

Poutziouris, P. Z. 2001. The views of family companies on venture capital: Empirical evidence from the UK small to medium-size enterprising economy. *Family Business Review*, 14: 277–291.

Praet, A. 2013. Family firms and the divestment decision: An agency perspective. *Journal of Family Business Strategy*, 4: 34–41.

Puranam, P., Powell, B. C., & Singh, H. 2006. Due diligence failure as a signal detection problem. *Strategic Organization*, 4: 319–348.

Ragozzino, R., & Reuer, J. J. 2010. The opportunities and challenges of entrepreneurial acquisitions. *European Management Review*, 7: 80–90.

Romano, C. A., Tanewski, G. A., & Smyrnios, K. X. 2001. Capital structure decision making: A model for family business. *Journal of Business Venturing*, 16: 285–310.

Salvato, C., Chirico, F., & Sharma, P. 2010. A farewell to the business: Championing exit and continuity in entrepreneurial family firms. *Entrepreneurship & Regional Development*, 22: 321–348.

Scholes, L., Westhead, P., & Burrows, A. 2008. Family firm succession: The management buy-out and buy-in routes. *Journal of Small Business and Enterprise Development*, 15: 8–30.

Scholes, L., Wright, M., Westhead, P., & Bruining, H. 2010. Strategic changes in family firms post management buyout: Ownership and governance issues. *International Small Business Journal*, 28: 505–521.

Scholes, L., Wright, M., Westhead, P., Bruining, H., & Kloeckner, O. 2009. Family firm buy-outs, private equity and strategic change. *The Journal of Private Equity*, 12: 7–18.

Scholes, M. L., Wright, M., Westhead, P., Burrows, A., & Bruining, H. 2007. Information sharing, price negotiation and management buy-outs of private family-owned firms. *Small Business Economics*, 29: 329–349.

Schulze, W. S., Lubatkin, M. H., & Dino, R. N. 2003a. Exploring the agency consequences of ownership dispersion among the directors of family firms. *Academy of Management Journal*, 46: 179–194.

Schulze, W. S., Lubatkin, M. H., & Dino, R. N. 2003b. Toward a theory of agency and altruism in family firms. *Journal of Business Venturing*, 18: 473–490.

Schulze, W. S., Lubatkin, M. H., Dino, R. N., & Buchholtz, A. K. 2001. Agency relationships in family firms: Theory and evidence. *Organization Science*, 12: 99–116.

Sharma, P. 2004. An overview of the field of family business studies: Current status and directions for the future. *Family Business Review*, 17: 1–36.

Sharma, P., Chrisman, J. J., & Chua, J. H. 1997. Strategic management of the family business: Past research and future challenges. *Family Business Review*, 10: 1–35.

Sharma, P., Chrisman, J. J., & Chua, J. H. 2003. Succession planning as planned behavior: Some empirical results. *Family Business Review*, 16: 1–15.

Sharma, P., Chrisman, J. J., Pablo, A. L., & Chua, J. H. 2001. Determinants of initial satisfaction with the succession process in family firms: A conceptual model. *Entrepreneurship Theory and Practice*, 25: 17–36.

Sharma, P., & Irving, P. G. 2005. Four bases of family business successor commitment: Antecedents and consequences. *Entrepreneurship Theory and Practice*, 29: 13–33.

Shen, J.-C., & Reuer, J. J. 2005. Adverse selection in acquisitions of small manufacturing firms: A comparison of private and public targets. *Small Business Economics*, 24: 393–407.

Silva, J. 2006. Venture Capital Investments in Family Firms. In J. E. Butler, A. Lockett, & D. Ucbasaran (Eds.), *Venture capital and the changing world of entrepreneurship*. Greenwich, CT: Information Age Pub, 239–247.

Sirmon, D. G., & Hitt, M. A. 2003. Managing resources: Linking unique resources, management, and wealth creation in family firms. *Entrepreneurship Theory & Practice*, 27: 339–358.

Strike, V. M. 2012. Advising the family firm: Reviewing the past to build the future. *Family Business Review*, 25: 156–177.

Tappeiner, F., Howorth, C., Achleitner, A. K., & Schraml, S. 2012. Demand for private equity minority investments: A study of large family firms. *Journal of Family Business Strategy*, 3: 38–51.

Thaler, R. H. 1993. *Advances in behavioral finance*. New York: Russell Sage Foundation.

Tranfield, D., Denyer, D., & Smart, P. 2003. Towards a methodology for developing evidence-informed management knowledge by means of systematic review. *British Journal of Management*, 14: 207–222.

Tsang, E. W. 2002. Learning from overseas venturing experience: The case of Chinese family businesses. *Journal of Business Venturing*, 17: 21–40.

Tyebjee, T. T., & Bruno, A. V. 1984. A model of venture capitalist investment activity. *Management Science*, 30: 1051–1066.

Upton, N., & Petty, W. 2000. Venture capital investment and US family business. *Venture Capital*, 2: 27–39.

Villalonga, B., & Amit, R. 2006. How do family ownership, control and management affect firm value? *Journal of Financial Economics*, 80: 385–417.

Wang, D. 2006. Founding family ownership and earnings quality. *Journal of Accounting Research*, 44: 619–656.

Wilson, N., Wright, M., Siegel, D. S., & Scholes, L. 2012. Private equity portfolio company performance during the global recession. *Journal of Corporate Finance*, 18: 193–205.

Wood, G., & Wright, M. 2009. Private equity: A review and synthesis. *International Journal of Management Reviews*, 11: 361–380.

Wright, M., Amess, K., Weir, C., & Girma, S. 2009. Private equity and corporate governance: Retrospect and prospect. *Corporate Governance: An International Review*, 17: 353–375.

Wright, M., & Robbie, K. 1998. Venture capital and private equity: A review and synthesis. *Journal of Business Finance & Accounting*, 25: 521–570.

Wulf, T., Stubner, S., Gietl, R., & Landau, C. 2010. *Private equity and family business: Can private equity investors add to the success of formerly owned family firms*. HHL-Arbeitspapier HHL Working Paper (87).

Zellweger, T. M., & Astrachan, J. H. 2008. On the emotional value of owning a firm. *Family Business Review*, 21: 347–363.

Zellweger, T. M., Kellermanns, F. W., Chrisman, J. J., & Chua, J. H. 2011. Family control and family firm valuation by family CEOs: The importance of intentions for transgenerational control. *Organization Science*, 23: 851–868.

Zellweger, T. M., Nason, R. S., & Nordqvist, M. 2012. From longevity of firms to transgenerational entrepreneurship of families introducing family entrepreneurial orientation. *Family Business Review*, 25: 136–155.

9

BUYOUTS OF FAMILY FIRMS

Company metamorphosis and the family management dyad

Carole Howorth and Nick Robinson

Introduction

Depending on the definition used, at least half – and in many countries three-quarters – of firms are family controlled businesses (IFERA, 2003; Howorth et al., 2010). The Institute for Family Business estimates that in the UK, family businesses represent two-thirds of all firms, that they contribute 47% of private sector employment, and 25% of GDP (IFB, 2017). One third of Fortune 500 firms are family controlled. Family businesses thus represent the dominant business ownership model across the world (IFERA, 2003).

Family firms tend to survive longer than firms under other models of ownership (Wilson et al., 2013). Much family business research emphasizes longevity, and many studies have provided models and recommendations of how families can successfully transfer their business from one generation to the next. Succession provides a critical juncture when the survival and future of the firm is at risk. Large numbers of family firms seek transfer of ownership to a new generation every year; estimates suggest that in the UK, 420,000 family firms will have an ownership succession in the next five years (IFB, 2017). However, there is no guarantee that firms will continue under family ownership, and family succession is not always the best strategy for particular firms or families (Wright, 2001; Niedermayer et al., 2010). Increasingly, management buyouts (MBOs) or buyins (MBIs) are providing a route for family owners to realize their assets (Scholes et al., 2009). Family firms account for a significant percentage of all buyouts (Scholes et al., 2009).

MBO/I research has paid little attention to family business deals (Cumming et al., 2007) and there are only a few relevant studies in the area of family MBO/Is. Two of these studies will be examined in detail in this chapter and will demonstrate that the concepts and circumstances relevant to family firm MBO/Is provide fertile ground for interesting research to not only inform understanding of family MBO/Is but also contribute to understanding MBO/Is in other circumstances. The chapter starts by examining what is different about family controlled businesses, examining available evidence and exploding some myths in order to establish relevant concepts that help explain approaches and behaviors in family firm MBO/Is. The reasons for family business MBO/Is will be explained, followed by an examination of the process for MBO/Is of family firms, with insights into variation in negotiation behaviors and implications for outcomes. Finally, the outcomes of family firm MBO/Is will be examined longitudinally, highlighting that MBO/Is can trigger an increase in firms' professionalization. Evidence will be produced to suggest that family firms can be rejuvenated through the influx of non-family talent and expertise. In the conclusion, we will suggest fruitful areas for further research.

Examining some family business myths

To start, we examine some widely held assumptions about family firms. Often it is assumed that family firms are small "mom and pop" local businesses – and certainly there are many family firms which fit that picture. However, there are also family firms across the size spectrum of businesses, and some of the largest firms in the world, like Walmart, Volkswagen, and Reliance Industries, are family-owned. Family firms are also not restricted to local markets and many are very active internationally (Kontinen & Ojala, 2010; Pukall & Calabrò, 2014). Active international family business networks, like FBN, provide advantages in linking family businesses across countries: studies have identified that families in business seek out other families to collaborate with (Pukall & Calabrò, 2014).

A further assumption might portray family firms as traditional and associate them with a lack of innovation. Certainly, family firms in some industries find a traditional family "born and bred" image helpful for their marketing (e.g., Warburtons Bakers, UK) but such branding does not preclude innovation. It is suggested that a family business brand evokes reliability and trustworthiness, and that family firms may seek an advantage by promoting their relational qualities (Binz et al., 2013). Competing via family branding does not mean that family firms lack innovation; there is variation in the levels of innovation by family firms, just as there is with other types of firms (Chrisman et al., 2015). Many family firms are at the forefront of their industries, and family firms can be extremely innovative through combining the best of innovation and tradition (De Massis et al., 2016). It has been suggested that family is the "oxygen that feeds the fire of entrepreneurship" (Rogoff & Heck, 2003).

The key point to note is that family firms are not a homogenous group, and we should avoid generalizing about the population of family firms (Westhead & Howorth, 2007). Moreover, family control of firms may not be immediately visible, and whereas some family firms emphasize their family ownership and heritage in their marketing, others profile a strong brand with little mention of the family ownership behind the brands (Binz Astrachan & Astrachan, 2015). For example, Pentland Brands is controlled by the Rubin family, but consumers will be much more familiar with their individual brands such as Speedo, Berghaus, Mitre, or Kickers – fashion brands that may not necessarily benefit from being associated with family business (Binz Astrachan & Astrachan, 2015).

Some of these misconceptions may explain the lack of emphasis, until recently, on family firms within MBO/I research. Family firms could mistakenly be assumed to be too small to be of interest for MBO/Is, or not provide sufficient income potential. It might also be assumed that families are only interested in intergenerational succession, and selling the firm is viewed as a failure or last resort. However, studies show that some families are not interested in passing the firm on to the next generation (Howorth et al., 2004), as we will see when we examine reasons for MBO/Is later in this chapter. The numbers and frequency of MBO/Is indicate that family firms account for the most significant and increasing proportion of deals (Scholes et al., 2009).

What's different about families in business?

To understand the reasons for – and process of – MBO/Is in family firms, it is important to identify how family firms differ from non-family firms. As noted earlier, family firms are not a homogeneous group (Westhead & Howorth, 2007), and we cannot generalize. However, we can gain an understanding of the particular influences that family owners might face, which are not (or not so much) an issue for non-family firms. The differences for family-owned firms compared to non-family-owned firms arise from the varying permutations of ownership, management, and family stakeholders who have an influence on the firm. A basic "three circles" model (Tagiuri & Davis, 1982) can be employed to map out the individuals involved in the firm, where family, ownership, or management interests might overlap and consider the formal and informal channels of communication that might influence decision-making in the family firm. An interesting aspect of family firms is that individuals, particularly those within the family circle, can have a strong psychological ownership (Pierce et al., 2001) perspective on the firm, even when they have no financial or legal ownership. Such individuals might have an influence on decision-making that can be powerful, either directly or indirectly, through their influence on other family members.

Shares in family firms, particularly firms that are three generations old or more, might be owned by a complex array of cousins, aunts, uncles, siblings, parents, and grandparents. Dispersed family shareholdings can create ownership issues as each generation swells the number of individual nuclear families within the branches of the family tree. Family shareholders who are distant from the firm might be more interested in dividends and financial returns than family owner-managers (Schulze et al., 2001). Occasionally, factions can develop within separate groups or branches of family members leading to tension, disputes or outright "family wars" (Gordon & Nicholson, 2010). Shares that have been gifted from another family member can evoke strong emotional attachment in the giftee and be valued highly (Kahneman et al., 1990), in line with the endowment effect (Thaler, 1980). Psychological ownership coupled with the endowment effect can lead to minority shareholders believing that they should have a greater say in the firm's future than might be expected of minority shareholders in other types of companies.

Family involvement and psychological ownership of the firm can lead to a range of competing objectives for family businesses. For example, family members may consider it important that the firm provides employment to family members, or that the CEO is a family member (Westhead & Howorth, 2006). Non-family managers may emphasize short-term financial returns, whereas family members might emphasize long-term investments (Westhead & Howorth, 2006; Corbetta & Salvato, 2012). Many family firms have a tendency not to separate ownership and management, which is especially noticeable in relation to succession, particularly in family-owned and managed companies. However, some family firms have agreed governance policies, processes, and structures (such as family councils, active boards, independent directors, family constitutions) that separate family and business decisions, aiming to ensure that an appropriate balance is maintained between family preferences and business needs (Westhead & Howorth, 2006).

Of particular relevance is that some family members might believe retaining ownership within the family is an incontrovertible objective, and therefore any sale of the business is complete anathema to them. Disagreements on this objective can lead to family conflict and delay – or even halt – negotiations in a sale or MBO/I. Niedermayer et al. (2010) identify that owning families might adopt a stakeholder approach where a range of financial and non-financial objectives could be at play, whereas potential buyers are likely to adopt a shareholder approach to business, emphasizing financial returns and short-term horizons. Niedermayer et al. (2010) suggest that families may prefer a "strategic buyer" over a financial investor, to align their aspirations for the firm and their utility from the sale. Strategic buyers might be expected to take a longer-term view and focus more on strategic vision and less on company value relative to financial investors (Lipman, 2001). Family members with strong psychological ownership of the firm are likely to care about the future of the firm post-sale and therefore perceive a more satisfactory deal where there is high goal alignment with a buyer in terms of the expected post-sale culture, development, and performance objectives (Graebner & Eisenhardt, 2004; Niedermayer et al., 2010).

MBOs and MBIs are likely to have different attractions for family-owned businesses. Some families may have a preference for MBO rather than MBI, because an MBO provides them with greater potential for continuity of the family ethos and continued involvement of themselves or family members, either in the MBO team or as advisors (Howorth et al., 2004). However, family members included in the MBO team are likely to have dual loyalties, to exiting family members and to the business going forward, which need to be recognized during negotiations.

Howorth et al. (2004) identify that in contrast to the presumed strong psychological ownership, some family owners have no desire or intention to continue in the business post-sale. Senior family members may also be ambivalent about the next generation becoming involved in the family business, particularly where their own experience has been negative (Howorth et al., 2016a). An MBI may be preferred because it provides a new management team without any ties to members of the family. Unlike other groups of investors who may have no future dealings with each other, family members have a shared future, and family relationships continue beyond their exit of the firm. Howorth et al. (2004) highlight that differences in expectations and powerful emotions can lead to a breakdown in the family relationship during the MBO process. One of the families in their study faced a rift between father and son during the MBO negotiations that was never mended.

The differences between family and non-family businesses thus originate from combining family relationships, ambitions, and emotions with business rationalities and objectives. These differences come to the fore during succession, and many studies have examined succession in family businesses to establish understanding and recommendations. Family owners who ignore succession risk the future of the business; family-owned business failures precipitated by the unexpected death of the owner are not uncommon, yet strong emotional attachments to the firm continue to generate resistance to succession (Morris et al., 1997). Retiring can be associated with admitting mortality, and it is recommended that succession plans consider proposals for the exitees which ensure that their role is clear and purposeful, whether their departure is through family succession, sale, or MBO/I (Sonnenfeld, 1988).

The numerous studies that have examined family business succession usually do so under the normative assumption that family succession is the ideal. Fewer studies have examined alternatives to family succession (Howorth et al., 2004). Niedermayer et al. (2010) examined family businesses that had been sold to non-family parties, providing an interesting assessment of the families' perspectives. Elsewhere in this book, vendors' reasons for a buyout are delineated. Reasons can be summarized as: business reasons that make the firm unsustainable in its present form or unable to satisfy expectations, and personal reasons relating to the life-stage or particular circumstances of the vendors, including illness and retirement, but also a desire to pursue alternative interests or business opportunities. Business-owning families might have additional, specific reasons to seek an MBO of their family firm. As mentioned earlier, family ownership becomes more dispersed through the generations: a greater number of family owners have smaller percentages of shares individually, and there might be a greater emphasis on short-term financial returns for many of these share owners, with less interest in the longer-term objectives of the firm. The dividend expectations of such family minority owners might diminish the firm's investment capability.

Family owners may be more vocal in their expectations for the firm than non-family shareholders in a public company, due to psychological ownership and family relationships that provide them with a platform for airing their views. Family members may be perceived by family managers as interfering excessively. It is not uncommon for older generations of family owners to press their views on younger generations after they have officially retired. Younger family members may be entrenched in previous generations' methods and beliefs. A unique characteristic of families is their shared past, and sometimes emotions and conflicts from the past can resurface in the context of business ownership. Confronting some or all of these issues might provoke conflict between minority family shareholders and family managers. For some family owner-managers, the solution is an MBO, to prune the family tree and reconfigure the ownership of the family business, as an alternative to a share buyback, providing an opportunity for entrepreneurial renewal (Wright, 2001).

Buyouts or buyins might therefore be sought as an alternative to family succession, either permanently or for a certain period. An MBO or an MBI can provide a transition stage for some business families until the next generation is experienced or old enough. Howorth et al. (2016b) demonstrated this, finding that an MBO/I can provide an important transitory phase that enables family firms to establish processes and systems that professionalize the firm. An experienced non-family CEO can work alongside potential family successors to develop their skills and experience. Howorth et al. (2004) provide examples of families turning to existing non-family managers to join next generation family managers in an MBO, in one case because the incumbent family owner CEO was ill and in another because the next generation were not deemed competent to undertake a leadership role. Not all families in business seek family succession. Senior family members might consider that the next generation would be better placed outside the family business, and/or next generation family members may express no interest in joining the family firm (Howorth et al., 2016a). However, Howorth et al. (2016a) highlight that next generation family members who have no interest in joining the firm in their teens or early twenties often change their minds later in their career.

Niedermayer et al. (2010) showed that business-owning families consider a different set of factors to non-family owners when contemplating the sale of their firm. Specifically, the family-owned sale takes longer than for a non-family-owned concern. For some business-owning families, the sale of their business might be considered a failure (Niedermayer et al., 2010), but a sale can also trigger a new wave of entrepreneurship for the family (DeTienne, 2010), providing funds and experience to invest in new ventures (Mason & Harrison, 2006). For the firms, a sale can generate entrepreneurial renewal (Wright, 2001) and professionalization (Howorth et al., 2016b).

Negotiation, trust, and conflict in the buyout process

The three main phases of the buyout process are pre-deal, doing the deal, and post-deal. Pre-deal is concerned with the motivation for buyout and the identification of interested parties, i.e., vendors and acquirers. Doing the deal involves all the stages of search, due diligence, negotiation, structure, and contracting (Wright & Robbie, 1998). Post-deal is concerned with performance, implications, and impact of the buyout (Wright & Robbie, 1998). Howorth et al. (2004) employed agency, trust, and negotiation theories in a complementary conceptual framework to examine the buyout process in family firms. Their evidence disputes the assumption that family firm buyouts likely progress more smoothly than other types of buyout due to fewer information asymmetries and closer working relationships between the buyout team and family owners. Some of the families in their study faced unresolved conflict during the buyout process, resulting in terminal breakdowns of family relationships. Only one of Howorth et al.'s (2004) eight cases exhibited the lower information asymmetries, higher levels of trust, and co-operative behavior that theoretically could be assumed to be associated with family firm MBO/Is.

Howorth et al.'s (2004) study examined MBO/Is that completed in the same year (1998), and adopted a rigorous dyadic approach to data collection, interviewing the former family owners (i.e., vendors) and the acquiring MBO/I teams, thereby providing valuable insights into the MBO/I process. Triangulation of responses from vendors and acquirers of the same firms strengthened the validity of the results. Drawing on qualitative data, Howorth et al. (2004) corroborated the varying reasons for buyouts detailed earlier. It was noted that family owners wishing to realize their assets may prefer an MBO/I over a trade sale because they believe that this would more likely retain the identity of the firm in which they have invested emotions and effort (Brundin & Härtel, 2014), and secure job prospects of employees and management with whom they might have an emotional attachment. An MBO might also be preferred by family owners wishing to maintain some involvement in the firm (Scholes et al., 2007). Personal circumstances (e.g., illness, divorce, remarriage) or owners' attitudes (e.g., towards offspring, finances) frequently trigger the MBO/I process in family firms.

Howorth et al. (2004) noted that agency theory would predict information asymmetry issues to be less prevalent in family firms, because the firms are frequently owner-managed and family members have close relationships with managers. However, information flows might be more complex due to the intertwining of family, business, and ownership systems (Tagiuri & Davis, 1982), and family priorities might have a strong influence on business decisions. Knowledge transfer may be a particular issue when the firm is reliant on tacit knowledge held within the family. Information asymmetries might be acute where the family system dominates, to the extent that an inside MBO team might have little informational advantage compared to an external MBI team. Information asymmetries were expected to influence the price of the firm and the perception of fairness of the price ex post.

The findings showed variations in information asymmetries across the cases, with high information asymmetries associated with weaker performance after MBO/I, due to the firm being over-valued and/or lack of knowledge transfer, particularly in relation to social capital. Perceptions of fairness were related to the level of trust between owners and managers, which also influenced information flows, in that high levels of trust between family owners and potential MBO/I teams were associated with lower levels of information asymmetry. However, unfamiliarity with the MBO/I process reduced levels of trust, particularly where trust was dependence based.

Negotiation theory provided insights into the behavior of the parties involved in the MBO/I process, including how the negotiation might play out and their post-deal relationship and behaviors. Close relationships between family and non-family members alongside commitments to the long-term success of the firm were expected to be associated with co-operative negotiations working towards a win-win solution. However, where individuals adopt a short-term perspective and aim to maximize individual gains, negotiations will be less co-operative and more opportunistic (Day & Klein, 1987).

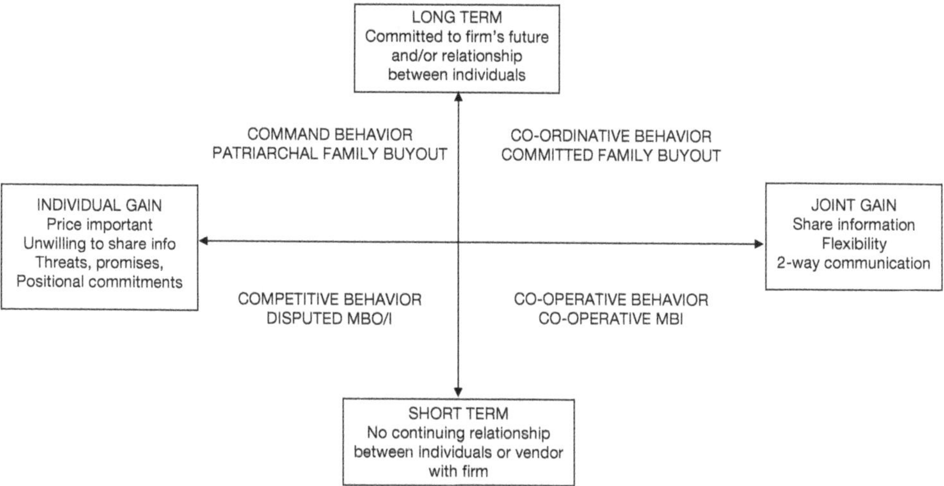

Figure 9.1 Negotiation behaviors

Source: Howorth et al. (2004), adapted from Dabholkar et al. (1994).

Figure 9.1 (reproduced from Howorth et al., 2004) provides a representation of the potential negotiating positions in a family MBO/I, based on Dabholkar et al. (1994) who proposed that negotiation behaviors can be classified according to the expected time dimension of the relationship and whether individual or joint gains were emphasized. Patriarchal family firm vendors are expected to exhibit "command" behavior (upper left quadrant), in which they aim to maximize their individual objectives, as well as being committed to the future of the firm. They likely have strong views on what they believe is best for the firm, which may include a continuing role for family members after the MBO/MBI deal. Where both vendors and purchasers take a short-term perspective, concerned only with maximizing their individual positions, "competitive" behaviors (lower left quadrant) are most likely, with a strong emphasis on price. In both cases, an unwillingness to share information is likely, and behaviors may include threats, promises, persuasive arguments, and positional commitments. Where both parties recognize the value of maximizing joint gains (i.e., win-win solutions), information asymmetries will be lower. Where joint gains and long-term relationships are important, "coordinative" behaviors (upper right quadrant) will be evident, characterized by flexibility and extensive information sharing. Because families are often committed to the long-term future of a firm, beyond their financial ownership, "coordinative" behavior may be more prevalent than in other types of MBO/I. A shared objective may be knowledge transfer, requiring a continuing role for one or more family members. "Co-operative" behavior (lower right quadrant) occurs where there is a short-term focus on joint gain; this may be present in MBIs where there is no relationship between the parties pre- or post-deal, and the focus is on co-operating to secure the best deal for vendors and acquiring teams.

Howorth et al.'s (2004) findings showed that information asymmetries provided an advantage in deal negotiations, but this was mitigated by good relationships and trust. Knowledge transfer was facilitated when the MBO/I was planned and part of a long-term strategy, rather than forced upon a firm through sudden illness or a change in circumstances.

Aside from the deal itself, there is the issue of the post-deal perspective. Niedermayer et al. (2010) develop a model that assesses family satisfaction immediately after the sale and retrospectively, based on a utility function of financial and non-financial factors. Niedermayer et al. (2010) propose that in line with procedural justice, satisfaction is increased where decision-making is democratic, in line with explicit agreed policies and not dominated by one individual. Most business-owning families consist of multiple shareholders from varying generations, which could result in protracted negotiations and test the patience of the buying team. The implications of this for the selling family in an MBO/I are that the process might take longer than for a non-family firm.

A major element in the buyout process is determining a price for the business. The endowment effect (Thaler, 1980) provides an explanation for why families might place a higher value on the business than the perceived market rate. The endowment effect, which identifies that an individual will place a higher value on something that they own than they would be willing to pay to acquire it, is enhanced when that item has been given to them (Kahneman et al., 1990), and we might expect that effect to be particularly extreme when the giver is someone with whom they have an emotional bond. Family businesses that have been passed down from generation to generation could therefore have a higher value placed on them by the current generation of family owners than might be perceived externally. Different models that have been proposed to capture the total value of a family business to the owning family include that by Astrachan and Jaskiewicz (2008), who proposed that total value of the business to the family was the sum of "emotional value" and financial value. Emotional value includes family involvement, educational opportunities, and independence, minus negatives such as family conflict and sibling rivalry. Gomez-Mejia et al. (2007) capture similar themes in their model of socio-emotional wealth, which highlights the value attached to the social and emotional benefits of family firms.

In addition to explaining negotiation behaviors, the concepts of psychological ownership, emotional value, and socio-emotional wealth all help to explain why families might find it especially difficult to step away from the business post-sale. Niedermayer et al. (2010: 301) suggest that "Leaving the company to new owners can be one of the most difficult transitions that a family has to face." Families may seek to retain influence over the company in some form, and psychological ownership may stimulate their interest for many years following a sale, even when they have no active involvement (Howorth et al., 2016b; Scholes et al., 2007). Family vendors may formally request to be kept informed about major changes affecting the company or they may seek information informally through contact with employees. Their influence on employees may continue post-sale and impact decision-making. Family vendors might also attempt to inject terms into the sale that allow their influence to continue (Scholes et al., 2007).

To summarize, while agency theory and particularly information asymmetries have some relevance to family business MBO/Is, the process is influenced by family factors, such as trust, relationships, and emotions, factors that are not captured by agency theory. The long-term perspective and emotional attachments associated with family-owned businesses help to explain why family owners may seek a high price and continuing post-deal involvement. However, variations were observed, highlighting the importance of not over-generalizing about the population of family firms. Figure 9.2 reproduces the conceptual framework that Howorth et al. (2004) produced to explain the MBO/I process. Figure 9.2 indicates that the structure of family, ownership, and management will influence the balance of information, trust, and relationships which in turn influence negotiation behavior. Negotiation behavior will affect deal outcomes that affect post-deal satisfaction and knowledge transfer. Howorth

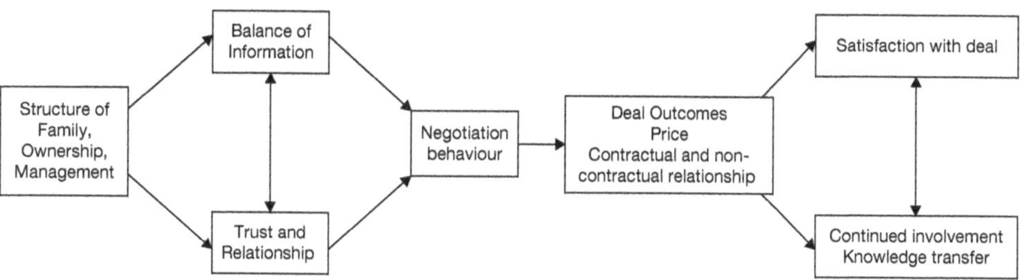

Figure 9.2 Influences on MBO/I process outcomes

Source: Howorth et al. (2004).

et al. (2004) intimated that knowledge transfer could be particularly important for the post-deal performance of the firm.

Professionalization through MBO/I in family firms

Howorth and colleagues followed up with further data collection and analysis of the same cases to explore the long-term impact of MBOs and MBIs on family firms. In their subsequent paper, Howorth et al. (2016b) provided a longitudinal analysis of six MBO/Is of family firms, from 1998–2014. Their study highlighted that in addition to providing an alternative to family succession and a means of restructuring family ownership, MBO/Is of former family firms could also provide an accelerator for the professionalization necessary for medium-sized companies to achieve their potential.

Howorth et al. (2016b) emphasize that professionalization is not a once and for all threshold development stage, as had previously been suggested in the literature, but is a multi-faceted ongoing process (Stewart & Hitt, 2012; Dekker et al., 2015). Howorth et al.'s (2016b) longitudinal analysis showed that professionalization was likely to occur in waves, triggered by changes in ownership and management, and that MBO/Is were particularly important triggers. The focus of professionalization activity was likely to vary at different points in the firm's development, contingent on firm-specific contexts and influenced by agency costs and stewardship relationships.

Figure 9.3 presents different phases of professionalization, alongside relevant explanatory theories, and demonstrates that the MBO/I process has a funneling effect, whereby diverse control systems converge into a standardized set of controls and governance mechanisms. Prior to the MBO/I, variation in the extent and specifics of control and governance mechanisms was observed. Entering into the MBO/I process was associated with formalization of policies and processes and structuring the firm for sale. If formal governance mechanisms, regular and frequent reporting systems, and planning and control systems were not already in place, the new ownership would implement them, resulting in standardization and convergence. Post-MBO/I, professionalization continued, but the actual mechanisms and controls diverged, contingent on firm-specific circumstances. Professionalization focuses on operations when stewardship relationships predominate, but on agency control mechanisms when there is increased potential for agency costs.

Figure 9.4 presents Howorth et al.'s (2016b) representation of the waves of professionalization. Professionalization develops from an ad hoc contingent approach through formalization and standardization triggered by the MBO/I process, followed by adaptation contingent

Figure 9.3 Funneling effect of MBO/I on professionalization

Source: Howorth et al. (2016b).

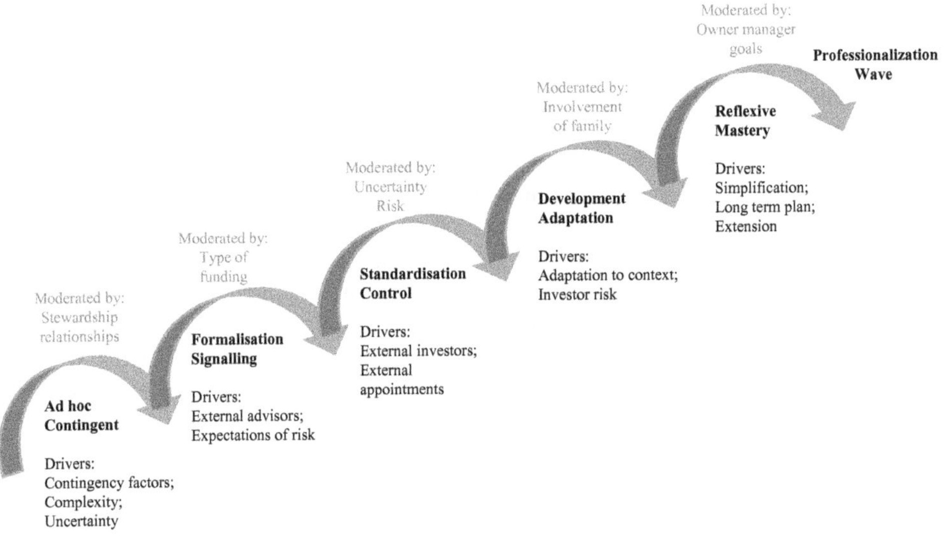

Figure 9.4 Waves of professionalization: drivers and moderators

Source: Howorth et al. (2016b).

on firm-specific needs towards mastery, characterized by reflexive management. Figure 9.4 presents the drivers and moderators of each wave of professionalization. Of particular note, the MBO/I process drives professionalization through the introduction of external advisors, investors, and appointments, alongside increased risk management.

Howorth et al.'s (2016b) study provides an important contribution in demonstrating that professionalization is a process occurring in waves, which intensify with firm ownership and management changes. The MBO/I is an important transitory phase requiring former family firms to introduce formalized management control systems; the buyout presents a funneling mechanism whereby systems and controls are standardized. Post-MBO/I increased variation in control systems and processes are contingent upon different types of ownership change, as well as levels of continuing family involvement associated with the relative importance of long- or short-term goals. This study of family firm MBO/Is contributes to an understanding of how successful MBO/Is can provide an important mechanism for ensuring the foundations are in place for regeneration and entrepreneurial renewal of firms (Wright, 2001; DeTienne, 2010).

Conclusions

This chapter has shown that MBO/Is of family firms are not just a means for family firms' shareholders to realize their assets. MBOs may be employed by family owners to reduce the influence or dispersion of family owners. Introduction of external management expertise may provide an important transitory phase for family-owned firms that wish to retain majority ownership within the family but have no suitable family successors available. This chapter has provided an insight into some of the specific issues that family MBO/Is might encounter. Recognition of some of the emotional and psychological factors that might influence the family MBO/I process helps to improve understanding of how negotiation and outcomes might vary.

Positive outcomes of an MBO/I of family firms include increased professionalization and entrepreneurial renewal, which provide the foundations for the firm to succeed in its next phase of ownership. Fresh skills can be introduced by incoming managers who might have different perspectives and a new vision for the family firm. Such benefits are not restricted to former family firms, and further research is required to establish the extent to which other types of firms, e.g., owner-managed firms, might achieve professionalization and entrepreneurial benefits from MBO/Is.

Further research is needed to investigate the extent to which MBOs are effective in pruning the family ownership tree. Interesting questions might investigate under what circumstances it is advantageous to rid the firm of distant family shareholders, and what the implications are for the family's entrepreneurial future and family relationships. Further longitudinal studies are required and would be particularly helpful in exploring how family owners might use an MBO as a transition phase to professionalize the firm and inject external influence, either during a succession gap or as an alternative to family management. The studies by Howorth et al. provided examples of firms that failed post-MBO/I and family relationships that were damaged during the MBO/I process. Further longitudinal studies could provide helpful insights into the pitfalls that families and MBO/I teams should avoid if they wish to have successful firms and positive relationships.

Studies suggest that an important reason for family owners considering MBOs over other forms of sale might be the expectation that the firm's ethos and the family heritage might continue. Further research is required to test this assumption and to examine how post-MBO/I performance is influenced by continuation, or rejection, of aspects of the family heritage. This research might also include exploration of the impact of the loss of the family owners' tacit knowledge and social capital following the buyout on the subsequent performance of the firm. There is some anecdotal evidence for example that buyouts of family firms are subsequently bought back by the family owners when the firms run into trading problems because of the loss of this knowledge. Finally, the issues that family firms bring to the MBO/I process may occur in other types of firms, particularly owner-managed firms. For example, other owner-managers may have strong psychological ownership of their firm that affects their behavior during the deal process and their expectations post-deal. Future studies could usefully explore the concepts and issues highlighted as relevant in MBO/Is of family firms to identify new insights into non-family firms.

Family firms are an important sector of the MBO/I market and by gaining a more complete understanding of their motivations, behaviors, and performance before and after a buyout, outcomes should be improved for all stakeholders.

References

Astrachan, J. H., & Jaskiewicz, P. 2008. Emotional returns and emotional costs in privately held family firms: Advancing traditional business valuation. *Family Business Review*, 21: 139–149.

Binz, C., Hair, J. F. Jr., Pieper, T. M., & Baldauf A. 2013. Exploring the effect of distinct family firm reputation on consumers' preferences. *Journal of Family Business Strategy*, 4: 3–11.

Binz Astrachan, C., & Astrachan, J. 2015. *Family business branding: Leveraging stakeholder trust.* London: IFB Research Foundation.

Brundin, E., & Härtel, C. E. J. 2014. Emotions in family firms. In L. Melin, M. Nordqvist & P. Sharma (Eds.), *The SAGE handbook of family business*. London: Sage, 529–548.

Chrisman, J. J, Chua, J. H., De Massis, A., Frattini, F., & Wright, M. 2015. The ability and willingness paradox in family firm innovation. *Journal of Product Innovation Management*, 32: 310–318.

Corbetta, G., & Salvato, C. 2012. *Strategies for longevity in family firms: A European perspective.* Basingstoke, UK: Palgrave MacMillan/Bocconi University Press.

Cumming, D., Siegel, D. S., & Wright, M. 2007. Private equity, leveraged buyouts and governance. *Journal of Corporate Finance*, 13: 439–460.

Dabholkar, P. A., Johnston, W. A., & Cathey, A. S. 1994. The dynamics of long term business-to-business exchange relationships. *Journal of the Academy of Marketing Science*, 22: 130–145.

Day, G. S., & Klein, S. 1987. Cooperative behavior in vertical markets: The influence of transactions costs and competitive strategies. In M. J. Houston (Ed.), *Review of marketing*. Minnesota, MN: American Marketing Association, 39–66.

Dekker, J., Lybaert, N., Steijvers, T., & Depaire B. 2015. The effect of family business professionalization as a multidimensional construct on firm performance. *Journal of Small Business Management*, 53: 516–538.

De Massis, A., Frattini, F., Kotlar, J., Petruzelli, A. M., & Wright, M. 2016. Innovation through tradition: Lessons from innovative family businesses and directions for future research. *Academy of Management Perspectives*, 30: 93–116.

DeTienne, D. R. 2010. Entrepreneurial exit as a critical component of the entrepreneurial process: Theoretical development. *Journal of Business Venturing*, 25: 203–215.

Gomez-Mejia, L. R., Haynes, K., Nuñez-Nickel, M., Jacobson, K. J. L., & Moyano-Fuentes, J. 2007. Socioemotional wealth and business risks in family-controlled firms: Evidence from Spanish olive oil mills. *Administrative Science Quarterly*, 52: 106–137.

Gordon, G., & Nicholson, N. 2010. *Family wars: Stories and insights from famous family business feuds*. London: Kogan Page.

Graebner, M. E., & Eisenhardt, K. M. 2004. The seller's side of the story: Acquisition as courtship and governance as syndicate in entrepreneurial firms. *Administrative Science Quarterly*, 49: 366–403.

Howorth, C., Parkinson, C., Stead, V., & Leitch, C. 2016a. *Next generation engagement in family businesses*. London: IFB Research Foundation.

Howorth, C., Rose, M., Hamilton, E., & Westhead P. 2010. Family firm diversity and development. *International Small Business Journal*, 28: 1–15.

Howorth, C., Westhead, P., & Wright, M. 2004. Buyouts information asymmetry and the family management dyad. *Journal of Business Venturing*, 19: 509–534.

Howorth, C., Wright, M., Westhead, P., & Allcock D. 2016b. Company metamorphosis: Professionalization waves, family firms and management buyouts. *Small Business Economics*, 47: 803–817.

IFB. 2017. *UK family business. Available at: www.ifb.org.uk/voice/uk-family-business.*

IFERA. 2003. Family businesses dominate. *Family Business Review*, 16: 235–240.

Kahneman, D., Knetsch, J. L., & Thaler, R. H. 1990. Experimental tests of the endowment effect and the coase theorem. *Journal of Political Economy*, 98: 1325–1348.

Kontinen, T., & Ojala, A. 2010. The internationalization of family businesses: A review of extant research. *Journal of Family Business Strategy*, 1: 97–107.

Lipman, D. L. 2001. *The complete guide to valuing and selling your business*. Roseville, CA: Prima Publishing.

Mason, C. M., & Harrison, R. T. 2006. After the exit: Acquisitions, entrepreneurial recycling and regional economic development. *Regional Studies*, 40: 55–73.

Morris, M. H., Williams, R. O., Allen, J. A., & Avila, R. A. 1997. Correlates of success in family business transitions. *Journal of Business Venturing*, 12: 341–422.

Niedermayer, C., Jaskiewicz, P., & Klein, S. B. 2010. 'Can't get no satisfaction?' Evaluating the sale of the family business from the family's perspective and deriving implications for new venture activities. *Entrepreneurship & Regional Development*, 22: 293–320.

Pierce, J. L., Kostova, T., & Dirks, K. 2001. Toward a theory of psychological ownership in organizations. *Academy of Management Review*, 26: 298–310.

Pukall, T., & Calabrò, A. 2014. The internationalization of family firms: A critical review and integrative model. *Family Business Review*, 27: 103–125.

Rogoff, E. G., & Heck, R. K. Z. 2003. Evolving research in entrepreneurship and family business: Recognizing family as the oxygen that feeds the fire of entrepreneurship. *Journal of Business Venturing*, 18: 559–566.

Scholes, M. L., Wright, M., Westhead, P., Bruining, H., & Kloeckner O. 2009. Family firm buyouts, private equity and strategic change. *Journal of Private Equity*, 12: 7–18.

Scholes, M. L., Wright, M., Westhead, P., Burrows, A., & Bruining. H. 2007. Information sharing, price negotiation and management buy-outs of private family-owned firms. *Small Business Economics*, 29: 329–349.

Schulze, W. S., Lubatkin, M. H., Dino, R. N., & Buchholtz, A. K. 2001. Agency relationships in family firms: Theory and evidence. *Organization Science*, 12: 99–116.

Sonnenfeld, J. 1988. *The hero's farewell: What happens when CEOs retire*. New York: Oxford University Press.

Stewart, A., & Hitt, M. A. 2012. Why can't a family business be more like a nonfamily business? Modes of professionalization in family firms. *Family Business Review*, 25: 58–86.

Tagiuri, R., & Davis, J. A. 1982. *Bivalent attributes of the family firm*. Working Paper. Cambridge, MA: Harvard Business School. Reprinted 1996 in Family Business Review 9(2): 199–208.

Thaler, R. 1980. Toward a positive theory of consumer choice. *Journal of Economic Behavior & Organization*, 1: 39–60.

Westhead, P., & Howorth, C. 2006. Ownership and management issues associated with family firm performance and company objectives. *Family Business Review*, 19: 301–316.

Westhead, P., & Howorth, C. 2007. 'Types' of private family firms: An exploratory conceptual and empirical analysis. *Entrepreneurship & Regional Development*, 19: 405–431.

Wilson, N., Wright, M., & Scholes, L. 2013. Family business survival and the role of boards. *Entrepreneurship Theory and Practice*, 37: 1369–1389.

Wright, M. 2001. Firm rebirth: Buyouts as facilitators of strategic growth and entrepreneurship. *Academy of Management Executive*, 15: 111–125.

Wright, M., & Robbie, K. 1998. Venture capital and private equity: A review and synthesis. *Journal of Business Finance & Accounting*, 25: 521–570.

10
BUYOUTS FROM FAILURE

Louise Scholes

Introduction

In times of recession there is always an increase in the number company bankruptcies (insolvencies) and therefore an accompanying increase in the number of management buyouts and management buyins[1] from these failed companies. Most buyouts from insolvency are purchases of parts of failed groups rather than attempts to rescue whole firms (Robbie et al., 1993; Scholes & Wright, 2009). A good example of this is the buyout of Denby from Coloroll. The parent company Coloroll ran into financial difficulties and was forced to sell Denby (see Case 2). The over-expansion of companies with debt-financed acquisitions when times are good is often the reason that these companies go into insolvency when times are not so good (Robbie et al., 1993). These failed companies have to shed their acquisitions, which are themselves often healthy entities. The acquired firms are then acquired again but by their own management team, an incoming management team, a private equity (PE)[2] firm, or a combination. Attempting to rescue whole failing firms may be a more complex task requiring significant strategic changes as well as management changes and restructuring. In these cases PE firms or incoming management teams need to have significant turnaround expertise if they are to succeed.

From a theoretical perspective buyouts have been explored mainly from an agency perspective but also more recently from an entrepreneurship perspective. The agency perspective of buyouts was initially proposed by Jensen (1989) and was based on PE buyouts of publicly listed firms. It suggested that agency cost reduction (i.e., the cost of persuading managers to act in the interest of owners) occurs as a result of three main changes that take place in a buyout. First, the management of the company become the new owners (along with PE firms) thus aligning objectives of owners and managers. Second, an increase in the amount of debt in the firm's financial structure means they must become more efficient to service the debt. Third, PE-imposed governance changes to the board, monitoring by PE, along with new managerial incentives, are aimed at ensuring performance improvements. By contrast the entrepreneurship perspective (Wright et al., 2000) considers buyouts as a catalyst for entrepreneurial activity which has already been shown to occur in buyouts of family firms (Scholes et al., 2010) and divestment buyouts from larger firms (Meuleman et al., 2009). In the case of buyouts from the receiver, those from failed independent companies may require significant restructuring and improvements in efficiency so may fit more with the agency perspective of buyouts proposed by Jensen. Those from failed parent companies may or may not require efficiency improvements but will certainly also have the opportunity to develop their company in new directions as they become free of the constraints imposed by the former parent company.

The following sections look at the general characteristics of these buyouts, PE involvement, post-buyout performance, three case studies, future research, and finally a summary.

General characteristics of buyouts from failure

The trend in the number and value of buyouts from insolvency from 1985 to 2016, taken from the Centre for Management Buy-out Research database[3] is shown in Figure 10.1. Buyouts from firms in insolvency initially peaked in the depth of the recession of the early 1990s, with 105 deals in 1991 accounting for 18.1% of the deal volume. A second, lower peak occurred in the much shallower recession of the early 2000s with 78 deals completed in 2002, accounting for 12.1% of deal volume. The deep recession of 2008 and 2009 saw a sharp increase in buyouts of companies from insolvency reaching 114 deals in 2009, accounting for this source's highest ever share of the market at 28.7% of deals. The total value of buyouts from insolvency reached its highest ever level in 2012 at £1.8 billion (10.3% of total deal value), but it was also significant in 2005 and 2009, when value reached £1.15 billion and £1.13 billion respectively (4.6% and 18.6% of total deal value respectively).

The relationship between the UK recessionary periods and the proportion of buyouts from insolvency is shown in Figure 10.2. It is clear that the proportion of buyouts from insolvency (in relation to all types of buyout) increases during recessions (represented by the falls in GDP) as firms in the general population fail.

Buyouts of firms from insolvency have occurred across a wide range of industries, being most numerous since the late 2000s in manufacturing, followed by retail, technology, media, and telecommunications (TMT), and business and support services (Table 10.1). However,

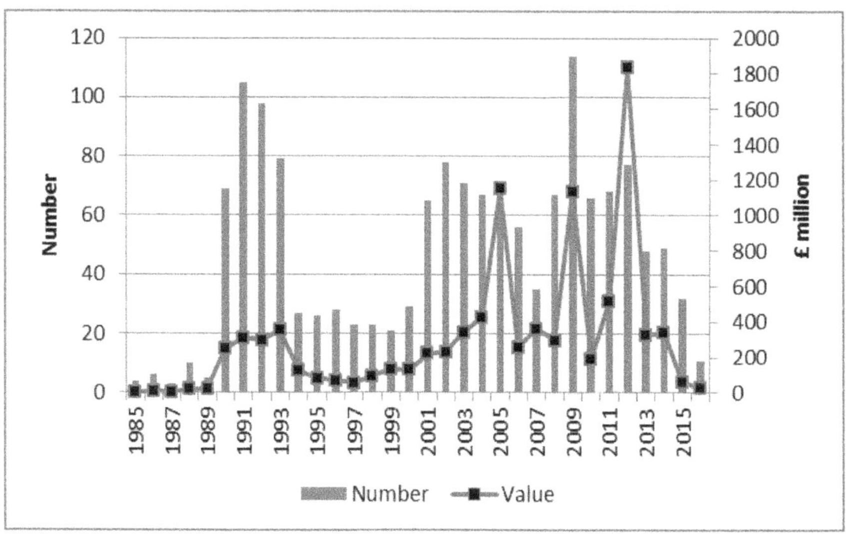

Figure 10.1 Buyouts of failure firms in the UK

Source: CMBOR/Equistone Partners Europe/Investec Bank.

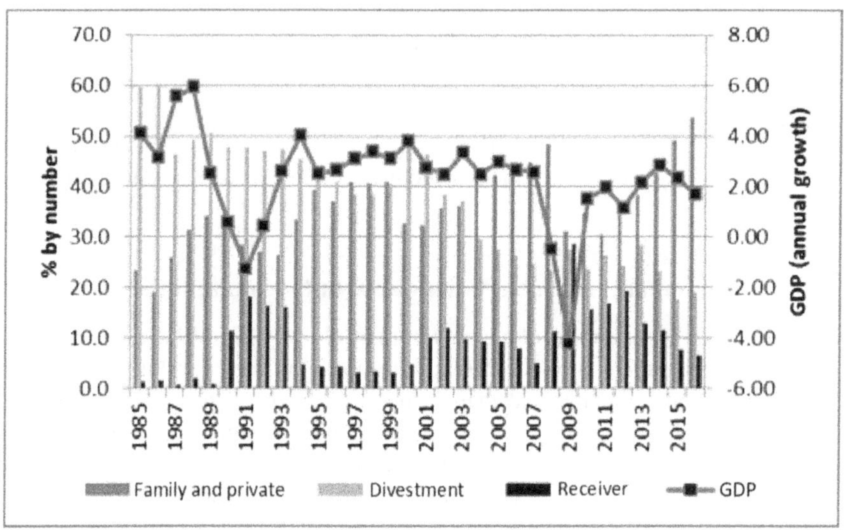

Figure 10.2 Source of buyouts from failed firms versus GDP[4] in the UK

Source: CMBOR/Equistone Partners Europe/Investec Bank.

Table 10.1 Sector distribution of buyouts from failed firms in the UK

Sector group	*2000–2014*	*2001–2003*	*2008–2012*	*2012–14*
Business and support services	95	15	45	19
Financial services	30	6	20	2
Food and drink	56 (15.5)	13 (13.8)	24 (28.6)	8 (18.6)
Healthcare	14	4	7	4
Leisure	80 (14.7)	9 (7.6)	42 (31.6)	21 (18.3)
Manufacturing	304	90	93	52
Other	76	13	29	12
Paper, print, publish	50	16	13	6
Property and construction	32 (8.0)	4 (4.1)	19 (19.0)	9 (22.0)
Retail	120 (20.2)	11 (9.2)	64 (36.6)	26 (34.2)
TMT	79 (7.38)	29 (10.2)	28 (10.2)	12 (7.6)
Transport and communications	19	4	8	3

Source: CMBOR/Equistone Partners Europe/Investec.

Note the percentage refers to the number of buyouts from failure in a particular sector divided by the number of all buyouts in that particular sector.

there are notable similarities between the earlier and later parts since 2000. The number of buyouts from failed firms in the TMT sector was high in the 2001–2003 period, reflecting the collapse of the dot.com boom, and high again in the most recent recessionary period (2008–2012). In the recent recession this was due to consolidation in the TV/radio/newspaper/magazine businesses as well as difficulties in the marketing sector. There are, however, some

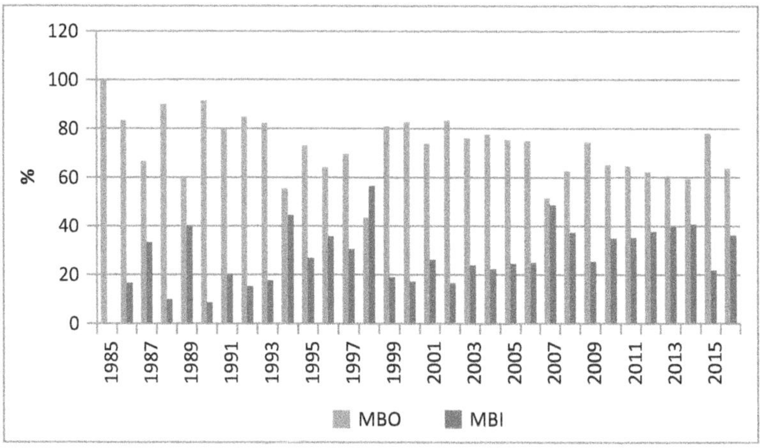

Figure 10.3 Buyouts versus buyins of failed firms in the UK

Source: CMBOR/Equistone Partners Europe/Investec Bank.

Table 10.2 Average deal structures for all UK buyouts, compared to PE-backed buyouts from failing firms (in parentheses)

Type of finance (average %)	*2000*	*2001*	*2002*	*2003*	*2004*
Equity	47.9 (85.9)	39.0 (45.0)	34.0 (51.0)	42.1	40.0 (49.5)
Mezzanine	4.7	3.6	3.1	2.5	4.2
Debt	41.7	46.6 (45.5)	49.7 (43.6)	48.9	48.7 (50.5)
Loan note	2.5	3.4	6.8	2.8	3.7
Other finance	3.5	7.4	6.4	3.7	3.4

Source: CMBOR/Equistone Partners Europe/Investec Bank.

differences across the period, which reflect the consequences of recession – specifically, that buyouts of failed firms in property and construction, food and drink, and retail and leisure sectors have been particularly prevalent recently compared to previous years. The property market experienced a significant decline after the banking collapse in 2008 due to falling confidence in lending and borrowing. The increase in failures in the food and drink sector reflect more selective buying that occurs in a recession particularly on necessities such as food. The increase in failures in the retail and leisure sectors is symptomatic of a fall in discretionary spending typical in recessionary times (Flatters & Willmott, 2009).

The majority of buyouts of firms from insolvency tend to be of the buyout type where the firm is bought by incumbent management. For example of the 69 deals from insolvency completed in 1990, the majority (92%) were buyouts rather than buyins. There is some evidence here that during recession the proportion of buyins increases and this could partly be due to an increase in the number of PE-backed deals (see Figure 10.3).

There is some evidence that PE-backed deals from failure have a greater proportion of equity in their deal structures and a lower proportion of debt compared to all buyouts, and that other types of finance like mezzanine and loan notes are not as likely to be used (Table 10.2).

Certainly, obtaining the traditional types of debt finance may be more problematic when firms are failing. PE firms may also prefer to invest in failing companies with intangible assets such as brand names or lists of customers, rather than/or in addition to physical assets, but there is no data yet to suggest that this is the case.

For the buyouts from failure (in parentheses) there is little data on structures, and only means from three or more data points have been included.

PE involvement

Failed independent firms, or firms attached to failed parent companies, present an opportunity not only for the incumbent management but also for PE firms to buy the company. This could be important for PE firms if they need to do deals, they still have funds to invest, but other sources of deals are hard to find (e.g., from family firms or divestment buyouts or de-listings from stock exchanges). For example traditional larger divestment-type deals could dry up in periods when debt is difficult to arrange (e.g., the recent recession). Larger deals may not be so easy to complete so smaller deals from insolvency may help to fill the gap. There is also a great deal of potential for PE firms in cases where the parent company is in trouble but the subsidiary is healthy, as was the case for Kingsmead Carpets (Case 1).

The problem of information asymmetry for PE firms exists, the PE firms do not have the same information as the incumbent management team, but if they are dealing with a healthy firm that was possibly constrained by the parent, there is a great deal of scope for improved efficiency and entrepreneurial activity (Wright et al., 2000; Meuleman et al., 2009; Scholes et al., 2010). In terms of buyouts of independent failing firms the experience and skills of the PE firm are even more important. Some PE firms not only provide finance and monitoring, as traditionally has been the case, but some also now have particular expertise in restructuring and turnarounds and it is these companies that will be most likely to succeed in turning failing companies around. For example Epic Private Equity (Case 3) is not only an equity provider but also an advisor to other PE firms. It can thus provide expertise on the restructuring of the businesses it buys, as well as to other PE firms. Endless LLP is another example of a PE firm with turnaround expertise and refers to itself as a "transformational private equity investor." It acquired Jones Bootmaker, one of the oldest brands in the shoe industry, for £11 million, in a so-called pre-pack deal in March 2017, an example of a failing independent firm that has to be restructured. The ability of PE firms to effect successful turnarounds is key to their successful involvement in all buyouts from failure but particularly in buyouts of failing independent companies.

According to CMBOR data, PE firms were most active in buying failing firms during the recessions of the 1990s, when there was a good supply of firms in insolvency and where bargains were to be found (Figure 10.4). In other periods, most noticeably since the end of the 2000s, PE firms have not been the main purchasers of these target firms. Nevertheless there is some evidence that during the most recent recession, PE firms were able to take advantage of the situation by buying failing companies (the proportion of PE-backed buyouts increased in the years 2012–2014).

The rise in the proportion of deals backed by PE firms in recent years may in part be due to the introduction of pre-pack deals (pre-pack administration) (Walton, 2009). Pre-pack deals appeared in the UK with the introduction of the Enterprise Act 2002, which was intended to be a mechanism where management could take over an insolvent company, allowing a firm to be sold to a new buyer as a going concern before the traditional administration process takes place, thus making the deal more favorable for PE firms. This speedy process prevents a company from being devalued by news of financial difficulties

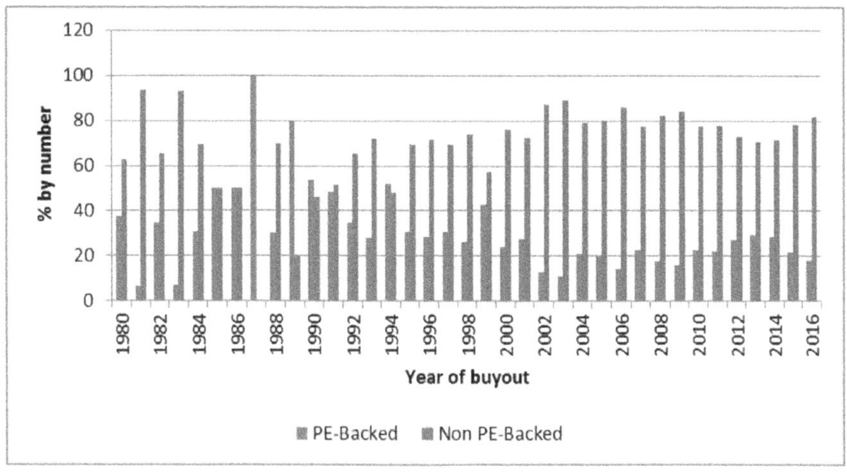

Figure 10.4 Buyouts from failed firms in the UK

Source: CMBOR/Equistone Partners Europe/Investec Bank.

that could affect customer and supplier loyalty and patronage. The proponents of pre-pack deals say that they speed up the process and save jobs, whereas critics suggest that creditors, particularly unsecured creditors, lose out but that the buyers, often the same managers, are able to buy back the more profitable assets at a knock-down price. This is in addition to the incentive managers already have to buy their own company, due to information asymmetries about the firm between themselves and the vendors, which may enable them to buy the firm at a price that is possibly too low. The pre-pack buyout for Jones Bootmaker was completed very quickly by PE firm Endless. It saved the majority of the 1000 jobs and nearly half of the firm's 170 stores, but all of its creditors lost out, unsecured creditor losing out the most. Some research suggests unsecured creditors get 1% return compared to 42% return for secured creditors (Frisby, 2007). Critics say that company directors are using pre-packs to get rid of large debts, unwanted shops, and even pension schemes.

Post-buyout performance

Although it is too early to assess the effects of buyouts from insolvency in the current recessionary period, our survey evidence from the last deep recession of the early 1990s, using a representative sample of 64 buyouts from insolvency, completed between 1990 and 1992, shows that major restructuring activities were needed to turn around the business (Robbie et al., 1993).

The study showed that the principal cause of insolvency was parent company related, including working capital failure, trading performance issues, acquisition policy, and market collapse (in the Whittard case performance issues and market collapse were dominant). Almost two-thirds (64%) had appointed new directors, 56% had not reappointed existing directors, 48% had reduced debtor days, 38% had reduced their vehicle fleet, and 34% had cash flow problems post-buyout (Table 10.3). The average employment level fell from 202 on buyout to 158 at the time of the survey. However, some 63% had not made job redundancies on buyout.

Between the buyout and the survey, 36% reduced employment further, 36% did not change employment levels, and the balance reported increases. In addition, in 19% of cases,

Table 10.3 Actions on or post-buyout (n=55–64)

Nature of action	%
Job losses at time of buyout	37
Sale of surplus land/buildings	13
Sale and leaseback of land/buildings	3
Vehicle fleet reduced	38
Refinancing of fixed assets	21
Creditor days extended	19
Debtor days reduced	48
Factoring of debtors	11
Company division sold	2
Existing directors not appointed	56
New directors appointed	64
Existing managers not appointed	29
New managers appointed	18
Cash flow problems post-buyout	34
Further finance required	34

Source: Robbie et al. (1993).

employment was above pre-buyout levels. Over a third of the firms in the sample had cash flow problems mainly because of failure to reach profit targets and large capital expenditure requirements, both outcomes indicative of corrections needed after the constraints imposed by failing parent firms. In a general assessment of performance, 75% of cases reported reasonable or good performance one year after the buyout. This raises the question of the importance of buyouts for acting as a catalyst for entrepreneurship and innovation activity (Wright et al., 2000). Current evidence is consistent with buyouts, i.e., incumbent management exploiting growth opportunities after being freed from the bureaucratic control of the parent company (Wright et al., 2000; Bacon et al., 2004). It highlights the differences between buyouts and buyins, the significant heterogeneity that exists among buyouts, and aligns with the earlier evidence already discussed suggesting that buyouts are possibly management buying their healthy company from a failing parent, whereas buyins may be external management (possibly PE firms alone) buying whole failing companies that are not particularly healthy entities needing significant restructuring post-deal.

In terms of the subsequent failure of buyouts from failed firms, evidence from deals completed between 1990 and 2005 shows that buyouts of firms from insolvency are slightly more likely to fail again than buyouts from other vendor sources. Taking all buyouts that failed up until June 2016, 24.5% of them were from insolvency originally compared to 22% from family/private, 17% from divestment buyouts, and 19% from secondary buyouts. However, when dividing the sample into PE-backed versus non-PE-backed there is a noticeable difference. PE-backed deals from insolvency are significantly more likely to fail again as are PE-backed deals of private/family buyouts (Table 10.4; Figures 10.5 and 10.6). Some reasons which help to explain this evidence are issues of information asymmetry and moral hazard for the incoming PE firms, along with a greater tendency to incorporate debt in the deal structure which may have repercussions in downturns when turnovers can fall. Some PE firms may also not have the specialist skills to turn companies around.

Table 10.4 Failures of buyouts from different sources (in the UK)

Source of deal	*Failure%*	
	PE	Non-PE
Family & private**	26.3	15.8
Divestment	18	15.3
Insolvency**	34.4	18.9
Secondary	20.7	17.1

Source: CMBOR/Equistone Partners Europe/Investec.
Statistical significance: **p < .01

Note: deals completed 1990–2005, exited by June 2016.

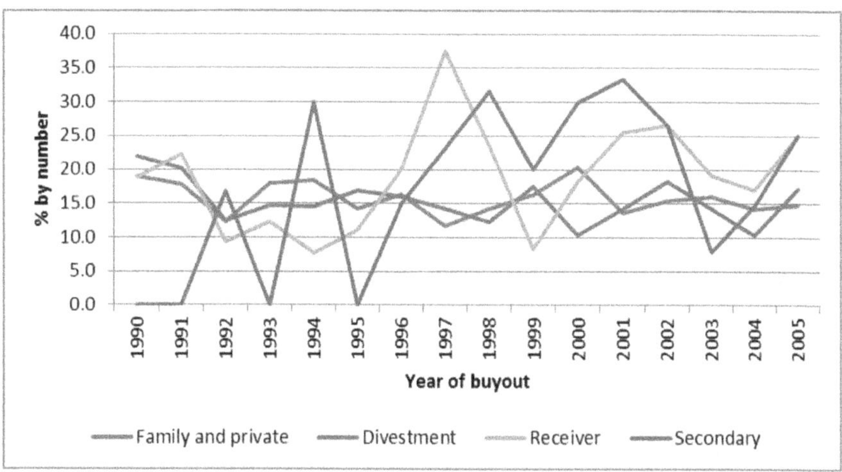

Figure 10.5 Creditor exits by source, non-PE-backed

Source: CMBOR/Equistone Partners Europe/Investec Bank.

Note: for example 36 deals completed in 1992 had creditor exits and 9.4% of these were sourced from insolvency.

Case studies

Case 1: Richards Group – Buyout to save parts of the company

Richards Group plc, a publicly quoted Aberdeen-based carpet manufacturer, went into insolvency in January 2002 after management disagreements and failed attempts at restructuring. It spawned several buyouts/buyins of parts of the company. Kingsmead Carpets based in Cumnock, Ayrshire, was sold to its management team saving 60 jobs. The sales and marketing director stated at that time that "Kingsmead used to be part of a large group which restricted who we could deal with and the products we manufactured. Now we are an independent we expect to be able to grow more quickly." The Northern Irish operation was sold to its management team and the Yorkshire-based floorcoverings subsidiary was subject to a trade sale. The remnant of Richards Group plc was sold as a management buyin to a local entrepreneur saving 145 jobs.

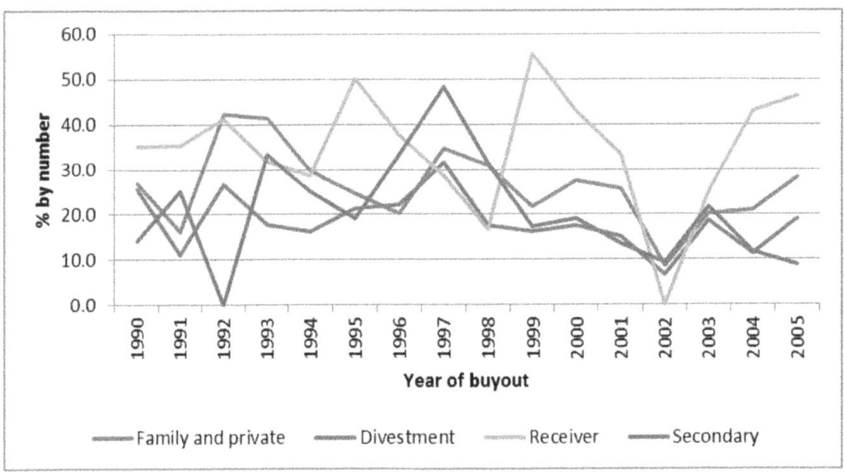

Figure 10.6 Creditor exits by source, PE-backed

Source: CMBOR/Equistone Partners Europe/Investec Bank.

Key lessons:

Management buyouts are a means of saving a firm and saving jobs.

Buyouts can act as a catalyst for entrepreneurial activity, particularly when it is the parent company that has failed (the entrepreneurship perspective).

Case 2: Denby – PE-backed buyout from an insolvent parent

The case of Denby highlights what can happen when a large parent organization goes into insolvency. A management buyout provides a means by which more viable divisions, like Denby, can survive. Denby was targeted by management and PE firms when the parent firm went into insolvency. It also became a target of later buyouts due to performance difficulties from over-expansion combined with difficulties in repaying debt (as a result of former buyouts).

Denby is a world-famous British pottery manufacturer based in Denby, Derbyshire, which started producing pottery in 1809. In June 1990, Coloroll, Denby's parent company, went into insolvency and Denby was purchased by its own management, backed by PE firm 3i, for a total of £7.4 million. Denby's managing director and three associates invested £140,000 for a 55% stake in the company, while 3i held the balance.

The firm began to sell its products in the US, and by the time it floated on the London Stock Exchange in 1994 it was valued at £43.4 million. It used some of the proceeds of the sale to repay its debts and continued its expansion abroad, updated its range of products, and opened a visitor center complex at Denby. The center became a major tourist attraction, with 300,000 visitors a year by the end of the century.

The company has since undergone many more management buyouts: the second in 1999 for £40.7 million involved a delisting from the stock exchange; the third in 2004 for £48 million was a management buyout. More recently, the firm had difficulty servicing its debts in tough retail conditions (particularly for the UK pottery industry) and had its fourth buyout in 2009 for £30 million led by the managing director and PE firm Valco Capital Partners, a specialist in restructurings. Half of the group's £72 million debt was written off as part of this transaction. Denby has added glassware and porcelain to its product range and continues to trade.

Key lessons:

Provides evidence of successful buyouts of more viable parts of failing businesses.

Debt, often associated with PE-backed buyouts, can be problematic in times of recession.

PE firms with the necessary restructuring skills to turn companies around are crucial.

Case 3: Whittards – Pre-pack deals and successful buyouts

Whittards of Chelsea provides an example of a deal using a pre-pack administration arrangement. It became a target for PE firms when profitability was poor and the recession hit its main financial backer. Whittards is a tea and coffee importer retailer and was established on Fleet Street (London) in 1886 by Walter Whittard. Timing was perfect as two years later tea that had been grown in India flooded into the UK. The firm remained in family hands until 1973 when it was sold to two PE firms for £2.2 million, eventually being listed on the AIM Stock Exchange in 1996 when the PE firms exited the business. After the flotation and accompanying equity injection, Whittards began to expand, building up to 120 stores in the UK and adding new retail capability through Kitchen Stores and factory outlets. It opened up tea bars called T-Zone in response to coffee outlets such as Starbucks and Costa Coffee with observers suggesting that this was too late and that they did not respond quickly enough. The firm also had a disastrous foray into internet selling with the cost of doing this far outweighing the profit from it. By 2001 the firm was having financial difficulties. They had some management changes, got rid of the internet side of the business, and started to focus again on the core tea and coffee business. After forming partnerships with retailers in the UK and the US (large supermarkets), they regained profitability temporarily. Whittards, still a listed company, was quickly struggling again financially and was bought by an Icelandic investment company Baugur Group in 2005 for £21 million, but in 2008 Baugur Group was hit hard by Iceland's financial collapse going into administration itself in that same year. Whittards was finally sold to Epic Private Equity in a pre-pack deal in 2008 for £0.6 million. Major restructuring has since taken place with the installation of a new management team, closure of 51 unprofitable stores, and improvements in in-store operations, point of sale, and merchandizing.

Key lessons:

Pre-packs can be used successfully as a means of buyout of a failing independent firm.

Independent failing firms are subject to efficiency improvements as a consequence of a buyout (the agency perspective).

Future research

Relatively little is known about buyouts from failed firms, so future research can be focused in several areas. Some of the suggestions here reflect the fact that buyouts are a very heterogeneous group, and there are substantial calls in the literature to recognize heterogeneity and context in this and other business-related fields of study (Zahra & Wright, 2011; Alperovych et al., 2013).

First, data shows that PE firms are not as successful at buying failed companies compared to management teams with no PE. Buying failed firms, especially during a recession, provides a great opportunity for PE firms to invest, and they are perhaps not making the most of this opportunity. What type of specialist turnaround skills are being employed, should this be different, and how do they overcome the problem of any limited time to assess the deal? In such situations what are the most valuable skills, are there any advantages to having relationships with the wider stakeholder community such as customers and suppliers, and would some form of legislation make a difference? Do they have in-house turnaround skills or do they have a network of turnaround specialists that they can use? Are any differences in shorter- or longer-term performance associated with the type and structure of the PE firm?

Second, what is the impact of pre-pack deals on buyouts from insolvency? Has this boosted the number of transactions, and, if so, what are the main factors associated with these deals that lead to easier transactions, and how controversial are they? Do deals arising from a pre-pack arrangement have a greater chance of success than others over time, what type of restructuring is involved, and does this give firms scope for growth over the longer term through capital investment, R&D, and innovation?

Third, there is little research on the type of entrepreneurial or innovation activity once the deal has been completed. Is it just firms that are bought by incumbent management teams that are innovative, just those that separate from a failing parent, and, if this is the case, what type of innovation do they engage in; is it exploitation or exploration (He & Wong, 2004), radical or incremental (Wright et al., 2000, 2001)? How well equipped are these firms to participate in different forms of innovation after potential serious constraints by parent companies, and what is the role of PE firms in entrepreneurship/innovation in these firms?

Fourth, there is certainly scope for a greater understanding of the differences between buyouts of a firm from a failed parent versus a buyout of a failed independent company. What are the performance differences between these two types of buyout from failure over time and especially during and after a recession? Does this relate to the health of the business at the outset, the extent of restructurings, the amount of debt, and what is the role of PE firms if they are involved?

Fifth, there is pressure on PE firms to use funds and invest in deals. Might there be a pecking order of deals? First, primary deals; second, if there is a lack of primary deals PE firms will invest in secondary buyouts; finally, if there are then insufficient secondary buyouts, will PE firms look at turning around failed businesses? Could investment in failed firms be a high risk part of a portfolio? Primary and secondary deals represent a lower risk part of the portfolio of investments while investment in turnaround is high risk. Do the potential rewards make it attractive to have a high-risk element in a portfolio of investments?

Sixth, there might be other general features of deals that are worth exploring. For instance, are PE targets from insolvency more likely to have physical assets or intangible assets (e.g., a list of customers or a trade name) since it might reduce the risk of the deal to the PE firm if these are valuable if the turnaround is unsuccessful? What are the sources and structure of finance for such deals? Presumably it is harder to secure loans, so does this mean that more equity is used in the deal? We have some evidence that the PE-backed deals have less debt and more equity, but this requires further investigation.

Finally, are MBOs from receivership more likely in regions where managers have fewer opportunities to find alternative employment? Are MBOs more likely in specific industries where managers have skills that cannot be easily transferred to employment in other industries?

Conclusions

Buyouts of distressed companies, whether in bankruptcy proceedings or close to them, are an important feature of the buyout market in general. These deals tend to come from viable parts of failed parent companies rather than failed independent businesses. They occur across a wide range of industries and are more prevalent during and just after recessions where supply is greatest. Reduced discretionary spend in times of recession can lead in particular to failures in the retail and leisure industry providing opportunities for management teams and PE firms to buy these companies at significantly reduced values. Management teams and PE firms with the right skills can take advantage of recessions and can, in doing so, help to stimulate the economy by rescuing ailing companies and even save national treasures like old-established former family firms such as Whittards and Denby (Cases 2 and 3). The majority of deals from insolvency are buyouts rather than buyins, an indication that the majority of deals are firms bought out by their own management from a failing parent. PE-backed buyouts from failure increase slightly during recessions but on the whole make up the minority of this type of deal. The main reasons for the failure of the group/ independent company are working capital failure, trading performance issues, acquisition policy, and market collapse. Post-buyout performance suggests that not all of these firms reduce employment; in fact this happens in only just over a third of cases. Among all of the PE-backed buyout failures, those from already failed companies make up the largest proportion and this proportion is significantly higher than for non-PE-backed deals.

Failing companies can be bought at discounted prices (enhanced recently by the introduction of controversial pre-packs), and if they involve viable parts of failed groups, it may be possible to make a purchase that is free of major parent liabilities giving the new firm a good chance of becoming a profitable business once again. These firms are often bought by incumbent management. Buying failed whole companies may be more complex, and it is possibly the case that PE firms are more likely to be involved in this type of buyout which may also explain why PE-backed firms from failed companies may be more likely to fail again. In these cases there will be a requirement for significant restructurings, changes in management teams, and changes in strategy in order to effect the turnaround successfully.

For both types of buyout from insolvency (whether from a group or independent), there is a need for considerable turnaround activity both on buyout and subsequently if a viable entity is to be created and maintained. PE firms can take advantage of the increased supply of failing firms during recessions provided that they have the necessary financial and management skills to turn the businesses around. In addition to finance and management skills, PE firms buying out failed companies will need to make investment decisions much more quickly than is generally the case, often with less scope for due diligence and with few, if any, warranties. There is a premium on PE firms that have expertise in a particular sector and experience of distressed deals that enable them to make a rapid assessment of prospective risks and returns.

"Timing is always tight … buy it in 4 weeks or company might run out of cash."

(John M. Collard, Chairman, Strategic Management Partners, Inc.)

The issue of timing and possible lack of crucial information may explain why among all of the PE-backed buyout failures, those from already failed companies make up the largest proportion. The more recent use of controversial pre-pack administration arrangements may make subsequent failure less likely for PE firms as the firm can be sold as a going concern before creditors are repaid. It is also important during this process to assess the calibre of incumbent management. If they are not a contributory factor to failure, their knowledge of the business may be crucial in avoiding any future pitfalls.

In the UK the number of PE firms that have very specific turnaround expertise has been increasing since the late 2000s, so this, combined with the advent of pre-pack administrations, may mean more buyouts from insolvency for PE firms and management teams in the future, and improved chances of longer-term success of these deals, along with more controversy.

Notes

1 From now on referred to as buyouts unless otherwise stated.
2 From now on private equity is shortened to PE.
3 The Centre for Management Buy-out Research (CMBOR), Imperial College Business School, London.
4 The annual growth in GDP is taken from the OECD (OECD.Stat).

References

Alperovych, Y., Amess, K., & Wright, M. 2013. PE firm experience and buyout vendor source: What is their impact on efficiency? *European Journal of Operational Research*, 228: 601–611.

Bacon, N., Wright, M., & Demina, N. 2004. Management buyouts and human resource management. *British Journal of Industrial Relations*, 42: 325–347.

Flatters, P., & Willmott, M. 2009. Understanding the post-recession consumer. *Harvard Business Review*, 87: 106–112.

Frisby, S. 2007. *A preliminary analysis of pre-packaged administrations*. Available at: www.r3.org.uk/what-we-do/publications/press/pre-pack-analysis.

He, Z.-L., & Wong, P.-K. 2004. Exploration vs. exploitation: An empirical test of the ambidexterity hypothesis. *Organization Science*, 15: 481–494.

Jensen, M. C. 1989. Eclipse of the public corporation. *Harvard Business Review*, 67: 61–74.

Meuleman, M., Amess, K., Wright, M., & Scholes, L. 2009. Agency, strategic entrepreneurship, and the performance of private equity-backed buyouts. *Entrepreneurship Theory and Practice*, 33: 213–239.

Robbie, K., Wright, M., & Ennew, C. 1993. Management buy-outs from receivership. *Omega*, 21: 519–529.

Scholes, L., & Wright, M. 2009. Leverage buy-outs and recession. In Various Authors (Eds.), *QFINANCE: The ultimate resource*. London: Bloomsbury Publications.

Scholes, L., Wright, M., Westhead, P., & Bruining, H. 2010. Strategic changes in family firms post management buyout: Ownership and governance issues. *International Small Business Journal*, 28: 505–521.

Walton, P. 2009. Pre-packin'in the UK. *International Insolvency Review*, 18: 85–108.

Wright, M., Hoskisson, R. E., & Busenitz, L. W. 2001. Firm rebirth: Buyouts as facilitators of strategic growth and entrepreneurship. *Academy of Management Executive*, 15: 111–125.

Wright, M., Hoskisson, R. E., Busenitz, L. W., & Dial, J. 2000. Entrepreneurial growth through privatization: The upside of management buyouts. *Academy of Management Review*, 25: 591–601.

Zahra, S. A., & Wright, M. 2011. Entrepreneurship's next act. *The Academy of Management Perspectives*, 25: 67–83.

11

JUST ANOTHER BUSINESS

Private equity in health services

Aline Bos and Paul Boselie

Introduction

Private equity (PE) activity has become a generally well-known phenomenon since the late 1980s, with its roots in the corporate US. During these years, PE firms have widened their geographical as well as their sectoral scope. This has involved increased activity in Europe and more deals in services compared to manufacturing (Guo et al., 2011). Especially since the 2008 financial crisis, PE firms have increasingly acquired organizations providing services that are central to the daily lives of citizens (Ivory et al., 2016), such as health services. This chapter therefore focuses on the role of PE firms in health services. We develop a conceptual model to explain why health services organizations are perhaps not "just another business" for PE investment, and use this model to explore the impact of PE in health services.

The health care sector accounts for approximately 12% of PE deal activity worldwide, as measured by the number of deals. Investment has surged in the health provider and related services subsector, totaling over half of the global deal value in health care for the year 2015. PE investment in so-called "healthcare-heavy assets," a label the firms apply to assets with meaningful exposure to reimbursement risk, continues to grow, with investors becoming more comfortable with reimbursement risk (Bain & Company, 2016: 8–10). In 2010, the first industry-specific PE trade association was established in the health care sector: the Healthcare Private Equity Association (HCPEA). The increasing pervasiveness of PE in healthcare is motivated by two developments. First, PE firms – having funds available – look for "deals that will not sour even if the economy does" (Evans, 2011). Second, PE is expanding to fill the health care gap as many governments are retreating from health services provision, and encouraging increased private sector involvement to attract capital and to deliver health services.

The largest proportion of health services PE deals occur in the US, in particular in nursing homes. For example, 4 out of 10 largest for-profit nursing home chains in the US were purchased by PE firms in the period 2003–2008 (Harrington et al., 2012). PE investors, however, also target other types of health services organizations such as US emergency services (Ivory et al., 2016). Health services providers in Western Europe have also been acquired, for example the Finnish healthcare service provider Terveystalo was acquired by the Swedish PE firm EQT partners in 2013, the Swedish health services company Capio was acquired by the PE firms Apax and Nordic Capital in 2006, and funding from several PE firms has backed small-scale nursing home facilities in the Netherlands.

The role of PE in such health services organizations raises a number of concerns. Their focus on financial performance can be at odds with the delivery of high quality health services. In the public as well as the academic debate, it is questioned whether PE interventions come at the expense of vulnerable patients (e.g., Duhigg, 2007; Pradhan et al., 2014: 4). For example, Ivory et al. (2016) report PE-owned health services organizations have implemented checklists named "Care to Cash," which may contradict key aims in health services such as providing "care to vulnerable patients." In line with this debate, this chapter develops a conceptual model to clarify how the nature of health services is fundamentally different from many other products or services, and suggests that health services are not "just another business" for PE firms. The specific nature of health services requires a multistakeholder and multidimensional performance approach to evaluate the impact of PE investment, which includes financial performance as well as employee, and client/ patient well-being. Subsequently, we consider the empirical evidence of the impact of PE in health services. Since specific research on this topic is relatively scarce, we draw from other sources to formulate propositions: this involves systematically analyzing evidence over the last 10 years on what we know about (a) the impact of for-profit nursing home ownership in comparison to not-for-profit ownership, and (b) the cross-sectoral impact of PE. The combination of both reviews enables us to formulate propositions on the impact of PE in health services. Finally, we identify certain knowledge gaps that could be addressed in future research.

Conceptual framework

By specifying the nature of health services, our conceptual framework aims to distinguish health services from manufacturing and services companies invested in by PE. For a full understanding of the specific health services context it is necessary to evaluate the impact of PE in health services from a stakeholder approach. Our focus is particularly on nursing home services, as nursing homes have been an important target of PE in health services thus far, and subsequently most available evidence is on this subsector.

Not "just another business"

To distinguish health services from other services and products, we introduce the market frame and the public value frame. The market frame starts from the idea that health services are a commodity. By treating health services as such, PE can apply general interventions for improving efficiency and maximizing profits. However, we argue that health services are not "just another business." Health services do not fit into the commodification logic that is attached to the market frame. The market frame therefore needs to be complemented or even replaced by a public value frame. We here present four arguments that underscore the need for this public value frame, as an alternative framework for exploring PE in health services. These four arguments are based on:

(a) the starting point for managing health services;
(b) perceptions of organizational success;
(c) perceptions of well-organized labor;
(d) perceptions of the client/ patient.

First, the *starting point* for managing health services can differ. The way in which nursing homes operate can be seen as a touchstone for how societies care for their elderly and for societal values more broadly. Delivering health services is therefore not only creating value for money by delivering commodities, but also creating public value by being part of people's lives, and the broader society. It relates to what Sandel (2000) calls "the moral limits of markets": when health services are commodified, that makes them a regular market exchange. This commodification may change the character of the service itself, as it may crowd out values worth caring about, such as accessible quality care for the elderly poor, human dignity, and happiness. From a market frame, health services commodities can be at a lower cost, as long as the care delivery fits within legal requirements; from a public value frame, the possibilities for lowering costs are related to public values that often transcend legal requirements.

Second, the view of economic value as the main indicator for *organizational performance* is too narrow. The client and the healthcare professional become intertwined in the nursing home service delivery. The "commodity" thus cannot be separated easily between provider and client, as the quality of the service is heavily dependent upon – often intense – interactions and relationships between clients and professionals. Health services delivery is "emotion work" (Hochschild, 1983), as it occurs in face-to-face interactions with clients. It uses emotions to influence patients' emotions, attitudes, and behaviors; and the display of emotions by professionals has to follow certain rules (Zapf, 2002). A market frame might overlook crucial aspects of the value creation process: the social capital that is built in micro action and relationships between staff and patients on a daily basis. Interventions from a market frame, such as the search for more efficiency, thus needs to be weighed against forms of social capital that are not easily measured, such as the quality of the relationships between patients and staff. For example, redeploying staff to improve efficiency can damage employee-client relationships that are essential for care quality.

Third, health services are labor-intensive, which puts emphasis on the importance of good *labor management*. The labor-intensity leads to Baumol's cost disease: there are limits to the growth of productivity over time, since productivity gains come mostly from improved capital and technology (Baumol & Bowen, 1966). Research shows how Baumol's cost disease applies to the US health care sector (Bates & Santerre, 2013). Productivity gains in the primary process – an important starting point for many PE firms in reorganizing their portfolio organizations (e.g., Wilson et al., 2012) – are thus restricted. Moreover, it can even be argued that many health services need some staff slack because of unforeseen events for which extra staff are required immediately (for example, patient falls and acute episodes of distress), and the high risks of understaffing at those moments.

Fourth, the commodification of health services can blur the difference between "ordinary clients" and nursing home *patients*. One difference relates to the fact that it is much harder for most nursing home patients than the "ordinary client" of regular commercial day-to-day services to "vote with their feet" when they are dissatisfied with the services delivered. Relocation to another nursing home will disconnect patients abruptly from relationships with staff and other patients, and is especially distressing for physically frail patients or those with other complicated health needs. In addition, places in other nursing homes can be scarce and might not be available directly. Another difference refers to the fact that it is relatively difficult for patients to identify care quality and to compare alternative nursing homes or care providers. This is partly because the quality of care is difficult to measure and assess compared to standard commodities, information is not readily accessible, and the most vulnerable patients are often least equipped to make the comparison at the times of highest

Table 11.1 Summary of the ideal type market frame and public value frame for health services

	"Just another business" *Market frame: health services as a commodity*	*Not "just another business"* *Public value frame: health services as a service in its own right*
Starting point	Building a financially successful business within legal requirements	Building a financially successful business within a legal context and in addition also respecting public values
Organizational performance	Economic value is key to nursing home success	Economic value and social capital are both key to nursing home success
Organizing labor	Labor needs to be organized as efficiently as possible	The nature of the service implies some staff slack
Client/patient	Dealing with the empowered client, who is making rational choices	Dealing with the dependent patient who needs protection

need. There is a huge difference of knowledge between the care provider and the patient, and information asymmetry may result in sub-optimal client choices of services and facilities. These issues highlight the dependency of the patient on the nursing home, including high transaction costs directly related to building and maintaining client relationships. They call for a certain level of protection of the patients by the organization, service commissioners, or the regulators responsible, and the restriction of socially undesirable profit-maximization (e.g., Hirschman, 1980: 436).

These four characteristics of the nature of health services can also be applied to, for example, education or child daycare services. Table 11.1 provides a summary of the characteristics, which can be categorized from a market frame and a public value frame.

From a shareholder approach to a stakeholder approach

What follows is a multidimensional performance perspective on health services organizations, as the delivery of health services implies the creation of value that goes beyond financial performance. Health service delivery also includes elements of public value, social capital, staff slack, and patient protection. Good performance in health services balances financial performance, employee well-being, and client well-being, as owners, employees, and clients are all affected by PE ownership (e.g., Freeman et al., 2010). Research on the impact of PE in health services therefore needs to start from a stakeholder approach, as opposed to the "traditional" shareholder approach. We argue that a stakeholder approach in combination with a multidimensional performance model fits health services better than a shareholder approach.

In the shareholder approach, principals (owners) and agents (managers) are challenged to optimize financial interests to ensure long-term organizational competitiveness (Jensen & Meckling, 1976). This approach is widely used in the buyout and PE literature. It can be characterized by a focus on a limited number of stakeholders and a one-dimensional performance orientation (i.e., organizational and financial performance). In contrast, the stakeholder approach (e.g., Freeman, 1984) starts from a multidimensional view of performance,

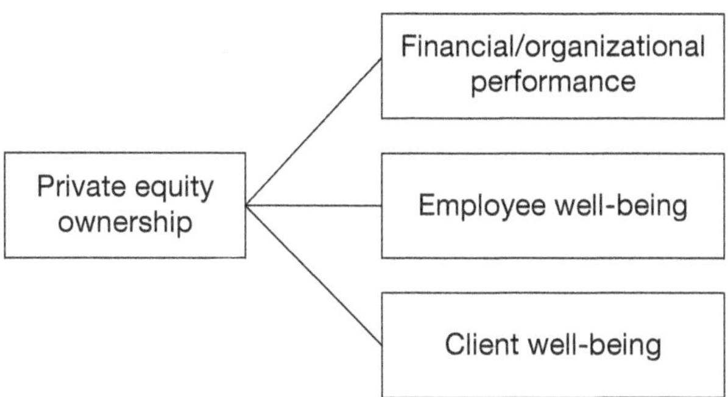

Figure 11.1 Multidimensional performance of PE in health services

Source: Authors.

with an emphasis on organizational outcomes, employee outcomes, and societal outcomes linked to the different stakeholders involved (see, for example, the Harvard model, Beer et al., 1984). In this chapter, we focus on three stakeholders in health services organizations: owners/employers, employees, and clients. While acknowledging that society as a whole has a stake in health service provisions and outcomes, society is not included in our review.

The stakeholder approach adds the possibility of dissimilar/conflicting outcomes for different stakeholders. Scholars identify a variety of potential outcomes from organizational decisions that range from conflicting outcomes to mutual gains outcomes (e.g., Van De Voorde et al., 2012). From the "conflicting outcomes perspective," the impact of PE ownership for different stakeholders is a zero-sum game: positive outcomes for one stakeholder come at the expense of another stakeholder. At the opposite end of the continuum, the "mutual gains perspective" assumes that decisions are possible that involve gains for all stakeholders. We will apply a multidimensional performance construct (see Figure 11.1), to explore which of these perspectives is most appropriate for describing the impact of PE ownership in health services. The goal of this chapter is to formulate propositions on the impact of PE in health services on organizational performance, employee well-being, and client well-being.

What we (do not) know about PE in health services

We argue that PE in health services needs specific attention in academic research. Lessons can also be learned for other public services sectors such as education and child daycare. Hitherto, research on PE has been mainly cross-sectoral, often using databases – such as the CMBOR database – that incorporate businesses in several sectors. Of the 62 papers included in our systematic review of the PE literature over 10 years, 79% presented cross-sectoral results (Bos et al., 2013). The few papers that focus on a specific sector are in nursing homes (8%) and retail (5%). We also found one paper for each of the following sectors: manufacturing, high technology engineering, telecoms, and the automobile industry.

Evidence on PE in nursing homes

The distinctive nature of health services calls for more sector-specific research on the impact of PE in health services. The first studies in this area have focused on nursing homes and the findings are inconsistent. Although Stevenson and Grabowski (2008) find lower staffing levels in US nursing homes following acquisition by a PE firm, they report that staffing levels were already reducing pre-purchase. No harm to care quality is reported as a consequence. In contrast, Harrington et al. (2012) find no significant changes in staffing levels for PE-owned nursing homes, but report higher levels of deficiencies post-buyout. Deficiencies are issued by the inspection when a nursing home does not meet minimal standards. A study by Pradhan et al. (2014) also reports significantly more deficiencies after PE deals in nursing homes. This study also finds lower staffing intensity of Registered Nurses (the higher educated nurses working in US nursing homes). Moreover, the number of higher educated professionals is reduced in relation to lower qualified care workers. With regard to financial performance, Pradhan et al.'s (2013) study reports improved financial performance of PE-owned nursing homes, while Cadigan et al. (2015) found little impact of private investment firms on the financial health of nursing homes. These studies all highlight one particular aspect of multidimensional performance. Given research on the impact of PE in health services is relatively scarce and focused on one dimension at a time (i.e., organizational performance, employee well-being or client well-being), we draw from related literatures to formulate propositions on the impact of PE in healthcare.

Drawing from related literatures

We narrow our focus to PE's impact on nursing homes in the US for three reasons. First, US nursing homes have been acquired by PE since 2000, and therefore there is relatively much experience in this area. Second, the very first studies on PE in health services, as presented in the previous paragraph, have been in US. Third, although research on PE in nursing homes is relatively scarce, there is a huge body of literature on the profit status of US nursing homes, which is indirectly informative. In contrast to many other industries PE invests in, nursing home ownership can also be not-for-profit or public. Research on the impact of for-profit status therefore provides insight into the question of what it means to deal with nursing home care delivery in a commercial way: as "just another business."

Starting from the stakeholder approach, we applied a multidimensional performance perspective on the available empirical evidence. We conducted two separate systematic reviews of the literature (see Bos et al., 2013, 2017). In a broad search of empirical evidence over the last 10 years, we systematically categorized all the evidence on the impact of PE, and profit versus not-for-profit nursing homes on the basis of whether studies report on financial/organizational performance, employee well-being, and client well-being. By combining what we know about the impact of for-profit nursing home ownership (step 1) and the cross-sectoral impact of PE (step 2), we aim to draw propositions on PE's impact in health services and to show knowledge gaps that need to be addressed by PE scholars.

The reviews resulted in respectively 62 relevant studies on the impact of PE across sectors, beyond health services, and 50 studies on the impact of a profit status in US nursing homes. After in-depth review of full texts, studies were classified according to the categories "organizational performance," "employee well-being," and "client well-being." For "financial/organizational performance," the following variables emerged from our review: profit margins, efficiency, and innovation. For employee well-being, we included staffing levels/employment and other working conditions.[1] For client well-being, we analyzed studies on product or service quality. For more details on the methods in the two separate reviews, we refer to the separate reviews (Bos et al., 2013, 2017).[2] Figure 11.2 provides an overview of the two analyses.

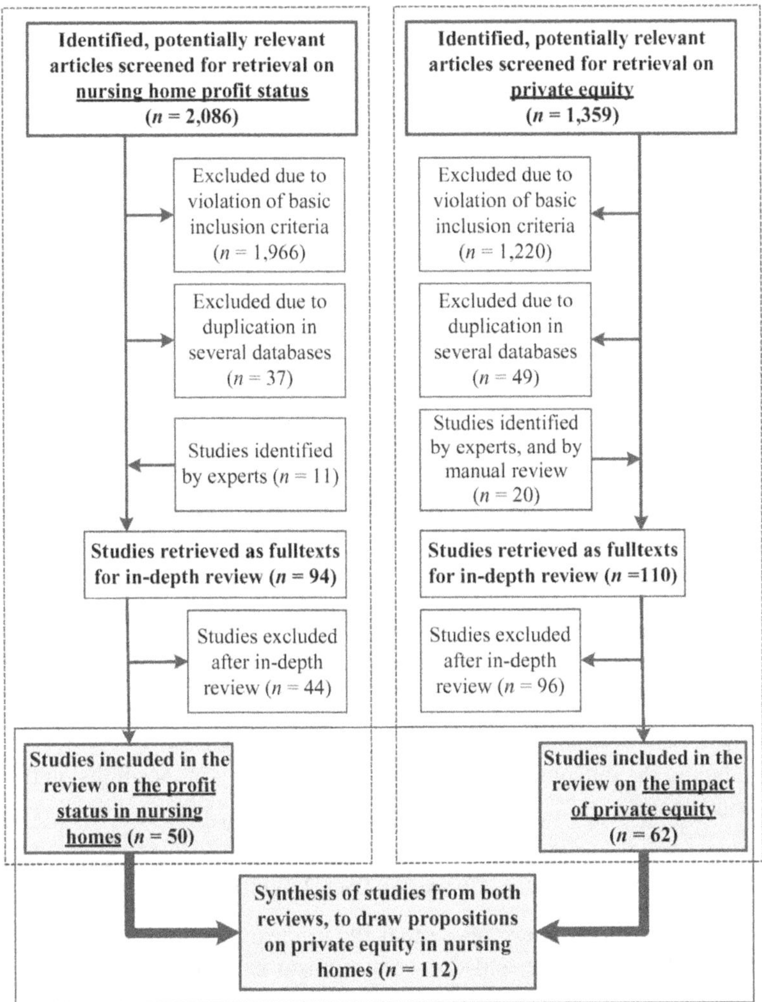

Figure 11.2 Overview of the steps taken in the systematic reviews that form the data for this chapter

Source: Authors.

Table 11.2 provides an overview of the findings from the review of the profit-status of nursing homes and the implications of PE ownership. The majority of research on the impact of PE focuses on variables of organizational/financial performance. More than one-third (profit status of nursing homes) and 4 in 10 (PE ownership) of the studies consider the implications for employee well-being. For the review of nursing homes, the majority of studies (over 6 in 10) concentrate on client well-being variables. This remarkable difference highlights the issues that PE firms are likely to be assessed against when acquiring health services. While the emphasis of PE scholars is on financial/organizational performance, health policy scholars accentuate care quality considerations. We now consider in turn the respective outcomes for organizational/financial performance, employee well-being, and client well-being.

Table 11.2 Overview of the results from the reviews[d]

	For-profit vs. not-for-profit nursing homes (n = 50)	*PE vs. non-PE ownership across sectors* (n = 62)
Organizational/financial performance	**12%**[a]	**74%**
Profit margins (profitability)	+[b]	+
Efficiency levels	+	+
Innovation (orientation)	0	0
Employee well-being	**36%**	**44%**
Employment/staffing levels	−	+/−
Other working conditions, including job satisfaction and benefits	−	+/−
Client well-being	**62%**	**7%**[c]
Quality	0/−	0/−

a The percentage of the studies included in the review that provide empirical data on organizational performance, employee well-being, or client well-being variables.

b − = decrease/worse, + = increase/better, 0 = no effect/difference

c Four papers, of which three are about PE in nursing homes

d The table only shows the variables that emerge in both reviews. The separate reviews contain more variables, such as bankruptcy rates, wages, industrial relations, turnover rates, hospitalization rates, and lawsuit/ complaint rates (see Bos et al., 2013, 2017).

By combining the outcomes from both reviews, we draw propositions on the impact of PE in nursing homes.

Organizational/financial performance

Based on the two reviews, we propose that PE in nursing homes will be largely beneficial for financial performance and does not seem to harm innovation. First, the review on the profit status of nursing homes shows that for-profit nursing homes tend to outperform not-for-profit nursing homes with regard to profit margins. The review on the impact of PE across sectors shows similar results: in general, PE-owned companies have higher margins than their industry counterparts which are not PE-owned. We therefore assume that PE increases the financial performance in PE-owned nursing homes. An initial study in this area (e.g., Pradhan et al., 2013) confirms this proposition, while a further study finds little impact of private investment firms on the financial health of nursing homes (Cadigan et al., 2015).

Second, efficiency is generally higher in for-profit nursing homes compared to not-for-profit nursing homes. Moreover, cross-sectoral research on PE shows that PE can generally be expected to increase efficiency. We therefore propose that PE ownership in nursing homes stimulates the efficiency of health services delivery.

Third, with regard to innovation PE investors are temporary owners with a potentially short-term time horizon that may reduce investment in new products and services. However, prior studies suggest PE ownership does not restrict innovation. Similarly, an initial study reports that the profit status of nursing home is not associated with changes in the orientation on innovation. We therefore propose that PE ownership will not hold back innovation in nursing homes. For financial/organizational performance, we therefore formulated the following propositions:

P_1: PE increases the profitability of nursing homes.
P_2: PE increases the efficiency in nursing homes.
P_3: PE does not change innovation in nursing homes.

Employee well-being

We propose a negative impact of PE's interventions on employment, i.e., staffing levels, in nursing homes. Research on the impact of PE on employment across the sector shows mixed results. Outcomes seem to be dependent on the characteristics and context of the portfolio company at the time of the acquisition. At the same time, the review on nursing homes indicates that for-profit nursing homes are associated with lower staffing levels than not-for-profit nursing homes. Moreover, an initial study reports lower employment levels in PE-owned nursing homes compared to other for-profit nursing homes in Florida. This study also finds reduced employment post-buyout when compared to the pre-buyout period of the nursing homes (Pradhan et al., 2014).

With regard to employee well-being, research on the impact of PE on working conditions is limited and shows mixed outcomes. In comparison, two studies report worse job benefits in for-profit nursing homes when compared to not-for-profit nursing homes (Kash et al., 2007; Haley-Lock & Kruzich, 2008). We expect that the mixed findings for PE across sectors on working conditions will bend to the negative side when it comes to PE in the nursing home sector. For employee well-being, we therefore formulated the following propositions:

P_4: PE reduces staffing levels in nursing homes.
P_5: PE diminishes general working conditions in nursing homes.

Client well-being

We earlier described the labor-intensity of nursing home services and argued that many health services need some staff slack to deal with unforeseen events. Understaffing is therefore potentially damaging for client/patient well-being in nursing homes and staffing levels are closely tied to client well-being, i.e., care quality (e.g., Schnelle et al., 2004). Apart from research on PE in nursing homes in particular, research on the impact of PE on product or service quality is limited (such as the case study of Palcic & Reeves, 2013). In contrast, the vast majority of studies on the impact of for-profit nursing home ownership focuses on the implications for care quality. Care quality is measured in different ways, ranging from the level of deficiencies, the number of inappropriate medication prescriptions, the incidence of resident pain, the use of physical restraints, the prevalence of pressure ulcers, to the loss of ability on daily tasks. The impact of for-profit nursing home ownership is associated with either no or worse care quality outcomes. Studies that directly addressed the impact of PE on nursing home care quality tend to show similar findings. While two studies report no harm to quality (Stevenson & Grabowski 2008; Cadigan et al., 2015: 192), two other studies find reduced quality levels (Harrington et al., 2012; Pradhan et al., 2014). The study of Pradhan et al. (2014) also reported several quality indicators that were not

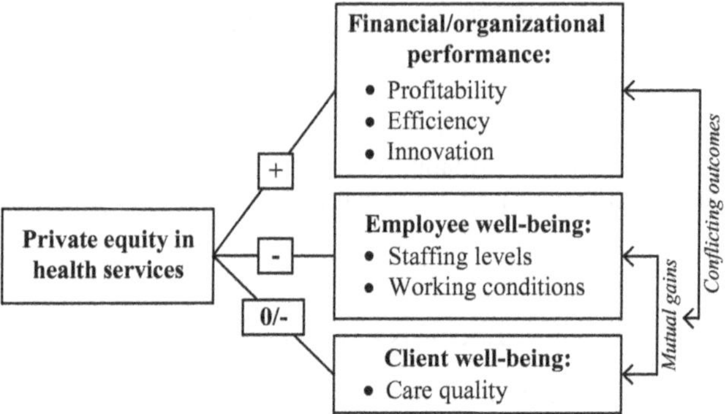

Figure 11.3 Propositions on PE in health services

Source: Authors.

influenced by PE. In line with these studies on care quality, as well as the intertwining of employee well-being and client well-being, we formulated the following proposition on client well-being:

P_6: PE has no impact or a slightly negative impact on care quality in nursing homes.

Summarizing our arguments, we predict that PE in nursing homes will be largely beneficial for financial performance and efficiency, and will not harm innovation. For employee well-being, we expect that PE ownership overall has a less positive impact. For client well-being, we predict that the impact of PE in nursing homes is either neutral or negative. By applying a multidimensional performance framework, we thus predict varied outcomes for different stakeholders. In terms of the conceptual framework, on conflicting outcomes and mutual gains, we therefore propose the following (see also Figure 11.3):

P_7: The conflicting outcomes perspective applies to the financial/organizational performance when related to employee well-being and client well-being.
P_8: The mutual gains perspective applies to employee well-being and client well-being.

Conclusions and future research opportunities

Conclusions

While we argued in our conceptual framework why health services are *not* just another business, PE investors nevertheless seem to treat health services as "just another business." Given the synthesis of the literature on both PE across sectors and for-profit nursing homes, we propose that PE owners are mainly successful from a market frame perspective. They are able to enhance financial/organizational performance in health services. Evidence also indicates that PE in health services can be associated with lower staffing levels, which is rather a signal of a labor process that is organized as efficiently as possible, than of a labor process that incorporates some staff slack with an eye on unforeseen events for which extra staff are required immediately. These outcomes go together with no or slightly negative consequences for patients/clients. The beneficial outcomes for employers/owners seems to be associated with less fortunate outcomes for employees and clients, which fits in the conflicting outcomes perspective. We suggest that PE owners, especially in nursing homes, should focus on a more strategic balance between organizational/financial performance, employee well-being, and client well-being, because such a balanced approach can lead to long-term organizational success (see also Oliver, 1997; Deephouse, 1999).

Future research opportunities

In addition to the conclusions and drawing on two systematic reviews, we identify two priorities for future research on PE.

First, the review on nursing homes' profit status shows that health policy researchers mainly focus on the impact of ownership on measures of client well-being. In contrast, scholars that examine the impact of PE ownership mainly concentrate on organizational and financial performance. Furthermore, the few papers that focus on the impact of PE on client well-being are almost exclusively carried out by health policy scholars, and focused on care quality in nursing homes. We therefore observe a knowledge gap with regard to the impact of PE on product and service quality. Some critics argue that PE investors focus on financial engineering rather than operational improvements (e.g., Appelbaum & Batt, 2014), let alone increasing products and/or service quality for clients. More research is required on the impact of PE acquisitions on client outcomes to evaluate a broader range of economic and social implications.

Furthermore, the public value frame underscores this need for more attention to measures of client well-being in PE research. Public services, such as care for the elderly, should not only be judged by their economic returns but also by their quality, or more broadly, by their contribution to social goals such as the overall health and well-being of citizens. Because health services organizations are an important target for PE firms, this is another reason for increasingly incorporating client well-being variables in scholarly work on PE.

Second, we found that results for employee well-being – and to a lesser extent client well-being – are mixed. Literature has not been able to provide clear explanations for such diverse findings. We assume this is due to context-specific factors, such as the type of PE investor, the type of portfolio organization, and the type of sector, including government interference in that sector. To uncover the mechanisms that explain the implications of PE ownership for different stakeholders, more qualitative research is needed. Instead of *what* the impact of PE ownership is, the attention needs to shift to *how* PE owners influence portfolio organizations. In this way, explanations can be found and deepened for the diverse outcomes, preferably with "longitudinal studies that chart the development and impact of changes" (Wright et al., 2009: 510–511). The focus then changes to understanding the *mechanisms* at work in PE-owned portfolio firms, and to building new theory.

Notes

1 Includes several variables such as employee consultation, trust in implicit contracts with employees, organizational uncertainty, institutional trust, CEO turnover, skill mix in nursing homes (indicating that higher educated professionals are replaced by lower educated and lower paid health care professionals), managerial discretion, and high commitment management practices, i.e., long-term investments practices that enhance employee well-being.

2 A list of all the articles included in the reviews is available from the authors.

References

Appelbaum, E., & Batt, R. 2014. *Private equity at work: When Wall Street manages Main Street*. New York: Russell Sage Foundation.

Bain & Company. 2016. *Global healthcare private equity and corporate M&A report 2016*. Boston, MA: Bain & Company.

Bates, L. J., & Santerre, R. E. 2013. Does the US health care sector suffer from Baumol's cost disease? Evidence from the 50 states. *Journal of Health Economics*, 32: 386–391.

Baumol, W., & Bowen, W. 1966. *Performing arts, the economic dilemma: A study of problems common to theater, opera, music, and dance*. New York: Twentieth Century Fund.

Beer, M., Spector, B., Lawrence, P., Mills, D. Q., & Walton, R. 1984. *Human resource management: A general manager's perspective*. New York: Free Press.

Bos, A., Boselie, P., & Trappenburg, M. 2017. Financial performance, employee wellbeing, and client wellbeing in for-profit and not-for-profit nursing homes: A systematic review. *Health Care Management Review*, 42: 352–368.

Bos, A., Trappenburg, M., & Boselie, P. 2013. *The impact of private equity ownership on organizational performance, employee well-being, and client well-being, a systematic review of the literature*. An earlier version of this paper was presented at the Utrecht School of Governance Research Day, Utrecht, The Netherlands.

Cadigan, R. O., Stevenson, D. G., Caudry, D. J., & Grabowski, D. C. 2015. Private investment purchase and nursing home financial health. *Health Services Research*, 50: 180–196.

Deephouse, D. L. 1999. To be different, or to be the same? It's a question (and theory) of strategic balance. *Strategic Management Journal*, 20: 147–166.

Duhigg, C. 2007. At many homes, more profit and less nursing. *New York Times*, 23 September.

Evans, M. 2011. Building equity. *Modern Healthcare*, 41: 32–33.

Freeman, E. 1984. *Strategic management: A stakeholder approach*. Boston, MA: Pitman.

Freeman, R. E., Harrison, J. S., Wicks, A. C., Parmar, B. L., & De Colle, S. 2010. *Stakeholder theory: The state of the art*. Cambridge, UK: Cambridge University Press.

Guo, S., Hotchkiss, E. S., & Song, W. 2011. Do buyouts (still) create value? *The Journal of Finance*, 66: 479–517.

Haley-Lock, A., & Kruzich, J. 2008. Serving workers in the human services: The roles of organizational ownership, chain affiliation, and professional leadership in frontline job benefits. *Nonprofit and Voluntary Sector Quarterly*, 37: 443–467.

Harrington, C., Olney, B., Carrillo, H., & Kang, T. 2012. Nurse staffing and deficiencies in the largest for-profit nursing home chains and chains owned by private equity companies. *Health Services Research*, 47: 106–128.

Hirschman, A. O. 1980. Exit, voice, and loyalty: Further reflections and a survey of recent contributions. *The Milbank Memorial Fund Quarterly. Health and Society*, 58: 430–453.

Hochschild, A. R. 1983. *The managed heart*. Berkeley, CA: University of California Press

Ivory, D., Protess, B., & Bennett, K. 2016. When you dial 911 and Wall Street answers. *New York Times*, June 25. www.nytimes.com/2016/06/26/business/dealbook/when-you-dial-911-and-wall-street-answers.html?_r=0.

Jensen, M., & Meckling, W. 1976. Theory of the firm: Managerial behavior, agency costs, and ownership structure. *Journal of Financial Economics*, 3: 306–360.

Kash, B. A., Castle, N. G., & Phillips, C. D. 2007. Nursing home spending, staffing, and turnover. *Health Care Management Review*, 32: 253–262.

Oliver, C. 1997. Sustainable competitive advantage: Combining institutional and resource-based views. *Strategic Management Journal*, 18: 697–713.

Palcic, D., & Reeves, E. 2013. Private equity leveraged buyouts in European telecoms: The case of Eircom. *Telecommunications Policy*, 37: 573–582.

Pradhan, R., Weech-Maldonado, R., Harman, J. S., & Hyer, K. 2014. Private equity ownership of nursing homes: Implications for quality. *Journal of Health Care Finance*, 42: 1–14.

Pradhan, R., Weech-Maldonado, R., Harman, J. S., Laberge, A., & Hyer, K. 2013. Private equity ownership and nursing home financial performance. *Health Care Management Review*, 38: 224–233.

Sandel, M. J. 2000. What money can't buy: The moral limits of markets. *Tanner Lectures on Human Values*, 21: 87–122.

Schnelle, J. F., Simmons, S. F., Harrington, C., Cadogan, M., Garcia, E., Bates, M., & Jensen, B. 2004. Relationship of nursing home staffing to quality of care. *Health Services Research*, 39: 225–250.
Stevenson, D. G., & Grabowski, D. C. 2008. Private equity investment and nursing home care: Is it a big deal? *Health Affairs*, 27: 1399–1408.
Van De Voorde, K., Paauwe, J., & Van Veldhoven, M. 2012. Employee well-being and the HRM–organizational performance relationship: A review of quantitative studies. *International Journal of Management Reviews*, 14: 391–407.
Wilson, N., Wright, M., Siegel, D. S., & Scholes, L. 2012. Private equity portfolio company performance during the global recession. *Journal of Corporate Finance*, 18: 193–205.
Wright, M., Bacon, N., & Amess, K. 2009. The impact of private equity and buyouts on employment, remuneration and other HRM practices. *Journal of Industrial Relations*, 51: 501–515.
Zapf, D. 2002. Emotion work and psychological well-being: A review of the literature and some conceptual considerations. *Human Resource Management Review*, 12: 237–268.

12

THE CHINESE STYLE MANAGEMENT BUYOUTS

Jun Du and Bach Nguyen

Introduction

A management buyout (MBO) is an acquisition in which a firm's equity is fully or partially acquired by the incumbent management team, often with the participation of private equity (PE) investors (Wright et al., 2001). MBOs originated in the US but later on occurred globally, for both private and public firms. The majority of the transactions are by divisional, secondary, private-to-private, and family-owned buyouts. Strömberg (2008) estimates that public-to-private MBOs account for less than 7% of total worldwide buyout transactions in terms of number of deals, and 28% in terms of value, which explains why the public-to-private MBO is not the dominant theme of the literature.

MBOs in China have specific characteristics that differ from other countries. Most of the Chinese MBOs happened during the era of enterprise reform in China (1998–2004), aiming to help state-owned enterprise (SOEs) to survive the sharply increased competition in the gradually marketized economy (Liu, 2008). MBOs, among several other means, were meant to transform the poorly performing SOEs into modern corporate organizations, often in private ownership. There are marked differences in the motivation of managers, private investors, and facilitators (in this case, local governments) in these buyouts from those that happened in the West. Without a deep understanding of the historical and institutional background in which Chinese MBOs took place, it would be difficult to understand the selection issues that occur in the process of MBOs, and evaluate the MBO performance found in the literature. This chapter provides a review of these issues by paying particular attention to the Chinese characteristics that define the MBOs in China.

In addition to the lack of in-depth analyses of the differences among Chinese MBOs, Western MBOs, and MBOs in other emerging or transitional economies, a main hurdle to studying China's privatization has been the lack of systematic data (Guo et al., 2008). As a result, there are only limited studies on this topic and hence inadequate insights could be drawn from the current literature. This chapter reviews the existing evidence, sets up the distinctive institutional background, and summarizes what we have learned about the fastest growing emerging economy in the world.

The remainder of the chapter is structured as follows. First, we provide a brief account of the historical background to China's privatization when public-to-private MBOs took place. Then, we review the literature to highlight the distinctive features of MBOs in China in comparison to those conducted in Western economies. We also discuss the financial and non-financial performance of MBO firms. Finally, we conclude the chapter with suggestions for future research.

Historical background

The first MBO case in China, Stone (四通) Group in 1998, turned a failing SOE into a well-known business success. Many similar dwindling SOEs followed the example and succeeded, while others eventually ended up being failures, some even leading to massive national asset losses. This brought huge controversy, which ultimately brought an end to the popularity of MBOs in 2004. To understand MBOs in China and their performance, it is essential to understand China's enterprise reform and SOE privatization in particular. This historical context not only provides pointers for understanding the motivations of the reform, but also the sources that determine their outcomes.

Privatization in China differs from that in other transitional economies in some important ways (Du & Liu, 2015). At the national level, in contrast to the mass privatizations in Russia and Central Eastern economies (CEE), where central governments pushed the privatization policy at the outset of liberalization, Chinese government delayed privatizing the state-owned sector as long as it could. Following China's earlier enterprise reform centered on the control rights reform prior to the mid-1990s, SOEs faced the waking market with the rapid entry of domestic private firms and foreign investors. A series of decentralization programs were implemented including government agencies' original function of managing SOEs, which was nearly dissolved, and the majority of the SOEs being degraded to the supervision of lower government affiliations (Liu, 2008). Then, the crucial reforms of the double-track price system[1] ended and the new financial accounting system and income tax law in 1994 became the turning point of China's enterprise reform and a new beginning for the marketized economy. This resulted in SOEs facing an unprecedented and devastating scale of loss-making in the state sector (Du & Liu, 2015). As a result, the government and the loss-making SOEs ended up with no choice but to implement radical reform. In this sense, both sides, SOEs (agents) and local governments (principals), gained momentum for the reform.

The external environment was already relatively developed for the subsequent enterprise reform. The sharply increased competition promoted by the marketized economy has served as a prerequisite for privatization, which is opposite from what has been observed elsewhere in the world (see Mickiewicz, 2009). China's institutional factors explain why the MBO was a promising option for SOE reform. Unlike the CEE countries, where at the time of mass privatization a strong institutional structure for product, labor, or financial markets had not been established, Chinese governments had significantly improved institutional infrastructure at the time of implementing *gaizhi*. In addition, financial markets had developed to a level that sufficiently supported leveraged MBOs (Xu et al., 2008). In addition to the external conditions, the Chinese government had a strategic plan and prioritized the buyout in the process of its execution.

While political control in China is highly centralized, there is regional economic decentralization to local governments. Local governments oversee whether and how to privatize SOEs within their jurisdictions, unlike in Russia and the CEE where it was entirely controlled by central government (Gan et al., 2010).This was an important contextual factor that explains the shared interests of the local governments and the failing SOEs when they opted for privatization as a solution, and chose a specific approach of privatization.

More specifically, provincial and municipal governments have relatively large freedom in setting up their own strategies and tactics of achieving the unified economic goal. In principle, SOEs may propose a restructuring plan themselves. Once approved by the local government, SOEs could carry out the restructuring plan as proposed, and select the specific approach and pace according to the circumstances (Du et al., 2014).

The large-scale privatization in China took place between the late 1990s and 2005. Gan (2009) estimates that between 1998 and 2005, more than 90,000 firms with more than 11 trillion RMB (US$1.4 trillion) worth of assets were privatized. As far as we know, there are no official statistics of the overall scale of MBOs in China during this period. The sporadic reports of the MBO statistics are all based on small surveys, which give us some indications of MBO size. However, the measures of the relative size of MBOs in different studies can be very different and thus hard to compare. For example, Gan et al. (2010) estimate that 47% of the privatized SOEs were through MBOs. Liu (2008) reports that 15% of the privatized SOEs' largest shareholders were managers and employees from the previous SOEs, and estimates that the majority of the wholly privatized SOEs might have been through MBOs or employee buyouts (EBOs).

While recognizing the advantages of MBOs as an approach to privatizing SOEs, there were considerable concerns about large losses of national assets around 2004. Specifically, the process of SOE property rights reform created legal loopholes which left opportunities for management to abuse the system for personal gain. In some cases, government officials and company management worked together to prevent real open and transparent bidding in order to secure under-priced sales to their own advantage. Some other financial scandals revealed cheating in financial reports to create deficit or hide increased value. MBOs were particularly singled out for business irregularities at the time, and aroused heated debate in economic and government circles (Nie, 2005).

In 2003, the State-owned Assets Supervision and Administration Committee (SASAC), the ultimate owner of state-owned assets, issued statements prohibiting the management of a company targeted for MBO from intervening in matters directly affecting the transfer of state-owned property rights. In the process of fundraising, management was prohibited from borrowing from state-owned and state-holding banks and enterprises, their own enterprises, or from using these enterprises' state-owned properties for the purposes of guarantee, mortgage, collateral, and discount. In 2004, the Ministry of Finance (MOF) stopped approving SOE share transfers to MBOs. In 2005, SASAC proclaimed a ban on MBOs in large-sized enterprises and required prudence to be taken in MBOs in small- and medium-sized enterprises (Kun-Chin & Shaofeng, 2013). The existing empirical findings indeed show that the peak of public-to-private MBOs in China was around 2003 and they were brought to a halt by 2006 (Guo et al., 2008).

Distinct characteristics of MBOs in China

Motivation of MBOs in China

One of the key distinct features of China's MBOs was that they were politically purposeful, and in most cases under the control of the state. As reviewed earlier, an MBO was one of the approaches devised by the government to save the ailing SOEs in the unprecedented crisis. These restructurings aimed to improve firm values and efficiency by changing SOEs' ownership structure from state-owned to partially or fully private-owned (Sun et al., 2010). It is noteworthy that it was restricted to non-strategic industries.

For small and medium SOEs, local governments were provided with sufficient autonomy to own and run local SOEs in their own ways (Gan et al., 2010). This was carried out under the State's development strategy under the slogan "retain the large, release the small" (*juada fangxiao*) and its exit from the competitive sectors (Du & Liu, 2015). For large SOEs, the State used a more hands-on approach, and carefully pushed forward reform in a veiled way of "transforming the system" and *gaizhi* due to political and ideological constraints (Garnaut & Song, 2005). Towards the end of 2004, a large proportion of Chinese SOEs were restructured under the strict three-year schedule placed by former Premier Zhu Rongji to turn around loss-making SOEs, some of which were through an MBO.

From the managers' viewpoint, opting for an MBO addressed the fundamental problem of incentive alignment. Under the old State's property right regime, managers were not compensated in line with their efforts and contributions. Managers could not take a dividend from (unlisted) SOEs by law, while their salaries and bonuses were only moderate, which was demotivating. The lack of entrepreneurial incentives was a key reason for organizational inefficiency and declines in profit margins in the face of rapidly increasing market competition (Zhang, 2006). Hence, privatization was considered the window of opportunity for new growth opportunities facilitated by a new ownership structure, such as a buyout (Wright et al., 2001).

Following MBOs, the concentrated ownership allows managers to create value and improve efficiency (Renneboog & Simons, 2005). This is particularly true for public-to-private transactions that suffer more from agency problems due to their dispersed ownership structure. Jensen (1986) argues that increased managerial ownership could improve firm performance because managers have greater stakes in value creation. Managers, having substantial ownership shares following buyouts, are motivated to work harder to maximize their share values.

In contrast, in Western countries, MBOs may occur for reasons other than incentive realignment. For example, low managerial equity firms are more frequently targeted by takeover attempts. Upon becoming the target of a takeover attempt, these managers might opt to undertake an MBO to maintain their position. High managerial equity firms are not concerned about hostile takeover attempts. The MBOs in high managerial ownership firms are more likely to be voluntary transactions (Halpern et al., 1999). Another situation is that in the absence of an insider (family member or manager) to succeed the retiring family, an external management team might acquire the business in an MBO transaction (Scholes et al., 2008). In general, it is noteworthy that MBOs in other contexts are not limited to solving principal-agent problems as they are in the context of China.

The role of PE investors

MBOs often occur with the participation of PE investors (Wright et al., 2009). In many cases, the ability of managers to self-finance a takeover is limited due to the large amounts of capital required. Thus, they often resort to external borrowing and seek financial support from buyout specialists (DeAngelo & DeAngelo, 1987). This is a typical case in Western countries. In China, however, even when management could not secure sufficient finance, there are two reasons why MBOs did not always have PE involvement.

First, due to incomplete accounting regulations, management could take risks to exploit their firms prior to the buyout transactions. This financial preparation could help the management team sufficiently to afford the buyout without PE investors. A typical example is the MBO of Yutong Bus. In the two years leading up to the MBO, the management team lifted the salary cap on senior managers and allocated handsome profit-sharing and dividend payouts to themselves, allowing them to raise money for the MBO (Kun-Chin & Shaofeng, 2013). Specifically, Yutong Bus decided to pay cash dividends of 6 RMB for every 10 shares to its shareholders, even though the company's earnings per share was only 0.72 RMB. After two years, the management had received a minimum of 28.2 million RMB, accounting for 20% of the costs of the subsequent buyout.

Second, Li et al. (2010) find that Chinese management usually bought on average less than 30% of the total equity through a newly established holding company wholly owned by the management or with employees. The management typically paid only around 10% of the total price on deal completion, with the remainder paid in instalments and obtained finance mainly from personal networks. Banks were strictly forbidden from providing loans for buyouts. However, in some buyouts of township and village enterprise (TVEs), the management obtained finance from local credit unions or other undisclosed sources.

One of the disadvantages of the gradual ownership transformation is that governments still have their control rights to the firms. This situation could reduce the incentives of the management team or become a constraint for them to operate within the strategic requirements of local authorities until they have collected sufficient ownership shares that allow them to make fully independent decisions. This situation is the reverse of that in the West, where buyout specialists typically hold a significant proportion of ownership shares in the transactions (Kats, 2008).

The participation of the PE investors is to ensure that ownership structure change is a one-off event. Since PE sponsors are repeat players in the buyout market, they may suffer a reputation loss if their investments are unsuccessful and underperform the market (Cao & Lerner, 2006). Thus, PE firms will actively join with the management to improve firm efficiency towards value maximization. Compared with the intervention of PE firms in the West, the intervention of governments in China is more unproductive and provides firms with less value-added services. However, there are some hard-to-neglect benefits that these firms could enjoy by maintaining a sustainable business-government alliance. They include: protection from political harassment, favorable access to scarce resources including land, "soft" loans from state-owned banks, independent export–import rights, and foreign exchange quotas (Sun & Tong, 2003).

The role of local authorities

The decentralization program gave local governments ownership rights to control and operate local SOEs, which assigned local governments a pivotal role in most of the MBOs. Gan et al. (2010) find that an MBO is a popular privatization approach in regions with a well-developed private sector (coastal provinces). Moreover, governments in interior regions tended to choose other privatization approaches. They also find that the local governments facing hard budget constraints or that have more fiscal surpluses tend to choose an MBO approach to privatization; and vice versa, for governments with soft budget constraints. The contingency of MBO as a means of privatization on the financial governance quality of local authorities suggests that provincial governments play a significant role in promoting/restricting MBOs at local markets.

In addition, there is evidence showing that local governments may have strong incentives to collude with the management team and support buyouts against the will of the central government (Kun-Chin & Shaofeng, 2013). A good example again is Yutong Bus. Local officials foresaw that the management would likely lose the motivation to run the firm efficiently if the MBO failed, but they also counted on Yutong management to promote local related enterprises, supply-chains, employment, and to expand local tax bases. Therefore, local governments decided to connive with the management and circumvent central government policies and regulations to facilitate the buyout in several ways such as strong lobbying activities, overlooking abnormal dividend payouts and high compensation for management, and awarding various honors and awards to the management even after the outcome of the Shanghai stock's investigation into the falsified accounts of the company. Therefore, it is evident that the legally contrived MBO could not have been completed without the tacit cooperation of local governments.

Because of the essential role of local authorities in the buyout process in the Chinese context, Sun et al. (2010) theorize the management–politician alliance by identifying two contrasting outcomes of management–politician alliances: first, successful privatization MBOs implying sustainable original alliances and, second, failed MBOs implying the collapse of the original alliances. Based on this setup, they suggest a range of factors that affect the stability of the business–government alliance in an MBO including rents' generation after the buyout, rents' appropriation away from the firm, distribution of appropriated rents, information asymmetry, regulation from central governments, and legitimacy of the MBOs. Unfortunately, there is little empirical evidence of the management–politician alliance in the context of MBOs.

Performance of Chinese MBO firms

Theoretical predictions and methodological issues

It is notable that the majority of the literature does not directly address the theoretical concerns of MBO performance per se, but discusses more broadly the outcomes of ownership change or privatization. While the theoretical literature on the effects of privatization is well established and provides evidence from different economies (reviewed by Megginson & Netter, 2001; Djankov & Murrell, 2002; Estrin et al., 2009), the empirical evidence is mixed. The focal argument of these theories is that establishing clear property rights through privatization provides economic incentives and better motivates improved economic performance of firms and economies (Estrin et al., 2009). Based on the theory of welfare economics, private ownership would bring more economic efficiency than the state ownership of production. Empirically, there is evidence of positive or marginally positive profitability effects (Song & Yao, 2004; Jefferson & Su, 2006; Rousseau & Xiao, 2008), but a few studies also report none or negative profitability effects (Calomiris et al., 2008). Jefferson and Su (2006) report significant increases in productivity post-ownership change, but insignificant changes in productivity, suggesting that where ownership change does not result in a decline in the level of asset ownership by the state, there remains the possibility for rent capture by either the state or local employees. Frydman et al. (1999) also find that privatization improves performance, but only when SOEs are acquired by outsiders. Most of these studies wrestle with the question of whether management performance improves after privatization.

The studies of the ownership change performance vary considerably in terms of their data and methodology, sample size, and findings. Also, due to data availability issues, the scope of the investigation can be limited. The identification of the ownership change effect is challenging for several reasons. For example, it is difficult to evaluate the effects of ownership change where the ownership structure is itself endogenous to the system that includes both political and performance goals (Megginson & Netter, 2001). In addition, accounting practice in China during the reform era was still not scrutinized, which means that the collusion with governments in overstating SOEs' pre-MBO performance was possible.

Many authors of empirical research try to apply appropriate econometric methods to treat the problem of endogenous variables, including a difference-in-difference approach with endogenous selection using the matching estimator technique (Bellak et al., 2006), an instrumental variable approach (Basu et al., 2004), 3SLS (Driffield et al., 2007) control function approach (Driffield & Du, 2007), and GMM method (Bennett et al., 2007; Hu & Izumida, 2008). However, the majority of the studies in the Chinese context fail to treat carefully the selection of privatization when evaluating its performance outcome. Du and Liu (2015) provide a detailed analysis of the patterns of selection in China's privatization. They find that the worst and the best performing SOEs tend to remain in the state sector, and these two extreme types of SOEs are privatized with less magnitude in private share holding when they are selected to privatize. In terms of timing, the worst and best performing SOEs also tend to be privatized later in time, if they are ever privatized.

Empirical evidence

Financial performance of MBOs

Xu et al. (2008) provide some simple statistics that could yield an informative comparison of MBO firms with other privatized SOEs, as well as firms before and after the buyout. By comparing with the mean and median of several financial variables before and after privatization, the findings suggest that, on average, after an MBO, firms increase assets and sale revenues while reducing debt burdens. These operational expansions in turn result in significant improvements in profitability. The statistics thus suggest that privatization works well for Chinese SOEs. On average, firms after privatization become larger and expand their sale operations subsequently. Thus, all three measures of profitability, including profit as a ratio of assets, as a ratio of sales, and as a ratio of number of employees appear significantly higher than before privatization.

It is noteworthy that MBO firms are smaller than the average privatized SOE in terms of assets and sales revenue. Their profitability before the buyouts is also lower than the average privatized SOE. However, after the buyout, all measures of profitability soar markedly to a level higher than the average. In addition, the significant improvement of labor productivity suggests that SOEs fail to improve their productivity because they cannot lay off redundant workers with permanent contracts with the government. Based on this finding, Gan et al. (2010) argue that the MBO is the best method to improve firm efficiency compared with other methods of privatization, at least for China.

Gan et al. (2010) argue that good firms may be selected for MBOs. Therefore, MBO firms cannot be directly compared with non-MBO firms to draw a conclusion that the MBO is a better privatization method. In order to deal with this issue, they use an instrumental variable estimator to control for the selection of MBO firms. The instrument variables they use include: the fiscal balance of the local government, the share of SOE in total industrial output of a city, whether the government provides a firm with land, whether privatization includes the land of a firm, and whether the government provides loan guarantees to the firm. They argue that these variables are correlated with the regressor MBO and are not correlated with the performance of local firms. Thus, they are valid instruments for the MBO variable. They find that the positive effects of MBOs on firm performance are statistically significant and economically more important using the instrumental variable approach.

Nonetheless, the too-good-to-be-normal effects of MBOs on firm performance raised another research question: is it the case that insider management deliberately manipulate firm performance before the buyout to reduce its sale value? The accounting manipulation hypothesis argues that ex-post MBO value gains do not represent real performance improvements since managers expropriate shareholders by using their private information and buy it below market value.

Lu and Dranove (2013) compare the performance of Chinese MBO firms to the performance of matched control firms. They find that MBO firms experience a significant decrease in profitability immediately prior to privatization and a return soon thereafter. The short-term reduction in profits is accompanied by a decrease in labor productivity, an increase in overdue accounts receivable, and an increase in R&D investment. They also claim that a similar pattern is not observed among firms acquired by outsiders. Thus, they conclude that insiders intentionally suppress the performance of their firms to acquire them at less than fair value.

Li (2003) proposes a solution for this moral hazard problem by suggesting reversing privatization as a screening mechanism. Specifically, the government's right to reverse privatized SOEs could be regarded as a call option on the firm with a strike price, X. If the firm value exceeds X in a pre-determined period after privatization, the government will exercise the call option and buy the firm back. If the firm value is below X, the government will not exercise it and allow the firm to remain private. This solution, however, may reduce the incentive of the management team to improve firm performance, or worse may even alleviate their buyout intention.

Finally, it is noteworthy that Chinese MBOs provide support for Kaplan and Strömberg's (2008) argument that performance-improving activities in MBOs tend to be one-off changes, and once they are implemented, benefits of future changes become relatively smaller. In particular, Xu et al. (2008) find that performance of Chinese MBO firms is negatively associated with the number of years after the buyout events. This finding raises a fundamental question about the phenomenal performance improvements immediately after the buyout. It is unclear whether significant efficiency improvements immediately after a buyout are due to management incentive alignment or the intentional manipulation of the management team to reduce the takeover price before the buyout. The discussion in the next section may provide some insights into this issue.

Non-financial performance of MBOs

One of the key non-financial changes after an MBO is the board transformation. Li et al. (2010) find that after buyouts, the size of the general board declines but cases of the duality roles of chairman and CEO increase. This ownership-management structure could facilitate incentive alignment, for example in the form of increased meeting frequency among members on the management board (Li et al., 2010). This finding is in line with the control hypothesis, suggesting that efficiency improvements in MBOs are largely due to the increased quality of monitoring because MBO boards convene more frequently (Grossman & Hart, 1980)

However, in their study, Li et al. (2010) reveal that the key issues addressed in board meetings are mostly related to MBO transactions, rather than other issues concerning firm operation and performance. This finding raises a fundamental concern about the sources of efficiency improvements. How could MBO firms improve performance after a buyout if the board does not work on it? This finding casts doubts on the validity of the management incentive alignment hypothesis in the context of China. It also suggests that the manipulation hypothesis may have a non-negligible explanatory power for the success of Chinese MBOs.

In terms of management compensation after buyouts, there is a consensus finding that executives' compensation is not tied to firm performance. This is interpreted in significantly different ways among scholars. Chen et al. (2010) argue that non-performance-based compensation structures tend to lead to entrenched insider managers further colluding with government officials and extracting firm assets. Therefore, they suggest that the Chinese government should consider exerting rigorous restrictions on executive shareholdings and MBO transactions. Transparent constraints would help reduce rent-seeking coalitions between managers and local politicians. By contrast, Gan et al. (2010) argue that MBO firms do not need to have performance-based pay to align executives' incentives. Their reason is that managers of MBO firms are owners, hence ownership and control are already aligned.

Finally, despite controversial opinions concerning the source of performance improvements, there is a consensus that Chinese MBO firms are moving towards greater levels of professionalization by introducing international accounting standards and independent auditors, as well as a board of directors (Xu et al., 2008; Li et al., 2010; Lu & Dranove, 2013). In contrast, firms that are privatized to outsiders are significantly less likely to establish a board of directors, to change the core management team, or to adopt international accounting standards. It is possible that the reason behind the professionalization of MBO firms is that they are considering listing and using the stock market as an exit platform.

Post-MBO firms detach from governments' control

There is another distinct characteristic between MBOs and other forms of privatization.

Unlike the privatized SOEs through IPO, in which the state still plays a non-negligible role and often retains rights to make decisions about firm's daily operations (Li et al., 2010), the government's control reduces much more in the case of MBOs. To some extent, the average intervention from governments after MBOs decreases to a level which is very close to that of regular private firms (Guo et al., 2008). For non-MBO privatized firms, the intervention remains almost nine times higher in comparison to MBO firms (Gan et al., 2010). This indicates that an MBO could completely change a firm's ownership structure in contrast to other privatization methods.

Another unusual feature of corporate governance in China is that almost all firms, including private and foreign firms, must have a committee of the Communist Party; and the party committee is involved in major decision-making within the firms. Gan et al. (2010) find that the party committee becomes less important after privatization; and this reduction is more substantial in MBO firms than in the firms privatized through other approaches. They also report that the average number of interventions made by the party committee in corporate decision-making is 16% of total decisions for MBO firms, significantly lower than firms that were privatized by selling to outsiders (25%), or by other methods (59%).

MBOs create concentrated ownership

Another non-financial feature of Chinese MBOs is that they create concentrated ownership. However, the level of concentration tends to be less severe than that in firms privatized by other methods. Gan et al. (2010) find that the ownership of the largest shareholder of MBO firms is significantly lower than for non-MBO privatized firms. The ownership by the second and third largest shareholders is also at the same levels with other firms. These statistics signal that ownership in MBO firms is not as highly concentrated as firms privatized using other methods. Nonetheless, it is noteworthy that the sum of the three largest shareholders in MBO firms on average exceed 50% of the total shares of a firm, which is a legal benchmark to obtain control rights.

A highly concentrated ownership structure has an advantage in reducing management costs because it alleviates heterogeneous decisions of the management board and prevents insider conflicts. Moreover, concentrated ownership also helps to align managerial interests with those of shareholders (Tseo et al., 2004). However, this kind of ownership also comes with a disadvantage, i.e., a small group of large shareholders has an absolute right of control over the firm and thus power to expropriate the resources of minority shareholders.

MBO firms suffer from less severe ownership concentration compared to firms privatized by other methods because one individual in the management team is typically unable to finance sufficient capital for the buyout. Therefore, several managers, sometimes with the participation of employees, together team up as a buyout crew, with a leading member who is usually the CEO of the firm (Tseo et al., 2004). This distinct feature of MBO firms allows management to have sufficient ownership concentration, but not over-concentrated in one member of the team. Therefore, MBO firms with average levels of ownership concentration could successfully align managerial incentives without an absolute power to expropriate outside shareholders (Gan, 2009).

Conclusion

This chapter provided a review of MBOs with Chinese characteristics that mostly occurred during 1998–2004. During this extraordinary enterprise reform period in China, a large number of MBOs took place so as to turn failing SOEs into profitable businesses. We reviewed the historical background and institutional context of these buyouts that are crucial to understanding their causes and consequences. Particular attention was paid to comparing and contrasting the differences in the incentives of the management involved in these buyouts, the role of PE investors, and the unique yet vital role of local governments.

The chapter also reviewed the performance of MBOs in China. Overall, the literature on this topic is sporadic and the data scarce. The intertwined relationship between business and government threads its way through the history of MBOs in China and, more generally, the evolution of Chinese enterprises. Much of the success of the reforms lies in the alignment of the entrepreneurs' incentives and government objectives.

Overall, there are only a few studies with any empirical data to examine the performance of different types of privatization including MBOs in China, which our existing knowledge is based upon. The confounding factors that may make MBOs particularly successful in SOE transition are still lack of theoretical considerations and sufficient empirical supports. Understanding more about the performance of MBO firms in comparison to other types of ownership change would help draw a larger picture of MBOs in China, and further understand better the Chinese economic transition.

Given the unique institutional setup of MBOs in China over this period, it would be very interesting to follow up the buyout companies for a longer period than the current literature has done. Contrasting and comparing the long-term performance of the firms that experienced MBOs and other types of privatization would highlight the effects of the alignment of entrepreneurs' incentives and government objectives on determining the success of the deal, and in particular the role of local governments in the process.

In addition to the well-researched public-to-private MBO type, it is also worth investigating other types of MBOs (private-to-private MBOs, foreign-to-domestic, domestic-to-foreign) that are largely left unexplored in the literature. We know relatively little about them and whether these cases are different from those in more advanced economies. China's private sector is rapidly growing more dynamic, and MBO transactions among private and foreign invested firms has become increasingly popular under the improved property rights protection from the governments.

Note

1 It was designed as a transitional price mechanism from a planned economy to a market economy.

References

Basu, S., Estrin, S., & Svejnar, J. 2004. *Wage determination under communism and in transition: Evidence from Central Europe*. IZA Discussion Paper No. 1276. Available at: SSRN: https://ssrn.com/abstract=586065.

Bellak, C., Leibrecht, M., & Römisch, R. 2006. On the appropriate measure of tax burden on foreign direct investment to the CEECs. *Applied Economics Letters Applied Economics Letters*, 14: 603–606.

Bennett, J., Lubben, F., & Hogarth, S. 2007. Bringing science to life: A synthesis of the research evidence on the effects of context-based and STS approaches to science teaching. *SCE Science Education*, 91: 347–370.

Calomiris, C., Fisman, R., & Yongxian, W. 2008. *Profiting from government stakes in a command economy: Evidence from Chinese asset sales*. NBER Working Paper No. 13774.

Cao, J., & Lerner, J. 2006. The performance of reverse leveraged buyouts. *Journal of Financial Economics*, 91: 139–157.

Chen, J. J., Xuguang, L., & Weian, L. 2010. The effect of insider control and global benchmarks on Chinese executive compensation. *Corporate Governance: An International Review*, 18: 107–123.

DeAngelo, H., & DeAngelo, L. 1987. Management buyouts of publicly traded corporations. *Financial Analysts Journal*, 43: 38–49.

Djankov, S., & Murrell, P. 2002. Enterprise restructuring in transition: A quantitative survey. *Journal of Economic Literature*, 40: 739–792.

Driffield, N., & Du, J. 2007. Privatisation, state ownership and productivity: Evidence from China. *International Journal of the Economics of Business*, 14: 215–239.

Driffield, N., Mahambare, V., & Pal, S. 2007. How does ownership structure affect capital structure and firm value? Recent evidence from East Asia. *Economics of Transition*, 15: 535–573.

Du, J., & Liu, X. 2015. Selection, staging and sequencing in the recent Chinese privatization. *Journal of Law and Economics*, 58(3): 657–682.

Du, J., Liu, X., & Zhou, Y. 2014. State advances and private retreats? Evidence from the decomposition of the Chinese manufacturing aggregate productivity decomposition in China. *China Economic Review*, 31: 459–474.

Estrin, S., Hanousek, J., Kočenda, E., & Svejnar, J. 2009. Effects of privatisation and ownership in transition economies. *Journal of Economic Literature*, 47: 699–728.

Frydman, R., Gray, C., Hessel, M., & Rapaczynski, A. 1999. When does privatisation work? The impact of private ownership on corporate performance in the transition economies. *Quarterly Journal of Economics*, 114: 1153–1191.

Gan, J. 2009. Privatisation in China: Experiences and lessons. In J. R. Barth, J. A. Tatom, & G. Yago (Eds.), *China's emerging financial markets: Challenges and opportunities*. New York: Springer, 581–592.

Gan, J., Guo, Y., & Xu, C. 2010. *Privatisation and the change of control rights: The case of China*. Working paper, School of Economics Peking University.

Garnaut, R., & Song, L. (eds). 2005. *The China boom and its discontents*. Canberra: ANU E Press.

Grossman, S. J., & Hart, O. D. 1980. Takeover bids, the free-rider problem, and the theory of the corporation. *The Bell Journal of Economics*, 11: 42–64.
Guo, Y., Gan, J., & Xu, C. 2008. A nationwide survey of privatised firms in China. *Seoul Journal of Economics*, 21: 311–331.
Halpern, P., Kieschnick, R., & Rotenberg, W. 1999. On the heterogeneity of leveraged going private transactions. *Review of Financial Studies*, 12: 281–309.
Hu, Y., & Izumida, S. 2008. Ownership concentration and corporate performance: A causal analysis with Japanese panel data. *Corporate Governance*, 16: 342–358.
Jefferson, G. H., & Su, J. 2006. Privatisation and restructuring in China: Evidence from shareholding ownership, 1995–2001. *YJCEC Journal of Comparative Economics*, 34: 146–166.
Jensen, M. C. 1986. *Agency costs of free cash flow, corporate finance, and takeovers*. University of Rochester, NJ: Managerial Economics Research Center, Graduate School of Management.
Kaplan, S. N., & Strömberg, P. 2008. Leveraged buyouts and private equity. *The Journal of Economic Perspectives*, 23: 121–146.
Kats, S. P. 2008. Earnings quality and ownership structure: The role of private equity sponsors. *The Accounting Review*, 84: 623–658.
Kun-Chin, L. I. N., & Shaofeng, C. 2013. The local government in corporate restructuring: Case studies in fractured bargaining relations. *Journal of Current Chinese Affairs*, 42: 171.
Li, H. 2003. Reversing privatisation as a screening mechanism. *Economics Letters*, 78: 267–271.
Li, Y., Wright, M., & Scholes, L. 2010. Chinese management buyouts and board transformation. *Journal of Business Ethics*, 95: 361.
Liu, X.-X. 2008. *The micro-foundation of China's market economy*. 30 years of China's reform studies series. Shanghai: Shanghai Renmin Press and Gezhi Press [in Chinese] (2008); Singapore: Cengage Learning Asia Pte. Ltd. [in English] (2009).
Lu, S. F., & Dranove, D. 2013. Profiting from gaizhi: Management buyouts during China's privatisation. *Journal of Comparative Economics*, 41: 634–650.
Megginson, W. L., & Netter, J. M. 2001. From state to market: A survey of empirical studies on privatisation. *Journal of Economic Literature*, 39: 321–389.
Mickiewicz, T. 2009. Hierarchy of governance institutions and the pecking order of privatisation. *Post-Communist Economies*, 21(4): 399–423.
Nie, S. 2005. Short history of reforms concerning Chinese state owned enterprises. *Shanghai Flash, Consulate General of Switzerland*, 2, February.
Renneboog, L., & Simons, T. 2005. *Public-to-private transactions: LBOs, MBOs, MBIs and IBOs*. TILEC Discussion Paper, Vol. 2005-023. Available at: urn:nbn:nl:ui:12-193351.
Rousseau, P. L., & Xiao, S. 2008. Change of control and the success of China's share-issue privatisation. *CHIECO China Economic Review*, 19: 605–613.
Scholes, L., Westhead, P., & Burrows, A. 2008. Family firm succession: The management buy-out and buy-in routes. *Journal of Small Business and Enterprise Development*, 15: 8–30.
Song, L., & Yao, Y. 2004. Impacts of privatisation on firm performance in China. *China Centre for Economics Research*, **E2004005**.
Strömberg, P. 2008. The new demography of private equity. *The Global Impact of Private Equity Report*, 1: 3–26.
Sun, P., Wright, M., & Mellahi, K. 2010. Is entrepreneur-politician alliance sustainable during transition? The case of management buyouts in China. *Management and Organization Review*, 1: 101–121.
Sun, Q., & Tong, W. H. S. 2003. China share issue privatisation: The extent of its success. *Journal of Financial Economics*, 70: 183–222.
Tseo, G., Hou, G. S., Zhang, P.-Z., & Zhang, L. 2004. Employee ownership and profit sharing as positive factors in the reform of Chinese state-owned enterprises. *Economic & Industrial Democracy*, 25: 147–177.
Wright, M., Gilligan, J., & Amess, K. 2009. The economic impact of private equity: What we know and what we would like to know. *Venture Capital*, 11: 1–21.
Wright, M., Hoskisson, R. E., & Busenitz, L. W. 2001. Firm rebirth: Buyouts as facilitators of strategic growth and entrepreneurship. *Academy of Management Executive*, 15: 111–125.
Xu, C., Gan, J., & Guo, Y. 2008. What makes privatisation work? The case of China. *NBER's Working Group on China 2008*.
Zhang, D. 2006. *A chronicle history of the Chinese state-owned enterprises reform*. Shanghai: China Worker Press.

PART III

Financing, structuring, and private equity firms

13

THE EVOLUTION AND STRATEGIC POSITIONING OF PRIVATE EQUITY FIRMS[1]

Robert E. Hoskisson, Wei Shi, Xiwei Yi, and Jing Jin

Introduction

General partners in private equity (PE) firms manage funds contributed by PE investors (limited partners, usually institutional investors) to acquire portfolio firms, most often using additional debt capital borrowed from banks or debt markets. As such, PE firms' general partners, limited partner investors, portfolio firms (or acquired firms, often labeled buyout firms), banks, and other debt providers are the main players in PE transactions (Stowell, 2010; Gilligan & Wright, 2014). Among the above five players, PE firms' general partners play the most important role as they solicit investor funds (limited partners), identify target portfolio firms, and initiate relationships with banks and other debt providers to finance buyout deals.[2]

Although PE firms' general partners are the key players in PE transactions, the majority of academic research on PE (for reviews see Harris et al., 2005; Cumming et al., 2007; Renneboog et al., 2007; and Wright et al., 2009) has focused on explaining performance disparities between PE portfolio firms and their peer publicly traded firms. The lack of a systematic examination of PE firms' strategies (when we speak of PE strategy we mean the overall portfolio strategy of general partners) hinders our understanding of competitive positioning among PE firms and its associated impact on buyout portfolio firms. To enrich our knowledge about PE firms' strategies, this chapter aims to provide a conceptual configuration of PE firms' strategic positioning (Doty & Glick, 1994).

To develop the foundation for our configuration model, we first review the evolution of PE firms through two historical waves of PE transactions (e.g., Kaplan & Strömberg, 2009). During the first wave, in the 1980s, PE firms focused on garnering the benefits of high financial leverage through leveraged buyouts (LBOs) of portfolio firms. In this wave, agency theory was foundational to explain the influence that PE firms had on buyout portfolio firms. After the first wave of PE transactions collapsed due to the over-issuance of junk bonds, the PE industry experienced a mild upward cycle in the 1990s. The second wave of PE transactions began at the end of the 1990s and peaked in 2007, but was interrupted by the 2008 global financial crisis. As the environment changed during the second wave and created a situation that goes beyond the explanations of agency theory, we argue that the combination of resource dependence theory and resource-based theory helps us better understand why

PE firms need to cultivate distinctly different competencies and capabilities and reorient their strategies to cope with increased environmental uncertainties and complexities. We will introduce these perspectives more fully in the second section as we analyze PE firms' strategic choices in relation to environmental changes and how such choices have resulted in divergent strategic positions.

Based on our review of the evolution of PE firms, we configure PE firms into four distinct strategic foci along two dimensions: financial structure emphasis and portfolio firm scope. The financial structure emphasis dimension refers to the level of financial leverage used by PE firms in restructuring the capital deployed among portfolio firms. This dimension indicates PE firms' preference for using debt versus equity financing in the capital structure of portfolio firms and reflects PE firms' short-term versus long-term investment horizon. To be clear, we are not talking about the central sourcing of overall capital, either debt or public equity, sought by general partners (for instance, Blackstone Group became publicly traded through an IPO in 2007). Rather, our focus is on how long- or short-term-oriented the overall deal structure that general partners apply to portfolio firms is.

The second dimension, portfolio firm scope, refers to the level of industry diversification among PE firms' portfolios of business. This dimension demonstrates how PE firms utilize their distinct resources and capabilities to choose different strategies and establish competitive advantages. After justifying these two dimensions, we categorize PE firms into four types: short-term efficiency niche players, niche players with long-term equity positions, diversified players with focused groups of portfolio firms, and short-term diversified efficiency-oriented players. We analyze the strategic focus and competitive advantage of each type of player and provide examples of PE firms associated with each type in the third section of the chapter. In addition, we analyze the dynamic movement of PE firms between types along the two dimensions, given opportunity for portfolio expansion and response to environmental change. In the final section, we discuss theoretical implications and future research opportunities using our proposed conceptual framework as well as managerial and public policy implications in regard to emerging trends in the PE industry. We start, however, by briefly reviewing the evolution of the PE industry.

Evolution of the PE industry

In this section, we review the evolution of PE firms by examining the previously mentioned two waves of PE transactions and comparing their distinguishing characteristics. In doing so, we provide an understanding of the PE firms' strategic advantages compared with other firms using agency theory in the first wave of PE transactions. We then apply resource dependence theory and the resource-based theory to explain how PE firms evolved to cope with environmental changes and external uncertainties during the second wave of PE transactions.

The first wave of PE firm transactions emerged during the 1980s. In 1981, Kohlberg Kravis Roberts (KKR & Co.) executed six LBO transactions, which encouraged other investors to engage in similar buyout transactions. Such investors typically acquired majority control of existing mature firms via increased financial leverage. Historically, the debt proportion of such portfolio buyout firms often ranged from 60% to 90% (Kaplan & Strömberg, 2009).

In regard to the first wave of PE firm transactions, the introduction of high leverage in PE portfolio firms as well as the adoption of incentive mechanisms as suggested by agency theory (Jensen & Meckling, 1976) better aligned the interests of portfolio firm managers to reduce agency costs (relative to publicly owned corporations) and thereby improved performance in buyout firms. In addition, high leverage results in capital structure changes and "tightens governance arrangements so as to reduce managerial discretion" (Wright et al., 1994: 217) and also boosts the return on equity for PE portfolio firms by deducting interest from profits before taxes (Kaplan, 1991; Wright et al., 2009; Lerner, 2011). According to agency theory, investors and owners are principals, and they hire managers to manage their businesses. To ensure that managers act in the interests of principals, firms establish boards of directors to monitor managers and use stock options to align the interests of shareholders and managers. A main conflict of interest between investors and managers in mature firms is managers' frivolous use of free cash flow. PE firms' prevalent use of high leverage is considered an effective strategy to discipline managers because the latter are obligated to meet interest payments. In other words, high levels of debt help reduce agency costs in portfolio firms (Jensen, 1986) because the need to pay back principal and interest compels managers to enhance firm performance and create value for shareholders.

While the use of high leverage has a number of advantages, it may also incur high risks. Later in the first wave of PE transactions, a large proportion of debt consisted of junior or unsecured loans financed by either high-yield bonds or "mezzanine debt" (Yago, 1991), which is subordinated to senior debt (Demiroglu & James, 2010). Issuing such junk bonds, while at first increasing capital liquidity and thereby stimulating a series of LBOs, generated high deal risks and finally led to the collapse of the first wave of buyout transactions.

Between the first and second waves of PE transactions in the early 1990s, as the PE industry gradually recovered from the junk bonds crisis, the industry experienced a mild upward cycle of LBO transactions. However, a second major wave of PE transactions emerged in the early 2000s. Specifically, from 1998 to 2005, PE buyouts increased at an annual rate of 13.22% (PricewaterhouseCoopers, 2006), primarily due to the low cost of capital. In the US, the value of PE transactions peaked in 2006, reflected in the delisting of many public firms. For example, the New York Stock Exchange (NYSE) recorded a net withdrawal of $38.8 billion in listed capital. NASDAQ recorded a net withdrawal of $11 billion as many public firms went private (Schneider & Valenti, 2010).

The second wave of PE transactions differs from the first wave in two ways. First, in the second wave the cost of being public became an additional reason for going private. Downward pressure on pay and the rising invasiveness of stakeholders decreased the attractiveness of being a public company for top executives (Kaplan, 2009). After 2002, the costs of being a public firm increased due to the requirements of the Sarbanes-Oxley Act (SOX). To avoid these costs and the short-term orientation caused by shareholder expectations associated with quarterly reports, PE firms took public firms private, allowing these firms to focus on better value creation, especially during periods of financial distress (Minns, 2010).

Second, in the second wave PE firms became more operations-oriented and focused on providing professional guidance (Matthews et al., 2009); in the first wave they had been keen on being "financial engineers," creating value for the focal firm through cost-cutting measures (e.g., significant layoffs). Since short-term cost-cutting strategy caused public resistance to PE firms, in the second wave more and more PE firms changed their role from "financial engineers" to "operational engineers" by providing professional managerial guidance to buyout firms to improve value and profitability. As a result, an increasing number of PE firms established their own professional advice teams (e.g., KKR and Bain Capital) and built partnerships with buyout firms to help them implement their strategic plans.

The revitalization of PE transactions in the 2000s was due partly to the need to shelter public firms from excessive governance costs and short-term pressure from investors as well as the cheaper cost of debt, but this renaissance was impeded by the global financial crisis that began at the end of 2007. The massive credit market crisis engendered by the global financial crisis posed a significant challenge to PE firms because inexpensive and readily available debt sources dried up. In addition, PE firms faced increasing normative pressure from public and government oversight, creating legitimacy concerns as media exposure depicted PE firms as excessively greedy during deteriorating macro-economic conditions (Blundell-Wignall, 2007). Hence, these adverse economic conditions complicated the profitability of the second wave of PE transactions.

Theoretical background: establishing PE firm positioning

To analyze how PE firms cope with emerging challenges such as the credit squeeze and exit difficulties we turn to resource dependence theory. Resource dependence theory (Pfeffer & Salancik, 1978; Hillman et al., 2009) contends that organizations, constrained by a web of interdependencies with other organizations, attempt to manage their external dependencies to reduce associated uncertainty and risks. Given the unfavorable social and financial environments confronting PE firms, it would follow that they would want to reexamine their relationships with external parties. Since the unfavorable financial market restrains available debt sources, higher levels of equity investment (mostly private ownership) tend to replace the dominant use of high debt in the financial structure of PE transactions. An increase in equity investment is not only a response to changed hostile business environments, but also an intentionally managed endeavor by PE firms to reduce uncertainty and strengthen the firm's independence from external parties. In addition, differentiated investment strategies reflect PE firms' efforts to reduce direct competition between firms for deals. In sum, resource dependence theory explains why, following the collapse of the first wave of PE transactions, PE firms would employ more equity investment among portfolio firms' capital structure instead of relying solely on riskier debt. In other words, some PE firms actively adapted their investment strategies to the changed external environment, as suggested by resource dependence theory.

This kind of environmental adaptation, however, is not the only means that PE firms have used to attract deals. Resource-based theory argues that sustained competitive advantages derive from the firm's valuable, rare, inimitable, and nonsubstitutable (VRIN) resources (Barney, 1991) and emphasizes the role of firms' embedded resources in shaping competitive advantage. From a resource-based perspective and in association with more competition for available capital, PE firms need to differentiate themselves and more clearly establish their competitive advantages to select targets and obtain capital. In addition, the shift from financial engineering that relied on retrenchment tactics in the first wave of PE transactions to operational engineering that emphasizes professional managerial guidance in the second wave of PE transactions also provides PE firms with the opportunity to consider their strategic identity. To comply with the trend to provide professional managerial guidance, some small- and medium-sized PE firms focus on a specialized field where their accumulated experience and professional teams can provide a competitive edge. Hence, the resource-based theory supports the emerging trend for PE firms to differentiate based on a narrow versus broad scope among portfolio firms. Also, PE firms that adopt more equity and less leverage may need to retain portfolio firms longer and develop skills to create value rather than relying on the short-term leverage effect coming primarily from a debt emphasis.

In sum, as PE firms intentionally manage environmental uncertainty and cultivate their core competencies, integrating resource dependence theory and resource-based theory into our conceptual framework will help unpack the theoretical rationales behind PE firm strategies.

Strategic configuration model of PE firms

As noted in the introduction, existing research regarding PE firms themselves has been rather limited, hindering our understanding of PE firms' overall strategic positioning and the associated impact on portfolio performance. As such, we seek to configure PE firms into a more coherent typological framework (Doty & Glick, 1994). Derived from our description of the evolution of PE firms, we configure PE firms into four distinct strategic foci along two dimensions, as previously noted: financial structure emphasis and portfolio firm scope. The financial structure emphasis dimension reflects the level of financial leverage used by PE firms in structuring their portfolio firms. The portfolio firm scope dimension refers to the level of industry diversification among PE firms' portfolios of business. We argue that these two dimensions capture configuration types among PE firms and that the combination of resource dependence theory and resource-based theory provides theoretical rationales for choosing these two dimensions.

For the *financial structure emphasis* dimension, the level of equity finance reflects PE firms' long-range investment horizons, in that equity holdings enable PE firms to reap sustained long-term profits from their equity positions and likewise create potential long-term incentives for portfolio firm managers and other equity partners (e.g., long-term institutional investors). In contrast, relying on debt finance encourages PE firms to restructure and exit their invested firms through initial public offerings (IPOs) as soon as possible to garner momentum profits from improved performance and to avoid potential bankruptcy associated with high leverage. For the *portfolio firm scope* dimension, a focused portfolio firm allows PE firms to nurture expertise in-house and thus provide buyout firms with professional guidance. However, in a diversified portfolio, operational expertise is more difficult to apply because a wider range of knowledge is more difficult to acquire, rendering the PE firm more likely to maintain financial engineering as its dominant skill.

We believe these two dimensions motivate PE firms to adopt distinct strategic foci for two reasons. First, the PE industry is facing a dramatically changed business environment, making sole reliance on high leverage to generate profits for investors more and more challenging (Kaplan, 2009). PE firms are commonly attacked for taking advantage of provisions in US tax law that treat carried interest from debt and ordinary income differentially (Wruck, 2008; *The Economist*, 2012a). Accordingly, some PE firms tend to increase their equity investment to demonstrate a longer-term commitment to buyout firms. Moreover, PE firms face a weak equity market that has not fully recovered from the 2008 global financial crisis and hence have difficulties divesting highly leveraged portfolio firms through IPOs. Consequently, some PE firms have to operate a business longer than normal because exit opportunities are limited. In addition, the recent credit crunch has inhibited PE firms from obtaining cheap debt from banks and other financial institutions. As a result, some PE firms have changed from a conventional strategy hinging on high leverage to engaging in more equity investment and an increased operational focus.

Second, PE firms need to position themselves differentially to satisfy the needs of distinct PE investors and to compete for high-value buyout firms. The financial crisis makes PE investors as well as other financial investors more risk averse; accordingly, PE investors (limited partners) exhibit a high level of caution when making investment decisions and choosing PE funds in which to invest. Although the depressed world economy has led to low

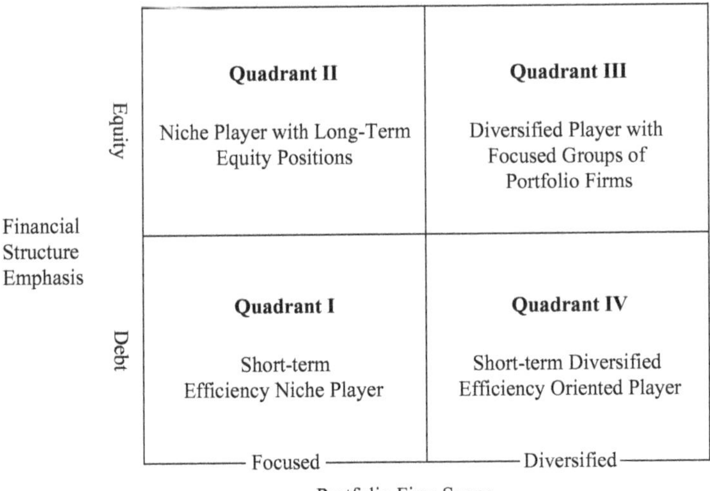

Figure 13.1 Strategic focus of PE firms: financial structure emphasis and portfolio firm emphasis
Source: Authors.

interest rates on borrowing, banks are becoming increasingly circumspect when assessing lending opportunities in the post-financial crisis era. Therefore, PE firms need to establish distinct competitive advantage to compete intensely for high-value investors, in particular pension funds (Nielsen, 2008) and lenders. Furthermore, given the large number of PE firms and limited number of buyout opportunities, PE firms face increased pressure in competing for portfolio firms with high potential (Gurung & Lerner, 2009; Lerner, 2011). Consequently, PE firms seek to differentiate themselves from one another to attract and retain institutional investors with comparable risk profiles and time horizons. Although most large PE firms have little difficulty raising funds thanks to their size and associated legitimacy and credibility, these firms (e.g., KKR and Blackstone) need to devote more attention to improving operational and managerial skills of portfolio firms (Rubenstein, 2010). For small- and medium-sized PE firms, the changed environment requires them to cultivate their core competitive skills and leverage their expertise in niche fields to compete for high-value PE limited partner investors and portfolio firms.

In sum, it is increasingly apparent that strategic choices of PE firms are diverging from each other to take advantage of their accumulated capabilities, expertise, and market power. Building on the dimensions of financial structure emphasis and portfolio firm scope, we illustrate our configuration framework in Figure 13.1. The horizontal axis differentiates PE firms by their portfolio firm scopes; the vertical axis differentiates PE firms by the financial structure emphasis of their portfolio firms. In the subsections that follow, we describe the four ideal types of PE firms and provide examples of PE firms associated with each quadrant in Figure 13.1.

Quadrant I: short-term efficiency niche players

PE firms in Quadrant I invest in a narrow scope of industry or firm types and have a typical financial structure that emphasizes debt over equity. This group of PE firms inherited the tradition of using high leverage as a tool to manage buyout firms and prefer to focus on a narrow set of industries and to provide professional performance improvement guidance for portfolio firms. In this chapter, we define this group of PE firms as short-term efficiency niche players. We will analyze strategic advantages of this group of PE firms from the two dimensions.

Using debt rather than equity in the financial structure refers to acquiring a company using a comparatively smaller portion of equity and a larger portion of external debt. As noted earlier, adopting high leverage as the financial structure of the portfolio firm has a variety of advantages. First, as mentioned, high leverage creates pressure on managers to fulfill the obligation to make principal and interest payments and improves the firm's corporate governance by reducing agency costs. Second, in the US and many other countries, high leverage increases the value of the firm through tax deductions on interest (Kaplan & Strömberg, 2009). Third, while high leverage poses great risks for public firms, portfolio firms that become private face less pressure from governance requirements (through SOX) and less obligation to meet short-term investor expectations. Hence, high leverage greatly enhances the short-term efficiency of PE transactions by aligning the interests of managers and investors.

The preference for a focused portfolio firm scope represents a commitment to value creation for the acquired firm as a niche player. Focusing on certain industries enables PE firms to recruit experienced industry experts, accumulate important industry knowledge and experience, and cultivate the specialized capabilities necessary to deal with particular industry requirements. In addition, industry experts create additional value for the acquired firms by providing focused talent and accumulated experience in that industry. A focused PE firm is able to target its resources and attention on certain industries and hence concentrate resources on research in those industries, leading to important accumulated industry knowledge.

Starting in the 1980s most PE firms had strategies that fit well within this quadrant. A recent example of a short-term efficiency niche player is Bain Capital, an asset management financial services company headquartered in Boston, Massachusetts.[3] Although Bain Capital has pursued deals internationally and now has subsidiaries in Europe, Asia, and India (Lopez-de-Silanes et al., 2009), it has relied mainly on capital raised from pension funds, insurance companies, endowments, high-net-worth individuals, sovereign wealth funds, and other institutional investors. The company is a typical short-term efficiency niche player, although it has traditionally focused on services industries (e.g., SunGard in business services and Dunkin' Brands in the dining industry) (McCarthy & Alvarez, 2006; Rozwadowski & Young, 2005). Benefiting from its focused strategy, Bain Capital is able to successfully implement corporate capital restructuring, operating earnings improvements, and acquisition development across countries.

Quadrant II: niche players with long-term equity positions

Niche players with long-term equity positions are the PE firms with a focused portfolio firm scope that deploy more long-run equity holdings in the financial structure of the buyout firms. To develop in-depth strategic and operational insights and to cultivate networks in these industries, these PE firms concentrate on a limited number of industry segments (Harper & Schneider, 2004). We further explain the main features of investment strategies of niche players using SCF Partners as an example.

In recognition of his clients' growing demands for PE investment, L. E. Simmons founded SCF Partners in 1989. Under Simmons' leadership, the firm has made more than $1.6 billion in PE capital investments in energy services and equipment companies and has created more than 10 public companies listed on the US and Canadian stock markets. By the end of 2010, SCF Partners managed approximately $1.5 billion in assets (SCF Partners, 2012). Nevertheless, SCF Partners is a small PE firm when compared to KKR, which managed more than $60 billion at the end of 2010 (Eccles et al., 2011). Unlike a typical PE firm that emphasizes debt financing, SCF Partners attaches prime importance to providing equity capital to buyout portfolio firms in the energy services, manufacturing, and equipment industry segments. In addition, SCF Partners not only gives its portfolio firms consistent professional support for their strategic growth but also injects capital incrementally to buttress the strategic acquisitions and growth plans of its firms. Examining SCF Partners' investment history reveals two features of its investment philosophy: the narrow investment focus and the reliance on equity investment.

First, the narrow investment focus enables SCF Partners to develop its expertise and cultivate its networks to build a solid reputation in its chosen industries. Its amassed experience and established reputation in these industries not only help SCF Partners provide portfolio firms with professional support but also aid in identifying future investment targets. Thanks to its industry knowledge, SCF Partners has a competitive edge in foreseeing industry trends and seeking firms with growth prospects in the energy services industry. Moreover, SCF Partners' in-depth industry expertise allows it to attract and win the confidence of investors with long-run investment horizons. A second feature of its investment philosophy finds SCF Partners using more equity capital to conduct its transactions because a high leverage ratio obligates buyout firms to service the debt rather than foster growth.

Unlike conventional PE practices that emphasize drastic organizational changes in the post-buyout period, SCF Partners collaborates with entrepreneurial owners of buyout firms to implement incremental "reforms." These owners, mostly private and often founder-dominated, have deep knowledge about and emotional connections with their ventures and are committed to growing their businesses. In other words, these entrepreneurial owners are the key to buyout businesses' successes. As a result, in the post-buyout period, most top executives remain in the firm, and the role of SCF Partners is to assist these executives in improving firm performance and boosting future growth through appropriate acquisitions and fostering co-operation.

For example, the rapid growth of the tar sands industry in Canada requires increased investment in infrastructure (e.g., roads and metal buildings to accommodate workers), as most tar sands resources are located in the Canadian wilderness. Recognizing opportunities associated with this boom, SCF Partners established Site Energy Services Ltd. to acquire small energy services firms, consolidating local infrastructure services firms in Calgary by partnering with top managers of these firms. Other examples of SCF Partners' investments include Rockwater Energy Solutions, which specializes in comprehensive fluids management services and environmental solutions, and Forum Energy Technologies (FET), which provides technologies and products to the energy industry.

Compared to Site Energy Services, FET is in a later stage of development. In partnership with SCF, FET has built businesses around deep-sea drilling services and sells remotely operated vehicles used for inspection and survey of associated deep-water well construction. In support of FET, SCF initiated an IPO in April 2012, not as an exit strategy but to provide continuing capital to pay down debt and support the growth of the company. Only about 20% of the company ownership was floated. SCF Partner has another portfolio company, Rockwater Energy Solutions, focused on services for horizontal drilling and associated hydraulic fracturing service where oil shale opportunities exist in the Bakken (North Dakota) and

Eagleford (West Texas) fields. SCF also has other businesses focused on drilling and well completion service products, intervention products, and services to get wells flowing.

The role of SCF Partners in its investments is to provide financial and strategic growth support to the owners of each individual firm, and deploy the resources of these firms in aggregate to negotiate larger contracts and offer a wider scope of infrastructure and environmental services. In this sense, SCF Partners provides a platform for owners of these services firms to co-operate with and complement each other and jointly explore potential markets. In addition, SCF Partners builds portfolio firms through incremental acquisitions. SCF Partners not only provides portfolio firms with capital to acquire related assets, but also helps them identify acquisition targets and integrate acquired firms.

SCF Partners' investment practices attest to a new trend in PE investments that departs from the emphasis on high leverage. The tenets of agency theory prescribe that high leverage leaves managers with little discretion and exerts pressure to avoid over-diversification (Wright et al., 2001). However, SCF Partners does not attempt to create value through reducing agency costs because most of its portfolio firms are small, private firms. Instead, it generates value by providing expertise and support to its portfolio firms. This position is supported by research by Castellaneta and Gottschalg (2016) who find the PE ownership fosters better performance the longer the portfolio firm is held, suggesting PE parent value-added rather than performance due to good target selection. We anticipate that more and more small- and medium-sized PE firms will adopt similar investment strategies and become niche players with long-term equity positions.

Quadrant III: diversified players with focused groups of portfolio firms

PE firms that emphasize relatively more equity investment and focus on a number of industries are defined as diversified players with focused groups of portfolio firms. Such PE firms are often relatively large PE funds with abundant resources and strong capabilities. These PE firms have developed expertise and knowledge in a number of related or unrelated industries and aim to exploit their expertise in chosen industries. Diversified players with focused groups of portfolio firms adopt relatively larger portions of equity investments because equity investments enable these PE firms to enjoy long-term returns associated with "patience capital" (Porter, 1992). In addition, facing a volatile equity market, highly leveraged buyout portfolio firms are subject to substantial bankruptcy risks, which is not in the interests of PE firms. Thus, diversified players with focused groups of portfolio firms have to adjust their profit-generating mechanisms from restructuring and a profitable quick exit to more consistent operational gains from equity holdings. In other words, consistent with the main principles of resource-based theory, diversified players with focused groups of portfolio firms proactively increase the portion of equity investment versus debt investment to exploit their capabilities in chosen industries. Diversified players with focused groups of portfolio firms choose to concentrate on a number of industries because having an in-depth understanding of a wide variety of industries is not only capital intensive but also consumes managerial time and energy. By nurturing expertise in a focused group of industries, PE firms in this quadrant develop their unique capabilities, providing a competitive distinction compared to other PE firms. To explain the uniqueness of PE firms in Quadrant III, we use Apax Partners as an example.

Apax Partners, headquartered in London, is an independent global PE firm that focuses solely on long-run investment in growth companies (Apax Partners, 2012). Although Apax managed $111.5 billion at the end of June 2011, it invests in only five industries (financial services, health care, media, retailing, and telecom). Apax believes that its experience, insight, and financial capital can help portfolio firms release their potential and generate significant growth. In spite of the dual roles that it plays – capital provider and catalyst for change – Apax attaches more importance to encouraging the growth of its buyout firms to maximize the value of its portfolios.

Its emphasis on growing buyout businesses is demonstrated by Apax's investment selection criteria. If a targeted firm is not within the five aforementioned industries, is not sustainable, or is not a market leader with great growth potential, Apax will not invest in it. In addition, Apax aims to add value to existing management and governance instead of reshuffling management teams and governance structures. Therefore, as it often co-operates with incumbent management teams of target firms in buyout deals, Apax finds it easier to align its interests with those of current top executives. Moreover, Apax not only sends professionals to assist portfolio firms' management teams but also sits on the boards of these firms to help top managers develop joint strategies. All these measures reflect Apax's commitment to portfolio firms and its willingness to maintain long-term equity positions.

For example, Apax Partners, together with Permira (another large UK PE firm), took over private UK fashion retailer New Look in 2003. The top executives of New Look, pressured by expectations to meet short-term performance as a listed firm, felt that the public markets did not provide the right environment to ambitiously grow their business, so they partnered with Apax and Permira to privatize the firm. Apax and Permira each took 30.1% of New Look, the founder and other top executives of New Look took 36.7%, and Dubai-based retail giant Landmark assumed the remaining 3.1% (Achleitner et al., 2010). With the support of Apax and Permira, New Look established a new distribution center, enlarged store formats, and embarked on a path to internationalization. Apax and Permira chose not to exit New Look at the end of 2007 in spite of a bull IPO market because their focus was to work with the top management team of New Look to deliver better performance results (Achleitner et al., 2010).

The example of New Look shows that Apax prioritizes improving the full potential of its invested businesses and is willing to maintain equity holdings of buyout firms for a longer period than other PE firms in Quadrants I and IV. Apax's long-term-focused, performance-oriented investment strategy is, in part, enabled by its own investors and relationships with banks. More than 46% of its funding comes from pension funds' investments (Apax Partners, 2012), which often have long-run investment horizons (Ryan & Schneider, 2002). The Apax example is also supported by research by Castellaneta (2016) who found that PE firms that adopt a "carrot and stick" incentive approach "improve the alignment of managerial and firm interests and, in turn, encourage capability building. The model shows how incentives act on capabilities in three areas: the leveraging of existing capabilities, the sourcing of capabilities internally and the sourcing of capabilities externally" (2016: 41).

Quadrant IV: short-term diversified efficiency-oriented players

PE firms that invest in diversified industries and adopt a high-leverage financial structure are defined as short-term diversified efficiency-oriented PE firms. Because of their large size, PE firms in this quadrant are often well known to the public, and many are publicly traded on the stock exchanges (e.g., KKR and Blackstone). Research comparing diversified PE firms to unrelated diversified multidivisional firms has suggested that one of the main differences of this firm type is resource allocation between portfolio firms and headquarters (Baker & Montgomery, 1994). Short-term diversified efficiency-oriented players might have invested in a narrow scope of industries by employing high leverage when they were small; however, as they grow in terms of committed capital and resources, this type of PE firm faces increased opportunity costs and risks should they maintain a narrow business focus because of the high risk associated with a narrow portfolio of industries. Generally, the number of deals in a specific industry is reduced over time, and large, successful PE firms with a significant amount of funds to invest must move to other industries to find sufficient deals to use their available capital. To diversify their risks and expand their opportunity set, PE firms in this quadrant may gain minority control of larger buyout firms or acquire single business units of large companies in industries outside their usual deal focus.

In spite of strained debt markets after the recent financial crisis, short-term diversified efficiency-oriented players still rely on debt investments for three reasons. First, PE firms in Quadrant IV are large, have solid reputations, and have more credibility in accessing debt markets. Second, several firms in this sector are publicly traded, allowing such PE firms to access funds through the equity market. Hence, PE firms in Quadrant IV are capable of raising large amounts of capital; however, they need to diversify investment risks by enlarging their investment portfolios. Extensive use of debt allows these PE firms to make investments in multiple projects simultaneously and to leverage available capital. Third, as already noted, many PE firms in Quadrant IV are publicly traded and face pressure to meet investors' short-term profit expectations; therefore, they need to exit portfolio firms as soon as possible through sell-offs or IPOs. Again, research by Castellaneta and Gottschalg (2016) suggest that these firms need to depend on selection (buy low and sell high) strategies because they take less time to restructure the portfolio firm and generally have less of an industry focus and expertise compared to Quadrant II and III players.

Similar to their counterparts, short-term diversified efficiency-oriented players have started to allocate more attention to operational improvements. However, unlike diversified players with focused groups of portfolio firms, short-term diversified efficiency-oriented players dedicate more efforts to operational enhancements to mitigate public criticism. In other words, diversified players with focused groups of portfolio firms proactively cultivate their expertise and knowledge in specific industries, whereas short-term diversified efficiency-oriented players attend to operational engineering as a reaction to external pressure to change the image of the PE industry as one based solely on financial engineering. Because they are the largest in the industry, short-term diversified efficiency-oriented players easily become targets of public criticism for using high leverage. In addition, relying solely on financial engineering cannot generate the expected benefits for PE firms (Kaplan, 2009); as a result, short-term diversified efficiency-oriented players need to pay more attention to operational improvements.

In sum, the motivation for PE firms in this quadrant to establish dedicated professional teams differs from that for PE firms in Quadrants II and III. PE firms with high-equity financial structures in Quadrants II and III establish professional teams to strategically and proactively pursue not only operational enhancements but also improved strategic positioning. Instead, PE firms with high debt in Quadrant IV use professional teams reactively because the exit option is limited; this is more in line with resource dependence theory.

Because PE firms have been perceived as burdening buyout firms with high levels of debt (*The Economist*, 2012b), some buyout firms may have used more equity than is typical, given the current social and economic trends (Bacon et al., 2013). Although this trend, as well as an increased operational orientation, may help deal with environmental pressure in the short run, once the depressed financial markets recovered these firms are seen to be refocusing on financial engineering.

We use KKR as an example to illustrate the attributes of short-term diversified efficiency-oriented PE firms. KKR is an American-based global PE company, founded in 1976 by Jerome Kohlberg, Henry Kravis, and George R. Roberts, that specializes in leveraged buyouts. As its committed capital rose from $31 million in 1977 to more than $17 billion in 2006, KKR invested in 11 different industries. During the 1990s, a vulnerable market prompted PE firms to change their tactics, especially for high-leverage PE firms. In reaction to the market downturn in 2000, Kravis and Roberts envisioned developing a dedicated operations team for KKR, later known as KKR Capstone, that would partner with management to protect their investors' interests (Eccles et al., 2011). KKR Capstone teams assist KKR deal teams during and after transactions. During a transaction, KKR Capstone teams help evaluate the operational efficiencies that could be achieved from a deal. More important, after the deal closes, two or more KKR Capstone professionals relocate to the portfolio company to achieve the improvements assumed in the pricing of the deal.

Although KKR uses industry expertise to help its portfolio firms, Capstone does not have deep specialized experience in a broad set of industries. Generally, given its diversified scope, KKR provides general management professionals to help restructure the portfolio firm in preparation for turnaround and exit. By consistently supporting and monitoring top executives in the portfolio firm, the on-site professional team makes sure the portfolio firm realizes the intended changes so the returns assumed in the pricing of the deal are achieved as soon as possible. In reaction to the environment change, KKR has to hold portfolio firms longer, consistent with the fact that privately owned holding periods have increased since the 1980s (Kaplan, 1991; Kaplan & Strömberg, 2009). However, compared to SCF Partners and Apax, which treat portfolio firms more as subsidiaries and exit less frequently, KKR, although it has become more operations-oriented because of environmental necessity, generally has shorter average holding periods.

Movements between quadrants' strategic positions

Although our PE firm configuration model provides evidence of differential strategic positioning, there is also evidence that PE firms gradually reposition their strategic directions and seek different buyout targets because of changes in both the exogenous environments and endogenous resources and capabilities. As described in the example of KKR, there was an evolution to more operational expertise in the establishment of Capstone. Although this does not establish a change in quadrants, it does suggest incremental change. The shift from one quadrant to another is not dramatic but takes place progressively, and the shift across the two dimensions – financial structure emphasis and portfolio firm scope – can be propelled by PE firms' attempts to maximize the value of their respective resources or to cope with new external uncertainties and risks. We propose that two basic strategic shifts capture the migration of PE firms across quadrants. The first shift is vertical movement caused by increasing equity investment; that is, from short-term efficiency niche players (Quadrant I) to niche players with long-term equity positions (Quadrant II) and from short-term diversified efficiency-oriented players (Quadrant IV) to diversified players with focused groups of portfolio firms (Quadrant III). The second shift is horizontal movement, which implies a more diversified portfolio; that is, from short-term efficiency niche players (Quadrant I) to short-term diversified efficiency-oriented players (Quadrant IV) and from niche players with long-term equity positions (Quadrant II) to diversified players with focused groups of portfolio firms (Quadrant III).These movements, whether vertical or horizontal, can appear the same but may be driven by different strategic intents: a proactive intent to utilize and to gain basic capabilities (using resource-based theory logic) or a reactive tactical logic in response to environmental change (using resource dependence theory logic).

The first shift suggests that short-term efficiency niche players (Quadrant I) and short-term diversified efficiency-oriented players (Quadrant IV) may increase their interest in equity investment. On the one hand, resource-based theory implies that PE firms in general need to cultivate their respective core competitive edges. For short-term efficiency niche players, they inevitably can deepen their insights into the focused set of industries in which they are heavily invested over time and accordingly nurture competitive advantages in these industries. For instance, one of Bain Capital's investment approaches is to make full use of its business intelligence from a related set of service industries. In a similar vein, in spite of the wide scope of industries in which short-term diversified efficiency-oriented players invest, these PE firms also pay heed to fostering their capabilities and resources in certain industries. For example, KKR focuses its attention mainly on 14 industries, although it does not exclude investment opportunities beyond these 14.

The capabilities that short-term efficiency niche players and short-term diversified efficiency-oriented players have built up in their chosen industries enable these PE firms to hold longer-term equity investments in those specific industries – knowledge that imparts confidence in making longer-term equity investments. On the other hand, the first shift can also be explained by the resource dependence theory logic that suggests that PE firms are motivated to decrease their dependence on external environmental change and thereby mitigate external uncertainties. For short-term efficiency niche players, given the consequences of the 2008 financial crisis, exiting buyout firms through an IPO is now more challenging. This suggests that short-term efficiency niche players need to transform their business models characterized by short turnarounds, which is more difficult and less likely under their original financial structures. As such, in order to solve such problems, short-term efficiency niche players may need to increase their equity investments.

Likewise, short-term diversified efficiency-oriented players are also subject to scarcer exit opportunities due to the depressed equity market. Moreover, short-term diversified efficiency-oriented players face increased public criticism and scrutiny with respect to their reliance on capital restructuring of buyout firms and taking advantage of debt-associated tax deductions. As a result, short-term diversified efficiency-oriented players have started to establish dedicated professional service teams, as illustrated by the example of KKR. Although these professional service teams were built by KKR as a reaction to external environments, they allow KKR to cultivate expertise and capabilities in certain industries, enabling KKR to hold equity investments with more confidence. Thus, the changed environments call for short-term efficiency niche players and short-term diversified efficiency-oriented players to take further actions to cope with increased exogenous risks by the need to hold portfolio firms for longer.

The second shift, which concerns an increase in the level of diversification for short-term efficiency niche players (Quadrant I) and niche players with long-term equity positions (Quadrant II), occurs for two reasons. First, the resource dependence logic suggests that PE firms are likely to expand into new industries in order to reduce uncertainties associated with particular industries and diversify risks as they grow in size. Niche players with long-term equity positions may be compelled to expand into other industries to diversify risks associated with a single industry as their funds grow in size. Similar arguments hold for short-term efficiency niche players as their fund size increases. Second, the resource-based theory suggests that firms need to constantly develop capabilities that can help them cope with new challenges and risks in the environment. As PE firms in Quadrants I and II grow in size and accumulate slack resources (Penrose, 1959), these firms have an incentive to cultivate new expertise and capabilities to effectively utilize their dormant resources. Resource-based theory logic would suggest that short-term efficiency niche players and niche players with long-term equity positions would have the incentive to use these capabilities to pursue a wider portfolio firm scope (Chatterjee & Wernerfelt, 1991). Consequently, PE firms in Quadrants I and II might migrate respectively to Quadrants IV and III to exploit their augmented set of resources.

We posit that diagonal movements across quadrants are less likely because of organizational path dependence. Organizational path dependence (Sydow et al., 2009) states that the set of decisions firms can make in a given situation are restricted by decisions made in the past. Therefore, PE firms in Quadrants I and IV are less likely to migrate to Quadrant III and Quadrant II, respectively, because such movements imply that these PE firms need to discard their previous investment strategies. Furthermore, it is their experience and past reputation for particular types of deals that allow them to raise new funds. By the same token, PE firms in Quadrants I and II are less likely to deviate sharply from previous investments in familiar industries but may expand gradually to new industries so as to ameliorate uncertainties and risks related to these new arenas. Therefore, we anticipate that PE firms will take an incremental approach to increase equity investments and toexpand portfolio firm scopes instead of engaging in diagonal movements, which requires simultaneous moves in both funding and diversified scope repositioning.

Our discussion suggests that the first shift (from debt investments to equity investments) and the second shift (from focused firm scope to broader diversified firm scope) represent both PE firms' proactive strategies and their reactions to external pressures. Taken together, the future landscape of the PE industry is jointly determined by external environments and the strategic choices among the four PE firm types.

Discussion

In this chapter, we argue that the PE firms are transforming themselves to embrace new challenges arising from changed business environments. Specifically, we contend that PE firms differentiate from each other in terms of financial structure and portfolio firm scope. As such, we argue that different types of PE firms develop heterogeneous capabilities and target different groups of investors and portfolio firms and have different debt provider relationships. The configuration of PE firms not only enables us to have a better understanding of the PE industry but also helps us to examine distinct ramifications of different PE firms. In this section, we first discuss theoretical perspectives that may facilitate and focus our research agenda on PE firms. We then address managerial and research implications that can be drawn from our configuration framework. Finally, we investigate public policy issues from the perspective we have put forward.

Theoretical implications

We have used agency theory, resource-based theory, and resource dependence theory to analyze the evolution of the PE industry. Generally, agency theory is the dominant theory to explain the emergence of PE transactions in the first wave. LBOs were the main form of the first wave of PE transactions. With a strong emphasis on financial leverage in these deals, the principles of agency theory suggest that with such leverage PE firms are able to constrain buyout firm managers' discretionary power through the pressure of interest payments, and hence solve the "free cash flow problem" (Jensen, 1986). This logic is pertinent to PE firms in Quadrants I and IV. Characterized by using high leverage as the dominant financial structure, these types of PE firms aim to play the role of financial engineers and garner the benefits derived from reduced agency costs.

As the PE industry evolves and the external environment changes, resource dependence theory and resource-based theory provide us with a more comprehensive perspective to explain the strategic positioning of firms in the PE industry. First, as PE firms accumulate resources and the competition in the PE industry becomes fiercer, PE firms find that it is important for them to establish their unique identity and core competence through improved resource orchestration and utilization. This is in accordance with resource-based theory logic that valuable, rare, inimitable, and nonsubstitutable resources provide sustainable competitive advantages for firms. Therefore, PE firms accumulating specific industry knowledge and expertise tend to choose a focused strategy by providing detailed and professional guidance to portfolio firms to create value (e.g., PE firms in Quadrant II), while PE firms focused on financial engineering tend to choose a diversified strategy since they need to diversify their scope to use their dominant capabilities as deals become difficult to find in previous industries of focus (e.g., PE firms in Quadrant IV). Hence, the resource-based theory not only explains the important characteristics of why a PE firm chooses to be a diversified player or a niche player subsequent to the second wave of PE transactions but also addresses why diversified players with focused groups of portfolio firms (Quadrant III) proactively establish their own professional teams.

Second, as the PE industry evolved and the lack of exit opportunities created fierce competition in the industry, the previous dominant form of LBOs put huge pressure on PE firms because they had been dependent on the debt market. To adapt to the new environment and reduce the firm's dependence on debt, as resource dependence theory suggests, PE firms in Quadrant I have used more equity investment. Likewise, Quadrant IV firms have received more capital from public equity markets and have used more equity investments in their portfolio firms as reactions to external environmental pressures. In addition, PE firms in Quadrant IV have been developing more operations-oriented teams to help manage the longer holding periods required by portfolio firms. Hence, resource dependence theory is useful in explaining PE firms' increasing use of equity investments and a higher level of operational orientation in working with portfolio firms.

Dynamic capabilities theory is an extension of the resource-based theory and complements it by addressing why and how firms maintain their competitive advantages in situations of rapid and unpredictable changes (Teece et al., 1997; Teece, 2007). As the operations of PE firms are subject to rapid changes as social and economic conditions evolve, how different PE firms "integrate, build, and configure internal and external competencies to address rapidly changing environments" is likely to be critical to their future successes (Teece et al., 1997: 516). Therefore, future research on PE firms might adopt the dynamic capabilities framework to address PE firms' migration among the four quadrants of our conceptual model to deal with changing environments.

Managerial and research implications

This chapter thus far has considered how changed social and economic environments have led PE firms to differentiate from each other and to develop their unique strategic foci. In this section, our discussion centers on how managers can better cope with the changing external environment from the perspectives of four key players (PE firms, investors, banks, and buyout firms) in PE transactions (Wright et al., 2010). Specifically, we examine the implications of globalization, the deal syndication among PE firms, the ramifications of institutional investors' different investment horizons (as limited partners) on the PE industry, the influence of distinct types of debt on PE firms' strategies, and the value of the PE industry for buyout firms' CEOs. In this section, we also provide some suggestions for future research in exploring these implications.

First, all four types of PE firms are engaged in different levels of internationalization. For diversified players with focused groups of portfolio firms and short-term diversified efficiency-oriented players, globalization of their businesses inevitably broadens their opportunity pools. New opportunities in emerging economies invariably attract diversified PE firms in Quadrants III and IV to embark on the path of internationalization. For example, KKR has a presence in 13 metropolitan areas ranging from New York to Beijing, and Apax has 10 offices around the world. Niche players with long-term equity positions and short-term efficiency niche players also seek to exercise their dedicated capabilities in certain industries on a global platform. Although Bain Capital has been exploring investment opportunities as far as Asia, it focuses on the industries in which it has expertise when making investment decisions. Similarly, SCF Partners has offices in Calgary, Canada, and Aberdeen, Scotland, in addition to Houston, US, and its portfolio firms can be found in New Zealand and the Middle East as well, although it remains focused on its original energy services, manufacturing, and equipment industry segments. Future research can examine the distinctions among internationalization strategies adopted by different PE firms.

Second, deal syndication is another promising strategy for PE firms. The Apax example shows the prevalence of deal syndication in the PE industry. Deal syndication is an interfirm alliance in which two or more PE firms invest jointly in firms and share payoffs from such investments (Lerner, 1994; Lockett & Wright, 2001; Sorenson & Stuart, 2001; Meuleman et al., 2009b). The purposes behind PE syndication are to enable a PE firm to invest in more industries to diversify risks (Cumming, 2006), to make high-quality decisions (Lerner, 1994), and to generate new deal opportunities (Lockett & Wright, 2001) without unbalancing its portfolio due to deal size. Without deal syndication, too much of Apax's capital might have been tied up with its investment in New Look. In this sense, alliances with Permira enabled Apax to make multiple deals at the same time and to reduce risks associated with relying on one particular deal.

Even though syndication may result in increasing agency and monitoring costs (Meuleman et al., 2009a), we suggest that it still could be a suitable strategy for all types of PE firms, but the underlying reasons and approaches may be different given the distinct strategic orientations. Future research can explore such syndication strategies from at least two aspects. First, syndications within the same quadrants allow PE firms with the same strategic orientations to reduce risks. It is of great importance for long-term-oriented PE firms (from Quadrants II and III) to diversify risks as they invest more equity capital in transactions. Risk diversification is also salient for short-term efficiency players (from Quadrants I and IV), especially when they invest in large transactions through high leverage. Second, syndications across quadrants might achieve complementary effects for both parties. For example, as it is difficult for short-term diversified efficiency-oriented players to have an in-depth understanding of a large number of industries, syndicating with niche players that focus on particular industries may be a plausible choice. Thus, it is likely that PE firms from different quadrants establish deal syndications to reduce risks, share operational expertise, and enhance short-term efficiency. More research is called for to untangle the different motivations behind PE firms' deal syndications as well as the consequences thereof.

Third, institutional investors should choose PE firms carefully by matching their investment horizons. As mentioned, PE firms have different preferences in terms of investment. Likewise, institutional investors adopt different investment strategies. For example, long-term institutional investors such as public pension funds favor long-run financial measurement of performance of their invested firms, whereas short-term institutional investors such as the majority of mutual funds and banks have more short-run financial parameters for their portfolio firms (Ryan & Schneider, 2002). Therefore, long-term institutional investors as limited partners should seek PE players with long-term-oriented positions – those in Quadrants II and III. In contrast, short-term institutional investors should focus on short-term efficiency players that turnover portfolio firms more quickly. Future research can examine how the compatibilities between PE firms and institutional investors influence strategic choices of buyout firms as well as of PE general partner firms.

Fourth, the changed landscape of the PE industry also has a significant impact on bank lending to PE firms. Managers of banks should be aware that PE firms with different strategic orientations have distinct strategies for debt and equity. Because short-term efficiency niche players rely on larger amounts of debt to finance deals but have short-term debt requirements, such PE firms may negotiate financing contracts with a number of banks to diversify their borrowing risks and to bargain for lower priced debt. Thus, when co-operating with short-term efficiency niche players, banks should carefully examine risks associated with short-term transactions and fast turnarounds. In contrast, banks can establish strategic partnerships with long-term-oriented PE firms (e.g., PE firms in Quadrants II and III) to reduce long-run transaction costs with these PE firms. Therefore, we suggest that banks should adopt different strategies to meet distinct borrowing needs of PE firms. More studies are needed to examine how PE firms' strategic orientations influence banks' lending behaviors. Likewise, more research is needed to study how different players would pursue public debt markets as an alternative to bank debt.

Last, the glamour of being a top executive of a public firm has reached a historically low level because of stakeholder pressure and public outcries about executive compensation (Kaplan, 2009). Simultaneously, a strengthening trend of privatization of public firms has emerged to allow potential portfolio firms to pursue opportunities not possible in public markets (Wright et al., 2001) and to maintain the value of their unique strategies (Shivdasani & Zak, 2007; Kaplan et al., 2011). In spite of the benefits of being a private firm and support from PE investors, top executives of buyout firms should be fully aware of vastly different strategies of distinct PE firms. Thus, we expect that managers of buyout firms with different foci (control rights versus long-term performance) may choose different types of PE firms. For example, if managers of buyout firms emphasize future control rights, they should collaborate with short-term efficiency-oriented players because they focus on relatively short-term investment horizons and seek "liquidity events" when the time is right (Wruck, 2008). However, if executives of buyout firms prefer long-term investors and do not attach much importance to control rights, they should seek investment from Quadrants II and III because these two types of PE firms are committed to buyout firms by assisting managers in developing the correct longer-term strategies. We believe that it is of the utmost importance to understand the implications of buyout firm managers' perceptions of PE investments in their co-operative strategies with PE firms through further studies across different institutional environments.

The above discussion suggests that the new environment requires managers of different PE firms to understand the nature of a globalization strategy and to seek deal syndications that fit their strategic intent. Correspondingly, managers of PE investors, banks, and portfolio firms should also choose an appropriate PE firm to match their goals and align the interests of both parties. Different strategic orientations of PE firms not only have a profound impact on managers of both PE firms and buyout firms but also reveal important implications for policy makers.

Public policy issues

The previous section discussed how managers can better cope with the changing environment in the PE industry. In this section, we discuss the implications of our conceptual framework for public policy makers in developed and emerging economies. In developed economies, one of the many public policy issues regarding the PE industry is whether tax benefits generated from high levels of debt should be monitored by regulators, as high levels of debt also generate high risks for portfolio firms. The past few years have witnessed increasing public criticism about how PE firms saddle portfolio firms with debt to take advantage of the tax code's treatment of debt (*The Economist*, 2012a) and may put portfolio firms at excessive risk. By revealing the variety and heterogeneity of PE firms, we suggest that public policy makers should avoid being overly influenced by public attitude and should be cautious relative to public accusations about PE firms. In fact, research by Wright et al. (2014) suggests that bankruptcies and recovery risks are no greater for PE firms than for other firms with similar capital structures.

As we revealed in the conceptual framework, PE firms differ from each other according to their financial structure emphasis and portfolio firm scope. For example, niche players with long-term equity positions (Quadrant II) and diversified players with focused groups of portfolio firms (Quadrant III) typically adopt a higher level of equity investments and are less likely to equip their portfolio firms with high levels of debt. Instead, they provide not only equity investment but also professional guidance to their portfolio firms. Therefore, public policy makers in developed markets should avoid succumbing to public pressures stemming from the belief that PE firms generate systematic risks for portfolio firms due to overuse of high leverage, and should avoid enacting restrictive regulation on PE firms. In fact, it is important for public policy makers in developed economies to realize that PE firms have in general shifted their focus from financial engineering in the 1980s to more focus on operational engineering. Also, recent research suggests that PE ownership and therefore involvement in a deal suggests deal quality to the market, especially in cross-border acquisitions (Humphery-Jenner et al., 2017). Not only PE firms in Quadrants II and III, which have relatively more equity investment, but also PE firms in Quadrants I and IV employ more professional talent to deal with environmental uncertainty. In sum, it is important for public policy makers in developed economies to conduct a thorough investigation and have a deep understanding of the heterogeneity of PE firms and their adaptation to the environment, and hence avoid making policy mistakes.

As an increasing number of PE firms embark on the path of internationalization, how public policy makers in emerging markets react to those large PE firms' foreign entrants becomes an important issue. Again, we emphasize how important it is for public policy makers in emerging markets to understand the heterogeneity among PE firms' strategic orientations (Klonowski, 2011). While they may be skeptical of PE firms in Quadrants I and IV, since these PE firms are short-term-oriented and focus on turning around distressed firms fast, we suggest that these policy makers need to consider the inherent advantages and disadvantages of each type of PE firm. For example, short-term efficiency niche players and short-term diversified efficiency-oriented players, due to their reliance on debt and their emphasis on reducing agency costs, play an indispensable role in "deepening and broadening the private sector" in emerging economies (Leeds & Sunderland, 2003: 113) and hence benefit mature firms in traditional manufacturing industries by enhancing the portfolio firms' corporate governance and reducing agency costs. They also need to be aware that some PE players are more long-term-oriented, with distinct operational capabilities in their specific or narrowly scoped industries (PE firms in Quadrants II and III). As such, they may provide more benefits for new ventures or growing firms in high-tech industries in emerging economies. By enacting policies that are flexible and therefore favorable to all PE firm types, their associated functions would be effective in realizing public policy makers' goals to stimulate healthy growth of domestic PE investments.

Another issue that needs further research is the influence of monetary policy on interest rates and how interest rates foster more or less development of the PE industry and their relative strategic positions. Given the different financial structures used by PE firms, easy money may not always foster PE firm demand with lower interest rates because some PE firms have a relatively high emphasis on equity versus debt.

Conclusion

Although a significant number of studies on PE investments have examined PE firm impact on portfolio firm performance, an assessment of the strategies pursued by independent PE firms was lacking. Therefore, the intent of this study was to examine the evolution of PE firms and specify the current nature of PE firms' strategic positioning. At the same time, we have sought to describe four ideal types of PE firms and provide examples of PE firms that represent positioning along two dimensions: financial structure emphasis and diversified portfolio firm scope. We also reviewed and discussed what theoretical perspectives might be helpful to enrich our insight into PE firms. In addition, we addressed the importance of considering heterogeneous strategic positioning among PE firms, for managers of PE firms and buyout firms as well as for public policy makers in developed and emerging economies. We hope that our treatise can represent a further step to enrich the understanding of PE firms as a financial service sector that is unique and critical to the global economy.

Notes

1 The chapter is adapted from an article originally published in the ***Academy of Management Perspectives*** (Hoskisson et al., 2013).
2 Note that we are focused on later-stage PE firms (formerly known as LBO associations) rather than on early-stage PE firms (often labeled venture capital firms).
3 In addition to PE business, Bain Capital has other investment businesses, such as early-stage venture capital. In this chapter, however, we focus on its late-stage PE business.

References

Achleitner, A.-K., Lutz, E., Herman, K., & Lerner, J. 2010. New look: Going private with private equity support. *Journal of Business Strategy*, 31: 38–49.

Apax Partners. 2012. www.apax.com.

Bacon, N., Wright, M., Ball, R., & Meuleman, B. 2013. Private equity, HRM and employment. *Academy of Management Perspectives*, 27: 7–21.

Baker, G. P., & Montgomery, C. A. 1994. *Conglomerates and LBO associations: A comparison of organizational forms* (Working Paper No. 10–024). Cambridge, MA: Harvard Business School.

Barney, J. 1991. Firm resources and sustained competitive advantage. *Journal of Management*, 17: 99–120.

Blundell-Wignall, A. 2007. The private equity boom: Causes and policy issues. *Financial Market Trends*, 1: 59–86.

Castellaneta, F. 2016. Building firm capability: Managerial incentives for top performance. *Journal of Business Strategy*, 37: 41–46.

Castellaneta, F., & Gottschalg, O. 2016. Does ownership matter in private equity? The sources of variance in buyouts' performance. *Strategic Management Journal*, 37: 330–348.

Chatterjee, S., & Wernerfelt, B. 1991. The link between resources and type of diversification: Theory and evidence. *Strategic Management Journal*, 12: 33–48.

Cumming, D. J. 2006. The determinants of venture capital portfolio size: Empirical evidence. *Journal of Business*, 79: 1083–1126.

Cumming, D. J., Siegel, D. S., & Wright, M. 2007. Private equity, leveraged buyouts and governance. *Journal of Corporate Finance*, 13: 439–460.

Demiroglu, C., & James, C. M. 2010. The role of private equity group reputation in LBO financing. *Journal of Financial Economics*, 96: 306–330.

Doty, D. H., & Glick, W. H. 1994. Typologies as a unique form of theory building: Toward improved understanding and modeling. *Academy of Management Review*, 19: 230–251.

Eccles, R. G., Serafeim, G., & Clay, T. A. 2011. *KKR: Leveraging sustainability* (Case No. 112–032). Cambridge, MA: Harvard Business School.

The Economist. 2012a. Private equity under scrutiny: Bain or blessing? January 28. Available at: www.economist.com.

The Economist. 2012b. Private equity: Monsters, Inc? January 28. Available at: www.economist.com.

Gilligan, J., & Wright, M. 2014. *Private equity demystified*, 3rd edition. London: ICAEW.

Gurung, A., & Lerner, J. 2009. The global economic impact of private equity report 2009. *Globalization of alternative investments working papers vol. 2*. New York: World Economic Forum USA.

Harper, N. W. C., & Schneider, A. 2004. Private equity's new challenge. *McKinsey Quarterly, August*. Available at: www.mckinseyquarterly.com/Private_equitys_new_challenge_1475.

Harris, R., Siegel, D. S., & Wright, M. 2005. Assessing the impact of management buyouts on economic efficiency: Plant-level evidence from the United Kingdom. *Review of Economics and Statistics*, 87: 148–153.

Hillman, A. J., Withers, M. C., & Collins, B. J. 2009. Resource dependence theory: A review. *Journal of Management*, 35: 1404–1427.

Hoskisson, R. E., Wei, S., Xiwei, Y., & Jing, J. 2013. The evolution and strategic positioning of private equity firms. *Academy of Management Perspectives*, 27: 22–38.

Humphery-Jenner, M., Sautner, Z., & Suchard, J. 2017. Cross-border mergers and acquisitions: The role of private equity firms. *Strategic Management Journal*, 38: 1688–1700.

Jensen, M. C. 1986. Agency costs of free cash flow, corporate finance, and takeovers. *American Economic Review*, 76: 323–329.

Jensen, M. C., & Meckling, W. H. 1976. Theory of the firm: Managerial behavior, agency costs and ownership structure. *Journal of Financial Economics*, 3: 305–360.

Kaplan, S. 2009. The future of private equity. *Journal of Applied Corporate Finance*, 21: 8–20.

Kaplan, S., Ferenbach, C., Bingle, M., Lipschultz, M., Canfield, P., & Jones, A. 2011. Morgan Stanley roundtable on the state of global private equity. *Journal of Applied Corporate Finance*, 23: 8–33.

Kaplan, S., & Strömberg, P. 2009. Leveraged buyouts and private equity. *Journal of Economic Perspectives*, 23: 121–146.

Kaplan, S. N. 1991. The staying power of leveraged buyouts. *Journal of Financial Economics*, 29: 287–313.

Klonowski, D. 2011. The evolution of private equity in emerging markets: The case of Poland. *Journal of Applied Corporate Finance*, 23: 60–69.

Leeds, R., & Sunderland, J. 2003. Private equity investment in emerging markets. *Journal of Applied Corporate Finance*, 15: 111–119.

Lerner, J. 1994. The syndication of venture capital investments. *Financial Management*, 23: 16–27.

Lerner, J. 2011. The future of private equity. *European Financial Management*, 17: 423–435.

Lockett, A., & Wright, M. 2001. The syndication of venture capital investments. *Omega: The International Journal of Management Science*, 29: 375–390.

Lopez-de-Silanes, F., Phalippou, L., & Gottschalg, O. 2009. *Giants at the gate: Diseconomies of scale in private equity*. American Finance Association 2010 Meetings Paper, Atlanta, GA.

Matthews, G., Bye, M., & Howland, J. 2009. Operational improvement: The key to value creation in private equity. *Journal of Applied Corporate Finance*, 21: 21–27.

McCarthy, J., & Alvarez, N. 2006. Private equity: Rolling on or rolling back. *Journal of Private Equity*, 9: 13–16.

Meuleman, M., Amess, K., Wright, M., & Scholes, L. 2009a. Agency, strategic entrepreneurship, and the performance of private equity-backed buyouts. *Entrepreneurship Theory and Practice*, 33: 213–239.

Meuleman, M., Wright, M., Manigart, S., & Lockett, A. 2009b. Private equity syndication: Agency costs, reputation and collaboration. *Journal of Business Finance & Accounting*, 36: 616–644.

Minns, S. E. 2010. Strategic change in firms following private equity acquisition: An ex post study of U.K. technology, industrial, and communications firms. *Journal of Private Equity*, 13: 22–29.

Nielsen, K. M. 2008. Institutional investors and private equity. *Review of Finance*, 12: 185–219.

Penrose, E. T. 1959. *The theory of the growth of the firm*. Oxford, UK: Oxford University Press.

Pfeffer, J., & Salancik, G. R. 1978. *The external control of organizations: A resource dependence perspective*. New York: Harper & Row.

Porter, M. E. 1992. *Capital choices: Changing the way America invests in industry*. Boston, MA: Harvard Business School Press.

PricewaterhouseCoopers. 2006. *Global private equity report*. Available at: www.pwc.com/extweb/pwcpublications.nsf/docid/A0777B94B3CC3741852572FA0071AEC9/$File/global_pe_report.pdf.

Renneboog, L., Simons, T., & Wright, M. 2007. Why do public firms go private in the UK? The impact of private equity investors, incentive realignment and undervaluation. *Journal of Corporate Finance*, 13: 591–628.

Rozwadowski, K., & Young, B. P. 2005. Buyout competition. *Journal of Private Equity*, 9: 67–73.

Rubenstein, D. 2010. *McKinsey conversations with global leaders: David Rubenstein of the Carlyle Group*. Available at: www.mckinseyquarterly.com/McKinsey_conversations_with_global_leaders_David_Rubenstein_of_The_Carlyle_Group_2605.

Ryan, L. V., & Schneider, M. 2002. The antecedents of institutional investor activism. *Academy of Management Review*, 27: 554–573.

SCF Partners 2012. Retrieved March 20, 2012. Available at: www.scfpartners.com.

Schneider, M., & Valenti, A. 2010. The effects of "going private" using private equity: The newly private corporation and the dimensions of corporate performance. *Business & Society Review*, 115: 75–106.

Shivdasani, A., & Zak, A. 2007. The return of the recap: Achieving private equity benefits as a public company. *Journal of Applied Corporate Finance*, 19: 32–41.

Sorenson, O., & Stuart, T. E. 2001. Syndication networks and the spatial distribution of venture capital investments. *American Journal of Sociology*, 106: 1546–1588.

Stowell, D. 2010. *An introduction to investment banks, hedge funds, & private equity: The new paradigm*. Burlington, MA: Academic Press.

Sydow, J., Schreyogg, G., & Koch, J. 2009. Organizational path dependence: Opening the black box. *Academy of Management Review*, 34: 689–709.

Teece, D. J. 2007. Explicating dynamic capabilities: The nature and microfoundations of (sustainable) enterprise performance. *Strategic Management Journal*, 28: 1319–1350.

Teece, D. J., Pisano, G., & Shuen, A. 1997. Dynamic capabilities and strategic management. *Strategic Management Journal*, 18: 509–533.

Wright, M., Amess, K., Weir, C., & Girma, S. 2009. Private equity and corporate governance: Retrospect and prospect. *Corporate Governance: An International Review*, 17: 353–375.

Wright, M., Cressy, R., Wilson, N., & Farag, H. 2014. Financial restructuring and recovery in private equity buyouts: The UK evidence. *Venture Capital*, 16:109–129.

Wright, M., Hoskisson, R. E., & Busenitz, L. W. 2001. Firm rebirth: Buyouts as facilitators of strategic growth and entrepreneurship. *Academy of Management Executive*, 15: 111–125.

Wright, M., Jackson, A., & Frobisher, S. 2010. Private equity in the U.K.: Building a new future. *Journal of Applied Corporate Finance*, 22: 86–95.

Wright, M., Robbie, K., Thompson, S., & Starkey, K. 1994. Longevity and the life cycle of management buyouts. *Strategic Management Journal*, 15: 215–227.

Wruck, K. H. 2008. Private equity, corporate governance, and the reinvention of the market for corporate control. *Journal of Applied Corporate Finance*, 20: 8–21.

Yago, G. 1991. *Junk bonds: How high-yield securities restructured corporate America*. New York: Oxford University Press.

14

ARE LOWER PRIVATE EQUITY RETURNS THE NEW NORMAL?

Eileen Appelbaum and Rosemary Batt

> Buyout fund returns have exceeded those from public markets in almost all vintage years before 2006. Since 2006, buyout fund performance has been roughly equal to those of public markets.
>
> Robert S. Harris, Tim Jenkinson, and Steven N. Kaplan (2015)

Introduction

Between 2013 and 2015, global private equity (PE) fundraising saw its best years since the 2008 financial crisis – raising over $300 billion each year. Fundraising in 2016 was still impressive, though down from the previous year. But is the enthusiasm of investors warranted? Do PE buyout funds deliver outsized returns to investors and will they do so in the future? This chapter answers this question by reviewing the most recent empirical evidence on buyout fund performance. The answer is no. The evidence we review draws on buyout funds because they represent by far the largest proportion of PE investment funds.

The PE industry grew rapidly from 2000 through the bubble years before collapsing in 2008–2009 during the financial crisis and great recession; but by 2010 it was on the mend, and since then its investments have surpassed its early growth period. Pension funds and other institutional investors are investing more now than ever in PE buyout funds. Between 2011 and 2015, global PE activity accelerated, with cumulative deal values of roughly $5.2 trillion, or $1 trillion annually (PitchBook, 2016e).

What has led to the boom in PE fundraising and activity in recent years? Notably, after several years of poor payouts during and after the financial crisis and recession, PE buyout funds were able to capitalize on a rising stock market to exit companies acquired before the crisis, and in turn make substantial distributions to investors after 2011. With distributions exceeding contributions, cash-rich pension funds and other institutional investors were again willing to plough money back into new PE funds. Fundraising in 2013–2015 was substantially higher than in the 2010–2012 period (PitchBook, 2016e). In the US alone, PE fundraising averaged 112% of fund targets and reached fund closings faster than at any time since 2006. Institutional investors are competing for opportunities to participate in funds that they view as more desirable. With their renewed bargaining power, PE buyout funds have explored new fee structures to enhance their own returns (Bain & Company, 2016: 5–7) – despite the fact that they already extract millions in fees from their limited partners (LPs) each year (Appelbaum & Batt, 2016). The average size of funds has also risen steadily, and mega-funds and mega-deals are back in play.

But is this enthusiasm warranted? Do PE buyout funds still deliver outsized returns to investors? Industry participants claim that these funds significantly outperform the stock market, but finance economists who study the industry have found considerably more modest results (see Appelbaum & Batt, 2014: 161–192). In this chapter, we analyze recent research by finance economists, which shows that the overall performance of PE funds *has been declining*. While PE buyout funds once beat the S&P 500, the median buyout fund has more or less matched the performance of the stock market since 2006 (Harris et al., 2015; L'Her et al., 2016; PitchBook, 2016a).

These findings raise serious questions about whether the recent investment explosion in PE buyout funds will pay off for pension funds and other institutional investors. Will newly-minted PE funds be able to acquire target companies that they can sell later at substantially higher prices? Changes in the competitive landscape cast doubt on their ability to do so. In the 1980s and 1990s, it was easy to make outsized returns on leveraged buyouts: a small number of buyout firms had many opportunities to break up large conglomerates and "unlock value." But by 2016, competition for acquisitions was fierce, with 4,100 PE firms headquartered in the US, and they had raised 696 buyout funds, according to the PE lobbying group, American Investment Council (2016) – formerly the Private Equity Growth Capital Council. The fall-off of deal-making in 2016 is one indicator of heightened competition. While global PE deal-making rose steadily from its low point in 2009 of $353 billion to a high of $1,243 billion in 2015, it fell by 20% in 2016 (PitchBook, 2016e). PE-backed company inventory has risen since the financial crisis, from 5,252 in 2010 to 6,201 in 2013 and 7,168 in 2016. Much of this is due to more recent acquisitions, but a significant number of portfolio companies have been held more than six years (Black, 2017). This contributed to a decline in PE exits in 2016, which fell by roughly 25% (PitchBook, 2016e).

Meanwhile, 2016 also saw a drop in global fundraising by 13%, linked to the fact that a large stockpile of "committed" capital has accumulated in global PE funds – so called "dry powder." Dry powder is capital that LPs have committed to PE buyout funds but has not been invested because these PE funds have not been able to acquire attractive buyout targets. Global dry powder reached a total of $852 billion in 2016 (PitchBook, 2016e: 10); dry powder in US PE funds reached $555.6 billion by the third quarter of 2017 (PitchBook, 2017a).

PE firms with too much cash on hand are also competing with publicly traded corporations that have deep cash reserves for strategic acquisitions. This has led to "sky-high acquisition prices," typically measured by "price multiples" – the ratio of the purchase price of a target company to its earnings or EBITDA (earnings before interest, taxes, depreciation, and amortization). Globally, price/EBITDA multiples have held at 8 times EBITDA in recent years but rose to 10 times EBITDA in the US by early 2015, and 11 times EBITDA in 2016 (PitchBook, 2016d). This is higher than the multiples for acquisitions in the bubble years.

Moreover, while the "strategics" benefit from investment-grade credit ratings that lower the cost of debt, PE firms face worsening credit conditions and weaker bank lending in light of new guidance set by bank regulators (Bain & Company, 2016: 12). Under these new guidelines, banks are strongly encouraged to limit lending for deals to no more than six times EBITDA (Board of Governors of the Federal Reserve System et al., 2013). Carlyle's 2016 acquisition of Veritas, the largest LBO in 2015, is a case in point. The deal was delayed six months while the banks negotiated to meet the new requirements and to address increased earnings uncertainty. Carlyle had to reduce leverage from 6.7 times to 5.8 times EBITDA and raise the equity portion of the deal from 33% to 40% of the purchase price (Davis & Natarajan, 2016).

This example is reflected in the overall trend data, which shows that PE firms have had to increase their equity contributions in PE buyouts from what was historically 30%, to 40% in the post-recession years, to over 50% in 2016 – a trend that is observed globally as well as in the US market (PitchBook, 2016d, 2016e). The lower leverage reduces future returns. In addition, as in the Carlyle case, due diligence processes are becoming lengthier and more costly because firms have to justify the amounts they are paying – again contributing to lower future returns.

Pulling together the recent evidence from PE-owned company inventory, fundraising, deal-making, and continued high purchase prices, industry analyst PitchBook predicted deal levels in 2017 will remain at their low 2016 level, and "a future return profile for the industry that is much lower than what we've grown accustomed to" (2016e: 4).

PE returns are also cyclical and mirror stock market trends, according to new research by finance economists, which we review in this report. PE distributions have been high in recent years because the stock market surged as the economy recovered from the recession. But buying companies when the stock market is at or near a peak and prices for target companies are high – as in the current period – yields substantially lower returns than buying at the trough when prices are low (Robinson & Sensoy, 2011, 2015).

In sum, the evidence from a wide set of industry indicators suggests that PE will face a more difficult future in its attempts to replicate the outsized returns it has historically promised. This is in addition to the evidence we review below that PE's fund performance over the last decade has been disappointing. This new research shows both that PE performance is cyclical, mirroring the stock market, and that it has a downward trajectory. It also shows that the past performance of a PE firm's general partners (GPs) is no longer a good predictor of future performance (Harris et al., 2014; Braun et al., 2015).

Thus, the new research that we review is critical for PE investors to consider. In the US in particular, it is noteworthy that fully a third of the capital in PE funds comes from US pension funds (Bain & Company, 2013). They are responsible for investing the savings of millions of Americans. Other major investors include university endowments, non-profit foundations, and insurance companies, whose fortunes rise and fall with their investment choices.

We begin by explaining the different ways in which PE returns are measured and why some are more appropriate than others. We then review new research on the performance outcomes of PE funds and their persistence over time.

Measuring the performance of PE funds[1]

"Measurement issues" in finance are often viewed as too technical or boring for the typical investor or public citizen to pay attention to. But they are central to understanding whether investing in PE funds is worthwhile. A central problem is that independent analyses of returns are difficult to carry out because of PE's notable lack of transparency and insistence on confidentiality. PE firms report net returns to their LP investors, but do not make this information available to others; neither do they tell their LP investors how they arrive at this measure of fund performance. Data available to researchers is improving, but no comprehensive, unbiased, and widely available data yet exists that can be used to evaluate PE performance. All studies of PE performance suffer from uncertainty about just how representative the data on fund returns actually is. As PE researchers Robinson and Sensoy (2015) note:

> Ultimately, however, the universe of private equity funds is not available, and summary statistics from [various sources] differ systematically from one another. Consequently, it is impossible to know whether any differences are a function of sample selection, self-reporting, and survivorship biases that creep into commercially available data sources, whether they reflect characteristics of the LP/GP matching process in private equity, or whether they are evidence of sample selection bias.
>
> *(2011, 2015: 13)*

Beyond the adequacy of data, three important measurement issues need to be addressed at the outset. The first concerns which *metric* is used to actually measure performance. While the PE industry has continued to report returns based on the "internal rate of return" (IRR), finance economists have shown why this metric is seriously flawed and should be replaced by a "public market equivalent" index, which takes into account the opportunity costs of investing in PE buyout funds versus other alternatives. The second issue concerns the measurement of *unrealized returns*, which arises because LPs typically make a commitment of capital to a PE fund and are locked into that commitment for the life of the fund – usually 10 to 12 years. But investors need to know about the returns to active funds in a more timely fashion. To do so, they must rely on estimates by the fund's GP of unrealized returns – that is, estimates of the value of companies still in PE portfolios. And GPs vary widely in the assumptions and methods they use to arrive at these estimates. A third issue is more intangible: how to evaluate the wide range of *risks* that the LPs assume when they invest in PE and how they should be compensated for that risk.

What is the appropriate measure of fund performance?

The IRR is widely used by PE industry participants as a measure of PE fund performance. The IRR is the interest rate (also known as the discount rate) that will bring a series of realized and future cash flows (positive and negative) to a net present value equal to the value of cash invested. The IRR formula can be very complex depending on the timing and variations in cash flow amounts. One of the disadvantages of using IRR is that all cash flows are assumed to be reinvested at the same discount rate, although in the real world these rates will fluctuate. The IRR suffers from three main flaws that make it a poor measure of fund performance.[2]

Computational difficulties. The calculation of the IRR is an iterative process carried out by a computer. Under certain conditions, either it does not converge to a value for IRR or it yields multiple results. This can happen if the cash flows used to compute the IRR change direction from positive to negative or negative to positive more than once over the time period under consideration. This is not uncommon in the case of PE.

IRR calculation assumes distributions are reinvested at the same IRR rate. In the calculation of the IRR, the high IRR earned from an early distribution is assumed to apply to these distributed funds in subsequent periods. That is, the mechanics of the IRR computation assume that the pension fund or other investor that receives the distribution has the opportunity to reinvest it at the same high IRR as the initial PE investment. As the CFA Institute explains, "IRR calculations assume that future investments will achieve the same returns as earlier investments. Realized cash distributions are assumed to keep earning the same returns in the future for the complete life of the fund or private investment" (McSwain, 2017). Thus the calculation exaggerates the return from PE investments during the life of the PE fund and does a poor job of predicting the actual return that will be realized when the fund reaches the end of its life span and is liquidated (Jenkinson et al., 2013: 14). McKinsey and Company recommends "that managers must either avoid using IRR entirely or at least make adjustments for the measure's most dangerous assumption: that interim cash flows will be reinvested at the same high rates of return" (Kelleher & MacCormack, 2004).

Opportunities to game the calculation. The IRR is sensitive to the timing of distributions from a PE fund. Early sales of high performing companies in the PE fund's portfolio raise the measured IRR. Decisions about when to sell portfolio companies and distribute the returns to investors are made by the fund's GP. The GP is typically a management committee drawn from the PE firm's partners. The GP manages the fund and makes all decisions; investors in the fund are LPs and have no decision-making power, including no say over the acquisition or subsequent sale of portfolio companies. This characteristic of the IRR provides GPs with an incentive to increase the fund's IRR by engaging in early sales of successful portfolio companies even when these sales do not make economic sense and/or are not in the best interests of LPs.

Averaging the IRR across multiple funds in an investor's portfolio or lining the funds up end-to-end and treating all of the investments and returns as if they were a single fund – from time zero when the first investment was made to the current year – can also lead to exaggerated results. This will occur if some funds in the portfolio have outsized returns while others, especially more recent vintages, perform poorly. The good performance of earlier vintages raises the overall IRR and masks the poor performance of recent vintages and may be misleading.

The public market equivalent

These well-known flaws in the IRR as a measure of PE fund returns led finance economists Steven Kaplan and Antoinette Schoar to develop an alternative method for calculating these returns – the public market equivalent (PME). In their seminal and widely cited study of PE returns, Kaplan and Schoar (2005) developed the PME, which compares returns from investing in PE with returns from comparable, and comparably timed, investments in the stock market, as measured by a stock market index, often the S&P 500. The PME is more useful than the IRR for the LP investors because they need to assess their returns relative to what investments in the stock market would yield. They care about two questions: how much money they get back by the end of the 10-year period (during which time they are locked into the PE fund) relative to their initial investment, and how that compares with the return they would have earned had they invested the same amount of capital in another way – say, in the shares of companies that trade on the stock market.

A PME equal to 1 means that the return from investing in the buyout fund just matches the return from an equivalent and similarly timed investment in the stock market. A PME greater than 1 indicates that the return from investing in the PE fund was greater than what it could have earned in the stock market; a PME less than 1 indicates a return from PE investments that is less than the stock market return. A PME of 1.27, for example, means that the PE fund outperformed the stock market by 27% over the life of the fund. If the fund has a life of 10 years, this implies an average annual outperformance of just over 2.4%.

The PME is the preferred metric of finance economists for evaluating fund performance. It avoids the problems associated with the use of the IRR for this purpose. It also produces interim results that more closely predict fund performance over the life of the PE fund.

An additional concern is that even when the public market equivalent is used, as it is in most of the studies we review later, researchers typically use the S&P 500 index to compute the PME. The S&P 500, however, is based on publicly traded corporations that are substantially larger than those typically acquired by PE buyout funds and has proven to be easier for buyout funds to outperform than other stock market indices. Small cap stock market indices may provide a better benchmark. Phalippou (2014) finds that buyout funds mainly acquire small companies and yield returns that are similar to the returns of small-cap indices. This suggests to us that LP investors would be able to achieve the same return with much less risk by investing in a small-cap stock market index fund.

Estimating the value of companies still in fund portfolios

In their 2005 study, Kaplan and Schoar examined fund returns over the period 1980–2001 in which all (or virtually all) portfolio companies had been sold and the fund had been liquidated. Thus, they based their calculations on *actual realized returns* to the LPs and not on subjective estimates by GPs of the value of companies still held in their fund's portfolio. In that study, Kaplan and Schoar found that the returns to LPs from these investments are highly variable and, on average, are slightly lower than what they would have earned by investing in the S&P 500 index (see also Driessen et al. (2012) who used a dynamic version of the IRR and found that PE underperformed). Kaplan and others have since raised questions about the quality of the data available for that study, so we will not dwell on the results. In the next section of this chapter, we report on the results of more recent studies of PE fund performance. What is important for the present discussion is that Kaplan and Schoar's (2005) study used data from funds that had been liquidated. Most other studies of PE fund performance include large numbers of active PE buyout funds and calculate fund returns by relying on interim valuations of the unsold portfolio companies held by these funds. The value of an active fund (its net asset value, or NAV) is calculated as the realized value of investments that have already been sold plus an estimate by the GP of the market value of unsold companies held in the fund's portfolio. In these cases, the calculation of PE fund performance necessarily relies on estimates by the GP of *unrealized returns*.

New accounting standards implemented in 2008 require PE funds to report the values of unsold companies in their portfolios at "fair value." This is defined as "the price that would be received to sell an asset or paid to transfer a liability in an orderly transaction between market participants as of the measurement date."[3]

The standard requires that unobservable inputs used in determining the fair value of an investment must incorporate the assumptions a market participant would use in developing an exit price. The PE fund can use its own data to develop the unobservable inputs used to arrive at the estimated fair value; but only the assumptions and not the data must be disclosed. Thus, a PE fund must outline a clear valuation process, but the fund's GP has full discretion in the choice of approach, which unobservable inputs are used, and the range of values for the inputs used to arrive at fair market value.

Thus, the standard gives the GP a lot of wiggle room in valuing companies in the fund's portfolio. Assumptions about key inputs – the discount rate, projected revenue growth, and profit margins among others – may lie within a reasonable range. But there is still a lot of guesswork embedded in assumptions about the range of values that each unobservable variable can take on, especially in determining where in this rather wide range the portfolio company falls. Choosing different values within that range for unobservable inputs can lead to wide differences in the valuation of the company. Clarification of the rules for Fair Value

Measurement issued in May 2011, cited in Gottlieb (2011), makes it clear that PE funds do not have to provide quantitative sensitivity disclosures to investors. That is, PE funds do not have to report to investors the potential impact of various assumptions on the valuation arrived at for the company. The GP simply presents its view of the value of companies in the PE fund's portfolio to the fund's LPs; the LPs have no way to evaluate independently the accuracy of the GP's estimates. This may be especially problematic for mature funds. Driessen et al. (2012) find that GPs' self-reported NAVs overstate the value of companies still held in a fund's portfolio and overstate the value of the PE fund.

It is important to recognize that calculations of industry-wide PE fund performance draw on estimates by GPs of the value of large numbers of unsold companies; reported gains are largely the unrealized gains attributed to these companies by GPs. For example, in 2015, the California Public Employees Retirement System (CalPERS) for the first time published what it pays to PE firms in performance fees (also known as carried interest); one-third of these fees were based on *unrealized carry* – that is, carry attributed to expected gains from sales of portfolio companies mostly acquired in the prior several years (Martin, 2015). These companies were acquired at very high price-to-earnings ratios. It is likely that GP estimates of the value of their PE funds reflect these high prices, and they may be difficult to match when these companies are resold.

How risky is investing in PE?

It is important to understand that investments in PE carry risks that are specific to this asset class. These include:[4]

Leverage risk: This is the potential for default and bankruptcy when portfolio companies are loaded with excessive amounts of debt. For example, PE-owned Caesar's Entertainment exemplifies how a portfolio company bought at a high multiple of earnings in a leveraged buyout with a high level of debt can become bankrupt, with investors losing the equity they invested in the company (Cohan, 2015).

Operating and business risk: Some companies acquired by PE funds may involve exceptional operating and business risks. Investments in oil and gas production, for example, may be subject to wild and unpredictable swings in energy prices. Energy Future Holdings, the largest leveraged buyout in history at $48 billion, went bankrupt because the PE owners bet on the price of natural gas rising and instead it collapsed (Appelbaum & Batt, 2014: 224–227).

Liquidity risk: Investments by LPs in PE funds are typically for a 10-year time period; funds cannot be withdrawn if there are economic changes that make it desirable to exit the investment. The secondary market generally provides limited opportunities for pension funds to sell their stakes in PE funds.

Commitment risk: The uncertain timing of capital calls and distributions, which are controlled by the PE fund's GP, is a risk for the LPs that invest in the fund. The LPs may face difficulties when commitments are called on short notice or when distributions they are counting on are delayed.

Structural risk: The potential for misalignment of interests between the PE fund's GP and its investors (including pension funds) can give rise to risks for the investors. For example, the GP collects monitoring and transaction fees from the portfolio companies owned by the PE fund; these fees enrich the GP but reduce the price at which the companies can be sold, and in turn, the returns to the LPs. In some cases, GPs have collected these fees from companies spiraling towards bankruptcy, exacerbating the financial crisis these companies face (Appelbaum & Batt, 2016).

Valuation risk: These risks are associated with the process that GPs use in computing the valuation of unsold companies in their funds' portfolios; the possibility exists that the valuation methodology may not be appropriate and the valuations may not be reasonable. In this case, interim calculations of the value of the portfolio may give a false impression of the actual returns investors will receive when the fund is liquidated.

Investors in PE funds need to earn a return that compensates them for the extra risk that these investments entail. That is, these investments should provide a return equal to what the investor could have earned in the stock market plus a risk premium. To be worth undertaking, PE investments should yield a return equal to an appropriate stock market index plus 300 basis points (3%), according to most financial advisors.

The performance of PE funds

The debate over whether PE funds yield returns that outweigh the risks to investors has occurred in the context of the recognized absence of unbiased data and questions about which performance metrics should be used. Nonetheless, serious studies have been published that attempt to deal with these issues in a variety of ways. Our earlier work reviewed the evidence on PE fund performance largely prior to the financial crisis (Appelbaum & Batt, 2014). In that evaluation, we examined reports provided by the PE industry itself which, based on the IRR, argued that PE buyout funds substantially outperformed the stock market. By contrast, the most credible research by top finance scholars did not rely on the IRR to measure performance and reached much more modest conclusions. Some of these studies showed that the median PE fund did not beat the stock market; others showed that returns for the median fund were slightly above the market. Most of these studies, however, used as the point of comparison, the S&P 500 index of large-cap stocks, which are larger than most PE fund portfolio companies and easier to beat. It would generally be more appropriate to use the Russell 3000 or stock market indexes tailored to the portfolio companies in PE funds. We concluded:

> The most positive academic findings for private equity compare its performance to the S&P 500: They report that the median fund outperforms the S&P 500 by about 1 percent per year, and the average fund by 2-to-2.5 percent. The higher average performance is driven almost entirely by the top quartile of funds – and particularly the top decile. With the exception of the top performing funds, returns do not cover the roughly 3 percent additional return above the stock market that is required to compensate investors for the illiquidity of PE investments. When PE funds are compared to indices of smaller publicly traded companies whose size is comparable to most PE-owned portfolio companies (the S&P 500 is comprised of much larger corporations), then the average PE fund barely performs better, and the median fund just matches stock market returns.
>
> *(Ibid., 2014: 11)*

Building on this review, below we analyze important new studies that rely on the PME to measure performance – some using the S&P 500 and others a more appropriate "tailored PME," as we explain later. The findings are generally consistent with what we previously found, with top quartile PE buyout funds outperforming the S&P 500 by a considerable margin. But the conclusions of the authors depend importantly on whether they focus on the *average* fund (skewed upward by better performing funds at the top) or the *median* fund (the typical fund), and whether they use a time horizon of 5 years or 10 years (the typical life of a fund is 10 years or longer).

The first study shows that at the median, and assuming the typical 10-year life span, half the funds outperformed the S&P 500 by less than 1% a year (0.87%), and many of these performed even worse than this and failed to beat the S&P 500 (Robinson & Sensoy, 2011, 2015). The authors also provide important evidence that PE fund returns are highly cyclical. A second study, based on funds launched between 1984 and 2010, reveals that PE buyout funds did beat the market over this time period; but performance declined over time. The median PE fund beat the S&P 500 by 1.75% annually in the 1990s and 1.5% annually in the 2000s, although this is well below the 3% return viewed as necessary to compensate investors for the added risk associated with PE investments. Importantly, the authors found that since 2006, PE buyout funds performed about the same as the S&P 500 (Harris et al., 2015). The analysis of PitchBook data, presented later, reaches similar conclusions.

Two other new studies consider the question of "persistence": Is the outperformance of an initial fund repeated in a follow-on fund managed by the same GP? Pension funds and other PE investors have generally assumed that they can reliably invest in a fund based on the track record of a GP, and indeed prior research showed this to be true (Kaplan & Schoar, 2005). But recent research that we review here (Harris et al., 2014; Braun et al., 2015) reverses the earlier findings. In her 2017 research, PE researcher Antoinette Schoar observes that the persistence of performance that she and Steven Kaplan identified in their seminal 2005 article no longer exists (White, 2017). These authors have found that the past performance of a GP does not predict future performance. This raises serious doubts about whether investors should continue to rely on a GP's past record as criteria for investing in a fund. And given a lack of persistence, investors and pension funds will be hard pressed to come up with other criteria for determining which PE buyout funds are likely to yield high returns.

Recent academic studies of PE fund performance

It is widely recognized that returns to PE buyout funds since about 2000 have not produced the outsized returns of the 1980s and 1990s when competition was scarce, hostile takeovers took Main Street companies by surprise, and many large conglomerates were ripe for dismantling. Subsequently, the remaining publicly traded companies became leaner, the number of PE firms rose dramatically in the 2000s, and choice targets became increasingly rare. Less clear is whether these investments are still worthwhile. The new research we review here is based in part on this new competitive environment and is therefore particularly relevant to the decisions of investors in the current period.

PE fund cyclicality and performance. Robinson and Sensoy (2011, 2015) examined the cyclical nature of PE fund performance. LPs in a PE fund commit a certain amount of capital to the fund; but GPs do not call on LPs to provide this capital until an attractive investment opportunity arises. Robinson and Sensoy analyzed the relationship between PE fund returns and the economic conditions that prevailed when the capital committed by LPs was called on for actual investments. Their main question is whether PE fund returns vary depending on when in the business cycle the investment occurs. Using a proprietary database of quarterly cash flows for 837 buyout and venture capital funds from 1984 to 2010, they found – as others have found – that funds raised when the economy is heating up tend to perform worse than those raised when economic conditions are poor.

They argue that it is particularly difficult for LPs to provide cash to the PE fund during periods of recession or financial turmoil. As a result, those investors that do provide capital calls during economic downturns should earn a liquidity premium – as compensation for the greater opportunity cost of providing capital for illiquid PE investments during recessions. Their empirical results support this argument. Robinson and Sensoy found that funds that call capital in bad economic times have higher returns and distributions to investors than other funds – a result that is consistent with a liquidity premium for supplying capital under difficult conditions.

More importantly, the authors assess whether PE buyout funds actually outperform the stock market or a public market equivalent index. To measure fund performance, they did not use the IRR because, as they observe, "it is a purely absolute measure of performance that makes … no attempt to account for the opportunity cost of private equity investments" (2015: 6). For this reason, they follow the lead of many academic researchers and use the public market equivalent to measure performance using both the S&P 500 and a "tailored PME," which is computed the same way as the standard PME but with alternative benchmark indexes. The tailored PME takes into account whether the fund is self-described as a small-cap, mid-cap, or large-cap buyout fund, using an index known as the "Fama-French size tercile index."

Robinson and Sensoy's summary statistics on fund performance are shown in Table 14.1. They are based on a total of 542 PE buyout funds: 174 active funds (those launched in recent years that have not been liquidated) and 368 liquidated funds (funds with a vintage year of 2005 or earlier that were effectively liquidated by the end of the sample period, June 30, 2010).

The data represents performance over the life of the fund – typically a 10-year period – although this can be extended by mutual agreement between the GP and the LPs. A PME of 1.09 for the median liquidated fund means that the typical PE fund outperformed the S&P 500 by 9% over the life of the fund. We used the data in this table to compute average *annual* returns to the fund, assuming a 10-year life span. Based on this assumption, an outperformance of 1.09 for the median fund translates into an average annual outperformance of less than 1% (0.87%); and many funds failed to beat the S&P 500 at all. Indeed, the bottom quarter of funds underperformed the S&P 500 by 18% over the fund's life, or an annual average underperformance of nearly 2% (1.96%). When returns to PE buyout funds are computed using the "tailored PME," which includes companies more comparable in size to particular PE fund portfolio companies, performance is even worse: the performance of the median buyout fund just matches this stock market index and half the funds underperform it.

The top performing funds – those in the top quartile of PE fund performance – outperformed the S&P 500 by a substantial margin – 46% over the 10-year life of the fund. That translates into an annual average outperformance of nearly 4% (3.86%). Thus the top quartile funds in this data set did deliver returns that make investing in PE attractive.

Table 14.1 PE fund performance compared to public market equivalent (PME)

	S&P 500 PME		*Tailored PME*	
	All funds	*Liquidated funds*	*All funds*	*Liquidated funds*
Average	1.19	1.18	1.08	1.10
Median	1.09	1.09	0.96	1.00
25th percentile	0.82	0.82	0.74	0.77

Source: Robinson and Sensoy (2015: 31, table 2).

Of course, most investors will not be in top quartile funds, although this is the goal of every pension fund and other PE LPs. Investors look at a GP's track record and use past performance as a guide to future investing in PE. But this may no longer be an effective strategy. As we show in the next section, in the period prior to 2001, a successful GP with a top quartile fund had a high likelihood that the next fund would also be top quartile. But this type of persistence in performance disappeared for funds launched after 2000.

In their paper, Robinson and Sensoy computed annual returns on investments in PE buyout funds in a different way – based on a 5-year "holding period" rather than the 10-year life span of the funds. It is unclear from the paper why they chose this method. Recall that the PME is designed to show *cumulative* earnings by the PE fund relative to a stock market index over the life of the fund. Thus it is appropriate to use the typical 10-year life span of a PE fund to compute average annual returns (Kaplan & Schoar, 2005; Phalippou & Gottschalg, 2009).

In their estimate of returns over five years, Robinson and Sensoy also used the *average* S&P 500 PME rather than the *median* PME. The average PME is pulled up by the outstanding performance of top quartile funds. The average S&P 500 PME in this data set is 1.18 or a cumulative outperformance of 18% over the life of the fund. Using the average performance for funds in the sample and a holding period of five years, the authors report higher returns to PE funds than what we calculated – a return of about 3% a year. They conclude that, "the average buyout fund in our sample has outperformed the S&P 500 by 18% over the life of the fund, or about 3% per year at an investment holding period of about five years" (2015: 10).

While the average return may be a useful figure for a very large pension fund or other institutional investor able to invest in a wide variety of PE buyout funds, it is not particularly relevant for the typical PE investor who invests in one or a few funds and is better served by knowing what the median return is. Moreover, the authors do not explain why investors in the fund would be interested in performance over a five-year average holding period for portfolio companies. We note that holding periods for portfolio companies have become longer since the great recession (Lewis, 2017). Research firm Preqin Ltd. estimates that funds launched in 2005 and earlier held about $115 billion in unrealized assets at the end of 2014 (Lim, 2016). GPs are asking investors for extensions to a fund's life span beyond the agreed upon 10 years to allow additional time for the GP to dispose of unrealized assets and avoid forced sales on unfavorable terms. Such extensions in the life of a fund reduce its average annual returns. What matters for LPs is the return on the capital they committed over the 10 or more years during which the GP controls capital calls and distributions, not whether the GP exits a particular investment in five years. In our view, from the perspective of investors in PE buyout funds, it makes more sense to calculate average annual returns based on the PME and the 10-year life span of the fund, as we propose. For the sample of funds in Robinson and Sensoy, and assuming a fund life span of 10 years, that figure would be 1.7% a year (rather than the 3% the authors report).

The performance of public and PE compared. The second recent study of PE fund returns compares the performance of public and PE (Harris et al., 2015). The authors used cash flow data from the holdings of almost 300 LPs that invested in 781 North American PE buyout funds plus data from 300 European buyout funds. Approximately 40% of the LPs in the data set are pension funds. The data includes PE buyout funds launched between 1984 and 2010; and the data ends in June, 2014. Thus, the authors were able to examine PE performance over a period that includes the economic boom of 2003 through 2007, the financial crisis of 2008–2009, and the post-crisis recovery to 2014. They estimated average returns net of fees and profit shares (carried interest). In addition to comparing the performance of PE and public equity, they also assessed the role that investment in top quartile funds plays in LP investment results.

Like Robinson and Sensoy, the authors did not use the IRR to measure performance, as it does not provide, "a direct way to assess how PE returns compare to those to public equity. We focus on Kaplan and Schoar's (2005) PME, which directly compares an investment in a PE fund to an equivalently timed investment in the relevant public market" (2015: 6).

The results of the analysis over the full time period were positive. The authors reported that, compared to the S&P 500, average and median PE fund performance for the entire period are positive:

> The weighted-average, average, and median PMEs also exceed 1.0 in all three decades. The weighted average buyout PME exceeds 1.0 for 25 of the 27 vintages from 1984 to 2010; the average for 23 and even the median PME exceeds 1.0 for 19 of 27 vintages. And, ignoring vintage years, the average fund in the entire sample has an average PME of 1.18 and a median PME of 1.09.
>
> *(2015: 9)*

They go on to show, however, that performance declined over time: "buyout fund returns have exceeded those from public markets in almost all vintage years before 2006. Since 2006, buyout fund performance has been roughly equal to those of public markets" (2015: 2).

Tables 14.2 and 14.3 below are extracts from tables II and IV in the Harris et al. study. Table 14.2 reports the average, median, and weighted average PMEs as of June 2014 for funds of different vintages compared to equivalent-timed investments in the S&P 500. Weighted averages use the capital committed to the funds as weights. Table 14.3 reports PMEs by performance quartile. In each vintage year, a fund is assigned to a quartile based on its PME relative to others in that year. Figures reported are the average PME across funds in that quartile.

In considering fund performance, most investors are interested in typical (median) performance because they are likely to be invested in a fund that performs at or around the median and have a 50% chance of doing worse than the median fund. Table 14.2 shows that the typical fund launched in the 1990s outperformed the S&P 500 by a cumulative 16% over the life of the fund, and by 19% for funds launched in the 2000s. The 16% median outperformance for the 1990s implies an average annual outperformance of 1.5%, relative to the S&P 500; the 19% median outperformance of funds in the 2000s implies an average annual outperformance of 1.75%.

Table 14.2 Buyout funds, S&P 500 public market equivalent (PME)

Vintage year	*Average*	*Median*	*Weighted average*
Average 1990s	1.23	1.16	1.25
Average 2000s	1.23	1.19	1.28
2005	1.26	1.12	1.26
2006	1.01	1.03	1.02
2007	1.01	0.97	0.99
2008	0.97	0.96	1.03
2009	0.96	0.92	1.01

Source: Harris et al. (2015: 30, table II).

Table 14.3 Buyout funds, S&P 500 public market equivalent (PME)

Vintage year	*Bottom (4th) quartile*	*3rd quartile*	*2nd quartile*	*Top (1st) quartile*
Average 1990s	0.54	0.94	1.32	1.91
Average 2000s	0.73	1.05	1.27	1.73
2005	0.77	1.04	1.29	1.89
2006	0.61	0.95	1.10	1.39
2007	0.66	0.92	1.05	1.41
2008	0.69	0.89	1.03	1.28
2009	0.72	0.88	0.97	1.23
2010	0.63	0.84	0.95	1.19

Source: Harris et al. (2015: 33, table II).

Note that PE fund performance in both the 1990s and 2000s is well below the 3% return that most investors in PE view as a reasonable premium for the added risk associated with these investments. An investor in a fund with average returns in either decade would experience an average annual outperformance of 2.1% – better, but still below the widely used "stock market plus 3%" benchmark. Funds launched in 2005 outperformed the S&P 500 by 12% over the period from 2005 to 2014. The performance of PE funds launched since 2006, however, has approximately matched the performance of the S&P 500 from their date of launch to 2014.

As we see in Table 14.3, *top quartile* funds did yield PME values that placed their cumulative returns far above the S&P 500 for all funds launched between 1994 and 1999, with the average annual return corresponding to a PME of 1.91, equal to 6.7%. Even second quartile funds in those vintage years (PME of 1.32) provided an average annual return that exceeded the S&P 500 by 2.8%. Even in the 1990s, however, funds in the third and fourth quartiles underperformed the S&P 500.

Fund performance over the 2000s for top and second quartile funds still looks strong: the PME of 1.73 for top quartile funds translates to an annual outperformance of 5.6%; the PME of 1.27 for second quartile funds implies an annual outperformance of 2.5%. However, these averages for the decade mask a dramatic decline in performance for funds launched after 2005. While not as strong as in the earlier period, top quartile funds launched in the second half of the decade continued to perform well. Top quartile funds in the 2007 vintage, for example, beat the S&P 500 by an estimated 3.5% a year and those launched in 2010 beat it by 1.75% a year. For vintages after 2005, however, funds not in the top quartile performed poorly relative to this stock market index.

Like Robinson and Sensoy, Harris et al. did not calculate average *annual returns* to investments in PE based on Kaplan and Schoar's PME metric. Instead, they computed annual returns using a different methodology (Gredit et al., 2014). The average PME across the 781 funds in their sample is 1.20 (2015: table II), or a cumulative outperformance of 20%. If we assume that funds have a 10-year life span, then the annual average outperformance is 1.8%. Using their alternative methodology, however, Harris et al. find an annual outperformance of 3.07% for the average fund and an outperformance of 2.40% for the median fund. As Harris et al. explained these results, "The average PME of about 1.20 and an average annual excess return of roughly 3 to 4 percent suggest that the typical duration of a buyout fund is on the order of five years, a duration lower than the typical fund's legal life of 10 to 13 years" (2015: 10). That is, to reconcile a 20% outperformance over the life of the fund (which implies an average annual outperformance of 1.8% over the typical 10-year life of a fund) with a 3 to 4% annual return requires that the return was actually earned over a five-year period.

This five-year period is labeled, by analogy with investments in bonds, as the "duration" of the fund.[5] But the analogy to investments in bonds is spurious. A bond is an instrument that pays interest and principal on pre-specified dates. Investors can calculate the duration for a bond because they know what the cash flows will be and the date at which they will be paid. This is clearly not the case for investments in PE funds where both the amount and timing of capital calls and distributions are uncertain. As we observed earlier, investors are obligated to pay 100% of the capital they have committed, but the cash flows – both capital calls and distributions – are decided by the GP. Investors in PE must manage their liquidity to accommodate capital calls by the GP. And GPs have the option of paying out distributions whenever they want to.

For pension funds and other investors in PE, the bottom line concern is how much extra money they can make over the life span of the fund compared to investing in the stock market over the same time period. This is what the PME is designed to measure. As noted earlier, it is becoming more common today for GPs to request an extension beyond the agreed upon 10 years. In 2016, for example, *The Wall Street Journal* reported that 2005 vintage Carlyle Partners IV received investor approval for a two-year extension to allow more time to exit two remaining investments (Lim, 2016).

Building stock market indexes tailored to the characteristics of PE buyout funds. A more recent study develops a much finer-grained approach to creating a stock market index of companies that more closely match the characteristics of PE portfolio companies (L'Her et al., 2016). The authors build on earlier research, including the studies by Robinson and Sensoy (2015) and Harris and colleagues (2015) discussed earlier. They begin by replicating prior approaches – calculating the risk-adjusted performance results of PE buyout funds, as compared to the PME based on the S&P 500 index. Their results are in line with those of the earlier studies. They find a similar level of outperformance by PE buyout funds for pre-2006 vintages, while post-2005 vintages just match the performance of the S&P 500.

L'Her and colleagues then go on to develop stock market indexes of publicly traded companies more closely tailored to the characteristics (i.e., firm size, sector, and leverage) of companies acquired by the PE buyout funds in their sample. They construct PME measures based on these stock market indexes. Using these more carefully tailored measures of performance, they find that the average returns of vintages of buyout funds post-2005 fail to outperform the market. PE fund performance relative to a stock market index grows worse as the companies in the index more closely resemble those in the PE buyout funds. Indeed, average returns over the full array of PE buyout funds in the 1986 to 2008 vintages fail to beat the tailored stock market indexes. Rather, their performance approximately matches the performance of these indexes.

The study by L'Her and colleagues included more years of data and a larger sample of PE buyout funds than the study by Harris et al. In the early years of a buyout fund, GPs are calling capital commitments from their LP investors and buying companies for the fund's portfolio. There are few to no returns to speak of. In the later years (years 6 to 10), the funds are typically selling the companies acquired earlier and providing investors with returns. The longer time period in the L'Her et al. study provides a greater opportunity for more recent vintages to exit investments and record returns. Thus the authors argue that it might be reasonable to expect to find that the 2005–2008 vintages in this study show higher returns than was the case for these vintages in Harris et al. (2015). But, as L'Her and colleagues report, that was not the case. Even with their larger sample and longer time period, the later vintages of funds in their sample fared no better than in the Harris et al. study. This, as they note, provides further evidence for the view that, on average, PE buyout funds have not outperformed their risk-adjusted stock market indexes.

The authors conclude, "After adjusting for appropriate risks, we found no outperformance of buyout funds vis-à-vis their public market equivalents on a dollar-weighted basis" (L'Her et al., 2016: 10). This finding is based on average, not median, performance of PE buyout funds when compared to appropriate stock market indexes. As we saw earlier, median fund performance is generally worse than average performance. Importantly, this finding suggests that even large pension funds and institutional investors that invest in a large number of PE buyout funds are unlikely, on average, to see investments in recently launched funds outperform the stock market.

Average and median returns for vintages since 2000 have been disappointing, especially for vintages after 2005, which have only slightly exceeded the S&P 500 and have barely matched or actually underperformed stock market indexes more closely tailored to match companies in PE fund portfolios. However, top quartile funds have been solid performers in that they have outperformed the S&P 500 by 1.75%–4%, depending on the estimate. Some, but not all, provide returns in excess of the 3% premium for liquidity risk. The question is whether LPs can be confident that they will earn high returns in the future by identifying GPs that have performed well in the past. In the next section, we examine this issue of "persistence" – whether follow-on funds of GPs with top quartile funds do in fact perform as well as their predecessors.

How persistent is the performance of PE buyout funds?

The question of persistence – the relationship between the final performance of an initial fund and a subsequent fund managed by the same GP – is critical to PE investors. They need criteria for deciding which PE fund to invest in; and often they have relied on the prior performance record of a GP. Research on this question was most convincingly answered in a widely-cited paper by Kaplan and Schoar (2005), who analyzed the performance of US venture capital and PE buyout funds with vintage years up to the late 1990s. They examined the performance of mature funds in which all (or nearly all) investments in portfolio companies had been exited. Ranking funds based on their performance using the PME, they divided the initial funds into terciles – the top third of performers, the middle third of performers, and the bottom third of performers. They then analyzed the likelihood that the subsequent fund managed by the same GP would be in the top, middle, or bottom tercile. Their results are summarized in Table 14.4.

Table 14.4 Buyout funds, S&P 500 public market equivalent (percent)

		Follow-on fund tercile		
		Top tercile	*Middle tercile*	*Bottom tercile*
Previous fund tercile	Top tercile	48	31	21
	Middle tercile	32	38	30
	Bottom tercile	20	31	49

Source: Kaplan and Schoar (2005).

These results show strong persistence of performance. In this sample of funds, GPs with funds in the top tercile have a much higher than one-third likelihood (48% compared with 33%) that their subsequent fund will also be in the top tercile. Similarly, GPs with funds in the bottom tercile have a much higher than one-third likelihood (49%) that their subsequent fund will be in the bottom tercile. Marquez et al. (2015) examine the reason for this persistence. They find that successful PE fund managers forego the opportunity to capture higher rents by increasing the size of their follow-on funds. Instead, they limit the number of portfolio companies acquired by the subsequent fund and focus on obtaining abnormally high returns for their investors. The advantage of this strategy is that high quality target companies prefer to be acquired by talented GPs who are likely to improve company performance, thus reinforcing the success of the GP.

Based on these findings for funds launched prior to 2000, pension funds and other investors in PE could conclude that investing with the "right" GP – one whose previous fund had performed well – would yield high returns. This view continues to be held today – it is common for investment staff to assure pension fund trustees that their investments in PE will outperform the stock market because their investments are with top performing GPs. The conventional wisdom is that PE investment is an exception to the adage that past investment performance is no guarantee of future earnings.

More recent research, however, has found that the persistence of performance by GPs has declined as the PE industry has matured. Two recent studies show that today, past performance of a fund managed by a particular GP is no longer a good predictor of how that GP will perform in the future. Using data that is net of all fees and carried interest, Harris et al. (2014) assessed the persistence of buyout fund performance of the same GPs across current and prior funds. They analyzed persistence for funds launched before 2001 and for those launched after 2000. They confirmed the earlier findings of strong persistence of performance for pre-2001 funds. For the post-2000 period, however, they did not find evidence of persistence except among the lowest performing GPs. The authors sorted PE funds by the quartile of their previous fund, as measured by the PME, and then the likelihood that their subsequent fund would be in each quartile. Their results are summarized in Table 14.5, where 1 is top quartile, 2 is second quartile, 3 is third quartile, and 4 is bottom quartile.

Based on this analysis, GPs with a top performing fund in the post-2000 period had a 22% probability that their subsequent fund would be top performing. A GP with a bottom performing fund had a 21% probability the subsequent fund would be top performing – not much different from that of a top performing GP. In other words, the probability is

Table 14.5 Persistence of PE fund GP performance, post-2000 (percent)

		Follow-on fund quartile			
		1 (top)	*2*	*3*	*4 (bottom)*
Previous	1 (top)	22	29	30	19
fund	2	24	23	32	21
quartile	3	15	28	39	18
	4 (bottom)	21	14	32	32

Source: Harris et al. (2014).

essentially random and indicates that past top performance is no longer a guide to future performance. While it is not possible to predict which GPs will have subsequent funds that are top performers, there is a tendency for poor performance to persist. A GP with a fund in the lowest quartile has a 64% chance that a subsequent fund will be below the median.

A second study using different data reached similar conclusions (Braun et al., 2015). This study used a sample of buyout fund deals that included both early and more recent funds; and they analyzed gross returns – before fees and profit shares (carried interest) have been subtracted. Their sample of deals is roughly split between the US and Europe and covers the period 1974 to 2012. The authors considered only buyout funds in which investments in all or most (more than 50%) of the portfolio companies had been exited. They partitioned their sample into an early period (through the end of 2000), and a later period, from 2001 forward.

Analyzing realized deals, they found that the persistence of GP performance has declined substantially as the PE industry has matured and competition has increased. They found a strong effect of the GP on performance in the pre-2001 period, but not in the post-2000 period. They reported that, "deal-level analyses found that performance persistence has largely disappeared in recent years" (2015: 6). While their regression analyses of the persistence of deal performance examined the earlier and later periods separately, their analysis of likelihood that a top performing *fund* will be followed by another top performing *fund* covers the full time period. Thus, we cannot separately observe the likelihood of persistence in the post-2000 sample of funds (see Table 14.6).

Nevertheless, it is possible to observe the decline in the persistence of performance at the fund level as compared to the earlier Kaplan and Schoar analysis. While differences in the data sets used in the two papers – in terms of region, years, and number and type of funds – can account for some of this difference, the authors conclude that "overall, the evidence we present suggests that performance persistence has largely disappeared as the PE market has matured and become more competitive" (2015: 7). In summarizing their results as compared to those of Kaplan and Schoar, they concluded, "We find that the probability of repeating top (bottom) tercile performance is lower in our sample: 39 percent (40 percent), and we can only reject the hypothesis of random transition probabilities at the 10 percent level" (2015: 13). That is, even considering the full sample of funds, including the early period in which performance was persistent, the likelihood that a top tercile fund will be succeeded by a top tercile fund may not be better than chance.

New research by Antoinette Schoar "shows that persistence of returns from private-equity funds in the last decade has gone down, undoing the seminal research she co-authored with Steve Kaplan" which found that top tercile PE fund managers had a high probability of

Table 14.6 Persistence of PE fund GP performance (funds launched 1974–2012) (percent)

		Follow-on fund tercile		
		Top tercile	*Middle tercile*	*Bottom tercile*
Previous fund tercile	Top tercile	39	30	31
	Middle tercile	29	37	34
	Bottom tercile	26	34	30

Source: Braun et al. (2015).

repeating that performance with their follow-on funds. Schoar attributes this decline in performance to the increase in fundraising, which has doubled both the capital under management and the number of funds. Both competition among funds and the concentration of assets in the biggest funds have increased. She finds that the marginal returns to capital go down, even among the top performers, as these funds become larger. This causes the difference in performance between top performers and other PE funds to decline (White, 2017; see also related findings of Lopez-de-Silanes et al., 2015 that it is not fund size per se that leads to lower returns, but rather that when PE firms hold a high number of investments simultaneously, the investments underperform substantially). Schoar's research shows that, since 2005, GPs with top quartile funds have less than a 25% probability of repeating that performance in a subsequent fund (Primack, 2017).

Pension funds, endowments, and other investors in PE have long relied on a belief in the persistence of returns when choosing which GPs to invest with. But recent research has found little or no persistence in the performance of fund managers. The conclusion to be drawn from these studies is that past performance cannot be used to predict the future. Like Schoar, Braun et al. (2015) conclude that their research has uncomfortable implications for PE investors – sticking with top-performing managers is no longer a recipe for success.

Many investors in PE buyout funds believe they can beat the odds by picking the right fund manager. They look to the larger PE firms for top quartile performance. These PE firms manage multiple PE funds; their large size and the number of funds they manage suggest to LPs that they must be successful at acquiring portfolio companies and securing high returns when they exit these investments. LPs compete to invest in funds managed by partners in these "name brand" PE firms. Once they gain entry to these funds, pension funds and other LPs tend to reinvest in subsequent funds sponsored by these fund managers. However, this confidence may be misplaced. A recent study examined the quartile rankings of funds managed by 18 of the largest PE firms[6] during the 1992 to 2013 vintage years and found surprisingly mediocre performance (Hooke & Yook, 2016). The authors note that during the last 10 vintage years (2006 to 2016) it is principally first quartile funds that beat the S&P 500; the bottom three quartiles (75% of funds) failed to beat this stock market index consistently.

Assigning a value of 1 to top quartile funds and 4 to bottom quartile funds, a family of funds managed by partners in a particular PE firm that performed no better than random would have an average quartile ranking of 2.5; a ranking *lower* than 2.5 means the PE firm's buyout funds perform *better* than this. The authors found that the average quartile ranking over the fund families managed by the 18 large, brand name PE firms was 2.16. This is better than 2.5 and suggests that the performance of these funds generally places them in the top half of funds. But, as Hooke and Yook note, "the 2.16 mean result is quite distant from a 1.00 first quartile ranking, where, in recent years, the bulk of the alpha occurs. These results throw the institutions [pension funds and endowments] continued dedication to these large family fund groups into question" (2016: 7). Of the 18 fund families, 4 – managed by partners at Goldman Sachs, KKR, Kohlberg, and Thomas H. Lee – had average quartile scores that were equal to or worse than a random result. The best performers, with an average quartile ranking less than 2, were Veritas, Berkshire Partners, Hellman & Friedman, and Apollo Global. This analysis includes funds launched in 1993 to 2013 and includes many funds launched prior to 2005, when the returns of even second quartile funds tended to beat the stock market. Looking at more recent fund vintages, the authors found that the average quartile ranking for funds launched by these PE firms in 2005 and later "was 2.50, exactly equal to an average, or random, result" (2016: 7).[7]

PE fund performance over time: comparing the PME and IRR

The performance of PE funds over time has also been tracked by PitchBook, an investment research and database firm that tracks PE and venture capital firms, their funds, LPs, and portfolio companies. The 2016 PitchBook Benchmarking and Fund Performance Report provides an analysis of annual PE fund performance between 2003 and 2013, comparing results using the PME measure and the IRR (PitchBook, 2016a). The results show the decline in performance of the typical PE fund launched in these years and largely mirror those of Harris et al. (2015), discussed earlier.

PitchBook uses the PME benchmark developed by Kaplan and Schoar (2005) to compare PE fund performance to the Russell 3000, a more appropriate benchmark index for PE buyout funds than the S&P 500, because the Russell 3000 is based on companies that are more similar in size to the companies found in PE fund portfolios. Figure 14.1 compares the performance of the typical (median) fund, from the year of its inception to March 31, 2016 with that of the Russell 3000 (PitchBook, 2016a).

The 1.59 value of the PME for the median PE fund launched in 2003 indicates an outperformance of 59% since the fund's inception 13 years earlier, or an average annual outperformance of 3.63%. Similarly, the 1.35 value of the PME in 2004 indicates an outperformance of 35% since the fund's inception – an annual outperformance of 2.53% since inception 12 years earlier. The typical fund launched a year later, in 2005, with a PME value of 1.27 beat the Russell 3000 index by a cumulative 27% over the 11 years since the fund's inception. This implies an average annual outperformance of 2.2%. These results are a far cry from the performance of the typical PE fund in 2001 (not shown in Figure 14.1), when the PME value since inception was over 1.60 – a 60% outperformance – and the average annual outperformance over 10 years[8] was 4.81%. Nevertheless, returns for funds launched in 2003 to 2005 are relatively strong and may justify the decision to invest in PE. That

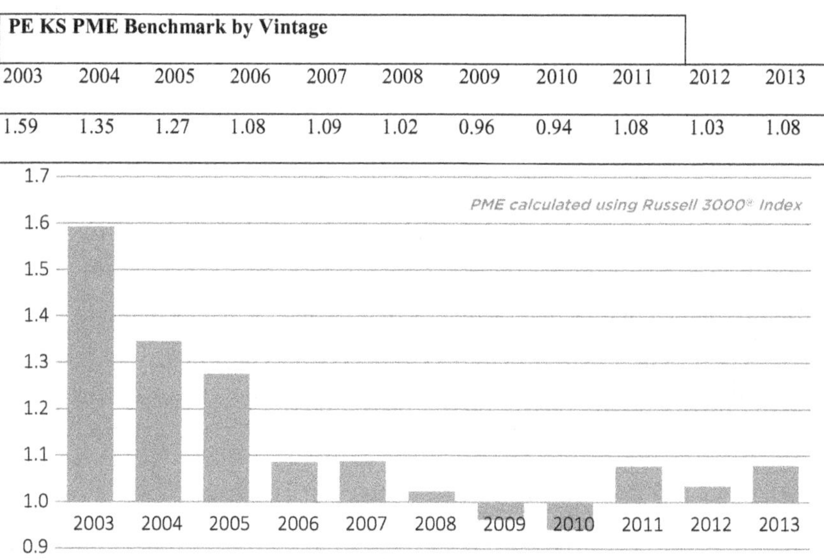

PE KS PME Benchmark by Vintage

2003	2004	2005	2006	2007	2008	2009	2010	2011	2012	2013
1.59	1.35	1.27	1.08	1.09	1.02	0.96	0.94	1.08	1.03	1.08

Figure 14.1 PE Kaplan and Schoar PME benchmark by vintage

Source: PitchBook (2016a: 5).

changed for funds launched after 2005; for those vintages the typical fund has more or less matched stock market returns, with some vintages slightly exceeding and others underperforming the Russell 3000. The PME of 0.94 for the typical fund launched in 2010, for example, means that the fund underperformed the Russell 3000 index by nearly 10% over the six years since inception – an average annual underperformance of 1.03%.

Despite its well-known weaknesses, the IRR has continued to be viewed as the gold standard of benchmarking by the PE industry. Its continued popularity is due in part to the fact that it tends to exaggerate PE fund performance. We can see how much better PE fund performance looks using the IRR in Table 14.7. Even using this metric, however, the failure in recent years of PE buyout funds to deliver the outsized returns promised by GPs is evident.

The median IRR for PE funds launched in 2001 was 21.5% according to PitchBook (2014). That means that the IRR for half the funds in that vintage exceeded 21%. The typical fund launched after 2004, however, failed to deliver on the PE industry's promise of a return of 20% or more. As of 2016, median returns were far below that mark and even top performing funds launched in 2005 or later have failed to deliver returns above 20%. Clearly, however, PE performance looks much better using IRR rather than PME to measure fund returns.

The median IRR reported for recent PE buyout funds may provide naïve investors who fail to risk adjust returns with the illusion that PE investments are worthwhile. But even apart from the well-known failings of the performance measure, absolute returns from investments in PE are an inappropriate guide to the payoff from this asset class. There are many additional risks associated with investing in PE and this performance measure does not adjust for that.

Pension funds and PE returns

Pension funds were early investors in PE; since 2000, they have become much larger and more significant investors in this asset class. In recent years, public and private pension funds have contributed over a third of the capital committed to PE funds. CalPERS and the California State Teachers Retirement System (CalSTRS) are regarded as leaders by other pension funds. This is due to their large size and long history of PE investing, their significant investments in PE, and the number of PE buyout funds in which they have invested.

These substantial commitments by pension funds to risky PE investments reflect several factors: the changing regulatory environment that freed up pension fund managers to invest

Table 14.7 Global PE IRR quartiles by vintage year

	2005	*2006*	*2007*	*2008*	*2009*	*2010*	*2011*	*2012*	*2013*
75th Percentile	13.5%	11.3%	14.8%	16.3%	18.7%	16.3%	18.3%	18.1%	19.5%
Median	8.3%	7.7%	9.3%	9.2%	10.1%	8.7%	11.2%	12.0%	7.3%
25th Percentile	3.3%	3.0%	4.5%	3.9%	6.3%	3.3%	6.9%	6.6%	−1.7%

*As of March 31, 2016

Source: PitchBook (2016a: 9).

in a wider range of financial products and the increased availability of those products; low treasury bond yields; changing guidelines under the Employee Retirement Income Security Act (ERISA) that encouraged more risky investments; and the increasing demand for payouts of benefits to an aging membership.

Pension funds are based in trust law and have a fiduciary duty that is higher than that imposed on corporations (Youngdahl, 2012: 115). The legal language that historically governed the actions of pension fund managers states that these fiduciaries must use "the entirety of their skill, care, and diligence" when exercising their authority; and must use their discretion in deciding whether or not to delegate authority and to whom (Hawley et al., 2011: 6–9; Youngdahl, 2012: 115). This meant investing in only the safest assets, such as government bonds. This approach was modified and replaced by the "prudent man rule," characterized as "how men of prudence, discretion and intelligence manage their own affairs, not in regard to speculation, but in regard to the permanent disposition of their funds" (Youngdahl, 2012: 122 and footnote 59). This broadened the range of permitted investments, but ruled out investments in speculative securities, purchase of securities in new enterprises, and purchase of land for resale (Youngdahl, 2012: 122).

Recognizing these changes, the 1974 Pension Act (ERISA) set only a general standard that offered pension trustees latitude to use their best "reasonable" judgment in the allocation of pension assets in a broad range of investment vehicles, including the stock market, speculative securities, and junk bonds (Hawley et al., 2011: 6). Economists, however, argued that "reasonable" should be interpreted in terms of "rational," individual self-interested behavior (Lydenberg, 2012: 3–5). Rational economic investment behavior was defined in terms of Modern Portfolio Theory (MPT), which assumes that markets are efficient, information is symmetric and able to correct temporary market imbalances, investors are risk averse, and risks can be minimized through diversification, securitization, and hedging (Lydenberg, 2012). In addition, rule changes by the Department of Labor in 1978 allowed this standard to be met by assessing risks on the portfolio-wide basis rather than an investment-by-investment basis.

In the face of these changes and financial innovations that offered a broader array of investment vehicles with potentially higher rates of return, the prior "prudent man" standard collapsed. MPT became the dominant approach for allocating pension fund assets and encouraged pension fund managers to invest in riskier individual financial products. In 1992, the assumptions of MPT were incorporated into trust law by replacing the language of the "prudent man rule" with the "prudent investor rule." The duty of loyalty became defined narrowly in terms of a fiduciary's duty to assess risk and return and diversify investments to limit losses (Youngdahl, 2012: 123). This was later reaffirmed and applied to investments in a wide range of risky products and for delegation of responsibilities to expert service providers (Hawley et al., 2011: 7).

Arguably, pension funds are under greater pressure than ever to enhance returns after the losses suffered during the 2008 economic crisis and to cover current retirement outlays without increasing beneficiary or taxpayer contributions. Many pension fund trustees and managers remain convinced of the soundness of MPT – that as long as risk is diversified across a large portfolio of investments, their risk exposure is sufficiently minimized. And, to the extent that PE investments do beat the market, the "prudent investor" rule can be interpreted as requiring fund managers to continue to invest in these funds. That rule requires, however, that pension funds evaluate the returns from investing in PE relative to the risks.

The legal understanding of fiduciary duty underwent large changes in the last half of the twentieth century, narrowing the duty of loyalty and permitting pension funds to delegate decision-making to advisors and to make risky investments. What remains of fiduciary duty, however, is that pension trustees must carefully weigh risks against returns when investing.

The requirement that investment returns should be commensurate with risk means that absolute returns are not an appropriate measure for trustees to use in evaluating returns from PE investments. An absolute return strategy simply seeks positive returns and is not evaluated in relation to alternative, less risky investments. The investment portfolio appropriate for such a strategy is not intended to outperform stocks and bonds when returns to these investments are positive (Putnam Investments, 2016). The lack of a benchmark means there is no weighing of returns against the risks of the investment. That is because the basic premise of an absolute return approach is simply its ability to preserve capital – not to earn returns commensurate with risk. Investment advisors who adopt an absolute return approach invest flexibly and diversify investments across asset classes; the successful ones are those who demonstrate skill in asset allocation (Maton, 2010). This is clearly not an option for investors in PE buyout funds. Thus, PE fund investments lack the characteristics required for an absolute return strategy.

Pension fund staff may find that eliminating the benchmark that is used to risk-adjust returns from risky investments is attractive as it lets them claim success in investing workers' retirement savings as long as these investments earn a positive return. In late 2015, the Board of Trustees of CalPERS debated using this kind of measure. CalPERS' staff brought forth a proposal at the pension fund's December 2015 board meeting to eliminate the requirement that its PE program's "strategic objective is to maximize risk-adjusted rates of return" (CalPERS, 2015a: 1). Had it passed, CalPERS would have substituted an inappropriate absolute returns standard, and returns from PE investments would no longer be risk-adjusted. Fortunately, the CalPERS board rejected this change.

More recently, at CalPERS' November Board meeting, the staff proposed a "technical" adjustment to its PE benchmark that lowered the bar and made it easier for the pension fund's PE returns to outperform its stock market benchmark. The old benchmark was two-thirds US stocks and one-third foreign to mirror the pension fund's public equity investment profile, plus 3% for the added risk. The new benchmark is an index of all global stocks that gives less weight to better performing US stocks, plus just 1.5% for the added risk (CalPERS, 2017). It is unlikely that CalPERS' staff believes that investing in PE has become less risky. More likely, this is an admission that returns will be lower in the future. The new benchmark may make PE investments look better but will do nothing to assure that these investments earn adequate returns.

PE is sold to pension fund trustees as a way to achieve high returns that outperform the stock market. In a recent report we noted that PE firms charge high fees directly to investors and indirectly via the monitoring fees that portfolio companies are often required to pay (Appelbaum & Batt, 2016). The rationale for these very high management, performance, and monitoring fees is precisely this promise of returns substantially above stock market returns. This has become increasingly difficult for PE to achieve.

Benchmarking PE returns

Pension funds use a variety of approaches for benchmarking PE performance. Few if any, however, use the PME that is preferred by finance experts who study the issue. Instead, pension funds typically use the IRR, despite its weaknesses, and benchmark the performance of PE investments against an appropriate stock market index plus 300 basis points (3%) to adjust for the greater risk inherent in PE investments. For example, public employee pension funds in Oregon and Washington – the Oregon Public Employees Retirement Fund (OPERF) and the Washington State Investment Board which manages a number of public employee pension funds in a Commingled Trust Fund (CTF) – benchmark the IRR measure of their PE returns against the Russell 3000 plus 3%. This benchmark is widely used by pension funds. Until recently, CalPERS also followed this approach. While not as accurate as using the PME to evaluate the performance of PE investments, these metrics do include a reasonable adjustment for the greater riskiness of these investments.

Surprisingly, however, some major public pension funds simply require their PE investments to yield a return above the median return of PE buyout funds. CalSTRS and the Teachers Retirement System of the City of New York (TSR), for example, both use the State Street Private Equity Index as their benchmark. The Pennsylvania State Education Retirement System (PSERS) uses the Burgiss median PE fund as its benchmark. The New York State and Local Retirement System (NYSLRS) uses the Cambridge US PE index. These benchmarks vary widely, however, raising questions about exactly what is captured by these indexes.

More fundamentally, however, measures that benchmark a particular fund against the average performance of a sample of funds do not compare PE returns with what could have been earned had the funds been invested in a different asset class. Economists call this "opportunity cost" and argue that to understand the true cost of a decision (including the decision to invest in PE), an investor must consider what is lost by not pursuing the next best alternative. This, in fact, is what occurs when PE returns are compared to returns from the stock market plus a risk premium. Pension funds would use this comparison in making decisions about whether to invest in PE funds or their next best alternative – public equities that trade on stock markets.

We can illustrate the secular decline in PE returns by analyzing CalPERS' PE performance. Since 2012, CalPERS has tracked PE returns separately from other alternative investments and implemented its former, risk-adjusted benchmark for PE performance. Thus, we have consistent results for CalPERS' PE performance beginning in June 2012.

Tables 14.8A and B and Figure 14.2 report CalPERS' average annual returns from its PE investments for 10-year periods ending on June 30 of the year indicated. Data are extracted from the pension fund's Comprehensive Annual Financial Reports (CAFR) for the years 2012 through 2016 (CalPERS, 2015b, 2016). In June 2012, CalPERS' 10-year average annual PE returns beat its benchmark by 1.5%. That is, it outperformed its stock market index by 4.5% (3 + 1.5). The 10 years preceding June 2012 would have included many funds launched before 2006 which, as we saw earlier, tended to outperform the stock market. Average annual returns for the 10-year period ending in June 2013 just exceeded the benchmark, outperforming CalPERS' stock market index by 3.2%. By June 2014, when most

Table 14.8A CalPERS' average annual returns for 10-year periods, 2012–2016 (percent)

	June 2012	*June 2013*	*June 2014*	*June 2015*	*June 2016*
CalPERS' PE	9.8	12.3	13.3	11.9	10.2
Benchmark	8.3	12.1	15.4	14.9	6.4

Benchmark = 67% FTSE USTMI + 33% FTSE AWEXUS + 3%.

Source: CAFR filings 2014, 2015, 2016.

Table 14.8B

	NAV (\$ mm)	*1 year*	*3 year*	*5 year*	*10 year*
CalPERS PE Program	25, 892	13.9	8.1	11.5	9.3
Policy Benchmark[4]		*20.3*	*9.9*	*13.7*	*13.0*
Excess vs. Policy Benchmark (%)		−6.4	−1.8	−2.2	−3.7

Source: CalPERS (2017), Agenda item 6b, Attachment 1, p. 3

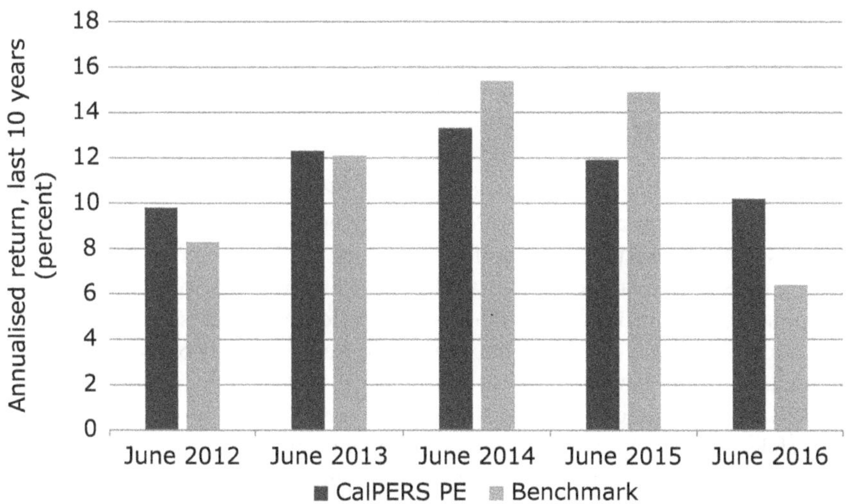

Figure 14.2 CalPERS' PE (net) vs. benchmark, 2012–2016 (percent)

Source: CalPERS' ***Comprehensive Annual Financial Report*** 2014, 2015, 2016.

of the earlier PE funds had been liquidated and were no longer included in the calculation of 10-year returns, CalPERS' PE returns slipped below its benchmark by 210 basis points (2.1%), beating the stock market by only 0.9% – not enough to justify investing in PE. In the 10-year period to June 2015, returns from CalPERS' PE investments just matched the performance of its stock market index and provided no risk premium (CalPERS, 2015b). CalPERS' PE performance improved markedly in the year to June 2016, exceeding its stock market benchmark by 380 basis points (3.8%) as volatility in the stock market depressed benchmark returns. But this improvement was short lived.

In 2017 CalPERS' investments in PE had a value of \$25.9 billion. The PE program's 1-year, 3-year, 5-year, and 10-year net returns did not meet its benchmark (Table 14.8B). The ten-year return (9.3%) underperformed the benchmark (13.0%) by 370 basis points or 3.7% and was 0.7% below the stock market return.

It is no wonder that in 2017, CalPERS changed its benchmark and lowered the bar to accommodate its expectation of lower PE returns in the future. While its PE investment performance failed to beat its old benchmark over the 10-year time period to 2017, it did manage to outperform its new one (CalPERS 2017, Agenda item 6b, Attachment 1, p. 3).

As noted earlier, the question of which stock market index pension funds should use in establishing the benchmark is also a matter of controversy. Recalling the opportunity cost argument – that the performance of investments in PE should be compared to the investor's next best alternative – suggests that the stock market index should reflect the range of publicly traded stocks in which the pension fund has invested. CalPERS' former benchmark, in use through 2017, did just that and employed an appropriate risk adjustment. The pension fund's new benchmark does not meet these criteria. It has proven easier to beat, but that is because it lowers the bar and not because it improves its performance.

PE buyout fund returns and pension fund investments in PE

Finance economists have demonstrated the superiority of the PME, which takes into account the timing and magnitude of actual cash flows, compared to the IRR as a measure of PE fund performance. Most pension funds (or their consultants) could calculate the PME and at least some do. Nevertheless, end-to-end IRRs are the PE industry's standard and are widely used by pension funds in reporting returns. This can obscure weaker performance by more recent PE fund vintages.

Academic studies suggest that most investors in PE buyout funds will find the superior performance PE firms promise elusive. Persistence of performance is also a thing of the past. With claims that PE investments outperform the stock market becoming less credible, GPs need a new sales pitch to attract investors. They have turned to PE's presumed low volatility as a major selling point. But claims of low volatility for investments in PE are misleading. Publicly traded stocks are essentially "marked to market" on a daily basis; their year-to-year valuations are publicly available and not self-reported. Not so with the valuations of unsold companies held in PE fund portfolios. Not only are the values of portfolio companies computed much less frequently, which alone would smooth any volatility, but the accuracy of GP self-reports of portfolio company's valuations has been called into question. A recent study (Hooke & Yook, 2017) concludes that marked-to-market estimates of the year-to-year value of these companies by GPs are unrealistic and exaggerate the value of both the companies in a PE fund's portfolio and the fund itself. Unrealistic valuations of portfolio companies also invalidate the industry's claim of low volatility. Indeed, Hooke and Yook find that PE buyout fund returns are more volatile than stock market returns – a finding predicted by finance theory. The greater use of debt by portfolio companies compared to publicly traded businesses means that portfolio company valuations should increase more in good times and fall further in bad.

In view of the negative impact on workers of leveraged buyouts – including the focus of buyout funds on cutting labor costs in their portfolio companies and the higher likelihood of bankruptcy of those portfolio companies due to the increased debt levels (documented in Appelbaum & Batt, 2014), employee pension funds, university endowments, and other investors with a broad public purpose require a compelling reason to invest in buyout funds. In the past, the promise of high returns and low volatility served to justify investing in PE buyout funds. Today, these promises are mostly empty.

Conclusion: what lies ahead for PE fund performance?

The mediocre performance of share prices of publicly traded PE firms has puzzled PE enthusiasts who continue to believe that PE investments yield exceptionally high returns. But it appears that stock market investors have been quick to recognize that volatility is higher and returns lower in PE than PE firms claim. Recent research provides further clarification. Jegadeesh et al. (2015: 3271) employ traditional asset pricing approaches to estimate returns to PE fund investments. This analysis yields estimates of abnormal performance of the PE funds of publicly traded firms that are in the "range from −0.5% to 0.25%. Essentially, the market anticipates that [publicly traded PE firm] funds will earn approximately zero abnormal returns."

Investors in publicly traded PE firms do not expect PE funds to provide high returns and outperform their stock market benchmarks during periods of financial weakness. This is evident in the sell-off of shares and sharp drop in share price of publicly traded PE firms in the first half of 2016. *The Financial Times* reported that shares of Apollo and Carlyle had fallen by two-thirds from their 2014 peaks, KKR's stock had fallen by half, and Oaktree's by 30% (Cotterill & Childs, 2016). Six of the nine publicly traded PE firms – American Capital, Apollo, Ares Management, Blackstone, Carlyle, and Fortress Investment Group – were trading below their IPO opening price as of May, 2016, according to a PitchBook analysis; only Main Street Capital, KKR, and Oaktree Capital were trading higher than their opening price (Dowd, 2016). As *The Financial Times* observed, this means "that investors are effectively entirely discounting their future performance fees, or the share of profit the [private equity] groups take alongside investors in their funds when they exit successful deals" (Cotterill & Childs, 2016). Performance fees – also known as carried interest – fuel the earnings of these PE firms and are used to pay dividends to shareholders. The sharp declines in share prices reflect the belief that future distributions and returns are likely to fall.

If a weak stock market is not good for PE, a strong stock market poses its own challenges. A recent analysis of PE returns found "that PE investments suffer from the same cyclicality as the public markets, with one major difference: Public equity investors benefit from run-ups whereas run-ups are a detriment to buyout funds" that acquire new portfolio companies at peak prices that will fall along with the decline in the stock market in a recession (PitchBook, 2017b: 1 and 6).

As the stock market reached new highs in the second half of 2016 and in 2017, prices of target companies that PE funds would like to buy have risen, with PE investors driven out of the buyout market by strategic acquirers (PitchBook, 2017a). Further complicating the PE returns picture is a decline in the use of debt; equity contributions have risen to nearly 50% (PitchBook, 2016c, 2017a). As PitchBook observed, "GPs are still able to raise ample amounts of capital, but the constant lack of targets to deploy that money continues to haunt many fund managers" (PitchBook, 2016b). The result has been a build-up of dry powder that raises the cost of PE investing (Braun & Stoff, 2016) and lowers returns.

Indeed, this is a view shared by leaders in the industry, who are hard at work trying to manage expectations down. Speaking at a Milken Institute conference in May 2016, a panel of PE titans – Leon Black of Apollo Global Management, Jonathan Nelson of Providence Equity Partners, David Rubenstein of The Carlyle Group, and Robert Smith of Vista Equity Partners – warned that returns will be lower than in the past, distributions back to investors will decrease, and new PE buyout funds may have lives as long as 20 years (Jacobius, 2016; see also Yves Smith, 2016a).

Yves Smith provides a cogent explanation for the dim view these PE firm GPs as well as public investors in PE firms have taken of unrealized, yet-to-be-earned, future profits and performance fees, which depend on successful exits from PE fund investments in portfolio companies. Smith highlights three developments that have transformed the tail winds that propelled PE firm profits in the post-financial crisis period into headwinds that may prove difficult to overcome (Yves Smith, 2016b):

1. Private equity has benefitted from a long-term trend of disinflation, from 1982 to 2008. It got an artificial extension due to central bank policies of ZIRP (zero interest rate policy) and QE [quantitative easing] giving them life beyond their natural sell-by date. Equity strategies, and even more, risky equity strategies like levered equity, as in PE, will do particularly well under this scenario.
2. Private equity EBITDA multiples (prices paid to acquire companies for PE fund portfolios relative to the earnings of these companies) in the fourth quarter of 2015 were higher even than at the peak of the last cycle in 2007.
3. It's hard to see how any scenario going forward will be good for PE. Central banks over the last six years have pushed investors into risky assets. Private equity will no longer have that tailwind. If interest rates go up (unlikely but not impossible) it will depress stock market valuations, increase the cost of borrowing, and make it harder to achieve high levels of leverage.

The upshot is that shareholders in publicly traded PE firms recognize that it will be difficult for PE to repeat the strong distributions of recent years. Credit to finance highly leveraged buyouts is likely to become more difficult to obtain as investors flee the junk bond market for high quality corporate and Treasury bonds, and banks become more cautious lenders. Prices of attractive target companies have been bid up by competition for them. The number of PE-backed exits in the US declined in 2017 for the second consecutive year as PE funds found it difficult to exit high-priced investments at a profit, and the average PE holding period for US-based companies has increased (Lewis, 2017).

By 2016, some PE firms were trying to shore up both share price and public confidence in their business model by buying back their own stock. In February 2016, Carlyle reported a 59% decline in fourth quarter profits in the prior year. The PE giant simultaneously announced that it would buy back $200 million worth of its shares. In this it joined Apollo and Fortress, which were buying back $250 million and $100 million worth of their own shares respectively, as well as Kohlberg Kravis Roberts & Company, which in October, 2015 pledged to buy back as much as $500 million worth of shares (Stevenson, 2016).

Unlike investors in publicly traded PE firms, pension plans and other institutional investors in PE funds continue to be lulled into these investments providing strong returns that warrant taking on the extra risks PE entails. Despite PE's poor performance relative to its benchmark and its excessive fees, pension plans and other investors continue to pour money into PE funds, fueling a record rise in PE firm assets under management (Jarzemsky, 2016). Unfortunately, these investors are likely to be disappointed.

This raises a number of questions for future research about the experiences of limited partners in PE funds. Why do these investors continue to make such large commitments to PE funds? Are the interests of GPs and LPs aligned? Or is the PE model designed to reward GPs even when LPs do not fare as well? How might a public pension fund or other LP determine the optimal commitment it should make to PE funds? Is there sufficient transparency about fees and net returns to LPs over the entire 10-year or longer commitment (as distinct from PE fund returns net of fees) to enable them to make this determination?

Notes

1 These issues are discussed at greater length in Appelbaum and Batt (2014).
2 For numerical examples that illustrate these points, see Appelbaum and Batt (2014: 168–171). For a detailed discussion, see Phalippou (2009).
3 In September 2006 the US Financial Accounting Standards Board (FASB) issued the Statement of Financial Accounting Standards SFAS) No. 157. Paragraph 5 of SFAS No. 157 (known today as ASC 820 in the updated FASB Codification) requires PE funds to report portfolio companies at fair value. Funds have had to report fair value since December 2008.
4 See, for example, the risk parameters listed in the California Public Employees' Retirement System Investment Policy for Private Equity (PE) Program, CalPERS (2015a), www.calpers.ca.gov/docs/policy-private-equity-program.pdf.
5 The duration of a bond is the point in time at which the amount paid for the bond and the cash flow received from the bond are equal.
6 The 18 PE firms, listed in alphabetical order, are Apollo Global; Bain Capital Partners; Berkshire Partners; Blackstone; The Carlyle Group; Clayton, Dubilier & Rice; Goldman Sachs & Co.; GTCR; Hellman & Friedman; KKR; Kohlberg & Co.; Madison Dearborn; Providence Equity; Silver Lake; Thomas H. Lee; TPG; Veritas; and Vestar Capital.
7 Hooke and Yook also examine the persistence of fund performance for these large fund families, but with respect to being in the top half rather than the top quartile of funds. They find that 52.5% of PE firms with a fund that ranks in the top half of funds has a follow-on fund that is also in the top half. This is just slightly better than random (50% would be expected to be in the top half on basis of chance). Of greater interest is the persistence of top quartile performance, since this is where the outperformance relative to the stock market occurs, but these results are not presented in their paper.
8 Most PE funds launched in 2001 had exited all, or nearly all, their investments by 2011. The PME performance of the typical PE fund launched in 2001 comes from the second quarter 2014 PitchBook benchmarking and fund performance report (PitchBook, 2014).

References

American Investment Council (formerly PEGCC). 2016. *PE by the numbers*. Washington, DC: American Investment Council.
Appelbaum, E., & Batt. R. 2014. *Private equity at work: When Wall Street manages Main Street*. New York: Russell Sage Foundation Press.
Appelbaum, E., & Batt. R. 2016. *Fees, fees and more fees: How private equity abuses its limited partners and U.S. taxpayers*. Washington, DC: Center for Economic and Policy Research.
Bain & Company. 2013. *Bain global private equity report 2013*. Boston, MA: Bain & Company.
Bain & Company. 2016. *Bain global private equity report 2016*. Boston, MA: Bain & Company.
Black, G. J. 2017. The current US PE company inventory still poses questions. January 27. Seattle, WA: PitchBook.
Board of Governors of the Federal Reserve System, Federal Deposit Insurance Corporation and Office of the Comptroller of the Currency. 2013. *Interagency guidance on leveraged lending*. Washington, DC: Board of Governors of the Federal Reserve System.
Braun, R., Jenkinson, T., & Stoff. I. 2015. *How persistent is private equity performance? Evidence from deal-level data. SSRN Working Paper*. Available at: http://ssrn.com/abstract=2314400.
Braun, R., & Stoff, I. 2016. The cost of private equity investing and the impact of dry powder. *The Journal of Private Equity*, 19: 22–33.
CalPERS. 2015a. *California public employees' retirement system investment policy for private equity (PE) program*. CalPERS December 14 Board Meeting, Agenda item 7a, Attachment 1. Sacramento, CA: CalPERS.
CalPERS. 2015b. *Comprehensive annual financial report*. Sacramento, CA: CalPERS.
CalPERS. 2016. *Comprehensive annual financial report*. Sacramento, CA: CalPERS.
CalPERS. 2017. *Private equity annual program review*. CalPERS November 13 Board Meeting, Agenda item 6a, Attachment 1, p.10. Sacramento, CA: CalPERS.
Cohan, W. D. 2015. A private equity gamble in Vegas gone wrong. *Fortune Magazine*, June 5.

Cotterill, J., & Childs, M. 2016. Private equity groups under pressure to buy own stock. *Financial Times*, February 7.

Davis, M., & Natarajan, S. 2016. Terms for Veritas LBO as loans reprice. *Bloomberg*, January 29.

Dowd, K. 2016. Private equity goes public: A history of PE stock performance. *PitchBook*, May 18.

Driessen, J., Lin, T.-C., & Phalippou, L. 2012. A new method to estimate risk and return of nontraded assets from cash flows: The case of private equity funds. *Journal of Financial and Quantitative Analysis*, 47: 511–535.

Gottlieb, J. 2011. Establishing a standard. *PE Manager*, June 8.

Gredit, O., Griffiths, B., & Stucke, R. 2014. *Benchmarking private equity: The direct alpha method.* SSRN Working Paper. Available at: http://ssrn.com/abstract=2403521.

Harris, R. S., Jenkinson, T., & Kaplan, S. N. 2015. How do private equity investments perform compared to public equity?" Darden Business School Working Paper No. 2597259. June 15. Forthcoming *Journal of Investment Management*. Available at: http://ssrn.com/abstract=2597259.

Harris, R. S., Jenkinson, T., Kaplan, S. N., & Stucke, R. 2014. *Has persistence persisted in private equity? Evidence from buyout and venture capital funds*. SSRN Working Paper. Available at: http://ssrn.com/abstract=2304808.

Hawley, J., Johnson, K., & Waitzer, E 2011. Reclaiming fiduciary responsibility balance. *International Journal of Pension Management*, 4: 4–16.

Hooke, J., & Yook, K. 2016. The relative performance of large buyout fund groups. *Journal of Private Equity*, 20: 25–34.

Hooke, J., & Yook, K. 2017. The curious year-to-year performance of buyout fund returns: Another mark-to-mark problem? *Journal of Private Equity*, 21: 9–19.

Jacobius, A. 2016. Private equity titans warn attendees to expect lower returns. *Pensions & Investments*, May 3. www.pionline.com/article/20160503/ONLINE/160509958/private-equity-titans-warn-attendees-to-expect-lower-returns.

Jarzemsky, M. 2016. Blackstone thinks it's time to buy. *Wall Street Journal*, January 28.

Jegadeesh, N., Kräussl, R., & Pollet, J. M. 2015. Risk and expected returns of private equity investments: Evidence based on market prices. *Review of Financial Studies*, 28: 3269–3330.

Jenkinson, T., Sousa, M., & Stucke, R. 2013. *How fair are the valuations of private equity funds*. SSRN Working Paper. Available at: http://ssrn.com/abstract=2229547.

Kaplan, S. N., & Schoar, A. 2005. Private equity performance, returns, persistence, and capital flows. *Journal of Finance*, 60: 1791–1823.

Kelleher, J. C., & MacCormack, J. J. 2004. *Internal rate of return: A cautionary tale*. New York: McKinsey & Company.

Lewis, A. 2017. PE hold times keep going up. *PitchBook*, November 15.

L'Her, J.-F., Stoyanova, R., Shaw, K., Scott, W., & Lai, C. 2016. A bottom-up approach to the risk-adjusted performance of the buyout fund market. *Financial Analysts Journal*, 72: 1–13.

Lim, D. 2016. Carlyle gets extension for boom-era fund. *Wall Street Journal*, March 10.

Lopez-de-Silanes, F., Phalippou, L., & Gottschalg, O. 2015. Giants at the gate: Investment returns and diseconomies of scale in private equity. *Journal of Financial & Quantitative Analysis*, 50: 377–411.

Lydenberg, S. 2012. *Reason, rationality and fiduciary duty*. New York: Investor Responsibility Research Center (IRRC).

Marquez, R., Nanda, V., & Yavuz, M. D. 2015. Private equity fund returns and performance persistence. *Review of Finance*, 19: 1783–1823.

Martin, T. W. 2015. Calpers' private-equity fees: $3.4 billion. *Wall Street Journal*, November 24.

Maton, B. 2010. Dissecting 'absolute returns' methods. *Financial Times*, October 10.

McSwain, P. 2017. Private equity presentations: Are some tall tales? *Enterprising Investor*, CFA Institute, October 30.

Phalippou, L. 2009. *The hazards of using IRR to measure performance: The case of private equity.* SSRN Working Paper. Available at: http://ssrn.com/abstract=1111796.

Phalippou, L. 2014. Performance of buyout funds revisited? *Review of Finance*, 18: 189–218.

Phalippou, L., & Gottschalg, O. 2009. The performance of private equity funds. *Review of Financial Studies*, 22: 1747–1776.

PitchBook. 2014. PitchBook 2Q 2014 global PE &VC benchmarking & fund performance report. Seattle, WA: PitchBook.

PitchBook. 2016a. PitchBook 1Q 2016 global PE &VC benchmarking & fund performance report. Seattle, WA: PitchBook.
PitchBook. 2016b. *PitchBook PE news, March 8, 2016*. Seattle, WA: PitchBook.
PitchBook. 2016c. *2016 annual US PE breakdown*. Seattle, WA: PitchBook.
PitchBook. 2016d. *PitchBook 2016 global PE deal multiples report III*. Seattle, WA: PitchBook.
PitchBook. 2016e. *2017 PE crystal ball report*. Seattle, WA: PitchBook.
PitchBook. 2017a. *3Q 2017 US PE breakdown*. Seattle, WA: PitchBook.
PitchBook. 2017b. *Is the risk worth the wait?* December 17. Seattle, WA: PitchBook.
Primack, D. 2017. *Pro Rata Newsletter*, Axios.com, November 21.
Putnam Investments. 2016. *Absolute return investing*. Boston, MA: Putnam Investments. Available at: www.putnam.com/individual/mutual-funds/investment-strategies/absolute-return-investing/different.
Robinson, D. T., & Sensoy, B. A. 2011, 2015. *Cyclicality, performance measurement, and cash flow liquidity in private equity*. Fisher College of Business, Ohio State University Working Paper Series. Dice Center WP 2010-021. Fisher College of Business WP 2010-03-021.
Smith, Y. 2016a. Smart money doing private equity in house as general partners warn of lower returns, dumb money pours in. *Naked Capitalism*, May 10.
Smith, Y. 2016b. Stock market investors abandon private equity, expect no profits overall from current deals. *Naked Capitalism*. February 8.
Stevenson, A. 2016. Carlyle Group reports drop in profit and announces stock buyback. DealBook, *The New York Times*, February 10.
White, A. 2017. Private equity persistence slips. *Top 1000 Funds*, November 9.
Youngdahl, J. 2012. The time has come for a sustainable theory of fiduciary duty of investment. *Hofstra Labor and Employment Law Journal*, 29: 115–139.

15

COLLABORATION DECISIONS IN PRIVATE EQUITY INVESTMENTS

Anantha Krishna Divakaruni

Introduction

Unlike venture capital (VC) firms that invest in risky, early-stage companies, private equity (PE) firms tend to invest in mature companies that have stable and recurring cash flows which can be used to repay the debt taken on the leveraged buyout (LBO) over time (Kaplan & Strömberg, 2009). The literature states that problems of asymmetric information and adverse selection are key issues that banks consider when evaluating prospective borrowers and determining the terms of lending (Petersen & Rajan, 1994; Boot & Thakor, 2000). Previous studies on buyouts have shown that PE firms and targets address these challenges by developing strong relationships with banks, which help them obtain LBO loans on cheaper terms (Ivashina & Kovner, 2011; Shivdasani & Wang, 2011; Fang et al., 2013). However, these findings do not recognize that bank-borrower relationships are characterized by power differentials in which borrowers could have more or less bargaining power over their relationship banks depending on their access to alternative sources of financing. Since LBOs are financed largely with debt, the power differentials between PE firms and their relationship banks, and between targets and their relationship banks, could have important implications on their decision to collaborate in the LBO and on their ability to negotiate financing terms of the transaction.

In addition, the LBO market consists of strong syndication networks among banks that facilitate the flow of information and capital. These syndication networks could be vital for resolving adverse selection and moral hazard problems with prospective borrowers and syndicate members. However, the implications of these bank syndication networks on the LBO deal structuring process are not well understood. The goal of this chapter is to contribute to our understanding of these aspects of the PE industry.

PE firms leading a buyout deal typically attempt to finance anywhere between 60% to 90% of the purchase price using external debt (Officer et al., 2010). For this purpose, the PE firm appoints one or more *lead banks* depending on the deal size and other considerations to arrange the debt financing. Typically, lead banks arrange these loans through *syndication* by inviting other banks within their network to participate, and can be seen as intermediaries between the demand side represented by LBO borrowers (i.e., PE firms and their targets), and the supply side represented by the participating banks. Since lead banks essentially control the flow of information and capital between the parties involved, they play a very important role in the LBO investment process.

Collaboration decisions in PE investments

Although the PE industry has grown in size and complexity, research on collaboration decisions in LBO transactions and their implications on deal financing is still very limited. Collaboration has been studied more extensively in other forms of financing including relationship lending, loan syndication, and VC syndication (Berger & Udell, 1998; Lockett & Wright, 1999; Sorenson & Stuart, 2001; Wright & Lockett, 2003; Elsas, 2005; Sørensen, 2007). The complexities associated with LBO deal structuring can be understood more accurately by examining each distinct form of collaboration between limited partners, targets, PE firms, and banks individually.

PE firms and limited partners

Since PE firms use the capital raised from their institutional investors (such as pension funds, endowments, and family offices) to invest in buyout opportunities, partnerships formed between PE firms and their investors are an important form of collaboration. PE firms typically raise capital through funds that are structured as limited partnerships and have a fixed term (usually 10–12 years). While there is a growing literature on the performance of PE funds and how it helps the PE firms raise follow-on capital (Kaplan & Schoar, 2005; Balboa & Marti, 2007; Metrick & Yasuda, 2010), there are no specific studies on the collaboration process between PE firms and investors or the basis on which investors commit capital to PE firms over successive funds. This limitation stems mainly from the lack of publicly available data on individual funds and their investors.

Table 15.1 provides an overview of studies that explore PE fundraising and performance.

PE firms and targets

Collaboration decisions between PE firms and targets are also particularly interesting because buyouts are essentially complex investments in targets that are informationally opaque. This is contrary to firms that are relatively transparent and obtain funding from the public equity and debt markets under contracts that are highly standardized and generic (Berger & Udell, 1998). Literature notes that PE firms address the information asymmetries associated with potential targets through screening and due diligence, which involves collecting information from the target and evaluating its business lines, market segments, assets that can be used as collateral for new loans, historical cash flows, and debt burden, and the quality of incumbent owners and management (Kaplan & Strömberg, 2009; Acharya et al., 2013; Gompers et al., 2016). PE firms use these details to value the target and establish contractual terms for the acquisition based on the financial characteristics and information problems associated with the target, as well as prospects for value improvement post-buyout. These terms are either negotiated directly with current owners/management or submitted in the form of a bid if the target is to be acquired through an auction (Boone & Mulherin, 2011). Targets with high free cash flows and assets that are mostly tangible are considered low-risk and can be acquired by the PE firm using large amounts of external debt. On the other hand, targets with high capital expenditures or intangible assets are less likely to attract debt financing, implying that the PE firm can either finance the entire deal using its own capital and face the prospect

Table 15.1 Collaboration between PE firms and limited partners

Authors & year	*Title*	*Research question(s)*	*Data & analysis*	*Main findings*
Kaplan & Schoar (2005)	Private equity performance: Returns, persistence, and capital flows	Does past performance influence the ability of PE firms to raise follow-on funds?	Archival data; 746 PE funds raised in the US between 1980 and 1996.	PE firms that outperform the industry in one fund are also likely to outperform in subsequent funds, and tend to raise larger follow-on funds. This persistence can be attributed to the heterogeneity in skill and quality of PE firms, whereby experienced PE firms perform much better than new entrants.
Balboa & Marti (2007)	Factors that determine the reputation of private equity managers in developing markets	Which factors determine the reputation of PE firms in developing markets?	Archival data; investment activity of 101 Spanish PE firms between 1991 and 2003.	PE firms use reputation-building mechanisms to minimize problems associated with information asymmetry that arise in their relationships with investors. PE firms that indulge in more investment activity, divest through IPOs and trade sales, and are members of national PE associations are perceived to be more reputable, and are consequently more successful in raising new funds.
Metrick & Yasuda (2010)	The economics of private equity funds	Is prior investment experience and track record important for PE firms to attract capital? Is it different in the case of VC firms?	Archival data; 144 PE funds and 94 VC funds raised between 1993 and 2006.	Experienced PE firms are more successful in attracting new capital and raise larger follow-on funds than VC firms. PE firms are also more scalable than VC firms and earn substantially higher revenue per partner.

of lower returns or abandon the transaction altogether (Opler & Titman, 1993; Axelson et al., 2009; Axelson et al., 2013). PE firms also collaborate with their targets post-buyout in order to monitor new management and implement the intended operational changes to improve firm value. In order to exert such control, PE firms usually take substantial positions on the boards of their targets and actively participate in their decision-making processes (Guo et al., 2011; Acharya et al., 2013).

Table 15.2 shows some studies that investigate the major aspects of collaboration between PE firms and targets.

Table 15.2 Collaboration between PE firms and targets

Authors & year	*Title*	*Research question(s)*	*Data & analysis*	*Main findings*
Halpern et al. (1999)	On the heterogeneity of leveraged going private transactions	Why do targets go private through a buyout, and which among these are likely to be acquired by PE firms?	Archival data; 126 US LBOs completed between 1981 and 1985.	Targets that go private through LBOs can be broadly distinguished into two categories: those in which managers hold an insignificant portion of the firm and those in which managers own a large portion of the firm. Targets in which managerial ownership is low face considerable takeover threats, forcing managers to consider a PE-led buyout. Such targets are eventually sold or taken public by PE firms to earn a return on their investment. In contrast, firms with substantial managerial ownership do not face takeover pressures and are more likely to be taken private by the managers themselves. Such targets tend to remain private under the new owner-managers unlike PE-led buyouts.
Ljungqvist et al. (2007)	The investment behavior of buyout funds: Theory and evidence	What drives the investment behavior of PE firms? Do the investment decisions of PE firms evolve over time?	Archival data; 2,274 buyout investments by 207 buyout funds between 1981 and 2000.	PE funds accelerate their investments as opportunities improve, when their bargaining power is high, and when debt is cheap and readily available. First-time funds are less sensitive to market conditions than established funds and tend to invest in riskier targets in a bid to build their track record. However, these early funds become more conservative following a period of good performance as they seek to preserve their reputation.

(*Continued*)

Table 15.2 (Continued)

Authors & year	*Title*	*Research question(s)*	*Data & analysis*	*Main findings*
Renneboog et al. (2007)	Why do public firms go private in the UK? The impact of private equity investors, incentive realignment and undervaluation	What are the sources of shareholder wealth gains in PE-backed buyouts?	Archival data; 177 PTPs in the UK between 1997 and 2003.	The extent to which target firms are undervalued, as reflected in the premiums paid, is a major source of shareholder wealth gains in UK PTPs. In addition, the level of managerial ownership in the pre-buyout target and subsequent incentive realignment is another important source of wealth gains. However, the premiums paid are lower if there is strong outside ownership in the target, as there is less scope for operational improvements in such firms.
Wright et al. (2007)	Irrevocable commitments, going private and private equity	Why do target firms issue irrevocable commitments to potential PE acquirers prior to making their bid public?	Archival data; 155 PTP transactions in the UK between 1998 and 2003.	Irrevocable commitments make it easier to take the firm private and increase with the bid premium, size of board shareholding in the firm, and reputation of the bidding PE firm. Such commitments are, however, reduced if there is speculation in the press about a potential takeover of the firm that can lead to competing takeover offers.
Mehran & Peristiani (2009)	Financial visibility and the decision to go private	Is financial visibility (and the costs associated with it) a major reason for firms to go private?	Archival data; 262 PTPs (including 169 LBOs) in the US between 1990 and 2007.	Firms that could not manage to gain sufficient financial visibility following their IPO are more likely to go private. This decision is driven by low analyst coverage and lack of interest among institutional investors, which result in equity mispricing and an illiquid stock. These findings are consistent with the view that close monitoring by analysts reduces agency conflicts between investors, owners, and managers of the firm.

Table 15.2 (Continued)

Authors & year	*Title*	*Research question(s)*	*Data & analysis*	*Main findings*
Bharath & Dittmar (2010)	Why do firms use private equity to opt out of public markets?	Which characteristics influence firms to go private via PE-backed buyouts? How do these compare for firms that continue to exist and listed entities?	Archival data; 1,377 US firms that went private via an LBO between 1980 and 2004. Comparison sample comprising 6,464 firms that remained public during this period.	Firms that have more concentrated ownership and less analyst coverage at the time of their IPO are more likely to go private via LBOs in the following years. Such firms also experience less share turnover, have high leverage, and low capital and R&D expenditures prior to their LBO. These findings suggest that the cost of information production, stock liquidity, and control issues determine a firm's decision to go private.
Fidrmuc et al. (2013)	When do managers seek private equity backing in public-to-private transactions?	Under what conditions do managers seek the help of PE firms to take their firm private?	Archival data; 54 MBOs and 75 PE-backed buyouts of UK public firms completed between 1997 and 2003.	Management-led buyouts are more likely if the target is relatively undervalued, if managers own large equity stakes in the target, if the target is relatively opaque to outside investors, and also if the target generates sufficient cash flows to support external financing. PE firms are invited to participate in these deals only if managers are constrained in financing the deal themselves.
Giot et al. (2014)	Are novice private equity funds risk-takers? Evidence from a comparison with established fund	Are novice PE firms that are new to the market more aggressive in risk-taking than established PE firms?	Archival data; 949 buyout and 5,766 VC funds raised in the US between 1986 and 2005.	Novice PE firms are more cautious than experienced PE firms, and tend to invest larger amounts in less-promising LBO opportunities than their experienced peers. Experienced PE firms become more aggressive following a successful IPO and invest in bigger deals than novice PE firms. These findings suggest that experience and reputation-building is a slow and risky process, and novice PE firms require at least a full fund cycle to gain sufficient investment experience.

(*Continued*)

Table 15.2 (Continued)

Authors & year	*Title*	*Research question(s)*	*Data & analysis*	*Main findings*
Arcot et al. (2015)	Fund managers under pressure: - Rationale and determinants of secondary buyouts	What are the motives for PE firms to invest or exit their investments via SBOs?	Archival data; 4,139 LBO exits comprising 1,219 SBOs in the US and 12 European countries.	PE funds that have substantial uninvested capital (dry powder) in the later stages of the fund cycle are more likely to participate in SBOs and pay more in such deals. PE funds under pressure use less leverage and syndication, suggesting that their primary objective is to invest their excess equity capital. On the sell side, PE funds with substantial unexited investments are also under pressure, and are more likely to sell to other PE firms at lower prices. PE firms face these buy and sell pressures because prospective investors (limited partners) look not only at their past performance but also at the track record of their current funds and investments.

PE firms and other PE firms

Collaboration also features prominently in PE syndicates where two or more PE firms co-invest in a given target to share risks and receive a joint payoff. Syndication is a popular form of collaboration where lead investors look for certain characteristics in the selection of non-lead partners. Syndication is very common in early-stage VC (Sorenson & Stuart, 2001; Manigart et al., 2006; Hochberg et al., 2007) and the phenomenon has become popular in later-stage buyouts through so-called *club* deals. Recent studies have identified a number of motives for why PE firms syndicate their deals. While the diversification of large or risky deals is certainly an important consideration, syndicates are also established when PE firms face capital constraints or need access to complementary skills and information (Bailey, 2007; Meuleman et al., 2010; Metrick & Yasuda, 2011). Syndication may also be a strategy to signal deal quality and raise loans on favorable terms, since it is much easier to obtain debt financing if several PE firms participate and attach their reputation to the deal (Officer et al., 2010). So far, studies have shown that PE syndicates are faced with at least two different types of agency problems. First, the collaboration of multiple investors and challenges of joint decision-making raise the issue of *horizontal* agency problems within the syndicate. Second, problems associated with information asymmetry and ex post monitoring of investments can lead to *vertical* agency problems with the target. Since trust among syndicate partners is key to resolving these issues, lead PE firms prefer investors with whom they have past interactions and who have a good track record. In addition, PE firms with proven experience in the target industry and having similar status and reputation as the lead PE firm are likely to be invited to join the syndicate (Meuleman et al., 2010; Huyghebaert & Priem, 2015).

Table 15.3 provides an overview of studies that focus on syndication among PE firms.

Table 15.3 Collaboration between PE firms and other PE firms (syndication)

Authors & year	*Title*	*Research question(s)*	*Data & analysis*	*Main findings*
Lockett & Wright (1999)	The syndication of private equity: Evidence from the UK	Why do PE firms tend to syndicate their buyout investments?	Surveys and in-depth interviews with 62 UK PE firms.	The primary objective for syndication among PE firms is to diversify risk rather than share information or access external resources. Selection of syndicate partners is driven by past relationships and the reputation of potential partners, and not on their financial characteristics or asset base. Syndication is less likely when there is excessive competition in the market.
Meuleman et al. (2009)	Private equity syndication: Agency costs, reputation and collaboration	What are the agency costs associated with syndication among PE firms? What are some key factors that facilitate or inhibit PE syndication?	Archival data; 1,122 buyouts completed by 80 UK PE firms between 1993 and 2006.	Syndication is less likely when agency costs associated with the target are high and require extensive ex post monitoring by the lead PE firm. Such agency issues are less problematic if the lead PE firm has a high reputation and is well networked in the buyout market.
Meuleman et al. (2010)	Partner selection decisions in interfirm collaborations: The paradox of relational embeddedness	Under what conditions are prior relationships a prerequisite for syndication among PE firms?	Archival data; 212 syndicated buyouts among UK PE firms between 1993 and 2003.	Prior relationships are less important for selecting syndicate partners when agency risks associated with the deal are low, allowing PE firms to expand their networks in search of new information and opportunities. In addition, the reputation of potential partners can partially offset information asymmetries despite the absence of prior relationships, resulting in. faster syndicate formation.

(*Continued*)

Table 15.3 (Continued)

Authors & year	*Title*	*Research question(s)*	*Data & analysis*	*Main findings*
Officer et al. (2010)	Club deals in leveraged buyouts	Are there major differences in the pricing and financing characteristics of club deals versus standalone PE investments?	Archival data; 4,031 acquisitions of US public firms between 1984 and 2007.	Target shareholders receive significantly lower premiums in club deals than in standalone LBOs or other types of M&A transactions. These effects are less prominent in targets with high institutional ownership, as such targets have more bargaining power and are able to solicit competing bids forcing the PE clubs to raise their price. No significant differences are observed in debt financing terms between club deals and standalone LBOs, suggesting that banks perceive similar levels of risk in both types of transactions.
Boone & Mulherin (2011)	Do private equity consortiums facilitate collusion in takeover bidding?	Do PE firms collude during the buyout bidding process to reduce competition and pay lower prices?	Archival data; 870 PE-backed takeovers of public targets between 2003 and 2007.	Collective bidding by PE firms does not suggest collusion and is instead associated with enhanced takeover competition. Prices paid by PE consortiums are similar to those paid by standalone bidders, implying that returns to target shareholders are unaffected as a result of the formation of consortiums. Additional evidence suggests that consortium formation is related to the scale and risks associated with the deal as well as the demand for shared expertise among constituent members.
Huyghebaert & Priem (2015)	How do lead financiers select their partners in buyout syndicates: Empirical results from buyout syndicates in Europe	What are the mechanisms through which lead PE firms select partners for their buyout syndicates?	Archival data; 366 European club deals over the period 1999–2009.	Lead PE firms prefer to select PE firms with whom they have a prior relationship, that have prior experience in the target industry, and have a similar reputation in the buyout market.

PE firms and banks

Research on collaboration in buyouts has mostly emphasized PE firms, the problems of adverse selection and moral hazard that PE firms confront when evaluating prospective targets, and the nature of contracts between PE firms and the targets they invest in. However, a common source of value creation in buyouts is the use of substantial debt in their financing structure. While it is known that the debt used in these *leveraged* buyouts boosts returns for PE investors through the tax deductibility of interest (Axelson et al., 2009; Guo et al., 2011), the mechanisms through which PE firms collaborate with banks to raise these LBOs were largely ignored until recently. A study of US LBOs by Demiroglu and James (2010) shows that PE firms with stronger reputation are able to borrow on more favorable terms (lower interest rate spreads, longer maturities, less covenant restrictions, etc.), and are better at timing their deal activity with conditions in the market. Similarly, Ivashina and Kovner (2011) argue that repeated interactions between PE firms and banks lower information asymmetries and create an environment of trust and reciprocity between them. Their evidence suggests that PE firms with strong bank relationships are able to acquire targets using debt that is both cheaper and contains less-restrictive covenants. A study by Fang et al. (2013) found that banks having strong past relationships with targets issue larger and cheaper loans to finance their acquisition via LBOs. These findings are consistent with the relationship lending literature which states that banks demand higher rates and collateral early in the relationship and ease the terms in later transactions depending on the quality of the borrower over the course of the relationship (Petersen & Rajan, 1994; Degryse & Van Cayseele, 2000; Elsas, 2005). The general conclusion in these studies is that strong relationships enhance collaboration between banks and borrowers by mitigating adverse selection and moral hazard problems and increasing the availability of loans.

Details of studies on collaboration decisions between PE firms, banks, and targets are available in Table 15.4.

Table 15.4 Collaboration between banks, PE firms, and targets

Authors & year	*Title*	*Research question(s)*	*Data & analysis*	*Main findings*
Opler & Titman (1993)	The determinants of leveraged buyout activity: free cash flow vs. financial distress costs	What are the key firm characteristics that motivate the use of debt financing for buyout transactions?	Archival data; 180 LBOs in the US between 1980 and 1990.	Firms with high free cash flows and low Tobin's q are more likely to initiate LBOs as it is easier for them to attract debt financing and repay their loans. On the other hand, firms with high capital expenditures are less likely to undergo an LBO, as they are deemed too risky and can potentially end up in financial distress with the use of leverage.

(*Continued*)

Table 15.4 (Continued)

Authors & year	*Title*	*Research question(s)*	*Data & analysis*	*Main findings*
Citron et al. (1997)	Loan covenants and relationship banking in MBOs	Does the use of financial covenants and relationship lending signal more risk in MBOs in comparison to traditional lending?	Surveys and in-depth interviews with 29 UK MBO lenders.	Banks perceive two sets of relationships: one with the PE investors and one with the post-buyout management of the target (prior relationships with target are virtually non-existent). Banks use more covenants in MBOs than in traditional corporate lending as a means to reduce monitoring costs, and place emphasis on short-term cash generation for reinvestment into the target and servicing of debt.
Cotter & Peck (2001)	The structure of debt and active equity investors: The case of the buyout specialist	What is the role of PE firms in structuring LBO transactions and in monitoring the post-LBO target?	Archival data; 763 US LBOs completed between 1984 and 1989.	LBOs are less likely to be financed with short-term and/or senior debt if the PE firm holds a majority stake in the post-LBO target. In such deals, PE firms also have greater board representation, suggesting that they actively monitor managers. This implies that superior monitoring by PE firms substitutes the need for imposing stringent loan terms to monitor LBO targets.
Demiroglu & James (2010)	The role of private equity group reputation in LBO financing	Does the reputation of PE firms influence the capital structure of LBO transactions?	Archival data; 180 PTP US LBOs completed between 1997and 2007.	Reputed PE firms are more capable of exploiting credit market conditions and use more leverage in their LBOs when lending conditions are favorable. Reputed PE firms pay lower interest rates, have longer loan maturities, and rely less on bank loans.
Braun et al. (2011)	The risk appetite of private equity sponsors	Does the investment and risk behavior of PE firms change over time? What drives these changes?	Archival data; 460 LBOs from Western Europe and North America completed between 1990 and 2005.	Reputation is an important competitive advantage that determines a PE firm's borrowing capacity. More experienced PE firms do not risk their reputation by taking excessive risks or majority ownership stakes in order to maintain their competitive advantage.

Table 15.4 (Continued)

Authors & year	*Title*	*Research question(s)*	*Data & analysis*	*Main findings*
Ivashina & Kovner (2011)	The private equity advantage: Leveraged buyout firms and relationship banking	How do prior relationships between PE firms and banks impact the financing terms of syndicated LBO loans?	Archival data; 1,590 LBOs completed between 1993 and 2005.	PE firms are able to reduce costly information asymmetries by developing strong relationships with their banks, and thus obtain better loan terms than standalone borrowers. The strength of PE firms' bank relationships is associated with lower LBO loan rates and less-restrictive covenants.
Achleitner et al. (2012)	Structure and determinants of financial covenants in leveraged buyouts	What determines the structure and restrictiveness of covenants in LBO loans?	Archival data; 130 German LBOs completed between 2000 and 2008.	The reputation of PE firms in the credit market lowers information asymmetries, and is acquired over time through repeated borrowing and a track record of past investments. Reputed PE firms receive better loan terms in the form of looser covenants and are less likely to invest in excessively risky targets. In addition, banks are more concerned about the reputation of PE firms than that of targets.
Fang et al. (2013)	Combing banking with private equity investing	Are banks capable of making superior equity investments in LBOs than independent PE firms? Are there any major differences in financing terms between bank-affiliated deals (banks provide equity financing only) and parent-financed deals (banks provide both equity and debt financing)?	Archival data; 2,105 US LBOs completed between 1993 and 2008.	Parent-financed deals have better financing terms than bank-affiliated deals, implying that banks are not superior equity investors than independent PE firms. These equity investments provide additional benefits to banks in terms of significant cross-selling opportunities. Evidence suggests that LBO loan terms are cheaper if banks and targets have prior borrowing relationships, but are not affected by the bank's reputation in the PE market.

International aspects of collaboration

PE has become a global phenomenon since the early 2000s as it has become a popular form of investment across Europe, Asia, and Australia, with Western Europe (including the UK) accounting for 48% of all transactions worldwide between 2000 and 2012. This suggests that PE is no longer a US-centric phenomenon since there has been more buyout activity outside the US in recent years.

An emerging strand of literature notes that the ongoing *internationalization* of PE has been driven in part by macro-economic factors and also due to gradual institutional reforms in various countries. Among the various institutional factors that could potentially affect a country's buyout market, legal institutions that define the quality of local corporate governance, ownership rights, and contractual enforcement have been identified as being of primary concern for investors (Globerman & Shapiro, 2003; Hernández & Nieto, 2015). For instance, Lerner and Schoar (2005) note that PE firms in countries with effective legal systems are less risk averse and invest using flexible contracts that shift control rights according to the performance of the target. On the other hand, PE firms in countries with weaker legal systems were found to demand greater control rights and majority ownership to compensate for the lack of effective legal enforcement. In a more elaborate study, Aizenman and Kendall (2008) find that cultural factors such as common language or past colonial ties foster greater institutional similarity and trust between countries, thereby encouraging greater cross-border flows of buyout capital between such countries. In addition, investments by foreign PE firms are greater into countries with better business and socio-economic environments. Other studies, such as Meuleman and Wright (2011), have sought to understand the strategies adopted by PE firms when entering foreign buyout markets. They find that PE firms initially rely on local PE firms to navigate the challenges associated with a foreign institutional environment, but gradually reduce their dependence on such local partnerships as they gain more operational experience in those environments.

Table 15.5 contains an overview of articles that explore PE investments at the international level.

Despite these important findings, academic research on PE investments outside the US has been limited mainly due to the scarcity of public data on such transactions. Consequently, the factors that facilitate such internationalization and influence the investment decisions of PE firms and banks in foreign buyout targets remain poorly understood.

Impact of collaboration on performance

While there is extensive literature on the performance of PE firms (both at the fund and firm levels), research attributing the performance of PE firms, banks, and targets to the collaboration decisions taken during deal structuring is generally lacking.

One of the earliest studies to investigate these effects is Groh and Gottschalg (2011), who compare the deal-specific risks borne by PE firms and banks and how these affect their performance. They find that PE firms are able to earn higher returns if they manage to transfer substantial parts of their risk to the banks that finance their deals or if they are able to reduce operational risks through superior monitoring. In addition, Groh and Gottschalg (2011) find that the systematic risk in LBOs changes over the holding period from high to low depending on how the debt is repaid gradually over time.

In another study of US LBOs, Guo et al. (2011) look at the effectiveness with which PE firms have been able to raise debt from banks over time. They observe that PE firms

Table 15.5 Collaboration in international buyouts (covers both non-US and cross-border deals)

Authors & year	*Title*	*Research question(s)*	*Data & analysis*	*Main findings*
Lerner & Schoar (2005)	Does legal enforcement affect financial transactions? The contractual channel in private equity	Does the quality of legal enforcement in a country affect the nature of investments by PE firms? Can PE firms overcome the deficiencies of legal enforcement and generate sufficient returns by using alternative contracts for their investments?	Archival data; 210 PE investments in developing countries.	PE firms tend to use convertible preferred stock with covenants when investing in countries with high legal enforcement and common law systems. In contrast, PE firms use a combination of common stock and debt to invest in countries characterized by weak enforcement and civil law systems, and depend on board control to generate value in their investments. As expected, valuations and returns on investment are significantly higher in countries with better legal systems.
Cumming & Johan (2007)	Regulatory harmonization and the development of private equity markets	Does regulation affect institutional investors' decision to invest in PE funds?	Surveys and archival data; 100 Dutch institutions that were actively investing or considering investing in PE funds between 2005 and 2010.	Perceived lack of regulation of the PE industry hinders institutional investment in PE funds. Weak regulation exacerbates the risk and illiquidity associated with PE investments, requiring additional monitoring and resource allocation by institutional investors that participate in PE funds.
Aizenman & Kendall (2008)	The internationalization of venture capital and private equity	What are the main factors that have contributed to the internationalization of the PE industry?	Archival data; cross-border flows of PE investments across 100 countries between 1990 and 2007.	Gravity analysis suggests that geographical distance, common language, strong business environment, and deep financial markets are important factors in attracting foreign PE capital. While PE activity was limited mainly to the US and UK until the 1990s, it has since expanded to other parts of the world due to increased cross-border participation by PE firms and the emergence of domestic buyout markets in many countries.

(*Continued*)

Table 15.5 (Continued)

Authors & year	*Title*	*Research question(s)*	*Data & analysis*	*Main findings*
Cumming & Zambelli (2010)	Illegal buyouts	How do changes in regulation affect LBO activity and deal structuring?	Surveys and in-depth interviews with 21 Italian PE firms that were actively investing in LBOs between 1999 and 2006.	LBO activity existed in Italy prior to 2004 although it was considered illegal back then by the country's legal system. A change in regulation in 2004 legalized LBOs, resulting in significant changes in the Italian buyout market. First, there is a marked increase in deal activity, coupled with greater involvement by PE firms in the control and management of their targets. Second, targets are screened more intensely and deals are structured using more convertible debt. These findings suggest that the legalization of LBOs has led to better deal structuring and incentivized PE firms to actively monitor their investments.
Groh et al. (2010)	The European venture capital and private equity country attractiveness indices	Explains the allocation of international PE investments within Europe using a composite measure of country attractiveness based on 42 institutional parameters	Institution-level data mainly from the World Bank, EUROSTAT, and the OECD spanning the period 2000–2005.	The level of investor protection, size and liquidity of capital markets, and quality of corporate governance are key factors that determine the attractiveness of a country's PE market. Differences across these factors explain why the UK has a much bigger and successful PE market in comparison to continental Europe.
Meuleman & Wright (2011)	Cross-border private equity syndication: Institutional context and learning	Why do PE firms rely on local partners when investing abroad?	Archival data; 685 buyout investments by 69 UK PE firms in continental Europe between 1990 and 2006.	Institutional context (represented by the availability of local PE firms) has an inverted U-shape effect on the likelihood that a cross-border deal will be

(*Continued*)

Table 15.5 (Continued)

Authors & year	*Title*	*Research question(s)*	*Data & analysis*	*Main findings*
				syndicated with local partners. In contrast, the availability of local investment banks and PE firms' international and country-specific experience reduce their dependence on local partners to invest in foreign LBO opportunities.
Cumming & Zambelli (2013)	Private equity performance under extreme regulation	What are the economic effects of extreme regulation on the supply of capital and returns to PE investors?	Archival data; 178 PE investments in the Italian market between 1999 and 2006.	LBOs were considered illegal in Italy between 2000 and 2004. During this period, there was less active involvement in monitoring and control by PE firms, suggesting inefficient allocation of control and cash flow rights in new target acquisitions. All these factors limited the scope of LBO activity in Italy during this period of illegality.
Cao et al. (2015)	Cross-border LBOs	Is there a relationship between cross-border LBO activity and creditor rights in the target country?	Archival data; 2,589 LBOs sponsored by domestic and cross-border PE firms between 1995 and 2007.	Cross-border LBO activity is stronger in target countries with better creditor protection, but the premium offered to target shareholders is lower in these countries. PE firms from countries with stronger creditor protection are more likely to invest abroad, especially in target countries with relatively weaker creditor protection. Although club deals are more likely to occur in target countries with weaker creditor rights, foreign PE firms are less likely to participate in them.

(Continued)

Table 15.5 (Continued)

Authors & year	*Title*	*Research question(s)*	*Data & analysis*	*Main findings*
Holloway et al. (2016)	Private equity firm heterogeneity and cross-border acquisitions	How does heterogeneity in the strategy and performance of PE firms influence LBO activity both at the domestic and cross-border levels?	Archival data; 8,107 buyouts by 1,504 PE funds completed between 1986 and 2013.	High-performing PE firms are more likely to acquire more cross-border targets than low-performing PE firms. In addition, PE firms that depend on active management of target firms are subject to bigger transaction costs associated with remote ownership, while those that pursue consolidation and growth strategies are more capable of generating value in foreign PE markets.

raised less leverage during the late 1990s and 2000s in comparison to deals completed during the 1980s. Guo et al. (2011) attribute these trends to the growing difficulty in raising leverage as the industry has matured since the late 1990s with new entrants and more competition among incumbent PE firms. They further note that PE firms are able to improve the performance and valuation of targets through operational improvements and/or acquisitions. In addition, they find evidence that the use of leverage provides generous tax shields which can be used to boost profitability and increase the cash flows available to PE firms and banks.

Table 15.6 provides additional details on studies related to this topic.

Emerging issues in collaboration and new evidence

Our review of the extant literature indicates that collaboration has received considerable attention both in domestic as well as cross-border LBO settings. Much of the theoretical and empirical evidence in this literature has emphasized that collaboration and investment decisions in the PE industry are driven by existing relationships among actors and their experience and reputation in the market. Relationships based on past interactions reduce information asymmetries and uncertainty between partners, resulting in a higher chance for collaboration between (i) PE firms and investors during fundraising, (ii) PE firms and targets during deal selection, (iii) PE firms during deal syndication, and (iv) PE firms and banks when arranging debt financing for the LBOs. While previous research offers interesting insights on the challenges, mechanisms, and outcomes of collaboration in LBO investments, there are major limitations in our understanding of the underlying mechanisms. We identify three areas in particular where emerging research contributes to our understanding of collaboration decisions in LBO financing.

Table 15.6 Implications of collaboration on ex post performance

Authors & year	*Title*	*Research question(s)*	*Data & analysis*	*Main findings*
Groh & Gottschalg (2011)	The effect of leverage on the cost of capital of US buyouts	How does the capital structure in LBOs affect the cost of capital in these transactions? Can the returns on LBO investments be estimated using a comparable public benchmark?	Archival data; 133 LBO exits in the US and UK between 1984 and 2004.	The systematic risk in LBOs changes over the holding period, whereby it is initially high due to the substantial leverage used in the transaction but decreases over time as the debt is repaid. The use of leverage allows PE firms to transfer much of the risk to the lenders. Taking these facts into consideration, it is estimated that the average cost of capital is lower by 3.29% than that of an equivalent S&P 500 index. These results suggest that using a public benchmark index to estimate the risk in PE investments can be misleading.
Guo et al. (2011)	Do buyouts (still) create value?	What are the mechanisms through which LBOs create value?	Archival data; 192 US LBOs completed between 1990 and 2006.	Compared to buyouts in the 1980s, LBOs during the sample period make use of less leverage, and premiums paid to shareholders are also relatively lower. These LBOs have subsequently experienced large increases in firm value due to operational improvements, a rise in industry and valuation multiples, and an increase in cash flows due to the tax shields provided by leverage. These outcomes are consistent with the view that debt can be instrumental in reducing agency costs.
Pe'er & Gottschalg (2011)	Red and blue: The relationship between the institutional context and the performance of leveraged buyout investments	How does institutional context affect deal activity and the performance of LBO investments?	Archival data; 10,476 US LBOs completed between 1980 and 2003.	Buyout activity and the success rate of LBO investments is higher in States dominated by the Republican party than in States dominated by the Democratic party. This is because the transaction costs associated with restructuring of targets and value creation are less expensive and more efficient in States aligned more towards Republican than Democratic norms.

(*Continued*)

Table 15.6 (Continued)

Authors & year	*Title*	*Research question(s)*	*Data & analysis*	*Main findings*
Chung et al. (2012)	Pay for performance from future fund flows: The case of private equity	How does past performance influence the ability of PE firms' general partners (GP) to raise future funds? How does it affect their income?	Archival data; 1,745 preceding and 1,469 follow-on funds raised by PE, VC, and real estate investment firms between 1990 and 2005.	Lifetime incomes of PE GPs are affected not just by the performance of their ongoing funds, but also by their perceived ability to raise follow-on funds. In fact, the likelihood of raising a follow-on fund and its size significantly affect the performance of the current fund. These findings indicate considerable heterogeneity in whether limited partners (LP) take performance into consideration when deciding to invest in subsequent funds raised by the PE firms. Additional results suggest that older GPs are more likely to raise follow-on funds.
Taussig & Delios (2015)	Unbundling the effects of institutions on firm resources: The contingent value of being local in emerging economy private equity	Can institutions have divergent/ competing influences on the performance of PE firms?	Archival data; 47 PE firms that have investments in 49 emerging and developing countries.	PE firms based in countries with weak contractual enforcement and foreign PE firms that have prior experience in such countries are able to enforce contracts through informal local networks. However, their performance is undermined by a lack of access to local financing options due to weak financial development in those countries.

The role of power differentials among prospective buyout participants

Understanding collaboration decisions on the basis of past relationships is lacking because traditional agency theory does not consider the influence of relative power of participants over each other. A power differential exists in the relationship if either of the actors depends more on the other or vice versa. Alternatively, the actors are in a state of balanced power if they are equally dependent on each other, and have no power over each other if they did not interact previously (Finkelstein, 1992; Hill & Jones, 1992; Chandler, 2015). Power differentials feature prominently in bank-borrower relationships and are important in the LBO context as both PE firms and targets often develop strong banking relationships. Since LBOs are financed mostly with debt, the extant power differentials between PE firms and their relationship banks, and between targets and their relationship banks, could have important implications on the LBO deal structuring process and its financing terms.

In general, bank-borrower relationships are characterized by power differentials due to several factors. While consistent borrowing from a single bank may strengthen the relationship, it also allows the bank to accumulate information on the borrower over the course of the relationship. Thus, the bank arguably has some power over the borrower given its exclusive access to information gained from the relationship that is unavailable to competing banks. The bank can use this information monopoly or hold-up to exploit the borrower and extract higher rents from the relationship (Petersen & Rajan, 1994; Berger & Udell, 1995). Moreover, inefficiencies and limited competition in the market imply that banks also derive power from considerable switching costs that make it expensive for a borrower to leave the relationship (Hill & Jones, 1992; Houston & James, 2001). Studies show that borrowers try to prevent such appropriation and maintain their bargaining power by engaging in multiple banking relationships (Diamond, 1991; Petersen & Rajan, 1995; Berger et al., 2008). Dependence on a single banking relationship is also risky as refusal of credit may send negative signals about the borrower to other banks in the market (Gopalan et al., 2011). To avoid such problems and ensure loan availability for future needs, firms typically maintain multiple banking relationships. In fact, firms with sufficient bargaining power may demand concessions on their loans or choose not to borrow from a given bank if they do not perceive such benefits in the relationship. Thus, power advantage on either side of a lending relationship can lead to appropriation of the less dependent actor.

While power differentials are easier to analyze under dyadic agency settings, they are far more complex in multiple agency settings such as LBOs that are essentially collaborative contracts between PE firms, banks, and targets. Multiple agency theory captures conflicts of interest between multiple principal-agent (PA) and principal-principal (PP) groups and resolves discrepancies over which principal's interests receive priority (Arthurs et al., 2008). The LBO deal structuring process represents a multiple agency setting comprising vertical PA ties between the target and investors (i.e., the PE firm and bank) and horizontal PP ties between the PE firm and bank. The presence of these multiple PA/PP dyads points towards a more complex power structure where each potential participant in the LBO may have varying levels of power advantage (or disadvantage) over other potential participants. This raises an important question whether these power differentials play a role in the deal structuring process, and whether participants use their power to appropriate each other when negotiating deal terms.

Analysis by Divakaruni et al. (2017) using US data shows that LBO financing costs are affected by whether banks hold a power advantage over PE firms and targets prior to a given transaction. They find that banks charge higher rates on LBO loans depending on the extent to which the PE firm and target involved in the transaction are dependent on that bank for their financing needs. In fact, banks seem to exploit their power even further by charging marginally higher rates when they hold a simultaneous power advantage over both participants. In addition, a bank's ability to exploit power depends on the degree to which the PE firm and target are locked into a borrowing relationship with that bank. LBO loan rates are marginally higher when the PE firms and targets are firmly entrenched to the bank, and marginally cheaper when it is difficult for banks to appropriate dependent borrowers that are less entrenched to the borrowing relationship. However, banks are forced to provide rate discounts in exchange for being able to finance an LBO when they do not have such power advantage over incumbent PE firms and targets. These discounts increase marginally depending on how committed the bank is to the PE firm and target based on past borrowing relationships between them.

Examining power differentials among prospective LBO participants and how they can be used by participants to negotiate the financing costs of the transaction highlight the importance of power not just in dyadic agency settings, but more importantly, in settings characterized by multiple agency among several stakeholders. Divakaruni et al.'s (2017) results show how multiple sources of power in these settings trade off against each other such that an actor's power over participants in one or more dyads may turn out to be inconsequential given its lack of power in other dyads within the setting.

The role of bank syndication networks

Agency theory which argues that prior relationships produce trust and limit adverse selection problems which might constrain opportunistic behavior among actors in subsequent partnerships, has been used to explain collaboration and partner selection decisions in buyouts. For instance, it is easier for PE firms to raise loans from banks with whom they have successfully collaborated in the past. Similarly, to restrict moral hazard problems within the syndicate, lead PE firms might seek investment partners with whom they have collaborated previously. However, relationships do not completely explain the mechanisms of collaboration in LBOs since such deals are formed even when these characteristics are weak or non-existent. This suggests that there could be other mechanisms of collaboration influencing the LBO deal structuring process that is not captured by relationships.

Most LBOs are financed with syndicated loans granted by a pool of lenders (Shivdasani & Wang, 2011). The syndication of LBO loans has become extremely popular given the benefits it provides to both lenders (risk diversification and access to deal flow) and borrowers (lower borrowing costs compared to loans from single lenders or public debt markets). Recent academic research attributes the formation of these syndicates to the experience and reputation of lead banks in the LBO market. Indeed, when a bank with a strong reputation decides to arrange financing for an LBO, then the bank's reputation serves as a strong signal to potential syndicate participants about the quality of the deal (Fang et al., 2013). Moreover, since lead banks are responsible for due diligence, loan allocation to syndicate members, and ex post monitoring of the target, participants will rely on the lead bank's reputation to decide whether to join the syndicate (Ross, 2010; Godlewski et al., 2012). Thus, banks with sufficient reputation and experience can reduce agency costs through better screening and monitoring of targets and by showcasing the merits of the deal to potential syndicate participants, which should result in better loan terms.

A bank's reputation in the LBO market could be influenced by its network of relationships within the market due to several reasons. First, the bank's reputation is closely related to the trust and reciprocity it develops with other banks in the market through repeated interactions. As the bank's network of relationships grows stronger and wider, so too does the likelihood that the bank will be able to invite others, or be invited, to join future syndicates. This is because banks place more trust on the monitoring and screening capabilities of fellow banks within their network (Sufi, 2007; Gadanecz et al., 2012). Second, banks with a large network of syndicate partners and those associated with more central partners might have better access to information about new investment opportunities that flows through the network (Godlewski et al., 2012). Third, banks that are more connected have high a reputation since they occupy prominent network positions in the LBO market. Such well-connected banks could be invited more often to join LBO loan syndicates since they provide legitimacy to the target, PE firm, and other banks associated with the deal. This certification effect might therefore be useful to signal the quality of LBO targets that are often informationally opaque and lack sufficient banking relationships.

These arguments suggest that bank syndication networks in the LBO market might be an important channel for reducing agency costs during deal formation. The position of a bank within these networks (centrality) signals not only its reputation and experience to potential syndicate members, but also its competence in screening potential targets (and PE firms) and in monitoring while the loan is outstanding. Since banks monitor each other's performance, the network position of a bank also signals its ability to form syndicates and lower agency conflicts among participants. This could have a direct influence on the efficiency of the syndication process and ultimately affect the costs and other financing terms of the LBO.

However, the role of bank syndication networks in LBO financing has received little academic interest even though these networks could play a crucial role in the entire loan syndication process. Differences in the network centralities of banks could have important implications for LBO financing for at least two potentially endogenous reasons. First, PE firms and targets may choose their lead bank based on the latter's network position. Second, the choice of lead bank and its network position could have a direct influence on the terms under which the LBO debt is issued.

Recent work by Alperovych et al. (2017) analyzing the impact of banks' network position on the choice of lead bank and on LBO loan terms suggests that banks that are well-connected within the syndicated LBO market are more likely to be selected as lead arrangers of LBOs. More central banks are preferred because this ultimately benefits PE firms and targets by granting them access to cheaper LBO debt with less collateral requirements. These findings suggest that bank syndication networks affect the asymmetric information among prospective LBO participants in at least three distinct ways. First, banks can use their syndication networks to access information on PE firms and targets and determine the quality and risks associated with a potential LBO investment. Second, well-connected banks are more capable of attracting participants to their loan syndicates and resolving ex post agency conflicts among syndicate members. Third, the presence of a well-connected bank as lead arranger sends a strong positive signal regarding the quality of the LBO deal to other banks in the market, thus attracting more participants and helping in the formation of syndicates more efficiently. Since relationship building and syndication are part of an active strategy pursued by both PE firms and banks, these networks seem likely to become more cohesive and sophisticated in the coming years and to continue to have a profound influence on the LBO deal structuring process.

The role of legal institutions and investor protection

Despite the growing internationalization of PE through cross-border LBOs, the mechanisms through which PE firms and banks invest in foreign LBO targets and gain experience and reputation in foreign buyout markets remain poorly understood.

The literature on cross-border acquisitions refers to the extent of similarity or dissimilarity of institutions between countries as a particular challenge to cross-border investments and ownership (Kostova, 1996; Meuleman & Wright, 2011). Since a country's legal institutions that define corporate governance, disclosure practices, and contract enforcement are of primary concern for foreign investors (Globerman & Shapiro, 2003), cross-country differences in legal investor protection have a strong influence on cross-border investments and collaboration between investors and targets (Mian, 2006; Bell et al., 2012; Cumming et al.,

2016). This suggests that investments by PE firms and banks in foreign LBO opportunities might be driven by differences in shareholder and creditor rights between their home and target countries (Bris & Cabolis, 2008; Bae & Goyal, 2009; Kang & Kim, 2010; Cumming et al., 2016).

However, the literature on cross-border investments suffers from two major problems. First, studies suggest that investing over large institutional distances is risky and expensive due to the difficulties in monitoring and controlling distant targets (Xu & Shenkar, 2002; Li et al., 2014; Tykvová & Schertler, 2014). A major problem with this argument is that institutional distance is typically measured in absolute terms, implying that prospects for cross-border investments between two countries are similar in either direction. However, investor protection in a target country may be better, similar, or worse than the investor's home country (Shenkar, 2001; Zaheer et al., 2012). For instance, while the US and China share the same legal distance[1] under the classical approach, US PE firms face far more risks in China due to its weak legal environment and are less likely to invest in Chinese LBO targets than Chinese PE firms investing in the US where legal investor protection is far superior. This illustrates that legal distance can have asymmetric effects on cross-border investments depending on whether the investor seeks to invest in a country with better or worse legal protection than its origin. Second, many studies have examined the quality of legal investor protection in different countries and its role in attracting foreign capital (Bris & Cabolis, 2008; Ferreira et al., 2009; Taussig & Delios, 2015), but have ignored the extent to which the target country legal system makes investors better or worse off relative to their home country. This is an important consideration since the decision to invest in a given country might be determined by the relative gain or loss in legal protection that is perceived by foreign investors.

These issues raise an important question whether differences in legal investor protection exert an asymmetric effect on the cross-border investment preferences of PE firms and banks. Cumming et al. (2017) hypothesize and show that both PE firms and banks prefer to invest in LBOs in countries with stronger legal investor protection than their origin, and are less likely to invest in countries that have weaker investor laws. These effects increase with the distance between investor and target countries, indicating that the relative gain or loss in legal protection for investors with respect to a target country plays a key role in cross-border LBO investment decisions. They also show that while cross-border experience acquired through repeat investments in foreign countries improves the scope for overseas LBO investments, PE firms and banks seem to use their cross-border experience in distinct ways. While PE firms continue to prefer target countries that offer better shareholder protection, banks seem less affected by the gain or loss in creditor protection as they gain more experience in the local buyout markets of other countries.

Cumming et al.'s (2017) findings address the "illusion of symmetry" that has been identified as an erroneous assumption in the treatment of institutional distance in past literature (Xu & Shenkar, 2002; Zaheer et al., 2012). By focusing on legal protection that is a key concern among foreign investors, they show that cross-country differences in legal protection have asymmetric effects on cross-border LBO investments depending on the relative change in legal protection experienced by PE firms and banks with respect to their home countries.

Conclusions: avenues for future research

This chapter presents some studies that explore collaboration decisions among participants and their outcomes in PE investments. Although the role played by PE firms as financial intermediaries and their ties to targets have been widely studied, research on the mechanisms that allow PE firms to raise equity capital from limited partners and debt capital from banks is quite lacking. More research is thus needed to fill the gaps in our current understanding of how buyouts are structured and how they perform.

Prior literature on PE and bank lending has argued that firms develop relationships with their capital providers with the prime purpose of establishing mutual trust and reciprocity. However, this ignores the reality that such relationships are also pursued with the objective of acquiring power and influence over each other. In addition, prior studies have focused mostly on dyadic relationships and how they influence agency costs, but have ignored the fact that buyouts often represent a multiple agency setting that depend on successful collaboration between two or more participants (e.g., multiple PE firms in *club* deals, banks investing in LBOs through loan syndication, and the joint provision of equity and debt financing by PE firms and banks (in LBOs), respectively). In fact, multiple agency settings are common in other interorganizational contexts such as joint ventures, VC syndicates, and IPOs. We therefore emphasize the use of more comprehensive frameworks in future studies that can delineate collaboration and interaction between multiple actors and determine their individual effects on LBO financing outcomes.

Lastly, unlike previous studies that use cross-sectional methods to explain how PE firms and banks invest (and co-invest) in certain LBO targets, it would be interesting to see how the dynamics of their interaction evolve during the post-LBO phase and over the course of multiple investments. Moreover, research on cross-border buyouts has been scarce despite the rapid internationalization of PE since the late 1990s. It would be interesting to see whether findings related to collaboration that are largely relevant to the Anglo-Saxon PE context would also apply to other regions such as Europe, Asia-Pacific, and the Middle East. Understanding the role of institutional and macro-economic factors on cross-border collaboration is highly necessary in this era of globalization wherein both PE firms and banks are looking to invest increasingly beyond their home markets.

Note

1 Legal distance represents the difference in legal investor protection between two countries.

References

Acharya, V. V., Gottschalg, O. F., Hahn, M., & Kehoe, C. 2013. Corporate governance and value creation: Evidence from private equity. *Review of Financial Studies*, 26: 368–402.

Achleitner, A. K., Braun, R., Hinterramskogler, B., & Tappeiner, F. 2012. Structure and determinants of financial covenants in leveraged buyouts. *The Review of Finance*, 16: 647–684.

Aizenman, J., & Kendall, J. 2008. *The internationalization of venture capital and private equity*. National Bureau of Economic Research. Paper No. 14344.

Alperovych, Y., Divakaruni, A. K., Manigart, S., & Meuleman, M. 2017. Do bank networks influence LBO financing? Available at SSRN: https://ssrn.com/abstract=2980709.

Arcot, S., Fluck, Z., Gaspar, J. M., & Hege, U. 2015. Fund managers under pressure: Rationale and determinants of secondary buyouts. *Journal of Financial Economics*, 115(1): 102–135.

Arthurs, J. D., Hoskisson, R. E., Busenitz, L. W., & Johnson, R. A. 2008. Managerial agents watching other agents: Multiple agency conflicts regarding underpricing in IPO firms. *Academy of Management Journal*, 51: 277–294.

Axelson, U., Jenkinson, T., Strömberg, P., & Weisbach, M. S. 2013. Borrow cheap, buy high? The determinants of leverage and pricing in buyouts. *The Journal of Finance*, 68: 2223–2267.

Axelson, U., Strömberg, P., & Weisbach, M. S. 2009. Why are buyouts levered? The financial structure of private equity funds. *The Journal of Finance*, 64: 1549–1582.

Bae, K. H., & Goyal, V. K. 2009. Creditor rights, enforcement, and bank loans. *The Journal of Finance*, 64: 823–860.
Bharath, S. T., & Dittmar, A. K. 2010. Why do firms use private equity to opt out of public markets? *The Review of Financial Studies*, 23(5): 1771–1818.
Bailey, E. 2007. Are private equity consortia anticompetitive? The economics of club bidding. *The Antitrust Source*, 6: 1–8.
Balboa, M., & Marti, J. 2007. Factors that determine the reputation of private equity managers in developing markets. *Journal of Business Venturing*, 22: 453–480.
Bell, R. G., Filatotchev, I., & Rasheed, A. A. 2012. The liability of foreignness in capital markets: Sources and remedies. *Journal of International Business Studies*, 43: 107–122.
Berger, A., & Udell, G. 1995. Relationship lending and lines of credit in small firm finance. *Journal of Business*, 68: 351–381.
Berger, A., & Udell, G. 1998. The economics of small business finance: The roles of private equity and debt markets in the financial growth cycle. *Journal of Banking & Finance*, 22: 613–673.
Berger, A. N., Klapper, L. F., Peria, M. S. M., & Zaidi, R. 2008. Bank ownership type and banking relationships. *Journal of Financial Intermediation*, 17: 37–62.
Boone, A. L., & Mulherin, J. H. 2011. Do private equity consortiums facilitate collusion in takeover bidding? *Journal of Corporate Finance*, 17: 1475–1495.
Boot, A., & Thakor, A. 2000. Can relationship banking survive competition? *The Journal of Finance*, LV: 679–713.
Braun, R., Engel, N., Hieber, P., & Zagst, R. 2011. The risk appetite of private equity sponsors. *Journal of Empirical Finance*, 18(5): 815–832.
Bris, A., & Cabolis, C. 2008. The value of investor protection: Firm evidence from cross-border mergers. *Review of Financial Studies*, 21: 605–648.
Cao, J. X., Cumming, D., Qian, M., & Wang, X. 2015. Cross-border LBOs. *Journal of Banking & Finance*, 50: 69–80.
Chandler, G. N. 2015. Control structures used in family business to manage wealth: Operationalization of antecedent and outcome variables. *Entrepreneurship Theory and Practice*, 39: 1305–1312.
Chung, J. W., Sensoy, B. A., Stern, L., & Weisbach, M. S. 2012. Pay for performance from future fund flows: The case of private equity. *The Review of Financial Studies*, 25(11): 3259–3304.
Citron, D., Robbie, K., & Wright, M. 1997. Loan covenants and relationship banking in MBOs. *Accounting and Business Research*, 27(4): 277–294.
Cotter, J. F., & Peck, S. W. 2001. The structure of debt and active equity investors: The case of the buyout specialist. *Journal of Financial Economics*, 59(1): 101–147.
Cumming, D., Divakaruni, A. K., & Meuleman, M. 2017. *The asymmetric effects of legal distance: Evidence from cross-border leveraged buyouts*. Working paper.
Cumming, D., & Johan, S. 2007. Regulatory harmonization and the development of private equity markets. *Journal of Banking & Finance*, 31(10): 3218–3250.
Cumming, D., Knill, A., & Syvrud, K. 2016. Do international investors enhance private firm value [quest] evidence from venture capital. *Journal of International Business Studies*, 47: 347–373.
Cumming, D., & Zambelli, S. 2010. Illegal buyouts. *Journal of Banking & Finance*, 34(2): 441–456.
Cumming, D., & Zambelli, S. 2013. Private equity performance under extreme regulation. *Journal of Banking and Finance*, 37(5): 1508–1523.
Degryse, H., & Van Cayseele, P. 2000. Relationship lending within a bank-based system: Evidence from European small business data. *Journal of Financial Intermediation*, 9: 90–109.
Demiroglu, C., & James, C. M., 2010. The role of private equity group reputation in LBO financing. *Journal of Financial Economics*, 96: 306–330.
Diamond, D. W. 1991. Monitoring and reputation: The choice between bank loans and directly placed debt. *Journal of Political Economy*, 99: 689–721.
Divakaruni, A. K., Meuleman, M., & Wright, M. 2017. *Power in multiple agency settings: The case of leveraged buyouts*. Working paper.
Elsas, R. 2005. Empirical determinants of relationship lending. *Journal of Financial Intermediation*, 14: 32–57.
Fang, L., Ivashina, V., & Lerner, J. 2013. Combining banking with private equity investing. *Review of Financial Studies*, 26: 2139–2173.
Ferreira, M. A., Massa, M., & Matos, P. 2009. Shareholders at the gate? Institutional investors and cross-border mergers and acquisitions. *Review of Financial Studies*, 23: 601–644.

Fidrmuc, J. P., Palandri, A., Roosenboom, P., & van Dijk, D. 2013. When do managers seek private equity backing in public-to-private transactions? *Review of Finance*, 17(3): 1099–1139.
Finkelstein, S., 1992. Power in top management teams: Dimensions, measurement, and validation. *Academy of Management Journal*, 35: 505–538.
Gadanecz, B., Kara, A., & Molyneux, P. 2012. Asymmetric information among lending syndicate members and the value of repeat lending. *Journal of International Financial Markets, Institutions and Money*, 22: 913–935.
Giot, P., Hege, U., & Schwienbacher, A. 2014. Are novice private equity funds risk-takers? Evidence from a comparison with established funds. *Journal of Corporate Finance*, 27: 55–71.
Globerman, S., & Shapiro, D. 2003. Governance infrastructure and US foreign direct investment. *Journal of International Business Studies*, 34: 19–39.
Godlewski, C. J., Sanditov, B., & Burger-Helmchen, T. 2012. Bank lending networks, experience, reputation, and borrowing costs: Empirical evidence from the French syndicated lending market. *Journal of Business Finance & Accounting*, 39: 113–140.
Gompers, P., Kaplan, S. N., & Mukharlyamov, V. 2016. What do private equity firms say they do? *Journal of Financial Economics*, 121: 449–476.
Gopalan, R., Udell, G. F., & Yerramilli, V., 2011. Why do firms form new banking relationships? *Journal of Financial and Quantitative Analysis*, 46: 1335–1365.
Groh, A. P., & Gottschalg, O. 2011. The effect of leverage on the cost of capital of US buyouts. *Journal of Banking & Finance*, 35: 2099–2110.
Groh, A. P., von Liechtenstein, H., & Lieser, K. 2010. The European venture capital and private equity country attractiveness indices. *Journal of Corporate Finance*, 16(2): 205–224.
Guo, S., Hotchkiss, E. S., & Song, W. 2011. Do buyouts (still) create value? *The Journal of Finance*, 66: 479–517.
Halpern, P., Kieschnick, R., & Rotenberg, W. 1999. On the heterogeneity of leveraged going private transactions. *The Review of Financial Studies*, 12(2): 281–309.
Hernández, V., & Nieto, M. J. 2015. The effect of the magnitude and direction of institutional distance on the choice of international entry modes. *Journal of World Business*, 50: 122–132.
Hill, C. W., & Jones, T. M. 1992. Stakeholder-agency theory. *Journal of Management Studies*, 29: 131–154.
Hochberg, Y. V., Ljungqvist, A., & Lu, Y. 2007. Whom you know matters: Venture capital networks and investment performance. *The Journal of Finance*, 62: 251–301.
Holloway, I., Lee, H. S., & Shen, T. 2016. Private equity firm heterogeneity and cross-border acquisitions. *International Review of Economics & Finance*, 44: 118–141.
Houston, J., & James, C. 2001. Do relationships have limits? Banking relationships, financial constraints, and investment. *The Journal of Business*, 74: 347–374.
Huyghebaert, N., & Priem, R. K. 2015. How do lead financiers select their partners in buyout syndicates? Empirical results from buyout syndicates in Europe. *European Management Review*, 12: 221–246.
Ivashina, V., & Kovner, A. 2011. The private equity advantage: Leveraged buyout firms and relationship banking. *Review of Financial Studies*, 24: 2462–2498.
Kang, J.-K., & Kim, J.-M. 2010. Do foreign investors exhibit a corporate governance disadvantage? An information asymmetry perspective. *Journal of International Business Studies*, 41: 1415–1438.
Kaplan, S. N., & Schoar, A. 2005. Private equity performance: Returns, persistence, and capital flows. *The Journal of Finance*, 60: 1791–1823.
Kaplan, S. N., & Strömberg, P. 2009. Leveraged buyouts and private equity. *The Journal of Economic Perspectives*, 23: 121–146.
Kostova, T., 1996. *Success of the transnational transfer of organizational practices within multinational companies*. Minneapolis, MN: University of Minnesota.
Lerner, J., & Schoar, A. 2005. Does legal enforcement affect financial transactions? The contractual channel in private equity. *The Quarterly Journal of Economics*, 120: 223–246.
Li, Y., Vertinsky, I. B., & Li, J. 2014. National distances, international experience, and venture capital investment performance. *Journal of Business Venturing*, 29: 471–489.
Ljungqvist, A., Richardson, M., & Wolfenzon, D. 2007. The investment behavior of buyout funds: Theory and evidence. Working Paper, New York University.
Lockett, A., & Wright, M., 1999. The syndication of private equity: Evidence from the UK. *Venture Capital: An International Journal of Entrepreneurial Finance*, 1: 303–324.

Manigart, S., Lockett, A., Meuleman, M., Wright, M., Landström, H., Bruining, H., Desbrières, P., & Hommel, U. 2006. Venture capitalists' decision to syndicate. *Entrepreneurship Theory and Practice*, 30: 131–153.
Mehran, H., & Peristiani, S. 2009. Financial visibility and the decision to go private. *The Review of Financial Studies*, 23(2): 519–547.
Metrick, A., & Yasuda, A. 2010. The economics of private equity funds. *Review of Financial Studies*, 23: 2303–2341.
Metrick, A., & Yasuda, A. 2011. Venture capital and other private equity: A survey. *European Financial Management*, 17: 619–654.
Meuleman, M., Lockett, A., Manigart, S., & Wright, M. 2010. Partner selection decisions in interfirm collaborations: The paradox of relational embeddedness. *Journal of Management Studies*, 47: 995–1019.
Meuleman, M., & Wright, M., 2011. Cross-border private equity syndication: Institutional context and learning. *Journal of Business Venturing*, 26: 35–48.
Meuleman, M., Wright, M., Manigart, S., & Lockett, A. 2009. Private equity syndication: Agency costs, reputation and collaboration. *Journal of Business Finance & Accounting*, 36(5–6): 616–644.
Mian, A. 2006. Distance constraints: The limits of foreign lending in poor economies. *The Journal of Finance*, 61: 1465–1505.
Officer, M. S., Ozbas, O., & Sensoy, B. A. 2010. Club deals in leveraged buyouts. *Journal of Financial Economics*, 98: 214–240.
Opler, T., & Titman, S. 1993. The determinants of leveraged buyout activity: Free cash flow vs. financial distress costs. *The Journal of Finance*, 48: 1985–1999.
Pe'er, A., & Gottschalg, O. 2011. Red and blue: The relationship between the institutional context and the performance of leveraged buyout investments. *Strategic Management Journal*, 32: 1356–1367.
Petersen, M. A., & Rajan, R. G. 1994. The benefits of lending relationships: Evidence from small business data. *The Journal of Finance*, 49: 3–37.
Petersen, M. A., & Rajan, R. G. 1995. The effect of credit market competition on lending relationships. *The Quarterly Journal of Economics*, 110: 407–443.
Renneboog, L., Simons, T., & Wright, M. 2007. Why do public firms go private in the UK? The impact of private equity investors, incentive realignment and undervaluation. *Journal of Corporate Finance*, 13(4): 591–628.
Ross, D. G. 2010. The "dominant bank effect:" How high lender reputation affects the information content and terms of bank loans. *Review of Financial Studies*, 23: 2730–2756.
Shenkar, O. 2001. Cultural distance revisited: Towards a more rigorous conceptualization and measurement of cultural differences. *Journal of International Business Studies*, 32: 519–535.
Shivdasani, A., & Wang, Y. 2011. Did structured credit fuel the LBO boom? *The Journal of Finance*, 66: 1291–1328.
Sørensen, M. 2007. How smart is smart money? A two-sided matching model of Venture Capital. *The Journal of Finance*, 62: 2725–2762.
Sorenson, O., & Stuart, T. E. 2001. Syndication networks and the spatial distribution of venture capital investments. *American Journal of Sociology*, 106: 1546–1588.
Sufi, A. 2007. Information asymmetry and financing arrangements: Evidence from syndicated loans. *The Journal of Finance*, 62: 629–668.
Taussig, M., & Delios, A. 2015. Unbundling the effects of institutions on firm resources: The contingent value of being local in emerging economy private equity. *Strategic Management Journal*, 36: 1845–1865.
Tykvová, T., & Schertler, A. 2014. Does syndication with local venture capitalists moderate the effects of geographical and institutional distance? *Journal of International Management*, 20: 406–420.
Wright, M., & Lockett, A. 2003. The structure and management of alliances: Syndication in the venture capital industry. *Journal of Management Studies*, 40: 2073–2102.
Wright, M., Weir, C., & Burrows, A. 2007. Irrevocable commitments, going private and private equity. *European Financial Management*, 13(4): 757–775.
Xu, D., & Shenkar, O. 2002. Note: Institutional distance and the multinational enterprise. *Academy of Management Review*, 27: 608–618.
Zaheer, S., Schomaker, M. S., & Nachum, L. 2012. Distance without direction: Restoring credibility to a much-loved construct. *Journal of International Business Studies*, 43: 18–27.

16

PRIVATE EQUITY IN EMERGING ECONOMIES

Which markets are sufficiently mature? Should investors wait or invest immediately?

Alexander Groh

Introduction

There is a major shift in the private equity (PE) landscape from "traditional" and mature markets towards emerging regions. Emerging countries attract investors by high economic growth opportunities. These growth opportunities stem from the economic catch up potential combined with the large populations that many emerging countries have (Hoskisson et al., 2000). Nevertheless, growth opportunities are not the only factor that renders countries attractive to investors. The existence of a prospering PE market infrastructure and investment environment requires many socio-economic and institutional prerequisites. However, as several emerging countries are not yet sufficiently mature in terms of their socio-economic development to support the PE business model, too early entrance in those countries might not be a beneficial strategy.

By entering into a "new market" firms can exploit significant growth opportunities without generating excess capacity (Spence, 1979). There are important advantages to being the first entrant in some sorts of markets (Schmalensee, 1982). First-mover advantages are expected for the pioneering firms with respect to gaining a head-start over rivals. This opportunity may occur because the firm possesses some unique resources or foresight (Lieberman & Montgomery, 1988). A first-mover advantage may also result from learning. Spence (1981) demonstrates that if learning can be kept proprietary, the learning curve can generate substantial barriers to entry.

Wright et al. (2005) and Hoskisson et al. (2013) discuss potential entry strategies in emerging markets. With respect to PE, emerging markets are "new markets" in the investors' universe and the entry pattern is from developed countries to the developing ones. First-movers might be able to benefit from untapped deal flow and gain a head-start over rivals. The emerging countries' economic growth requires substantial funding. Early-movers could capitalize on the growth opportunities, thereby achieving local experience and building up networks. For limited partners (LPs) of emerging market PE funds there is a widespread argument to commit capital early. Access to the top general partners (GPs) might be restricted after they prove a successful track record. Their follow-on funds will be oversubscribed and therefore not accessible by LPs who had no relationship with them in the pioneering phase. This motivates institutional investors to move quickly into emerging regions and to develop strategic partnerships with local fund managers.

On the downside, early-movers have no prior experience with the country they invest in and they cannot also build on the experience of others. Hence, there is no possibility for syndication (Lockett & Wright, 1999; Wright & Lockett, 2003; Manigart et al., 2006; Meuleman et al., 2009) but GPs first need to establish and run the business for their LPs. However, these GPs need to adapt to local conditions and cannot transfer their "recipes" from developed to emerging countries (Wright et al., 2002). LPs therefore have to evaluate the investment environment and need to overcome potential knowledge deficits with respect to new markets. They gather data and meet local GPs to analyze the determinants they deem important before allocating to a particular country. Unfortunately, this country due diligence is time-consuming and costly. Additionally, the pace of economic development of many emerging countries makes the selection of those that meanwhile support PE activity more and more cumbersome. It would therefore be beneficial if a rating of emerging markets existed which allows an assessment of their capabilities to support the PE business model and deal-making. In joint research, we developed a composite indicator to assess the attractiveness of countries for LPs who seek international diversification of their PE portfolio. This country attractiveness index can support allocation decisions across a large number of countries. However, it cannot clearly determine the best timing when LPs should start allocating capital to emerging markets. It remains an unsolved question when a particular country actually becomes investible. The LPs have to weigh the benefits of entering early, establishing a network, and gaining experience against the disadvantage caused by lacking local experience and eventually not yet mature investment environments. It remains challenging to assess the non-pecuniary benefits and disadvantages of early entry for the long term. Nevertheless, one can analyze the direct monetary success of emerging market PE transactions and may draw conclusions from how improvements of the socio-economic environment in developing countries and gaining local experience affect the returns to emerging market PE investors.

In this chapter, I present my research on emerging PE markets. In the first part, I propose a composite measure that benchmarks the attractiveness of 125 countries to receive PE allocations from institutional investors.[1] The intention is to serve the investment community, preparing and analyzing a large quantity of socio-economic data. Subsequently, I use this composite measure to assess if early-movers in emerging PE markets gained advantages from their early entry with respect to the returns earned. I draw on Groh (2017) which deals with first-mover benefits in emerging PE markets. Based on 1,157 emerging market PE transactions in 86 host countries between 1973 and 2009, the evidence presented in this chapter shows that "waiting and learning pays." Controlling for different definitions of the opportunity cost of capital, for cross-currency rate fluctuations, for real GDP growth during the transaction holding period, for liquidity of the exit market, and for socio-economic determinants, such as a country's innovation capacity, its legal quality, its human capital and labor market protection, Groh (2017) reveals that early transactions underperform the later ones. The internal rate of return of emerging market PE transactions has increased over time since the pioneering investment. This effect is consistent with benefits from learning and improvements of PE deal-making conditions. I therefore conclude that there are no directly measurable early-mover advantages and that it is preferable for investors to delay their emerging market PE allocations until the particular countries are mature enough to establish vibrant PE markets.

Factors that shape a country's attractiveness for limited partners

Wright et al. (1992) describe three decisive factors which are important for the establishment of a vibrant PE market. These factors include the generation of deal opportunities, the infrastructure to complete transactions, and opportunities to realize gains. These three criteria can be broken down into better measurable determinants which assess, in the first instance, the determination of deal opportunities, and second, the expectation of an efficient deal-making environment which allows matching with the supplied capital and divesting. Numerous research contributions discuss the criteria and they can be grouped into six key drivers of international PE activity:

1. Economic activity
2. Depth of capital market
3. Taxation
4. Investor protection and corporate governance
5. Human and social environment
6. Entrepreneurial culture and deal opportunities.

Economic activity

Evidently, the state of a country's economy affects its PE attractiveness. An economy's size and employment levels are proxies for prosperity, the number and diversity of corporations, and general entrepreneurial activity, and therefore also for expected deal flow. Economic growth expectations require investments and provide the rationale to enter many emerging countries. Gompers and Lerner (1998) argue that more attractive PE investment opportunities exist if an economy is growing quickly. Romain and van Pottelsberghe de la Potterie (2004) find that PE activity is cyclical and significantly related to GDP growth. Wilken (1979) highlights the fact that economic prosperity and development facilitate entrepreneurship, as they provide a greater accumulation of capital for risky investments. Economic size and growth are certainly very important criteria to assess expected deal opportunities and PE country attractiveness. However, economic growth itself is also a result of many other criteria discussed within the subsequent key drivers.

Depth of capital market

Black and Gilson (1998) discuss major differences between bank-centered and stock market-centered capital markets. They argue that well-developed stock markets, which allow general partners to exit via IPOs, are crucial for the establishment of vibrant PE markets. In general, bank-centered capital markets are less able to produce an efficient infrastructure of institutions that support PE deal-making. They affirm that it is not only the strong stock market that is missing in bank-centered capital markets; it is also the secondary institutions in place, including bankers' conservative approach to lending and investing, and the social and financial incentives that reward entrepreneurs less richly (and penalize failure more severely), that compromise entrepreneurial activity. Jeng and Wells (2000) stress that IPO activity is the main force behind cyclical PE swings because it directly reflects the returns to investors. Kaplan and Schoar (2005) confirm this. Similar to Black and Gilson (1998), Gompers and Lerner (2000) point out that risk capital flourishes in countries with deep and liquid stock markets. Similarly, Schertler (2003) uses the capitalization of stock markets or the number of listed companies as measures for stock market liquidity and finds that they significantly impact PE investments.

As well as the disadvantages of bank-centered capital markets, Green (1998) emphasizes that low availability of debt financing is an obstacle for economic development, especially for start-up activity in many countries. Corporations and entrepreneurs need to find backers – whether banks or PE funds – who are willing to bear risk. Cetorelli and Gambera (2001) provide evidence that bank concentration promotes the growth of those industrial sectors that have a higher need for external finance by facilitating credit access to companies.

To summarize, the state of a country's capital market evidently affects its PE activity. There is a direct link between the quoted capital market, banking activity, and the unquoted segment. Banks are required for transaction financing and credit facilities. The size of the IPO market indicates the potential for the preferred exit channel, and IPOs likewise spur entrepreneurial spirit because they reward entrepreneurs. This is analogous to the size of the M&A market, which also incentivizes entrepreneurial managers and presents the second preferred PE divestment channel, as well as deal sourcing opportunities. Therefore, the liquidities of the M&A, banking, and public capital markets provide good proxies for PE activity because they assess the quality of the PE deal-making infrastructure. In countries with a strong public capital market, M&A, and banking activity, we also find the professional institutions, such as investment banks, accountants, lawyers, M&A boutiques, and consultants which are essential for successful PE deal-making.

Taxation

Bruce (2000, 2002), and Cullen and Gordon (2002) reveal that tax regimes matter for business entry and exit. Djankov et al. (2010) show that direct and indirect taxes affect entrepreneurial activity. Poterba (1989) builds a decision model showing the advantages of becoming an entrepreneur, driven by taxation incentives. Bruce and Gurley (2005) explain that increases in personal income tax can raise the probability of becoming an entrepreneur: large differences between personal income tax rates and corporate tax rates provide an incentive for start-up activity.

While it is much discussed in economic literature and reasonable to predict that taxation of income drives corporate activity and new venture creation, it is more difficult to detect a direct link with PE investments. There are countries with relatively high corporate income tax rates but also very large PE investments at the same time. On the other hand, there are many (especially emerging) countries with low corporate tax rates where no remarkable PE investments are reported. In general, developed countries have higher tax brackets, but also more PE investments. This signals that the levels of taxes themselves do not strongly affect PE activity. It also points to the characteristic reliance of the PE asset classes on tax transparent fund and transaction structures that neutralize the differentials across tax regimes. Therefore, the index focuses on the incentives for new venture creation provided by the spread between personal and corporate income tax rates as suggested by Bruce and Gurley (2005) and reward tax regimes with low administrative burdens and requirements.

Investor protection and corporate governance

Legal structures and the protection of property rights strongly influence the attractiveness of PE markets. La Porta et al. (1997, 1998) confirm that the legal environment determines the size and extent of a country's capital market and local companies' ability to receive outside financing. They emphasize the differences between statutory law and the quality of law enforcement. Roe (2006) discusses and compares the political determinants of corporate governance legislation for the major economies and focuses on the importance of strong shareholder protection to develop a vibrant capital market. Glaeser et al. (2001) and

Djankov et al. (2003, 2005) suggest that parties in common-law countries have greater ease in enforcing their rights from commercial contracts.

Cumming et al. (2006) find that the quality of a country's legal system is even more closely related to facilitating PE-backed exits than the size of a country's stock market. Cumming et al. (2010) extend this finding and show that cross-country differences in legality, including legal origin and accounting standards, have a significant impact on the governance of investments in the PE industry. Desai et al. (2006) show that fairness and property rights protection largely affect growth and the emergence of new enterprises. Cumming and Johan (2007) highlight the perceived importance of regulatory harmonization with respect to investors' commitments to the asset class. La Porta et al. (2002) find a lower cost of capital for companies in countries with better investor protection, and Lerner and Schoar (2005) confirm these findings. Johnson et al. (1999) show that weak property rights limit the reinvestment of profits in start-up companies. Finally, and more broadly, Knack and Keefer (1995), Mauro (1995), and Svensson (1998) demonstrate that property rights significantly impact investments and economic growth.

The numerous studies cited here illustrate the importance of the quality of a country's legal system for its capital market, be it in terms of the quoted or unquoted segment. Nevertheless, what is important for financial claims is equally valid for any claim in the corporate world. Doing business becomes costly without proper legal protection and enforcement possibilities. PE is strongly exposed to this circumstance because it is based on long-term relationships with institutional investors, where the investment source and host countries can be distant and different. Investors rely on their agents, and the general partners themselves rely on the management teams they back. If investors are not confident that their claims are well protected in a particular country, they will refuse to allocate capital.

Human and social environment

Black and Gilson (1998), Lee and Peterson (2000), and Baughn and Neupert (2003) argue that cultures shape both individual orientation and environmental conditions, which may lead to different levels of entrepreneurial activity. Megginson (2004) argues that, in order to foster a growing risk capital industry, education with respect to schools, universities, and research institutions plays an important role.

Rigid labor market policies negatively affect the evolution of a PE market. Lazear (1990) and Blanchard (1997) discuss how protection of workers can reduce employment and growth. It is especially important for start-up and medium-sized corporations to respond quickly to changing market conditions. Black and Gilson (1998) argue that labor market restrictions influence PE activity, though not to the same extent as the stock market.

Djankov et al. (2002) investigate the role of several societal burdens for start-ups. They conclude that the highest barriers and costs are associated with corruption, crime, a larger unofficial economy, and bureaucratic delay. This argument is of particular importance in some emerging countries with high perceived levels of corruption.

Entrepreneurial culture and deal opportunities

The expectation regarding access to viable investments is probably the most important factor for international risk capital allocation decisions. Particularly for the early stage segment, the number and volume of investments is likely to be related to the innovation capacity and research output in an economy. Gompers and Lerner (1998) show that both industrial and academic research and development (R&D) expenditure significantly correlate with venture capital activity. Kortum and Lerner (2000) highlight that the growth in venture capital fundraising in the mid-1990s may have been due to a surge of patents in the late 1980s and 1990s. Schertler (2003) emphasizes that the number of both R&D employees and patents, as an approximation of the human capital endowment, has a positive and highly significant influence on venture capital activity. Furthermore, Romain and van Pottelsberghe de la Potterie (2004) find that start-up activity interacts with the R&D capital stock, technological opportunities, and the number of patents. However, innovations and R&D are not only important for early-stage investments. Without modernization and sufficient R&D, it will be impossible for established businesses to maintain brand names and strong market positions, factors which attract later-stage PE investors.

Despite the innovative output of a society, Djankov et al. (2002) and Baughn and Neupert (2003) argue that bureaucracy in the form of excessive rules and procedural requirements, multiple institutions from which approvals are needed, and cumbersome documentation requirements, may severely constrain entrepreneurial activity. Lee and Peterson (2000) stress that the time and money required to meet such administrative burdens may discourage new venture creations.

Summary on the determinants of vibrant PE markets

The available research emphasizes the difficulty of identifying the most appropriate parameters for the attractiveness of countries for PE investors. There is no consensus about a ranking of the criteria. While some parameters are more comprehensively discussed and certainly of high relevance, it remains unclear how they interact with others. For example, it is arguable whether the PE activity in a country with a high quality of investor protection is affected more by the liquidity of its stock market or by its labor regulations.

While an IPO exit is, in principle, possible at any stock exchange in the world, the labor market frictions in a particular country can hardly be evaded. On the other hand, many of the criteria are highly correlated with each other. Black and Gilson (1998) call it a "chicken and egg" problem: it is impossible to detect which factor causes the other. One line of argument is that modern, open, and educated societies develop a legislation that protects investors' claims, which favors the output of innovation and the development of a capital market. This leads to economic growth and to demand for PE. However, the causality might be the reverse: economic growth spurs innovation and the development of modern educated societies. There is a third suggestion: only competitive legal environments allow the development of the societal requirements that support innovations, economic growth, the capital market, and activity. Finally, there is a fourth alternative, which may also be relevant: low taxes attract investors who provide financing for growth, which in turn leads to modern and educated societies.

All lines of argument are reasonable and validated by the economic development of selected countries in different historic periods. Nevertheless, it seems to be the combination of all these factors which need to improve in parallel to increase PE attractiveness of countries. For this reason, the subsequently proposed index does not rely on a selection of only a small number of parameters. For a country to receive a high index rank, it needs to achieve a high score on all of the individual criteria. Unfortunately, none of these six key drivers is directly measurable, so it requires data series that adequately express their character. Hence, it uses best proxies for the aforementioned drivers of PE attractiveness. An important constraint is that these proxies must be available for a large number of countries. This rules out the use of particular data series, which might be available for developed economies but do not exist for several of the emerging countries.

Building the PE Country Attractiveness Index

Assessing six latent key drivers

The most important principle of the composite index is to assess the six latent drivers of PE attractiveness outlined earlier.

Latent drivers are criteria that are not directly observable, but driven by others which can be measured. While in a first step the PE attractiveness of a country is determined by

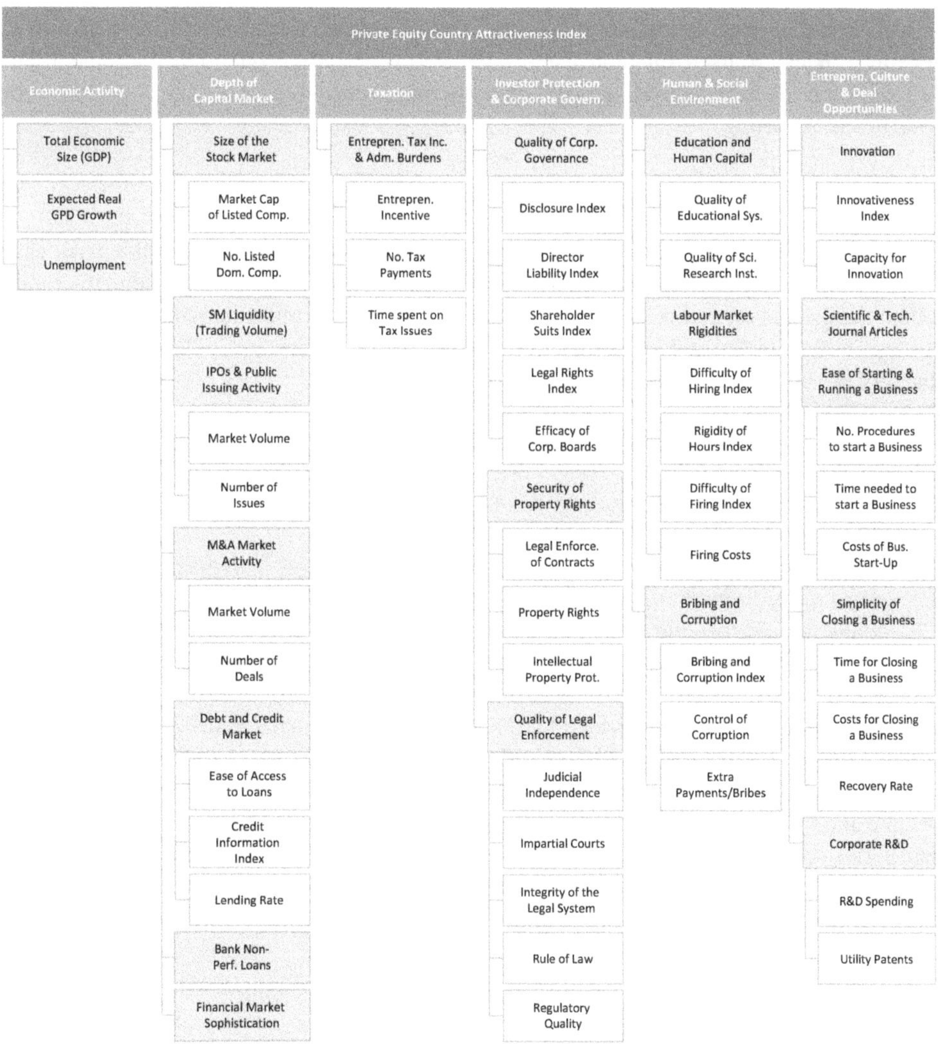

Figure 16.1 PE Country Attractiveness Index: construction scheme

Source: Author.

six key drivers, the key drivers themselves are not measurable but need to be estimated. For example, ideally the quality of the deal-making environment in a country would be expressed by the number of investment banks, M&A boutiques, law firms, accountants, and consultants. Unfortunately, while it might be possible to obtain these data for a selected number of developed countries, such data does not exist on a global scale. The only alternative is to gather more general information, for example, on the level of debt provided by the banking sector, or estimates about the perceived sophistication of the financial system. These criteria should affect the latent key driver, the depth of the capital market. However, even if they are not perfect proxies, one expects that in countries where these criteria are better developed, the capital market will be deeper, and more deal-supporting institutions will exist to facilitate PE activity. Hence, the latent key drivers are assessed with observable data. This principle is maintained at all individual levels for the index construction. An unobservable criterion is assessed with several proxy parameters. In principle, the attractiveness of a country is expressed via the six key drivers. However, several proxies are used for their assessment not to be reliant on single individual data series, which might be biased by different gathering procedures across the countries or by insufficient reporting.[2]

Disaggregating the six key drivers

In accordance with the principle of assessing latent key drivers with observable data, each key driver is further disaggregated into sub-categories. These sub-categories are either individual data series or, again, latent drivers dependent on determinants named "level-2 constructs." For example, as documented in Figure 16.1, the key driver "2. Depth of the capital market" is split into seven sub-categories:

2. Depth of capital market:
2.1. Size of the stock market;
2.2. Stock market liquidity (trading volume);
2.3. IPOs & public issuing activity;
2.4. M&A market activity;
2.5. Debt & credit market;
2.6. Bank non-performing loans to total gross loans;
2.7. Financial market sophistication.

Data series 2.2 and 2.6 are provided by the World Bank and data series 2.7 results from a survey initiated by the World Economic Forum (WEF). However, the other indicators are constructs themselves. For instance, "2.3 IPOs and public issuing activity" is assessed by volume and by number of issues. This approach has two major advantages. First, individual data series do not gain too much weight when they are grouped, and this limits the impact of outliers. Second, the overall results can be traced to more granulated levels which provide complete transparency and better interpretation.

Weighting scheme and country coverage

Since its first edition in 2007 the index has received several revisions with respect to the data structure and the weighting scheme. The currently optimized structure proposes applying equal weights for all data series when aggregated to the level-2 constructs and equal weights for the level-2 constructs to aggregate them on the next higher level of the six key drivers. Finally, the individual weights for the six key drivers depend on the number of their level-2 constructs. For example, "1. Economic activity" consists of three level-2 constructs, "2. Depth of capital market" of seven, while "3. Taxation" consists of only one. Overall, 22 level-2 constructs are used, and hence, "1. Economic activity" receives a weight of 3/22, which is 0.136, while the weight of "2. Depth of capital market" is 7/22, which is 0.318, and for "3. Taxation" it is 1/22, which is 0.046, respectively.

The advantage of this weighting scheme is that the key drivers which include more level-2 constructs, and hence data series, gain more weight. First, this represents their actual importance for PE attractiveness as revealed by our own analyses, and second, the effect of potential outliers in the data diminishes. Any statistical "more sophisticated" technique does not improve the index quality. The weighting scheme assigns appropriate emphasis according to the explanatory power of the individual key drivers.

The index covers as many countries as possible, and the inclusion of a particular country is dependent only on data availability. Since the first index edition, the availability and quality of data has continuously improved so that it now includes the 125 countries presented in Table 16.1.

Table 16.1 Countries covered by the Country Attractiveness Index

Region (number of countries covered)	*Countries*
Africa (31)	Algeria, Angola, Benin, Botswana, Burkina Faso, Burundi, Cameroon, Chad, Côte d'Ivoire, Egypt, Ethiopia, Ghana, Kenya, Lesotho, Madagascar, Malawi, Mali, Mauritania, Mauritius, Morocco, Mozambique, Namibia, Nigeria, Rwanda, Senegal, South Africa, Tanzania, Tunisia, Uganda, Zambia, Zimbabwe
Asia (22)	Armenia, Azerbaijan, Bangladesh, Cambodia, China, Hong Kong, India, Indonesia, Japan, Kazakhstan, Korea South, Kyrgyzstan, Malaysia, Mongolia, Pakistan, the Philippines, Russia, Singapore, Sri Lanka, Taiwan, Thailand, Vietnam
Australasia (2)	Australia, New Zealand
Eastern Europe (21)	Albania, Belarus, Bosnia-Herzegovina, Bulgaria, Croatia, Czech Republic, Estonia, Georgia, Hungary, Latvia, Lithuania, Macedonia, Moldova, Montenegro, Poland, Romania, Slovakia, Slovenia, Turkey, Ukraine, Serbia
Latin America (17)	Argentina, Bolivia, Brazil, Chile, Colombia, Dominican Republic, Ecuador, El Salvador, Guatemala, Jamaica, Mexico, Nicaragua, Panama, Paraguay, Peru, Uruguay, Venezuela
Middle East (10)	Bahrain, Israel, Jordan, Kuwait, Lebanon, Oman, Qatar, Saudi Arabia, Syria, United Arab Emirates
North America (2)	US, Canada
Western Europe (20)	Austria, Belgium, Cyprus, Denmark, Finland, France, Germany, Greece, Iceland, Ireland, Italy, Luxembourg, Malta, Netherlands, Norway, Portugal, Spain, Sweden, Switzerland, UK

Table 16.2 The PE Country Attractiveness Index ranking

Country	*Rank/Trend*		*Score*	*Country*	*Rank/Trend*		*Score*	*Country*	*Rank/Trend*		*Score*
US	1	–	100.0	Iceland	43	↓	63.2	Uganda	85	↑	42.8
UK	2	↑	95.5	Estonia	44	↑	62.6	Pakistan	86	↓	42.6
Canada	3	↓	94.3	Mauritius	45	↑	62.4	Nigeria	87	↓	41.8
Singapore	4	–	93.3	Romania	46	↑	61.0	Tanzania	88	↓	41.2
Hong Kong	5	↑	92.7	Hungary	47	↓	60.1	Ghana	89	↑	40.2
Australia	6	↓	91.9	Vietnam	48	–	59.5	Kyrgyzstan	90	↑	40.1
Japan	7	–	91.8	Kazakhstan	49	↑	59.4	El Salvador	91	–	38.4
New Zealand	8	↑	88.7	Slovenia	50	↑	59.1	Kenya	92	↑	38.2
Germany	9	↓	88.6	Bahrain	51	↓	58.8	Namibia	93	↓	36.7
Switzerland	10	↑	85.7	Latvia	52	↑	58.7	Bangladesh	94	↓	36.0
Malaysia	11	↑	85.6	Peru	53	↓	58.7	Belarus	95	–	33.7
Denmark	12	↓	85.4	Brazil	54	↓	58.3	Malawi	96	↓	33.4
Norway	13	↑	85.2	Bulgaria	55	↑	58.0	Ivory Coast	97	↑	33.1
Finland	14	–	85.2	Czech Republic	56	↑	57.6	Bosnia-Herzegovina	98	↓	32.9
Sweden	15	↓	84.6	Sri Lanka	57	↓	56.4	Dominican Republic	99	↑	32.3
Netherlands	16	–	84.4	Morocco	58	↓	55.8	Rwanda	100	↑	32.0
Ireland	17	↑	82.2	Jordan	59	↑	54.8	Bolivia	101	↓	31.8
Belgium	18	↓	81.6	Oman	60	↓	54.3	Moldova	102	↓	31.7
Israel	19	↓	81.3	Slovakia	61	↑	54.2	Guatemala	103	↓	31.5
Korea, South	20	↑	80.8	Argentina	62	↓	54.0	Azerbaijan	104	↑	29.1
France	21	↓	80.3	Georgia	63	↑	53.8	Cambodia	105	↑	29.0
Taiwan	22	↓	79.4	Zambia	64	↑	53.3	Paraguay	106	↓	28.3
Austria	23	↓	78.5	Tunisia	65	↓	53.2	Albania	107	↓	26.4
China	24	↓	77.1	Greece	66	↑	53.2	Algeria	108	↑	26.0
Poland	25	↑	73.7	Cyprus	67	↓	52.7	Cameroon	109	↑	25.0
Spain	26	–	73.7	Qatar	68	↓	50.1	Ethiopia	110	↑	24.7
Chile	27	↓	73.0	Malta	69	↓	50.0	Nicaragua	111	↓	24.6
Thailand	28	↑	71.5	Egypt	70	↓	50.0	Senegal	112	↓	24.1
India	29	–	69.9	Ukraine	71	↑	50.0	Madagascar	113	↑	24.0
Luxembourg	30	↑	68.9	Mongolia	72	↑	49.1	Mali	114	↓	23.7
Portugal	31	↑	68.6	Macedonia	73	↑	47.5	Mozambique	115	↓	23.4
South Africa	32	↓	67.5	Ecuador	74	↑	47.3	Lesotho	116	↑	22.4
Turkey	33	↑	67.2	Armenia	75	↑	47.2	Zimbabwe	117	↓	22.3
Italy	34	↓	67.0	Uruguay	76	↓	46.9	Burkina Faso	118	↓	20.7
Saudi Arabia	35	↓	66.8	Serbia	77	↑	46.1	Benin	119	↓	20.5
Colombia	36	↓	66.3	Panama	78	↑	46.1	Venezuela	120	↓	19.2
United Arab Emirates	37	↑	65.2	Lebanon	79	↓	46.0	Syria	121	↓	17.3
Indonesia	38	↑	64.9	Croatia	80	↓	46.0	Mauritania	122	–	15.3
Mexico	39	↑	64.6	Jamaica	81	↑	45.3	Burundi	123	–	15.0
Lithuania	40	↑	64.0	Montenegro	82	↓	44.8	Chad	124	↑	13.4
Russian Federation	41	↑	63.5	Botswana	83	↓	44.8	Angola	125	↓	11.5
The Philippines	42	↑	63.4	Kuwait	84	↓	44.1				

Note: ↑ indicates a rank increase over a five-year period. ↓ indicates a rank decrease over a five-year period.

The PE Country Attractiveness Index ranking

Using the latest available data (i.e., from 2016) and an economic outlook yields the US remaining the most attractive country for PE allocations, retaining its ranking from all previous index editions. The US score is rescaled to 100, allowing to directly benchmark it against all other countries. Its two immediate followers, the UK and Canada, achieve scores of 95.5% and 94.3% respectively.

Table 16.2 presents the ranking of The PE Country Attractiveness Index. The table is open to debate. Some readers might argue that particular countries are ranked too high, others too low. However, the index ranking is the result of commonly available, transparent, aggregated socio-economic data, which describes relevant characteristics for investors in PE assets. The results can be traced to the level of the individual data series and, hence, can be reconciled.

Several countries, e.g., among the BRICS or other emerging markets currently receive strong investor attention and record levels of PE activity. One could criticize the index ranking which hardly reflects this trend. It is certain that the capital absorption capacity in many emerging markets allows quick transaction making and large volumes. So one might be attempted to increase the importance of GDP growth or of the economic activity key driver to reflect investors' appreciation of these fast growing markets. However, the weights are an optimized result of comprehensive cross-sectional and longitudinal analyses. Increasing the weight of GDP growth, for example, can produce awkward rankings which do not correspond with the fact that many of the "traditional" markets still provide the best deal-making, value-adding, and exit opportunities for PE investors. It is not evident from today's perspective that the shift of investors' attention towards emerging countries will result in increased levels of successful transactions in the long run, and hence, satisfying returns to investors in the future. The index assesses a "probability for success" from the institutional and socio-economic perspective. This probability increases with better developed key driving forces as defined earlier, and vice versa.

Historic comparison and allocation recommendations

In order to demonstrate shifts in the PE country attractiveness, I compare the latest (2016) and the 2012 rankings. Figure 16.2 shows the current country ranks (ordinate) and the historic rank changes (abscissa – positive to the right and negative to the left) between the two indices. It provides interesting insights and reveals strong increases of PE attractiveness for certain countries, and the impact of financial and economic crises on others.

It needs to be stressed that according to the methodology of the index calculation, every country's score is calculated relative to all other sample countries. This means that those countries gaining or losing ranking positions did not necessarily improve or worsen their investment conditions in absolute terms. They may simply have outperformed or been outperformed by others in the international competition to attract capital resources.

Figure 16.2 allows valuable insights interpreting the four quadrants of the graph. Obviously, all countries on the left-hand side of the figure should be carefully observed by investors, in particular the lower their current rank. It seems reasonable to recommend to investors avoidance of the countries in the lower left quadrant. Contrarily, on the right-hand side of the ordinate we find the countries with promising development. The countries in the right upper quadrant can be considered highly attractive investment hosts. Several emerging PE markets have shown very strong improvements of their attractiveness to foreign

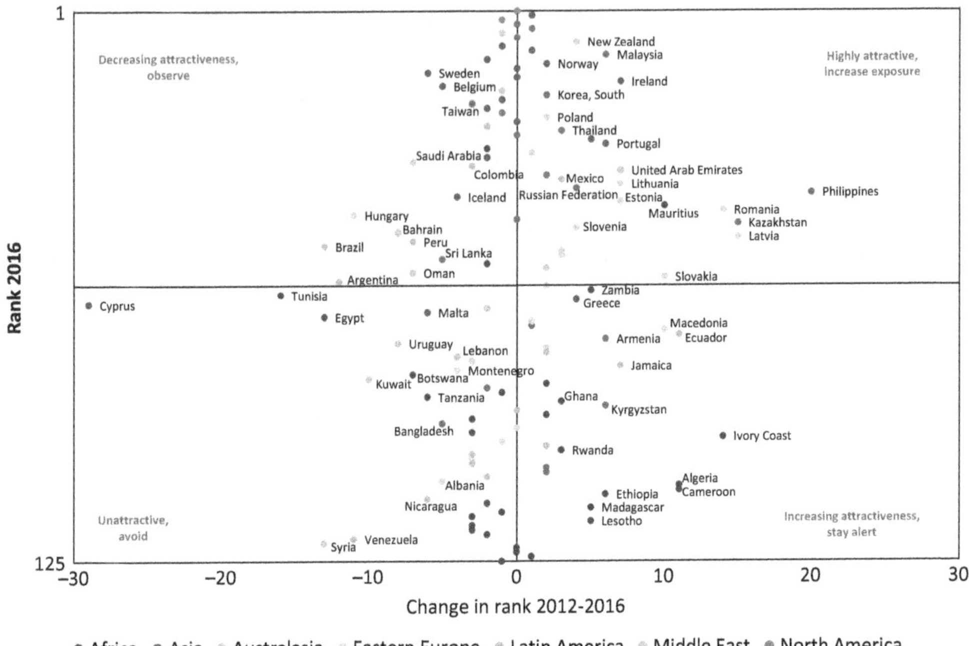

Figure 16.2 Current ranks and rank changes between index version 2012 and 2016
Source: Author.

investors and have now reached this quadrant, most notably the Philippines, Kazakhstan, and Mauritius. The lower right corner groups the countries with increasing but yet moderate levels of attractiveness. The further down we get in the graph the lower the maturity of these countries to support PE transactions. However, investors should stay alert not to miss the right time to enter.

The BRICS, Turkey, Mexico, Indonesia, the Philippines, and Nigeria

The BRICS (Brazil, Russia, India, China, and including South Africa) have received substantial attention and PE flows in recent years. PE investment data from commercial data providers, such as Thomson One, reveals that China is ranked the second most active country in 2016, right behind the US, and that India and Brazil rank 8 and 20 in a global comparison. This investment activity ranking is not equivalent to the fundamental investment conditions as assessed by the composite index. However, one should note that Brazil has substantially improved investment conditions and South Africa was already high ranked due to its ties with the UK and the establishment of a similar legal and capital market-oriented culture. Only Russia lags behind her peers, which is most probably related to some of the factors set out in the subsequent figures. Nevertheless, investors meanwhile look beyond the BRICS and search for new emerging and frontier markets for allocations. Similar to the experiences with the BRICS, the race winning countries will probably be those with large populations and strong economic catch-up potential, notably Mexico, Indonesia, the Philippines, Nigeria, and Turkey. The size of a population combined with

Region	*Index rank*	*Index score*	*1 economic activity*	*2 Depth of capital market*	*3 Taxation*	*4 Investor protection and corporate governance*	*5 Human and social environment*	*6 Entrepreneurial culture and deal opportunities*
China	24	77.1	108.4	86.7	110.6	57.8	50.9	75.9
India	29	69.9	103.0	79.5	84.7	62.7	43.7	62.9
South Africa	32	67.5	60.8	79.2	108.7	80.9	35.7	68.8
Turkey	33	67.2	89.5	75.0	107.5	64.1	46.4	56.9
Indonesia	38	64.9	95.6	75.6	66.7	55.3	40.4	60.4
Mexico	39	64.6	94.3	69.1	104.1	63.4	30.3	68.0
Russia	41	63.5	81.7	73.3	97.8	53.5	30.9	69.7
Philippines	42	63.4	93.4	72.1	84.2	52.7	54.2	48.8
Brazil	54	58.3	81.1	77.5	21.3	53.3	33.2	57.9
Nigeria	87	41.8	75.9	28.9	49.7	52.8	27.3	53.0

Figure 16.3 The six key drivers for the BRICS, Turkey, Mexico, the Philippines, Indonesia, and Nigeria

Source: Author.

expected economic growth is a simple indicator for deal opportunities. Nevertheless, this combination is necessary for emerging countries but not sufficient to guarantee appropriate PE investment conditions. All of the defined key drivers should be taken into account. I compare the BRICS, Turkey, Mexico, the Philippines, Indonesia, and Nigeria in Figures 16.3 to 16.5.

Investors seek to capitalize on the combination between expected growth and the large populations. The graphs reveal that not only the economic soundness of the presented emerging countries is excellent but also that China, India, South Africa, Turkey, and Brazil have developed a financial market infrastructure which ranks ahead of many of the developed countries. However, the figure also reveals the disequilibrium among the key driving forces of PE attractiveness. Emerging PE markets are characterized by peaks towards their economic activity. Despite meanwhile deep capital markets, the other important key drivers "Investor protection and corporate governance," "Human and social environment," and "Entrepreneurial culture and deal opportunities" are poorly developed for most of them. This effect can be reconciled by considering the level-2 constructs.

Figures 16.4 and 16.5 present the scores of the level-2 constructs for the BRICS, Turkey, Mexico, the Philippines, Indonesia, and Nigeria. They reveal the expectations of growth and the deep capital markets. However, they also point to general concerns about emerging market PE in general. Corporate governance indicators (with the exception of South Africa) and investor protection still remain obstacles. Further, perceived bribery and corruption levels are high, while innovations and corporate R&D remain relatively low. We know from the BRICS and other emerging countries that growth and development are mainly concentrated in particular hubs or certain regions, but are not widespread. We also know that the benefit of wealth creation is often allocated among small elite groups and not larger parts of the population. This presents not only socio-economic and political challenges in those countries

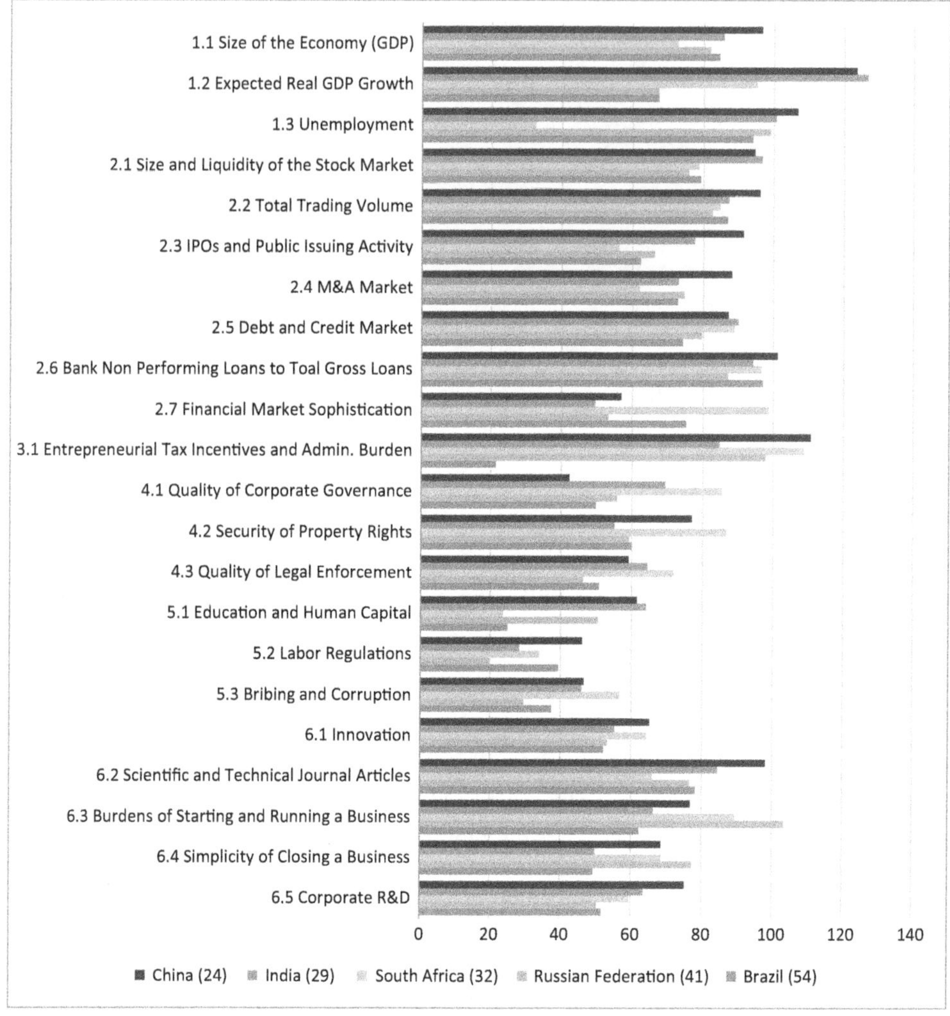

Figure 16.4 Level-2 constructs for the BRICS

Source: Author.

but also affects their PE attractiveness. If the countries cannot transfer the wealth effects of growth to a broader part of their population, this is unlikely to improve the other key driving forces of PE attractiveness, and if the pace of economic growth slows down, the countries will be less attractive for PE investors.

In summary, the BRICS and the other emerging markets provide many investment opportunities and have strong financing requirements for their expected economic growth. However, it is more challenging in several emerging countries to get access to high quality deals because of the relative immaturity of the institutional deal-supporting environment. Where corruption is present, it might be the case that the most promising transactions are negotiated among small groups of local elites while lemons are broadly auctioned. Hence, deal flow could be cumbersome and costly. Furthermore, if the protection of investors is insufficient, and if bribery and corruption are high, then the net returns to investors can suffer.

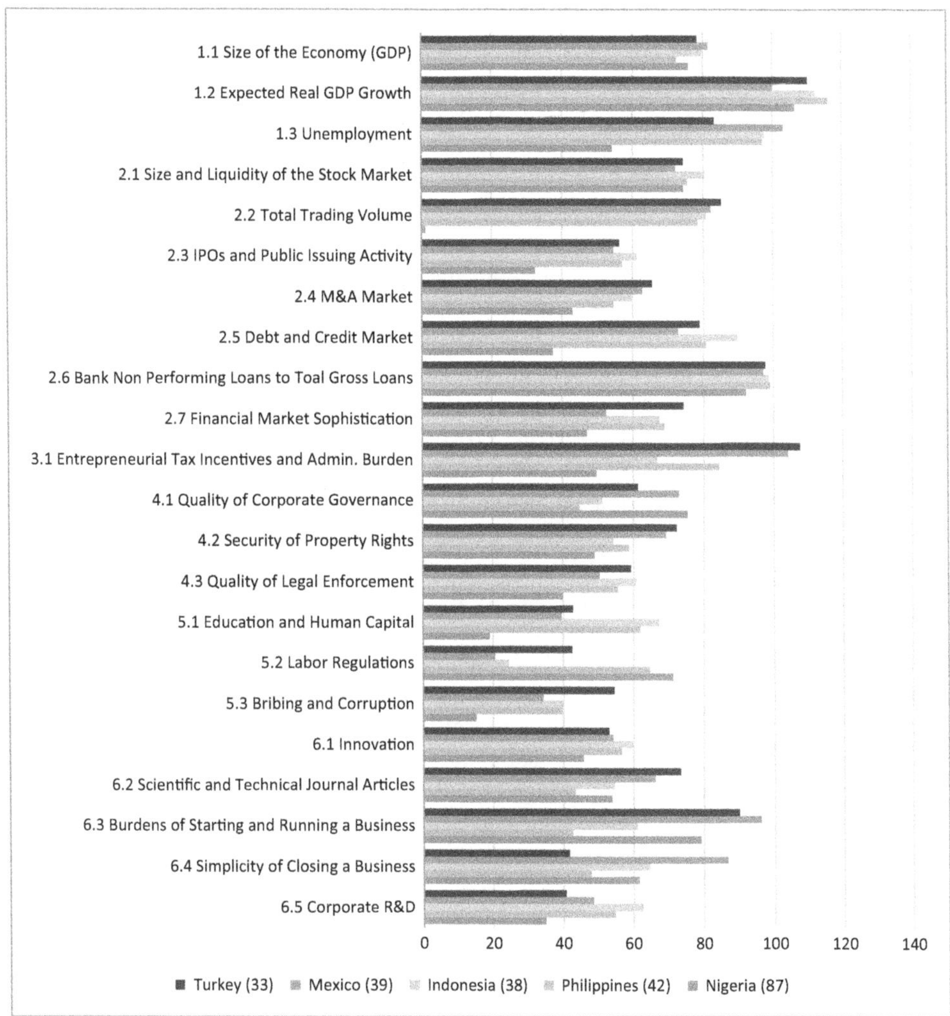

Figure 16.5 Level-2 constructs for Turkey, Mexico, the Philippines, Indonesia, and Nigeria

Source: Author.

Limited partners should carefully consider the advantages and disadvantages of the emerging opportunities as the exceptional growth comes at a certain cost.

First-mover disadvantages

Subsequent to the discussion of the required favorable socio-economic conditions for successful PE deal-making and to the proposition of the PE Country Attractiveness Index, I can address the question whether internationally acting institutional investors should commit capital to various emerging PE markets. Several emerging countries, e.g., China, India, and Brazil, host large amounts of PE investment volumes. From others we do not know yet about any remarkable activity, and the question arises whether investors should start committing capital to these markets. As revealed by the Country Attractiveness Index, many of them have probably not yet reached the level of economic development to support the PE business model and therefore, it might not be easy for the pioneers to gain access to good deals. It could rather be beneficial to wait until these countries' states of development facilitate PE deal-making.

Despite the required level of socio-economic development of a country to support PE activity, research has provided evidence on the value drivers in PE transactions and on appropriate target company characteristics. It is commonly understood that PE sponsors can add value to their portfolio companies by reducing agency costs, exploiting debt tax shields, and by added-value advice to exploit new markets. Active monitoring, incentive structuring, and bonding may lower the agency costs of free cash flow. Improvements in operating efficiency, focusing on core activities and selling off non-core assets, creates more competitive entities (e.g., Wright et al., 2000; Cumming et al., 2007, Nikoskelainen & Wright, 2007; Meuleman et al., 2009; Gilligan & Wright, 2014). The benefit of PE is assumed to be largest for corporations with high agency costs of free cash flow, namely high operating cash flows but missing investment opportunities. Jensen (1989) notes that "desirable leveraged buyout candidates are frequently firms or divisions of larger firms that have stable business histories and substantial free cash flow (i.e., low growth prospects and high potential for generating cash flows) – situations where agency costs of free cash flow are likely to be high."

The index reveals that the required socio-economic environment for successful PE deal-making has not yet been established in many emerging PE markets. One can expect that creating deal flow is cumbersome there too because potential target firms probably do not fulfill the appropriate characteristics of ideal PE candidates with potential high agency costs of free cash flow. It is doubtful that companies in rapidly growing markets provide these opportunities because they have high capital expenditures. The necessity to exploit the growth potential in a short time should also not leave much room for operational improvement. Further, as the opportunity cost of capital is usually high in emerging countries, other investment channels, such as portfolio and corporate foreign direct investment, could be better suited to capitalize on the growth anticipations. As a result, one would not expect first-mover advantages from early entry in emerging PE markets. There is no need to be among the first investors because PE deal-making conditions are not sufficiently developed at the time the pioneers enter.

If this is true, then we can expect improving deal-making conditions in emerging countries over time. These improving conditions should yield a higher value creation on the target company levels and, hence, improve the returns of the financial sponsors gradually over time.

Literature on emerging market PE returns

Kaplan and Strömberg (2009) note that PE activity strongly spread to new parts of the world between 2001 and 2006, particular to Asia, where deal size almost tripled during that period. Lerner and Schoar (2005) argue that systematic data on emerging market PE returns is hard to come by but submit that returns in these nations appear to have been far lower than in the US and Europe. They conclude that the experience of PE funds in the developing world poses interesting issues, which have been little explored in academic research so far.

Leeds and Sunderland (2003) underscore the notion of inferior returns to investors from emerging market PE activities and discuss potential determinants of underperformance. They argue that the PE industry evolved gradually in the US over a 40-year period which was increasingly conducive to this type of financing and point to a sympathetic public policy environment, a reliable legal system, stability, a well-developed financial market, and, finally, demand from co-operative entrepreneurs. In particular, they identify low standards of corporate governance, limited legal recourse, and dysfunctional capital markets impeding PE activity in emerging markets. Nahata et al. (2014) elaborate on these assumed deficiencies and reveal that indeed, the quality of legal rights and investor protection, and the general development of stock markets, are inhibitors. Cumming and Walz (2009) and Cao et al. (2015) confirm the role of legal protection for PE sponsors in emerging countries. Lopez de Silanes et al. (2015) find that emerging market PE transactions have slightly longer durations and exhibit statistically significantly poorer performance across several measures, with the exception of bankruptcy rates. However, the authors expected the opposite due to higher assumed cost of capital in these countries. The lower returns could be the result of costly learning, poor legal environments, and illiquid exit markets. They also find lower degrees of leverage of developing country PE transactions and suggest this as another reason for smaller returns on equity.

Chemmanur et al. (2016) add to the research on the liability of foreignness of PE investors. They find that syndicates composed of international and local investors are more successful than syndicates of either exclusively international or exclusively local funds. Both groups of investors have comparative disadvantages: international PE firms lack proximity but local funds might have less investment experience. The benefits of mixed syndicates are stronger in emerging regions, which is consistent with the notion that difficulties in monitoring and deficiencies in local knowledge faced by international investors are more severe there.

Reddy and Blenman (2014) analyze LBO transactions in different growth phases of the investees and compare developed and developing economies. They find that the returns achieved by the financial sponsors are on average higher for transactions in the developed countries. However, in periods of strong economic growth, the returns are higher in the emerging economies.

All these contributions highlight the importance of addressing the question about performance of PE investments in emerging countries and motivate the subsequent analyses.

Dataset and descriptive statistics

General sample characteristics and dependent variable

The literature review and the earlier discussed mismatch between the fundamental investment conditions and the actual PE activity in some emerging countries gives rise to the research question whether early entry into these countries was really beneficial for the LPs. To address this question, I obtained in Groh (2017) a sample of 1,157 emerging market PE transactions collected from Private Placement Memoranda (PPMs) and extracted from the data used in Lopez de Silanes et al. (2015). The dataset offers a broad pool of variables describing each single investment but, most importantly, information on the timing of the transactions, the host countries of the targets, and their success expressed by the internal rate of return (IRR) of the underlying cash flow stream. The IRRs are calculated gross of management fees and are therefore comparable across time, countries, and general partners.

The sample comprises investments in 86 host countries by 73 different general partners between 1973 and 2009 with exit/reporting dates ranging from 1975 to 2009 and durations from 1 month up to 18.5 years. Table 16.3 presents these primary sample characteristics.

Table 16.3 Primary characteristics of the sample of transactions

Country	*Obs.*		*Closing year*		*Exit/reporting year*		*Duration*			
	Obs.	*in %*	*Min*	*Max*	*Min*	*Max*	*Mean*	*Median*	*Min*	*Max*
Algeria	1	0.10	2003	2003	2007	2007	4.0	4.0	4.0	4.0
Angola	2	0.20	2004	2005	2008	2008	4.0	4.0	3.5	4.5
Argentina	40	3.50	1992	2008	1998	2008	8.9	8.8	0.5	16.5
Bangladesh	1	0.10	1999	1999	2003	2003	4.0	4.0	4.0	4.0
Benin	5	0.40	1993	2002	2008	2008	12.1	12.5	6.5	15.5
Bolivia	8	0.70	1990	2001	2008	2008	12.6	13.5	7.5	18.5
Botswana	3	0.30	1990	2005	2008	2008	9.8	7.5	3.5	18.5
Brazil	83	7.20	1990	2007	1995	2008	7.8	7.5	0.5	18.5
Bulgaria	14	1.20	1997	2007	2002	2007	3.5	1.7	0.4	8.4
Burkina Faso	3	0.30	1998	2004	2007	2008	8.0	10.5	3.0	10.5
Cameroon	1	0.10	2004	2004	2008	2008	4.5	4.5	4.5	4.5
Chile	17	1.50	1990	2008	2001	2008	9.9	9.5	0.5	18.5
China	79	6.80	1994	2009	1998	2009	3.4	2.7	0.1	11.5
Colombia	25	2.20	1991	2008	2008	2008	5.6	4.5	0.5	17.5
Congo, Dem. Rep.	8	0.70	1996	2008	2007	2008	3.6	2.5	0.5	12.5
Costa Rica	5	0.40	1991	2008	2008	2008	10.5	9.5	0.5	17.5
Côte d'Ivoire	11	1.00	1990	2002	2008	2008	12.2	12.5	6.5	18.5
Croatia	8	0.70	2000	2004	2003	2007	4.6	4.3	2.8	7.0
Czech Republic	14	1.20	1997	2005	2001	2008	4.1	4.9	0.4	8.1
Dominican Republic	5	0.40	1990	2008	2008	2008	10.1	11.5	0.5	18.5
Ecuador	3	0.30	1999	2000	2008	2008	9.2	9.5	8.5	9.5
Egypt	2	0.20	2002	2006	2007	2007	3.1	3.1	1.3	5.0
El Salvador	6	0.50	1994	2005	2008	2008	8.5	8.5	3.5	14.5
Eritrea	1	0.10	1998	1998	2008	2008	10.5	10.5	10.5	10.5

Estonia	13	1.10	1996	2006	1997	2006	3.5	3.0	0.4	8.0
Gambia	2	0.20	1991	1991	2008	2008	17.5	17.5	17.5	17.5
Georgia	1	0.10	1997	1997	2007	2007	9.8	9.8	9.8	9.8
Ghana	10	0.90	1990	2008	2007	2008	10.2	7.3	0.5	18.5
Guatemala	3	0.30	1994	2000	2008	2008	10.5	8.5	8.5	14.5
Guinea	1	0.10	1996	1996	2008	2008	12.5	12.5	12.5	12.5
Guinea-Bissau	4	0.30	1990	2000	2008	2008	14.3	15.0	8.5	18.5
Guyana	2	0.20	2001	2006	2008	2008	5.0	5.0	2.5	7.5
Haiti	1	0.10	2000	2000	2008	2008	8.5	8.5	8.5	8.5
Honduras	2	0.20	1995	2008	2008	2008	7.0	7.0	0.5	13.5
Hong Kong	25	2.20	1973	1995	1975	2007	5.0	4.0	0.4	13.0
Hungary	10	0.90	1997	2004	1999	2007	3.9	3.5	0.9	9.1
India	59	5.10	1998	2007	1999	2008	3.3	2.3	0.2	9.0
Indonesia	51	4.40	1993	2005	2001	2007	3.7	3.4	0.2	13.3
Jamaica	3	0.30	1997	2004	2008	2008	7.5	6.5	4.5	11.5
Kazakhstan	1	0.10	1997	1997	2007	2007	10.3	10.3	10.3	10.3
Kenya	23	2.00	1990	2008	2007	2008	6.9	4.0	0.5	18.5
Korea, South	1	0.10	1993	1993	2003	2003	10.5	10.5	10.5	10.5
Kuwait	1	0.10	1998	1998	2007	2007	9.0	9.0	9.0	9.0
Latvia	6	0.50	2002	2005	2006	2006	2.2	2.0	1.0	4.0
Lithuania	12	1.00	1996	2005	1999	2006	3.3	2.5	1.0	6.0
Madagascar	4	0.30	1992	2008	2008	2008	8.3	8.0	0.5	16.5
Malawi	3	0.30	1995	2000	2008	2008	10.8	10.5	8.5	13.5
Malaysia	16	1.40	1995	2005	2001	2007	3.3	2.6	0.3	11.0
Mali	2	0.20	1995	1998	2008	2008	12.0	12.0	10.5	13.5
Mauritania	2	0.20	1991	1998	2008	2008	14.0	14.0	10.5	17.5
Mauritius	3	0.30	1990	1992	2008	2008	17.5	17.5	16.5	18.5
Mexico	45	3.90	1990	2008	1993	2008	7.9	7.5	0.4	18.5

(Continued)

Table 16.3 (Continued)

Country	*Obs.*		*Closing year*		*Exit/reporting year*		*Duration*			
	Obs.	*in %*	*Min*	*Max*	*Min*	*Max*	*Mean*	*Median*	*Min*	*Max*
Morocco	1	0.10	2008	2008	2008	2008	0.5	0.5	0.5	0.5
Mozambique	5	0.40	1998	2006	2007	2008	7.8	9.0	2.5	10.5
Namibia	2	0.20	1999	2002	2008	2008	8.0	8.0	6.5	9.5
Nicaragua	1	0.10	1999	1999	2008	2008	9.5	9.5	9.5	9.5
Nigeria	20	1.70	1993	2007	2007	2008	5.3	3.3	0.7	15.5
Panama	4	0.30	2000	2008	2008	2008	5.8	7.0	0.5	8.5
Peru	12	1.00	1994	2008	2008	2008	6.0	4.0	0.5	14.5
Philippines	7	0.60	1996	2005	2002	2008	6.1	5.7	3.3	10.4
Poland	123	10.60	1992	2006	1999	2008	7.0	6.3	0.1	13.8
Romania	23	2.00	1996	2005	2000	2006	5.3	5.4	1.0	10.0
Russian Federation	14	1.20	1995	2004	2002	2007	8.0	9.1	0.8	12.0
Rwanda	2	0.20	2004	2008	2007	2008	1.8	1.8	0.5	3.0
Saudi Arabia	1	0.10	1998	1998	2003	2003	5.4	5.4	5.4	5.4
Senegal	5	0.40	1994	2004	2007	2008	9.0	9.5	3.0	14.5
Serbia	2	0.20	2003	2003	2007	2007	3.7	3.7	3.5	3.9
Singapore	2	0.20	1996	1997	2006	2007	10.4	10.4	10.2	10.7
Slovakia	7	0.60	2000	2005	2005	2006	3.9	4.3	0.5	5.3
Slovenia	2	0.20	2000	2000	2005	2005	4.9	4.9	4.9	4.9
South Africa	153	13.20	1990	2008	1993	2008	5.3	5.5	0.5	13.6
Sri Lanka	3	0.30	1997	2006	2004	2007	5.0	7.0	1.0	7.1
Swaziland	3	0.30	1990	2001	2008	2008	13.8	15.5	7.5	18.5
Taiwan	1	0.10	1996	1996	1998	1998	2.8	2.8	2.8	2.8
Tanzania	10	0.90	1994	2008	2008	2008	10.7	12.0	0.5	14.5
Thailand	36	3.10	1989	2006	1992	2008	2.1	1.1	0.2	6.4

Togo	4	0.30	1991	2001	2008	2008	12.8	13.0	7.5	17.5
Trinidad and Tobago	1	0.10	1990	1990	2008	2008	18.5	18.5	18.5	18.5
Tunisia	2	0.20	1997	2005	2007	2008	6.8	6.8	2.0	11.5
Turkey	2	0.20	2003	2006	2006	2008	2.6	2.6	2.0	3.3
Uganda	9	0.80	1993	2006	2007	2008	10.4	12.5	0.7	15.5
Ukraine	14	1.20	1996	2002	2004	2007	7.4	8.1	2.2	11.5
Uruguay	2	0.20	1990	2002	2008	2008	12.5	12.5	6.5	18.5
Venezuela	11	1.00	1991	2002	2008	2008	13.0	14.5	6.5	17.5
Zambia	6	0.50	1998	2008	2007	2008	7.8	9.5	0.5	10.5
Zimbabwe	16	1.40	1991	2002	2007	2008	11.7	11.5	4.7	17.5
Total/mean/min/max	1,157	100.00	1973	2009	1975	2009	6.3	5.3	0.1	18.5

The origins of the investors are not as broadly diversified as the host countries of the investees. This corresponds with the typical pattern of emerging market PE transactions being originated in financial centers. Almost 50% of the sample transactions are sponsored by general partners based in the US. 11% are undertaken by UK GPs. Other hubs are in Poland, Finland, the Netherlands, the Czech Republic, the Russian Federation, and in Greece serving the Central and Southern Eastern European and the Commonwealth of Independent States PE markets (for approximately 16% of the sample transactions). GPs from financial centers in China, India, Hong Kong, and Malaysia provide financing for 10% of the transactions mainly located in South Eastern Asia. South Africa serves as a hub for 108 African transactions, which represent approximately 9%, and Argentina and Brazil for 49 Latin American deals, which represent approxiamtely 4% of the sample. From this geographic distribution of investor locations we realize that 73% of the transactions are sourced across a border while 27% are local deals, i.e., emerging country investors investing in the same country's investees.

Independent and control variables

Analyzing the returns of PE transactions in an international comparison is a challenging task, as described in Manigart et al. (2002). However, to address the question if early entry into emerging PE markets is an advisable strategy for institutional investors, I need to describe the investment conditions at the time of the transactions. Therefore, I require a set of independent and control variables which capture investors' experience in the host countries and their deal-making environment. One of the key variables of interest is therefore a proxy for the experience that investors have in the various host countries. Since we do not know detailed information about the sponsors at the time of the transactions, e.g., their staff's emerging market experience or their tenure/experience in general, I refer to simple proxies that can be determined from the data collection. The first stylized measure for experience in a particular country uses the sample's first transaction entry date. The pioneering observation in every investment host country sets the cut-off entry date and all subsequent transactions are related to this date. The key variable (i) "Time since first investment in the host country" takes the value of the difference of the closing dates between a particular transaction and the pioneering one in the same country. Obviously, for the initial transactions in every country this variable has a value of zero. This proxy therefore captures the experience that the overall investment community has in an individual country. It can also be interpreted from another perspective as it likewise serves as a proxy for the development and state of the PE market and characterizes the awareness of the asset class in a country's society and professional investment community. However, the variable needs to be interpreted with some caution because I am unaware if the first observation is indeed the pioneering deal in a particular country. Therefore, the proxy might be biased towards too small values. Several other independent variables control for the investment environment and for valuation effects, i.e., the public market equivalents (PMEs).

Table 16.4 presents the key measures of experience and all other independent and control variables that I use in Groh (2017) for multivariate analyses. Public stock markets have an important signaling effect for the unquoted equity market. PE investors usually use public peer group multiples when valuing unquoted investees. Therefore, stock market valuations strongly drive target values and, hence, the returns of PE transactions (Lopez de Silanes et al., 2015). However, it is not clear which stock markets serve to determine peer group valuations for emerging market PE transactions. Market participants could

Table 16.4 Independent variables

Indicators	*Dimension*	*Explanation*	*Source(s)*
(1) Time since the first investment in the host country	Years	Measure for the experience gained in general in a particular emerging country. The first observed transaction in every country of our sample sets the cut-off date and receives a value of 0 for this variable. All other closing dates of the transactions in the same country (if any) use this offset. The years of experience are the difference between transaction closing and the first closing date.	My data set
(2) Time-matching S&P 500 return	[%]	Public market equivalent return which is measured by the geometric average growth rate of the S&P 500 index over the same time as the holding period of the PE transaction.	Bloomberg
(3) Time-matching local or regional stock market return	[%]	Public market equivalent return of a local benchmark index. The calculation is the same as for indicator (3) but using local emerging stock market indices instead of the S&P 500 as benchmarks. For every particular country, the most important/representative stock market index is used. If such an index is not available, or was not available at the closing of the PE transaction, then a neighboring country or regional stock market index is used as an alternative. A detailed list of the benchmark stock market indices and their alternatives is provided in Table 16.5.	Bloomberg
(4) Time-matching GDP growth	[%]	The transaction holding period-matching real GDP growth in the host country of the investment. Corresponds to the geometric average growth rate of a host country's GDP between closing and exit of the PE transaction. The indicator's accuracy is calculated on the level of months with the annual GDP observation broken down accordingly.	International Monetary Fund, International Financial Statistics, and World Economic Outlook/UN/ national statistics
(5) Aggregated IPO proceeds in host country in the year of exit	[billion USD]	This indicator aggregates the annual proceeds of IPO volumes (including green shoe options) in a particular country for the exit year of the PE transaction.	Thomson One Banker
(6) Host country's property rights index	#	The Property Rights Index is an assessment of the ability of individuals to accumulate private property, secured by clear laws that are fully enforced by the state. The index ranges from 1 to 10, with higher values indicating higher protection of property rights. We regard this index as time-invariant and use the 2007 observations.	Fraser Institute

either refer to peers traded in the US or locally. Variable (2), the time-matching S&P 500 return, is therefore used to determine the benchmark return if valuations follow US peers; and variable (3), the time-matching local or regional stock market return, determines the public market equivalent return if peers are selected from local (emerging) stock markets. However, several of the investee host countries do/did not (at the transaction date) have a public stock market or a representative benchmark index. For these countries, I refer to close neighbors or regionally representative indices to determine the alternative benchmark returns. The use of these two benchmark definitions can also be motivated from a different perspective. Contingent on an investor's perspective, one can refer to the S&P 500 or a local stock market index as a measure for the opportunity cost of capital. Using either benchmark will affect the performance of a particular PE transaction. I include both alternative cost of capital measures to show that the results hold, whatever the preferred performance attribution of a particular investor might be. Alternatively, one could use special regional or global emerging stock market indices. However, referring to such alternative benchmark definitions would probably not change the results meaningfully as the benchmark returns are expected to range somewhere between the S&P 500 and the local stock market indices.

Variable (4), the time-matching GDP growth, captures the real growth of the GDP in the investment host country over the holding period of the transaction. The rationale for using this variable is similar to that for using a PME. GDP growth is a fundamental driver of PE performance and the most important motivation for allocations to emerging PE markets in the first place. The GDP growth is annualized and extrapolated according to the exact (month-end) closing and exit days. Variable (5), the aggregated IPO proceeds in the investment host country in the year of exit, captures the liquidity of the exit market at the time of divestment. Several countries do not have public stock markets/IPO activity and hence, consistently zero proceeds. Variable (6), a host country's Property Rights Index, controls for legal quality in the investee country.

Variable (6) indexes are often not available for years prior to 2000 and do not change meaningfully over time either. They are therefore considered time-invariant and are replaced by their 2009 values. All other variables either match the duration of the sample transactions or correspond with the exit year observation.

Multivariate analyses

In the first specification in Table 16.5, I regress the winsorized IRR in USD on the experience measure "Time since the first investment in the host country," a constant and controls include country, GP, industry fixed effects, and the legal quality indicator. The number of observations is 1,157, and the adjusted R^2 is 22.74%.

The coefficient of the independent variable in the first line of Table 16.5 is 0.013 and statistically significant at the 1% level. The second line (0.119) represents the standardized parameter coefficient, i.e., the estimate if all variables are transferred into their z-scores. The third line [0.005] is the estimate's standard error.

The economic magnitude of the parameter estimate can be interpreted as follows: Every year of waiting until a transaction has been closed led to an increase in the IRR of 1.3 percentage points on average. This effect is strong and meaningful for investors and we can attribute it to two factors. The first is the experience that market participants gained in the particular emerging country. The second is the simple result of further development of the deal-making conditions that facilitate PE transactions in this country.

Table 16.5 PE transactions' IRR determinants from a USD investor's point of view

Specification:	*A*	*B*	*C*	*D*	*E*
Independent variables:	*β (Std.β) [S.E.]*	*β (Std.β) [S.E.]*	*β (Std.β) [S.E.]*	*β (Std.β) [S.E.]*	*β (Std.β) [S.E.]*
Time since the first investment in the host country	0.013*** (0.119) [0.005]	0.029*** (0.265) [0.006]	0.026*** (0.235) [0.006]	0.015*** (0.136) [0.004]	0.014*** (0.125) [0.004]
Time-matching S&P 500 return		1.150*** (0.273) [0.176]	0.980*** (0.232) [0.185]	0.729*** (0.173) [0.156]	0.744*** (0.176) [0.153]
Time-matching local or regional stock market return			0.143*** (0.089) [0.054]	0.145*** (0.090) [0.053]	0.120** (0.074) [0.051]
Time-matching GDP growth				2.509*** (0.132) [0.742]	2.003*** (0.105) [0.760]
Aggregated IPO proceeds in the host country in the year of exit					0.006*** (0.118) [0.002]
Constant	1.107*** [0.211]	0.817*** [0.226]	0.779*** [0.229]	0.198 [0.132]	0.147 [0.135]
Controls:					
Country fixed effects	yes	yes	Yes	no	no
GP fixed effects	yes	yes	Yes	yes	yes
Industry fixed effects	yes	yes	Yes	yes	yes
Legal quality	yes	yes	Yes	yes	yes
N	1,157	1,157	1,157	1,157	1,157
adj. R^2 in %	22.74	26.55	26.94	22.66	23.18

Specifications B to E add independent variables and alter the set of control variables. Specification B includes the transaction period-matching S&P 500 benchmark return as independent variable. As expected, the global stock market benchmark has a strong impact on valuations in the non-quoted emerging markets and, hence, on the PE returns. A 1% increase in the benchmark return over the holding period increases the transactions' returns by 1.15%, on average. The standardized parameter coefficient (0.273) is slightly larger than that of the experience measure, signaling that the public stock market has a stronger effect on PE performance than the experience measure. The adjusted R^2 of this regression increases from 22.74% to 26.55% compared to specification A.

Specification C adds the transaction time-matching local benchmark return as independent variable. Its parameter 0.143 is significant at the 1% level, indicating that investors not only refer to the US to determine valuation multiples but also to local stock markets. Alternatively, one could argue that the local stock market indices provide more appropriate information about the local economic conditions than the S&P 500 index. However, the local benchmarks' standardized coefficient is smaller than that of the other variables, suggesting that the local benchmark returns have less impact on emerging market PE returns than experience or the S&P 500 levels. It is furthermore surprising that both variables gain, respectively keep significance in this and the subsequent regressions, and do not cancel out each other. One could assume that controlling for the standard benchmark index performance (i.e., the S&P 500 index) is sufficient to explain emerging market PE returns.[3]

In specifications D and E, country-specific properties are included and therefore, country fixed effects are dropped to avoid multicollinearity. The first country-specific characteristic is the holding period-matching real GDP growth in D. This yields a decrease of the adjusted R^2 from 26.94% to 22.66%, compared to specification C. The regression reveals that the GDP growth's parameter coefficient is significant at the 1% level. Economic growth is the underlying source of value creation in the investee corporations and therefore strongly drives the transactions' returns. The impact of GDP growth is substantial. A 1% increase of the real GDP growth improves the average transaction performance by 2.5%.

Specification E adds the IPO proceeds in the country in the transaction's exit year to the set of independent variables. The coefficient for the proxy of exit market liquidity is significant at the 1% level and highlights its importance for the asset class.

Interpretation

The analyses reveal a strong effect of waiting on the performance of emerging market PE transactions. The positive parameter coefficient of the elapsed time since the pioneering investment in a host country is economically and statistically significant throughout all of the regressions and robust with respect to the effect of alternative benchmark indices, cross-currency rate changes, potential over-representation of sample countries, non-observation of the "really pioneering" investment, and to the fact that it cannot last forever. All these robustness checks and additional analyses are reported in Groh (2017). We may interpret this as evidence of learning benefits and of the improvement of the deal-making conditions. However, as measured by the key variable "Time since the first investment in the host country," these effects are not proprietary to a single general partner. All market participants benefit from gaining experience and improving deal-making conditions at the same time.

I aim to control for deal-making conditions, using benchmark index performance, GDP growth, exit market liquidity, and cost of debt at the same time of the transaction. However, I cannot completely cover the improving socio-economic conditions during the holding period over a particular deal. The reason is that the indicators for innovation capacity, the quality of educational systems, or for labor market rigidities are sticky over time and not correctly tracking gradual improvements. Furthermore, since these indicators are not available for many of the sample countries for the respective transaction periods, I use the 2009 observations of these indicators for all countries and treat them time-invariant. For this reason, I cannot completely disentangle learning effects from improving socio-economic conditions.

The analyses replicate previous findings, proving that several independent variables have the expected economic effects on PE performance. I confirm, for example, the impact of

GDP growth, exit market and socio-economic conditions on the value generation in emerging market PE transactions. I also show the importance of stock market valuations thereby differentiating a global standard (the S&P 500 index) and local benchmark indices. It is not unexpected that each of the two measures for opportunity cost has an individual and alternative contribution to explain PE returns. However, it is rather surprising that both measures remain significant in the regressions if kept simultaneously. This highlights the notion that emerging market PE valuations follow global benchmarks but underlie specific conditions at the same time, which are well expressed by superimposed local emerging stock market conditions.

A potential limitation of this research is caused by the dataset. It is possible that the sample of transactions does not include the "real first-movers." These might have been extraordinary successful transactions caused by privileged access to superior untapped deal flow by the pioneer. In general, I believe to have collected the most comprehensive and accurate sample of (early) emerging market PE transactions. Nevertheless, I cannot rule out that I do not precisely track entry and early followers in every particular country. However, the institutional investors who provided PPMs for this research are prominent players, especially for emerging PE markets. PPMs are marketing instruments for fundraising. If one of the general partners in the fundraising process had originated one of the potentially extraordinary pioneering transactions, we could expect it not to be missing in its PPM. Therefore, I would rather believe it better to miss some of the early less successful transactions in the sample instead of the popular ones. Since in general, the coverage of transactions improves over time, this potential sample selection bias works towards the results and not against them.

Discussion and conclusions

This chapter proposes a composite measure that determines the attractiveness of 125 countries to receive capital allocations from investors in the PE asset class. The composite measure is based on six main criteria: economic activity, depth of the capital markets, taxation, investor protection and corporate governance, the human and social environment, and entrepreneurial culture and deal opportunities. The six criteria are not directly observable. Therefore, we may use proxy variables to assess them for each country. As a result, we obtain a country ranking and provide detailed analyses on the strengths and weaknesses of the particular nations and information on the historic development of the criteria.

I find a general pattern if I compare country characteristics. There is considerable dispersion with respect to the six key drivers. Some countries attract investors with tax incentives. Many countries show strong entrepreneurial culture and deal opportunities. There is great dispersion in economic activity, especially with respect to emerging markets and in the human and social environment. However, the two key criteria, depth of capital markets, and investor protection and corporate governance, make the difference across the large sample. Common law countries dominate the others regarding these criteria. I observe that strong investor protection and corporate governance rules favor deep and liquid capital markets. These elicit the required professional community to secure deal flow and exit opportunities for PE funds, which affect a country's attractiveness for institutional investments in the PE asset class.

Emerging market PE provides interesting opportunities to investors. However, it is the discussed lack of balance of the key driving forces that renders emerging PE allocation decisions challenging. Exceptional growth opportunities come at the cost of disadvantageous conditions with respect to investors' protection, usually less liquid exit markets, lower innovation capacity, and higher perceived bribery and corruption.

This raises the question about the entry timing in an emerging PE market. There are several good reasons to justify early entry. Many emerging countries are large in terms of their population and have enormous economic catch up potential. This eventually results in high demand for risk capital and favorable economic growth. One may consider this an optimal environment for PE investors. However, sophisticated relationships between investors, general partners, and investee firms require certain legal standards, enforcement opportunities, and, briefly, a socio-economic development level which might not yet have been reached in many emerging countries. Additionally, in strongly growing economies deal flow of "ideal investees" with high agency cost of free cash flows and appropriate debt capacity might not emerge.

The analyses summarized here show that the returns to investors from emerging market PE transactions gradually increased over time. Investors would have therefore been better off if they had waited with their commitments. This finding is strong and robust with respect to a variety of possible concerns, which are comprehensively discussed in Groh (2017). We can interpret it as the result from learning and improving deal-making conditions. I control for deal-making conditions but the availability of data does not allow me to completely disentangle the two effects.

Early entry might still be beneficial for investors to build up relationships with local general partners, allowing further allocations and increased returns in the future. This is a widely used argument in practice. It is valid if the experience the general partners gain increases their success rates at later stages. However, the analyses also show that emerging PE market experience cannot be kept proprietary. All investors benefit from waiting, thus ruling out an important principle of gaining first-mover advantages.

Hence, I may conclude that there are probably interesting opportunities in emerging PE markets. However, there is no need to be among the first investors who invest in countries newly arising on the map of investable markets. Waiting pays because socio-economic conditions improve and market participants gain their experience. Nevertheless, positive effects from early moves might materialize in fund vintages subsequent to the coverage of the sample – when these emerging PE markets gain maturity. This conjecture should be addressed in additional research, when performance figures of more recent vintage years become available. Furthermore, in expansion of Meuleman and Wright (2011), it would be interesting to learn about the role of international syndication in emerging markets. Experience effects and learning could be improved with local partners. Foreignness and cultural distance can be bridged in international syndicates. Such syndicates would also open foreign product, service, labor, and exit markets to emerging country investees. Hence, syndication in emerging market PE deals could be even more beneficial than it is the case for mature markets. However, analyzing this challenging research question requires a comprehensive data set of both emerging and developed PE market syndicated transactions.

Notes

1 This composite measure is available at http://blog.iese.edu/vcpeindex/ and follows the principles discussed in Groh et al. (2010).

2 A detailed description of the data and all sources is available at http://blog.iese.edu/vcpeindex/.

3 This assumption and the impact of the benchmark indices is comprehensively discussed in Groh (2017).

References

Baughn, C. C., & Neupert, K. E. 2003. Culture and national conditions facilitating entrepreneurial start-ups. *Journal of International Entrepreneurship*, 1: 313–330.

Black, B., & Gilson, R. 1998. Venture capital and the structure of capital markets: Banks versus stock markets. *Journal of Financial Economics*, 47: 243–277.

Blanchard, O. J. 1997. The medium run. *Brookings Papers on Economic Activity*, 2: 89–158.

Bruce, D. 2000. Effects of the United States' tax system on transition into self-employment. *Labor Economics*. 7: 545–574.

Bruce D. 2002. Taxes and entrepreneurial endurance: Evidence from the self-employed. *National Tax Journal*. 55: 5–24.

Bruce, D., & Gurley, T. 2005. Taxes and entrepreneurial activity: An empirical investigation using longitudinal tax return data. *Small Business Research Summary*, 252: 1–51.

Cao, J. X., Cumming, D., Qian, M., & Wang, X. 2015. Creditor rights and LBOs. *Journal of Banking and Finance*, 50: 69–80.

Cetorelli, N., & Gambera, M. 2001. Banking market structure, financial dependence and growth: International evidence from industry data. *The Journal of Finance*, 56: 617–648.

Chemmanur, T. J., Hull, T. J., & Krishnan, K. 2016. Do local and international venture capitalists play well together? A study of international venture capital investments. *Journal of Business Venturing*, 31(5): 573–594.

Cullen, J. B., & Gordon, R. H. 2002. *Taxes and entrepreneurial activity: Theory and evidence for the U.S.* NBER Working Paper 9015.

Cumming, D., Fleming, G., & Schwienbacher, A. 2006. Legality and venture capital exits. *Journal of Corporate Finance*, 12: 214–245.

Cumming, D., & Johan, S. 2007. Regulatory harmonization and the development of private equity markets. *Journal of Banking and Finance*, 31: 3218–3250.

Cumming, D., Schmidt, D., & Walz, U. 2010. Legality and venture capital governance around the world. *Journal of Business Venturing*, 25(1): pp. 54–72.

Cumming, D., Siegel, D., & Wright, M. 2007. Private equity, leveraged buyouts and governance. *Journal of Corporate Finance*, 13: 439–460.

Cumming, D., & Walz, U. 2009. Private equity returns and disclosure around the world. *Journal of International Business Studies*, 41(4): 727–754.

Desai, M., Gompers, P., & Lerner, J. 2006. *Institutions and entrepreneurial firm dynamics: Evidence from Europe*. Havard NOM Research Paper 03-59.

Djankov, S., Ganser, T., McLiesh, C., Ramalho, R., & Schleifer, A. 2010. The effect of corporate taxes on investment and entrepreneurship. *American Economic Journal: Macroeconomics*, 2(3): 31–64.

Djankov, S., La Porta, R., Lopez-de-Silanes, F., & Shleifer, A. 2002. The regulation of entry. *Quarterly Journal of Economics*, 117: 1–37.

Djankov, S., La Porta, R., Lopez-de-Silanes, F., & Shleifer, A. 2003. Courts. *Quarterly Journal of Economics*, 118(2): 453–517.

Djankov, S., La Porta, R., Lopez-de-Silanes, F., & Shleifer, A. 2005. *The law and economics of self-dealing*. NBER Working Paper 11883.

Gilligan, J., & Wright, M. 2014. *Private equity demystified*, 3rd edition. London: ICAEW.

Glaeser, E. L., Johnson, S., & Shleifer, A. 2001. Coase vs. the coasians. *Quarterly Journal of Economics*, 116: 853–899.

Gompers, P., & Lerner, J. 1998. What drives venture fundraising? *Brooking Papers on Economic Activity, Microeconomics*, 1998: 149–192.

Gompers, P., & Lerner, J. 2000. Money chasing deals? The impact of funds inflows on the valuation of private equity investments. *Journal of Financial Economics*, 55: 281–325.

Green, P. G. 1998. Dimensions of perceived entrepreneurial obstacles. In P. Reynolds (Ed.), *Frontiers of entrepreneurship research*. Babson Park: Center for Entrepreneurial Studies, Babson College, 48–49.

Groh, A. P. 2017. *You needn't be the first investor there: First-mover disadvantages in emerging private equity markets*. Unpublished working paper. Available at SSRN: https://ssrn.com/abstract=2839215.

Groh, A. P., Liechtenstein, H., & Lieser, K. 2010. The European venture capital and private equity country attractiveness indices. *Journal of Corporate Finance*, 16: 205–224.

Hoskisson, R. E., Lorraine, E., Lau, C. M., & Wright, M. 2000. Strategy in emerging economies. *Academy of Management Journal*, 43: 249–267.
Hoskisson, R. E., Wright, M., Filatotchev, I., & Peng, M. W. 2013. Emerging multinationals from mid-range economies: The influence of institutions and factor markets. *Journal of Management Studies*, 50: 1295–1321.
Jeng, L. A., & Wells, P. C. 2000. The determinants of venture capital funding: Evidence across countries. *Journal of Corporate Finance*, 6: 241–289.
Jensen, M. C. 1989. Eclipse of the public corporation. *Harvard Business Review*, 67: 61–74.
Johnson, S. H., McMillan, J., & Woodruff, C. M. 1999. *Property rights, finance and entrepreneurship*. SSRN Working Paper 198409.
Kaplan, S. N., & Schoar, A. 2005. Private equity performance: Returns, persistence, and capital flows. *Journal of Finance*, 60: 1791–1823.
Kaplan, S. N., & Strömberg, P. 2009. Leveraged buyouts and private equity. *Journal of Economic Perspectives*, 23(1): 121–146.
Knack, S., & Keefer, P. 1995. Institutions and economic performance: Cross-country tests using alternative institutional measures. *Economics and Politics*, 7: 207–228.
Kortum, S., & Lerner, J. 2000. Assessing the contribution of venture capital to innovation. *Rand Journal Economics*, 31: 674–692.
La Porta, R., Lopez-de-Silanes, F., Shleifer, A., & Vishny, R. 1997. Legal determinants of external finance. *Journal of Finance*, 52: 1131–1150.
La Porta, R., Lopez-de-Silanes, F., Shleifer, A., & Vishny, R. 1998. Law and finance. *Journal of Political Economy*, 106: 1113–1155.
La Porta, R., Lopez-de-Silanes, F., Shleifer, A., & Vishny, R. 2002. Investor protection and corporate valuation. *Journal of Finance*, 57: 1147–1170.
Lazear, E. P. 1990. Job security provisions and employment. *Quarterly Journal of Economics*, 105: 699–726.
Lee, S. M., & Peterson, S. J. 2000. Culture, entrepreneurial orientation and global competitiveness. *Journal of World Business*, 35: 401–416.
Leeds, R., & Sunderland, J. 2003. Private equity in emerging markets: Rethinking the approach. *Journal of Applied Corporate Finance*, 15: 111–119.
Lerner, J., & Schoar, A. 2005. Does legal enforcement affect financial transactions? The contractual channel in private equity. *Quarterly Journal of Economics*, 120: 223–246.
Lieberman, M. B., & Montgomery, D. B. 1988. First-mover advantages. *Strategic Management Journal*, 9: 41–58.
Lockett, A., & Wright, M. 1999. The syndication of private equity: Evidence from the UK. *Venture Capital: An International Journal of Entrepreneurial Finance*, 1: 303–324.
Lopez de Silanes, F., Phalippou, L., & Gottschalg, O. 2015. Giants at the gate: Diseconomies of scales in private equity. *Journal of Financial and Quantitative Analysis*, 50(3): 377–411.
Manigart, S., De Waele, K., Wright, M., Robbie, K., Desbrières, P., Sapienza, H., & Beekman, A. 2002. Determinants of required return in venture capital investments: A five-country study. *Journal of Business Venturing*, 17: 291–312.
Manigart, S., Lockett, A., Meuleman, M., Wright, M., Landström, H., Bruining, H., Desbrières, P., Hommel, U. 2006. Venture capitalists' decision to syndicate. *Entrepreneurship Theory and Practice*, 30: 131–153.
Mauro, P. 1995. Corruption and growth. *Quarterly Journal of Economics*, 110: 681–712.
Megginson, W. 2004. Toward a global model of venture capital? *Journal of Applied Corporate Finance*, 16: 89–107.
Meuleman, M., Amess, K., Wright, M., & Scholes, L. 2009. Agency, strategic entrepreneurship, and the performance of private equity-backed buyouts. *Entrepreneurship Theory and Practice*, 33: 213–239.
Meuleman, M., & Wright, M. 2011. Cross-border private equity syndication: Institutional context and learning. *Journal of Business Venturing*, 26: 35–48.
Meuleman, M., Wright, M., Manigart, S., & Lockett, A. 2009. Private equity syndication: Agency costs, reputation and collaboration. *Journal of Business Finance and Accounting*, 36: 616–644.
Nahata, R., Hazarika, S., & Tandon, K. 2014. Success in global venture capital investing: Do institutional and cultural differences matter? *Journal of Financial and Quantitative Analysis*, 49(4): 1039–1070.

Nikoskelainen, E., & Wright, M. 2007. The impact of corporate governance mechanisms on value increase in leveraged buyouts. *Journal of Corporate Finance*, 13: 511–537.
Poterba, J. 1989. Venture capital and capital gains taxation. In L. Summers (Ed.), *Tax policy and the economy*. Cambridge, MA: MIT, 47–67.
Reddy, N., & Blenman, L. 2014. Leveraged buyout activity: A tale of developed and developing economies. *Journal of Financial Markets, Money and Institutions*, 2(2): 157–184.
Roe, M. 2006. *Political determinants of corporate governance*. Oxford, UK: Oxford University Press.
Romain, A., & van Pottelsberghe de la Potterie, B. 2004. *The determinants of venture capital: A panel analysis of 16 OECD countries*. Université Libre de Bruxelles Working Paper WP-CEB 04/0154.
Schertler, A. 2003. *Driving forces of venture capital investments in Europe: A dynamic panel data analysis*. European Integration, Financial Systems and Corporate Performance (EIFC) Working Paper No. 03-27, United Nations University.
Schmalensee, R. 1982. Differentiation advantages of pioneering brands. *American Economic Review*, 72(3): 349–365.
Spence, A. M. 1979. Investment strategy and growth in a new market. *Bell Journal of Economics*, 10(1): 1–19.
Spence, A. M. 1981. The learning curve and competition. *Bell Journal of Economics*, 12(1): 49–70.
Svensson, J. 1998. Investment, property rights and political instability: Theory and evidence. *European Economic Review*, 42: 1317–1341.
Wilken, P. H. 1979. *Entrepreneurship: A comparative and historical study*. Norwood, NJ: ABLEX.
Wright, M., Hoskisson, R. E., Busenitz, L. W., & Dial, J. 2000. Entrepreneurial growth through privatization: The upside of management buyouts. *Academy of Management Review*, 25: 591–601.
Wright, M., Hoskisson, R. E., Filatotchev, I., & Peng, M. W. 2005. Strategy research in emerging economies: Challenging the conventional wisdom. *Journal of Management Studies*, 42: 1–33.
Wright, M., & Lockett, A. 2003. The structure and management of alliances: Syndication in the venture capital industry. *Journal of Management Studies*, 40: 2073–2102.
Wright, M., Lockett, A., & Pruthi, S. 2002. Internationalization of western venture capitalists into emerging markets: Risk assessment and information in India. *Small Business Economics*, 19: 13–29.
Wright, M., Thompson, S., & Robbie, K. 1992. Venture capital and management-led, leveraged buyouts: A European perspective. *Journal of Business Venturing*, 7: 47–71.

17

PRIVATE EQUITY INVESTMENT IN ENTREPRENEURIAL COMPANIES

Selection & performance

Na Dai and Andrew McAlpine

Introduction

Venture capital funds (VCs) and buyout funds (PEs) typically have very different investment objectives, styles, and geographic target areas.[1] For instance, VCs often focus on small, young, and high-growth private firms, while most buyout funds focus on larger and more mature companies, among which many are already public companies. The early stage investment in Google by Kleiner Perkins Caufield & Byers is clearly a VC type investment, and the leveraged buyout of Hilton Hotels by Blackstone represents a typical buyout transaction. Over the years, however, there has been an increasing interest of PEs in entrepreneurial companies, which overlaps with investments that have traditionally been made by VCs. These raise several interesting questions: How do PEs select and invest in entrepreneurial companies? How do they perform? How do they interact with VCs? There is a large literature on VC and buyout activities, respectively. However, every little is studied about PE involvement in high growth entrepreneurial companies.

Using a sample of investments in entrepreneurial companies made between January 1990 and December 2014, we examine the characteristics of PE investments in entrepreneurial firms in comparison to VCs. Specifically, we look into what type of entrepreneurial companies PEs prefer to invest, the investment size, valuation, and the exit performance of the portfolio companies when a PE fund is involved.

Venture capital, buyout, and growth equity

Metrick and Yasuda (2011: 3) define a venture capitalist (VC) as follows:

- A VC is a financial intermediary, meaning that it takes investors' capital and invests it directly in portfolio companies.
- A VC invests only in private companies.
- A VC takes an active role in monitoring and helping the companies in its portfolio.

- A VC's primary goal is to maximize the financial return by exiting through a sale or IPO.
- A VC invests to fund the internal growth of companies.

This definition is quite broad, as the first four criteria also apply to buyout funds. While both VC and buyout funds are typically organized as limited partnerships, invest in illiquid and high-risk assets, play active roles in monitoring and advising, and exit through IPO or a sale, they are quite different from each other in terms of scale, the types of companies they invest, their investment styles, and capital structure.

The first consideration is scale. VC firms, which invest in small and young start-up companies requiring intensive active involvement, raise small funds, typically less than $1 billion. According to National Venture Capital Association (NVCA) 2016 yearbook, the average VC fund size is $135 million. Buyout firms, on the other hand, often raise funds of at least $1 billion and would find it inefficient to provide the intense oversight required by early-stage companies and to deal with many small companies.

The second difference is the type of companies VCs and buyout funds traditionally invest in. VCs primarily invest in start-up companies which are characterized by significant intangible assets, a high level of information asymmetry and uncertainty, and years of negative earnings and cash flow. Buyout funds traditionally invest in troubled companies that need to undergo restructurings. Most of these companies are later-stage mature companies. Although both types of companies represent high-risk, potentially high-reward investments, the expertise needed to help the company succeed is clearly different.

VCs and buyout funds are also different in terms of their investment styles. While VCs typically only obtain minority ownership of their portfolio companies, buyout funds almost always purchase majority ownership of their portfolio companies. The majority of VCs are attracted to technology related industries. On the other hand, buyout funds invest across all industries. VCs rarely use debt. In contrast, buyout funds always use a combination of equity and debt in their investment. Returns by buyout funds are heavily dependent on financial leverage.

Since the late 1990s, there has been a noticeable emergence of so-called growth equity (NVCA, 2016). As defined by NVCA, growth equity investments are made in companies that have rapidly growing revenues, positive cash flow, and are founder-owned or managed. Investors typically obtain minority ownership and do not use or only use light leverage. The deal stage of growth equity investment includes expansion, later stage, acquisition for expansion, acquisition, LBO, mezzanine, MBO, recap or turnaround, secondary buyout, and secondary purchase. As the investment time horizon for venture-backed companies has grown, so too has the need for continued financing of these emerging growth companies in the longer run-up to their exits. In 2015, growth equity investments totaled $20.6 billion across 463 deals with the industry mix being very similar to that of VCs and reaching a 15-year high (NVCA, 2016). Buyout funds are increasingly interested in investing in these founder-owned private companies with high growth potential (Evans, 2013).

There is a large body of literature on VC and buyouts (see the review article by Cumming et al., 2007), respectively. However, very few studies focus on the growth equity or the buyout funds' side interest in entrepreneurial firms. While many firms in our sample fall into the growth equity investment category, we do not restrict our study to growth equity only. In addition to the growth equity space, we notice buyout funds are also actively involved in early-stage investments, although with a much smaller weight.[2] Our focus in this chapter is PE participation in the full spectrum of the entrepreneurial world. While the differences between investments traditionally made by PEs and VCs are well documented, the characteristics and performance of PE investment in entrepreneurial firms have been less studied. We attempt to fill this void and identify some of those differences, with a focus on investment size, company valuation, and exit performance.

Empirical analysis

Data and sample

We obtained data on US PE and VC investments in entrepreneurial companies between 1990 and 2014 from Thompson Financial's VentureXpert. We categorized buyout funds, generalist PE funds, and other PE funds as the PE group. For the VC group, we only keep independent partnership VC funds for a "like-for-like" comparison. Our sample consisted of 76,465 investment rounds involving 29,752 investee companies. For each observation, we obtained portfolio company name, industry, development stage at a specific investment round, investor fund name, investor fund type (PE or VC), date of the investment round, round size, number of investors participating, and equity amount invested by the investor, among others.

Figure 17.1 documents the total amount of capital and number of portfolio companies invested by the PE group over the 25-year period, in comparison to the VC group. PE funds invested about $68 billion in entrepreneurial firms at different development stages, which is about 16% of the total amount invested by the VC funds. Over 6,000 entrepreneurial companies received funding from PE funds, representing 22% of the sample.

As shown in Figure 17.2 and Table 17.1, the trend of PE investment in entrepreneurial companies is very much consistent with the overall pattern of VC investment. The peak year was 2000 when the PE group invested about $10 billion in entrepreneurial companies. It declined substantially in the years that followed and has been quite stable at around $2–3 billion in recent years.

Summary statistics

In Table 17.2, we categorize each financing round into those with PE participation and those without PE participation. PE participation is defined as at least one PE fund investing in

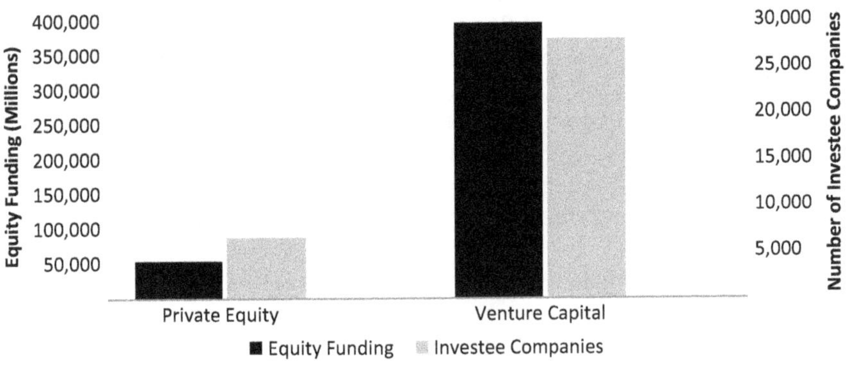

Figure 17.1 Funding by investor type

Source: Authors, adapted from Thomson Financial VentureXpert.

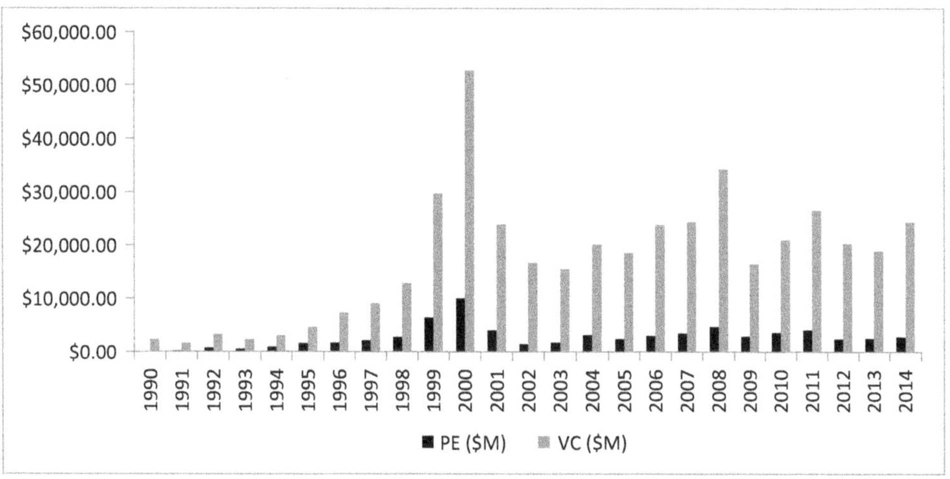

Figure 17.2 Funding by year, 1990–2014

Source: Authors, adapted from Thomson Financial VentureXpert.

Table 17.1 Year distribution of PE investment in growth companies, 1990–2014

Year	*PE ($m)*	*VC ($m)*	*Total ($m)*
1990	119.72	2,300.48	2,404.70
1991	149.76	1,679.84	1,829.80
1992	677.79	3,267.50	3,371.90
1993	467.89	2,314.74	2,751.40
1994	817.82	3,028.53	3,679.80
1995	1,469.11	4,655.84	5,629.60
1996	1,640.41	7,388.94	8,683.40
1997	2,101.61	9,119.43	11,119.70
1998	2,667.54	12,890.99	15,099.50
1999	6,446.19	29,691.00	33,076.80
2000	9,977.17	52,712.39	59,976.20
2001	3,933.23	23,860.28	27,064.30
2002	1,387.76	16,740.58	16,910.00
2003	1,677.52	15,486.19	16,069.40
2004	3,060.03	20,117.22	20,072.10
2005	2,314.45	18,622.82	20,093.40
2006	2,925.37	23,799.55	23,573.60
2007	3,414.83	24,349.34	26,046.70
2008	4,586.34	34,150.18	24,909.90
2009	2,842.16	16,449.27	17,437.00
2010	3,569.89	20,980.29	20,184.50
2011	4,052.78	26,482.80	24,628.40
2012	2,297.25	20,347.96	21,194.40
2013	2,440.94	18,952.74	20,197.10
2014	2,754.77	24,312.63	24,455.30
Total	67,792.33	433,701.53	450,458.90

a specific round. Out of the 76,465 financing rounds from 1990–2014, we find PE funds participated in 10,544 rounds, or 13.8% of all financing rounds.

The comparison between rounds with PE participation and those without shows that PE funds exhibit some distinct investment preferences and styles. First, PE funds prefer expansion and later-stage investments. Almost 70% of the financing rounds with PE participation are associated with expansion stage (47%) and later-stage (22%) ventures, 20% more than the rounds without PE participation. Second, PE funds are more likely to invest in non-high-tech firms than VC funds. While only 13% of rounds without PE participation are non-high-tech ventures, about 23% of rounds with PE participation are associated with non-high-tech ventures. Third, PE funds are more willing to invest in areas outside of California. About 67% of rounds with PE participation are not located in California, in comparison to 59% of rounds without PE participation. Fourth, rounds with PE participation often involve more investors and the round size is significantly larger. The mean number of investors of rounds with PE participation is three and the average round size is $16 million. In contrast, the mean number of investors of rounds without PE participation is two and the average round size is $8 million. Fifth, rounds with PE participation have significantly higher valuations. The average valuation for rounds with PE participation is $94 million while it is $57 million for rounds without PE participation.[3]

We also observe significant differences in the probability of exits. Firms with PE investment appear to be more likely to exit through an IPO, but less likely to exit through a M&A.

Table 17.2 Characteristics of PE investments in growth companies

Panel A: Rounds with PE participation vs. rounds without PE participation

	With PE participation	*Without PE participation*	*p-value*
N of observations	10,544	65,921	
Company stage			
Seed-stage	6.74%	9.98%	0.000***
Early-stage	20.99%	28.68%	0.000***
Expansion-stage	47.31%	33.09%	0.000***
Later-stage	22.29%	17.23%	0.000***
Other	2.67%	11.02%	0.000***
Industry			
Computer-related	39.30%	45.01%	0.000***
Biotechnology	5.45%	8.69%	0.000***
Communications and media	16.12%	13.77%	0.000***
Medical/health/life science	9.71%	12.90%	0.000***
Semiconductors	5.97%	6.93%	0.000***
Non-high-tech	23.43%	12.70%	0.000***
California	32.70%	40.50%	0.000***
Round size ($m)	15.96	8.30	0.000***
N of investors	2.77	2.06	0.000***
Valuation ($m)[4]	94.20	57.36	0.000***
IPO exit	6.88%	5.46%	0.000***
M&A exit	19.83%	21.12%	0.003***
Total successful exit	26.72%	26.58%	0.774***

(*Continued*)

Table 17.2 (Continued)

Panel B: Rounds with PE as the lead investor vs. rounds with VC as the lead investor

	PE lead investor	*VC lead investor*	*p-value*
N of observations	6,469	69,996	
Company stage			
Seed-stage	7.00%	9.77%	0.000***
Early-stage	20.25%	28.30%	0.000***
Expansion-stage	48.76%	33.78%	0.000***
Later-stage	19.89%	17.74%	0.000***
Other	4.10%	10.41%	0.000***
Industry			
Computer-related	35.97%	44.99%	0.000***
Biotechnology	3.86%	8.65%	0.000***
Communications and media	14.96%	14.02%	0.000***
Medical/health/life science	8.95%	12.78%	0.000***
Semiconductors	4.95%	6.97%	0.000***
Non-high-tech	31.3%	12.60%	0.000***
California	27.18%	40.53%	0.000***
Round size ($m)	14.91	8.84	0.000***
N of Investors	1.92	2.18	0.000***
Valuation ($m)[5]	90.92	61.20	0.000***
IPO exit	6.92%	5.63%	0.336***
M&A exit	16.71%	21.34%	0.003***
Total successful exit	22.63%	26.97%	0.000***

Our sample consists of 76,465 financing rounds in high growth companies made by PE funds and VC funds between 1990 and 2014. The table compares all financing rounds that include PE participation to rounds in which there is no PE participation. Investment characteristics include the number of investee companies, company stage, company industry, average investment round size, average number of investors, and exits through IPO and trade sales. Significance is marked with *** at 1%.

If we consider both IPO and M&A as successful exits, the overall probability of successful exits is similar among firms with PE investments and those without.

In 6,469 financing rounds, PE funds take the role as the lead investor. We define lead investor has the one that has invested the largest amount of equity capital in a specific financing round. In Table 17.2 Panel B, we further compare rounds where PE funds are the lead investor to those where VC funds are the lead investor. Generally speaking, the pattern is very similar to what we find in Panel A with two exceptions. First, the number of investors is less when the PE fund is the lead investor. Second, the probability of IPO exit of rounds led by PE funds is not different from, while the total successful exit rate is significantly lower than, those where VC funds are the lead investor.

Regression analysis

In this section, we examine three aspects of PE investments in entrepreneurial firms in the multivariate setting, investment size, valuation, and the exit performance, respectively.

Investment size and valuation

In analyzing round size and company valuations of PE investments, four linear regressions are run at the investment round level. *Ln (Round size)* and *Ln (Valuation)* are our dependent variables. The key independent variable of interest includes *With PE* dummy, which is equal to one if at least one PE fund participates in a specific round, and zero otherwise, and the *PE Lead* dummy, which is equal to one if a PE fund is the lead investor of a specific round, and zero otherwise. In all specifications, we control for company development stage at the time of financing, company industry, company geographic location, the number of investors, and the year fixed effect. The detailed definitions of the key variables are provided in Appendix A.

Table 17.3 shows the results pertaining to round size and company valuation in financing rounds with PEs participation. In Panel A, the key variable of interest is *With PE* which is set equal to 1 if at least one PE participates the investment round and 0 otherwise. In Panel

Table 17.3 Regression analysis: round size and valuation

Panel A: PE participation

	LnValuation	*LnRoundSize*
With PE	***0.4595*** (0.0000)***	***0.2666*** (0.0000)***
Ln(N investors)	1.0239*** (0.0000)	0.4110*** (0.0000)
Seed-stage	−0.6285*** (0.0000)	−1.8040*** (0.0000)
Early-stage	−0.2595*** (0.0000)	−1.2516*** (0.0000)
Expansion-stage	−0.0044 (0.8150)	−0.4748*** (0.0000)
Later-stage	−0.0274 (0.1820)	−0.1652*** (0.0000)
Biotechnology	0.0203 (0.3670)	0.1255*** (0.0000)
Computer-related	−0.1855*** (0.0000)	−0.0265 (0.3370)
Communications/media	−0.0318 (0.1010)	0.2272*** (0.0000)
Medical/health/life science	−0.1355*** (0.0000)	−0.0723** (0.0240)
Semiconductors	−0.1670*** (0.0000)	0.1326*** (0.0000)
California	0.2259*** (0.0000)	0.1489*** (0.0000)
Constant	−0.7188 (0.0000)	2.6930 (0.0000)
Year fixed effect	Yes	Yes
N of observations	76,162	17,902
Adj R-squared	0.2985	0.3952

Panel B: PE funds as the lead investor

	LnRoundSize	*LnValuation*
PE lead	***0.5584*** (0.0000)***	***0.3289*** (0.0000)***
Ln(N investors)	1.0764*** (0.0000)	0.4487*** (0.0000)
Seed-stage	−0.6216*** (0.0000)	−1.7987*** (0.0000)
Early-stage	−0.2543*** (0.0000)	−1.2461*** (0.0000)
Expansion-stage	0.0022 (0.9070)	−0.4668*** (0.0000)
Later-stage	−0.0194 (0.3430)	−0.1573*** (0.0000)
Biotechnology	0.0219 (0.3310)	0.1242*** (0.0000)
Computer-related	−0.1815*** (0.0000)	−0.0282 (0.3090)

(*Continued*)

Table 17.3 (Continued)

	LnRoundSize	*LnValuation*
Communications/media	−0.0282 (0.1460)	0.2256*** (0.0000)
Medical health/life science	−0.1355*** (0.0000)	−0.0771** (0.0160)
Semiconductors	−0.1629*** (0.0000)	0.1281*** (0.0010)
California	0.2240*** (0.0000)	0.1457*** (0.0000)
Constant	−0.7494*** (0.0000)	2.6599*** (0.0000)
Year fixed effect	Yes	Yes
N of observations	76,162	17,902
Adj R-squared	0.2984	0.3944

B, the key variable of interest is *PE Lead*, which is set equal to 1 if a PE is the lead investor of a specific investment round and 0 otherwise. In each specification we control for company stage, company industry, number of investors, and investment year. Variable definitions can be found in Appendix A. Standard errors are reported under the coefficients. Significance is marked with *** at 1%.

The empirical results are reported in Table 17.3. We find that PE participation is significantly and positively correlated with round size and valuation, consistent with the univariate test. Specifically, the coefficient of *With PE* in the regression of *LnRoundSize* is 0.4595, significant at the 1% level. The coefficient of *With PE* in the regression of *LnValuation* is 0.2666, also significant at the 1% level. The results are also economically significant. On average, round size is approximately $1.58 million larger and the valuation is $1.31 million higher with PE participation.

Panel B of Table 17.3 considers the case where PE funds are the lead investor. We find *PE Lead* is also significantly and positively correlated with round size and valuation. Specifically, the coefficients of *PE Lead* in the regression of *LnRoundSize* is 0.5584, and 0.3289 in the regression of *LnValuation*. Both are significant at the 1% level. They are also economically significant. On average, round size is approximately $1.75 million larger and the valuation is $1.39 million higher when PE funds lead the financing round.

Exit performance

In this section, we analyze whether PE participation in high growth companies makes a difference in terms of companies' exit performance. Specifically, we consider the probability of IPO and M&A, and the probability of IPO alone. In a subsample of companies that have successfully exited, we further analyze PE funds' preference for IPO vs. M&A. Similar to the preceding section, *With PE* and *PE Lead* are the independent variables of interest. In all regressions, we further control for company development stage at the time of financing, company industry, company geographic location, the number of investors, and the year fixed effect.

Table 17.4 shows results of probit regressions pertaining to company exits when PEs participate. In Panel A, the key variable of interest is *With PE* which is set equal to 1 if at least one PE participates in the investment round and 0 otherwise. In Panel B, the key variable of interest is *PE Lead* which is set equal to 1 if a PE is the lead investor of a specific investment round and 0 otherwise. In each specification we control for company stage, company industry, number of investors, and investment year. Variable definitions can be found in Appendix A. Standard errors are reported under the coefficients. Significance is marked with *** at 1%.

The empirical results are reported in Table 17.4. Regardless of whether PE funds simply participate in a round or lead the round, we find a significantly lower probability of successful exits when PE is involved. However, the probability of a IPO is significantly higher when PE is involved. Specifically, when a PE is involved (participates or as lead), the probability of successful exits is 2.3–3.4% lower, while the probability of an IPO is about 1% higher. In a further analysis with the subsample of companies that have successfully exited, we find that when PE is involved, the probability of an IPO is 5–7% higher. These results suggest that PE investors do not appear to add more value to portfolio companies (lower successful

Table 17.4 Regression analysis: exit performance

Panel A: PE participation

	Probability of successful exits	*Probability of IPOs*	
	Full sample	*Full sample*	*Subsample*
With PE	***−0.0726*** (0.0152)***	***0.0825*** (0.0232)***	***0.1752*** (0.0317)***
Ln(N investors)	0.2657*** (0.0128)	0.2322*** (0.0194)	0.0921*** (0.0261)
Seed-stage	0.0262 (0.0238)	−0.4800*** (0.0361)	−0.8479*** (0.0522)
Early-stage	0.0943*** (0.0199)	−0.3958*** (0.0294)	−0.7429*** (0.0436)
Expansion-stage	0.1861*** (0.0193)	−0.1668*** (0.0272)	−0.4770*** (0.0409)
Later-stage	0.3046*** (0.0211)	0.0743** (0.0296)	−0.2219*** (0.0435)
Biotechnology	0.5440*** (0.0237)	0.9599*** (0.0343)	0.8535*** (0.0514)
Computer-related	0.5474*** (0.0177)	0.2396*** (0.0296)	−0.1616*** (0.0429)
Communications/media	0.5210*** (0.0204)	0.3858*** (0.0330)	0.0600 (0.0473)
Medical/health/l ife science	0.3857*** (0.0214)	0.4676*** (0.0334)	0.2182*** (0.0487)
Semiconductors	0.4924*** (0.0246)	0.3593*** (0.0400)	0.0038 (0.0553)
California	0.0620*** (0.0104)	0.2027*** (0.0165)	0.2539*** (0.0223)
Constant	−1.3321*** (0.0406)	−1.5725*** (0.0531)	0.0926 (0.0794)
Year fixed effect	Yes	Yes	Yes
N of observations	76,465	76,465	20,341
Pseudo R-squared	0.0656	0.1448	0.1884

Panel B: PE fund as lead investor

	Probability of successful exits	*Probability of IPOs*	
	Full sample	*Full sample*	*Subsample*
PE lead	***−0.1110*** (0.0191)***	***0.0847*** (0.0291)***	***0.2211*** (0.0407)***
Ln(N investors)	0.2524*** (0.0126)	0.2472*** (0.0191)	0.1257*** (0.0255)
Seed-stage	0.0260 (0.0238)	−0.4775*** (0.0361)	−0.8445*** (0.0522)

(*Continued*)

Table 17.4 (Continued)

	Probability of successful exits	*Probability of IPOs*	
	Full sample	*Full sample*	*Subsample*
Early-stage	0.0945*** (0.0199)	−0.3937*** (0.0294)	−0.7400*** (0.0435)
Expansion-stage	0.1870*** (0.0193)	−0.1637*** (0.0272)	−0.4741*** (0.0408)
Later-stage	0.3053*** (0.0211)	0.0776*** (0.0296)	−0.2180*** (0.0435)
Biotechnology	0.5413*** (0.0237)	0.9584*** (0.0343)	0.8521*** (0.0514)
Computer-related	0.5445*** (0.0177)	0.2385*** (0.0296)	−0.1630*** (0.0429)
Communications/media	0.5187*** (0.0204)	0.3846*** (0.0330)	0.0573 (0.0472)
Medical/health/ life science	0.3835*** (0.0214)	0.4657*** (0.0334)	0.2161*** (0.0487)
Semiconductors	0.4896*** (0.0246)	0.3579*** (0.0400)	0.0006 (0.0553)
California	0.0617*** (0.0104)	0.2020*** (0.0165)	0.2540*** (0.0223)
Constant	−1.3164*** (0.0406)	−1.5883*** (0.0531)	0.0556 (0.0793)
Year fixed effect	Yes	Yes	Yes
N of observations	76,465	76,465	20,341
Pseudo R-squared	0.0657	0.1447	0.1883

rates); however, PE investors seem to prefer IPO exits over M&A exits. Please note, in this chapter, we do not deal econometrically with the potential endogeneity problem. There is a possibility that PE investors choose to invest in companies with a higher probability of going public.

Discussion and conclusion

While PEs have historically had very different investment strategies and styles from VCs, recent trends show that more and more PEs are becoming interested in investing in entrepreneurial companies. While past literature has studied the differences in investments by buyout funds and VC funds separately, little academic research has been done on PE investments in the growth equity space. This chapter shows some characteristics of PE investments, as well as their performance, in what has traditionally been VC territory.

This chapter analyzed 76,465 PE and VC investment rounds in entrepreneurial companies between 1990 and 2014. We showed that investment round size as well as company valuation at the time of the investment are positively correlated with PE participation. These relationships are even stronger when the PE fund that participates acts as the lead investor. With regards to the exit performance, we find successful exit (either IPO or M&A) is less likely when a PE participates or leads, but companies are more likely to exit through an IPO as opposed to a trade sale when PE participation is present.

PE's active participation in financing young and high-growth entrepreneurial firms has some important implications for the dynamic of the VC industry. First of all, given that PE funds in general are larger than VC funds and are willing to invest larger rounds of financing, entrepreneurial firms will have better access to private capital, especially at later stages. One direct consequence is that they can choose to stay private for longer if the exit window is not promising. This is exactly what the industry has been observing over recent years.

Second, given the high level of dry power in the PE sector in recent years, the influx of PE capital in the VC territory will further boost the valuations of private firms. The emergence of the so-called "unicorns" could be a side effect of the influx of these non-traditional VC funds.

Appendix A: Variable definitions

Variables	*Definitions*
Ln (Round Size)	The natural logarithm of total dollar amount for a financing round.
Ln (Valuation)	The natural log of the company dollar valuation for a financing round.
With PE	A variable which is equal to 1 if at least one private equity fund participates in the financing round, and 0 otherwise.
PE Lead	A variable which is equal to 1 if the lead investor is a private equity fund, and 0 otherwise.
Ln (# of investors)	The natural logarithm of the number of investor's in a round of financing.
PE-VC Syndication	A variable which is equal to 1 if both a private equity and venture capital fund participate in the financing round, and 0 otherwise.
Seed-stage	A dummy variable which is equal to 1 if the financing occurs within a company currently in seed stage, and 0 otherwise.
Early-stage	A dummy variable which is equal to 1 if the financing occurs within a company currently in early stage, and 0 otherwise.
Expansion-stage	A dummy variable which is equal to 1 if the financing occurs within a company currently in expansion stage, and 0 otherwise.
Later-stage	A dummy variable which is equal to 1 if the financing occurs within a company currently in later stage, and 0 otherwise.
Biotechnology	A dummy variable which is equal to 1 if the company operates in the biotechnology industry, and 0 otherwise.
Computer-related	A dummy variable which is equal to 1 if the company operates in the computer-related industry, and 0 otherwise.
Communications and Media	A dummy variable which is equal to 1 if the company operates in the communications or media industry, and 0 otherwise.
Medical/Health/Life Science	A dummy variable which is equal to 1 if the company operates in the medical, health, or life science industry, and 0 otherwise.
Semiconductors	A dummy variable which is equal to 1 if the company operates in the semiconductor industry, and 0 otherwise.
California	A dummy variable which is equal to 1 if the company being financed is located in California, and 0 otherwise.

Notes

1 Throughout this chapter, we use PE and buyout interchangeably.
2 We discuss this in detail in the data section.
3 The number of observations for valuation is much smaller. We have valuation data for 17,902 financing rounds, among which 3,006 rounds have PE participation, and 14,896 rounds do not.
4 The number of observations for valuation is much smaller. We have valuation data for 17,902 financing rounds, among which 3,006 rounds have PE participation, and 14,896 rounds do not.
5 The number of observations for valuation is much smaller. We have valuation data for 17,902 financing rounds, among which 1,414 rounds are led by PE funds and the rest by VC funds.

References

Cumming, D., Siegel, D., & Wright, M. 2007. Private equity, leveraged buyouts and governance. *Journal of Corporate Finance*, 13: 439–460.
Evans, B. 2013. As exit runways grow, so does growth equity. *PE Hub*. New York.
Metrick, A., & Yasuda, A. 2011. *Venture capital and the finance of innovation, 2nd edition*. New York: Wiley.
National Venture Capital Association Yearbook. 2016. Washington, DC: NVCA.

18

HEDGE FUNDS AND PRIVATE EQUITY

Features, diversity, and regulations

Douglas Cumming and Geoffrey Wood

Introduction

Alternative investors have become much more prominent in the global financial ecosystem. Four of the most prominent categories include private equity (PE), hedge funds, sovereign wealth funds, and venture capital. Although none has escaped controversy, the former two have come under particular scrutiny for their possible effects on target firms. PE explicitly seeks to change how the firm is run in terms of scale and scope of operations, extent of assets, work and employment relations, and/or relative debt leverage; interventions form the basis of returns. While hedge funds may similarly promote new managerial strategies, they may also adopt a more hands-off approach, basing returns on the time period of retention of shares; at the same time, aggressive and short-term buying and selling of shares may impact on the firm's relative well-being and on managerial behavior.

Hedge funds represent an alternative investment vehicle that seeks to secure superior returns; although they have historically engaged in traditional hedging strategies, making use of offsetting investments that seek to compensate for adverse market trends and take advantage of short-term price fluctuations, their main aim is returns, rather than commitment to a particular methodology. Given this, they can invest in almost anything, using a big range of financial instruments, but the primary focus on this review is on when they buy shares in listed firms.

Hedge funds differ from other activist investors in that there is a preference to target more profitable firms (Klein & Zur, 2009). Hedge funds typically increase their relative ownership through the use of debt, derivatives, and options (Clifford, 2008). Unlike PE, they do not usually seek to change quotidian managerial practice, and concentrate on broad questions of corporate governance and control, focusing in on cash flow agency cost issues, rather than longer-term investment strategies (Kahan & Rock, 2007; Klein & Zur, 2009). They are generally subject to considerably less regulation than mutual funds, and investing in them is not open to the general public (Kahan & Rock, 2007). Activist hedge funds are distinct in that not only do they seek to have a closer and more immediate impact on target firms, but they are also associated with longer notification periods for withdrawals and lock-up periods (Clifford, 2008). Activist hedge funds are particularly focused on short-term returns; more controversial is whether such short term is damaging to the long-term good of corporates or not (Kahan & Rock, 2007). As with private equity, they are most commonly limited partnerships, with relatively high investment criteria, and with a specified lock-up time frame.

PE represents limited partnerships, raising capital for closed-end funds, with clear strategies for investment (Cumming et al., 2015). PE typically consists of a limited partnership, which seeks to target firms believed to have the potential for releasing greater amounts of value to owners; following takeover, they impose new managerial strategies aimed at achieving this. Although typical transactions involve a complete takeover and delisting of the firm in order to attain this, there are many instances of PE taking part ownership of a firm, with the aim of promoting specific patterns of managerial practice. PE takeovers usually involve relatively high amounts of debt leverage, and often have an envisaged limited period of ownership; thereafter the target firm is sold on.

In this chapter, we review key strands of the literature on both hedge funds and PE funds, and draw out the implications for theory. We begin by documenting the relative research interest in hedge funds and PE funds by reference to data from Google Scholar. Thereafter, we explain differences in hedge funds and PE funds in respect of performance, activism, and diversification. Finally, we offer some insights into regulation of both hedge funds and PE funds, and to the development of theory.

Research interest in hedge funds and PE funds

Figure 18.1 presents Google Scholar trends data from 2000 to 2017 on articles that discuss hedge funds, PE, and both hedge funds and PE.

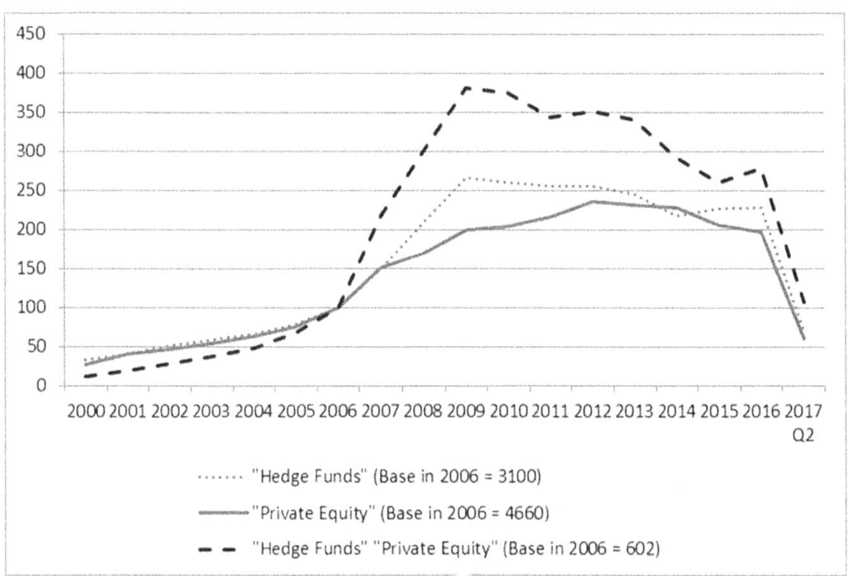

Figure 18.1 Google Scholar hits to hedge funds and PE

This figure reports Google Scholar hits to "hedge funds" and "private equity," and "hedge funds" "private equity," over the years 2000-2017(Q2). The hits are indexed to 2006 at 100. The number of hits in 2006 for each search term is indicated in the legend.
Source: Google Scholar.

Early research on hedge funds was facilitated by the availability of data from data vendors including TASS and CISDM (Agarwal et al., 2015). However, much of the hedge fund literature focuses on a limited range of topics, centering on rates of return, with some studies exploring fund manager skill, differences in outcomes according to type of fund, their effects on asset prices, and the risks posed to both hedge fund investors and the financial system at large (Ibid.). In contrast, the contradictory findings on work on hedge fund performance represent to a large extent differences in methodological approaches (c.f. Kat & Brooks, 2001; Fung & Hsieh, 2004; Baquero et al., 2005).

There is a considerable, but very heterogeneous literature on PE. In part, this diversity reflects differences in the data individual researchers have been able secure on the latter, but also in terms of definitions (some scholars conflate PE with venture capital), scope, and underlying theoretical assumptions.

Controversies in performance: hedge funds versus PE funds

Hedge funds

There has been a long-standing strand of literature that casts doubt on whether hedge funds perform any better than other investment vehicles, and, indeed, suggests that this is often worse. It has also been argued that there is little evidence that hedge fund managers exhibit exceptional skill. As early as 1999, Brown et al. (1999) evaluated the performance of the offshore fund industry, and found that funds did not always match the stock market, were characterized by high levels of attrition, and that there was little sign of differential managerial skill. A further issue is the relative reliability of voluntary disclosures. Patton et al. (2015) find that hedge funds regularly revise their historical returns; such corrections do not appear to be simply the correction of plausible errors. Moreover, underperforming funds tend to be the worst offenders, regularly making downward adjustments to past performance data. This might suggest the need for closer regulatory scrutiny in this area.

In contrast, Bebchuk et al. (2015) concluded that, even over a five-year time period, hedge funds did not leave firms worse off; again early increases in stock price at the time of the takeover tended to persist, as did stock performance.

Similarly, Brav et al. (2008) argue that when they adopt an activist approach, hedge funds drive higher rates in CEO turnover, operating performance, and returns to shareholders. They further argue that this reflects the extent to which hedge funds represent an effective device for better monitoring of managers and closer alignment with shareholder value agendas. Although they suggest that this effect persists one year after hedge fund intervention, it could be argued that, over a longer period of time, these effects may reverse themselves and leave the target organization worse off.

Edwards and Caglayan (2001) concluded that there was a great deal of heterogeneity in hedge fund performance, and that there was a similar degree of persistence in the track record between superior and poorly performing funds; much of this diversity depends on the investment style of fund managers. However, they argue that fund manager incentive fees represent an important predictor of performance, and that higher incentives result in superior performance in terms of returns; however, it could be argued that this may be detrimental to the medium- to long-term well-being of target organizations.

The findings of Edwards and Caglayan (2001) are echoed by Agarwal et al. (2009), who argue that greater fund managerial incentives – including high water mark provisions, higher fund manager ownership levels, and incentive fee contracts – drive better results, rather than incentive fee percentage rates per se. They suggest that when fund managers have higher discretion, they are likely to be more effective (Ibid.). However, there are three limitations to this argument. The first, would be to argue that it is inconsistent to suggest that hedge funds are effective as they help solve agency issues, when at the same time arguing for modes of fund management that might open up a new set of agency problems that weaken the rights and control of investors. The second is that a wider range of incentives may encourage excessive risk-taking. The third is the question of causality; Liang (2001) argues that poor performing funds compensate by charging lower incentive fees, rather than vice versa. Lim et al. (2015) note that in the case of the average hedge fund, indirect incentives were relatively high, but that this was particularly the case in the instance of more scalable, younger funds.

Fung et al. (2015) found that multiproduct hedge funds underperformed single-product hedge funds, but were able to secure higher fee revenues. Hedge fund firms that were able to launch follow-up funds were also able to attract greater levels of investment, and set tougher terms of redemption. This has meant that, despite sub-optimal performance, multiproduct hedge fund firms are becoming increasingly dominant in the hedge fund ecosystem.

Kat and Brooks (2001) found that hedge fund indexes exhibit unusually pronounced levels of kurtosis, and that, when this is taken into account, their properties are much less attractive than a simple analysis in mean variance terms would suggest. How investors approach hedge funds represents very much a product of the tools and techniques they use to evaluate their performance (Ibid.).

There appears to a significant political dimension to hedge fund performance. Gao and Huang (2016) found that a number of US-based hedge funds could gain informational advantages flowing from close ties to lobbyists. This enabled advance information of likely policy developments; hedge funds that were politically well connected exhibited superior performance. While the passing on of political information may benefit a wide range of players in the financial services industry, hedge funds appear particularly well placed to capitalize on such information.

PE funds

The theory and evidence from PE indicates that PE investors may add value through sitting on boards of directors, offering strategic, operating, and human resource advice, and enabling networks of contacts that improve firm performance (Kaplan & Schoar, 2005; Jelic & Wright, 2011). There is not only substantial value added, but also superior selection abilities of PE fund managers through many weeks of due diligence (Cumming & Zambelli, 2017). In other words, there are both selection and value-added effects, and empirical studies in PE control for selection effects when assessing the value of the advice provided to investee firms.

In addition to the varying effects of different fund types, an important variation in performance outcomes may reflect how PE fund managers report the performance of deals not yet sold to institutional investors. That is, PE investors typically invest two to seven years prior to selling their investments as IPOs, acquisitions, or secondary sales. Early work presumed that the yet-to-be-sold deals were reported at cost (Kaplan & Schoar, 2005). However, as first shown at the deal level (Cumming & Walz, 2010) and confirmed at the fund level (Phalippou & Gottschalg, 2009), PE fund managers often exaggerate the performance of their yet-to-be-sold investments in order to improve their fundraising success for their follow-up funds. Cumming and Walz (2010) provide empirical evidence that this effect is more pronounced in countries with poor legal and accounting standards, among first-time fund managers, and for deals that are more opaque such as high-tech and early-stage deals where there are more plausible alternative explanations for value changes.

Investor activism: hedge funds versus PE funds

Hedge funds

It could be argued that hedge funds have much more effect on firms in terms of their ability to readily buy shares or exit, than in terms of seeking control; in many instances, they appear to exhibit non-confrontational approaches to managerial teams (Brav et al., 2008). However, in recent years, there has been a trend towards hedge funds assuming a more activist role (Coffee & Palia, 2016). On the one hand, it could be argued that more activist hedge funds provide an effective mechanism for representing the interests of smaller and more dispersed shareholders; on the other, it could be argued that such activities are disruptive, without adding to value (Ibid.). Coffee and Palia (2016) concluded that activist hedge funds added to the productivity and performance of target firms, but diminished the stockholder wealth of average competitors. However, when rivals faced a high threat of a hedge fund intervention, then they upped their own game and seemed to respond effectively to such challenges. They noted that these effects were particularly pronounced in dispersed industries and those with low entry barriers (Ibid.).

Aslan and Kumar (2016) similarly encountered significant industry-wide spillover effects among competing firms in terms of productivity, market share, and returns. Nonetheless, they found much diversity in such spillover effects reflecting considerable differences in post-activism changes in managerial practice and the relative competitiveness of the industry in question (Ibid.). Interestingly, financial markets appeared to anticipate spillover effects and reacted accordingly (Aslan & Kumar, 2016). However, it could be argued that spillover effects may deflect firms to greater short termism, and to adopt measures such as share buybacks that may burden the corporation with unnecessarily high levels of debt.

Brown et al. (2001) argue that a key issue with hedge funds is not only rate of return but also the risks associated with them. Past performance may provide some measure of risk, but fund survival also depends on the levels of volatility and the age of funds. As is the case with PE, it may be that superior performance by a limited number of larger established players may eclipse weak performance by a larger number of smaller funds with less experienced managers. Jagannathan et al. (2010) argue that path dependence in fund performance is more closely associated with superior performing funds than inferior ones; the latter are rather more volatile in how they do.

Indeed, Amin and Kat (2003a) find that smaller and weaker performing funds have relatively high failure rates, as is the case with heavily leveraged funds. Given this, funds of hedge funds also yield relatively inferior results. Again, as fund of funds impose a double fee regime, they generally represent a poor investment (Amin & Kat, 2003b). As an asset class, this would suggest that survivor bias may result in the systematic overestimation of returns and the underestimation of failure, leading to an over-allocation of investment capital into hedge funds (Amin & Kat, 2003a). Indeed, Amin and Kat (2003b) argue that at best, hedge funds have a mediocre risk-return profile. Again, writing as early as 1999, Edwards (1999) argues that existing risk management policies were ineffective in taking account of real levels of risk and argued for more stringent regulation; however, it could be argued that subsequent regulatory interventions remain insufficiently robust.

Goetzmann et al. (2003) find hedge fund performance fees are particularly lucrative to money managers, and may constitute quite a high claim on investor wealth. Bessler et al. (2015) concluded that, in Germany, hedge funds increased shareholder value, but this was through taking advantages of opportunities in weakly governed firms; however, the performance of more aggressive funds was poor, and they conclude that they sought to expropriate existing shareholders by exiting at temporarily induced share price peaks.

Liang (2001) concluded that through the 1990s, hedge funds yielded inferior results when compared to the S&P 500. Again, although over the decade, the S&P was more volatile, the effect of shocks in global financial markets was greatly magnified in the case of hedge funds. In looking at the 1990s and 2000s, Boyson et al. (2010) find similar evidence that hedge funds are particularly prone to contagion; again, they argue that while liquidity shocks severely affect hedge fund performance, these shocks are not properly captured by existing ways of modeling hedge fund returns. Getmansky et al. (2015) concluded that in the absence of lock-ins, the performance of hedge funds was broadly similar to mutual funds.

A major limitation of the existing literature on hedge funds is the primary focus on rates of return; there is very much less on how hedge fund activities may affect the firm, managers, employees, and other stakeholders (c.f. Baquero et al., 2005). A rare exception is that of Brav et al. (2015); they conclude that investments by hedge funds improve productivity, particularly through an overhaul of business strategies. However, this is also associated with a stagnation in working time and wages; they suggest that a major cause of value release is the redeployment of capital. In looking at the impact of activist hedge funds on innovation, Brav et al. (2016) found that target firms improved their relative innovative efficiency; even if R&D expenditure was tightened, innovation appeared to increase. This seemed to be neither the result of the effective stock picking by such funds nor voluntary changes in managerial practice (Ibid.).

Shawky et al. (2012) show that there is a positive relation between hedge fund performance and diversification across sectors and asset classes. However, diversification across geographies does not have a significant impact on hedge fund performance, and diversification across styles ("jack of all trades" fund manager) negatively affects hedge fund returns.

PE funds

In the context of PE, Knill (2009) shows that pure play strategies are bad for performance, and likewise excess diversification is also bad for performance. As such, it is important for institutional investors to clarify the fund strategy and goals at the time the fund is established.

As with the hedge fund ecosystem, there is much diversity within the PE ecosystem. While there are many different types of fund, according to sources of funding, sectoral focus, and the types of organization they target, a key distinction first of all, is whether the fund is venture capital or PE per se (Wood & Wright, 2009). Although these two categories are often conflated (Wood & Wright, 2009), there are a number of key distinctions between them, and this will impact on the type of practices they impose on target firms. While both types of investor seek to change or enhance particular managerial practices, a key distinction is that, in the case of venture capital, the target firm is one that is early in its organizational life cycle, and, hence usually with a more limited range of assets against which debt can be leveraged (Gompers & Lerner, 2004). Venture capital targets relatively new firms with potential for success, and seeks to strengthen managerial capabilities (Sahlman, 1990). While promising start-ups may have excellent business concepts and/or be highly innovative, they often lack experience of the practicalities of management in a particular industry

(Gompers & Lerner, 2004). The latter is the value added by the venture capitalist, who typically enters into a co-ownership arrangement with the original entrepreneur; typically, VCs retain some equity stake after the IPO, and retain board seats on portfolio firms, maintaining an effective monitoring role (Barry et al., 1990). It could be argued that venture capital has the potential to make a real contribution to the attainment of organizational ambidexterity, supplementing the explorative knowledge and capabilities of the original entrepreneur with exploitative knowledge and capabilities (Hill & Birkinshaw, 2006). Given the strong interest of governments and regional development authorities in supporting new business development, there have been numerous incidences of direct or indirect state support for venture capital (Jeng & Wells, 2000). Again, this has made venture capital much less controversial than PE; trade unions are often hostile to the latter, but can be much more accommodating of the former (Coe et al., 2004). Although it is recognized that venture capital represents an important component of the alternative investor ecosystem, for the reasons set out earlier we remain convinced that it should be treated as quite a distinct category to PE. However, at the same time, we are skeptical of the view that venture capital is always benign, and PE similarly malign. Not only are there several different types of PE fund, but venture capitalists vary greatly in terms of their relative effectiveness and outcomes. As with any type of investor, venture capitalists are by no means uniformally competent. Small players may lack sufficient capital to make a real difference, and inexperienced ones may similarly lack access to networks and the managerial expertise to enhance the performance of target firms and/or be over-stretched in terms of the demands placed on them (Hochberg et al., 2007). Indeed, it could be argued that the *chain saw principle* holds true; just because an individual is possessed with such a device does not make her/him trained or equipped to perform tree surgery, undocumented claims of such a status or capability notwithstanding. Again, by no means all venture capitalists have the knowledge, resources, or competence to make a positive difference, despite the positive aura attached to the title. However, the primary focus of this review is on PE, given, as with hedge funds, the degree of interest and controversy their activities have attracted. On the one hand, it could be argued that PE tends to treat organizations in an overly instrumental fashion; as vehicles from which value can be captured, taking excessive debt and selling off assets, benefitting financial intermediaries who risk a relatively small part of their own capital, yet leave stakeholders and the target firm very much worse off (Folkman et al., 2007).

Within the broad PE category, an important distinction is between managerial buyouts (MBOs), managerial buyins (MBIs), and institutional buyouts (IBOs). Again, there is a regrettable tendency in strands of the literature to conflate these categories when there is evidence of very different core principles, focus, and outcomes (Wood & Wright, 2009). In the case of MBOs, an existing managerial team works with PE to take over an existing organization, typically ending up owning a significant component of equity, using debt to access further finance (Wood & Wright, 2009). Not only does this resolve any agency challenges, but existing managers bring with them their detailed knowledge and understanding of a particular firm and industry; it is also easier for them to accurately cost the worth of their human assets. Bacon et al. (2004) concluded that such MBOs brought with them new possibilities to forge entrepreneurial deals with staff, unlocking human potential. Based on industry wide survey evidence, they conclude generally superior outcomes in this instance.

MBIs represent an outside managerial team working with PE, again to take over an organization, making usage of debt leverage, with a view to bringing about changes in practice. They may infuse new managerial skills when the existing management team is weak, but excessive debt may bring with it problems of its own. In comparing MBOs and MBIs,

Robbie et al. (1992) found that MBIs tended to perform worse than MBOs, given that it was easier for outsiders to misjudge the problems facing the target firm. Robbie and Wright (1995) argue that although MBIs may result in an optimally incentivized managerial team, there are challenges in ensuring the optimal mix of entrepreneurs and firms, monitoring, and strategy implementation. There is, once more, the possibility of the chain saw principle: a self-professed manager may or may not have managerial expertise and industry relevant knowledge and capabilities. It is likely that such takeovers would lead to a rebalancing of the resources accruing to managerial vis-à-vis line staff (see Brewster et al., 2017).

In the case of an IBO, a PE partnership takes over a firm and either replaces the existing managerial team, or subordinates it to a new agenda; typically, managers do not own significant shares (Goergen et al., 2014). Also typically, the process involves heavy debt leverage. It is this category of takeover that has become controversial. As those controlling firms are outsiders, it is easier to renege on implicit contracts (Shleifer & Summers, 1988). In comparing IBOs with a control group of firms, Goergen et al. (2014) found that over a five-year period, employment, productivity, and performance dropped vis-à-vis the control group. They ascribed this to an inability of outsiders to accurately cost the worth of a firm's human assets and their capabilities as a collective. While restructuring may enable the leverage of further debt and the liquidation of assets, this appears to negatively damage sustainability of the firm.

There are a number of general critiques of PE; typically such studies make usage of limited panels of case studies (Froud & Williams, 2007a, 2007b). Again, this work concludes that employees and other stakeholders tend to be left very much worse off, even if value is released in the process. A focus on high returns encourages repressive HR policies, with there being many documented examples of PE-owned firms following this path (Clark, 2007). Ernst et al. (2013) suggest that target firms are often overvalued, as the primary aim is to liquidate accumulated assets.

There are two strands of thinking that see more beneficial effects. The first suggests that job cuts represent a positive sign, demonstrating that excessive managerial empire building is reigned in, and the sale of assets leads to capital being redirected to more optimal paths (Jensen, 2006). Again, Baker and Anderson (2010) argue that PE may introduce a much needed objectivity into managerial processes, and a clearer focus on the bottom line. A second strand of thinking suggests that within specific types of takeover, the employment effects may be positive, rather than negative, and, indeed, employees may benefit from the efficiencies released by reduced agency costs (Bacon et al., 2010). However, Bacon et al. (2013) note that the PE ecosystem is a diverse one, and that not all PE investors have short-termist investment horizons.

Regulation of Hedge Funds and PE Funds

Table 18.1 summarizes a number of studies pertinent to the regulation of hedge funds and PE funds. In respect of hedge funds, early theory (Verret, 2007) and evidence (Brown et al., 2009) from the US shows that there can be value to mandatory registration of funds and simple due diligence screens that investors can put onto funds. In particular, the due diligence that is possible with a simple form ADV in US registration enables substantial performance improvements with hedge funds (Brown et al., 2009) by not investing into funds that have more pronounced operational risk, such as having a prior criminal record. However, this registration requirement is not the only thing that should work in theory, as there could be components of self-regulation that might enhance the value of registration and disclosure

Table 18.1 Overview of studies on hedge fund and PE fund regulation

Author(s)	*Data source(s)*	*Country samples*	*Time period*	*Dependent variables*	*Main explanatory variables*	*Main findings*
Hedge funds						
Verret (2007)	Not applicable	US	2006	Not applicable	Not applicable	The author examines the registration requirement for hedge funds in the US that was in place for a short period in 2006 before it was struck down by the Supreme Court in the Goldstein decision. The author argues that future attempts at hedge fund regulation should accommodate a self-regulatory system.
Cumming & Johan (2008)	CISDM	Many countries	1994–2005	Hedge fund forum shopping	Market conditions, hedge fund variables, investee variables	The data offers scant support for the view that hedge fund managers pursuing riskier strategies or strategies with potentially more pronounced agency problems systematically select jurisdictions with less stringent regulations. For the most part, fund strategies are not systematically and statistically related to different regulations observed in different jurisdictions. In fact, to the extent that there is evidence of forum shopping, it is for the most part suggestive that funds pursuing riskier strategies or strategies with greater potential agency problems select jurisdictions with more stringent regulations. We may infer from the evidence that forum shopping by fund managers in relation to fund strategic focus is not consistent with a race to the bottom where funds select jurisdictions with scant regulation such that regulators have incentives to offer limited regulation. Rather, the data suggests hedge funds select jurisdictions that are in fund investors' interests in order to facilitate capital raising by the hedge fund.

Brav et al. (2008)	SEC 13 D Filings	US	2001–2006	Targeting dummy, abnormal returns	Type of activism, firm-specific characteristics	Activist hedge funds in the US propose strategic, operational, and financial remedies and attain success or partial success in two-thirds of the cases. Hedge funds seldom seek control and in most cases are nonconfrontational. The abnormal return around the announcement of activism is approximately 7%, with no reversal during the subsequent year. Target firms experience increases in payout, operating performance, and higher CEO turnover after activism.
Bollen & Pool (2009)	Center for International Securities and Derivatives Markets (CISDM)	Many countries	1994– 2005	Return discontinuity for marginally negative and marginally positive returns	Firm investment strategies, risk factors, audit periods, managerial skill	There is a significant discontinuity in the pooled distribution of reported hedge fund returns: the number of small gains far exceeds the number of small losses. The discontinuity is present in live funds, defunct funds, and funds of all ages, suggesting that it is not caused by database biases. The discontinuity is absent in the three months culminating in an audit, funds that invest in liquid assets, and hedge fund risk factors, suggesting that it is generated neither by the skill of managers to avoid losses nor by nonlinearities in hedge fund asset returns. A remaining explanation is that hedge fund managers avoid reporting losses to attract and retain investors.
Brown et al. (2009)	Lipper TASS and SEC Form ADV filings	US	1994–2005	Fund operational risk, fund survival	Year dummy variables, fund strategies, fund operational risk	Using a complete set of US SEC filing information on hedge funds (Form ADV) and data from the Lipper TASS Hedge Fund Database, the study reported here developed a quantitative model called the omega-score to measure hedge fund operational risk. The omega-score is related to conflict-of-interest issues, concentrated ownership, and reduced leverage in the Form ADV data. With a statistical methodology, the study further related

(*Continued*)

Table 18.1 *(Continued)*

Author(s)	*Data source(s)*	*Country samples*	*Time period*	*Dependent variables*	*Main explanatory variables*	*Main findings*
						the omega-score to such readily available information as fund performance, volatility, size, age, and fee structures. Finally, the study demonstrated that although operational risk is more significant than financial risk in explaining fund failure, a significant and positive interaction exists between operational risk and financial risk.
Cumming & Dai (2010b)	CISDM	Many countries	1994–2005	Return discontinuity for marginally negative and marginally positive returns	Hedge fund regulation variables, market conditions, hedge fund variables, investee variables	We find strong evidence that differences in hedge fund regulation significantly affect the propensity of fund managers to misreport monthly returns. Returns are less likely to be misreported among jurisdictions that permit distributions via investment managers, which reflects active external monitoring of reported returns. By contrast, monthly returns are more likely to be misreported among jurisdictions which permit distribution channels via wrappers, banks, and private placements, as well as among jurisdictions which have higher minimum capitalization requirements, and jurisdictions that restrict the location of key service providers. Further, the data indicates fund managers that operate more than one fund are more likely to misreport returns. The findings are robust to selection effects and various other robustness checks. We show misreporting significantly affects capital allocation, and calculate the wealth transfer effects of misreporting and relate this wealth transfer to differences in hedge fund regulation.

Cumming & Dai (2010a)	CISDM	Many countries	1994–2005	Hedge fund returns, hedge fund fees	Hedge fund regulation variables, market conditions, hedge fund variables, investee variables	The data indicates restrictions on the location of key service providers and permissible distributions via wrappers are associated with lower fund alphas, lower average monthly returns, and higher fixed fees. Further, restrictions on the location of key service providers are associated with lower manipulation-proof performance measures, while wrapper distributions are associated with lower performance fees. As well, the data shows standard deviations of monthly returns are lower among jurisdictions with restrictions on the location of key service providers and higher minimum capitalization requirements.
Cumming & Dai (2009)	CISDM	Many countries	2003-2005	Hedge fund flows	Hedge fund regulation variables, market conditions, hedge fund variables, investee variables	The data indicates that distribution channels in the form of private placements and wrappers mitigate the impact of performance on fund flows. Distribution channels via investment managers and fund distribution companies enhance the impact of performance on fund flows. Funds registered in countries which have larger minimum capitalization requirements for funds have higher levels of capital flows. Funds registered in countries which restrict the location of key service providers have lower levels of capital flows. Further, offshore fund flows and calendar effects evidenced in the data are consistent with tax factors influencing fund flows.

(*Continued*)

Table 18.1 *(Continued)*

Author(s)	*Data source(s)*	*Country samples*	*Time period*	*Dependent variables*	*Main explanatory variables*	*Main findings*
Cumming et al. (2012)	CISDM	Many countries	1994–2008	Hedge fund performance persistence	Hedge fund regulation variables, market conditions, hedge fund variables, investee variables	The data show evidence of three types of regulation influencing performance persistence: (1) minimum capital restrictions, which restrict lower quality funds and hence increase the likelihood of performance persistence, (2) restrictions on location of key service providers, which restrict human capital choices and hence tend to mitigate performance persistence, and (3) distribution channels, which make fund performance more opaque and decrease the likelihood of performance persistence. We do not find evidence that distribution channels that promote fund presence to institutional investors, enhance performance persistence. Finally, we show differences in the effect of regulation on persistence by fund quartile ranking.
Kaal et al. (2014)	Morningstar Direct	US	January 2012 – October 2012	Hedge fund performance	Dodd-Frank Act	Based on regression discontinuity analysis, the authors find that there was no long-term impact of the Dodd-Frank Act on US hedge fund performance.
Cumming et al. (2015)	Lipper/TASS	US	1994–2010	Hedge fund fees, contractual terms with institutional investors, performance, flows, liquidation, risk shifting	Delaware hedge fund registration, market conditions, hedge fund variables, investee variables	Delaware hedge funds exhibit significant differences in contractual structure in terms of higher management and incentive fees. Delaware funds are more likely to use high water mark provisions and less likely to invest their personal capital. Both the redemption notice periods and lock up periods are significantly longer for Delaware hedge funds. While Delaware hedge funds do not outperform or underperform funds registered elsewhere, fund flows are more sensitive to Delaware funds' prior performance

						and Delaware funds are more likely to be liquidated due to poor performance. Further, Delaware funds are more likely to increase risk after poor absolute performance.
Coffee and Palia (2016)	Not applicable	US	Not applicable	Not applicable	Not applicable	Engagements by activist hedge funds appear to be producing a significant externality: severe cut-backs in long-term investment (and particularly a reduction in investment in R&D) by both the targeted firms and other firms not targeted but still deterred from making such investments. The authors review prior studies on the impact of activism, looking successively at (1) who are the targets of activism? (2) does hedge fund activism create real value? (3) what are the sources of gains from activism? and (4) do the targets of activism experience post-intervention changes in real variables? They find the evidence decidedly mixed on most questions. Finally, they examine the policy levers that could encourage or curb hedge fund activism and consider the feasibility of reforms (including with respect to the law on insider trading).
Cumming et al. (forthcoming)	Lipper/TASS	Many countries	2007–2015	7-factor alpha, 9-factor alpha, stdev of monthly returns, Idiosyncratic Risk (7-factor model), Idiosyncratic Risk (9-factor model), IR (7-factor model), IR (9-factor model)	Dodd-Frank regulation, market conditions, hedge fund variables, investee variables	Relative to non-US hedge funds, US hedge funds that are regulated under Dodd-Frank have lower alphas, lower risk, and lower information ratio in the post-Dodd-Frank implementation period. We find evidence that investors become more sensitive to performance of US hedge funds after the implementation of Dodd-Frank. We show some differences in these findings depending on fund size and strategy. The findings are robust to difference-in-differences analyses comparing US to non-US funds.

(*Continued*)

Table 18.1 *(Continued)*

Author(s)	*Data source(s)*	*Country samples*	*Time period*	*Dependent variables*	*Main explanatory variables*	*Main findings*
Private equity funds						
Kaplan & Schoar (2005)	Venture economics	US	1980–2001	IRRs, probability raising a new fund	Size, vintage year, market conditions	There is a large degree of heterogeneity among fund returns. Returns persist strongly across funds raised by individual PE partnerships. The returns also improve with partnership experience. Better performing funds are more likely to raise follow-on funds and raise larger funds than funds that perform poorly. This relationship is concave so that top performing funds do not grow proportionally as much as the average fund in the market. At the industry level, market entry in the PE industry is cyclical. Funds (and partnerships) started in boom times are less likely to raise follow-on funds, suggesting that these funds subsequently perform worse. Aggregate industry returns are lower following a boom, but most of this effect is driven by the poor performance of new entrants, while the returns of established funds are much less affected by these industry cycles. Several of these results differ markedly from those for mutual funds.
Wright et al. (2009)	CMBOR (Centre for Management Buyout Research)	Many countries	1998–2006	Not applicable	Not applicable	PE firms are heterogeneous in their characteristics and activities. Nevertheless, a corporate governance structure with PE involvement provides incentives to reduce agency and free cash flow problems. Additionally, PE enhances the efficacy of the market for corporate control. PE investment is associated with performance gains, with such gains not simply being a result of transfers from other stakeholders. In the short term, the benefits appear clear to outgoing owners and to the

						new owners and management, while in the longer term the benefits are less clear. While non-financial stakeholders argue that other stakeholders suffer in the short and long term, the evidence to support this view is at best mixed.
Cumming & Zambelli (2010)	Hand-collected sample comprising 84% active Italian PE funds	Italy	1999–2006	Frequency of LBO transactions, cash flow and control rights, due diligence	Legal variables pertaining to the illegality of LBO transactions, market conditions, other investee-specific and PE-fund specific variables	Legislation that prohibited LBOs was ineffective. LBOs still were common, except with inefficient structures: fewer cash flow and control rights to the investor, and due diligence was geared towards the agreeableness of target management and not the business plan, market conditions, or the financial strength of the deal.
Cumming & Walz (2010)	CEPRES	Many countries	1971–2003	Realized IRRs and reported unrealized IRRs to institutional investors	Legal conditions, market conditions, PE fund specific variables, investee specific variables, and transaction specific variables	Stronger legal conditions enable higher returns to realized PE transactions. To obtain more funds from the institutional investors, PE fund managers may report inflated valuations of private investee companies that are not yet sold. However, such overvaluations may result in a reputational cost when those investments are realized. The data indicates significant systematic biases in managers' reporting of fund performance. These biases depend on the accounting and legal environment in a country, and on proxies for the degree of information asymmetry between institutional investors and PE fund managers.
Jelic & Wright (2011)	CMBOR	UK	1980–2009	Post-buyout operating performance: probability and efficiency	Market conditions, firm-specific and transaction-specific variables	The univariate and panel data analysis of post-buyout performance conclusively shows positive changes in output. It also finds strong evidence for improvements in employment and output and a lack of significant changes in efficiency and profitability following initial public offerings (IPO) exits. IPOs from the main London Stock Exchange (LSE) market outperform their counterparts from the Alternative Investment

(*Continued*)

Table 18.1 *(Continued)*

Author(s)	*Data source(s)*	*Country samples*	*Time period*	*Dependent variables*	*Main explanatory variables*	*Main findings*
						Market (AIM) only in terms of changes in output. For secondary MBOs (SMBOs), performance declines during the first buyout but in the second buyout performance stabilizes until year three, after which profitability and efficiency fall while employment increases. Although PE-backed buyouts do not exhibit either post-buyout or post-exit underperformance, they fail to outperform their non-PE-backed counterparts. In the subsample of buyouts exiting via IPOs on the AIM, PE firms do not outperform non-PE buyouts. The findings highlight the importance of tracing the overall performance of buyouts over a longer period and controlling for sample selection bias related to the provision of PE backing.
Cao et al. (2015)	DEALOGIC	Many countries	1995–2007	Cross-border deals, syndication, deal premiums	Creditor rights, anti-director rights, firm-specific characteristics, market conditions	Cross-border LBO investment is more common from strong creditor rights countries to weak creditor rights countries. Club deals are less common in countries with stronger creditor rights, and less common in cross-border LBOs. Premiums are lower in countries with stronger creditor rights, and among cross-border deals.
Renneboog & Vansteenkiste (2017)·	SDC Thompson	US, UK, Continental Europe	1985–2016	Not applicable	Not applicable	This paper provides an exhaustive literature review of the motives for public-to-private LBO transactions. First, the paper develops the theoretical framework for the potential sources of value creation from going private: a distinction is made between the reduction in agency costs, stakeholder wealth transfers, tax benefits, transaction costs savings, takeover defense strategies, and corporate undervaluation. The paper then reviews and summarizes whether and

how these theories have been empirically verified in the four different strands of literature in LBO research. These strands of literature are categorized by phase in the LBO transaction: Intent (of a buyout), Impact (of the LBO on the various stakeholders), Process (of restructuring after the leveraged buyout), and Duration (of retaining the private status). Then, the paper shows that in the first half of the 2000s, a public-to-private LBO wave re-emerged in the US, UK, and Continental Europe, whose value vastly exceeded that of the 1980s US LBO wave. Finally, the paper provides suggestions for further research.

This table summarizes various papers that focus on hedge fund and PE fund regulation. The authors, data sources, countries, time periods, variables, and main findings are summarized. The main findings are largely paraphrased and/or copied from the abstracts of the papers to best and succinctly represent the authors' contributions, but are not meant to exhaustively represent all of the findings from the papers.

(Verret, 2007). Early work by Brav et al. (2008) shows that activist funds have substantial improvements in the financial performance of investee firms, but other work has questioned the effects on other firm stakeholders (Coffee and Palia, 2016).

Cumming and Johan (2008) and Cumming et al. (2013) show that there are substantial differences in the ways in which hedge funds are regulated around the world, including restrictions on the location of key service providers, permissible distribution channels, and minimum size requirements. However, they also show that hedge fund managers are not subject to a "race-to-the-bottom" in the sense that they pick the jurisdiction with the worst regulations to enable more pronounced agency problems associated with their fund.

Bollen and Pool (2008, 2009) show that hedge funds misreport returns from month-to-month in order to avoid reporting negative monthly returns, thereby improving their capital flows into the fund. This misreporting is more pronounced among funds registered in jurisdictions with wrapper distributions where performance is less clear-cut as financial products are comingled with one another (Cumming & Dai, 2010b). Also, this misreporting is more pronounced when there are restrictions on the location of key service providers, as it appears that such service providers are of lower quality in jurisdictions where these restrictions are in place (Cumming & Dai, 2010a). Restrictions on location and wrapper jurisdictions further enable capital flows into worse performing funds (Cumming & Dai, 2009) and the persistence of poor quality of funds over time (Cumming et al., 2012). Within the US, evidence is consistent with the view that Delaware hedge funds have substantial advantages in respect of the clarity of obligations with their institutional investors, albeit there are no differences in overall performance (Cumming et al., 2015).

A few studies have examined the impact of Dodd-Frank legislation on US hedge funds. Early work from a sample of nine months in 2012 shows no discernible impact of US hedge fund performance (Kaal et al., 2014). However, more recent evidence with a longer time period from 2007 to 2015 shows that funds subject to Dodd-Frank have lower returns, but also low risks (Cumming et al., forthcoming).

PE funds have experienced relatively scant regulation in the US. The dearth of regulation appears to be appropriate, as there is substantial evidence showing that PE funds achieve substantial returns (Kaplan & Schoar, 2005) and value-improvements with investee firms (Wright et al., 2009; Jelic & Wright, 2011), with few scandals or other investor harms.

Some European countries, by contrast, have imposed substantial regulations on PE funds, and overall, the evidence shows these regulations have not enhanced the quality of the market (Cumming & Zambelli, 2010, 2013, 2017; Renneboog & Vansteenkiste, 2017). In Italy, for example, LBOs were prohibited from 1999 to 2004, which in turn did not eliminate LBOs but instead changed their deal structures and the activist investment that could have brought about improved deal values (Cumming & Zambelli, 2010, 2013, 2017).

Comparing across countries, regulatory systems that protect investors, particularly creditors in LBOs, are important to PE investors (Cao et al., 2015). Likewise, institutional investors are made better off by legal and accounting standards that improve reporting quality of PE funds (Cumming & Walz, 2010). The bulk of the literature on PE takeovers has been conducted in the US and the UK. Important exceptions are represented by Bacon et al. (2012) and Boselie and Koene (2010). The former suggested that overseas investors did adapt to realities in the host institutional regime. Meanwhile, the latter found that PE from liberal markets appeared more likely to introduce hardline HRM policies into coordinated ones (Boselie & Koene, 2010). In looking at PE takeovers in France, Brewster et al. (2017) found job losses when foreign PE was involved; however, French PE appeared to behave the same way as any other French investor. They ascribe this to the active state role in the indigenous PE industry, which promotes the kind of takeovers that would support regional development objectives (Ibid.).

Theoretical implications

Agency approaches would view hedge funds and PE in a broadly similar light, in that both represent mechanisms for solving agency problems and realigning managerial interests with owner agendas (see Jensen, 2006). Downsizing or debt leverage would be viewed as releasing capital to more productive paths (Ibid.). There are three broad limitations to such approaches. The first is that there is a conflation of the interests of property owners and intermediaries; however, as the earlier review of hedge fund activities would suggest, these cannot always be conflated. The second is that investors may have quite diverse agendas; not all will operate according to the same time periods; this is reflected, for example, in the different manifestations of PE. The third is that it accords insufficient attention to context (albeit that developments of such approaches recognize the effect of institutions on the choices made by actors; La Porta et al., 2000). However, empirical evidence would suggest diversity and that this is bound up not just with formal regulation, but also informal conventions and the density of ties between key players (Deeg & Jackson, 2007; Wood et al., 2014).

An alternative, socio-economic explanation would be to recognize common features of the global financial ecosystem, but be skeptical of the possibility of a single optimal path in regulation or practice (Wood et al., 2014). In turn, this would suggest that any category of investment may have beneficial and negative consequences, but that in specific settings and times, some may result in much better (or worse) outcomes than others. Although the relationship between institutions and social action remains an open-ended debate, we would argue for a more nuanced understanding not only of the former, but also of the latter. As noted earlier, there is an informal dimension to institutions and associated rules (Hollingsworth & Boyer, 1997; Deeg & Jackson, 2007; Wood et al., 2014). Again, although it is increasingly recognized that rational action is bounded, there remains a tendency to see agents as broadly competent in seeking to realize their agendas. Much diversity in the outcomes of both hedge funds and PE would suggest that competence is sometimes lacking, that poor performing funds may still succeed in attracting investments for sustained periods of time, and there remains an element of uncertainty as to what might be the optimal intervention in any setting. Finally, as the checkered progress of PE in Germany and hedge funds in Japan would evidence, the viability of particular alternative investment strategies depends a great deal on how other players in the financial ecosystem respond to them.

Conclusions

Hedge funds and PE funds are active value-added investors that show massive performance potential but also substantial differences in performance across funds. Unfortunately, delegated asset management through hedge funds and PE funds involves a number of potential agency problems. These agency problems include, but are not limited to, misreporting fund returns to investors in hedge funds (Bollen & Pool, 2009) and PE funds (Cumming & Walz, 2010). The evidence in this chapter shows substantial value associated with investors that carry out due diligence before investing in these funds (Brown et al., 2008), and value associated with regulations that enable transparency and better monitoring. The evidence reviewed in this chapter provides insights into the similar economics underlying hedge funds and PE funds. As these funds evolve over time and around the world, there will be significant opportunities to explore additional empirical issues with measuring the costs and benefits with delegated asset management under different institutional contexts.

References

Agarwal, V., Daniel, N. D., & Naik, N. Y. 2009. Role of managerial incentives and discretion in hedge fund performance. *The Journal of Finance*, 64: 2221–2256.

Agarwal, V., Mullally, K. A., & Naik, N. Y. 2015. The economics and finance of hedge funds: A review of the academic literature. *Foundations and Trends in Finance*, 10: 1–111.

Amin, G. S., & Kat, H. M. 2003a. Welcome to the dark side: Hedge fund attrition and survivorship bias over the period 1994–2001. *Journal of Alternative Investments*, 6: 57–73.

Amin, G. S., & Kat, H. M., 2003b. Hedge fund performance 1990–2000: Do the "money machines" really add value? *Journal of Financial and Quantitative Analysis*, 38: 251–274.

Aslan, H., & Kumar, P. 2016. The product market effects of hedge fund activism. *Journal of Financial Economics*, 119: 226–248.

Bacon, N., Wright, M., Ball, R., & Meuleman, M. 2013. Private equity, hrm, and employment. *Academy of Management Perspectives*, 27: 7–21.

Bacon, N., Wright, M., & Demina, N. 2004. Management buyouts and human resource management. *British Journal of Industrial Relations*, 42: 325–347.

Bacon, N., Wright, M., Meuleman, M., & Scholes, L. 2012. The impact of private equity on management practices in European buy-outs: Short-termism, anglo-saxon, or host country effects? *Industrial Relations: A Journal of Economy and Society*, 51: 605–626.

Bacon, N., Wright, M., Scholes, L., & Meuleman, M. 2010. Assessing the impact of private equity on industrial relations in Europe. *Human Relations*, 63: 1343–1370.

Baker, K., & Anderson, R. 2010. An overview of corporate governance. In K. Baker, & R. Anderson (Eds.), *Corporate governance: A synthesis of theory, research and Practice*. Hoboken, NJ: Wiley, 3–18.

Baquero, G., Ter Horst, J., & Verbeek, M., 2005. Survival, look-ahead bias, and persistence in hedge fund performance. *Journal of Financial and Quantitative Analysis*, 40: 493–517.

Barry, C. B., Muscarella, C. J., Peavy, J. W., & Vetsuypens, M. R. 1990. The role of venture capital in the creation of public companies: Evidence from the going-public process. *Journal of Financial Economics*, 27: 447–471.

Bebchuk, L. A., Brav, A., & Jiang, W. 2015. *The long-term effects of hedge fund activism* (No. w21227). National Bureau of Economic Research.

Bessler, W., Drobetz, W., & Holler, J., 2015. The returns to hedge fund activism in Germany. *European Financial Management*, 21: 106–147.

Bollen, N. P. B., & Pool, V. K. 2008. Conditional return smoothing in the hedge fund industry. *Journal of Financial and Quantitative Analysis*, 43: 267–298.

Bollen, N. P. B., & Pool, V. K. 2009. Do hedge fund managers misreport returns? Evidence from the pooled distribution. *Journal of Finance*, 64: 2257–2288.

Boselie, P., & Koene, B. 2010. Private equity and human resource management: 'Barbarians at the gate!' HR's wake-up call? *Human Relations*, 63: 1297–1319.

Boyson, N. M., Stahel, C. W., & Stulz, R. M. 2010. Hedge fund contagion and liquidity shocks. *The Journal of Finance*, 65: 1789–1816.

Brav, A., Jiang, W., & Kim, H. 2015. The real effects of hedge fund activism: Productivity, asset allocation, and labor outcomes. *Review of Financial Studies*, 28: 2723–2769.

Brav, A., Jiang, W., Ma, S., & Tian, X. 2016. *How does hedge fund activism reshape corporate innovation?* (No. w22273). National Bureau of Economic Research.

Brav, A., Jiang, W., Partnoy, F., & Thomas, R. 2008. Hedge fund activism, corporate governance, and firm performance. *The Journal of Finance*, 63: 1729–1775.

Brewster, C., Guery, L., Stevenot, A., & Wood, G. 2017. The impact of private equity on employment: The consequences of fund country of origin - New evidence from France. *Industrial Relations: A Journal of Economy and Society*, 56: 723–750.

Brown, S. J., Goetzmann, W. N., & Ibbotson, R. G. 1999. Offshore hedge funds: Survival and performance, 1989–95. *Journal of Business*, 72: 91–117.

Brown, S. J., Goetzmann, W. N., Liang, B., & Schwarz, C. 2008. Lessons from hedge fund registration. *Journal of Finance*, 63: 785–815.
Brown, S. J., Goetzmann, W. N., Liang, B., & Schwarz, C. 2009. Estimating operational risk for hedge funds: The -Score. *Financial Analysts Journal*, 65: 43–53.
Brown, S. J., Goetzmann, W. N., & Park, J. 2001. Careers and survival: Competition and risk in the hedge fund and CTA industry. *The Journal of Finance*, 56: 1869–1886.
Cao, J., Cumming, D. J., Qian, M., & Wang, X. 2015. Cross border LBOs. *Journal of Banking and Finance*, 50: 69–80.
Clark, I. 2007. Private equity and HRM in the British business system. *Human Resource Management Journal*, 17: 218–226.
Clifford, C. P. 2008. Value creation or destruction? Hedge funds as shareholder activists. *Journal of Corporate Finance*, 14: 323–336.
Coe, N. M., Hess, M., Yeung, H. W. C., Dicken, P., & Henderson, J. 2004. 'Globalizing'regional development: A global production networks perspective. *Transactions of the Institute of British Geographers*, 29: 468–484.
Coffee Jr, J. C., & Palia, D. 2016. Wolf at the door: The impact of hedge fund activism on corporate governance. *Annals of Corporate Governance*, 1: 1–94.
Cumming, D. J., & Dai, N. 2009. Capital flows and hedge fund regulation. *Journal of Empirical Legal Studies*, 6: 848–873.
Cumming, D. J., & Dai, N. 2010a. A law and finance analysis of hedge funds. *Financial Management*, 39: 997–1026.
Cumming, D. J., & Dai, N. 2010b. Hedge fund regulation and misreported returns. *European Financial Management*, 16: 829–867.
Cumming, D. J., Dai, N., Hass, L. H., & Schweizer, D. 2012. Regulatory induced performance persistence: Evidence from hedge funds. *Journal of Corporate Finance*, 18: 1005–1022.
Cumming, D. J., Dai, N., & Johan, S. A. 2013. *Hedge fund structure, regulation and performance around the world*. Oxford, UK: Oxford University Press.
Cumming, D. J., Dai, N., & Johan, S. A. 2015. Are hedge funds registered in Delaware different? *Journal of Corporate Finance*, 35: 232–246.
Cumming, D. J., Dai, N., & Johan, S. A. forthcoming. Dodd-Franking the hedge funds. *Journal of Banking and Finance*.
Cumming, D. J., & Johan, S. A. 2008. Hedge fund forum shopping. *University of Pennsylvania Journal of Business Law*, 10: 783-–831.
Cumming, D. J., & Walz, U. 2010. Private equity returns and disclosure around the world. *Journal of International Business Studies*, 41: 727–754.
Cumming, D. J., & Zambelli, S. 2010. Illegal buyouts. *Journal of Banking and Finance*, 34: 441–456.
Cumming, D. J., & Zambelli, S. 2013. Private equity performance under extreme regulation. *Journal of Banking and Finance*, 37: 1508–1523.
Cumming, D. J., & Zambelli, S., 2017. Due diligence and investee performance. *European Financial Management*, 23: 211–253.
Deeg, R., & Jackson, G. 2007. Towards a more dynamic theory of capitalist variety. *Socio-Economic Review*, 5: 149–179.
Edwards, F. R. 1999. Hedge funds and the collapse of long-term capital management. *Journal of Economic Perspectives*, 13: 189–210.
Edwards, F. R., & Caglayan, M. O. 2001. Hedge fund performance and manager skill. *Journal of Futures Markets*, 21: 1003–1028.
Ernst S., Koziol C., & Schweizer, D. 2013. Are private equity investors boon or bane for an economy? A theoretical analysis. *European Financial Management*, 19: 180–207.
Folkman, P., Froud, J., Johal, S., & Williams, K. 2007. Working for themselves: Financial intermediaries and present day capitalism. *Business History*, 49: 552–572.
Froud, J., & Williams, K. 2007a. Private equity and the culture of value extraction. *New Political Economy*, 12: 405–420.
Froud, J., & Williams, K. 2007b. New actors in a financialized economy and the remaking of capitalism. *New Political Economy*, 12: 339–347.
Fung, W., & Hsieh, D. A. 2004. Hedge fund benchmarks: A risk-based approach. *Financial Analysts Journal*, 60: 65–80.

Fung, W., Hsieh, D. A., Naik, N. Y., & Teo, M. 2015. *Growing the asset management franchise: Evidence from hedge fund firms*. Available at SSRN 2542476.

Gao, M., & Huang, J., 2016. Capitalizing on Capitol Hill: Informed trading by hedge fund managers. *Journal of Financial Economics*, 121: 521–545.

Getmansky, M., Liang, B., Schwarz, C., & Wermers, R. 2015. *Share restrictions and investor flows in the hedge fund industry*. Available at SSRN: https://ssrn.com/abstract=2692598.

Goergen, M., O'Sullivan, N., & Wood, G. 2014. The employment consequences of private equity acquisitions: The case of institutional buy outs. *European Economic Review*, 71: 67–79.

Goetzmann, W. N., Ingersoll, J. E., & Ross, S. A. 2003. High water marks and hedge fund management contracts. *The Journal of Finance*, 58: 1685–1718.

Gompers, P. A., & Lerner, J. 2004. *The venture capital cycle*. Cambridge, MA: MIT Press.

Hill, S. A., & Birkinshaw, J. 2006. Ambidexterity in corporate venturing: Simultaneously using existing and building new capabilities. *Academy of Management Proceedings*, 1: C1–C6.

Hochberg, Y. V., Ljungqvist, A., & Lu, Y. 2007. Whom you know matters: Venture capital networks and investment performance. *The Journal of Finance*, 62: 251–301.

Hollingsworth, J. R., & Boyer, R. 1997. Coordination of economic actors and social systems of production. In J. R. Hollingsworth & R. Boyer (Eds.), *Contemporary capitalism: The embeddedness of institutions*. Cambridge, UK: Cambridge University Press.

Jagannathan, R., Malakhov, A., & Novikov, D. 2010. Do hot hands exist among hedge fund managers? An empirical evaluation. *The Journal of Finance*, 65: 217–255.

Jelic, R., & Wright, M. 2011. Exits, performance, and late stage private equity: The case of UK management buyouts. *European Financial Management*, 17: 560–592.

Jeng, L. A., & Wells, P. C. 2000. The determinants of venture capital funding: Evidence across countries. *Journal of Corporate Finance*, 6: 241–289.

Jensen, M. C. 2006. Morgan Stanley roundtable on private equity and its import for public companies. *Journal of Applied Corporate Finance*, 18: 9–37.

Kahan, M., & Rock, E. B., 2007. Hedge funds in corporate governance and corporate control. *University of Pennsylvania Law Review*, 155: 1021–1093.

Kaplan, S. N., & Schoar, A. 2005. Private equity performance: Returns, persistence, and capital flows. *Journal of Finance*, 60: 1791–1823.

Kat, H. M., & Brooks, C. 2001. *The statistical properties of hedge fund index returns and their implications for investors*. Cass Business School Research Paper. London: City University.

Kaal, W. A., Luppi, B., & Paterlini, S. 2014. *Did the Dodd-Frank Act impact hedge fund performance?* University of St. Thomas Legal Studies Research Paper No. 14-09.

Klein, A., & Zur, E., 2009. Entrepreneurial shareholder activism: Hedge funds and other private investors. *The Journal of Finance*, 64: 187–229.

Knill, A. 2009. Should venture capitalists put all their eggs in one basket? Diversification versus pure-play strategies in venture capital. *Financial Management*, 38: 441–486.

La Porta, R., Lopez-de-Silanes, F., Shleifer, A., & Vishny, R. 2000. Investor protection and corporate governance. *Journal of Financial Economics*, 58: 3–27.

Liang, B., 2001. Hedge fund performance: 1990–1999. *Financial Analysts Journal*, 57: 11–18.

Lim, J., Sensoy, B. A., & Weisbach, M. S. 2015. Indirect incentives of hedge fund managers. *The Journal of Finance*, 25: 871–918.

Patton, A. J., Ramadorai, T., & Streatfield, M. 2015. Change you can believe in? Hedge fund data revisions. *The Journal of Finance*, 70: 963–999.

Phalippou, L., & Gottschalg, O. 2009. The performance of private equity funds. *Review of Financial Studies*, 22: 1747–1776.

Renneboog, L., & Vansteenkiste, C. 2017. Leveraged buyouts: Motives and sources of value. *Annals of Corporate Governance*, 2: 291–389.

Robbie, K., & Wright, M. 1995. Managerial and ownership succession and corporate restructuring: The case of managerial buy-ins. *Journal of Management Studies*, 32: 527–549.

Robbie, K., Wright, M., & Thompson, S. 1992. Management buy-ins in the UK. *Omega*, 20: 445–456.

Sahlman, W. A., 1990. The structure and governance of venture-capital organizations. *Journal of Financial Economics*, 27: 473–521.

Shawky, H. A., Dai, N., & Cumming, D. J. 2012. Diversification in the hedge fund industry. *Journal of Corporate Finance*, 18: 166–178.

Shleifer, A., & Summers, L. 1988. Breach of trust in hostile takeovers. In A. J. Auerbach (Ed.), *Corporate takeovers: Causes and consequences*. Chicago, IL: University of Chicago Press.

Verret, J. W. 2007. Dr. Jones and the raiders of lost capital: Hedge fund regulation, Part II, A self-regulation proposal. *Delaware Journal of Corporate Law*, 32: 799–841.

Wood, G., Dibben, P., & Ogden, S. 2014. Comparative capitalism without capitalism, and production without workers: The limits and possibilities of contemporary institutional analysis. *International Journal of Management Reviews*, 16: 384–396.

Wood, G., & Wright, M. 2009. Private equity: A review and synthesis. *International Journal of Management Reviews*, 11: 361–380.

Wright, M., Gilligan, J., & Amess, K. 2009. The economic impact of private equity: What we know and what we would like to know. *Venture Capital*, 11: 1–21.

PART IV

Post-MBO firm behavior

19

INNOVATION IN PRIVATE EQUITY LEVERAGED BUYOUTS

Fabio Bertoni

Introduction

Private equity (PE) leveraged buyouts (LBOs) are financial transactions through which an acquirer (i.e., a PE fund) buys a controlling stake in a company using a substantial amount of debt, with the objective of selling it after a few years for a profit (Kaplan & Strömberg, 2009; Wright et al., 2009). The objective of this chapter is to illustrate how LBOs affect innovative activity at target companies. Specifically, the aim is threefold: first, I want to illustrate how the effect of LBOs on innovative activity can be described using two complementary theories, and how these theories reflect the characteristics of different LBO waves. Second, I want to discuss how the literature has focused mostly on technological innovation, paying relatively less attention to managerial innovation. Third, I want to illustrate some possible avenues for future research on this topic.

A key objective of an LBO is to increase the valuation of the target company between the day on which the company is acquired and the day on which it is sold (e.g., at initial public offering, to an industrial acquirer through a trade sale, or to another LBO investor through a secondary sale) (Kaplan & Schoar, 2005). This increase in valuation, which is amplified by the use of leverage, is what makes the transaction profitable for an LBO investor (e.g., a PE firm). In order to obtain this increase in valuation, LBO investors will perform a number of activities including: changing the corporate governance of the company, restructuring its production process, changing the perimeter of its activities (e.g., liquidating unprofitable divisions), accelerating its expansion, boosting efficiency, and introducing new management practices (Cumming et al., 2007; Gompers et al., 2016). We can categorize these activities into three groups: financial engineering, governance engineering, and operational engineering (Kaplan & Strömberg, 2009). Most of these activities are likely to affect directly or indirectly, innovation in target companies in profound ways, which requires a multidimensional conceptual framework (Berg & Gottschalg, 2005). In order to conceptualize how LBOs may affect innovation, we need a theory linking these activities and their relative importance to the innovation process itself.

Two main theoretical frameworks link LBOs to the performance in general – and the innovation in particular – of target companies: agency theory and strategic entrepreneurship theory. The two theories differ both with respect to the relative importance and the role played by PE funds in performing to financial, governance, and operational engineering. The agency theory of LBOs stems from the seminal works on the relationship between shareholders and managers (Jensen & Meckling, 1976; Fama & Jensen, 1983; Jensen, 1986). According to this theory, the main value driver of an LBO is its ability to transform a company in which managers have weak incentives to maximize firm value and cash flows in excess of investment opportunities, into a company in which managers have high-powered incentives and no excess cash flow to spare. This transformation is performed mostly through a combination of a change in governance (especially management compensation) and an increase in leverage, which – according to this view of the LBO – is not only a mechanism to boost the return for LBO investors but also a factor that plays a fundamental role in the success of the transaction (Kaplan, 1989a, 1989b), especially for large LBO targets (Lahmann et al., 2017). According to agency theory, the result of the LBO will then be a better use of resources and an increased pressure towards efficiency. The renovated pressure on efficiency will also affect the innovation process. Accordingly, agency theory would predict that the process of technological innovation should focus on efficiency and become more efficient itself. It is important to notice that agency theory does not necessarily predict that a company will innovate more – or less – because of the LBO, but rather focuses on what type of innovative activity (efficiency-driven innovation) is being performed and on how efficient the innovation process is. The agency view is consistent both with more innovation being produced using the same resources and with fewer resources being used to produce the same amount of innovation. However, because LBOs in the period in which the agency theory was first formalized were mostly in low-tech sectors, where technological innovation was less crucial as a driver of competitive advantage, the prevalent view was that the LBO would not result in a boost of innovation activity, but rather in a more streamlined and efficient innovation process. As we will discuss later, some scholars have argued that the cost-cutting pressure of LBOs could actually cause short-termism and managerial myopia, which would hurt innovation (Hitt et al., 1991). This argument builds upon some elements of agency theory but does not descend directly from it. Interestingly, this argument has received very resonant media attention despite the fact that the empirical evidence largely rejects it.

The second theoretical framework that can be used to describe the impact of LBOs on innovative activity is strategic entrepreneurship theory (Wright et al., 2001a; Meuleman et al., 2009b). Both agency theory and strategic entrepreneurship theory view increased incentives as a fundamental aspect of LBOs. However, whereas in agency theory the focus is mostly on how this increase in incentives reduces inefficiency in firms with excess cash flows, the strategic entrepreneurship theory focuses on how it combines with the expansion of the firm's resources and capabilities to boost the target firm performance. This difference in focus is partly due to the different theoretical underpinnings of the two theories, and partly due to a change in the prevailing characteristics of LBOs across different waves. Agency theory builds on the principal-agent theory, which studies the optimal mechanisms to reduce the inefficiencies arising from the delegation of a task from a principal (shareholders) to an agent (the managers), hence its focus on efficiency improvements. Strategic entrepreneurship theory is instead based on the resource-based view of the firm (Meuleman et al., 2009a). This theory focuses on how the competitive advantage of a firm depends on its unique resources and competences (Ireland et al., 2003). The role of an LBO is thus to enhance the resource and competence base both directly (e.g., managerial competences, financing), and indirectly (e.g., facilitating alliances). The historical reasons why the strategic entrepreneurship theory became increasingly more used is that targets of recent LBO waves were more often high-tech companies with underexploited growth opportunities rather than low-tech companies in mature industries and poor growth opportunities, which was the case in the early waves (Kaplan & Strömberg, 2009). Moreover, besides public-to-private buyouts, a number of different LBOs types (e.g., divisional LBOs, private-to-private) have become common in recent years (Alperovych et al., 2013).

Clearly, the perspective of strategic entrepreneurship theory is radically different when it comes to the expected impact of LBOs on innovative activity. The focus of this theory is more on the extent to which LBOs may boost innovation by providing additional resources and competences rather than on the efficiency of the firm and its innovation process. To this extent, the two views are complementary, because they focus on different aspects of the LBO process, and which one is most appropriate will depend on the circumstances and the object of the analysis (Makadok, 2003).

A second aspect that I want to highlight in this chapter is that whereas innovation is a very broad concept, the literature has paid a disproportionate attention to one specific aspect: technological innovation. A number of input and output measures of technological innovation have been proposed, each capturing a specific aspect of the phenomenon (Hagedoorn & Cloodt, 2003). In terms of output, we may define technological innovation as the introduction of new products or services or the improvement of the processes needed to produce products and provide services. In terms of inputs, technological innovation is often measured in terms of R&D expenses. Somewhere between inputs and outputs, patents are also often used to gauge technological innovation. Technological innovation is an extremely important form of innovation, especially in high-tech sectors. However, technological innovation is not the only type of innovation. Management innovation includes a number of significant changes in key non-technological aspects of the company, including its strategy, organization, management practices, or the design of its products (Birkinshaw et al., 2008; Mol & Birkinshaw, 2009, 2014). All these aspects are part of a broad definition of innovation; however, they have received limited attention in the literature. One possible explanation of this phenomenon is that, whereas technological innovation is relatively easy to measure (e.g., patents and R&D expenses can be obtained using commercial databases for a large number of companies across a large number of countries), managerial innovation can essentially only be gauged using survey data (OECD, 2005). However, the extent to which we understand the effect of LBOs on technological and management innovation is still very different.

This consideration naturally leads me to the third contribution of this chapter, which is to illustrate possible avenues of future research. One, of course, is to shed light on management innovation. However, there are several other aspects of the innovation process that have not yet been fully explored including: how LBOs affect the process of innovation to make it more efficient, how innovations differ (e.g., in how radical or incremental they are) in LBO companies, and how the path of innovation evolves after an LBO (e.g., if a company's reliance on previous innovation is reduced after an LBO). This aspect can be particularly interesting because the effectiveness of LBOs can be particularly high when innovation is more about experimenting than exploiting (Ferreira et al., 2014). In summary, while we tend to know a lot about "how much" innovation LBO companies produce, we know relatively little about "how" they do that and "how effective" this innovation is.

In the rest of this chapter I will elaborate the concepts that I briefly illustrated in this introduction. I will begin, in the next section, by illustrating the different theoretical frameworks to analyze LBOs and the extent to which the empirical literature supports their predictions. Next, I will discuss differences between technological and managerial innovation and how LBOs can be expected to affect them according to the theoretical framework used. Finally, I will illustrate some possible avenues for future research.

Two complementary theoretical frameworks to study innovation in LBOs

Agency theory

We can trace the agency theory of LBOs back to the seminal works on ownership and governance (Jensen & Meckling, 1976). The theoretical framework describes a company owned by one shareholder who decides to sell part of her or his equity to an external shareholder. The reduced incentives of the incumbent shareholder because of the reduced stake in the firm cause an increased incentive to extract non-pecuniary benefits from the company at the expense of the new shareholder. A number of mechanisms (monitoring, bonding, incentives) may reduce but not completely offset this effect, leaving the company and its shareholders with a residual loss.

To some extent, we can think of an LBO as a transaction that is the reverse of what we just described. This is especially the case for public-to-private LBOs, in which a company that was previously listed (and hence with a high separation between ownership and control) is taken private by means of an LBO. The result is then the concentration of ownership and the reduction of the incentives for the controlling shareholder of extracting non-pecuniary benefits and hence causing an increase in the value of the company. The extent of the non-pecuniary benefits that can be extracted from a company depends on a series of characteristics, the most important of which is the presence of free cash flows, which are the cash flows from operations in excess of the investment opportunities of a company (Fama & Jensen, 1983; Jensen, 1986). When free cash flows are high, managers have more leeway for using them for investments from which they receive gratification, status, reputation, or visibility but that do not create value for shareholders. For this reason, we would expect LBOs to target profitable companies (i.e., high cash flow from operations) in mature industries (i.e., limited investment opportunities), with dispersed shareholdings (i.e., high potential gain from concentrating ownership through an LBO) (Harris et al., 2005). Put differently, efficiency-oriented buyouts generally occur in mature and stable industries where the lack of innovation is less likely to cause a competitive disadvantage (Wright et al., 2001a).

It is interesting to note that the agency theory of LBOs does not derive the efficiency focus from its theoretical underpinnings: the principal-agent theory. This theory discusses how, in a very general setting, contractual arrangements can be used to minimize the cost for a principal (in this case, external shareholders) of delegating a task to an agent (in this case, the shareholder-manager). Principal-agent theory provides a very broad set of recommendations and studies a large number of deviations from first-best equilibria. For instance, standard moral hazard models are typically described in terms of incentive for the agent to exert effort (Laffont & Martimort, 2009), which is a rather different setup than what is used by agency theory of LBOs, which focuses on how incentives affect the extraction of private benefits. In conclusion, the relatively narrow perspective of the agency theory of LBOs does not derive from its foundation on the principal-agent theory, but is rather the reflection of the historical development of the theory itself. When the agency theory of LBOs was developed, LBOs were mainly public-to-private transactions in low-tech industries (Kaplan & Strömberg, 2009). In this setting, the governance-improvement perspective of agency theory was appropriate to describe the key issues for value creation. As we will discuss in the next section, as LBOs changed their nature, new theoretical perspectives became an important addition to agency theory.

Leverage is a fundamental disciplining element in the agency theory of LBOs. Accordingly, it could be expected that changes in aggregate availability of credit affect the functioning of LBOs. This prediction is confirmed by Axelson et al. (2013), who find that buyout leverage is unrelated to the cross-sectional factors and is, instead, strictly related to variation in economy-wide credit conditions. This result suggests that cheap credit is a fundamental driver of the leverage decision in LBOs. Moreover the authors show that leverage is associated with higher transaction prices and lower buyout fund returns, suggesting that acquirers overpay when access to credit is easier.

We can identify several ways in which agency theory can be utilized to predict the impact of LBOs on innovative activity. The first and most direct application is with respect to the efficiency of the innovation process itself. To the extent to which LBOs reduce the incentive of managers to use cash flows for unproductive uses, including unproductive investment in innovation (e.g., pet projects), the innovation process should become more efficient. This means that more innovation output should be produced per unit of innovation input. Whereas there is a large literature studying increases in economic performance after an LBO (Lichtenberg & Siegel, 1990; Smith, 1990; Harris et al., 2005; Guo et al., 2011; Alperovych et al., 2013; Scellato & Ughetto, 2013), the specific evidence about innovation is limited but overall consistent with the hypothesis that innovation is more efficiently conducted after an LBO (Lerner et al., 2011).

The second way in which agency theory could be used to predict how LBOs affect innovation is by combining it with management myopia. After an LBO, the stress created by the increased leverage might lead managers to adopt a stricter regime for the use of capital, as confirmed by the fact that – contrary to what happens for venture capital (VC) – capital investments are more dependent on internal capital after an LBO (Bertoni et al., 2010a, 2013, 2015). Accordingly, even the productive expenditure in R&D could be foregone because managers care more about their short-term costs than their long-term benefits (Hitt et al., 1990). Moreover, LBOs may divert managers' attention and distract them from other strategic matters, including innovation (Hitt et al., 1991; Long & Ravenscraft, 1993). Following this line of reasoning, one could argue that LBOs should cause a decline in innovation and, especially, a decline in capital-intensive technological innovation. Intriguingly, this view resonates with concerns commonly heard from the public opinion about PE being a "locust investor."[1] Quite interestingly, the empirical literature largely rejects this view. Ughetto (2010) studies the patenting activity of European manufacturing LBOs between 1998 and 2004 using a panel dataset of 681 LBOs, 200 of which have patents. She finds that LBO targets file more patents per year after the LBO (1.59) than before the LBO (1.06).

Lerner et al. (2011) also examine patenting activity in LBO companies and find no evidence that LBOs sacrifice long-term investments. Conversely, and consistently with the view that LBO companies become more efficient, they find that LBO patents are more cited and become more concentrated in the important areas of companies' innovative portfolios.

Finally, LBOs can affect the incentives to innovate in a more subtle way. Ferreira et al. (2014) show that the incentives to innovate, and the type of innovation they generate, depend on a company's ownership structure. More specifically, their model can be used to contrast LBOs to public companies. The logic of their model is that LBOs are less transparent to outside investors than are public firms and that this lack of transparency essentially generates a put option for insiders (who can time the market by choosing an early exit strategy). This put option makes insiders more tolerant of failures and more inclined to invest in innovative projects. The consequence is that it is optimal for a firm to be public when exploiting existing ideas, whereas it is optimal for a firm to go private when exploring new ideas. Following this logic, exploitation/exploration phases of the innovation cycle (Benner & Tushman, 2003) should be reflected in LBO/IPO cycles.

Strategic entrepreneurship theory

Strategic entrepreneurship theory focuses on the role of LBOs as vehicles for facilitating innovation (Wright et al., 2001b). The theory is based on the resource-based view of the firm, which recognizes the role of resources and competences in exploiting growth opportunities and creating a sustainable competitive advantage (Barney, 1991; Mahoney, 2001; Ireland et al., 2003). It is important to note that strategic entrepreneurship and agency theories are not competing theories, but rather two theories that complement each other (Makadok, 2003). Whereas agency theory focalizes on the contractual aspects of an LBO, strategic entrepreneurship theory focuses on the provision of additional resources and competences (Hendry, 2002). Important synergies may exist between improved governance and additional competences (Makadok, 2003). These synergies may be so critical that governance improvement may not be sufficient, on its own, to guarantee a competitive advantage (Barney, 2002). It should also be highlighted that, to the extent to which governance engineering allows a better alignment of interests, it may also improve a firm's ability to pursue competitive advantage (Gottschalg & Zollo, 2007).

A number of complementary resources can be provided to LBO targets by PE firms, including valuable intangible resources such as financial, strategic, and operational industry knowledge, reputation, and networks (Castanias, 1991; Coff, 1999; Arthurs & Busenitz, 2006). LBOs may also complement the existing competences of the management team (Zahra & Filatotchev, 2004). Due to these additional resources and competences, LBOs can stimulate strategic changes, enable growth opportunities, and create entrepreneurial opportunities that lead to revitalization and strategic innovation (Wright et al., 2001a; Meuleman et al., 2009a).

Strategic entrepreneurship theory offers a more direct framework for studying how LBOs affect innovation. One way LBOs may foster innovation is through the interaction between the managers of the target company and the investment team (Berg & Gottschalg, 2005). New products and services can be developed building on the improved ability to identify new markets (Meuleman et al., 2009a). Moreover, LBOs may improve the capability to take advantage of new technologies (Balkin et al., 2000). An LBO may also favor non-technological innovation (Schmidt & Rammer, 2007) because of the industry knowledge and business experience of PE (Kaplan & Strömberg, 2009).

A number of studies have embraced a strategic entrepreneurship perspective before the theory was formalized. Bull (1989) showed that the performance of LBOs increased after the buyout besides what could be explained by financial optimization and tax savings. Based on a number of interviews with LBO participants, the author concluded that no explanation for the increased performance of LBO targets was more persuasive than the introduction of entrepreneurial management. This conclusion is mostly based on anecdotal evidence that the introduction of entrepreneurial management contributed to creating value besides the reduction of agency costs alone. Malone (1989) studied smaller-company LBOs and showed that the target companies were typically in slow growth sectors, that layoffs and asset stripping were infrequently observed, and that the pressure due to the increased debt level actually

Table 19.1 Key features of agency and strategic entrepreneurship theories

	Agency theory	*Strategic entrepreneurship*
Driver of performance	High-powered incentives	Resources and competences
Main mechanism	Improved governance Disciplining leverage	Complementary resources Entrepreneurial opportunities
Possible effects on innovation	Efficiency-driven innovation Efficient innovation process Short-termism	New products and services Managerial innovation Corporate entrepreneurship
Selected papers using the theory	Long and Ravenscraft (1993) Ughetto (2010) Lerner ct al. (2011)	Zahra (1995) Wright et al. (2001a) Meuleman et al. (2009a)

more often caused a pronounced shift away from salaried compensation and a stronger focus on revenue-generation efforts (e.g., increased sales and marketing).

Zahra (1995) was the first to explicitly document the changes in corporate entrepreneurship after an LBO and link them to changes in performance. The study compared pre- and post-LBO commitment to corporate entrepreneurship (innovation and venturing) and performance levels on a sample of 47 LBO companies. The results confirmed that LBO companies: increased their commitment to developing new products, placed greater emphasis on commercializing their technology, intensified their new venture efforts, and enhanced the quality and size of their R&D function without a significant change in R&D spending. The results also showed that post-LBO company performance was significantly higher than pre-LBO levels and especially so in companies in which corporate entrepreneurship was more pronounced.

More recent studies, such as the one by Guo et al. (2011), illustrate that whereas LBOs have changed over time, increase in operating performance is still as important and financially value-added. The authors show that LBO pricing and leverage were more conservative between 1990 and 2006 than in the 1980s, and that returns equally derive from increases in industry valuation multiples, realized tax benefits, and operating gains.

Boucly et al. (2011) study the change in corporate behavior following an LBO. They find that LBO targets become more profitable, grow faster, and increase their capital expenditures. Their results suggest that this evidence is consistent with the idea that PE creates value because it allows the exploitation of otherwise unexploited growth opportunities.

Link et al. (2014) find that PE investments in firms funded by the Small Business Innovation Research (SBIR) result in significantly increasing their licensing and selling their technology rights. Moreover, these firms are also more likely to do collaborative research and engage in development agreements. The results highlight the role of PE in accelerating the development and the commercialization of research-based technologies.

Davis et al. (2014), show that LBOs bring productivity gains at target firms, mainly through accelerated exit of less productive establishments and greater entry of highly productive ones.

Comparison of the two theories

In Table 19.1, I briefly summarize the main features of agency theory and strategic entrepreneurship theory.

Technological and management innovation

So far, I have discussed the impact of LBOs on innovative activity, but I have been very generic about what type of innovation I was referring to. Innovation is a very broad concept that ranges from the development of new products using novel technologies (e.g., the use of 3D printing) to the introduction of new management techniques (e.g., lean production). A first basic distinction is the one between technological innovation and managerial innovation. Technological innovation is the introduction of new products or production processes that embody inventions from the industrial arts, engineering, applied sciences, and/or pure sciences (Garcia & Calantone, 2002). Generally speaking, the literature has predominantly studied technological innovation (Birkinshaw et al., 2008), especially in relation to early-stage VC investment (Hall & Lerner, 2010). The case for a link between VC and innovation is somewhat straightforward, especially when VC invests in high-tech start-ups for which technological innovation is a key value driver. The literature has highlighted that VC investment is positively related at the macro level to technological innovation in terms of patents (Kortum & Lerner, 2000; Popov & Roosenboom, 2012), total factor productivity (Hirukawa & Ueda, 2011), and R&D (Brown et al., 2009). Studies at the micro level generally confirm this evidence (Baum & Silverman, 2004; Engel & Keilbach, 2007; Bertoni et al., 2010b) but point out that different types of VC investors may have profoundly different effects on technological innovation, especially with respect to corporate VC (Dushnitsky & Lenox, 2005, 2006; Chemmanur et al., 2014) and governmental VC (Bertoni & Tykvová, 2015). Most studies argue that VC boosts innovation by alleviating firm's financial constraints (Hall & Lerner, 2010).

PE targets, which tend to be larger and more mature than VC targets, should be less affected by financial constraints (Bertoni et al., 2013) and, if anything, financial constraints should be accentuated, rather than alleviated, because of the increase in leverage. The accentuation of financial constraints should be especially pronounced during times of crisis (Bertoni et al., 2014), amplifying the cyclicality of R&D cycles (Aghion et al., 2012). The literature on technological innovation by LBOs is hence mostly based on strategic entrepreneurship and on the ability of PE to revitalize firms' innovative ability (Wright et al., 2001a, 2001b; Amess et al., 2016) and reinstate an entrepreneurial orientation in mature companies (Bruining & Wright, 2002). However, what is more interesting is that this set-up actually makes an even stronger argument if used for management, rather than technological, innovation. Using a narrow definition, management innovation can be defined as the invention and implementation of a management practice, process, structure, or technique that is new to the state of the art and is intended to further organizational goals (Birkinshaw et al., 2008). A somewhat broader definition is the one suggested by the Oslo manual (OECD, 2005) and implemented by the community innovation survey throughout Europe, which includes within management innovation any substantial change in the firm's: strategy, management practices, organization, and marketing.

Four perspectives can be identified in the study of management innovation (Birkinshaw et al., 2008): the institutional perspective, the fashion perspective, the cultural perspective, and the rational perspective. The institutional perspective focuses on the socioe-conomic conditions in which management innovation is conducted. The fashion perspective focuses on the role of providers of management ideas and in their interaction with users of management ideas. The cultural perspective focuses on how the introduction of a new management practice generates a reaction in an organization. Finally, the rational perspective focuses on how management innovation results in performance improvement. Each of these perspectives can be used to study management innovation brought by LBOs. The institutional perspective can be useful to assess how institutional characteristics (Groh et al., 2010) result in different PE conducts (Meuleman & Wright, 2011) that in turn affect management innovation in target firms. The fashion perspective can focus on the extent to which the diffusion and propagation of management ideas (Abrahamson, 1996) are facilitated by the presence of PE. The cultural perspective may be used to understand how PE shapes and is shaped by the management culture inside an organization, starting from its board of directors (Acharya et al., 2009).

However, the rational perspective is probably the most natural starting point for analyses on management innovation and buyouts, because the motivation of the introduction of management innovation by PE follows a rational perspective. Mol and Birkinshaw (2014) examine the role of external involvement in the creation of management innovation. They argue that external involvement in the process of management innovating can occur in different ways. First, they describe the process through which internal change agents (the employees of the innovating company) and external change agents (independent consultants, academics, or management gurus) interact through the phases of management innovation (motivation, invention, implementation, and theorization). The role of external change agents is to give credibility to a management innovation in the invention phase, to act as a sounding board during the implementation phase, and to support the theorization phase. PE can directly promote management innovation by operating as an external change agent (because of its management competences) or indirectly accelerate management innovation by hiring external consultants it has close relationships with, a practice that has become more common in recent years (Kaplan & Strömberg, 2009). These sources of external knowledge can be used both to generate new ideas and to improve the chances of success of innovation effort (Weitz & Shenhaav, 2000). PE can thus be a very powerful external change agent in fostering management innovation in LBO companies because of their skills, their ability to complement managers with external support (Acharya et al., 2013), and the formal authority they acquire by sitting in – and often controlling – the board of directors (Cumming et al., 2007).

Wright et al. (2001a) were among the first to set up a comprehensive theoretical setting linking LBOs with management innovation. The authors argue that LBOs can create entrepreneurial opportunities, allow upside growth, and lead to revitalization and strategic innovation. More generally, PE can be seen as a facilitator for firms crossing a strategic threshold in their life cycle (Filatotchev et al., 2006), which will be accompanied by a change in the firm's organization, management, and strategy. Management control systems will play a very important role in determining how the competitive strategy is formulated, implemented, and modified after an LBO (Bruining et al., 2004).

In summary, the case for a link between LBOs and management innovation is very strong, and possibly stronger than the link between LBOs and technological innovation. The empirical literature, however, has so far only paid marginal attention to this aspect, which naturally leads us to the next section, in which I discuss avenues for future research.

Avenues for future research

The academic literature started analyzing LBOs soon after they first developed in the US in the 1980s, which means scholars worldwide have now been studying LBOs for several decades. As a whole, LBOs are thus definitely not a frontier topic, as confirmed by the large number of studies surveyed by literature reviews on the subject (Kaplan & Strömberg, 2009;

Wright et al., 2009). However, some aspects of LBOs are still poorly understood and require closer scrutiny. In general, the impact on innovative activity is among the lesser studied aspects of LBOs, especially by the finance literature.[2]

Within the general topic of LBOs and innovation, the literature has focused on quantitative aspects of innovation (e.g., how much innovation is produced by LBOs). One aspect that has received less attention is how this innovation is produced. First, the literature seems to suggest that innovation could be more efficient in LBOs, but we do not know how this is achieved. What are the key competences and practices that allow LBO targets to produce technological innovation using fewer resources? Second, how does this technological innovation differ from technological innovation before the LBO? We know from the literature (Lerner et al., 2011) that patents filed by LBO companies receive more citations and cover fewer core areas, but there are a number of other characteristics that we do not know about. Is radical innovation (as opposed to incremental innovation) less common in LBOs (Ferreira et al., 2014)? Are LBOs bringing new technological skills to their portfolio companies or rather changing the process through which these skills are combined? Relatedly, we know from the literature that recipients of SBIR grants accelerate the commercialization of research-based technologies (Link et al., 2014). To what extent do LBOs have a similar effect?

Relatedly, we know very little about how valuable and effective LBO innovation is. Generally, we know that the value of a patent is proportional to parameters such as citations and family size, but even after controlling for these factors, the value of patents varies enormously (Shane & Klock, 1997; Harhoff et al., 2003; Hirschey & Richardson, 2004; Trajtenberg, 2010). Clearly, innovation that is not patentable (or that, despite being patentable, uses a different intellectual property protection mechanism) is even harder to evaluate. As a result, our understanding of the actual value of innovation conducted by LBO firms is still limited.

Management innovation is, as I mentioned previously, a very interesting aspect of LBOs' value-creation process and, yet, it is relatively under-researched. The few studies on this topic point out that LBOs are followed by a spree of management innovations, especially in strategy. But what types of strategic changes are caused by LBOs? To what extent, and under which dimensions, is the new strategy different from the pre-LBO strategy?

Another interesting topic for future research is how management innovation is identified and implemented in LBO companies. We know that PE partners have the business expertise and the experience in restructuring companies, and that they often partner with consultancy companies to complement their skill set. But how is this knowledge used to drive management innovation within LBO targets? How does the incumbent top and middle management of the company manage the interface between the inside (existing management practices) and the outside (now management ideas)? And how does the LBO company cope with the loss of this external knowledge source once the PE exits the company? Does the LBO leave an imprint on the company that lasts after the PE firm has left?

At an aggregate level, the role of PE as channel through which management innovation is diffused is an interesting avenue for research. We know PE waves are related to R&D cycles (Brown et al., 2009), but an equally interesting question is how they are related to the diffusion of management practices. The process can go both ways. On the one hand, a new management fashion can create business opportunities for LBOs, as was the case for the dismantling of conglomerates in the 1980s. On the other, PE can be an instrumental factor in accelerating the speed at which these new practices are adopted.

Table 19.2 What we know and what we would like to know about LBOs and innovation

General topic	*We know about*	*We would like to know about*
Types of innovation	Technological innovation	Management innovation
Post-LBO technological innovation	How much innovation Patents Technological focus	How innovation is produced Radical vs. incremental Innovation strategy
Value of technological innovation	Citations Family size	Commercialization Licensing
Management innovation	Strategic rebirth	Implementation of new strategy Knowledge transfer Imprinting
Knowledge diffusion	R&D cycles and LBOs	LBOs and management practices

Finally, an interesting dimension that deserves attention by future research is the heterogeneity among LBOs, which I have not discussed here for the sake of brevity. Not only are LBOs conducted in companies with different characteristics (e.g., size, maturity, performance, technology intensity) but PE investors vary enormously in terms of their general and specific experience, assets under management, time horizon, and strength of their relationships with financial and non-financial partners. All these parameters may fundamentally affect their impact on innovative activity in a way that has not yet been fully addressed.

I summarize these avenues for future research in Table 19.2. For each macro-topic that I discussed in this section I identify the aspects we know more about, and those that I see as promising avenues for future work in this field.

Conclusions

In this chapter I gave an overview of the theoretical framework and the main empirical results about LBOs and innovation. Whereas I tried to give a comprehensive and coherent view about this topic, it is fair to acknowledge that the literature is neither comprehensive, as I pointed out in the previous section, nor entirely coherent. The reason is twofold. The first reason is the long time through which this literature extends. Since the late 1980s, the nature of LBOs, the characteristics of their targets, and the value levers used by PE firms have all evolved, making LBOs a moving target. Moreover, during the same period, our understanding of what we mean by – and how we measure – innovation has also evolved (Fagerberg, 2005).

The second reason is that, as is often the case with innovation, the literature is highly multi-disciplinary but, unfortunately, the existence of different perspectives results in a fragmented literature. Specifically, there seems to be a divide between the finance literature and the innovation literature. Part of this divide is due to the different emphasis given to the different terms in "LBO and innovation." Simplifying, the finance literature mostly cares about "LBOs and innovation" because of "LBOs" whereas the innovation literature cares about it because of "innovation." The result is that a finance paper and an innovation paper on the same aspects of "LBOs and innovation" will pay a substantially different attention to the two elements. The two fields also tend to have different narrative styles, reference journals, and – to a large extent – reference papers. Our understanding of the phenomenon is clearly not helped by this state of facts, which I hope will become less pronounced in the future.

On the positive side, the combination of the institutional differences across countries, the multi-faceted aspects of innovation, the differences among PE investors, the evolution of LBOs over time, and the moderating role of regional and temporal characteristics result in a very rich set of interesting research questions that are still only partly explored. I believe that studying innovation in LBO companies is an interesting, relevant, and far from exhausted topic for future research, and I hope that future scholars will answer some – if not all – of the questions that we still have on this subject.

Notes

1 See e.g., *The Economist* (May 26, 2005), "Locust versus locust: German business and private equity."

2 The literature review by Kaplan and Strömberg (2009), for instance, does not have a specific section on innovative activity.

References

Abrahamson, E. 1996. Management fashion. *Academy of Management Review*, 21: 254–285.

Acharya, V. V., Gottschalg, O. F., Hahn, M., & Kehoe, C. 2013. Corporate governance and value creation: Evidence from private equity. *Review of Financial Studies*, 26: 368–402.

Acharya, V. V., Kehoe, C., & Reyner, M. 2009. Private equity vs. PLC boards in the U.K.: A comparison of practices and effectiveness. *Journal of Applied Corporate Finance*, 21: 45–56.

Aghion, P., Askenazy, P., Berman, N., Cette, G., & Eymard, L. 2012. Credit constraints and the cyclicality of R&D investment: Evidence from France. *Journal of the European Economics Association*, 10: 1001–1024.

Alperovych, Y., Amess, K., & Wright, M. 2013. Private equity firm experience and buyout vendor source: What is their impact on efficiency? *European Journal of Operational Research*, 228: 601–611.

Amess, K., Stiebale, J., & Wright, M. 2016. The impact of private equity on firms' patenting activity. *European Economic Review*, 86: 147–160.

Arthurs, J. D., & Busenitz, L. W. 2006. Dynamic capabilities and venture performance: The effects of venture capitalists. *Journal of Business Venturing*, 21: 195–215.

Axelson, U., Jenkinson, T., Strömberg, P., & Weisbach, M. S. 2013. Borrow cheap, buy high? The determinants of leverage and pricing in buyouts. *Journal of Finance*, 68: 2223–2267.

Balkin, D. B., Markman, G. D., & Gomez-Mejia, L. R. 2000. Is CEO pay in high-technology firms related to innovation? *Academy of Management Journal*, 43: 1118–1129.

Barney, J. 1991. Firm resources and sustained competitive advantage. *Journal of Management*, 17: 99–120.

Barney, J. 2002. *Gaining and sustaining competitive advantage*. Upper Saddle River, NJ: Prentice Hall.

Baum, J. A. C., & Silverman, B. S. 2004. Picking winners or building them? Alliance, intellectual, and human capital as selection criteria in venture financing and performance of biotechnology startups. *Journal of Business Venturing*, 19: 411–436.

Benner, M. J., & Tushman, M. L. 2003. Exploitation, exploration, and process management: The productivity dilemma revisited. *Academy of Management Review*, 28: 238–256.

Berg, A., & Gottschalg, O. F. 2005. Understanding value generation in buyouts. *Journal of Restructuring Finance*, 2: 9–37.

Bertoni, F., Colombo, M. G., & Croce, A. 2010a. The effect of venture capital financing on the sensitivity to cash flow of firm's investments. *European Financial Management*, 16: 528–551.

Bertoni, F., Croce, A., & D'Adda, D. 2010b. Venture capital investments and patenting activity of high-tech start-ups: A micro-econometric firm-level analysis. *Venture Capital*, 12: 307–326.

Bertoni, F., Croce, A., & Guerini, M. 2015. Venture capital and the investment curve of young high-tech companies. *Journal of Corporate Finance*, 35: 159–176.

Bertoni, F., Ferrer, M. A., & Martí, J. 2013. The different roles played by venture capital and private equity investors on the investment activity of their portfolio firms. *Small Business Economics*, 40: 607–633.

Bertoni, F., Le Nadant, A.-L., & Perdreau, F. 2014. Innovation and R&D investments by leveraged buyout companies in times of crisis. *Economic Bulletin*, 34: 856–864.

Bertoni, F., & Tykvová, T. 2015. Does governmental venture capital spur invention and innovation? Evidence from young European biotech companies. *Research Policy*, 44: 925–935.

Birkinshaw, J., Hamel, G., & Mol, M. 2008. Management innovation. *Academy of Management Review*, 33: 825–845.

Boucly, Q., Sraer, D., & Thesmar, D. 2011. Growth LBOs. *Journal of Financial Economics*, 102: 432–453.

Brown, J. R., Fazzari, S. M., & Petersen, B. C. 2009. Financing innovation and growth: Cash flow, external equity, and the 1990s R&D boom. *Journal of Finance*, 64: 151–185.

Bruining, H., Bonnet, M., & Wright, M. 2004. Management control systems and strategy change in buyouts. *Management Accounting Research*, 15: 155–177.

Bruining, H., & Wright, M. 2002. Entrepreneurial orientation in management buy-outs and the contribution of venture capital. *Venture Capital*, 4: 147–168.

Bull, I. 1989. Financial performance of leveraged buyouts: An empirical analysis. *Journal of Business Venturing*, 4: 263–279.

Castanias, R. P. 1991. Managerial resources and rents. *Journal of Management*, 17: 155–171.

Chemmanur, T. J., Loutskina, E., & Tian, X. 2014. Corporate venture capital, value creation, and innovation. *Review of Financial Studies*, 27: 2434–2473.

Coff, R. W. 1999. When competitive advantage doesn't lead to performance: The resource-based view and stakeholder bargaining power. *Organizational Science*, 10: 119–133.

Cumming, D., Siegel, D. S., & Wright, M. 2007. Private equity, leveraged buyouts and governance. *Journal of Corporate Finance*, 13: 439–460.

Davis, S. J., Haltiwanger, J., Handley, K., Jarmin, R., Lerner, J., & Miranda, J. 2014. Private Equity, jobs, and productivity. *American Economic Review*, 104: 3956–3990.

Dushnitsky, G., & Lenox, M. J. 2005. Corporate venture capital and incumbent firm innovation rates. *Research Policy*, 34: 615–639.

Dushnitsky, G., & Lenox, M. J. 2006. When does corporate venture capital investment create firm value? *Journal of Business Venturing*, 21: 753–772.

Engel, D., & Keilbach, M. 2007. Firm-level implications of early stage venture capital investment: An empirical investigation. *Journal of Empirical Finance*, 14: 150–167.

Fagerberg, J. 2005. Innovation: A guide to the literature. In J. Fagerberg, D Mowery, & R. R. Nelson (Eds.), *The Oxford handbook of innovation*. Oxford, UK: Oxford University Press.

Fama, E. F., & Jensen, M. C. 1983. Agency problems and residual claims. *Journal of Law and Economics*, 26: 327–349.

Ferreira, D., Manso, G., & Silva, A. C. 2014. Incentives to innovate and the decision to go public or private. *Review of Financial Studies*, 27: 256–300.

Filatotchev, I., Toms, S., & Wright, M. 2006. The firm's strategic dynamics and corporate governance life-cycle. *International Journal of Managerial Finance*, 2: 256–279.

Garcia, R., & Calantone, R. 2002. A critical look at technological innovation typology and innovativeness terminology: A literature review. *Journal of Product Innovation Management*, 19: 110–132.

Gompers, P., Kaplan, S. N., & Mukharlyamov, V. 2016. What do private equity firms say they do? *Journal of Financial Economics*, 121: 449–476.

Gottschalg, O. F., & Zollo, M. 2007. Interest alignment and competitive advantage. *Academy of Management Review*, 32: 418–437.

Groh, A. P., von Liechtenstein, H., & Lieser, K. 2010. The European venture capital and pivate equity country attractiveness indices. *Journal of Corporate Finance*, 16: 205–224.

Guo, S., Hotchkiss, E. S., Song, W. 2011. Do buyouts (still) create value? *Journal of Finance*, 66: 479–517.

Hagedoorn, J., & Cloodt, M. 2003. Measuring innovative performance: Is there an advantage in using multiple indicators? *Research Policy*, 32: 1365–1379.

Hall, B. H., & Lerner, J. 2010. The financing of R&D and innovation. In B. H. Hall & N. Rosenberg (Eds.), *Handbook of the economics of innovation*. Amsterdam: Elsevier-North Holland.
Harhoff, D., Scherer, F. M., & Vopel, K. 2003. Citations, family size, opposition and the value of patent rights. *Research Policy*, 32: 1343–1363.
Harris, R., Siegel, D. S., & Wright, M. 2005. Assessing the impact of management buyouts on economic efficiency: Plant-level evidence from the United Kingdom. *Review of Economics and Statistics*, 87: 148–153.
Hendry, J. 2002. The principal's other problems: Honest incompetence and the specification of objectives. *Academy of Management Review*, 27: 98–113.
Hirschey, M., & Richardson, V. J. 2004. Are scientific indicators of patent quality useful to investors ? *Journal of Empirical Finance*, 11: 91–107.
Hirukawa, M., & Ueda, M. 2011. Venture capital and innovation: Which is first? *Pacific Econonomic Review*, 16: 421–465.
Hitt, M. A., Hoskisson, R. E., & Ireland, R. D. 1990. Mergers and acquisitions and managerial commitment to innovation in M-form firms. *Strategic Management Journal*, 11: 29–47.
Hitt, M. A., Ireland, R. D., Harrison, J. S., & Hoskisson, R. E. 1991. Effects of acquisitions on R&D inputs and outputs. *Academy of Management Journal*, 34: 693–706.
Ireland, R. D., Hitt, M. A., & Sirman, D. G. 2003. A model of strategic entrepreneurship: The construct and its dimensions. *Journal of Management*, 29: 963–989.
Jensen, M. C. 1986. Agency costs of free cash flow, corporate finance, and takeovers. *American Economic Review*, 76: 323–329.
Jensen, M. C., & Meckling, W. H. 1976. Theory of the firm: Managerial behavior, agency costs and ownership structure. *Journal of Financial Economics*, 3: 305–360.
Kaplan, S. 1989a. Management buyouts: Evidence on taxes as a source of value. *Journal of Finance*, 44: 611–632.
Kaplan, S. 1989b. The effects of management buyouts on operating performance and value. *Journal of Financial Economics*, 24: 217–254.
Kaplan, S. N., & Schoar, A. 2005. Private equity performance: Returns, persistence, and capital flows. *Journal of Finance*, 60: 1791–1823.
Kaplan, S. N., & Strömberg, P. 2009. Leveraged buyouts and private equity. *Journal of Economic Perspectives*, 23: 121–146.
Kortum, S., & Lerner, J. 2000. Assessing the contribution of venture capital to innovation. *RAND Journal of Economics*, 31: 674–692.
Laffont, J-J., Martimort, D. 2009. *The theory of incentives: The principal-agent model*. Princeton, NJ: Princeton University Press.
Lahmann, A. D. F., Stranz, W., & Velamuri, V. K. 2017. Value creation in SME private equity buyouts. *Qualitative Research in Financial Markets*, 9: 2–33.
Lerner, J., Sorensen, M., & Strömberg, P. 2011. Private equity and long-run investment: The case of innovation. *Journal of Finance*, 66: 445–477.
Lichtenberg, F. R., & Siegel, D. 1990. The effect of ownership changes on the employment and wages of central office and other personnel. *Journal of Law and Economics*, 33: 383–408.
Link, A. N., Ruhm, C. J., & Siegel, D. S. 2014. Private equity and the innovation strategies of entrepreneurial firms: Empirical evidence from the small business innovation research program. *Managerial and Decision Economics*, 35: 103–113.
Long, W. F., & Ravenscraft, D. J. 1993. LBOs, debt and R&D intensity. *Strategic Management Journal*, 14: 119–135.
Mahoney, J. T. 2001. A resource-based theory of sustainable rents. *Journal of Management*, 27: 651–660.
Makadok, R. 2003. Doing the right thing and knowing the right thing to do: Why the whole is greater than the sum of the parts. *Strategic Management Journal*, 24: 1043–1055.
Malone, S. C. 1989. Characteristics of smaller company leveraged buyouts. *Journal of Business Venturing*, 4: 349–359.
Meuleman, M., Amess, K., Wright, M., & Scholes, L. 2009a. Agency, strategic entrepreneurship, and the performance of private equity-backed buyouts. *Entrepreneurship Theory & Practice*, 44: 213–240.
Meuleman, M., & Wright, M. 2011. Cross-border private equity syndication: Institutional context and learning. *Journal of Business Venturing*, 26: 35–48.

Meuleman, M., Wright, M., Manigart, S., & Lockett, A. 2009b. Private equity syndication: Agency costs, reputation and collaboration. *Journal of Business Finance and Accounting*, 36: 616–644.

Mol, M. J., & Birkinshaw, J. 2009. The sources of management innovation: When firms introduce new management practices. *Journal of Business Research*, 62: 1269–1280.

Mol, M. J., & Birkinshaw, J. 2014. The role of external involvement in the creation of management innovations. *Organization Studies*, 35: 1287–1312.

OECD. 2005. *Oslo manual: guidelines for collecting and interpreting innovation data. The measurement of scientific and technological activities*. Paris: OECD Publishing.

Popov, A. A., Roosenboom, P. 2012. Venture capital and patented innovation: Evidence from Europe. *Economic Policy*, 27: 447–482.

Scellato, G., & Ughetto, E. 2013. Real effects of private equity investments: Evidence from European buyouts. *Journal of Business Research*, 66: 2642–2649.

Schmidt, T., & Rammer, C. 2007. *Non-technological and technological innovation: Strange bedfellows?* Available at SSRN: https://ssrn.com/abstract=1010301.

Shane, H., & Klock, M. 1997. The relation between patent citations and Tobin's Q in the semiconductor industry. *Quantitative Finance*, 9: 131–146.

Smith, A. J. 1990. Corporate ownership structure and performance. The case of management buyouts. *Journal of Financial Economics*, 27: 143–164.

Trajtenberg, M. 2010. A penny for your quotes : Patent citations and the value of innovations. *RAND Journal of Economics*, 21: 172–187.

Ughetto, E. 2010. Assessing the contribution to innovation of private equity investors: A study on European buyouts. *Research Policy*, 39: 126–141.

Weitz, E., & Shenhaav, Y. 2000. A longitudinal analysis of technical and organizational uncertainty in management theory. *Organizational Studies*, 21: 243–266.

Wright, M., Gilligan, J., & Amess, K. 2009. The economic impact of private equity: What we know and what we would like to know. *Venture Capital*, 11: 1–21.

Wright, M., Hoskisson, R. E., & Busenitz, L. W. 2001a. Firm rebirth: Buyouts as facilitators of strategic growth and entrepreneurship. *Academy of Management Executive*, 15: 111–125.

Wright, M., Hoskisson, R. E., Busenitz, L. W., & Dial, J. 2001b. Finance and management buyouts: Agency versus entrepreneurship perspectives. *Venture Capital*, 3: 239–261.

Zahra, S. A. 1995. Corporate entrepreneurship and financial performance: The case of management leveraged buyouts. *Journal of Business Venturing*, 10: 225–247.

Zahra, S. A., & Filatotchev, I. 2004. Governance of the entrepreneurial threshold firm: A knowledge-based perspective. *Journal of Managerial Studies*, 41: 885–897.

20

BUYOUTS AND INVESTMENT

Dirk Engel and Joel Stiebale

Introduction

The effects of buyouts on investment of portfolio firms are a central topic in the literature on private equity (PE). Seminal theoretical contributions argue that public corporations characterized by a separation between ownership and control are inefficient due to over-investment by managers which tend to waste free cash flow on unprofitable investment projects (e.g., Jensen, 1986). Debt bonding, managements' equity stakes, and the presence of active investors often contribute to overcome this problem (Jensen, 1986, 1989), and PE firms can induce empire-building managers to reduce over-investment after buyouts and focus on profitable investment opportunities (e.g., Kaplan & Strömberg, 2009). While the literature focusing on buyouts of large public firms has also emphasized cost-cutting more generally (e.g., Kaplan, 1989; Smith, 1990; Aslan & Kumar, 2011), a more recent literature (e.g., Wright et al., 2001) argues that some buyout transactions can also accelerate entrepreneurial activity and contribute to identifying investment opportunities.

Although PE firms play a prominent role in several efforts to accelerate entrepreneurial activity as well as to reduce over-investment (e.g., Gorman & Sahlman, 1989; Gompers & Lerner, 1998), their growing importance as financiers in many countries has led to controversial debates among practitioners, policy makers, and researchers. Examples are the US Dodd-Frank Act from June 2010, a White Paper by the European Commission (2006), the UK Financial Services Authority's 2006 paper (FSA, 2006), and a famous speech by Germany's former vice chancellor Franz Müntefering, who equated PE investors with locusts and stated that these investors hollow out companies for their own benefit (e.g., Ferran, 2007). Most of these concerns are implicitly due to the perception that PE firms amplify financing constraints or have a negative impact on long-run investment. Portfolio firms are typically acquired via a leveraged buyout (LBO) in which the PE firm will raise debt finance, secured by the portfolio firms' assets and future cash flows, in order to facilitate the transaction (Gilligan & Wright, 2014). Policy makers are often concerned that these LBOs make portfolio firms over-indebted. They are also concerned that PE investors have a short-term planning horizon and therefore cut investments, especially those with a long-term character.

In this chapter, we discuss the existing empirical evidence on the effects of buyouts on investment and financial constraints. Particularly, we assess the following questions:

i) What do we know about the impact of PE firms on portfolio firms' investment and financial constraints?
ii) Do the results differ across different types of portfolio firms and investors?
iii) What are the methodological problems of empirical studies?
iv) Which are the most promising areas for future research?

A growing number of empirical studies analyze post-buyout performance with respect to productivity (Harris et al., 2005), firm growth (Amess & Wright, 2007) and other outcome variables and provide mixed results which seem to differ across countries (e.g., Davis et al., 2011; Amess & Wright, 2012). In this chapter, we focus on the part of this literature that has analyzed the effect of buyouts on capital expenditures (Kaplan, 1989; Smith, 1990), other types of investment (e.g., Lerner et al., 2011), and financing constraints (e.g., Boucly et al., 2011). We discuss the theoretical background, methodology, and data used by these empirical studies and the results they have produced.

The rest of this chapter is organized as follows. In the next section we summarize the effects of buyouts on investment from a theoretical point of view. Then we introduce the empirical methodology employed by empirical studies and present related findings. Thereafter, we discuss methodological problems in the existing literature and suggestions for future research, and the final section concludes.

Buyouts, investment, and the role of PE firms from a theoretical point of view

The role of PE investors in buyouts

The role of PE firms in buyouts has mainly been developed from the perspectives of agency theory (e.g., Jensen, 1986, 1989) and entrepreneurship theory (e.g., Wright et al., 2001). Agency theory analyses over-investment in targets of buyouts and how PE firms reduce this problem. The entrepreneurship perspective argues that buyouts induce entrepreneurial investment and growth in portfolio firms. In contrast to these positive views, PE firms might have an incentive to cut investment in order to increase short-term profit because they usually have to repay fund investors' capital, along with any profit generated, about 5 to 10 years after a buyout. Further, due to the high amount of leverage typically used to finance the transaction, which is usually secured by portfolio firms' assets or future cash flows, cash is used to service the debt rather than make investments that yield a longer-term payoff (e.g., Rappaport, 1990; Kaplan, 1991).

It is well documented that capital markets are characterized by information asymmetries, and suppliers of finance are confronted with an adverse selection problem leading to the rationing of finance and under-investment (Stiglitz & Weiss, 1981; Hubbard, 1998). Whether leveraged buyouts have positive or negative effects on portfolio firms' ability to exploit profitable investment opportunities therefore depends on PE firms' ability to deal with these capital market imperfections. Several theories argue that PE firms' activities, which include screening, contracting, monitoring, providing financial expertise, hands-on management, providing access to external finance, and their indirect signaling effects towards external investors, reduce information asymmetries (e.g., Gorman & Sahlman, 1989; Berger & Udell, 1998; Gompers & Lerner, 1998). The improvement in corporate governance via LBOs can help to overcome moral hazard problems, providing creditors with the confidence that funds are used productively. Further, PE firms' financial expertise is a reassurance to creditors, making it more likely they will provide funds for investment. Consequently,

PE firms might relax growth barriers and financial rationing in their portfolio firms. Corporate governance structures implemented by PE firms and the necessity to service debt generated by the buyout transaction can induce managers to focus on the most profitable investment projects (e.g., Jensen, 1986). Therefore, PE firms can contribute to reducing under-investment in firms with growth perspectives and reducing over-investment in firms with managers that tend to waste free cash flow.

PE firms' heterogeneity with respect to their active role

Different types of PE investors might have different strategic goals and incentive structures, which can result in different monitoring and governance activities (see, for instance, Chen et al., 2007). Further, PE firms are a heterogeneous group of financial intermediaries, and it is an important question which characteristics of PE firms and deals are favorable to achieve economic efficiency and to exploit growth opportunities. The literature of financial intermediation postulates that active involvement of PE firms can be identified along several dimensions (e.g., monitoring, hands-on management) which affect the behavior of portfolio firms (e.g., Hart, 2001) as well as their performance (e.g., Amit et al., 1998).

The role of PE investors is also influenced by country-specific conditions. As argued by La Porta et al. (1998, 2000), there are considerable differences across countries in governance mechanisms dealing with agency conflicts. Bottazzi et al. (2009) develop a theoretical model to link investor protection to the extent of PE firms' involvement in portfolio firms. In this model, PE firms have stronger incentives to provide value-added support and to develop value-adding competencies in a legal system with higher investor protection. This arises because low investor protection implies a higher probability that portfolio firms' managers will find a weakness in the legal system that allows them to divert cash into their own pockets, which reduces the expected return for PE firms' efforts. The empirical results of Bottazzi et al. (2008, 2009) are in line with their theoretical predictions. The frequency of interactions with portfolio firms, as a proxy for the extent of value-added support, is higher for companies in countries characterized by a common law than for companies in countries characterized by civil law. Further empirical studies confirm this pattern. Schwienbacher (2008) shows that US investors are engaged in syndicated deals and replace the management team in their portfolio firms more often than European PE firms. Different activity levels of PE firms in their portfolio firms therefore potentially lead to heterogeneous buyout performance across countries.

Buyout firm characteristics and their role in the extent of agency costs and entrepreneurial opportunities

Portfolio firms are arguably not uniformly affected by over- and under-investment before buyouts take place. They are heterogeneous with respect to several characteristics which affect the extent of agency costs and entrepreneurial opportunities. Meuleman et al. (2009: 8) point out that "the vendor source of the buyout may also vary, with consequences for pre-buyout agency issues". Two main agency problems matter: (1) agency problems between owner and manager and (2) agency problems between different owners, particularly blockholders versus shareholders with small equity shares. Several studies differentiate between family-controlled and non-family controlled firms to operationalize the relationship between agency costs and investment patterns. Family firms are characterized by the entity of ownership, management, and control, which allows them to avoid over-investment in a better way than in public firms (e.g., Villalonga & Amit, 2006 for details). Listed corporations should experience few financing constraints due to relatively high collateral, strict reporting requirements, which reduce information asymmetries between firms and financiers, and access to equity markets. In contrast, the difficulty in conveying information to providers of finance make it more likely that private firms have to rely on internal financial resources and have limited access to bank loans, which can imply under-investment due to financing constraints (Carpenter & Petersen, 2002; Behr et al., 2013). Similarly, financing constraints are usually more severe for small firms with low levels of collateral and younger firms which do not have an established track record (Carpenter & Petersen, 2002). Hence, PE firms have higher potential to reduce financing constraints in private-to-private rather than in public-to-private transactions and in portfolio firms of relatively low size and among young firms.

Another theoretically interesting issue is the case of divisional buyouts. On the one hand, a divisional organization structure might be more effective in allocating financial resources than the financial market (Williamson, 1975, 1985). On the other, divisional structures in conglomerates can be affected by information asymmetries between divisional managers and headquarters, which have control over financial resources (Williamson, 1985; Seru, 2014). This problem is arguably particularly severe for investments with uncertain payoffs such as innovation activities. Roth and O'Donnell (1996) point out three important factors for the extent of agency costs. Agency costs rise with the cultural distance between headquarters and division, the level of decision-making authority of divisions, and the goal incongruence between headquarters and division. The net effect of divisional buyouts by PE firms on investment is therefore ambiguous from a theoretical point of view.

The type of investment in portfolio firms is also likely to play a role in the severity of financial constraints. For instance, research and development (R&D) and other types of intangible investments are typically associated with lower collateral value but higher riskiness and asymmetric information problems compared to tangible investment. This implies that financial constraints are particularly severe for the financing of innovation (e.g., Brown et al., 2012; Hsu et al., 2014), which has been confirmed by robust empirical evidence (see, for instance, Stiglitz & Weiss, 1981; Aghion et al., 2012; Hottenrott & Peters, 2012). The potential of PE firms to reduce financing constraints is therefore arguably higher in firms with innovation potential.

The literature has also differentiated between management buyouts (MBOs), where the incumbent management team buys shares, management buyins (MBIs), where an external management team takes over the portfolio firm, investor-led buyouts (IBOs), which include friendly or hostile takeovers, and hybrid forms between MBO/MBI and IBO. There is evidence that MBOs are associated with higher involvement of the existing management in succession planning compared to MBIs (see Scholes et al., 2008: 19). This implies that information asymmetries might be lower and entrepreneurial opportunities are more likely to be exploited through MBOs. Therefore, MBOs might induce higher investment levels than MBIs.

Main empirical findings

Existing empirical studies on the effects of PE on investment and financial constraints can be broadly divided into three groups. First, direct measures of financing constraints in PE-backed firms via investment cash flow (ICF) sensitivities (e.g., Bertoni et al., 2013; Engel & Stiebale, 2014; Ughetto, 2016). Second, empirical analyses providing indirect evidence by estimating heterogeneous effects of buyouts among firms that are likely to face financing constraints (e.g., Boucly et al., 2011; Chung, 2011; Amess et al., 2016) or during periods of financial distress (e.g., Hotchkiss et al., 2014). And third, evidence on (different types of) investment in general (e.g., Smith, 2015; Agrawal & Tambe, 2016).

Investment cash flow sensitivities

Since portfolio firms might not be selected randomly, descriptive patterns of pre- and post-buyout levels of investment might not tell us much about the causal effects of buyouts. Empirical analyses in the first group exploit investment theory and knowledge about determinants of investment to model an investment equation. According to Bond and van Reenen (2007), financial constraints describe a situation where a "windfall" increase in the availability of internal funds, i.e., an increase which conveys no information about the profitability of investment, causes higher investment spending. Researchers measuring financial constraints have mostly operationalized this definition by regressing firm-level investment on a measure of investment opportunities and a measure of internal finance, usually a firm's cash flow:

$$I_{it} = \alpha_i + F(x_{it}) + \beta \cdot CF_{it} + \varepsilon_{it} \quad (1)$$

where I_{it} measures investment of firm i in period t (sometimes normalized by the capital stock), x is the vector of control variables, CF denotes a measure of cash flow, α captures unobserved firm heterogeneity, and ε is an error term. If investment opportunities are sufficiently controlled for via $F(x_{it})$, the coefficient β, the ICF sensitivity, measures the degree of financial constraints. The reasoning is as follows. In neoclassical investment models, firms choose investment such that the marginal product of capital equals its user costs. In a perfect capital market, the user costs of capital are constant and independent of the source of financing according to the Modigliani-Miller theorem. In contrast, in imperfect capital markets, firms have a preference for internal financing since there is a cost premium for external finance. Hence, firms with limited internal finance might not undertake some investment projects with an expected return that lies between the costs of external and internal finance but will increase investment if additional cash becomes available. The higher the cost premium for external finance, the more financially constrained are firms with profitable investment projects, and the higher is their preference for internal finance. The sensitivity of investment to cash flow is thus associated with the degree of financing constraints. To evaluate effects of buyouts on investment, researchers have augmented equation (1) to include an indicator of post-buyout periods and an interaction term with cash flow:

$$I_{it} = \alpha_i + F(x_{it}) + \beta \cdot CF_{it} + \gamma \cdot PE_{it} + \theta \cdot CF_{it} \cdot PE_{it} + \varepsilon_{it} \quad (2)$$

where PE_{it} takes on a value of 1 for portfolio firms after a buyout. Scholars have based their estimates on various theories which imply different controls for investment opportunities, $F(x_{it})$, related to different specifications of adjustment costs and expectation formation. The investment literature mostly applies standard neoclassical models with convex costs of adjustment (see, for instance, Cooper & Haltiwanger, 2006). The *Q-model* and the *Euler equation* specification are structural models which are explicitly derived from this theory.

The Q-model is based on the idea that investment equals the ratio of the shadow value of capital to its purchase price for an additional unit, known as marginal Q. In empirical applications, marginal Q is often approximated by the observed market-to-book ratio known as average Q or Tobin's Q. This measure is usually constructed from stock market valuations and, thus, unquoted firms are not the subject of these studies. Since targets of buyouts are often not listed on the stock market, this model is not very well suited for studying the effects of LBOs. The empirical implementation of the *Q*-model critically hinges on the assumption that stock market prices reflect expected discounted future profits. Among others, Schiantarelli (1996) and Hubbard (1998) argue that stock markets might not be efficient and stock price data could therefore be a very imprecise proxy of investment opportunities.

Due to the potential problems of the *Q*-model (see Bond & van Reenen, 2007 for further details) and its non-applicability to unquoted firms, many researchers prefer alternative econometric approaches which avoid the use of stock price data. One example of such a model is the Euler equation which can be constructed from standard balance sheet items and usually assumes convex adjustment costs (see Bond & Meghir, 1994 for an empirical application). Many empirical studies find, however, large and extremely complex adjustments in firm-level data and, thus, this assumption might be violated (Cooper & Haltiwanger, 2006; Bond & van Reenen, 2007). Flexible *accelerator models* (e.g., Harhoff, 1998; Mairesse et al., 1999) overcome this limitation by specifying dynamic models with simple partial adjustment – usually based on lagged values of investment, capital, and sales – which can be seen as an approximation of a more complex adjustment process (Bond et al., 2003). The model can be applied for investments in tangible fixed assets or for R&D spending as an indicator for long-run investments (e.g., Bond et al., 2005). The validity of all these specifications critically depends on their ability to control for investment opportunities and adjustment costs.

Bertoni et al. (2013) estimate a Euler investment equation extended by interactions between cash flow and pre- and post-buyout dummies. The authors estimate their model for a sample of 78 buyouts in Spain between 1995 and 2004. They estimate a statistically insignificant ICF sensitivity for pre-buyout periods and a significantly positive ICF sensitivity in post-buyout periods. The authors interpret this finding as evidence that buyouts create growth opportunities and portfolio firms lack internal funds to exploit these opportunities. However, they do not analyze how the level of investment changes.

Engel and Stiebale (2014) apply a dynamic version of a sales accelerator model with indicators of buyouts and their interaction with cash flow. They estimate their empirical model separately for a sample of 7,543 UK firms including 315 buyout firms, and 18,095 French firms subject to 277 buyouts that take place between 1999 and 2007. The authors find that the ICF sensitivities of portfolio firms are positive and similar to other firms before PE financing starts but are reduced significantly after buyouts in the UK. These firms also display higher levels of investment in post-buyout periods. The increase in investment and the reduction of financial constraints is concentrated among small firms, which are arguably more likely to face financial constraints a priori. In contrast, they find that the level of investment and financial constraint are not significantly affected by buyouts in France.

Some empirical studies have also analyzed differences in distinctive characteristics discussed in the previous section (vendor source, type of buyout, and investor), and estimated heterogeneous effects. For instance, Crocea et al. (2013) address family-controlled businesses and differentiate between first generation venture capital (VC) backed firms (i.e., founding firms acquire VC) and descendant generation PE-backed firms which include both expansion financing as well as buyout financing. The authors estimate a Euler equation for a sample of 469 privately-held Spanish firms including 151 firms with initial VC investment between 1995 and 2006. They find that descendant generation PE-backed firms do not show a statistically significant ICF sensitivity in the pre-investment period and, in contrast to other studies, find no significant change in the post-investment period. However, the heterogeneity of Crocea et al.'s sample might explain these findings, since changes in ICF sensitivities might differ between expansion financing and buyouts.

Ughetto (2016) also applies the Euler equation methodology and takes characteristics of PE firms and buyouts and interactions with cash flow into account. The equation is estimated on a sample of 206 low- and medium-technology firms (including 108 buyouts) from the UK, France, Italy, and Spain. In contrast to Engel and Stiebale (2014), she estimates a significantly positive effect of buyouts on ICF sensitivity for French legal origin firms (France, Italy, Spain). For UK firms, the effects on ICF sensitivities are even more pronounced, and she also finds negative effects on the level of investment independent of cash flow. Further, the estimates suggest that higher cash flow sensitivities and lower investment levels are concentrated in buyouts with independent rather than captive investors. This finding is in principle in line with the view that independent PE firms are more active investors than non-independent ones.[1]

In contrast to the role of independent versus captive investors, we know relatively little about the effects of governmental buyouts on investment. Most studies focus on new-technology based firms (e.g., Grilli & Murtinu, 2011; Bertoni & Tykvová, 2015) whereas the role of governmental PE buyouts has so far been neglected.

With respect to the vendor source, Pindado et al. (2011) show that family-owned firms have lower ICF sensitivities than other firms. The result suggests that family control reduces both financing constraints as well as unproductive use of free cash flow due to managerial discretion. Ellul et al. (2010) find that investments in family-controlled firms are lower in countries with strict inheritance laws after a succession. As pointed out by Jaskiewicz et al. (2015), imprinting the entrepreneurial legacy helps such that the successor does not fear the paying out of other heirs and, thus, entrepreneurial opportunities can be exploited to a greater extent.

Indirect evidence on PE firms and financing constraints

A small but growing literature investigates the effect of PE firms on investment and financial constraints indirectly without specifying an investment equation. The idea behind this strand of literature is that if buyouts affect investment via affecting credit constraints, the effects of buyouts should be most pronounced in industries in which financial constraints potentially play a more important role and among firms which are a priori more likely to be financially constrained. The most common industry-level indicator of the importance of external finance across industries is the Rajan and Zingales (1998) measure of financial dependence. It measures the share of investment that cannot be financed from internal cash flow for the median listed US firm within industries. This measure is based on the assumption that listed firms in the US operate in a relatively unconstrained financial environment, and therefore this figure captures the technological dependence on external finance across industries. Boucly et al. (2011) investigate the effects of LBOs on French portfolio firms allowing for heterogeneous effects of PE firms across industries that depend on external finance to a different extent. For this purpose, they estimate difference-in-differences (DiD) regressions comparing the performance of firms that have been taken over in an LBO to other firms:

$$Y_{ijt} = \beta_1 \cdot post_t + \beta_2 \cdot post_t \cdot LBO_i + \beta_3 \cdot post_t \cdot FD_j + \beta_4 \cdot post_t \cdot FD_j \cdot LBO_i + \eta_i + u_{ijt}$$

In this specification, Y_{ijt} indicates the outcome of firm *i* active in industry *j* at time *t*. *post* takes on a value of 1 in post-buyout periods for portfolio firms and their control observations, FD_j, is the measure of financial dependence and LBO_i indicates buyout firms. $post_t \cdot FD_j \cdot LBO_{ij}$ thus measures how the effects of buyouts vary across industries with different levels of financial dependence. The authors use various outcome variables to show that positive growth effects of buyouts are indeed higher in industries with high levels of dependence on external finance, which is in line with buyouts alleviating financial constraints. They also provide evidence that positive effects of buyouts are concentrated among initially private firms and small firms which are arguably more likely to be credit constrained.

Amess et al. (2016), who investigate the effect of buyouts on innovation in UK portfolio firms, use a related identification strategy. To control for endogeneity of buyouts, the authors use propensity score matching to identify an adequate control group. Using the matched sample, they estimate a DiD specification allowing for heterogeneous effects for firms which are a priori more likely to be financially constrained. The case of innovation is of particular importance for assessing financial constraints since R&D is typically associated with lower collateral value but higher riskiness and asymmetric information problems compared to tangible investment. This implies that financial constraints are particularly severe for the financing of innovation (Brown et al., 2012; Hsu et al., 2014), which has been confirmed by robust empirical evidence (e.g., Stiglitz & Weiss, 1981; Aghion et al., 2012; Hottenrott & Peters, 2012). In line with PE firms relaxing credit constraints for innovation, Amess et al. (2016) indeed find that buyouts have more pronounced effects among portfolio firms which are a priori more likely to be financially constrained, such as private firms, firms with low pre-buyout credit ratings, and firms operating in financially dependent industries. Chung (2011) also estimates positive effects of buyouts on firm growth for private but not for large public firms which are characterized by a separation of ownership and control.

Buyouts and different types of investment

A growing literature investigates the effects of buyouts on different types of investments. Early studies focused on the effects of buyouts on capital expenditures and have provided evidence that these expenditures fell after buyouts of large publicly listed firms (Kaplan, 1989; Smith, 1990). In contrast, Boucly et al. (2011) and Smith (2015) find that capital expenditures increase after buyouts in France and India and that these effects are concentrated in relatively small private firms. In line with these results, a recent study using industry-level data by Bernstein et al. (2016) finds evidence for increasing capital stocks in industries that attract high levels of PE across many different countries.

Meuleman et al. (2009) focus on the role of distinctive characteristics of PE firms to explain performance differences within a sample of 238 PE financed buyouts in the UK. One of their main findings is that experience of PE funds, measured by the cumulative number of buyout investments from the early 1980s onwards, is positively related to the growth of PE-financed buyouts. Furthermore, PE-financed buyouts of independent PE firms also achieve significantly higher growth rates in sales and employment. However, the level of growth is significantly negatively related to the number of investments which are handled by one investment executive. While Meuleman et al. (2009) do not directly analyze investment outcomes, their results indicate that distinctive characteristics of PE firms accelerate the exploitation of entrepreneurial opportunities and, thus, they are likely to enhance investment activity as well.

Of particular interest has been the effect of buyouts on investment with a long-run character such as innovation, as this measure is directly related to the concern that PE firms focus on short-term performance. Tåg (2010) summarizes the empirical evidence and points out that results of studies in the 1990s are rather mixed. For instance, Long and Ravenscraft (1993) estimate negative effects of buyouts on R&D intensity, Lichtenberg and Siegel (1990) find insignificant effects, whereas the study of Wright et al. (1992) provides evidence for positive effects which are in accordance with the view of strategic entrepreneurship. Earlier studies were mostly limited to buyouts of large listed companies and may thus not be representative of the market for LBOs.

More recently, Lerner et al. (2011) study 472 PE-based US LBO transactions between 1986 and 2005 and find that patents of portfolio firms are more cited after a buyout occurs, which suggests that the quality of innovation output increases in post-buyout periods. The evidence with respect to the level of patent activity shows a decline in patenting activity after a buyout, although the authors suggest interpreting the result with caution. For instance, the time lag from application to patent filing is about 30 months and the possibility that the decline is mainly driven by innovation activity before the buyout occurs cannot be ruled out. Ughetto (2010) provides first evidence for Western Europe based on a sample of 681 buyouts in manufacturing between 1998 and 2004. She finds that the average number of patents increases by around 50% after a buyout relative to the pre-buyout period. The estimated change in patenting varies with characteristics of the LBO. In particular, syndicated buyouts and buyouts with a specialized or experienced lead investor, tend to be buyouts where patenting activity increased the most. Both studies are, however, rather descriptive, as their evidence is based on a before-after comparison of buyout firms without a control group. Thus, it is not clear whether the results reflect the causal effect of buyouts or rather the selection of portfolio firms with certain innovation performance.

Amess et al. (2016) use propensity score matching to identify a suitable control group from a large sample of firms in the UK which they compare to their sample of 407 portfolio firms. They combine their matching approach with a DiD estimator to estimate the causal effect of buyouts on innovation measured by patenting. The results show that the absolute number of patents as well as citation-weighted patents increase upon buyouts. There is also evidence that buyouts can induce other types of investments and technology upgrading. For instance, Agrawal and Tambe (2016) show that post-buyout, portfolio firms increase their investment in information and communication technologies. Further, evidence suggests that PE firms induce divestment and investment in subsidiaries (e.g., Davis et al., 2011).

Discussion and suggestions for future research

All in all, our overview of the existing literature shows that while an increasing number of studies investigates the relationship between buyouts and investment of portfolio firms, the evidence is far from conclusive. The relationship between buyouts and investment is ambiguous from a theoretical perspective. On the one hand, leverage ratios of portfolio firms usually increase after a buyout transaction, which might limit their ability to exploit investment opportunities. On the other, several studies point out the potential for the creation and exploitation of entrepreneurial opportunities. We believe that a conceptual framework with respect to (1) the type of buyout, (2) the vendor source, and (3) the main characteristics of acquirer/financier might be helpful to understand under which circumstances the exploitation of entrepreneurial opportunities, the alleviation of financial constraints, and the reduction of investment are most likely to occur.

Given the mixed results of previous studies on buyouts and investment, it is natural to ask whether results of some studies are more reliable than others. As discussed in Chapter 19, a significant part of previous studies have relied on ICF sensitivities to identify financial constraints in portfolio firms. The validity of ICF sensitivities as a measure of financial constraints is controversial in the literature. For instance, Kaplan and Zingales (1997) point out that ICF sensitivities may not increase monotonically with the cost premium for external finance. They show that in a static demand setting, the sensitivity of investment to (a windfall change in) the availability of internal funds may be lower for firms with a higher cost premium for external finance if the marginal product of capital is sufficiently convex. Bond and Söderbom (2013), who show that this result only applies to unconditional sensitivities in a static setting without adjustment costs, have recently challenged this conclusion. They argue that ICF sensitivities increase monotonically conditional on investment opportunities in the presence of adjustment costs. However, the interpretation of ICF sensitivities still relies on a correct specification of the adjustment cost process and adequate control for investment opportunities. For instance, Cummins et al. (2006) show that ICF sensitivities among US listed firms are affected by a measurement error in investment opportunities when these are proxied by stock market valuations, and that sensitivities disappear once this measurement error is assessed by using analysts' earnings forecasts as a measure of investment opportunities. This result has, however, been obtained from a sample of US listed firms, which are arguably not the most likely to be financially constrained.

Another critical aspect of ICF sensitivities is that cash flow is arguably endogenous to investment and not all studies have accurately controlled for this issue. Due to a lack of external instrumental variables, the more convincing analyses have used lagged variables as instruments in a system- or difference-generalized method of moments (GMM) framework. The validity of lagged variables as instruments, however, critically hinges on correct model specification and the validity of the assumed autocorrelation structure. Overall, the validity of ICF sensitivities remains controversial, and results of existing studies have to be interpreted cautiously. Given the difficulties in measuring financial constraints, it will be interesting to see whether different measures of financial constraints will yield different results in future studies.

The few empirical studies that have estimated heterogeneous effects of LBOs on firms that are a priori likely to face financial constraints to a different extent seem to have produced a more consistent picture. Although they are less sensitive to the econometric and measurement issues affecting ICF sensitivities, they critically hinge on assumptions about which firms are a priori likely to be financially constrained. However, the results obtained by these studies so far are quite intuitive. PE firms seem to induce growth, investment, and innovation mainly in external finance-dependent industries, in private firms, small firms, and firms with relatively low initial credit ratings, hence, in situations where financial factors arguably play an important role. Most estimates of negative effects on the level of investment largely stem from earlier studies that were limited to a sample of large public corporations. Future research will show whether these results remain robust in different contexts and samples studied.

Another important issue in research on PE and investment (and other outcome variables) is the lack of exogenous variation in buyouts. Many studies compare post-buyout performance of LBO firms to non-PE backed firms, controlling for some observable industry or firm-level characteristics. These studies therefore implicitly assume that targets of buyouts are randomly selected. However, PE firms have industry expertise and might base their investment decisions on firm characteristics unobservable to the researcher. Similar to studies of other acquisition events, it is extremely difficult, to obtain valid instrumental variables or sources of (quasi-)experimental variation (e.g., Braguinsky et al., 2015). Some empirical analyses have partly addressed selection issues using a (propensity score) matching approach combined with a DiD estimator which controls for observed time varying and unobservable time-invariant characteristics. The approach can be convincing if the relevant determinants of the outcome variables, including past growth rates of outcomes, are adequately controlled for. Nevertheless, time-varying unobservable characteristics would bias the estimated effects of buyouts. Furthermore, matching procedures seem to be the best one can do to circumvent the problem that acquired firms are not a random subset of the population. For this reason, this method is also frequently used in M&A research (e.g., Guadalupe et al., 2012).

Another approach, frequently used in the finance literature, is to compare acquired firms to targets of announced M&As that were not completed for reasons that are unlikely to be related to the outcome variables of interest (e.g., Bena & Li, 2014; Seru, 2014). A similar idea is exploited by Smith (2015) who analyses a sample of PE-backed firms in India which he compares to the performance of firms that will receive PE in the future. The author complements this evidence with data from a specific PE firm that enables him to identify firms initially selected for PE investments that were finally not acquired. This reduces endogeneity concerns, which potentially affect many studies on buyouts and investment. The results obtained from this identification strategy suggest that, among other things, portfolio firms increase their investments, indicated by a growth of assets, after buyouts. Studies that exploit a similar empirical strategy as Smith (2015) are a promising area for future research. Since this study is limited to Indian firms, it will be interesting to see whether a similar identification strategy affects results obtained for portfolio firms in the US and Europe which have been the subject of most empirical research on buyouts.

Besides methodological issues, a potential explanation for varying results across studies and countries are differences in the share of family-controlled firms and divisional buyouts as well as differences in entrepreneurial legacy and inheritance laws. Another interesting direction for future research is thus to investigate these issues in more detail.

Meuleman et al. (2009) address differences between divisional and non-divisional buyouts in the UK. They find that divisional buyouts are characterized by significantly higher changes in profitability and employment growth compared to non-divisional buyouts. A study which addresses the effect of buyout transactions on investment and financing constraints in divisional and non-divisional buyouts by considering different investors, is still missing however.

Many divisions of large (industrial) multinational enterprises (MNEs) were targets of buyout transactions. Questions remain about the role of corporate investors in these transactions compared to PE firms. It is a well-documented empirical fact that subsidiaries of MNEs outperform other firms with respect to many indicators (e.g., Helpman et al., 2004; Chang et al., 2013). Further, MNEs are usually active investors that often shift resources and economic activity across different locations (e.g., Berry, 2010, 2013). Some of these shifts might also include buyout transactions at the location of divestment, and we know little about the evolution of these entities after divestments such as their growth, productivity, investments, and innovation performance.

As we have discussed in the previous section, there is evidence that buyouts can induce R&D and patenting and that some of this increase seems to stem from PE firms relaxing financing constraints. While the level of R&D expenditures and patenting are interesting outcomes, they do not tell us much about the efficiency with which innovation activity is performed if they are studied in isolation. An important question for future research is thus whether portfolio firms are able to generate higher innovation output *conditional* on innovation input.

Although patents are a commonly used measure of innovation output, it is well known that they only capture part of firms' innovation activities and sometimes reflect a firms' innovation strategy (e.g., Ziedonis, 2004). To gain a more complete picture on the effects of buyouts on innovation it would thus be interesting to study additional variables such as process innovations and the introduction of new or improved products. Another important question in this context is whether buyouts lead to changes in the management of innovation processes and whether these contribute to higher innovation efficiency. Further, an interesting area for future research is whether buyouts affect other variables that reflect productivity-enhancing investments in a broader sense such as vertical and lateral integration and investments in product quality.

Conclusion

In this chapter, we have summarized the literature on the effects of buyouts by PE firms on the investments and financial constraints in their portfolio firms. From a theoretical point of view, the net effect of PE firms on investment is ambiguous. The earlier literature has focused on buyouts in large public organizations in which PE firms are likely to reduce the over-investment by empire-building managers and improve investment efficiency. A newer strand of literature has, in contrast, focused on entrepreneurial buyouts, which might relax growth constraints in portfolio firms. However, since higher leverage after buyouts might limit portfolio firms' ability to exploit investment opportunities, the net effect of PE firms ultimately boils down to an empirical question.

While overall the findings of empirical studies are mixed, a significant part of the more recent literature has found that buyouts can induce both tangible investment as well as investment in innovation and new technologies. One of the channels that seems to drive this result is a reduction of financing constraints, especially in private firms, small firms, and firms operating in industries with high dependence on external finance. Our survey shows that the effects of buyouts is not uniform but depends on portfolio firm characteristics, the type of investor, country characteristics, and time periods studied. Evidence on investment and financial constraints of PE-backed firms during the financial crisis is still limited.

We have also discussed methodological issues of existing empirical studies and argued that more evidence on investment and financing constraints is needed that is based on credible control groups of firms that are unaffected by buyouts. Given the difficulty in measuring financing constraints, it will also be interesting to see whether the results of existing studies are robust if new and different methods for identifying credit constraints are applied.

From a policy point of view, it seems that the perception that PE firms over-indebt portfolio firms and negatively affect their investment activities, seems on average not to be supported by empirical evidence. The results of studies surveyed in this chapter, however, suggest that the benefits of buyouts crucially depend on the type of investor, portfolio firms, and country characteristics.

Note

1 The differentiation between independent and captive investors results from the fact that detailed information about the activity level is missing. Bottazzi et al. (2008) find that independent VCs have a higher probability of being involved in recruiting senior management, in hiring outside directors, and in raising external funds. The major implication of Bottazzi et al.'s result is that differentiation between independent and captive funds is a suitable proxy to differentiate between more and less active PE firms.

References

Aghion, P., Askenazy, P., Berman, N., Cette, G., & Eymard, L. 2012. Credit constraints and the cyclicality of R&D investment: Evidence from France. *Journal of the European Economic Association*, 10: 1001–1024.

Agrawal, A., & Tambe, P. 2016. Private equity and workers' career paths: The role of technological change. *Review of Financial Studies*, 29: 2455–2489.

Amess, K., Stiebale, J., & Wright, M. 2016. The impact of private equity on firms patenting activity. *European Economic Review*, 86: 147–160.

Amess, K., & Wright, M. 2007. The wage and employment effects of leveraged buyouts in the UK. *International Journal of the Economics of Business*, 14: 179–195.

Amess, K., & Wright, M. 2012. Leveraged buyouts, private equity and jobs. *Small Business Economics: An Entrepreneurship Journal*, 38: 419–430.

Amit, R., Brander, J., & Zott, C. 1998. Why do venture capital firms exist? Theory and Canadian evidence. *Journal of Business Venturing*, 13(6): 441–466.

Aslan, H., & Kumar, P. 2011. Lemons or cherries? Growth opportunities and market temptations in going public and private. *Journal of Financial and Quantitative Analysis*, 46: 489–526.

Behr, P., Norden, L., & Noth, F. 2013. Financial constraints of private firms and bank lending behaviour. *Journal of Banking and Finance*, 37: 3472–3485.

Bena, J., & Li, K. 2014. Corporate innovations and mergers and acquisitions. *Journal of Finance*, 69: 1923–1960.

Berger, A. N., & Udell, G. F. 1998. The economics of small business finance: The roles of private equity and debt markets in the financial growth cycle. *Journal of Banking and Finance*, 22: 613–673.

Bernstein, S., Lerner, J., Sorensen, M., & Strömberg, P. 2016. Private equity and industry performance. *Management Science*. Available at: http://dx.doi.org/10.1287/mnsc.2015.2404.

Berry, H. 2010. Why do firms divest? *Organization Science*, 21: 380–396.

Berry, H. 2013. When do firms divest foreign operations? *Organization Science*, 24: 246–261.

Bertoni, F., Ferrer, M., & Marti, J. 2013. The different roles played by venture capital and private equity investors on the investment activity of their portfolio. *Small Business Economics: An Entrepreneurship Journal*, 40: 607–633.

Bertoni, F., & Tykvová, T. 2015. Does governmental venture capital spur invention and innovation? Evidence from young European biotech companies. *Research Policy*, 44: 925–935.

Bond, S., Harhoff, D., & van Reenen, J. 2005. Investment, R&D and financial constraints in Britain and Germany. *Annales d'Économie et de Statistique*: No. 79/80 (July/December), Contributions in memory of Zvi Griliches: 433–460.

Bond, S., & Meghir, C. 1994. Dynamic investment models and the firm's financial policy. *Review of Economic Studies*, 61: 197–222.

Bond, S., & van Reenen, J. 2007. Microeconometric models of investment and employment. In J. J. Heckman & E. E. Leamer (Eds.), *Handbook of econometrics*, vol. 6A. Amsterdam: Elsevier, 4417–4498.

Bond, S. R., Elston, J. A., Mairesse, J., & Mulkay, B. 2003. Financial factors and investment in Belgium, France, Germany, and the United Kingdom: A comparison using company panel data. *Review of Economics and Statistics*, 85: 153–165.

Bond, S. R., & Söderbom, M. 2013. Conditional investment–cash flow sensitivities and financing constraints. *Journal of the European Economic Association*, 11: 112–136.

Bottazzi, L., Da Rin, M., & Hellmann, T. 2008. Who are the active investors? Evidence from venture capital. *Journal of Financial Economics*, 89: 488–512.

Bottazzi, L., Da Rin, M., & Hellmann, T. 2009. What is the role of legal systems in financial intermediation? Theory and evidence. *Journal of Financial Intermediation*, 18: 559–598.

Boucly, Q., Sraer, D., & Thesmar, D. 2011. Growth LBOs. *Journal of Financial Economics*, 102: 432–453.

Braguinsky, S., Ohyama, A., Okazaki, T., & Syverson, C. 2015. Acquisitions, productivity, and profitability: Evidence from the Japanese cotton spinning industry. *The American Economic Review*, 105: 2086–2119.

Brown, J. R., Martinsson, G., & Petersen, B. C. 2012. Do financing constraints matter for R&D? *European Economic Review*, 56: 1512–1529.

Carpenter, R. E., & Petersen, B. C. 2002. Is the growth of small firms constrained by internal finance? *Review of Economics and Statistics*, 84: 298–309.

Chang, S. J., Chung, J., & Moon, J. J. 2013. When do foreign subsidiaries outperform local firms? *Journal of International Business Studies*, 44: 853–860.

Chen, X., Harford, J., & Li, K. 2007. Monitoring: Which institutions matter? *Journal of Financial Economics*, 86: 279–305.

Chung, J. W. 2011. *Leveraged buyouts of private companies*. Available at SSRN: https://ssrn.com/abstract=1904342 or http://dx.doi.org/10.2139/ssrn.1904342.

Cooper, Russell W., & Haltiwanger, J. C. 2006. On the nature of capital adjustment costs. *The Review of Economic Studies*, 73: 611–633.

Crocea, A., Martíb, J., & Rottke, O. M. 2013. Investment-cash flow sensitivity in family-controlled firms and the impact of venture capital funding. *SSRN Electronic Journal*, 48: 420–430.

Cummins, J. G., Hassett, K. A., & Oliner, S. D. 2006. Investment behavior, observable expectations, and internal funds. *The American Economic Review*, 96: 796–810.

Davis, S. J., Haltiwanger, J. C., Jarmin, R. S., Lerner, J., & Miranda, J. 2011. *Private equity and employment* (No. w17399). National Bureau of Economic Research.

Ellul, A., Pagano, M., & Panunzi, F. 2010. Inheritance law and investment in family firms. *The American Economic Review*, 100: 2414–2450.

Engel, D., & Stiebale, J. 2014. Private equity, investment and financial constraints: Firm-level evidence for France and the United Kingdom. *Small Business Economics*, 43: 197–212.

European Commission. 2006. *White Paper on enhancing the single market framework for investment funds*, 686 final, Brussels.

Ferran, E. 2007. *Regulation of private equity-backed leveraged buyout activity in Europe*. ECGI – Law Working Paper No. 84/2007.

Financial Services Authority (FSA). 2006. *Private equity: A discussion of risk and regulatory engagement*, DP06/6, London.

Gilligan, J., & Wright, M. 2014. *Private equity demystified*. London: ICAEW.

Gompers, P. A., & Lerner, J. 1998. What drives venture capital fundraising? *Brookings Papers on Economic Activity, Microeconomics*, 1: 149–192.

Gorman, M., & Sahlman, W. A. 1989. What do venture capitalists do? *Journal of Business Venturing*, 4: 231–248.

Grilli, L., & Murtinu, S. 2011. *Turning European new technology-based firms into "gazelles": The role of public (and private) venture capital*. In VICO Final Conference, Stresa, Italy, June.

Guadalupe, M., Kuzmina, O., & Thomas, C. 2012. Innovation and foreign ownership. *American Economic Review*, 102: 3594–3627.

Harhoff, D. 1998. Are there financing constraints for R&D and investment in German manufacturing firms? *Annales D Économie Et De Satistique*, 49/50: 421–456.

Harris, R., Siegel, D., & Wright, M. 2005. Assessing the impact of management buyouts on economic efficiency: Plant-level evidence from the United Kingdom. *The Review of Economics and Statistics*, 87: 148–153.

Hart, O. 2001. Financial contracting. *Journal of Economic Literature*, 34: 1079–1100.

Helpman, E., Melitz, M. J., & Yeaple, S. R. 2004. Export versus FDI with Heterogeneous Firms. *American Economic Review*, 94: 300–316.

Hotchkiss, E. S., Strömberg, P., & Smith, D. C. 2014. *Private equity and the resolution of financial distress*. ECGI - Finance Working Paper No. 331/2012. Available at SSRN: https://ssrn.com/abstract=1787446.

Hottenrott, H., & Peters, B. 2012. Innovative capability and financing constraints for innovation: More money, more innovation? *Review of Economics and Statistics*, 94: 1126–1142.

Hsu, P. H., Tian, X., & Xu, Y. 2014. Financial development and innovation: Cross-country evidence. *Journal of Financial Economics*, 112: 116–135.

Hubbard, R. G. 1998. Capital-market imperfections and investment. *Journal of Economic Literature*, 36: 193–225.

Jaskiewicz, P., Combs, J. G., & Rau, S. B. 2015. Entrepreneurial legacy: Toward a theory of how some family firms nurture transgenerational entrepreneurship. *Journal of Business Venturing*, 30: 29–49.

Jensen, M. C. 1986. Agency costs of free cash flow, corporate finance and takeovers. *The American Economic Review Papers and Proceedings*, 76: 323–329.

Jensen, M. C. 1989. The eclipse of the public corporation. *Harvard Business Review*, 67: 61–74.
Kaplan, S. 1989. The effects of management buyouts on operating performance and value. *Journal of Financial Economics*, 24: 217–254.
Kaplan, S. 1991. The staying power of leveraged buyouts. *Journal of Financial Economics*, 29: 287–313.
Kaplan, S., & Strömberg, P. 2009. Leveraged buyouts and private equity. *Journal of Economic Perspectives*, 23: 121–46.
Kaplan, S. N., & Zingales, L. 1997. Do investment-cash flow sensitivities provide useful measures of financing constraints? *The Quarterly Journal of Economics*, 112: 169–215.
La Porta, R., Lopez-de-Silanes, F., Shleifer, A., & Vishny, R. W. 1998. Law and finance. *Journal of Political Economy*, 106: 1113–1155.
La Porta, R., Lopez-de-Silanes, F., Shleifer, A., & Vishny, R. W. 2000. Investor protection and corporate governance. *Journal of Financial Economics*, 58: 3–27.
Lerner, J., Sorensen, M., & Strömberg, P. 2011. Private equity and long run investment: The case of innovation. *The Journal of Finance*, 66: 445–477.
Lichtenberg, F. R., & Siegel, D. 1990. The effects of leveraged buyouts on productivity and related aspects of firm behavior. *Journal of Financial Economics*, 27: 165–194.
Long, William F., & Ravenscraft, D. J. 1993. LBOs, debt and R&D intensity. *Strategic Management Journal*, 14: 119–135.
Mairesse J., Hall, B. H., & Mulkay, B. 1999. Firm-level investment in France and the United States: An exploration of what we have learned in twenty years. *Annales d'Economie et de Statistique*, 55/56: 27–69.
Meuleman, M., Amess, K., Wright, M., & Scholes, L. 2009. Agency, strategic entrepreneurship, and the performance of private equity-backed buyouts. *Entrepreneurship Theory and Practice*, 33: 213–239.
Pindado, J., Requejo, I., & de la Torre, C. 2011. Family control and investment–cash flow sensitivity: Empirical evidence from the Euro zone. *Journal of Corporate Finance*, 17: 1389–1409.
Rajan, R. G., & Zingales, L. 1998. Financial dependence and growth. *The American Economic Review*, 88: 559–586.
Rappaport, A. 1990. The staying power of the public corporation. *Harvard Business Review*, 68: 96–104.
Roth, K., & O'Donnell, S. 1996. Foreign subsidiary compensation strategy: An agency theory perspective. *Academy of Management Journal*, 39: 678–703.
Schiantarelli, F. 1996. Financial constraints and investment: Methodological issues and international evidence. *Oxford Review of Economic Policy*, 12: 70–89.
Scholes, L., Westhead, P., & Burrows, A. 2008. Family firm succession: The management buy-out and buy-in routes. *Journal of Small Business and Enterprise Development*, 15: 8–30.
Schwienbacher, A. 2008. Venture capital investment practices in Europe and the United States. *Financial Markets and Portfolio Management*, 22: 195–217.
Seru, A. 2014. Firm boundaries matter: Evidence from conglomerates and R&D activity. *Journal of Financial Economics*, 111: 381–405.
Smith, A. J. 1990. Corporate ownership structure and performance: The case of management buyouts. *Journal of Financial Economics*, 27: 143–164.
Smith, T. D. 2015. *Private equity investment in India: Efficiency vs expansion*. SIEPR Discussion Paper 15-011. In 2015 Fall Conference: The Golden Age of Evidence-Based Policy. Appam, India.
Stiglitz, J., & Weiss, A. 1981. Credit rationing in markets with imperfect information. *The American Economic Review*, 71: 393–410.
Tåg, J. 2010. *The real effects of private equity buyouts*. IFN Working Paper No 851. Available at SSRN: http://dx.doi.org/10.2139/ssrn.1674759.
Ughetto, E. 2010. Assessing the contribution to innovation of private equity investors: A study on European Buyouts. *Research Policy*, 39: 126–140.
Ughetto, E. 2016. Investments, financing constraints and buyouts: The effect of private equity investors on the sensitivity of investments to cash flow. *The Manchester School*, 84: 25–54.
Villalonga, B., & Amit, R. 2006. How do family ownership, control and management affect firm value? *Journal of Financial Economics*, 80: 385–417.
Williamson, O. E. 1975. *Markets and hierarchies: Analysis and antitrust implications*. New York: Free Press.

Williamson, O. E. 1985. *The economic institutions of capitalism: Firms, markets and relational contracting*. New York: Free Press.
Wright, M., Hoskisson, R., & Busenitz, L. 2001. Firm rebirth: Buyouts as facilitators of strategic growth and entrepreneurship. *Academy of Management Executive*, 15: 111–125.
Wright, M., Thompson, S., & Robbie, K. 1992. Venture capital and management-led, leveraged buy-outs: A European perspective. *Journal of Business Venturing*, 7: 47–71.
Ziedonis, R. H. 2004. Don't fence me in: Fragmented markets for technology and the patent acquisition strategies of firms. *Management Science*, 50: 804–820.

21
ENTREPRENEURSHIP, CONTEXT, AND BUYOUTS

Mike Wright

Introduction

Leveraged buyouts (LBOs) and private equity (PE)-backed buyouts are typically associated with improving firm efficiency through reducing agency costs, restructuring, cost cutting, divestments, employment reductions, etc. Yet some buyouts have also pursued significant entrepreneurial and innovative trajectories (Wright et al., 2001a; Loihl & Wright, 2002).

This chapter sets out to provide a review and synthesis of the theory and systematic empirical evidence relating to entrepreneurship in management buyouts (MBOs). We adopt a Schumpeterian view of entrepreneurial activity, which encompasses new product and market development, product and service innovation, and asset and organizational restructuring (Schumpeter, 1934; Thompson & Wright, 1988). We then develop themes for further research before concluding with some implications for practice.

Theory and entrepreneurship

Agency theory and the strategic entrepreneurship perspective provide complementary bases for the theoretical understanding of entrepreneurship in buyouts (Meuleman et al., 2009). The strategic entrepreneurship perspective emphasizes the importance of an entrepreneurial mindset in identifying and exploiting opportunities and of entrepreneurial leadership in managing the firm's resources and capabilities (Ireland et al., 2003).

Wright et al. (2000, 2001a) develop a conceptual framework to understand the mindsets of managers and entrepreneurs involved in MBOs. They identify four types of buyouts (Figure 21.1).

The traditional control and incentive mechanisms associated with buyouts that aim to address agency cost problems may generate efficiency enhancements, giving rise to *efficiency buyouts* (Quadrant 1). Significant equity ownership in a buyout introduces high powered managerial incentives, high leverage in the deal provides pressure to perform so as to service interest payments, while active monitoring by PE backers provides a complementary system that is particular applicable to mature firms with significant agency problems and free cash flows that would otherwise be diverted to inefficient diversification. In these cases, enhanced monetary incentives lead executives to improve the efficiency of the firm.

	INDIVIDUAL MINDSET	
	Managerial Mindset	*Enterpreneurial Mindset*
- Pre-Buyout Context and Decision Mindset	Quadrant 1: Efficiency Buyout Agency problems; low risk. Decisions based primarily on systematic data and financial criteria. Post-buyout: High leverage and financial control	Quadrant 4: Buyout Failure Mismatch of mindset, incentives and governance. Post-buyout: High leverage and financial control
- Pre-Buyout Context and Decision Mindset	Quadrant 2: Revitalization buyout Bureaucratic procedures stifle innovation and investment needed to be competitive; moderate risk. Decisiosns to renew competitive capabilities via innovations are based on their already proven success among key competitors. Post-buyout: Flexible monitoring by private equity firms	Quadrant 3: Entrepreneurial Buyout Bureaucratic procedures stifle radical innovations associated with uncertainty and limited information; or technology-based buisnesses headed in the wrong direction; high risk. Heuristic-based logic can lead to strategic innovations and efficient decision-making. Post-buyout: Flexible leverage; financial monitoring and technical skills of private equity firms

Figure 21.1 Buyout typology
Source: Adapted from Wright et al. (2001a).

Large diverse corporations typically develop bureaucratic measures based on objective information to ensure performance of their various divisions. While these measures may help in coordination, they likely constrain entrepreneurial activity related to innovation and experimentation which relies on more subjective information. Divisions of state-owned corporations may also be constrained, especially if they are peripheral parts of a loss-making firm that is heavily cash constrained (Thompson et al., 1990; Wright et al., 1993, 1994; Wieser et al., 1997). These problems may be exacerbated by the socio-political goals imposed on state-owned corporations that restrict their ability to expand and diversify their customer base. Similarly, local government service providers may be constrained if they are prevented from taking advantage of opportunities to expand their client base by local government control (Robbie & Wright, 1996). Separating a division from the private sector parent or through privatization from the state sector by means of a buyout may relax these restrictions. These aspects may be writ large in former centrally planned economies where buyouts were an important mechanism associated with the evolution to a market economy (Karsai & Wright, 1994; Wright, 1994).

Even though a PE investor may put in place its own monitoring, the buyout results in management having greater degrees of freedom in deciding the direction of the business firm, rather than having to adopt the corporate controls designed to optimize parental goals.

If the new owner-managers have a managerial mindset, they may engage in only incremental or catch-up entrepreneurial activities, creating *revitalization buyouts* (Quadrant 2). Buyouts from state-owned firms have been found to engage in this type of entrepreneurial activity, such as in the case of Unipart (Wright et al., 2000). Incentivized through direct ownership following a privatization buyout, employees are also reported to identify and communicate entrepreneurial opportunities to access new customers that they did not do previously (Bradley & Nejad, 1989).

In contrast to the previous quadrants, an entrepreneurial cognition or mindset means that managers buying out may be able to pursue entrepreneurial opportunities through the use of heuristics that they had identified under the previous ownership regime, but which they were unable to exploit because the constraints of a larger corporation meant that they would need to provide systematic evidence relating to the opportunity which may not have been available in the uncertain context associated with entrepreneurship. The resultant buyouts are *entrepreneurial buyouts* (Quadrant 3) and involve managers with idiosyncratic skills who may be able to process such incomplete information in contrast to those managers who respond well to close monitoring to prevent shirking. Examples of this type of buyout may arise in technological sectors where in contrast to division managers, parent corporation managers lack the capability to understand or manage the technology, but where divisional management do. There is quite strong survey evidence that demonstrates that managers are motivated to undertake the buyout as it affords them the scope to be able to develop strategic opportunities stymied under the previous owners, as well as to control their own destiny (Wright & Coyne, 1985). In the US, managers of the clothing store chain Kohl's acquired the business out of BAT, a large diversified conglomerate, following the purchase with the introduction of a range of innovations such as new store design as well as transforming it into a hybrid discounter/department store.

A variant of Quadrant 3 involves cases where entrepreneurial owner-managers have the capabilities and incentives to pursue entrepreneurial activities from start-up through to and beyond IPO, but where control mechanisms fail to develop at the same pace. Such firms may subsequently encounter financial problems, generating the opportunity for a busted tech buyout. That is, a buyout can be negotiated to introduce the appropriate governance mechanisms to better monitor and control the continued or renewed exploitation of entrepreneurial opportunities. In 2000, the struggling disk drive company Seagate Technology underwent a public-to-private buyout so that, away from the short-term demands of stock market analysts, it would be able to restructure and develop new innovative products with higher margins. By 2002, Seagate returned to the stock market, and by August 2003 was named the number one company for innovation and enterprise in disc drives by *VAR Business Magazine*.

Entrepreneurial buyouts may need a degree of leverage below the norm for buyouts in mature sectors in order that it can use cash flow to develop new opportunities rather than to service interest payments. These buyouts may also need a PE investor with significant expertise in being able to help the buyout be entrepreneurial, rather than just the traditional monitoring skills. However, a mismatch may arise between the availability of opportunities, the governance mechanisms provided by the PE firm, and the financing structure, as well as the mindset of managers, leading to a *buyout failure* case (Quadrant 4).

As we have seen elsewhere in this volume (Howorth and Robinson, Chapter 9 and Ahlers et al., Chapter 8) buyouts can be used to facilitate the continuance of a family firm. Controlling ownership in the family firm can be acquired by non-family managers. An MBO may preserve the family identity and culture of the firm, perhaps in a transformed manner (Howorth et al., 2016) and the psychic income of the former family owners can be maintained if they secure continuing involvement in the buyout such as providing networking links with suppliers and customers that the family has traded with for many years. Non-family managers may be able to identify and pursue entrepreneurial opportunities resisted prior to the buyout by family owner-managers who may have been more focused on agendas linked to family lifestyle instead of enhancing efficiency and profitability (Wright et al., 2001b). As such, the buyout may be essential to ensure the continued survival of the firm as an entity. When dominant family owners have not developed a strong non-family managerial cadre, managerial talent from outside the firm may be required (Wright et al., 2016). In buyout terms, this may mean acquisition by means of an MBI so as to pursue entrepreneurial opportunities that were being missed. However, there are potential pitfalls, such as failure to recognize that it is the founder who has the tacit knowledge required to make the business successful and that once s/he has departed entrepreneurial opportunities may be extremely challenging. Buybacks by founders of companies that have struggled after a buyout because of this problem are not uncommon.

The strategic entrepreneurship perspective also emphasizes the importance of the resources necessary for opportunities to be exploited. These resources relate to the human and social capital of the managers leading the buyout as well as the finance and human and social capital of PE backers relating to strategy, operations, marketing, and mergers and acquisitions (Meuleman et al., 2009), as well as sector expertise (Cressy et al., 2007). It may be necessary to bring in outside managers who possess the tacit knowledge and idiosyncratic skills required to seize new opportunities (Hendry, 2002). PE firms play an important role in identifying such individuals as well as providing the benefits of their networks and relationships with potential new customers and suppliers. Buyouts with entrepreneurial opportunities may need greater involvement from the PE investor to help develop entrepreneurial competencies through establishing new ventures/acquisitions, broadening market focus, and reviewing R&D, budgets, and marketing plans (Bruining & Wright, 2002).

The more experienced PE firms are through undertaking and successfully exiting deals, the more likely they are to develop a depth and breadth of their knowledge and networks relating to markets. Research from the venture capital sector has shown that such contacts provide privileged access to expert advice which might contribute to the identification and realization of entrepreneurial opportunities (Hochberg et al., 2005).

Buyouts with entrepreneurial potential may also need more intense PE involvement to enable them to identify and exploit such opportunities. PE firms may differ in the size of an investment executive's portfolio. All else being equal, the greater the number of investments in a PE firm's portfolio for a given number of executives, the more difficult it will likely be to devote sufficient time to providing the specialist knowledge required to develop new opportunities. PE investors seeking to provide added entrepreneurial value, therefore, may need to limit the size of their investment portfolio. Alternatively, they may need to recruit a larger, more experienced team, which may presents major challenges in the thin labor market in PE for such expertise (Wright et al., 2010).

Previous investment experience and intensity of involvement by PE firms may be particularly important in divisional buyouts that have been constrained by parental policies, since it means that PE firms are likely to have developed the expertise to monitor investees and help identify and exploit entrepreneurial opportunities.

The framework for understanding the different entrepreneurial mindsets and types of buyouts is a static one and says little about the temporal dynamics involved in the development of entrepreneurial activities. Bacon et al. (2013) distinguish short- and longer-term approaches to the development of growth following buyout, which may involve different entrepreneurial strategies.

Firms that remain with a buyout structure for a short period before exiting through a trade sale or IPO may provide scope to obtain capital and know-how for rapid growth. What Bacon et al. (2013) call "rapid rebounders," these buyouts grow quickly by expanding current business activities. For example, the secondary buyout of Gondola engaged in entrepreneurial activities involving shared management services, the introduction of a professional marketing department and a commercially-oriented accounts department, the creation of a common supply chain, and rapid increases in the number of restaurants.

Some PE-backed buyouts create value from a long-term approach to ownership and an emphasis on organizational growth to increase value. PE firms allocate capital to better and more entrepreneurial executives and managers who introduce superior strategic and operational knowledge to improve performance. These buyouts require a long-term perspective since it takes time for entrepreneurial actions to raise the exit value of the buyout (Tåg, 2012).

Evidence on entrepreneurship in buyouts

Besides improvements in financial, economic, and employment performance resulting from efficiency improvements, reviewed in other chapters in this volume, evidence shows that MBOs may also have an impact on the entrepreneurial activities of portfolio firms (Wright et al., 2000, 2001a; Meuleman et al., 2009). In this section we review the evidence relating to entrepreneurial growth, which includes new product and market development as well as growth by acquisition, exporting, and innovation. We include evidence on the role of PE investors in facilitating entrepreneurial activity.

Entrepreneurial growth

Studies relating to the early wave of buyouts have shown that PE backing oftentimes results in an increase in new product development and extension of products into new markets (Wright & Coyne, 1985; Wright et al., 1992; Zahra, 1995), with buyouts engaging in asset and organizational restructuring to a greater extent than non-buyouts (Wiersema & Liebeskind, 1995). The evidence on the impact of buyouts on CAPEX and R&D expenditure is mixed (Lichtenberg & Siegel, 1990; Long & Ravenscraft, 1993), but there is some evidence that it is maintained in more innovative sectors and that better use is made of the expenditure that is made (Zahra, 1995). Divisional buyouts previously constrained by their parents particularly show evidence of entrepreneurial growth (Wright et al., 2000). Divisional buyouts that trade with their former parent typically are able to reduce their dependence on the former parent following buyout as they have greater discretion to seek new customers and markets (Wright, 1986).

The resources provided by PE firms' experience are a significant driver of higher growth in divisional buyouts (Meuleman et al., 2009). Further, the intensity of PE involvement in portfolio companies is associated with higher growth.

The rationale for secondary mangeemnt buyouts (SMBOs) is oftentimes argued to be that a further buyout is required to exploit entrepreneurial growth opportunities as the benefits from efficiency improvements have largely been exhausted in the first buyout. In an SMBO, new PE investors may be introduced who believe they have the expertise to help grow the business, for example through internationalizing activities. Emerging evidence suggests that

SMBOs struggle to achieve entrepreneurial growth unless backed by experienced PE firms (Degeorge et al., 2013) and oftentimes this is achieved through acquisitions rather than through organic growth (Wang, 2012). The classic buyout incentive and control mechanisms are not associated with growth in SMBOs (Zhou et al., 2014).

More recent evidence has attempted a more fine-grained assessment of the expertise of PE investors in helping the SMBO to grow. SMBOs with PE directors with high-level business education are significantly and positively associated with growth performance, while PE directors with complementary human capital to selling PE directors through high-level business education have better profitability/growth (Jelic et al., 2018).

Exporting

Exporting is an important entrepreneurial activity, typically involving different levels of risk compared with home markets (Wright et al., 2007). Studies of buyouts and PE have devoted little attention to exporting, yet the buyout may provide the conditions that both release a firm from the governance, risk orientation, and financing constraints imposed by a previous ownership regime (George et al., 2005), as well as providing monitoring and value-adding resources that help such firms to begin or increase exporting (Pruthi et al., 2003; Zahra et al., 2007).

Shortcomings in internal monitoring prior to the buyout may have led to sub-optimal internationalization behavior. Management may have been constrained by the former owners' head office strategies and financial controls (Wright et al., 2000) that adversely impacted their ability to engage in export markets. They may also have opted for the easier option of home markets even though these may not have been the most profitable or may have not fully exploited international market opportunities. The buyout provides the ownership incentive and PE firm monitoring to encourage the new owner/managers to be both more entrepreneurial in seeking out new revenue sources from international markets as well as being more efficient in using their existing internal resources. Post-buyout the investors may introduce onto the board directors with wider networks and experience of export markets who can bring their relationships with corporate partners at home and overseas. The introduction of external PE monitoring resources will improve financial discipline in the firm and may help to overcome previous organizational inertia regarding exporting. PE firms may also be able to provide expertise and contacts that can facilitate exporting.

An initial study of exporting in PE-backed firms was based on a cross-sectional mailed questionnaire survey. Lockett et al. (2008), in a European study of 340 VC-backed firms that included PE-backed buyouts in the UK, argue and find support for the hypothesis that monitoring as opposed to value-adding inputs by PE firms will be more important for buyouts than for early stage VC-backed firms in assisting the international expansion of the business.

Building on general arguments and evidence from the exporting literature (Love & Roper, 2015), the introduction of PE investment may mean that better performing firms now select into exporting and/or the PE investor acts to increase the export intensity of buyout firms that already have some export experience via both further increases in efficiency and the exploitation of the PE representatives' wider networks of relationships overseas.

Wilson and Wright (2017) explore exporting using a panel dataset covering the period 1998–2013 and involving 2.6 million company-level observations including PE-backed buyouts and other firms in the UK of which around 10% are actively engaged in exporting. Among the PE subsample around 23% were actively engaged in exporting and, on average, around 10% of sales were exported, higher than the population average. Controlling for other factors, they find that PE-backed buyouts are more likely to be internationalized (*export propensity*) than the control sample of non-buyouts. They find a positive and significant relationship between total factor productivity (TFP) and *export propensity* with firms with more know-how, innovation, and expertise being more likely to be exporters (Wilson & Wright, 2017).

With respect to *export intensity* (the share of sales that are exported), Wilson and Wright (2017) find a positive and significant coefficient on PE backing and a negative sign on a dummy variable relating to pre-PE investment, indicating an uplift in export performance of firms post-PE investment. Firms with PE backing appear to have a percentage export differential of 2–3% over the control group of non-PE-backed firms. The PE-backed buyouts were found to have a growth rate of 6.2% in export sales post-buyout compared to 5.9% in the same period for non-buyouts that were regular exporters. Moreover some 15% of buyouts that were not exporting pre-buyout became exporters. Interestingly, among PE backed buyouts, the mid-size range firms with an asset value of £10–£50m had a higher export intensity compared to larger PE-backed firms. The percentage of foreign nationals on the board has a positive and significant effect along with the average age and experience of the board directors on both *export propensity* and *export intensity*.

Innovation

Although covered in more detail in this volume in the chapter by Bertoni, MBOs can have an entrepreneurial impact in terms of changes to the firm's innovative activities. The early evidence on R&D activity is mixed, but more recently, studies have also examined the impact of PE backing for buyouts on innovation activity as measured by the effectiveness of patenting activity (Ughetto, 2010; Lerner et al., 2011).

The study by Ughetto (2010) of the number of patents granted by the European Patent Office and the likelihood of filling at least one successful patent application in a sample of European buyouts, is interesting, because it shows that the innovation activity of buyouts is contingent on contextual factors relating to the characteristics of firms and different types of lead investors and their associated different goals and attitudes to risk and investment. There is also evidence that PE backing of buyouts leads to a release of financial constraints on patenting activity, notably in relation to patent citations (Amess et al., 2015), and that this shift is most pronounced in divisional and family firm buyouts.

Further research

We have identified evidence of the importance of MBOs in increasing entrepreneurial activity regarding both the propensity and intensity of exporting by the firms involved. Although we showed that board characteristics are influential regarding exporting, more refined analysis of board diversity and networks is needed to assess the added value of PE involvement. Further, the evidence on exporting lacks detail on the countries involved and further analysis is required. In particular, as yet, we have no insights into whether the increase in export intensity is due to an increase in exporting in countries where buyouts are already present or whether they enter new countries. Evidence is also needed on the exporting activity of different types of buyouts and buyouts from different vendor sources.

We showed theoretically that different types of buyouts may be expected to involve variations in cognition by the managers involved, notably whether they have a managerial or entrepreneurial mindset. However, at present we lack studies that measure empirically how the cognitive approach of these managers differs. Further, more fine-grained work is also needed to explore differences between managers involved in MBOs, management buyins, and SMBOs, and between these managers and other entrepreneurs such as those starting a venture.

In the general entrepreneurship literature there has been a heated debate on the extent to which entrepreneurial opportunities are discovered or created or involve elements of both (Alvarez & Barney, 2007; Busenitz et al., 2017). Research on entrepreneurial buyouts has yet to explore discovery and creation processes.

Although there have been recent developments in understanding entrepreneurial processes in traditional start-up ventures and academic spin-offs (Vohora et al., 2004; Rasmussen et al., 2014), we know little about the entrepreneurial process in MBOs. Bruining (this volume) considers resource orchestration processes in case studies of MBOs based on the constructs identified by Sirmon et al. (2007) in respect of corporations. However, the same constructs may not be appropriate for all types of ventures. For example, Baert et al. (2016) identify the resource orchestration constructs of sharing, transforming, and harmonizing in the context of portfolio entrepreneurship compared to larger corporations. In the context of MBOs, there is therefore a need to explore whether and to what extent distinctive resource orchestration constructs are present. Further, given our identification of different levels and types of entrepreneurial behavior, additional research may also seek to identify whether there are distinctive resource orchestration constructs associated with each.

Further extending this research lies the question of how buyouts change their resource orchestration processes from before the buyout compared with post-buyout. The different types of buyouts may also vary in this respect. A key question concerns which actor(s) initiate and lead the orchestration, that is, whether management or PE firms are the prime movers. From the perspective of the PE firm, an interesting issue concerns whether and to what extent they have a "template" approach that they apply to all of their portfolio or whether they adapt their approach as they learn from prior portfolio firm investments.

Process aspects introduce a temporal dimension to entrepreneurship in buyouts. We have referred to short- and long-term aspects of buyouts but, although there is extensive evidence on the longevity of buyouts (see the chapter by Jelic et al. in this volume), we still lack analysis of the contribution of entrepreneurial activities to the longevity of the buyout form. Further, it is unclear to what extent too much or too little entrepreneurial activity increases the likelihood of failure.

MBOs represent one type of entrepreneurial ownership mobility (Wright, 2016), that is organizational forms where changes in ownership may impact the ability of the actors to exploit entrepreneurial opportunities. Other types of entrepreneurial ownership mobility involve the spin-offs of inventions from universities by faculty scientists (Vohora et al., 2004; Wennberg et al., 2011), the transfer of ownership between generations of family firms (Miller et al., 2015), the geographical ownership mobility of returnee (Wright et al., 2008) and transnational entrepreneurs (Drori et al., 2009; Pruthi & Wright, 2017), the ownership mobility by habitual entrepreneurs as they create more ventures in their portfolio or sell one venture to create or acquire a subsequent one (Westhead & Wright, 2016), and the spinning off by employees of larger corporations to create new ventures. While there is a developing body of research on the entrepreneurial activities of these different types, additional research is warranted that attempts to synthesize and compare the relative impact of each type. With respect to buyouts, for example, to what extent are entrepreneurial opportunities more incremental than the entrepreneurial opportunities pursued through the other forms of entrepreneurial mobility? To what extent do the entrepreneurial opportunities in buyouts vary depending on whether managers are proactive in proposing a buyout or whether they are reacting to a decision by the parent to divest or close the division?

There is growing recognition that entrepreneurship may have a dark side in terms of its impact at societal and individual levels (Zahra & Wright, 2011). At the societal level entrepreneurship may have adverse impacts on the environment, on working conditions, etc. At the individual level, entrepreneurship may be associated with stress, family tension, and break-ups, etc. The debate involving PE-backed buyouts that exploded during the first and second waves of the phenomenon considered dark side questions about the potential adverse impacts on employment, investment, and R&D in particular based on notions of short-termism and cost efficiencies. Further research is needed regarding the extent to which board involvement by investors in buyouts can constrain excessive entrepreneurial risk-taking by management. While there are well-recognized agency costs of debt, especially for managers with little equity ownership, managers taking on high levels of corporate debt in a buyout as well as potentially second mortgages on their homes and guarantees may be under greater personal and family stress than they were as employees. To what extent does this impact the nature of their entrepreneurial risk-taking exploiting entrepreneurial opportunities? How can PE firms address these concerns? Do managers become more risk averse or less able to focus on identifying and exploiting opportunities? To what extent are the dark sides of buying out for managers greater than in the case of start-up entrepreneurs and top management in larger corporations?

Finally, a potential dark side to entrepreneurial activities in buyouts concerns the extent to which managers buying out exploit information regarding entrepreneurial opportunities by not disclosing this to pre-buyout owners. These concerns have been heightened in respect of buyouts that are exited within very short periods after deal completion. This has been especially an issue with respect to buyouts of formerly state-owned enterprises. On the one hand, this may mean that managers effectively buy the firm at below its "true cost." On the other, to the extent that the perceptions of these opportunities are subjective, they may be viewed as returns to managers' human capital that are not being recognized by current owners. These issues may potentially be greater in peripheral divisions of large conglomerates and state-owned firms, the latter especially in weak institutional environments. There has been some discussion of the potential ethical problems in buyouts in relation to pricing (Sun et al., 2010). Auctions and clawback mechanisms have been proposed as potential solutions to this problem, rather than allowing management to be the preferred or even sole bidder. However, such processes may do little to solve asymmetric information problems that serve to advantage management insiders at the expense of vendors and competing bidders, especially in respect of sales of divisions that did not have separate accounts prior to the sale. Further more fine-grained research is needed that focuses on "unproductive" entrepreneurial behavior in this context.

Conclusions

In this chapter we have explored the theoretical and empirical evidence relating to entrepreneurial aspects of MBOs. We have also shown that the nature of entrepreneurship in buyouts may be contingent on the particular context, notably the vendor context, from which the deal emanated. In particular, buyouts from divisions and family firms seem to fare better than secondary buyouts and, especially during the second wave of buyouts, public-to-private buyouts (Guo et al., 2011).

The studies reviewed in this chapter have important implications for buyout practice. The scope for entrepreneurial activities suggests that practitioners may be able to generate significant returns in buyout deals rather than relying simply on efficiency gains. This route may offer interesting options for investors in the light of evidence of declining portfolio returns (Kaplan & Sensoy, 2015). However, caveats are in order. First, there is a need to develop expertise in the buyouts themselves but also in the PE backers that have the capability and level of involvement to undertake entrepreneurial actions. Such expertise relates particularly to board members with sector, exporting experience, and networks. Second, the ability to generate high returns from entrepreneurship in secondary buyouts appears, on average, to be particularly difficult. This is a specific concern given that the value of secondary buyouts completed annually exceeds that for primary buyouts. A major challenge therefore for investors concerns their ability to be able to identify sufficient primary buyouts with entrepreneurial potential.

References

Alvarez, S., & Barney, J. 2007. Discovery and creation: Alternative theories of entrepreneurial action. *Strategic Entrepreneurship Journal*, 1: 11–26.

Amess, K., Stiebale, J., & Wright, M. 2015. The impact of private equity on firms' innovation activity. *European Economic Review*, 86: 147–160.

Bacon, N., Wright, M., Ball, R., & Meuleman, M. 2013. Private equity, HRM and employment. *Academy of Management Perspectives*, 27: 7–21.

Baert, C., Meuleman, M., Debruyne, M., & Wright, M. 2016. Portfolio entrepreneurship and resource orchestration. *Strategic Entrepreneurship Journal*, 10: 346–370.

Bradley, K., & Nejad, A. 1989. *The NFC buyout*. Cambridge, UK: Cambridge University Press.

Bruining, H., & Wright, M. 2002. Entrepreneurial orientation in management buy-outs and the contribution of venture capital. *Venture Capital*, 4: 147–168.

Busenitz, L., Dimov, D., Fiet, J., McMullen, J., Gregoire, D., & Wright, M. 2017. Debate about the nature of entrepreneurial opportunities. In C. Léger-Jarniou & S. Tegtmeier (Eds.), *Opportunity formation*. Cheltenham, UK: Edward Elgar.

Cressy, R., Malipiero, A., & Munari, F. 2007. Playing to their strengths? Evidence that specialization in the private equity industry confers competitive advantage. *Journal of Corporate Finance*, 13: 647–669.

Degeorge, F., Martin, J., & Phalippou, L. 2013. *The consequences of secondary buyouts for private equity investors*. Paper presented at the Coller Institute Conference on Private Equity, London Business School.

Drori, I., Honig, B., & Wright, M. 2009. Transnational entrepreneurship: An emergent field of study. *Entrepreneurship Theory and Practice*, 33: 1001–1022.

George, G., Wiklund, J., & Zahra, S. A. 2005. Ownership and the internationalization of small firms. *Journal of Management*, 31: 210–233.

Guo, S., Hotchkiss, E., & Song, W. 2011. Do buy-outs (still) create value? *Journal of Finance*, 66: 479–517.

Hendry, J. 2002. The principal's other problems: Honest incompetence and the specification of objectives. *Academy of Management Review*, 27: 98–113.

Hochberg, Y., Ljungqvist, A., & Lu, Y. 2005. Whom you know matters: Venture capital networks and investment performance. *Journal of Finance*, 62: 251–301.

Howorth, C., Wright, M., Westhead, P., & Allcock, D. 2016. Company metamorphosis: Professionalization waves, family firms and management buyouts. *Small Business Economics*, 47: 803–817.

Ireland, R. D., Hitt, M. A., & Sirmon, D. G. 2003. Strategic entrepreneurship: The construct and its dimensions. *Journal of Management*, 29: 963–989.

Jelic, R., Zhou, D., & Wright, M. 2018. Sustaining the buyout governance model: Inside secondary management buyout boards. *British Journal of Management*, forthcoming.

Kaplan, S., & Sensoy, B. 2015. *Private equity performance: A survey*. Charles A. Dice Center Working Paper No. 2015-10.

Karsai, J., & Wright, M. 1994. Accountability, governance and management buy-outs in Hungary. *Europe-Asia Studies*, 46: 997–1016.

Lerner, J., Sørensen, M., & Strömberg, P. 2011. Private equity and long-run investment: The case of innovation. *The Journal of Finance*, 66: 445–477.

Lichtenberg, F., & Siegel, D. 1990. The effect of leveraged buyouts on productivity and related aspects of firm behavior. *Journal of Financial Economics*, 27: 165–194.

Lockett, A., Wright, M., Burrows, A., Scholes, L., & Paton, D. 2008. Export intensity of venture capital backed companies. *Small Business Economics*, 31: 39–58.

Loihl, A., & Wright, M. 2002. *Seagate Technology Case*. CMBOR, Nottingham University Business School.

Long, W. F., & Ravenscraft, D. 1993. LBOs, debt and R & D intensity. *Strategic Management Journal*, 14: 119–135.

Love, J., & Roper, S. 2015. SME innovation, exporting and growth: A review of existing evidence. *International Small Business Journal*, 33: 28–48.

Meuleman, M., Amess, K., Wright, M., & Scholes, L. 2009. Agency, strategic entrepreneurship and the performance of private equity backed buyouts. *Entrepreneurship Theory and Practice*, 33: 213–240.

Miller, D., Wright, M., Lebreton-Miller, I., & Scholes, L. 2015. Resources and innovation in family businesses: The Janus-face of family socio-emotional preferences. *California Management Review*, 58: 20–40.

Pruthi, M., & Wright, M. 2017. Social ties, prior experience and venture creation by transnational entrepreneurs. *International Journal of Entrepreneurship and Small Business*, DOI: 10.1504/IJESB.2019.10010772..

Pruthi, S., Wright, M., & Lockett, A. 2003. Do foreign and domestic venture capital firms differ in their monitoring of investees? *Asia Pacific Journal of Management*, 20: 175–204.

Rasmussen, E., Mosey, S., & Wright, M. 2014. The influence of university departments on the evolution of entrepreneurial competencies in spin-off ventures. *Research Policy*, 43: 92–106.

Robbie, K., & Wright, M. 1996. Local authorities, compulsory competitive tendering and buy outs. *Local Government Studies*, 22: 127–146.

Schumpeter, J. 1934. *The theory of economic development: An inquiry into profits, capital, credit, interest and the business cycle*. Piscataway, NJ: Transaction Publishers.

Sirmon, D. G., Hitt, M., & Ireland, R. D. 2007. Managing firm resources in dynamic environments to create value: Looking inside the black box. *Academy of Management Review*, 32: 273–292.

Sun, P., Wright, M., & Mellahi, K. 2010. Is entrepreneur-politician alliance sustainable during transition? The case of management buyouts in China. *Management & Organization Review*, 6: 101–122.

Tåg, J. 2012. The real effects of private equity buyouts. In D. Cumming (Ed.), *The Oxford handbook of private equity*. Oxford, UK: Oxford University Press, 271–299.

Thompson, S., & Wright, M. 1988. *Internal organization, efficiency and profit*. Deddington, UK: Philip Allan.

Thompson, S., Wright, M., & Robbie, K. 1990. Management buy-outs and privatisation: Organisational form and incentive issues. *Fiscal Studies*, 11: 71–88.

Ughetto, E. 2010. Assessing the contribution to innovation of private equity investors: A study on European buyouts. *Research Policy*, 39: 126–140.

Vohora, A., Wright, M., & Lockett, A. 2004. Critical junctures in spin-outs from universities. *Research Policy*, 33:147–175.

Wang, Y. 2012. Secondary buyouts: Why buy and at what price? *Journal of Corporate Finance*, 18: 1306–1325.

Wennberg, K., Wiklund, J., & Wright, M. 2011. The effectiveness of university knowledge spillovers: Performance differences between university spinoffs and corporate spinoffs. *Research Policy*, 40: 1128–1143.

Westhead, P., & Wright, M. 2016. *The habitual entrepreneur*. London: Routledge.

Wiersema, M., &. Liebeskind, J. 1995. The effects of leveraged buyouts on corporate growth and diversification within large firms. *Strategic Management Journal*, 16: 447–460.

Wieser, O., Wright, M., & Robbie, K. 1997. Austrian buy-outs from the public sector. *Annals of Public and Cooperative Economics*, 68: 689–712.

Wilson, N. & Wright, M. 2017. *Private equity and exporting*. Report prepared for British Venture Capital Association.

Wright, M. 1986. The make-buy decision and managing markets: The case of management buy-outs. *Journal of Management Studies*, 23: 443–464.

Wright, M. (ed.) 1994. *Technical note on management and employee buy-outs in Central and Eastern Europe*. EBRD/CEEPN, January 1994.
Wright, M. 2016. The conquest of interestingness: Entrepreneurial ownership mobility. In D. Audretsch & E. Lehmann (Eds.), *Companion to makers of modern entrepreneurship*. New York: Routledge.
Wright, M., & Coyne, J. 1985. *Management buyouts*. Beckenham, UK: Croom Helm.
Wright, M., DeMassis, A., Scholes, L., Kotlar, J., & Hughes, M. 2016. *Entrepreneurship and family business*. London: Institute for Family Business.
Wright, M., Filatotchev, I., Buck, T., & Robbie, K. 1994. Accountability and efficiency in privatisation by buy-out in CEE. *Financial Accountability and Management*, 10: 195–214.
Wright, M., Hoskisson, R., & Busenitz, L. 2001a. Firm rebirth: Buyouts as facilitators of strategic growth and entrepreneurship. *The Academy of Management Executive*, 15: 111–125.
Wright, M., Hoskisson, R., Busenitz, L., & Dial, J. 2000. Entrepreneurial growth through privatization: The upside of management buyouts. *Academy of Management Review*, 25: 591–601.
Wright, M., Hoskisson, R., Busenitz, L., & Dial, J. 2001b. Finance and management buy-outs: Agency versus entrepreneurship perspectives. *Venture Capital*, 3: 239–261.
Wright, M., Jackson, A., & Frobisher, S. 2010. Private equity: Building the new future. *Journal of Applied Corporate Finance*, 22: 86–95.
Wright, M., Liu, X., Buck, T., & Filatotchev, I. 2008. Returnee entrepreneur characteristics, science park location choice and performance: An analysis of high technology SMEs in China. *Entrepreneurship Theory and Practice*, 32: 131–156.
Wright, M., Thompson, S., & Robbie, K. 1992. Venture capital and management-led leveraged buy-outs. *Journal of Business Venturing*, 7: 47–71.
Wright, M., Thompson, S., & Robbie, K. 1993. Financial control in privatisation by management buy-out. *Financial, Accountability and Management*, 9: 75–99.
Wright, M., Westhead, P., & Ucbasaran, D. 2007. Internationalisation by SMEs: A critique and policy implications. *Regional Studies*, 41: 1013–1030.
Zahra, S. 1995. Corporate entrepreneurship and financial performance: The case of management leveraged buyouts. *Journal of Business Venturing*, 10: 225–247.
Zahra, S., Neubaum, D. O., & Naldi, L. 2007. The effects of ownership and governance on SMEs' international knowledge-based resources. *Small Business Economics*, 29: 309–327.
Zahra, S., & Wright, M. 2011. The other side of paradise: Examining the dark side of entrepreneurship. *Entrepreneurship Research Journal*, 1: 1–5.
Zhou, D., Jelic, R., & Wright, M. 2014. SMBOs: Buying time or improving performance? *Managerial and Decision Economics*, 35: 88–102.

22

RESOURCE ORCHESTRATION POST-MANAGEMENT BUYOUT

Hans Bruining

Introduction

Financial expertise, negotiation skills, insights into debt markets, and experience in optimizing capital structure are all important drivers of value creation for private equity (PE) investors. However, for the purpose of value generation in buyouts, PE investors cannot do without capable management who take actions to restructure, revitalize, and grow the business. In fact, managerial knowledge of operational and industry requirements is crucial to buyout success. In this chapter we show how buyouts of mature firms are managed to create value drawing on the concept of resource orchestration (Sirmon et al., 2011). More specifically, we look at the actions taken by new owners to better manage the company's resources and capabilities post-buyout from three levels. First, we consider the post-buyout changes to strategy described in the buyout literature (Gilligan & Wright, 2014) and the consequences for the resources they acquire, accumulate, and divest. Then we review buyout studies to identify management initiatives to improve the efficiency of existing capabilities, and to enrich or acquire new capabilities, in order to improve a firm's competitive position. Finally, we trace organizational changes in buyouts that help coordinate capabilities to support the implementation of strategies to improve firm performance. Implementing strategies to improve buyout performance requires management and organizational changes that improve existing, extend current, and build new capabilities, and coordinate them post-buyout to create value.

Usually it is a significant advantage if managers know pre-buyout how the business must be conducted after the buyout. This involves understanding the resources and capabilities required to exploit post-buyout opportunities. Sometimes adjustments have already been put in motion before the buyout and gain momentum after the buyout. In other cases, the necessary adjustments emanate from buyout negotiations with the PE investors. We argue that without appropriate and timely implemented changes in management, organization, and strategy, the responsible management team cannot manage the firm's resources adequately and thus cannot create an efficient, adaptive, and innovative firm that generates value. To make sufficient progress with these changes in buyouts, management and investors need to balance managerial as well as entrepreneurial mind sets and incentives (Wright et al., 2000). PE investors can play an important role in creating an ambidextrous mix of administrative and entrepreneurial management (Bruining et al., 2013). This supports the firm to adapt to the dynamics of the industry by simultaneously developing new products, creating operational efficiency, increasing organizational collaboration, and enhancing the strategic distinctiveness of the buyout firm, with each of these offering potential for value creation.

In this chapter we use the resource management model from Sirmon et al. (2007) to explore the resource management process in buyouts stemming from four main sources: divisional buyouts, family firm/private buyouts, secondary buyouts (SBOs), and buyouts from receivership. We adapt the model for buyouts and illustrate how new owners orchestrate their resources and capabilities to create value by improving exploitation of existing opportunities and creating new entrepreneurial opportunities – a process that involves changing the firm's strategic focus (Morrow et al., 2007). Drawing on case studies of buyouts from each of these sources we outline resource-related actions of managers/owners in PE-backed buyouts and capture the associated changes in management, organization, and strategy post-buyout. This helps them to anticipate the actions required in terms of firm resource management to improve performance. Anticipating these changes should help managerial-investor alignment and further clarify the expected contributions of each. The structure is as follows. First, we define buyouts and present different buyout sources. Second, we review the buyout literature (Gilligan & Wright, 2014) identifying what we know about post-buyout changes to strategy, management, and organization. We link the findings for the changes to the resource management model of Sirmon et al. (2007) and adapt the model to cover the reported changes following buyout. Third, drawing on buyout cases from four main sources we illustrate how new owners transform resources and capabilities post-buyout by taking action with regard to four aspects of resource management, specifically strategy, structuring resources, bundling resources, and leveraging capabilities. Fourth, we analyze the findings across the case studies and present differences and similarities in post-buyout resource management. Finally, we draw conclusions for the successful orchestration of resource management for managers and PE investors and discuss implications.

Definition and sources of buyouts

According to Wright et al. (2000) a buyout is an acquisition of a firm by a group of individual managers and investors. Buyouts involve new ownership and governance structures. These take the form of managerial equity ownership, commitment to create new growth opportunities, pressure to service debt, and in many cases ownership and active involvement by the PE investor. The PE investors, before committing themselves, conduct due diligence and consider strategic plans by gathering privileged information from discussions with management and trusted external sources. A due diligence report screens the firms' resources and capabilities and its position in the market. For example, it seeks to establish whether products/services are new and uncontested or just introduced, or already settled or declining. It also considers if resources and capabilities are in line with needs, redundant, or require developing. In addition, it considers whether the firm's organizational configuration is in a good or bad shape, whether staff reduction is necessary, or current staff skills require development.

In each buyout the new owners are strongly motivated to further the economic development of the firm and managers/employees require courage to personally invest in the firm. By doing this, they align with the PE investor's goals and communicate a sense of urgency to do what is best for the company in the short and the long term. In addition to a managerial mind set to improve existing capabilities, adopting an entrepreneurial mind set (Wright et al., 2000) is indispensable to the effective implementation of changes that tap into new opportunities for value creation post-buyout. This requires restructuring of the resource portfolio and expansion or skills renewal, as we will explain later. In larger deals, PE firms have a majority of the equity and monitor performance to stay in control of value generation, providing strategic advice to guide the long-term development of the buyout firm.

Buyout sources

Looking at the total value (equity and debt of the deals) of the market for buyouts and buyins, SBOs take nearly half of the total value, followed by divisional buyouts stemming from local and foreign parent firms (30% of total value), while private/family firm buyouts account for only 18%. However, in terms of numbers, the main buyout source is private/family firm buyouts (44%), followed by buyouts from local or foreign parent firms (25%), and SBOs (23%) (CMBOR, 2015). Buyouts, especially those backed by PE, can lead to significant changes in a firm's ownership composition and subsequent rate of growth (Scholes et al., 2010). This is reflected in strategy, organizational, and management practices.

Bringing about changes is not a "one size fits all" exercise for all buyouts. No buyout is the same. In the case of divisional buyouts some firms have been denied access to financial resources for growth and modernization for a long time because the parent firm was financially troubled. Other divisional buyouts did not belong to the core business of the parent firm, although timely divestment may not have deprived them of resources for a prolonged period. The possible consequences may vary from catch up investment to a refocus of strategy and entering new markets following buyout (Wright et al., 2001). Buyouts from other sources like family firms, which are characterized by succession problems, may have suffered from under-investment by risk-averse and aging founders. Another issue, also often affecting buyouts of family firms, is that the authoritarian style of leadership of founders may also have encouraged managerial and staff disengagement (Ball et al., 2008). Catch up investment and changes in managerial style and organization culture are therefore often required post-buyout. Changes in SBOs are less clear. SBOs may require financial backing by a PE industry expert to further focus on efficiency to reduce costs or growth to improve revenues. In buyouts from receivership, turnaround often requires substantial changes in resources and capabilities to improve business processes and implement the strategy successfully.

The next section examines and links the evidence from the strategy, management, and organizational changes after the buyout to the resource management model of Sirmon et al. (2007).

Buyout literature

Strategy changes

The business plans of buyouts mobilize the identification of resources and capabilities needed to exploit market opportunities based on external and internal analyses, as well as investments needed in new capabilities to develop new products/services. They are a vital tool for any company seeking any type of investment funding, because they document a company's management, business concept, and goals (Gilligan & Wright, 2014), and lay the foundation for a shared value creation focus between management and PE investor (Acharya et al., 2009). Once they are analyzed on readiness to exploit opportunities in current and adjacent markets and verified by the PE investor's due diligence process, it can be decided which resources should be divested, acquired, and/or accumulated to develop new capabilities and new markets.

New owners often change the strategic focus of buyouts by reviewing the firm's resource portfolio. The buyout literature since the late 1990s (Gilligan & Wright, 2014) suggests this involves buyouts acquiring, accumulating, and divesting resources. Growth-oriented buyout deals use acquisitions and joint ventures (Gottschalg, 2007) to develop new markets and products. Acquisition capabilities of PE investors are important drivers of profitability and growth in divisional buyouts and of post-buyout efficiency improvement (Cressy et al., 2007; Meuleman et al., 2009; Alperovych et al., 2013). Buyouts accumulate resources by increased alertness to opportunities for creating wealth (Bull, 1989) such as developing new but related products (Wright et al., 1992; Seth & Easterwood, 1993; Phan & Hill, 1995), new product development, and improvements to marketing and cost control (Malone, 1989; Zahra, 1995; Bruining & Wright, 2002). Divestment is also an important issue, for example, Muscarella and Vetsuypens (1990) reported that US leveraged buyouts, which are relatively more diversified than EU buyouts, improved strategic focus by acquisitions in 25% of cases and by divestment and reorganization in more than 40% of cases. In the UK, 18% of buyouts sell surplus land and buildings and 21% sell surplus equipment (Wright et al., 1992). Other studies of US buyouts report cost-cutting by asset sales and disposals that lower capital expenditure (Kaplan, 1989). The strategies that buyouts implement reduce diversification (Wiersema & Liebeskind, 1995), with one-third of buyouts selling both related and unrelated assets within six years (Kaplan, 1991; Seth & Easterwood, 1993). The following sections examine empirical evidence with regard to how a change in strategic focus post-buyout translates into management initiatives that combine firm resources to construct and alter capabilities, and in organizational actions to coordinate and deploy capabilities to implement new strategies after the buyout.

Management changes

In the early development of the buyout market, previous research focused primarily on efficiency-enhancing buyouts, which emphasize quick and strong improvement of bundling or combining existing resources. The management effort was primarily directed towards improving the existing business execution, thus stabilizing the firm on a solid economic basis as quickly as possible. The managers focused on: decreased overhead, increased operational productivity, cost-cutting programs, improved capacity utilization, improved planning and logistics, decreased working capital, reorganization of operations, and employment reduction (Wright & Coyne, 1985; Baker & Wruck, 1989; Thompson & Wright, 1989; Muscarella & Vetsuypens, 1990; Bruining, 1992). Several studies report more effective management and higher plant productivity in LBOs than in comparable firms (Lichtenberg & Siegel, 1990; Amess, 2002; Davis et al., 2009), often following significant reductions in employment (Harris et al., 2005). We conclude that management changes post-buyout report the improvement of existing operational capabilities with immediately positive effect on the efficiency of buyout firms. However, buyouts are heterogeneous and literature has highlighted other sources of performance improvement which require extending current capabilities or the creation of new capabilities. For example, by lifting the restrictions imposed by former parent firms, the buyout firm managers may focus on growth opportunities and engage in catch up expenditure on new equipment and plant, and develop new products and markets (Wright et al., 1992; Bruining & Wright, 2002). Such expenditure may help to explain higher revenue growth in buyouts than in industry comparators (Singh, 1990), increased cash flow to sales ratio (Opler, 1992), and higher cash flow and return on investment (Bruining, 1992). The specialist role of the PE investor is also highlighted, with frequent interaction between investors and executives during the first 100 days to improve strategic planning (Acharya et al., 2008). Wilson and Wright (2013) report that PE investors specialized in the industry of the target, compared to non-PE-backed private companies, show significant positive cumulative average growth rates. Some platform buyouts, operating in fragmented markets, use "build-up" or "roll-up" strategies for growth, with PE investors specialized in selecting acquisitions consolidating markets through acquisitions (Gottschalg, 2007; Wright et al., 2010). Such buyouts show increased profitability during three consecutive years (Cressy et al., 2007) and higher growth in divisional buyouts (Meuleman et al., 2009). PE involvement in buyouts helps improve performance as the duration of the buyout increases and when economic conditions are more adverse (Castellaneta & Gottschalg, 2016). Other studies report more focused patent portfolios after PE investment (Lerner et al., 2008) and more patenting post-buyout (Ughetto, 2010). These studies suggest PE investors help to develop and enrich the capabilities of buyout firms, for example by providing expertise to develop new products and markets or by creating new capabilities through learning from firms that are acquired. Castellaneta and Gottschalg (2016) find that they differ in capabilities of value addition to buyouts, and LeNadant and Perdreau (2014) point out the financial leverage constraints.

Organizational changes

Buyouts also introduce organizational changes by improving coordination of capabilities as reported in early wave buyouts in the 1980s and 1990s. Divisional buyouts seek to improve communication by shorter lines of communication between top management and operations, and encourage employee participation in decision-making through the introduction of flexible working practices (Wright & Coyne, 1985). Bruining (1992) also reports divisional buyouts hiring product development specialists to release operations staff to concentrate on production, reducing senior management to decentralize decisions to line managers, decreasing contracting out to control product quality, and increased feedback to improve operations. To better use their capabilities to create value, divisional buyouts reorganize because independence from parent firms encourages greater operational autonomy, with operational and marketing decisions decentralized and increased participation in decision-making to improve firm performance (Green, 1992). Managers in divisional buyouts work alongside PE investors in making critical financial decisions rather than having to seek approval from parent firms (Baker & Wruck, 1989). New accounting control and strategic control systems are often introduced that better meet targets and allow entrepreneurial growth (Baker & Wruck, 1989; Jones, 1992; Bruining et al., 2004). Operational decentralization increases with management equity stakes in the firm (Phan & Hill, 1995). Later wave buyout studies confirm this decentralization trend and report higher levels of employee commitment (Pendleton et al., 1998), more commitment-oriented employee policy (Bacon et al., 2004), increases in training and employee empowerment (Bruining et al., 2005), and more discretion for craft and skilled workers over their work practices (Amess et al., 2007). The impact of high performance work practices in buyouts is affected by the length of the PE investment relationship (Bacon et al., 2012).

To support coordination of the chosen strategy, buyouts physically use capability configurations. For example, changes are made to how top managers are monitored, evaluated, and advised. In order to implement the buyout's strategic plans, PE investors join the (supervisory) board and meet with the CEO and the management team to control policy, and to talk over personnel matters and strategic topics facing the firm. Supervisors with proven experience from "networks of former entrepreneurs" are often hired (Acharya et al., 2009; Wright et al., 2010). Boards can be equipped with insiders with operating experience and outsiders with entrepreneurial skills to capitalize on growth opportunities. PE investors set higher standards for performance management, and managers lacking specialized knowledge or underperforming are replaced (Baker & Wruck, 1989). In many cases, PE investors can be seen as an organizational refocusing device that simultaneously increases entrepreneurial and administrative management (Bruining et al., 2013).

To summarize, given the business plans, buyouts mobilize a reconfiguration of firm capabilities to exploit market opportunities. Post-buyout decentralization helps improve working practices and increase participation in changes to improve performance. Board recomposition introduces new knowledge to reconfigure the balance between capabilities to improve operations and exploit entrepreneurial opportunities. We suggest in the next section that this is usefully framed by the resource management model.

Resource management model for buyouts

In many firms which are candidates for a buyout, managers have paid insufficient attention to updating operations, coordinating structures, and capabilities. In this section we explain how the strategic emphasis of CEOs and PE investors is operationalized in strategic resources and capabilities in buyout firms. We apply and adapt Sirmon et al.'s (2007) resource management model of value creation for mature firms that go through a buyout and link the findings of the resource-related actions from and across four case studies to the components in this model; specifically: strategy, structuring, bundling, and leveraging of resources. Compared to the buyout literature, the resource management model examines the orchestration of value creation in a coherent way. With this model (see column 1 of Table 22.1) we explore a comprehensive process of strategy, structuring, bundling, and leveraging of the buyout firm's resources with the purpose of creating value for customers and competitive advantages for the firm. From the literature we conclude that strategy, management and organization changes post-buyout cover conceptually the components of the adapted resource management model of Sirmon et al. (2007).

Orchestration in buyouts starts with mobilizing the firm's strategy, as new owners need to identify the capabilities required to support the organizational changes necessary to exploit and explore market opportunities before investing money. It is an outcome of the pre-buyout strategizing process and therefore a realistic starting point for resource management post-buyout. We place this component at the front of the Sirmon et al. model, whereas the other components have been taken over unchanged.

The second component of the resource management model includes top management actions of acquiring, accumulating, and divesting resources, labelled "structuring" or management of the resource portfolio. The structuring component follows strategy, containing processes of purchasing, developing, and divesting firm resources, and in what products and markets the new owners want to invest and compete and where they want to stay out of or withdraw from. How they will do this is also considered; for example, this may involve developing their own product-development resources such as R&D facilities or by selecting acquisitions to purchase resources.

The third component, "bundling" of resources, focuses on three types of actions, the ones that stabilize existing capabilities, those that enrich current ones, and the group representing new capabilities. The management change part of the literature embodies the bundling component, the way the firm combines resources to stabilize, enrich, and create capabilities. Stabilizing aims at making improvements of existing capabilities to recover efficiency and stabilize the firm post-buyout. Improving efficiency may also require enriching or extending the firm's current capabilities with regard to quality management for example. New capabilities may be required if the business plan involves development of new products and entry of new markets in environments that are highly uncertain. Developing entrepreneurial potential requires new capabilities related to product and market innovations.

The fourth component, "leveraging", consists of coordinating actions to integrate identified capabilities and physically using capability configurations to support strategy post-buyout. Both steps are needed to implement strategy. For integrating the identified capabilities into an effective configuration we look at organizational changes post-buyout, often characterized by reducing the bureaucratic organizational structure, redefining the entrenched organizational culture, and appointing new managers or board members to develop new products and markets. Changes therein facilitate quicker decision-making and a proactive stance among their employees towards customers to improve market responsiveness. Such leveraging processes support distinctive competences in the post-buyout strategy that can create competitive advantage.

We list these components in this order in column 1 of Table 22.1, showing at a glance which strategic choices management and investors in alignment make and how they purchase, develop, and shed resources and develop capabilities to create value post-buyout. Some buyouts stand for the first time on their own feet, such as divisional buyouts, or need to change entrenched relationships, as in the case of family buyouts, or make a fresh start after receivership, or are SBOs. This will have consequences for the timing and content of bundling resources, the processes of coordinating and integrating capabilities into configurations, and deploying them physically to exploit opportunities. New owners are keen on making changes, but literature also shows that the PE investor can be seen as a capability configuration to implement post-buyout strategy. They were challenged after the 1990s recession and the dot.com bubble to develop from a passive to an operational active investor (Denis, 1994; Cornelli & Karakas, 2008; Bruining et al., 2013) who could facilitate or initiate enrichment of current capabilities and creation of new capabilities to coordinate a chosen market opportunity strategy. Some were more successful than others.

To understand how the new owners post-buyout arrange this process to create value, we need to know to which resource-related actions they give priority post-buyout. Possessing resources is not enough to understand what happens with resources managed post-buyout (Sirmon et al., 2007). We illustrate how new owners/managers transform resources post-buyout to create value and the path followed in buyouts that emanate from different sources. We describe resource-related actions at the levels of strategy, structuring, bundling, and leveraging illustrated by case studies, and report our findings to illustrate how top managers and PE investors may regard their active role in prioritizing and synchronizing these actions. In this way we get an idea of how they orchestrate the different components of the resource management model. The next section describes these actions in different areas of resource management in each of the four buyout sources. Table 22.1 presents an overview of the findings.

Table 22.1 Overview of the resources management findings in four types of buyout[1]

Buyout type	*Divisional buyout*	*Family buyout*	*Secondary buyout*	*Receivership buyout*
Cases	Draka Holding	Royal Peijnenburg	Grozette	Vialle
Strategy:	From mass telecom market to focus on world markets in glass fibers and electrical wiring with high value-adding resources. Business plan: identification of sources and capabilities needed	Strategy first aimed at broadening market in A-brands. Later, new marketing focus on branding for repositioning. Business plan: identification of sources and capabilities needed	Strategy focus on niche markets with higher value added in Buy-out 2. Business plan: identification of sources and capabilities needed	Business plan with identification sources and capabilities needed in 2002 (IBO) with focus on EU countries and 2003 (MBO): expanded with supply in licensed deals to South Korea, China, and India
Structuring:				
Accumulating resources	Learning from acquisitions; management development	Pre-MBO: innovative snacks: bio-based, healthy, quick breakfasts. Post-MBO: developing branding resource to bring innovative products quicker to market	Buyout 2: developing internally resources for new product development (R&D) in ready meal niches worldwide	Product leader pre-MBO: innovative LPI injection module
Acquiring resources	25 acquisitions (1989/1997) in glass fibers/ electric cables	Proposed acquisition cancelled due to high price	None in buyout 2	Post-IBO: acquiring resources from PE: personnel, finance, production and logistics, ERP. Post MBO: alliance with BK Gas (Shell) for handling safety issues and ANWB to promote "drive clean" nationally
Divesting resources	Production for extreme competitive markets (high voltage telecom cables)	Not applicable	Cheese trading activity in buyout 2	Divestment old vaporizer technique and license contracts to Indian car manufacturer; cancelling R&D bus project

(*Continued*)

Table 22.1 (Continued)

Buyout type	*Divisional buyout*	*Family buyout*	*Secondary buyout*	*Receivership buyout*
Bundling:				
Stabilizing	Efficiency management; cutting costs, margin improvement, renegotiating supplier contracts	Efficiency management, cutting overhead, lower labor costs, improving contribution margin and productivity	Efficiency management, cutting overhead and costs, improving contribution margin and productivity	Post-IBO: turnaround and restructuring by PE; severe staff reduction from 180 to 106 fte Post-MBO: decrease costs of tubes, improve margin, further labor reduction to 50 fte
Enriching	New layout, rationalizing production with new machines, optimal production	Profit optimization, quality control, use of benchmarks, optimal use raw material	Buyout 1: professionalizing procurement, quality control, distribution systems on customer specification (private label)	Production planning and logistics, ERP system, working capital, ISO certificate
Pioneering	R&D and sales four times higher than pre-buyout; innovative solutions in glass fibers and electric wiring	New marketing: re-branding and repositioning; building brand loyalty, marketing campaigns; logo and commercials	Buy-out 2: market research, new market and product development: home-made salad, pizza factories, supermarkets; developing Middle East market (Islamic dietary meals)	Pre-buyout: technological pioneer Post-IBO: ISO certificate LPI installer and new marketing approach based on customer intimacy (23 new marketing people employed)
Leveraging:				
Coordinating	Fewer management layers, faster decision-making; management development in subsidiaries: cultural change to enhance self-management and	Fewer management layers, faster decision-making; cultural change: entrepreneurial and profit orientation (promoting intrapreneurship)	Fewer management layers, faster decision-making, direct communication on work floor	Post-IBO: set up new marketing department with 23 new employees; direct supply to automotive industry Post-MBO: network

(*Continued*)

Table 22.1 (Continued)

Buyout type	*Divisional buyout*	*Family buyout*	*Secondary buyout*	*Receivership buyout*
Coordinating	profit consciousness leading principle in restructuring of acquired firms			of dealers and assembling spots in Asia to install LPI module
Deploying	Employee ownership; outsourcing technical service & catering; AEX Stock Exchange listing; decentralization: subsidiaries as autonomous strategic business units	Brainstorm sessions between directors, plant and marketing managers: penetration by product positioning projects to exploit current opportunities; be first in new opportunities, 10% turnover from new opportunities. Job appraisal and reward system matched with marketing strategy	Industry expert supervisory board, monitoring and facilitating new product development in adjacent markets	Post-IBO: hiring specialists from PE; combined selling efforts CEO and PE Post-MBO: alliances with BK (supplier LPG Shell tank stations)

Orchestrating divisional buyouts

One of the central questions in divisional buyouts is whether the company is ready to function independently or whether certain functions such as administration, finance, and purchasing should be brought up to strength. The divested firm must stand alone to operate independently from all support provided by the former parent. With regard to mobilizing strategy, due diligence checks focus on whether the buyout can stand alone in terms of business strategy, market, firm resources and capabilities, the management, and organization.

The classic scope for performance improvement depends on lifting the split between ownership and management of the corporate assets and the use of appropriate control and incentive mechanisms by the PE investor (Fama & Jensen, 1983; Hill, 1985; Thompson & Wright, 1987) which were lacking pre-buyout. Agency controls like monitoring and rewarding of the management by the PE investor, goal alignment between PE investor and management based on equity participation, and incentives for mutual monitoring by members of the management team, will lead to a more efficient and profitable allocation of resources. By having claims more closely tied to the performance of the unit under their control, managers can be expected to improve their performance (Hite & Vetsuypens, 1989) and carry out plans that are in the best interests of the firm.

We illustrate the resource management implications of divisional buyouts drawing on Draka Holding N.V., a divisional buyout from electronics parent company Royal Philips as summarized in column two of Table 22.1.

Draka Holding NV

Strategy

In response to the 1973 and 1979 oil crises, Philips concentrated on its core activities such as consumer electronics, light, and medical systems and decided to divest the cable firm Draka in 1986. Draka had negative results and no major investments during the period 1975–1985. Managers participated in inefficient and time-consuming intercompany meetings and non-constructive competition within the Philips cable group. With a turnover of €100 million Draka was sold in 1986 for an undisclosed sum to its management and employees, each with 5% of the equity, with the rest contributed by PE firm Parcom (at the time a subsidiary of the Dutch ING Group) and PE investor Flint Beheer (a PE company owned by a wealthy investor). Philips' strategy had involved vertical integration, internal growth, and targeting products at a broad range of applications. After a divisional buyout, Draka changed this strategic focus and opted for a focus strategy of development, production, and marketing of electrical wire and optical fiber on an international scale for buildings, industry, transport (cars and airplanes), and original manufacturing companies. This strategy was chosen to withstand severe international competition from Siemens, Alcatel, BICC, and ABB. In the glass fibers sector, Draka became one of the largest global players, securing one of two exclusive contracts to supply cables to Airbus and a successful cable business supplying the computer industry. It took somewhat more than two years to become a leading expert in the electronic cable sector.

Structuring

Post-buyout, Draka divested its high voltage and telecommunication cables business. After a few years it embarked on an expansion program of 25 international acquisitions in glass fibers and electrical wiring between 1989–1997 at a cost of €240 million, as well as maintaining new investments in existing operations amounting to €90 million in this time period. Finding, screening, and selecting acquisition candidates were extremely important PE investor capabilities given strong competition from Pirelli, among others. R&D expenses increased development of resources fourfold compared to the period before the buyout.

Bundling

Simultaneously, Draka improved post-buyout efficiency in existing operations at the Amsterdam plant and also enriched skills with new machines and a new lay-out for approximately €32 million. It reduced overhead and labor costs, improved working capital and cash management, and optimized quality control and material use. Furthermore, supplier contracts were renegotiated to decrease costs by approximately 20%. This also applied to the companies purchased. Shortly thereafter followed pioneering new skills from R&D and newly acquired firms yielding innovative solutions in glass fibers and electric wiring. The combined efficiency drive, improved operational and innovative capabilities signaled to Draka workers that the buyout team was confident about the future of the firm. Restructuring and expansion was initially funded by cash flows and financial backing from Parcom and Flint.

Leveraging

According to the CEO, the new shareholders demonstrated commitment to Draka employees, and combined with employee ownership encouraged discretionary effort. Further restructuring involved relocating support staff outside Draka (including 100–150 employees in the catering and technical services department) mainly by redeployment to subcontractors. Coordination improved with greater responsibility for decision-making in autonomous subsidiaries and managerial delayering with a small corporate office.

Profitability consciousness programs were introduced for the workforce to decrease costs by approximately 20%. This also applies to the companies purchased. Top management encouraged cultural change from a "wait and see" attitude towards greater self-management through an increased expenditure on training and management development for middle subsidiary management. Speed of action became very important for the firm to compete with Alcatel, Regem, and BICC.

To finance these transactions the company went public in 1991, listing on the AEX Stock Exchange. In 2009 the company was acquired by the Prysmian group, an Italian multinational in Milan and world market leader in cables.

Orchestrating family buyouts

Succession is a central issue in family business survival. In private or family firms, buyouts often facilitate ownership change to address the lack of adequate successors. Family businesses are therefore a hot market for buyout investors (Reinebach, 2007; CMBOR, 2015).

One of the most prominent features of a family business is often the emotional involvement of the family. For the family, the company is not only the place where they perform work during the week, but is much more a part of life that keeps them always busy. Emotional involvement stems from the fact that the company is not only a source of income but also a status determinant of the family. Employee commitment to family owners can provide a significant competitive advantage. The negative view of family business suggests that family buyouts have opportunities to address the negative effects of informal management, entrenched family relationships, and autocratic leadership styles.

In contrast to the challenge facing divisional buyouts to stand alone, family firm buyouts are accustomed to operating independently. The scope for performance improvement post-buyout depends not so much on agency controls as in divisional buyouts, but on the degree of professionalization of management (Howorth et al., 2015), the effectiveness of management control systems, and on deferred investment in innovation due to increased risk aversion of an aging founder (Meuleman et al., 2009). A necessary condition for improving operational efficiency and stimulating growth is thus the presence of the founder and absence of non-family managers with equity stakes and non-executive directors pre-buyout (Scholes et al., 2010). Non-family managers and directors may have forced family firms to professionalize management and increase investment. A contrasting argument is that family businesses may focus on long-term investments to benefit future generations rather than short-term gain, stimulating innovation and firm growth. In such cases, post-buyout gains may stem from efficiency savings. We now consider how the new owners may orchestrate their resources to realize value creation post-family buyout as summarized in column three of Table 22.1.

Royal Peijnenburg b.v.

Strategy

In 2000, Royal Peijnenburg Biscuit Factories, with a turnover of €45 million and 213 employees was sold by the Peijnenburg family for an undisclosed sum to Gilde Participaties

(77%), specialists in the food industry, and incumbent management (23%). The lack of family successors and weak liquidity that hindered investment triggered the sale. Prior to the buyout it had grown organically in existing market segments for bread substitutes by maintaining market share. Following the management buyout (MBO), it focused on broadening the strategy to sell other A-brands in addition to gingerbread and to grow externally by acquisition, merger, or strategic collaboration. New marketing and coordinating capabilities were needed to develop more innovative products and bring them faster to the market.

Structuring

Pre-buyout, the firm accumulated scarce innovative resources to produce biologically-based biscuit products, e.g., healthy snacks and quick breakfasts for children. It also engaged in co-creation with ingredient suppliers in order to finetune products to consumer preferences. To withstand competition the firm needed further and above all faster growth. The PE investor identified a firm for acquisition, a former chocolate sprinkles subsidiary of Dutch food company CSM; however, this was cancelled because the deal price was too high for Royal Peijnenburg. There were no divestments of resources.

Bundling

The firm, certified for preventive food safety, had a strong market position in a mature market and supplied A-brands for food products in coffee and tea and in-between meals. However, under family ownership, the firm had lacked a commitment to profit optimization. Therefore, post-buyout, management focused on improving labor efficiency, overhead reduction, contribution margin, and higher productivity, stabilizing their financial management capabilities. One of the measures involved removing a complete management layer in all four factories, resulting in shorter lines of communication, quicker decision-making, and improved cash flow. The PE investor introduced tight controls over cash flow, brought in brand strengthening processes, installed clear rules over investment decisions, and sharpened the focus on turnover, costs, and margin. For example, 10% of turnover should come from new products and investment decisions required an ROI target of 20%. The introduction of a quality management system with strict food processing guidelines delivered improved hygiene and optimized the use of raw material and maintenance, thus extending capabilities. To stimulate further growth, the firm needed to improve coordination between R&D, production, and marketing functions. As a result, the PE investor introduced new marketing expertise to build brand loyalty, creating new logos and commercials.

Leveraging

The most far-reaching change post-MBO was the change in organizational culture to overcome parochialism and the strict separation between office and production operations that had limited staff engagement. For leveraging innovative resources in the marketplace more effectively, a major coordinating change was necessary to transform a closed family firm culture into an open culture stimulating a proactive entrepreneurial management style to exploit current and adjacent market opportunities. The CEO sought to break open the closed culture, a heritage of prolonged paternalistic leadership of family owners, through increased training and management development to create a results-oriented attitude. Training concentrated on entrepreneurship, creativity, decisiveness, persuasiveness, leading, and customer orientation. Input came from brainstorming sessions between directors, plant managers, and marketing, using benchmarking with competitors and research from scan information. This resulted in product repositioning projects and renovation of the production floor. After the MBO, a new bonus-related appraisal system for managers was deployed, which connected firm goals, department goals, and personal goals. In June 2006 the company was sold to Lotus Bakeries (Belgium).

Orchestrating SBOs

The total value of SBOs in Europe accounted for nearly 50% of PE-backed transactions and represented one-quarter of all PE transactions (CMBOR, 2015). Buying portfolio firms from other PE investors became popular, because corporate restructuring programs were on the decline. In an SBO the first buyout deal is refinanced with a new ownership structure, including a new set of PE financiers, while the original financiers and possibly some of the management have exited. The central question in these buyouts is whether there is still upside potential left after the first PE investor has left. Literature offers contrary findings. Some studies argue that all the "low-hanging fruit" is harvested (Brinkhuis & de Maeseneire, 2009; Wang, 2012), and SBOs perform worse than primary buyouts (Bonini, 2012; Freelink & Volosovych, 2012; Smit & Volosovych, 2013; Zhou et al., 2014). In contrast, other studies report that SBOs have similar (Achleitner et al., 2012) or better value creation potential compared to primary buyouts (Jelic & Wright, 2011). Below we consider how a new composition of owners, including a PE partner specialized in the industry of the buyout firm, may orchestrate their resources to realize value creation post-SBO as summarized in column four of Table 22.1.

Grozette b.v.

Grozette b.v., founded in 1963, produces a variety of fresh as well as dried grated cheeses for the food industry, foodservice, and retail. In addition to the Grozette brand, the firm also manufactures products under private labels. Grozette is a household name in the Netherlands and an established international company with activities in more than 30 countries.

Primary buyout

In 1996, the founding families de Groot and van Zijl decided to sell the company to Gilde Investors (50%) and a private investor, owner of Kaascentrale (50%), who distributes fresh cheese on behalf of Albert Heijn, a large Dutch supermarket chain. The latter shareholder had cheese production and trading interests and hoped to achieve synergies with this portfolio. In the years following the family buyout, Gilde Investors and management made concerted efforts to professionalize management systems, introducing up-to-date procurement, quality control, and distribution systems. However, gradually Grozette's directors felt that the private investor regarded Grozette as a cash cow, limiting new project development. Growing differences in opinion and private investor interference in management had a negative impact on morale and management effectiveness. Finally, Grozette's shareholders attempted a sale and agreed the €4.3 million price of an SBO in November 2003. At the time of the SBO the company had 70 employees and €25.0 million annual turnover.

Secondary buyout

Strategy In 2001, "Parmesan" was granted trademark protection restricted to producers in specified Italian regions, triggering a supermarket price war that reduced Grozette's turnover and resulted in low to zero profits. Therefore management wanted to change the strategy focus of the firm to offering customized products (for example, ready made salads), yielding higher value with increased margins on low volumes. If Grozette could be the first to enter these niche markets, they would benefit from first-mover advantage. The SBO made possible a refocus on the drying and grating business. Incumbent managers had six weeks to raise the necessary funds and accepted a bid that granted PE investor Antea a minority stake over other investors that wanted a majority stake.

Structuring The focus on niche markets with lower volumes and higher value-added after the SBO required divestment of unprofitable trading activities with low profit margins and required increased storage and transportation capacity. With an annual volume of only 7,000 tons, Grozette's small trading business was divested. To accumulate resources, Grozette's SBO invested in market research and product development by investing in R&D to open new product opportunities in domestic and foreign markets. Due to limited cash flow, no resources were purchased from acquisitions.

Bundling Grozette bundled resources and stabilized existing capabilities to improve performance by cutting overhead and labor costs, and improving productivity and efficiency using their contribution margin. Divesting the trading business reduced the workforce, with redundancies avoided by not extending short-term (one-year) contracts. Reduction of inventory costs following the divestment of the trading business, and reduction of reserves and cash-in-hand produced more efficient cash flow management. Fixed assets decreased in line with the reorganization and disposals of equipment previously used in trading. Two years after the SBO, operating costs had significantly decreased. Each product sold contributed more to earnings then previously, with better net profit and quick ratio (liquid assets, cash, and receivables) signifying an improved debt service ability.

Market research activities extended current capabilities to identify market niches. Pioneering skills in new product development helped to secure business from pizza factories, pasta ready-meal producers, supermarkets, and the Middle East market. Grozette became a big private-label producer of customized products such as mini-sachets (from 7–60 g) of different kinds of cheese used in pre-made salads, and in cheese products that comply with Islamic dietary laws. It exported to more countries (increasing from 30 to 50), and taking into account the divestment of the trading business, turnover increased from €25 million in 2004 to €30 million in 2008.

Leveraging After the SBO, the bureaucracy of having to consult with the private shareholder was removed, leading to a leaner production and sales operation. An informal culture developed with direct communication between MBO directors and lower-level management and workers and higher levels of engagement. Antea also provided solid contacts in the industry with one of their investors coming from a major customer, Friesland Foods. This industry expert joined the supervisory board of Grozette b.v. after the SBO was finalized in February 2004. The case provides an example of a successful deployment of a PE investor with industry-specific experience on the supervisory board to support the chosen market opportunity strategy in adjacent markets. After four years, Antea sold Grozette b.v. in 2008 to another PE investor, Astor Participaties.

Orchestrating receivership buyouts

In 2012, 5% of the total number of buyouts stemmed from receiverships, representing nearly 0.5% of the total buyout value (CMBOR, 2012), subsequently declining sharply to approximately 0.5–1.0% per year since then. In receivership buyouts from insolvency extensive changes are usually required. Following liquidation there is a small chance that the firm can be taken over by incumbent or interim managers and PE investors. The latter are usually hands-on turnaround specialists and must believe that the firm may become viable and the right management team is available to realize this. Below we present a buyout from receivership that highlights the capability problems that lead to bankruptcy and the actions required for turnaround following bankruptcy. Column five in table 22.1 summarizes these changes.

Vialle Alternative Fuel Systems BV

Vialle started as an importer of liquid petroleum gas (LPG) equipment in 1967. It was the first company to invent and patent liquid propane injection in the 1980s. Despite its market and technological leadership in LPG automotive systems in the Netherlands and despite the attractiveness of promising foreign markets like China, the firm did not succeed in developing and implementing a successful strategy to profitably market its LPG fuel system. Numerous unsuccessful projects targeting distant markets and a shrinking home market in Europe created a very high cost structure and severe losses. It operated in a declining niche market due to the negative image of LPG among car drivers and government transport policies with regard to LPG at the beginning of 2000. The successful introduction of a liquid propane injection (LPI) system with higher output efficiency compared to older vapor-based technologies was not without start-up problems, as was the conversion to the next generation systems. Vialle's strong focus on research and testing enabled the firm to complete the development of its LPI system in 2001, but this had drawn resources away from sales and marketing. The firm was trapped in a situation with ample opportunities but high losses.

Strategy

By 2001, the majority shareholder PE investor Antea hired an interim manager to develop a business plan to rescue the company. He approached PE investor and turnaround specialist Nimbus and presented a strategy to make the company profitable. The new business plan aimed to focus Vialle on selling products, entering markets in selected countries, and downsizing the workforce from 180 to 106 employees. Since the firm had a unique position in a technologically highly qualified product, it was decided to focus on the marketing of the LPI system to car manufacturers in Europe to install LPI injection systems in the production of cars and to dealers who offer to install a second fuel system in cars.

After five weeks of due diligence by Nimbus and close co-operation with the interim manager, Antea agreed to invest with an agreed plan of action. The original intention of Nimbus was to buy the firm as a "going concern", but Vialle's liquidity crisis was too serious to prevent receivership. Following liquidation on January 8, 2002, Vialle was acquired by PE investor Nimbus and other PE investors Antea, NesBic, and Foresta. The interim manager stayed on as managing director with a relatively small shareholding of 5%.

Structuring

The old LPG technique of vaporizer systems was withdrawn from the market, the Asian expansion cancelled, and the development and marketing of heavy applications suspended. Vialle acquired resources from PE investor Nimbus to enable a restart after the turnaround with up-to-date resources of financial management, operation management, and information technology.

Bundling

To stabilize the firm financially, the workforce was further decreased by 50, and 4 Nimbus investment managers were appointed as specialists to key positions and realized the turnaround in 11 months. They took care of restructuring and associated personnel issues, debt restructuring, financial control, and the improvement of working capital. The specialists extended Vialle's current capabilities and implemented a new ERP system, improved the firm's logistics and production planning system, and relocated the firm. With ISO certification of the LPI production processes, new capabilities were created to provide the automotive industry with guarantees related to LPI installation and problem-solving. These capabilities were essential emerging from bankruptcy to commercialize its technically superior LPI module. Vialle became a preferred supplier of LPI systems, and effective marketing increased turnover, with 23 new employees hired and trained to market LPI installation and increase operating capacity. Within a couple of months, the first original equipment manufacturing contracts with Hyundai were signed, yielding a 50% increase in turnover per month.

Leveraging

To build a new company and integrate the required capabilities, Nimbus concentrated on reducing costs and restructuring the organization, and the managing director concentrated on customers and marketing. The PE investor accompanied the CEO on trips to large potential customers. After one hectic year of turnaround activities, Vialle recorded above average profitability and a strong balance sheet. PE investor Nimbus negotiated an MBO with the managing director, which was announced June 3, 2003. The new shareholders were PE investor Antea (12%), key managers of Vialle (8%), and the managing director (80%). All Nimbus managers were replaced by newly-appointed managers from Vialle.

Although improved marketing to increase turnover remained the top priority, the new owners post-MBO sought to decrease costs and further improve margins. This involved reducing the variety of liquid gas tubes offered to a few standard tubes. Directly supplying the automotive industry in other countries boosted turnover significantly, with 180,000 LPI systems sold in a licensed deal to Hyundai taxis in Seoul (Korea), and the total German market developed to 70,000 LPI systems. Compared to 13,000 systems for the saturated Dutch market, these numbers indicated significant growth potential in foreign markets, with local assembly facilities sought in China and India. Finally, Vialle created alliances with other firms successful in improving acceptance of LPG products, such as BK, a former subsidiary of Royal Dutch Shell, and specialized in LPG distribution.

Resource management across different buyout sources

These four cases illustrate the shift in strategic emphasis of CEOs and PE investors post-buyout, the successive consequences for the firm's resource portfolio, the development of resources to construct and alter capabilities, and the process of integrating capabilities to support value creation strategies. These involve orchestrating resource management in the period after the buyout and illustrate how orchestration depends on buyout source characteristics, showing how top managers and PE investors may regard and outline their active roles in prioritizing and synchronizing these actions. The general conclusions are as follows.

Strategy

The resource management process in buyouts starts with the strategy, e.g., the identification of the capabilities needed and of the organizational configuration to exploit market opportunities, usually defined in a business plan or management plan pre-MBO. Draka and Grozette left highly competitive mass markets and shifted strategic focus to higher value-adding resources to realize growth. Vialle and Peijnenburg emphasized in particular new marketing strategies to market their innovative products more effectively.

Structuring

After the SBO, Grozette advanced internal R&D resources to develop new products, concentrating on accumulating. Draka implemented a growth strategy by decentralizing R&D facilities and undertaking numerous acquisitions to acquire pioneering capabilities that address the competition in the glass fiber and electronic wiring markets. PE investors backed the accumulation and acquisition of their resource portfolio.

After the proposed acquisition was cancelled to broaden the market with A-brands, Peijnenburg's new owners concentrated on developing branding resources for new products. Vialle, product leader pre-buyout, acquired resources for ERP, logistics, production, personnel, and finance from the PE to build a new company through a turnaround. Divestment of unprofitable businesses (Draka's high voltage telecom cables, Vialle's vaporizer technology, and Grozette's cheese trading) did not harm future value creation, and PE investors brought skills varying from selection to value-adding to help buyouts focus on profitable business activities that created value within a three- to five-year timescale.

Bundling

Stabilizing actions by managers to improve financial management capabilities post-buyout helped decrease operating costs in all four types of buyouts. Stabilizing existing financial management capabilities helps to retain and update the healthy core of the firm. This assists in addressing pre-buyout problems such as low margins, high cost-levels, high overhead of the parent firm, lack of professional management by founders, low productivity, and absence of profit consciousness. However, stabilizing is not sufficient for creating value over the longer term. Draka invested in enriching capabilities through rationalization and modernization of existing operations, and in learning and creating new capabilities from acquisitions, while Grozette accumulated internal resources for market research and new product and market development. Enriching capabilities with new marketing programs took place at Peijnenburg and Vialle. Top management and PE investors in Peijnenburg first enriched the firm's skills to optimize profit, quality control, and use of raw material. Gradually, the bundling of resources shifted to creating new marketing capabilities to increase sales by building brand loyalty, new marketing campaigns, logos, and commercials to create quicker entry into the market. Top management and PE investors in Vialle agreed to focus on the effectiveness of the new marketing approach and develop capabilities to secure ISO certification. This marketing capability was further developed after the buyout.

Leveraging

Draka, Peijnenburg, and Grozette all improved coordinating post-buyout involving decentralized decision-making and management delayering to encourage quicker decision-making and direct communication with the shop-floor. The CEOs from Draka and Peijnenburg sought to create a more entrepreneurial culture that focused on innovation and customer requirements. Management development programs were introduced at Draka's strategic business units to achieve self-management and profit consciousness, which were seen as necessary to building leadership in electrical cable and glass fibers. Vialle built a new marketing department which maintained strong links with supply channels, dealer networks, and assembly sites to install LPI modules in cars. Grozette integrated capabilities organized around the core business with R&D for ad hoc product development teams.

Different physical capability configurations are deployed to support the chosen firm strategies. To be able to operate on a global scale, Draka transformed subsidiaries into strategic business units, responsible for profit and costs per product-market combination, thus leveraging its key resources focused on certain markets. This supports the use of capabilities to sustain a market opportunity strategy. To sustain growth by acquisition, the firm went public in 1991 and listed on the AEX Stock Exchange. Saying goodbye to the legacy of low staff involvement in innovation in the past, Peijnenburg's brainstorming sessions, job appraisals, and reward systems provided feedback and formed a capstone for integrating entrepreneurial capabilities into an effective configuration of capabilities, thus leveraging key resources to sustain penetration by product positioning to exploit current opportunities and develop new products in adjacent markets.

In the secondary MBO of Grozette, the PE investor appointed an expert in the food industry to the supervisory board to monitor and support exploring and exploiting opportunities in new markets. To help improve the image of LPG, Vialle cooperated with BK, at the time a liquid gas subsidiary of Shell. The temporary employment of PE specialists in production planning and logistics, enterprise resource management systems, and turnaround enhanced human capital to turn the company around and readied Vialle to implement a market opportunity strategy.

Conclusions

There is a lack of empirical literature that specifically focuses on resource management in buyouts from different sources. With this chapter we offer a resource management framework for buyouts, to identify and explain the resource management actions of the new owners and their implications for performance. Analytically our findings confirm the scarce observations that buyouts emerge as an efficient and effective means of needed organizational change (Wright et al., 2001) and that heterogeneity of buyout types offers considerable opportunity for entrepreneurial pursuits (Meuleman et al., 2009). To draw general conclusions, we argue that buyout companies in similar circumstances as the cases discussed here, may be facing the same resource orchestration challenge.

- The buyout resource management model shows a coherent view on resources-related actions following buyouts. Noticeable is that despite low or high uncertainty in the environment, nearly all buyouts structure the resource portfolio and divest non-profitable activities and combine resources to stabilize the firm's efficiency.

- The cases offer insight into the differences in scope for improvement for buyouts from diverse sources. Initial conditions of the buyout source determine resource management priorities to implement strategy post-buyout. In the divisional buyout entrepreneurial opportunities may have been stifled by parental control. The buyout gives leeway to decrease agency costs, extend current capabilities by rationalization and modernization of existing operations, and create new capabilities from acquisitions. In a receivership buyout tasks to rebuild the company are divided. The PE investor sets the decisive steps for the turnaround and the director focuses on getting customers. To enhance entrepreneurial and profit orientation in a family buyout, management demands cultural change. For improving market positioning and new product development, a new match of incentives and mindset between management and a PE investor with an appropriate advisory source is needed in an SBO.
- Insights into the value of the capabilities inherited on buyout are essential for developing effective value creation strategies. For each different buyout source, buyouts develop different capability configurations where the PE investors are actively involved because new knowledge is transferred into the firm. To penetrate new markets, a food industry specialist from the PE network can be appointed to the supervisory board of an SBO. To grow fast in new markets, integrating well-selected acquisitions by the PE investor in the organization of the divisional buyout is indispensable. In case a planned takeover is cancelled, PE can support further professionalization of the marketing function in a family buyout to defend and conquer market share. To turn the company around after bankruptcy the PE investor can deliver key personnel and assist the CEO in obtaining customers.
- Indebtedness in buyout firms requires managers to work closely with investors who can provide experienced human capital. The role of the PE investor is therefore of great importance in decisions with regard to orchestrating resources.

Note

1 The author would like to thank the CEOs, CFOs, and the PE investors of the buyout companies for their cooperation and Arjen Mulder, M. Dijkman, R. Hendriks, M. Kessels, N. Pourel, A. Sewbalak, F. Elfring, M. Guimares, S. Heidepriem, and L. Bennet Leyers for their case study research assistance. The author is also grateful for the valuable comments of Nicolas Bacon.

References

Acharya, V., Hahn, M., & Kehoe, C. 2009. *Corporate governance and value creation evidence from private equity*. Available at SSRN: https://ssrn.com/abstract=1324016.

Acharya, V., Kehoe, C., & Reyner, M. 2008. The voice of experience: Public versus private equity. *The McKinsey Quarterly*, 28: 1–7.

Achleitner, A. K., Bauer, O., Figge, C., & Lutz, E. 2012. The case for secondary buyouts as exit channel. *Journal of Applied Corporate Finance*, 24: 102–111.

Alperovych, Y., Amess, K., & Wright, M. 2013. Private equity firm experience and buyout vendor source: What is their impact on efficiency? *European Journal of Operational Research*, 228: 601–611.

Amess, K. 2002. Management buyouts and firm-level productivity: Evidence from a panel of UK manufacturing firms. *Scottish Journal of Political Economy*, 49: 304–317.

Amess, K., Brown, S., & Thompson, S. 2007. Management buyouts, supervision and employee discretion. *Scottish Journal of Political Economy*, 54: 447–474.

Bacon, N., Wright, M., & Demina, N. 2004. Management buyouts and human resource management. *British Journal of Industrial Relations*, 42: 325–347.

Bacon, N., Wright, M., Meuleman, M., & Scholes, L. 2012. The impact of private equity on management practices in European buy-outs: Short-termism, anglo-saxon, or host country effects? *Industrial Relations: A Journal of Economy and Society*, 51: 605–626.

Baker, G. P., & Wruck, K. H. 1989. Organizational changes and value creation in leveraged buyouts: The case of the OM Scott & Sons Company. *Journal of Financial Economics*, 25: 163–190.

Ball, R., Burrows, A., Howorth, C., Kloeckner, O., Scholes, L., Westhead, P., & Wright, M. 2008. *Private equity in family firms*. CMBOR-Nottingham University Business School, Nottingham, Jun 1:51.

Bonini, S. 2012. *Secondary buyouts*. Working Paper, University of Bocconi.

Brinkhuis, S., & De Maeseneire, W. 2009. *What drives leverage in leveraged buyouts? An analysis of European LBO's capital structure*. Working paper, Vlerick Leuven Gent Management School, Gent.

Bruining, H. 1992. *Performance improvement post-management buy-out*. PhD dissertation, Erasmus University Rotterdam. Available at: https://repub.eur.nl/pub/22413.

Bruining, H., Bonnet, M., & Wright, M. 2004. Management control systems and strategy change in buyouts. *Management Accounting Research*, 15: 155–177.

Bruining, H., Boselie, P., Wright, M., & Bacon, N. 2005. The impact of business ownership change on employee relations: Buy-outs in the UK and The Netherlands. *The International Journal of Human Resource Management*, 16: 345–365.

Bruining, H., Verwaal, E., & Wright, M. 2013. Private equity and entrepreneurial management in management buy-outs. *Small Business Economics*, 40: 591–605.

Bruining, H., & Wright, M. 2002. Entrepreneurial orientation in management buy-outs and the contribution of venture capital. *Venture Capital: An International Journal of Entrepreneurial Finance*, 4: 147–168.

Bull, I. 1989. Management performance in leveraged buyouts: An empirical analysis. *Journal of Business Venturing*, 3: 263–278.

Castellaneta, F., & Gottschalg, O. 2016. Does ownership matter in private equity? The sources of variance in buyouts' performance. *Strategic Management Journal*, 37: 330–348.

Center for Management Buy-Out Research. 2012. *CMBOR report, Winter 2011*. Equistone Partners Europe Limited, Newsletter, Imperial College Business School, London.

Center for Management Buy-Out Research. 2015. *CMBOR report, Winter 2014*. Equistone Partners Europe Limited, Newsletter, Imperial College Business School, London.

Cornelli, F., & Karakas, O. 2008. Private equity and corporate governance: Do LBOs have more effective boards? In J. Lerner & A. Gurung (Eds.), *The global impact of private equity report 2008: Globalization of alternative investments*. Working Papers Volume 1, World Economic Forum, 65–84.

Cressy, R., Munari, F., & Malipiero, A. 2007. Playing to their strengths? Evidence that specialization in the private equity industry confers competitive advantage. *Journal of Corporate Finance*, 13: 647–669.

Davis, S., Lerner, J., Haltiwanger, J., Miranda, J., & Jarmin, R. 2009. Private equity, jobs and productivity. In A. Gurung & J. Lerner (Eds.), *The global impact of private equity report 2009: Globalization of alternative investments*. Working Papers Volume 2, World Economic Forum, 25–46.

Denis, D. J. 1994. Organizational form and the consequences of highly leveraged transactions: Kroger's recapitalization and Safeway's LBO. *Journal of Financial Economics*, 36: 193–224.

Fama, E. F., & Jensen, M. C. 1983. Separation of ownership and control. *Journal of Law & Economics*, 26: 301–325.

Freelink, S., & Volosovych, V. 2012. *Do secondary buyouts create value? Evidence from the United Kingdom*. Working Paper, School of Economics, Erasmus University.

Gilligan, J., & Wright, M. 2014. *Private equity demystified: An explanatory guide*. Institute of Chartered Accountants in England and Wales, Centre for Business Performance.

Gottschalg, O. 2007. *Private equity and leveraged buyouts*. Study IP/A/ECON/ IC/2007-25, European Parliament, Policy Department: Economic and Scientific Policy.

Green, S. 1992. The impact of ownership and capital structure on managerial motivation and strategy in management buyouts: A cultural analysis. *Journal of Management Studies*, 29: 513–535.

Harris, R., Siegel, D. S., & Wright, M. 2005. Assessing the impact of management buyouts on economic efficiency: Plant-level evidence from the United Kingdom. *The Review of Economics and Statistics*, 87: 148–153.
Hill, C. 1985. Internal capital market controls and financial performance in multidivisional firms. *The Journal of Industrial Economics*, 37: 67–83.
Hite, G. L., & Vetsuypens, M. R. 1989. Management buyouts of divisions and shareholder wealth. *The Journal of Finance*, 44: 971.
Howorth, C., Wright, M., & Westhead, P. 2015. *Succession, professionalization and the staying power of familiness: A longitudinal study of MBOs of family firms*. Working paper, UK.
Jelic, R., & Wright, M. 2011. Exits, performance, and late stage private equity: The case of UK management buy-outs. *European Financial Management*, 17: 560–593.
Jones, C. S. 1992. The attitudes of owner-managers towards accounting control systems following management buyout. *Accounting, Organizations and Society*, 17: 151–168.
Kaplan, S. 1989. The effects of management buyouts on operating performance and value. *Journal of Financial Economics*, 24: 217–254.
Kaplan, S. N. 1991. The staying power of leveraged buyouts. *Journal of Financial Economics*, 29: 287–313.
LeNadant, A-L., & Perdreau, F. 2014. Ex-post innovation profile of LBO targets: Evidence from CIS data for the Netherlands. *Strategic Change*, 23: 93–105.
Lerner, J., Strömberg, P., & Sørensen, M. 2008. Private equity and long-run investment: The case of innovation. In J. Lerner & A. Gurung (Eds.), *The global impact of private equity report 2008, globalization of alternative investments*. Working Papers Volume 1, World Economic Forum, 27–42.
Lichtenberg, F. R., & Siegel, D. 1990. The effects of leveraged buyouts on productivity and related aspects of firm behavior. *Journal of Financial Economics*, 27: 165–194.
Malone, S. 1989. Characteristics of smaller company leveraged buyouts. *Journal of Business Venturing*, 4: 349–359.
Meuleman, M., Amess, K., Wright, M., & Scholes, L. 2009. Agency, strategic entrepreneurship, and the performance of private equity-backed buyouts. *Entrepreneurship Theory and Practice*, 33: 213–239.
Morrow, J. L., Sirmon, D. G., Hitt, M. A., & Holcomb, T. R. 2007. Creating value in the face of declining performance: Firm strategies and organizational recovery. *Strategic Management Journal*, 28: 271–283.
Muscarella, C. J., & Vetsuypens, M. R. 1990. Efficiency and organizational structure: A study of reverse LBOs. *The Journal of Finance*, 45: 1389–1413.
Opler, T. C. 1992. Operating performance in leveraged buyouts. *Financial Management*, 21: 27–34.
Pendleton, A., Wilson, N., & Wright, M. 1998. The perception and effects of share ownership: Empirical evidence from employee buy-outs. *British Journal of Industrial Relations*, 36: 99–123.
Phan, P. H., & Hill, C. W. 1995. Organizational restructuring and economic performance in leveraged buyouts: An ex post study. *Academy of Management Journal*, 38: 704–739.
Reinebach, A. 2007. Family matters. *Mergers and Acquisitions*, 42: 4.
Scholes, L., Wright, M., Westhead, P., & Bruining, H. 2010. Strategic changes in family firms post management buyout: Ownership and governance issues. *International Small Business Journal*, 28: 505–521.
Seth, A., & Easterwood, J. 1993. Strategic redirection in large management buyouts: The evidence from post-buyout restructuring activity. *Strategic Management Journal*, 14: 251–273.
Singh, H. 1990. Management buyouts and shareholder value. *Strategic Management Journal*, 11: 111–129.
Sirmon, D. G., Hitt, M. A., & Ireland, R. D. 2007. Managing firm resources in dynamic environments to create value: Looking inside the black box. *Academy of Management Review*, 32: 273–292.
Sirmon, D. G., Hitt, M. A., Ireland, R. D., & Gilbert, B. A. 2011. Resource orchestration to create competitive advantage: Breadth, depth, and life cycle effects. *Journal of Management*, 37: 1390–1412.
Smit, H. T., & Volosovych, V. 2013. *Secondary buyout waves*. Working paper, School of Economics, Erasmus University Rotterdam.
Thompson, R. S., & Wright, M. 1987. Markets to hierarchies and back again: The implications of MBOs for factor supply. *Journal of Economic Studies*, 14: 15–22.

Thompson, R. S., & Wright, M. 1989. Bonding, agency costs and management buyouts: A note. *Bulletin of Economic Research*, 41: 69–76.
Ughetto, E. 2010. Assessing the contribution to innovation of PE investors: A study on European buyouts. *Research Policy*, 39: 126–140.
Wang, Y. 2012. Secondary buyouts: Why buy and at what price? *Journal of Corporate Finance*, 18: 1306–1325.
Wiersema, M. F., & Liebeskind, J. P. 1995. The effects of leveraged buyouts on corporate growth and diversification in large firms. *Strategic Management Journal*, 16: 447–460.
Wilson, N., & Wright, M. 2013. *A convenient truth: Private equity and portfolio company growth*. Available at SSRN: https://ssrn.com/abstract=2290983.
Wright, M., & Coyne, J. 1985. *Management buy-outs*. Beckenham, UK: Croom Helm.
Wright, M., Hoskisson, R. E., & Busenitz, L. W. 2001. Firm rebirth: Buyouts as facilitators of strategic growth and entrepreneurship. *The Academy of Management Executive*, 15: 111–125.
Wright, M., Hoskisson, R. E., Busenitz, L. W., & Dial, J. 2000. Entrepreneurial growth through privatization: The upside of management buyouts. *Academy of Management Review*, 25: 591–601.
Wright, M., Jackson, A., & Frobisher, S. 2010. Private equity in the US: Building a new future. *Journal of Applied Corporate Finance*, 22: 86–95.
Wright, M., Thompson, S., & Robbie, K. 1992. Venture capital and management-led, leveraged buy-outs: A European perspective. *Journal of Business Venturing*, 7: 47–71.
Zahra, S. A. 1995. Corporate entrepreneurship and financial performance: The case of management leveraged buyouts. *Journal of Business Venturing*, 10: 225–247.
Zhou, D., Jelic, R., & Wright, M., 2014. SMBOs: Buying time or improving performance? *Managerial and Decision Economics*, 35: 88–102.

23

THE POLITICAL ECONOMY OF FINANCE-LED CAPITALISM

Connecting financialization, private equity, and employment outcomes

Ian Clark

Introduction

Observers of comparative political economy have outlined changes in the nature of capitalism that have since the late 1970s. It is suggested that full-employment capitalism was replaced by a finance-led capitalism centered on neo-liberalism (Harvey, 2007; Crouch, 2011). The financial crisis of 2008 reinforced the trajectory of finance-led capitalism and neo-liberalism. Central to this change is a process whereby the principles of deregulation and privatization were further embedded in the institutional framework of countries such as the UK. Recent contributions to this literature link together economic restructuring, associated neo-liberalism, and the emergence of finance-led capitalism. It is suggested that these changes represent a social revolution from above, designed to restore the power of capital over labor (Cox & Nilsen, 2014: 136; Srnicek & Williams, 2015: 52–67).

A literature on financialization (a particular outcome of finance-led capitalism) subsequently emerged that asserts capital markets increasingly regulate firm-level behavior. Financialization involves three processes. First, the ascendency of shareholder value that prioritizes the interests of investors at the expense of other firm-level stakeholders (van der Zwan, 2014). Second, the emphasis on shareholder value legitimizes a more aggressive management of corporate assets to prioritize financial objectives, for example high stock prices and maximizing the release of cash flows to investors, at the expense of other stakeholders (Thompson, 2011). Third, it popularizes a range of financial techniques whereby investors extract the gains from corporate restructuring and divestment rather than re-investing savings in the firm or sharing the gains with other stakeholders. Although these processes are described at an abstracted level, the consequences for work and employment at firm level are less clear.

The main arguments developed in this chapter are that the UK played a key role in facilitating the transition to finance-led capitalism and financialization, and that the financial instruments popularized by private equity (PE) through leveraged buyouts spill over to affect the corporate sector more broadly. The chapter is divided into three sections. The first section provides a theoretical framework which outlines the emergence of finance-led capitalism, the associated diffusion of financialization in the UK economy, and its potential effects on labor. The following section outlines the negative implications for work and employment as PE instruments enable and encourage investors to appropriate value from firms. The final section illustrates the arguments with empirical material drawn from two detailed case studies relating to the AA under PE ownership and the collapse of the British Homes Stores (BHS) pension scheme.

Full-employment capitalism to finance-led capitalism

From the end of the Second World War until the early 1970s the UK operated within a broader Western economic system in which fixed exchange rates facilitated international trade in manufactured goods. This system involved Keynesian state intervention to deliver sustained economic growth and improved welfare provision (Ruggie, 1982; Harvey, 2007). Western economies balanced a commitment to the market economy with intervention to promote full employment and social welfare. This capital–labor compromise was designed to avoid the economic collapse and associated depression of the 1930s that contributed towards the Second World War (Harvey, 2007: 11–12). In the UK, this compromise took the form of capital controls, nationalization, a commitment to the welfare state, and trade union representation. However, economic growth up until the 1960s obscured long-run relative economic decline (Gamble, 1988). From the 1970s onwards, neo-liberals proposed to reverse economic decline by an alternative policy agenda focused on anti-inflation, balanced budgets, reducing union militancy, and curtailing the drag effects on the market of welfare expenditure and state monopolies. The subsequent sterling crisis in 1976 followed by increases in industrial action led to successive Conservative governments (1979–1997) that focused on financial deregulation and privatization to shift the balance of the economy from manufacturing to financial services (Harvey, 2007: 19–30; Crouch, 2011). These changes were consistent with the demise of the Bretton Woods fixed exchange rate system which underpinned the expansion of export trade between developed nations. Financial markets expanded with the beginnings of what became a globally unregulated international financial system (Eichengreen, 2008).

By the City "Big Bang" in 1986, the increasing size of the financial sector positioned the UK economy center stage in global capitalism. New financial actors such as global asset management for hedge funds, PE firms, and sovereign wealth funds dominated the City of London (Augar, 2009). The presence of support services for these intermediaries in the City and neo-liberal governments removed regulatory obstacles to international capital movements and foreign ownership of UK firms (Harvey, 2007: 62, 70–73; Pendleton & Gospel, 2014: 88). From the late 1990s, the financialization of the UK economy had involved the deregulation of capital markets and legal restrictions on industrial action by the labor force. The systematic financialization of UK capitalism required managers to prioritize shareholder value and downgraded relationships with other stakeholders such as the labor force (Lapavitatas, 2013: 15). From the late 1970s, financial market actors have developed and diffused innovations to increasingly extract value from firms.

The transition to finance-led capitalism was achieved by financial deregulation and international integration which readjusted UK capital into a global form. This reworking legitimized the central concern of capital markets, with the market for corporate control exerting discipline on managers that did not seek to maximize shareholder value (Münnich, 2016: 285). The consequences for UK labor included higher job insecurity, increased wage inequality, and the dismantling of collective representation. The connection to the labor process and the broader political economy of labor is therefore clear. Finance-led capitalism and the market for corporate control require a relentless search for investor value that ruptures established relations between capital and labor. This has most notably involved the decline in wages as a share of national income from 61% in the 1970s to less than 56% since 1982 (OECD, 2015). The wage share is defined to include wages and non-wage benefits such as pensions and national insurance contributions, which represent reproduction costs for labor. This represents a breach of the post Second World War social contract between employers, labor, and the state. New business models aimed to cheapen labor to boost short-term profits, through increased labor flexibility (Atkinson, 1984), privatization, and management buyouts (Wright et al., 2000, 2002). The "take private" PE business model highlighted the extent to which capital was no longer willing to make continuous commitments to labor or even firm ownership. More recently so-called "gig economy" firms such as Uber, Deliveroo, and Airbnb that are associated with "platform capitalism" (often funded by venture capital and PE) have focused more determinedly on the externalization of employment (Srnicek, 2015).

The movement to finance-led capitalism re-purposed the UK state towards restoring opportunities for profitable capital investment, notwithstanding low levels of productivity in manufacturing and services. Indeed, since the late 1970s, the privatization (often in the form of buyouts) of utilities, housing, transport, health, education, and infrastructure were key acts by which neo-liberalism pumped profitability back into the private sector (Mason, 2015: 278). A particular firm level outcome of this transition is that managers are more likely to respond to the demands of financial markets than labor markets. Neo-liberalism undermines alliances between the state, managerial elites, and organized labor at its heart. Restoration of profitability depended on breaking organized labor and a re-commodification of labor (Cox & Nilsen, 2014: 141–147). This was achieved by monetary policy which allowed unemployment to fluctuate and restricted organized labor and welfare state expenditure (Glyn, 2006: 27–31). The following section focuses on the role of PE as an instrument of finance-led capitalism.

Private equity: an instrument of finance-led capitalism

The previous section highlighted the role of state policy in the transition to finance-led capitalism. Therein structural innovations in capital markets – the market for corporate control and a relentless search for investor value – disrupt established relations between capital and labor. A disdain for customers, employees, and attachment to locality are hallmarks of a globalized approach to business that disconnects circuits of capital and labor (Appelbaum et al., 2013). Accordingly, this section briefly defines PE, explains how mega "take private" PE funds became a macro instrument of finance-led capitalism under the UK's New Labour government (1997–2010), and then details how the micro instruments of PE challenged established workplace employment relations settlements.

Private equity

PE is an asset class that is funded by investors who commit monies to an investment fund for a defined numbers of years, usually fewer than ten. Professional fund managers invest these monies on behalf of investors in organizations which become portfolio firms either owned outright or majority controlled by PE fund partners. So a PE fund is a fund management company either in the form of a limited partnership or a plc business that actively manages the pool of money. The limited partnership model is the favored vehicle for two reasons. First, a limited partnership has no legal personality yet individual partners can operate collectively. Second, both managing partners in a partnership and limited partners who provide the bulk of investment funds are taxed as individuals whereas the partnership itself has no liability to taxation. Accordingly, the taxation liability of managing and limited partners, as a result of financial engineering, is often reduced to a level less than the taxation levied in the UK by booking income as a capital gain, utilizing none-domiciled status, offshoring a portfolio firm, or writing off interest against borrowing.

The PE sector is broad in scope and includes venture capital, which is a form of capital typically provided by professional institutionally backed outside investors who support the growth of new businesses. In addition to venture capital and mid-market PE funds which take stakes in an established business to help it roll out nationally, larger, multinational PE funds acquire plc firms or divisions of plc firms by buying all the shares or a controlling percentage of the shares which are listed on a public stock market such as the London Stock Exchange. The purchase of a controlling percentage of the available shares is often the first move to complete control, and once a fund has control of all the shares in a portfolio company then it becomes the single or majority shareholder and the firm is no longer a publicly traded plc company; this is what is referred to as the take private, PE business model. So venture capital, mid-market funds, and mega-funds which specialize in taking listed firms private are different factions of PE capital, but what they do have in common is the manner in which funds are raised – on private rather than public markets. But how did the take private model deployed by mega-funds come to prominence in the UK?

Private equity under New Labour: a macro instrument of finance-led capitalism?

The New Labour government (1997–2010) further rebalanced the economy towards finance-led capitalism by promoting the interests of financial capital, in particular hedge funds, PE funds, and financial capital asset managers (Augar, 2009). This rebalancing operated in two ways, by taxation and fiscal policy. With regard to taxation, New Labour's 1998 budget exempted business assets held initially for ten years from capital gains tax, but then very quickly, business assets held for only two years. This exemption was designed to stimulate venture capitalists and small business start-ups, but the deregulation was drafted so loosely that it created a tax break available to all capital. Hedge funds and PE funds which specialized in buying "asset rich" listed firms took advantage of the regulations to fund these acquisitions with massive levels of leverage, up to 70% in some cases. After the 1998 budget changes, chargeable gains were tapered against the length of time an asset was held with the taper applied to net gains that were chargeable after the deduction of any allowances including interest on loans secured to buy an asset. This produced the lowest possible charge. Considering business assets held for two years, only 25% of the gain would be chargeable creating an effective higher rate taxation at 10% (IFS, 2008: 214; Seely, 2010: 3). In benign economic conditions and with rising asset values these assets were realized relatively quickly at a massive gain to vicarious investors in these funds and the limited partners who put the deals together.

With regard to fiscal policy, from the 1998 budget onwards New Labour's policy on financial regulation legitimized the argument that firms were only accountable to vicarious rentier, investor-owners, associated asset managers, and shareholders. This commitment secured an alliance with finance and the City that extended over three general election victories (Heyes et al., 2014). Hence the financialization of government fiscal policy involved serving the interests of venture capital and business, and served the interests of newer more innovative factions of financial capital – asset managers, hedge funds, and PE funds. These factions while operative and in some cases registered in the UK, are internationalized operations which act in the interests of global financial capital.

Theoretically, the development and growth of PE (the take private variant in particular) as an instrument of finance-led capitalism lies within the growth of corporate finance as an academic discipline and the associated theory of efficient capital markets (Jensen, 2007). The theory of efficient capital markets contains an efficient-contracting orientation to the firm, that is (capital) markets allocate resources to investments that secure the highest returns. The attraction of PE funds, particularly those that specialize in take private buyouts is the comparatively high rates of return which averaged between 15% and 20% prior to the financial crisis (BVCA, 2008).

These returns led academic supporters and practitioners to argue that PE-backed firms secured higher returns for investors and shareholders, had higher productivity, and created more jobs than equivalent plc firms, (Bacon et al., 2004, 2008, Bruining et al., 2005; BVCA, 2008). In many cases the business model did secure the benefits identified in these claims and the studies that supported them; however, below the survey method that the majority of these studies employed there is far less evaluation of the effects of PE ownership at firm or workplace level other than reference to the benefits of active ownership, rapid organizational change, and powerful management incentives.

The logic behind PE, like many other business models associated with finance-led capitalism, sees a business as a bundle of assets that can be managed on a contractual and transactional basis. The ultimate purpose is to generate cash flow and profit streams over short-term time horizons by financial and organizational manipulation returning these revenue streams to investors. So while PE as a faction of capital claims to be a long-term investor, it is the long-term interests of the fund that they refer to not the portfolio firms that they control. Rather, portfolio firms are viewed as short-term investments from which significant value can be appropriated and redistributed to investors. So in what ways do the micro instruments of the take private business model both enable and encourage investors to appropriate value from what become portfolio firms?

Micro instruments of PE and the appropriation of value from portfolio firms

At firm level the instruments of a PE buyout operate in several ways including share buybacks, corporate restructuring, asset sales, and the securitization of firm-level assets, pension scheme contribution holidays for employers, and contractual approaches to managing a company pension scheme. Each instrument detaches from firm-level performance and the development of core operational capability in a business. The application of these instruments represents a strategic choice for a new owner to either appropriate value from a business and return it to investors and new owners in interim dividends and payments, or invest money in developing the business (House of Commons, 2016: 6). Share buybacks for example are designed to reduce the pool of shareholders, raise the price of shares, and facilitate the return of monies to investors and are often deployed just prior to a firm being taken private. Securitization may also enable corporate restructuring by divesting firm-level assets and then managing them through contractual rather than in-firm relational methods. Securitization and associated lease back arrangements take value bearing but less liquid assets such as buildings, equipment, transport fleets, and sometimes pension schemes and through financial engineering transpose assets into a security. For example, a mortgage-backed security is secured by a collection of mortgages or ownership rights to premises or vehicles. Cash flows are generated as financial institutions and non-financial firms use securitization to immediately realize the value of a revenue-generating asset such as buy-to-let mortgages or the value of investments and payments which fund a defined benefit pension scheme. These instruments are frequently used by non-financial firms too, which illustrates the diffusion of particular techniques and instruments associated with finance-led capitalism into the non-financial economy.

In the case of defined benefit pension schemes securitization is further complicated by the availability of insurance company buyouts of pension schemes. Specialist pension management firms buy up final salary pension schemes usually on the proviso that they are sold to them "closed" to new members and some current members. However, in some cases such as the buyout of BHS and then the secondary sale of BHS to Retail Acquisitions, it can prove difficult to secure a pension scheme sale (House of Commons, 2016: 20). It may be the case that following an employer pension scheme payment holiday instigated by a new PE-backed owner that the scheme is in substantial deficit and by association that the Pensions Regulator will not allow a sale to proceed (House of Commons, 2016: 14–19). The implications of a business failure for the workforce are dramatic and as the cases at Comet Electrical stores, Jessops the camera retailer, and MG Rover previously demonstrated, resulted in significant write-downs in the value of pension contributions for the workforces and those already retired (Bailey et al., 2010). More significantly the liability for pension protection in cases of a business in administration is transferred to the pension protection fund. This is a fund levied on all final salary pension funds, many of which are significantly smaller than those in these larger funds which were written down as a result of the application of unsustainable business models. It is true that all forms of firm can enter administration, but as the recent Work and Pensions Department inquiry into the collapse of the BHS fund concluded, in some cases of acquisition by PE-supported investors, pension payment holidays are one method by which such investors strategize "taking money out of a business" and redistributing it to investors (House of Commons, 2016: 55–56).

As an instrument of PE acquisitions employer pension contribution payment holidays enable financialized business models to "mine" firm-level assets. Often expressed in the term "recapitalizations", the monies previously allocated to employer pension scheme contributions are instead returned to investors. Consideration of recapitalizations which divert employer pension payments is important because pension payments represent reproduction costs for labor which many new investor-owner models that are emblematic of finance-led capitalism seek to minimize if not avoid.

Some instruments that are designed to appropriate value under PE ownership, such as corporate restructuring and associated dividend and debt recapitalizations, operate within approaches to corporate governance developed under finance-led capitalism. These approaches work in the specific interest of capital and seek to minimize liability to taxation and transparency by delisting firms ("taking them private") and in the use of offshore registration for now private firms. Private firms and those which are offshored are not subject to the same transparency requirements or related codes of conduct as publicly listed firms. Indeed it is often the case that the stated purpose of taking a firm private is to reduce both transparency requirements and liability to taxation in the country where it was previously listed. Alliance Boots, for example, is no longer a UK firm; it was bought in 2007 in a deal fronted by KKR PE which led six other PE investors where the firm was re-domiciled as a private Swiss company substantially reducing its liability to taxation. In 2012 Walgreens, the US drug store retailer, bought 45% of the business and in 2014 confirmed its option to acquire the rest of the business in 2015; hence Alliance Boots is now a UK-based, Swiss-registered, US-owned multinational firm.

The logic of going private and offshoring is further reinforced if a firm-level final salary pension scheme is in deficit as a result of employer payment holidays or where the deficit is so large that it potentially undermines the business as a going concern. As the next section of the chapter illustrates, detailed case study evidence strongly suggests that a central reason for deficits in the era of finance-led capitalism is that monies allocated for employer pension fund contributions are frequently diverted to pay down debt or are paid to owner investors as dividend recapitalizations. At firm level these claims flow towards investors who position themselves as new claimants to value, both its appropriation from the labor process and its extraction from contracts which new owners choose to default on (Lazonick & Mazzucato, 2013: 1096). The appropriation of value by PE owners which have taken a firm private may be enacted directly by investor activism, leveraged buyouts, and associated restructures which lead to intensification of the labor process (Clark, 2011, 2016). It is the case too that these instruments can operate retrospectively, as managers acting on behalf of capital appropriate, sell, or take contribution holidays from restructured pension schemes – the previously earned-deferred income of labor (Grady, 2013).

Redundancy

A clear-cut instrument designed to appropriate value for PE investors is the use of redundancy. Again critics of the argument developed in this chapter will argue that all firms involved in merger and acquisition undertake some consolidation; clearly that is true but PE-backed acquisitions have specific advantages over listed businesses and listed business acquisitions. At the height of the take private boom in 2007 many PE firms denied that they were in fact an employer but that instead they represented many smaller scale investor-owners who were in fact the real owners of a business. The Treasury Select Committee, which investigated the PE sector in 2007–2008, held that such arguments were disingenuous (House of Commons Library, 2008). It is, however, the case that PE acquisitions which remain a publicly listed firm or those taken private are classed as a change of majority shareholder not a transfer of undertaking protected by the UK's TUPE – transfer of undertaking protection of employment regulations. This enables PE investors to disregard agreements unilaterally formulated by previous owners or those negotiated between a recognized trade union and an employer in collective bargaining. This derogation from the legislation allows PE owners to lawfully deny some "employer responsibilities" in respect of information and consultation prior to acquisition and deny and de-recognize any existing collective bargaining agreements more easily than traditional employers. In cases where a portfolio firm does not have a recognized trade union and therefore no collective bargaining arrangements, these changes can amount to unilateral employer action. While unilateral changes to pay rates, holiday entitlement, and pension provision represent serious breaches of contract, those affected by them may be asked to agree to such changes or find their job subject to potential redundancy. This leaves many workers subject to unilateral changes with no option but to accept them or accept them but seek to minimize the effects of any unilateral change.

The AA and BHS under private equity

At the start of this chapter it was argued that finance-led capitalism and its associated motives and instruments in PE required state sponsorship to enable the transition to financial capitalism. Deregulation of financial services abolished established rules covering specific privately owned exchanges and financial enterprises. As the previous sction explained, in the case of incentives for PE, these rules were replaced by capital-friendly government regulations. The employment implications will now be outlined in two case studies. Developments at the AA highlight the direct impact of PE buyouts on employment. A further important impact of financialization is the spillover of the instruments developed in PE buyouts that affect labor in the broader corporate sector. This impact is explained by considering the pension scheme at BHS.

Private equity at the AA

The AA was formed in 1905 following a meeting of motoring enthusiasts who were concerned about the deployment of speed traps by the police. The group operated as a campaigning pressure group on road safety and road signs. After the Second World War, the AA campaigned against the continuation of petrol rationing and in 1949 it introduced a breakdown and recovery service. Insurance services were rolled out and in the early 1970s AA "roadwatch" began reporting details of traffic congestion and roadworks on commercial radio stations. In 1973 the AA introduced AA Relay, a service which undertook to transport all occupants of any covered vehicle to any destination in the UK in the event that a vehicle could not be repaired or restarted at the road side. By the mid 1990s the AA had over 8 million members and was ranked first in the *Which* surveys of roadside assistance providers. The AA website claimed that in 2007 the group had 15 million members. In 1999 AA members voted to de-mutualize the company and AA managers sold the company to Centrica, the holding company owners of British Gas for £1.1 billion, gifting each fully paid up member of the breakdown service a £100 payment. In 2004 Centrica sold the AA to two PE firms CVC and Permira for £1.75 billion. In 2007 the AA merged with the Saga group, which was owned by a third PE group Charterhouse. A new holding company, Acromos Holdings, was created which was owned by CVC, Permira, Charterhouse, and Charterhouse staff. The deal secured £3.35 billion for the AA and at the time valued the combined group at £6 billion, placing it as the 20th biggest company in the UK.

Union recognition at the AA

The GMB trade union held sole recognition rights at the AA. The union had a substantive agreement with the AA over collective bargaining for pay and working time and a procedural agreement over job security and redundancy, termed a "job security and business development agreement". The latter included a collective agreement on redeployment and severance terms, which in turn was incorporated into individual contracts of employment. In comparison to statutory terms the details of this agreement were well developed; for example, AA staff liable to redundancy were subject to a four-month notice period and within this in the first instance, if staffing levels had to be reduced, volunteers were sought to avoid the need for compulsory redundancies. Moreover, all staff subject to redundancy were offered alternative employment opportunities which, if on a lower pay rate, were protected by pay red circling. Lastly, statutory severance payments for voluntary or compulsory redundancies were supplemented in the AA-GMB agreement by an additional one month's salary for each year of service up to a maximum of 25 months. Redundant staff were able to leave the AA with full entitlement to severance pay immediately on notification. The agreement was signed by the AA group managing director and the group personnel director, the GMB national chairman, and the GMB national secretary and covered all AA staff in post before January 1, 1996 and remained operational until the AA was acquired by Permira. In 2004 the GMB's membership density stood at 70%.

Union recognition under PE

The GMB was de-recognized by the AA in 2005, and the union was denied all access to the workplace, and check-off arrangements for collection of union subscriptions was terminated. The GMB senior organizer stated that GMB members were told that a new section of the GMB was in consultation with the AA. From February 2005 the applicability of all GMB AA substantive and procedural agreements came to an end. The staff association was in fact the AA Democratic Union (AADU), which changed its name to the Independent Democratic Union (IDU) in October 2007. The IDU is registered with the certification officer as an independent trade union under the Trade Union and Labor Relations (Consolidation) Act, 1992. Since 2005, the IDU is the only union recognized for the purpose of collective bargaining at the AA, and its rule book is only available by written request of members and is not available in any form on the IDU website (www.idu.org.uk). In March 2007 the IDU General Secretary claimed to have more union members at the AA than the GMB (1,500) which still claimed to have 2,300 members, many of whom it was still acting for either as employees or former employees in unfair dismissal cases (www.gmb.aa.org.uk). In April 2007 the IDU claimed 70% union membership across the AA, when the AA's Human Resources director declared the company to be satisfied with relations with the IDU in the context of negotiating and agreeing a 4.5% pay award (Berry, 2007).

Even though the IDU has a certificate of independence, the GMB national organizer maintained that it was and remains a "scab" organization which was founded by a disgruntled GMB official (who is now the IDU General Secretary) in collusion with AA management and their PE owners. The evidence suggests that the AA's PE owners wanted to de-recognize the GMB union and that they had the assistance and capability of local staff to enable them to do so (Clark, 2011, 2016). Recognition of the AADU/IDU aligned PE owner interests with those of the workforce by enabling management, on behalf of PE owners, to downgrade the financial scale and scope of substantive and procedural agreements. By retaining collective bargaining integrity to these agreements AA management and their PE owners were able to claim the GMB de-recognition and the recognition of the IDU was an inter-union dispute and nothing to do with them.

Impact on AA employees

Within a month of recognizing the AADU in 2005 the AA PE owners commenced a restructure by initiating a performance management program via letters sent to all patrol staff informing them that they would be placed in one of two categories: those meeting or exceeding expectation and those whose performance does not meet expectations. Patrol staff who met expectations were awarded a £2,000 bonus. Those who did not were called to one-to-one roadside meetings without representation from the AADU or the GMB and offered £18,000 to leave the AA or accept placement on an improvement program which would lead to summary dismissal if they did not accept this change to their terms and conditions to which the AADU had agreed (GMB archive 1).

Through this process 3,400 patrol workers (50% of the patrol force) left the firm. These departures were not redundancies but voluntary resignations recorded on an AA RSS Patrol decision form. In the decision box AA employees are given two options: either "I wish to accept a mutual termination of my employment" or "I wish to continue my employment with the AA as an RSS patrol" (GMB archive 2). In addition, these resignations were covered by an "authority to advise on compromise agreements" (GMB archive 3).

> I hereby authorize xxxxxxxx xxxxxxx to advise me regarding the compromise agreement between myself and the AA. I understand the rules of the union representation/advice in connection with this compromise agreement is given by the AADU national secretary or representative nominated by the AADU national secretary on condition that 1, I will remain a member of the AADU and continue to pay the normal contribution rate while the proceedings continue and 2, I will cooperate fully with the representative nominated by the AADU, act upon their advice and provide as far as possible, all relevant information. I understand that if I fail to comply with conditions or wilfully provide false information to the union or my representative, representation may be withdrawn by the AADU.
>
> The £18,000 exit award was far lower than those previously agreed between the now de-recognized GMB union and the AA, which on average could see a patrol worker retire or take voluntary redundancy with a payment of around £30,000 and in some cases up to £50,000 for long serving workers. The firm also intensified working by the introduction of the "last job of shift" which could significantly lengthen a worker's shift. "Last jobs" could be called within the final 30 minutes of an 8-hour shift, which could potentially lengthen working time by as much as a further 5 hours. Third, the firm introduced 195 annual "standby hours", which in effect equated to unpaid overtime. These individual developments were recently rolled up into new contracts which cut core earnings but inserted incentives for jobs completed to compensate for last job of shift and stand-by hours and further incentives for sales commissions, for example on membership upgrades.

While remaining de-recognized in 2016, the GMB retains over 800 members in the AA's current workforce of 4,000, giving it a density of 20%. The majority of these members work in the patrol service where 2,300 workers are currently employed. Although the GMB's aim is to secure re-recognition, this may prove hard to secure other than if patrol workers are taken as an initial bargaining unit, which would give the GMB an approximate density of 30%. The GMB has scored regular successes in employment tribunal cases where the union represented AA workers as individuals and has now secured the right under the Employment Relations Act 1999 for GMB shop stewards to represent union members on individual issues which the AA previously denied them. The AA agreed that its position that AA workers could not be accompanied by a certified GMB representative did not reflect the procedural position laid out in legislation.

The financialization of the AA

In 2014 the AA and Saga were de-merged with both firms re-listed on the London Stock Exchange. The cost of the de-merger and all associated flotation costs were placed on the AA balance sheet (Automobile Association, 2013). This marked the acceleration of financialization at firm level. The ownership structure employed by the AA PE owners – the limited partnership – enabled them to become the firm's new investor-owners via a change of majority shareholder and continue to run the firm as it was before they acquired it. This allowed the new owner to place any costs associated with its acquisition of the firm and any further costs associated with any restructure on the balance sheet of the business. Debts associated with leverage and any loans or dividend payments to themselves, consultancy fees, and accumulated debt interest can be charged to the portfolio firm (the AA), which Acromas Holdings owned. That is, the AA was mined for returns to investors and shareholders and then charged for the direct and indirect costs of this appropriation of value. The original purchase by PE partnerships CVC and Permira was highly leveraged with loans of £1.3 billion or 75% of the £1.75 billion purchase price secured against the AA's assets. The following year the owners increased their loans by a further £1 billion, 50% of which they appropriated as an interim payment. Two years later in 2007 Acromas Holdings funded the merger of the AA and Saga via a refinancing deal which resulted in £4.8 billion of debt on the AA/Saga balance sheet. Some £3 pounds was used to buy back existing debt at the AA and Saga while the remainder of the debt was used to make a further interim payment to management and PE investors in Acromas. The 2014 de-merger was refinanced with a further £3 billion loan secured against the AA's assets and future revenue streams. A management team at the AA bought 70% of the firm with backing from 10 City fund managers for approximately £1 billion to fund an accelerated stock market listing valued at £1.4 billion.

At the time of its stock market listing the accumulated debt on the AA's balance sheet was roughly twice the value of its listing valuation. In March 2015 the AA announced plans to raise a further £1 billion to help improve its finances and repay "PIK" (payment in kind) notes in an effort to reduce annual financing interest costs of £195 million. In June 2015 the AA's market capitalization value was £2.32 billion. Since flotation the AA has been headed by a new chief executive, who previously headed a rival car recovery service, Green Flag, a business run on a franchise model. Interviews with the GMB national organizer, senior southern region organizer, and regional organizers suggest that this model may be one that the new management team may seek to diffuse at the AA, that is, retreat from an employment-based model to one of self-employment.

The collapse of BHS

The acquisition of BHS by Sir Phillip Green and the Taveta Investment Group followed by its sale to Retail Acquisitions illustrates the regulatory weaknesses in the UK's finance-led capitalism. In particular the BHS case highlights permissive governance in private investment vehicles modelled on the take private, PE business model and its associated acquisition methods and practices. These arrangements have significant implications for the regulation of defined benefit pension schemes. The retailer was bought by Sir Phillip Green for £200 million in May 2000 and was immediately sold to Taveta Number Two Investments for the same amount of money in a deal which was 100% leveraged over eight years, that is Taveta put no money into the deal. The BHS group paid £423 million in dividends and lease back deals for property in the period until 2004, £307 million of which went directly to the Green family (House of Commons, 2016: 5). However, by 2014 BHS was in a financially precarious position and was effectively kept in business by loans from the Green family totaling £250 million. Sir Phillip Green made a strategic choice to appropriate considerable value from BHS in its earlier profitable years and made no attempt to increase investment in the firm to sustain its competitive edge. More specifically Taveta Number Two Investment was a 100% leveraged offshore investment vehicle. To reduce taxation and transparency liability, it combined with another offshore firm, Carmen, owned by the Green family, which too reduced taxation liabilities on its revenues from leases on BHS properties.

At the same time as extracting and appropriating value from BHS, via the application of instruments pioneered in PE, under Sir Phillip Green's leadership the firm declined to make the necessary employer pension contributions to retain the sustainability of the pension fund. By 2009 the deficit on the two BHS pension schemes was £166 million, whereas in 2000 when the firm was acquired the two schemes had a surplus of £43 million. It is clear from the deliberations of the DWP inquiry into the collapse of the BHS pension schemes that Sir Phillip Green sought to avoid these payments. Moreover, some of the monies which should have gone into the pension schemes went into dividend payments, management charges, sale and leaseback payments and associated charges, inter-firm loans, and use of BHS shares as collateral for loans to fund company purchases. The Pensions Regulator asked for this material to be provided but BHS declined to do so (House of Commons, 2016: 16). The pension scheme deficit prevented the sale of the firm to an appropriate and credible buyer; for example, Sports Direct declined to buy the firm for precisely these reasons.

By 2012 the BHS pension scheme deficit was £233 million and Sir Phillip Green began seeking a buyer for the business. After several abortive attempts including the one with Sports Direct in 2015, BHS was sold to Retail Acquisitions for £1. The firm was sold as a going concern that had financial support from the Taveta Investment Group and, according to the BHS 2013–2014 annual report, was capable of trading without threat of liquidation for 12 months (BHS, 2013, 2014). To establish credibility Retail Acquisitions had to provide £35 million of equity to BHS and secure working capital from Farallon, a US-based PE and investment firm. On the basis that Retail Acquisitions had both the equity and the working capital, the deal went ahead; however, the purchaser had neither. The £35 million was supposed to come from the sale of the BHS headquarters building in Marylebone but failed to transpire. In contrast Farallon Capital issued only a non-binding term-sheet offer to Retail Acquisitions which set out the details of a possible loan which was subject to satisfactory resolution of BHS pension liabilities with The Pensions Regulator. The funding was in fact three £40 million loans, each of which was payable after the repayment of the previous loan. The only working capital that Retail Acquisitions was able to secure was a £25 million loan facility from Sir Phillip Green. Despite this, Retail Acquisitions appropriated £7 million on its first day of ownership to pay advisors, its board, associated salary costs, and transaction management fees. Moreover, Retail Acquisitions removed all profitable assets from BHS and placed them under its ownership and appropriated £11 million in fees and salary costs in its 13-month ownership of BHS. Retail Acquisitions assumed full responsibility for the BHS pension scheme deficit but made no payments into the scheme, and by April 2015 when BHS was wound up by HMRC the deficit stood at £345 million. The 20,000 current and former BHS employees faced an uncertain future as the pension scheme liabilities were passed to the pension protection scheme, which proposed write downs on pension payouts of up to 31% where the average across the BHS schemes was 25%. However, in May 2016, Sir Phillip Green agreed to pay £363m to insolvent BHS pension funds, and the proposal is that staff get on average 80% of full benefits. The 9,000 scheme members with pension pots of less than £18,000 will be offered cash settlements and the other 10,000 members will receive top-ups (of between 80–88% of original entitlements) in a new scheme. In the end Green decided to offer these payments because of the reputational damage associated with the inappropriate use of pension payment holidays – diverting monies to investors and owners. At the time when these payments were made, it remained lawful to sell a firm as a going concern despite The Pensions Regulator having moral hazard concerns on any proposed restructure. That is, Green knew The Pensions Regulator would discover what came out in the DWP inquiry but sought to sell out to Retail Acquisitions to legally absolve his investment vehicles of any legal responsibility. Accordingly, in this voluntary arrangement scheme, members will still lose at least 12% of their deferred income.

Conclusions

As many contributions in this volume illustrate, management buyouts are often very successful and lead to innovative sustainable businesses where owners, managers, and employees all share in financial returns. There are though cases where the very success of the take private business model and the deregulation which surrounds it has significant firm-level distributional consequences. The two cases examined here are not necessarily typical of all PE buyouts. However, each illustrates that the state acting in capital's interest has created conditions whereby both finance-led capitalism and financialization extract value from firms at labor's expense. It is within the current framework of finance-led capitalism that the instruments of PE and management buyouts operate. The cases do present worst cases scenarios of how deregulation in the UK context can lead to deteriorating employment relations settlements for labor following on from buyouts. Indeed the AA case in particular and the trade union media campaign which surrounded it led directly to a Treasury Select Committee examination into the sector. Moreover, the publicity which surround the AA buyout and the Parliamentary investigation into the sector resulted in many PE-backed owners and managers moderating their previously aggressive behavior towards labor and agreeing to work with trade unions in a process of managed change. The BHS case illustrates the diffusion of micro instruments associated with PE into non-financial firms. It also illustrates the scope of deregulation when a firm in financial distress is potentially supported by PE investors in a secondary sale. The argument demonstrates how state-facilitated finance-led capitalism enables the priorities, motives, and instruments of financialization to assert the interests of capital over labor. PE investors, in particular larger so-called mega-funds, which often launch buyouts for listed firms, became in the late twentieth and early twenty-first centuries a key instrument in finance-led capitalism actively supported by the state.

References

Appelbaum, E., Batt, R., & Clark, I. 2013. Implications for employment relations research: Evidence from breach of trust and implicit contracts in private equity buy-outs. *British Journal of Industrial Relations*, 51: 498–518.

Atkinson, J. 1984. Manpower strategies for flexible organizations. *Personnel Management*, August: 28–31.

Augar, P. 2009. *Chasing alpha – How reckless growth and unchecked ambition ruined the city's golden decade*. London: Boodle Head.

Automobile Association. 2013. *Base prospectus, £5,000,000,000 multicurrency programme for the issuance of Class A Notes*. June 24, 2013.

Bacon, N., Demina, N., & Wright, M. 2004. HRM in management buyouts. *British Journal of Industrial Relations*, 42: 325–348.

Bacon, N., Wright, M., Demina, N., Bruining, H., & Boselie, P. 2008. Human resource management in management buyouts in the UK and the Netherlands. *Human Relations*, 61: 1399–1433.

Bailey, D., Clark, I., & De Ruyter, A. 2010. Private equity and the flight of the phoenix four: The collapse of MG Rover. *The Cambridge Journal of Regions, Economy and Society*, 3: 1–15.

Berry, M. 2007. Members of the AA Democratic Union accept 4.5% pay rise. *Personnel Today*, 27th April.

British Home Stores Annual Report. 2013. London: BHS.

British Home Stores Annual Report. 2014. London: BHS.

British Venture Capital Association. 2008. *UK private equity returns outperforming over long term.* London: BVCA.
Bruining, H., Boselie, P., Wright, M., & Bacon, N. 2005. Business ownership change and effects on the employee relationship: An exploratory study of buyouts in the UK and the Netherlands. *International Journal of Human Resource Management*, 16: 345–363.
Clark, I. 2011. Private equity, union recognition and value extraction at the AA. *Industrial Relations Journal*, 42: 36–50.
Clark, I. 2016. Financialization, ownership and employee interests under private equity at the AA, part two. *Industrial Relations Journal*, 47: 328–353.
Cox, L., & Nilsen, A. 2014. *We make our own history: Marxism and social movements in the twilight of neo-liberalism*. London: Verso.
Crouch, C. 2011. *The strange non-death of neo-liberalism*. London: Polity.
Eichengreen, B. 2008. *Globalizing capital*. Princeton, NJ: Princeton University Press.
Gamble, A. 1988. *The free economy and the strong state*. London: Macmillan.
Glyn, A. 2006. *Capitalism unleased*. Oxford, UK: Oxford University Press.
GMB Archive 1. *Letter from AA director of road operations to all road operation staff*. April 8, 2005. The letter details the two categories at length and in terms of the consequences of allocation to each category.
GMB Archive 2. *AA RSS patrol decision form*. Numerous examples in the archive some used in later employment tribunal cases. Date on one original April 21, 2005.
GMB Archive 3. *AADU authority to advise on compromise agreements published by the AADU*. Compromise agreement between AA and terminated workers runs to 18 pages and contains an exit offer pack which includes decision form, two copies of the agreement and information on pensions quotes.
Grady, J. 2013. Trade unions and the pensions crisis: Defending member interests in a neo-liberal world. *Employee Relations*, 35: 294–308.
Harvey, D. 2007. *A brief history of neo liberalism*. Oxford, UK: Oxford University Press.
Heyes, J., Lewis, P., & Clark, I. 2014. Varieties of capitalism re-considered: Learning from the great recession and its aftermath. In M. Haupemeier, & M. Vidal (Eds.), *The comparative political economy of work and employment relations*. London: Palgrave Macmillan.
House of Commons. 2016. *BHS: First report of the Work and Pensions Committee and the fourth report of the Business, Innovation and Skills committee session, 2016–2017*. House of Commons, Work and Pensions, Business, Innovations and Skills Committee, HC54. July 25, London.
House of Commons Library. 2008. *Private equity (transfer of undertakings and protection of employment) bill 2007–2008*. HCL Research paper 08/23 March.
Institute for Fiscal Studies. 2008. CGT, IFS 212–237. Available at: www.ifs.org.uk/budgets/gb2008/08chap10.pdf.
Jensen, M. 2007 *A theory of the firm: Governance, residual claims and organizational forms*. Cambridge, MA: Harvard University Press.
Lapavitatas, C. 2013. *Profiting without producing: How finance exploits us all*. London: Verso.
Lazonick, W., & Mazzucato, M. 2013. The risk-reward nexus in the innovation-inequality relationship: Who takes the risks? Who gets the rewards? *Industrial and Corporate Change*, 22: 1095–1127.
Mason, P. 2015. *Post capitalism: A guide to our future*. London: Allen Lane.
Münnich, S. 2016. Re-adjusting imagined markets: Morality and institutional resilience in the German and British bank bailout of 2008. *Socio-Economic Review*, 14: 283–307.
OECD. 2015. *The labor share in G20 economies*. Employment Working Group, February. Paris: OECD.
Pendleton, A., & Gospel, H. 2014. Financialization, new investment funds and weakened labour: The case of the UK. In H. Gospel, A. Pendleton, & S. Vitols (Eds.), *Financialization, New Investment Funds and Labour*. Oxford, UK: Oxford University Press.
Ruggie, J. 1982. International regimes, transactions and change: Embedded liberalism in the post-war economic order. *International Organization*, 10: 379–415.
Seely, A. 2010. Capital gains tax: Background history. House of Commons Library, UK. Standard note SN860.
Srnicek, N. 2015. *Platform capitalism*. London: Verso.
Srnicek, N., & Williams, A. 2015. *Inventing the future: Post capitalism and a world without work*. London: Verso.

Thompson, P. 2011. The trouble with HRM. *Human Resource Management Journal*, 21: 355–367.
van der Zwan, N. 2014. "State of the art": Making sense of financialization'. *Socio-Economic Review*, 12: 99–129.
Wright, M., Buck, T., & Filatotchev, I. 2002. Post-privatization effects of management and employee buy-outs. *Annals of Public and Cooperative Economics*, 73: 303–352.
Wright, M., Hoskisson, R., Busenitz, L., & Dial, J. 2000. Entrepreneurial growth through privatization: The upside of management buyouts. *Academy of Management Review*, 25: 591–601.

24
HRM PRACTICES

Nick Bacon and Kim Hoque

Introduction

Although management buyouts (MBOs) are often studied from a purely financial perspective, their impact on employees has attracted significant levels of interest among academics, policy makers, and the public in recent years. Indeed, debates around the implications of buyouts and private equity (PE) for employees have begun to appear relatively frequently in the mainstream and financial press, and there is now perhaps as much public interest in the impact of buyouts on employees as in the impact of other forms of corporate restructuring such as privatization, mergers, and acquisitions. This is also reflective of the fact that MBOs have become a global phenomenon, having risen to prominence first in the US during the early 1980s, thereafter becoming prevalent in the UK, and then more recently in mainland Europe.

This chapter reviews what is currently known about the impact of buyouts on employees, focusing in particular on the implications for human resource management (HRM). We define HRM as the overall approach taken to employee management (in terms of whether the firm adopts an HRM strategy that seeks to develop workforce skills and loyalty, or seeks to minimize employment costs), and the implications of this overall approach for three broad interconnected policy areas: employment relations (which includes practices covering training, reward systems, and managing employment change); work relations (which relates to the organization of labor such as team-based organization, levels of task discretion, and the management of health and safety); and industrial relations (which covers institutions for worker voice such as the role of trade unions and collective bargaining) (Gospel, 2010).

The chapter draws on this framework to summarize what is currently known about the impact of buyouts on HRM. It then considers the influence of buyout heterogeneity on HRM, exploring: buyouts led by insiders as opposed to buyins led by outsiders, the role of PE funds, short-hold buyouts, and levels of indebtedness incurred by the firm. Reflecting the emergence of buyouts as a global phenomenon, the international evidence is considered where available, focusing in particular on the investor's country of origin and the national institutional context in which the buyout is located. Finally, we outline an agenda for future research and consider some of the methodological challenges.

HRM strategy

This section considers whether buyouts are associated with an overall approach to HRM strategy that seeks to develop workforce skills and loyalty, or seeks to minimize employment costs. In doing so, it explores: the perceived importance of HRM issues, resources devoted to managing employees, and the extent of adoption of high-performance work systems that indicate an investment orientation.

The perceived importance of HR issues and resources devoted to managing employees in buyouts

The impact of buyouts on HRM may be assessed by considering any subsequent changes to the overall approach or philosophy that managers in a firm adopt towards employee management and practices. One key issue here is the impact of buyouts on the perceived importance of HR issues within the firm, given that this may in turn affect the levels of expenditure and resources devoted to managing employees. With regard to this matter, a survey of managers in 148 UK buyouts completed in the period 1994–1997 reported that in over half (54%) of buyouts the approach or philosophy to managing employees was significantly different post-buyout (Bacon et al., 2004: 334), with a majority reporting that the importance of HRM issues had increased (51%) or stayed the same (46%), and only 4% reporting it had decreased. The implications appeared to be generally positive for employees, with 44% of respondents indicating an increase in resources devoted to managing employees, 47% indicating that resources had stayed the same, and only 9% indicating a decrease. This new and significant emphasis on HRM involved an increase in employee involvement, flexibility, and training. As such, HRM changes following buyouts appear reflective of an emphasis on investment and growth rather than on seeking efficiencies to improve the performance of the firm via restructuring and cost reduction.

Notable, however, is that an increased emphasis on HRM tends not to be the result of buyout investors becoming directly involved in HRM decision-making. For example, where PE-backed buyouts are concerned, investors are mainly involved in the monitoring of financial and operating performance, and in developing the buyout's business strategy. Operational HRM issues remain the responsibility of the buyout's managers who work closely with investors to ensure that performance targets are met. Accordingly, managers report limited PE investor involvement in decisions such as employment levels and payroll budgets, and only rare involvement in negotiations with trade unions (EVCA, 2008: 3).

High-performance work systems

An alternative way of assessing the impact of buyouts on overall HRM strategy is to consider the adoption of high-performance work systems (HPWS) aimed at improving firm performance by increasing employee abilities, motivation, and opportunities to contribute (Appelbaum et al., 2000). Practices associated with such systems include selective hiring, extensive training, employee involvement, and teamworking, with extensive research conducted over the past 20 years having identified a positive relationship between the adoption of an integrated set of such practices and firm performance (Combs et al., 2006). HPWS practices require a long-term approach to investing in employees and are unlikely to be adopted by firms with a short-term approach that seeks to minimize employment costs. Therefore, if such practices are abandoned or eschewed after buyout, this will provide a useful indicator of whether buyouts encourage a short-term cost-minimization approach to HRM.

Much of the evidence suggests, however, that buyouts have a positive impact on the adoption of HPWS, with research based on the aforementioned study of 148 UK buyouts and also on 45 buyouts in the Netherlands suggesting increases in HPWS practices such as training, team-based working, and shared decision-making (Bacon et al., 2004, 2008; Bruining et al., 2005). Although these studies lack a control group of non-buyouts and rely on data from management respondents alone, the findings are consistent with a global study that indicates PE-owned buyouts are well-managed compared to other ownership forms in terms of using performance incentives to reward high-performing employees, and retraining or moving underperformers (Bloom et al., 2015).

Similar findings were also reported by EVCA's (2008) survey of 190 PE-backed buyouts from across Europe between 2002 and 2006. Increases were reported in a range of HPWS practices after buyout, including: regular team briefings (which increased from 71% to 90%); internal promotion as the norm to fill vacancies (increased from 72% to 81%); work organized around team-working for the majority of staff (increased from 68% to 78%); and a formal grievance procedure allowing employees to raise problems with management (increased from 70% to 79%).

However, these studies also suggest that the impact of buyouts on HPWS adoption is affected by institutional context. In the UK/Netherlands surveys cited here, the increase in the rate of uptake of HPWS following buyout was greater in the UK (Bacon et al., 2004, 2008; Bruining et al., 2005). EVCA's (2008) pan-European survey found that seven of the HPWS practices assessed increased significantly following buyouts in liberal market economies (the UK and Ireland) and six increased in Mediterranean Europe (France, Italy, Portugal, and Spain). This compared with increases in the use of only two HPWS practices in coordinated market economies (Austria, Belgium, Germany, the Netherlands, and Switzerland) and no significant changes in Nordic countries (Denmark, Finland, Norway, and Sweden). These findings suggest that buyouts may have the effect of addressing the under-investment in HPWS practices in less regulated countries (liberal market economies) while maintaining such investments in more regulated countries (coordinated market economies) where such practices are often legally required or are more common practice.

Overall, therefore, the evidence suggests that buyouts, in their efforts to improve performance, encourage investments in HPWS rather than seeking to adopt a cost-minimization approach. These findings are consistent with arguments that buyouts release firms from financial constraints, thereby enabling them to grow and to modernize by adopting technological and operational upgrades (Boucly et al., 2011). The following sections consider whether these conclusions are also reflected in the research that has focused on the impact of buyouts on the three related HRM policy areas outlined earlier (employment relations, work relations, and industrial relations).

Employment relations

Turning first to the impact of buyouts on employment relations, we concentrate here on training provision, pay systems, and the management of employment change.

Training provision

Agency theory suggests that buyouts will reduce inefficient expenditure (Jensen, 1989). Expenditure on workforce training may fall into this category if it is regarded as unlikely to add value for current owners or represents rent-seeking by employees. Similarly, wealth transfer arguments suggest that buyouts will seek to improve short-run financial performance by reducing training expenditure (Shleifer & Summers, 1988: 33; Appelbaum et al., 2014: 58). From this perspective, buyouts are regarded as hostile takeovers in which new owners are willing to abrogate long-term contracts between managers and employees with regard to the expectation of continued training and development. This contrasts with the situation in public corporations in which it is assumed that managers will seek to secure employee loyalty and discretionary effort by spending retained earnings on training and development, and promoting employees within internal labor markets. Buyouts are thus regarded by critics as a short-term approach to ownership, in contrast to the long-term horizon required by firms to invest in skilled employees and improve productivity (Haves et al., 2014: 149).

Reflecting these theoretical arguments, reductions in training have been highlighted in a number of case studies of buyouts. For example, Ireland's largest telecommunications provider Eirecom is reported to have reduced training following a buyout in 2005 (ITUC, 2007: 29–30). Consistent with these arguments, politicians and trade unions have expressed concerns about the implications of buyouts for workforce training (PSE, 2007: 97). Trade unions have concluded that following buyouts, new owners stop investing in training in order to divert cash out of the firm (IUF/UITA/IUL, 2007: 16), while government regulators and accounting bodies have expressed concern over the potential impact of buyouts on long-term investments in training (House of Commons Treasury Committee, 2007: 13–14).

The evidence on the impact of buyouts on training investment is, however, somewhat limited. Notwithstanding the case study accounts above of reduced training investment following buyouts, few studies to date have explored this matter systematically within the population of buyouts. Exceptions are the aforementioned studies of 148 UK and 45 Netherlands buyouts. These studies found managers reported increased training following buyouts alongside increases in other complementary HPWS practices such as team-based working and shared decision-making (Bacon et al., 2004, 2008; Bruining et al., 2005). Specifically, across both studies, 55% of buyouts reported that the amount of training employees received had increased, 39% that it had stayed the same, and only 6% that it had decreased (Bacon et al., 2004: 335). Training provision increased in buyouts in both countries (Bruining et al., 2005) although it increased to a greater extent in UK buyouts than in Dutch buyouts, reflecting lower levels of training provision in the UK firms to begin with (Bacon et al., 2008). Broadly similar findings are reported by the aforementioned EVCA (2008) survey, which found that 45% of buyouts had increased expenditure on non-managerial employee training (adjusted for inflation) and just 3% had reduced expenditure.

These studies have some limitations, given that they rely on managers' rather than employees' reports of training levels following buyouts, and they do not contain a control group of non-buyouts. However, in a recent study that drew on non-employer data and included a useful comparison between buyouts and a non-buyout control group, Bernstein and Sheen (2016) identified 118 PE buyouts affecting 3,342 individual restaurants in Florida between 2002 and 2012. Drawing on longitudinal health inspection data from the Florida Department of Business and Professional Regulation, the study identified increased store-level training in buyouts compared to non-buyouts.

As such, there is no evidence within the more representative quantitative studies to suggest that, overall, buyouts result in reductions in workforce training. One possible explanation is that buyouts seek to improve performance in part by reducing hierarchical layers and removing tiers of middle management (Lichtenberg & Siegel, 1990). In such cases, increased training and ongoing development are required to enable shop-floor employees to take on duties previously performed by supervisors, and also to increase employees' awareness of customer and business requirements (Van Neerven et al., 1996). Commensurately, shop-floor employees in buyouts report less supervision and increased discretion over work tasks (Amess et al., 2007). A further potential explanation relates to technological change. Agrawal and Tambe (2016) find that buyouts help address under-investment in information technologies. This in turn is likely to require employee training in the use of such technologies. Either way, the increase in workforce skills training in buyouts identified in the research outlined earlier appears to be in stark contrast to the lack of skills development in listed public companies traditionally attributed to short-term stock market fluctuations and quarterly reporting requirements.

Pay systems

The research on the impact of MBOs on wage levels is reviewed in detail by Kevin Amess in this volume. Summarizing the main findings here, prior studies that draw on wage data from annual reports indicate a relative reduction in wages and lower average wages in PE-backed buyins (Amess & Wright, 2007). This might be viewed as commensurate with the adoption of a cost-minimization HRM approach. However, a focus on the impact of buyouts on average wage levels obscures other important features of pay systems, such as the distribution of pay and benefits between employees at different grades and pay award criteria (Storrie, 2014: vi). There is a paucity of studies exploring these broader issues.

Lichtenberg and Siegel's (1990) study is, however, an important exception. This study considers changes in wage levels for different occupational subgroups. Drawing on the US Census Bureau's Longitudinal Research Database containing annual data for over 20,000 manufacturing establishments in the years 1972–1986, the analysis shows that wages for non-production employees fell by 5.4% compared to a 3.6% increase in wages for production employees following buyouts. They attribute these changes to technological and operational upgrades that increase shop-floor participation in decision-making and facilitate the removal of bureaucratic layers. Similarly, Antoni et al.'s (2015) study of all employees in Germany linked to data on buyout deals to identify 190,000 employees affected by buyouts in the years 2002–2008 suggests that the negative wage effects of buyouts is concentrated in managerial grades (particularly among middle managers) – buyouts may address managerial rent-seeking. It would be of greater concern if reductions in wages disproportionately affected less-skilled workers. However, the two studies described here suggest that this is not the case. More studies are nevertheless required before firm conclusions on the impact of buyouts on non-managerial and lower-paid employees can be reached.

As well as affecting pay rates, buyouts may also impact on pay systems within firms (Gospel & Pendleton, 2014: 42). However, little is known about this matter. Arguably, buyouts will prefer performance-based incentive pay systems (Thornton, 2007: 4) to help address underperformance by ensuring competent employees are rewarded properly (Cuny & Talmor, 2007: 631) and to avoid general wage increases that raise future labor costs. In line with this argument, prior studies have found an emphasis on performance monitoring and performance-related pay in buyouts (Malone, 1989; Bacon et al., 2004). For example, the aforementioned survey of 148 UK buyouts indicated that: the number of staff whose performance was appraised increased in over 4 in 10 buyouts, a similar proportion reported an increase in the number of staff receiving merit pay, and one-quarter of respondents (those in management-led employee buyouts) reported increases in the proportion of non-management employees owning shares (Bacon et al., 2004: 335). Similarly, the pan-European

EVCA (2008) survey of 190 PE-backed buyouts identified the widespread introduction of incentive pay schemes including payment by results and profit-related pay, especially in buyouts in liberal market economies (the UK and Ireland). These findings are broadly consistent with those of Bloom et al. (2009: 9) that indicate PE-backed buyouts focus on performance incentives to reward high-performing employees.

It must be kept in mind, however, that the introduction of incentive pay systems may go hand-in-hand with a reduction in the overall wage bill, given that such systems can be used to reward a small number of high-performing employees while keeping across-the-board wage increases to a minimum. For example, Appelbaum et al. (2013: 505) report reduced discretion for managers in buyouts to reward employees in performance evaluation systems as a result of downward pressure on the payroll. Little research has been conducted on this matter, however. More studies of performance-related pay in buyouts are thus required that focus not just on the adoption of incentive pay schemes but also on whether such systems are used to control wage costs.

Finally, EVCA's (2008) survey provides some notable observations on pension provision, showing that buyouts do not have negative implications for occupational pension schemes. Indeed, the proportion of LBOs offering such schemes increased from 76% pre-buyout to 81% post-buyout. Although pension schemes post-buyout have evolved more towards open defined contribution money purchase schemes and away from defined benefit salary-related schemes, this reflects the trend across all firms. EVCA's (2008) survey also found that the terms of occupational pension schemes did not generally deteriorate following buyouts, with only 1.4% of LBOs reporting a material reduction of the security of pensions in the event of hypothetical insolvency.

Managing employment change

While the impact of buyouts on employment levels is considered elsewhere in this volume, less attention has been paid to how changes in employment levels are managed. Employers are generally encouraged to avoid compulsory redundancies when adjusting staffing levels and to provide help to employees if such redundancies are necessary. There is little evidence to date to suggest that buyouts deviate from this approach. Almost three-quarters of the 190 European PE-backed buyouts surveyed by EVCA (2008: 4) had made no redundancies. Where redundancies had been made, 65% of buyouts offered enhanced severance packages, 46% provided counselling, and 46% offered outplacement assistance (Ibid.). The research conducted to date on redundancies does not therefore suggest the existence of an overt cost-minimization approach within buyouts.

However, a number of further factors might also be important in assessing the management of employment change in buyouts. These include: the use and impact of redundancy consultation, the replacement of permanent with non-permanent employment contracts, outsourcing, and dismissal rates. No prior research has been conducted on these matters. Relatedly, prior studies have also not sought to assess employee perceptions of job insecurity in buyouts. Future studies may usefully address such matters to enhance current understanding of the management of employment change in buyouts.

Overall, therefore, where employment relations practices are concerned, there is no evidence to suggest that buyouts have negative implications for employee training, and no consistent evidence of negative implications for pay systems and the management of employment change. Although more research is needed on these latter two issues (particularly in terms of whether the use of incentive pay systems in buyouts is aimed at controlling wage costs, and on whether the manner in which redundancies and workforce change is handled), there is nothing within the existing research on employment relations practices in LBOs to suggest the adoption of a cost-minimization approach to HRM.

Work relations

The second of the three broad HRM policy areas outlined earlier on which buyouts might have an influence is work relations (the organization of labor such as team-based organization, levels of task discretion, and the management of health and safety, for example). As suggested earlier, buyouts appear to result in shop-floor reorganization (Lichtenberg & Siegel, 1990) with HPWS practices such as team-based working and shared decision-making being increasingly adopted post-buyout (Bacon et al., 2004; Bruining et al., 2005). EVCA's (2008) pan-European survey reported increased use of regular team briefings, team-working for the majority of staff, flexible job descriptions, and flexible working time arrangements for most employees to balance work and family life. As noted earlier, these changes were particularly evident in liberal market countries and Mediterranean Europe where such practices are less commonly adopted in the economy overall.

In terms of the implications of the greater adoption of such practices in buyouts for employees, there has been considerable debate in the broader HRM literature over whether these practices result in improved job quality or an increase in work intensity and stress (Ramsay et al., 2000). It is similarly open to debate whether an increased adoption of such practices in buyouts is reflective of a cost-minimization approach to HRM which might be expected to have negative employee outcomes.

However, as critics of buyouts themselves acknowledge (Appelbaum & Batt, 2014: 194) there is a paucity of representative quantitative data on this matter. Critics have instead relied on selected case studies to argue that where buyouts divest from less profitable operations, this results in the adoption of work relations practices that breach long-term contracts between managers and employees with regard to the conditions of work (Appelbaum et al., 2013). As such, employees, fearful for their jobs, might be expected to accept changes that result in work intensification and a deterioration of working conditions (ITUC, 2007: 28; Thornton, 2007; Watt, 2008: 557; Appelbaum et al., 2014: 61; Gospel & Pendleton, 2014: 26; Clark, 2016). According to the ITUC (2007: 29), this may involve accepting extra shifts and the forfeit or postponement of annual leave (ITUC, 2007: 29). Workers at the Kion buyout, for example, reportedly worked extra shifts each week to increase the utilization of production lines (PSE, 2007: 111). Changes to work relations practices in buyouts may therefore be suggestive of a calculative, cost-minimization HRM approach in buyouts. To explore this matter further, in the following discussion we consider four different work relations practices in buyouts: task discretion, control over the pace of work, participation in decision-making, and health and safety.

Turning first to task discretion, Rodrigues and Child (2010: 1331) predict that buyouts may result in "an intensification of work and moves towards low-discretion work roles" for non-management employees. In support of this, where managerial grades are concerned, buyout critics highlight cases in which task discretion has reduced for managers, such as more limited discretion for line managers to reward exceptional contribution in performance evaluations systems at Mervyns, and reduced discretion for repertoire managers and artists at EMI (Appelbaum et al., 2013: 505 and 508).

There is, however, limited evidence that this has occurred for non-management employees. For example, drawing on UK-matched data from 1,959 firms and 27,263 employees,

Amess et al. (2007) examined the impact of buyouts on task discretion and supervision. Task discretion was defined as the amount of influence an employee perceives they have over their range of tasks, pace of work, and how they do their work. Employees in buyouts reported higher task discretion than their counterparts in non-buyouts (although this was limited to workplaces with a higher proportion of craft and skilled service workers). These findings may be explained by an increase (as outlined earlier) in decision-making responsibility being devolved to employees as a result of reductions in the number of supervisory staff (Lichtenberg & Siegel, 1990).

Turning to employees' control over the pace of work, this might be expected to reduce in buyouts given that workforce reductions are likely to require the remaining employees to take on extra job tasks (Rodrigues & Child, 2010: 1327). Following the buyout at the AA, for example, it is reported that workloads and unpaid overtime increased, the time for toilet trips and meal breaks was restricted, and last job working time was extended for roadside rescuers (Rodrigues & Child, 2010: 1328; Clark, 2016: 249). However, these findings do not concur with research undertaken on the broader population of buyouts, with Amess et al. (2007), as reported earlier, showing that employee control over their pace of work appears greater in buyouts than non-buyouts, at least for craft and skilled service workers.

Participation in decision-making might also be expected to change following buyouts. Critics of buyouts suggest that new owners often make key decisions without discussion with the affected employees (Appelbaum et al., 2013: 515). However, at the shop-floor level this is not easily reconciled with the evidence outlined earlier that employees in buyouts perceive themselves to have greater influence (Amess et al., 2007). It is possible, therefore, that employee participation increases in relation to decisions affecting their job tasks on the shop-floor, but decreases in relation to decisions concerning the future of the firm made at higher levels.

Employee health and safety and well-being may also suffer as a result of the uncertainty and stress generated by ownership change and restructuring. For example, the buyouts of Telemig in Brazil, and Debenhams and the AA in the UK are described as having resulted in "unbearable stress for some employees" (Rodrigues & Child, 2010: 1327). However, no systematic nationally representative studies have been conducted to assess whether employees in buyouts report lower levels of work-related well-being. With regard to health and safety, the only available nationally representative study does not support the arguments within the case studies reported here as it reports that workplace injury rates decline following buyouts of publicly traded firms (Cohn et al., 2016). Furthermore, studies based on nationally representative US data (Cohn et al., 2016: 14) suggest that buyouts do not result in longer working hours that may have negative implications for stress or workplace health and safety.

It is evident from this discussion that greater research on the impact of buyouts on work relations is needed in a number of areas. For example, there is little explanation currently for why buyouts appear to engender greater task discretion for non-managerial employees but lower task discretion for managers/professionals. Similarly, only limited research has been conducted on employees' control over the pace of work (and the implications of this for work intensification and time pressure), and the research that has been undertaken reveals inconsistent results. Additional studies are also required on employee participation (exploring in particular employee participation in decisions taken at different organizational levels following buyouts) and on employee well-being. However, beyond the conclusions drawn from selective case studies, and notwithstanding this need for further research, there is little evidence within the research conducted to date to suggest that changes in work relations in buyouts reflect a cost-minimization approach to HRM or have negative overall effects for employees.

Industrial relations

The third HRM policy area under exploration here on which buyouts might have an impact is industrial relations. With regard to this issue, trade unions are among the most vocal critics of buyouts, and they have suggested that buyouts seek to marginalize their influence by downgrading arrangements for joint consultation and collective bargaining (IUF/UITA/IUL, 2007: 5; Watt, 2008: 557; Gospel & Pendleton, 2014: 26), thereby threatening the European social model of worker participation (Vitols, 2008). Union de-recognition is even considered by some critics to be an important motivation for PE buyouts (ITUC, 2007; Work Foundation, 2007: 26). Frequently cited examples of de-recognition following buyouts include the withdrawal from collective bargaining and union recognition disputes at the AA, NCP, and Kettle Chips (ITUC, 2007; TUC, 2007; Evans & Habbard, 2008; Clark, 2009a, 2009b, 2016).

These examples contrast, however, with other cases where PE has worked closely with union representatives in US and Australian buyouts (Beeferman, 2009; Westcott, 2009) and to rescue UK firms in distress during the 1970s and 1980s (Wright, 1984). They also contrast with survey evidence suggesting that buyouts do not typically have negative implications for union representation, with few changes to representation being reported in the first wave of UK buyouts (Wright et al., 1990, 2009; Bacon et al., 2004). EVCA's (2008) pan-European survey also reports little change regarding union recognition, membership density, management attitudes to trade union membership, the terms and conditions subject to joint regulation, and the frequency of consultation. For example, two-thirds of managerial respondents stated that they were either in favor or neutral towards union membership, and on average, the terms and conditions subject to joint regulation increased following PE-backed buyouts, specifically with regard to distributive issues such as rates of pay, hours of work, and staffing plans (Ibid.). Additionally, use of consultative committees increased from 50% before the buyout to 63% after the buyout. Managers also reported an increase in the influence of consultative committees following buyouts.

There are, therefore, considerable differences in the conclusions drawn from the case study and survey evidence regarding the impact of buyouts on industrial relations. While the case study evidence suggests that the changes that have occurred in industrial relations might be viewed as commensurate with a cost-minimization approach to HRM, this is not the case where the survey evidence is concerned. This suggests that more nationally representative studies are required that include a non-buyout control group to help distinguish between the impact of buyouts and the broader decline of union influence in many countries.

Summarizing the chapter thus far, the representative evidence gathered to date does not, on balance, indicate that buyouts result in a cost-minimizing HRM approach. Although individual cases may highlight some negative changes to certain aspects of employment relations, work relations, and industrial relations, these do not appear to be the case for the average firm subject to a buyout in the broader population of firms. It is possible, however, that the implications for employees may differ between types of buyouts, according to the investor's country of origin, or in specific institutional contexts. The following section explores this possibility.

Different types of buyouts, investor country of origin, and institutional context

Buyout types

Turning first to buyout heterogeneity, while buyouts overall may not be associated with a cost-minimizing approach to HRM, buyouts with specific features may have particularly negative implications. Sources of buyout heterogeneity include whether the buyout is: investor or non-investor led, PE-backed, short- or long-term, and has a high or low debt ratio.

The most frequently considered aspect of the impact of buyout heterogeneity on HRM relates to the contrast between insider and outsider buyouts. Insider buyouts include MBOs, management-employee buyouts, and employee buyouts. Outsider buyouts include investor-buyouts and management buyins. These different forms of buyouts may vary considerably in terms of their implications for HRM. From a theoretical point of view, the wealth transfer perspective suggests that outsiders will lack an established relationship with employees and will therefore be more likely to abrogate long-term contracts between managers and employees (Shleifer & Summers, 1988). By contrast, incumbent managers in insider buyouts appear to be more inclined to continue established relationships with employees, and hence the approach they take to employee management is less likely to change post-buyout. Supporting this argument, Bacon et al. (2004: 336) demonstrate that MBOs are indeed less likely to make changes in their approach to managing employees than outsider buyouts. In addition, employment reductions are more marked in outsider than insider buyouts (Amess & Wright, 2007).

However, not all the evidence suggests that outsider buyouts have more negative HRM implications than insider buyouts. For example, Bacon et al. (2008: 1423) show that outsider buyouts are more likely than insider buyouts (MBOs and management-employee buyouts) to adopt new HPWS practices. Thus, the conclusions drawn from the research on the implications of insider and outsider buyouts on HRM remain inconsistent.

Turning to a second feature of buyout heterogeneity, buyouts conducted by PE firms have attracted particular attention in recent debates, with several studies having sought to compare the effects of PE-backed and non-PE-backed buyouts. These studies are particularly helpful given that much of the recent policy debate has concerned the regulation of PE funds rather than buyouts per se.

In theorizing why the effects of PE-backed and non-PE-backed buyouts on HRM may differ, PE funds are often portrayed as active investors who are involved in developing strategic plans, taking seats on the board, and monitoring strategy implementation. Investor activism is central to explaining how buyouts may address agency problems in public corporations and help improve firm performance. Such activism might take at least three forms, all of which have potential consequences for HRM. The first relates to direct investor involvement in financial control (e.g., monitoring financial performance and restructuring debt financing). The second relates to involvement in talent management to improve leadership (e.g., firing underperforming managers and hiring serial entrepreneurs known to the PE firm). The third relates to investor involvement in operational HR issues (e.g., payroll budgets and the implementation of incentive pay systems).

However, it is less clear whether these forms of investor activism that characterize PE-backed buyouts will result in a cost-minimization approach to HRM or a more developmental approach. The empirical evidence on this is mixed, with some research suggesting that the effect is largely neutral. For example, Bacon et al. (2008) report that PE-backed buyouts are less likely than non-PE-backed buyouts to report increased use of HPWS practices. However, they do not on average reduce the usage of these practices, and they do adopt additional HPWS practices in instances where investors are more heavily involved in HRM issues. Furthermore, financial monitoring of buyouts is positively associated with increases in the perceived importance of HRM issues after the buyout. This finding could be considered surprising given that financial monitoring might be expected to result in downward pressure on employment costs. Where investor involvement in talent management is concerned, this may have both positive and negative effects. Hiring serial entrepreneurs may have positive knowledge transfer effects as new managers may introduce more sophisticated HRM practices. In line with this argument, investor involvement in talent management is positively associated with the percentage of employees working in formally designated teams (Ibid.). In contrast, negative effects may follow from hiring managers that have less loyalty to employees, with evidence that investor involvement in talent management is negatively associated with employee involvement practices and the percentage of employees receiving profit-related pay (Bacon et al., 2004: 337–340).

As such, the HRM implications of the investor activism typical to PE buyouts appear somewhat mixed. While some of the evidence suggests that active PE investors provide buyouts with managerial skills and expertise on HRM issues beyond the provision of financial acumen (and this may result in a more developmental HRM approach being taken), not all of the research supports this argument.

Turning to the HRM implications of short-term ownership, less research has been conducted on this matter. However, critics have argued that buyouts are a short-term form of ownership with a corresponding "disinclination to invest in longer-term, intangible assets such as human resources" (Gospel & Pendleton, 2014: 27). This might particularly be the case for short-hold "quick flip" buyouts in which investors seek to exit from the buyout within a short time period. In accordance with this argument, Bacon et al. (2012) found that a longer intended time to exit at the time of the buyout deal is positively associated with the adoption of HPWS practices. No further studies have, however, addressed this issue.

Finally, in terms of aspects of buyout heterogeneity, buyout critics have highlighted the negative effects of high debt levels incurred in buyouts. High leverage encourages an emphasis on efficiencies rather than investment and growth (Kaplan & Strömberg, 2008), given that debt repayment limits free cash flow for investment (Jensen, 1989). As such, high debt levels commit reserves that may otherwise "be used for investment in the sustainable development of the enterprise and innovation or human resource management and training" (PSE, 2007: 20). However, although debt is frequently highlighted as a key aspect of buyouts, no prior studies have considered the implications of buyout debt levels for HRM.

Overall, therefore, there is no consistent evidence that the forms of buyouts that critics argue have particularly deleterious effects (investor-led buyouts, PE-backed buyouts, short-term buyouts, and high debt ratio buyouts) are associated with a cost-minimization approach to HRM. The research is limited, however, suggesting further studies are needed before firmer conclusions can be reached.

Country of origin and institutional context

As buyouts have become a global phenomenon, many investors now operate beyond their country of origin and acquire firms in a wide range of national institutional contexts. However, only rare assessments have been conducted of whether the impact of buyouts on HRM varies depending on the investors' country of origin. Foreign investors may be more likely than domestic investors to introduce changes in buyouts for a range of reasons, including: different frames of reference with regard to management ideas, greater distance from employees and hence potentially less identification with them, and reduced susceptibility to host country norms or established practice. In addition, investors from specific countries may carry greater threat to employees. For example, Anglo-Saxon investors (e.g., from the US or UK) might be expected to threaten the established practices of the firms they acquire in coordinated market economies in mainland Europe. Current evidence suggests, however, that Anglo-Saxon and foreign investor involvement are not significantly related to a change in HPWS practices after buyout (Bacon et al., 2012). Although the involvement of Anglo-Saxon investors is positively associated with the extension of performance-related pay schemes to cover more employees, this is less likely when the buyout occurs in non-Anglo-Saxon countries (Ibid.: 621).

Also with regard to institutional context, as mentioned earlier, the main increases in the uptake of HPWS practices post-buyout appear to be in liberal market countries (EVCA, 2008) in which stock market pressure may have deterred the widespread adoption of such practices, and a more permissive set of labor laws have not required firms to adopt them (Bruining et al., 2005; Bacon et al., 2008, 2012). In countries where HPWS practices are more commonly adopted there is no evidence that buyouts lead to a reduction in their use (EVCA, 2008).

A recent study of the impact of PE on employment in France reached different conclusions (Guery et al., 2017). Drawing on data from the nationally representative Enquête Relations Professionnelles et Négociations d'Entreprise (REPONSE), the analysis revealed that establishments owned by foreign PE investors were more likely to report employment decline in the previous three years, specifically declines in non-production workers, when compared to establishments owned by French PE investors and non-PE-owned establishments. These findings are attributed to the role of state involvement in French PE firms, with public investment groups adopting social as well as financial objectives. It is also possible, however, that the findings reflect selection effects whereby foreign investors may be more likely to acquire firms that needed turning around.

Future research

As the above discussion suggests, considerable additional research is needed in several areas to further understanding of the implications of buyouts for HRM. Turning to the first of the three HRM policy areas (employment relations), few studies have, as outlined earlier, systematically evaluated the implications of buyouts for training provision. Further studies on this issue would provide a useful test of the willingness of buyouts to make long-term investments. Any reductions to training provision may be particularly concerning from a public policy perspective given the goal of most governments to increase skill levels in the labor market. To enhance the validity of the findings, studies should also assess training provision reported by employees rather than just employers to guard against potential response bias.

Additional studies are also required with regard to pay systems. These studies need to compare the adoption of incentive pay systems in buyouts and non-buyouts, given that the adoption of incentive pay following buyouts identified in the extant research may merely reflect increased usage of such practices among firms as a whole. Further research is also needed to identify whether incentive pay systems are being used in buyouts to control overall wage levels. Incentive pay systems potentially also allow management to exercise control over wage costs by shifting risk onto employees. During the good times bonuses are paid out, while during bad times bonuses are not paid out. The other side of the argument is that lower wage costs during bad times means there is less pressure on management to shed jobs. The impacts on incentive pay on employees therefore needs careful assessment.

There also remains a paucity of research on the management of employment change in buyouts. While studies to date have focused on the implications of buyouts for employment levels, future studies also need to assess the manner in which workforce reductions in buyouts are handled (whether via redundancy and dismissal as opposed to natural wastage, for example), and also whether buyouts increase the use of non-permanent employment contracts and outsourcing.

With regard to the second of the HRM policy areas outlined earlier (work relations), as demonstrated, additional research is required to extend knowledge on the impact of buyouts on task discretion, the pace of work, participation in decision-making, and health and safety. An assessment of these matters would facilitate greater understanding of the broader impact of buyouts on employee job quality.

With regard to the third HRM policy area (industrial relations), future studies might explore whether there are changes in the issues on which management normally negotiate, consult, or inform worker representatives. These studies should ideally combine data collected from employers and worker representatives in order to verify whether the perceptions of increased consultation reported by managers in prior studies are shared by worker representatives. Studies should also include a non-buyout control group to help distinguish between the impact of buyouts and broader secular changes (the decline of union influence, for example).

Across many of the issues outlined earlier on which further research is required, greater consideration is needed of whether managers and non-managerial employees are equally affected by changes in HRM following buyouts. Any negative changes that disproportionately affect less-skilled and low wage workers would be concerning as their prospects for future employment and earnings are lower (Appelbaum & Batt, 2014: 199). Important issues from this perspective include: whether buyouts have differential effects on training provision for managerial and non-managerial employees, whether a greater proportion of non-managerial than managerial pay is at risk under incentive schemes, and whether non-managerial as opposed to managerial employees are particularly at risk of job insecurity and reductions to intrinsic job quality.

In addition, little is known about the impact of buyouts on employee attitudes. This is surprising given that the wealth transfer perspective highlights the potential for breaches of both explicit and implicit long-term contracts (Shleifer & Summers, 1988). Future studies on employee attitudes might therefore include: consideration of whether employees perceive sufficient opportunities for training and development; whether they are satisfied with their pay; whether they feel adequately represented at work; and their satisfaction with levels of job security, job quality, and opportunities to influence decisions.

Future studies should also consider these effects in different types of buyouts. While a number of studies have sought to provide comparisons between insider and outsider buyouts, the findings reached by these studies on the impact of such buyouts on HRM is inconclusive, suggesting further research is warranted. The more limited research on PE-backed buyouts and short- versus long-hold buyouts is similarly inconclusive, thus suggesting a need for further research. Also, no prior research has explored the implications of buyout debt ratios for HRM, suggesting this would be a fruitful avenue for future studies. In addition, future studies should also continue to explore country of origin effects and the role of institutional context.

Many of these issues pose significant challenges in terms of the collection and analysis of available data. Whereas it is possible to draw on existing datasets to consider overall employment and pay data, most HRM issues are not consistently or routinely included in annual reports. Prior studies have therefore relied on surveys of buyouts completed by a management respondent. However, low response rates and response bias may affect the findings, while case studies appear a poor substitute given their lack of representativeness. One way forward would be to make greater use of government surveys that cover HRM issues and include matched employer-employee data. Examples include the British Workplace Employment Relations Survey and the French REPONSE. Buyouts may be identified by linking these data to existing buyout datasets. As these buyout datasets also include data on buyout characteristics, they also provide the potential to explore HRM issues in different types of buyouts.

The impact of buyouts on the HRM outcomes covered in this chapter such as training, pay, job security, and job quality, is likely to remain of interest given the importance of these outcomes from economic and social perspectives. It is to be hoped that future studies as called for here will provide an increasingly reliable basis on which to inform public policy debates on the impact of buyouts on these outcomes.

References

Agrawal, A., & Tambe, P. 2016. Private equity and workers' career paths: The role of technological change. *Review of Financial Studies*, 29: 2455–2489.

Amess, K., Brown, S., & Thompson, S. 2007. Management buyouts, supervision and employee discretion. *Scottish Journal of Political Economy*, 54: 447–474.

Amess, K., & Wright, M. 2007. The wage and employment effects of leveraged buy-outs in the UK. *International Journal of the Economics of Business*, 14: 179–195.

Antoni, M., Maug, E., & Obernberger, S. 2015. *Private equity and human capital risk*. Available at: https://papers.ssrn.com/sol3/papers.cfm?abstract_id=2602771.

Appelbaum, E., Bailey, T., Berg, P., & Kalleberg, A. 2000. *Manufacturing advantage: Why high-performance work systems pay off*. Ithaca, NY: ILR Press.

Appelbaum, E., & Batt, R. 2014. *Private equity at work: When Wall Street manages Main Street*. New York: Russell Sage Foundation.

Appelbaum, E., Batt, R., & Clark, I. 2013. Implications of financial capitalism for employment relations research: Evidence from breach of trust and implicit contracts in private equity buyouts. *British Journal of Industrial Relations*, 51: 498–518.

Appelbaum, E., Batt, R., & Lee, J. E. 2014. Financial intermediaries in the United States: Development and impact on firms and employment relations'. In A. Pendleton, H. Gospel, & S. Vitols (Eds.), *Financialization, new investment funds, and labour: An international comparison*. Oxford, UK: Oxford University Press, 53–86.

Bacon, N., Wright, M., & Demina, N. 2004. Management buyouts and human resource management. *British Journal of Industrial Relations*, 42: 325–348.

Bacon, N., Wright, M., Demina, N., Bruining, H., & Boselie, P. 2008. The effects of private equity and buy-outs on human resource management in the UK and the Netherlands. *Human Relations*, 61: 1399–1433.

Bacon, N., Wright, M., Scholes, L., & Meuleman, M. 2012. The impact of private equity on management practices in European buy-outs: Short-termism, Anglo-Saxon or host country effects? *Industrial Relations*, 51: 605–626.

Beeferman, L. 2009. Private equity and American labor: Pragmatic responses mirroring labor's strengths and weaknesses. *Journal of Industrial Relations*, 51: 543–556.

Bernstein, S., & Sheen, A. 2016. The operational consequences of private equity buyouts: Evidence from the restaurant industry. *Review of Financial Studies*, 29: 2387–2418.

Bloom, N., Sadun, R., & Van Reenen, J. 2015. Do private equity owned firms have better management practices? *American Economic Review: Papers & Proceedings*, 105: 442–446.

Bloom, N., Van Reenen, J., & Sadun, R. 2009. Do private equity owned firms have better management practices? In A. Gurung & J Lerner (Eds.), *Globalization of alternative investments working papers volume 2: The global economic impact of private equity 2009*. New York: World Economic Forum USA, 1–10.
Boucly, Q., Sraer, D., & Thesmar, D. 2011. Growth LBOs. *Journal of Financial Economics*, 102: 432–453.
Bruining, H., Boselie, P., Wright, M., & Bacon, N. 2005. The impact of business ownership change on employee relations: Buy-outs in the UK and The Netherlands. *The International Journal of Human Resource Management*, 16: 345–363.
Clark, I. 2009a. Owners and managers: Disconnecting managerial capitalism? Understanding the private-equity business model. *Work, Employment and Society*, 23: 775–786.
Clark, I. 2009b. Private equity in the UK: Job regulation and trade unions. *Journal of Industrial Relations*, 51: 489–500.
Clark, I. 2016. Financialisation, ownership and employee interests under private equity at the AA, part two. *Industrial Relations Journal*, 47: 238–252.
Cohn, J., Nestoriak, N., & Wardlaw, M. 2016. *How do employees fare in private equity buyouts? Evidence from workplace safety records*. Working Paper. University of Texas-Austin.
Combs, J., Liu, Y., Hall, A., & Ketchen, D. 2006. How much do high-performance work practices matter? A meta-analysis of their effects on organizational performance. *Personnel Psychology*, 59: 501–528.
Cuny, C. J., & Talmor, A. 2007. A theory of private equity turnarounds. *Journal of Corporate Finance*, 13: 629–646.
Evans, J., & Habbard, P. 2008. From shareholder value to private equity – The changing face of financialisation of the economy. *Transfer*, 14: 63–75.
EVCA. 2008. *The impact of private equity-backed buyouts on employee relations*. Brussels: European Venture Capital Association.
Gospel, H. 2010. Human resource management: A historical perspective'. In A. Wilkinson, N. Bacon, T. Redman, & S. Snell (Eds.), *The SAGE handbook of human resource management*. London: Sage, 12–30.
Gospel, H., & Pendleton, A. 2014. Financialization, new investment funds, and labour. In A. Pendleton, H. Gospel, & S. Vitols (Eds.), *Financialization, new investment funds, and labour: An international comparison*. Oxford, UK: Oxford University Press, 1–52.
Guery, L., Stevenot, A., Wood, G. T., & Brewster, C. 2017. The impact of private equity on employment: The consequences of fund country of origin- new evidence from France. *Industrial Relations*, 56: 723–750.
Haves, J., Vitols, S., & Wilke, P. 2014. Financialization and ownership change: Challenges for the German model of labour relations. In A. Pendleton, H. Gospel, & S. Vitols (Eds.), *Financialization, new investment funds, and labour: An international comparison*. Oxford, UK: Oxford University Press, 148–175.
House of Commons Treasury Committee. 2007. *Private equity: Tenth report of session 2006–07*. London: The Stationery Office Limited.
ITUC. 2007. *Where the house always wins: Private equity, hedge funds and the new casino capitalism*. Brussels: International Trade Union Confederation.
IUF/UITA/IUL. 2007. *A workers' guide to private equity buyouts*. Geneva: International Union of Food, Agricultural, Hotel, Restaurant, Catering, Tobacco and Allied Workers' Associations.
Jensen, M. C. 1989. Eclipse of the public corporation. *Harvard Business Review*, 67: 61–74.
Kaplan, S. N., & Strömberg, P. 2008. *Leveraged buyouts and private equity*. Working Paper 14207, National Bureau of Economic Research, July, Cambridge, MA.
Lichtenberg, F., & Siegel, D. 1990. The effect of ownership changes on the employment and wages of central office and other personnel. *Journal of Law and Economics*, 33: 383–408.
Malone, S. 1989. Characteristics of smaller company leveraged buyouts. *Journal of Business Venturing*, 4: 349–359.
PSE. 2007. *Hedge funds and private equity: A critical analysis*. Brussels: Socialist Group in the European Parliament.
Ramsay, H., Scholarios, D., & Harley, B. 2000. Employees and high performance work systems: Testing inside the black box. *British Journal of Industrial Relations*, 38: 501–531.

Rodrigues, S. B., & Child, J. 2010. Private equity, the minimalist organization and the quality of employment relations. *Human Relations*, 63: 1321–1342.

Shleifer, A., & Summers, L. H. 1988. Breach of trust in hostile takeovers. In A. J. Auerbach (Ed.), *Corporate takeovers: Causes and consequences*. Cambridge, MA: National Bureau of Economic Research, 33–68.

Storrie, D. 2014. Preface. In A. Pendleton, H. Gospel, & S. Vitols (Eds.), *Financialization, new investment funds, and labour: An international comparison*. Oxford, UK: Oxford University Press, v–vii.

Thornton, P. 2007. *Inside the dark box: Shedding light on private equity*. London: The Work Foundation.

TUC. 2007. *Private equity – A TUC perspective*. Trades Union Congress Evidence to the Treasury Committee Inquiry, May.

Van Neerven, T., Bruining, H., & Paauwe, J. 1996. Managing without traditional owners. In P. C. Flood, M. J. Gannon, & J. Paauwe (Eds.), *Managing without traditional methods*. Wokingham, UK: Addison-Wesley, 105–146.

Vitols, S. 2008. The evolving European system of corporate governance: Implications for worker participation. *Transfer*, 14: 27–43.

Watt, A. 2008. The impact of private equity on European companies and workers: Key issues and a review of the evidence. *Industrial Relations Journal*, 39: 548–568.

Westcott, M. 2009. Private equity in Australia. *Journal of Industrial Relations*, 51: 529–542.

Work Foundation. 2007. *Inside the dark box: Shedding light on private equity*. London: Work Foundation.

Wright, M. 1984. Management buyouts and trade unions: Dispelling the myths. *Industrial Relations Journal*, 15: 45–52.

Wright, M., Bacon, N., & Amess, K. 2009. The impact of private equity and buyouts on employment, remuneration and other HRM practices. *Journal of Industrial Relations*, 51: 503–517.

Wright, M., Chiplin, B., Thompson, S., & Robbie, K. 1990. Management buy-outs, trade unions and employee ownership. *Industrial Relations Journal*, 21: 136–146.

PART V

Performance and life cycle

25

THE IMPACT ON PRODUCTIVITY OF MANAGEMENT BUYOUTS AND PRIVATE EQUITY

Yan Alperovych

Introduction

A management buyout (MBO) is a form of transaction in which management teams acquire a firm or its division(s) from its current shareholders. As managers often lack sufficient financial resources, these operations are executed with the help of financial backers known as private equity (PE) firms. The transaction is typically financed with a mixture of equity and debt, the latter being a larger proportion of the total deal value than the former.[1]

Buyouts first attracted academic attention in the middle of the 1980s. The seminal paper by Jensen (1986) proposed that at the heart of this phenomenon lies the problem of agency costs of free cash flows (FCF). The latter are defined as excess cash that remains within a firm after it has financed all positive net present value projects.

The underlying mechanism of the agency conflict arising from these cash flows is based on the hypothesis that corporate managers could pursue objectives that might be prestigious/beneficial to them but do not necessarily maximize shareholders' wealth (Jensen & Meckling, 1976; Hart, 1995). For instance, managers face strong incentives to let their firms grow beyond their optimal size as it increases their power. A way to align the interests of managers with those of shareholders is to provide the former with an equity stake and introduce pay-for-performance compensation structures (e.g., grant them stock options) in the firms they manage. However, these mechanisms may be insufficient when companies are able to generate abundant FCFs. Available present and future cash can still allow managers to engage in all kinds of investment policies even though the latter may not earn the marginal required rates of return. In the absence of FCFs, pursuing these policies would require managers to raise funds from external sources and these will obviously be more expensive than those internally available. As a consequence, corporations with substantial current or future cash flow generation capacity could be fraught with an internal conflict of interest over the FCFs. Managers would have a strong incentive to retain FCFs and thus increase resources at their disposal.[2] Shareholders, on the other hand, would prefer this cash to be distributed, as this will limit the managers' power and provide further discipline to eliminate organizational inefficiencies and wasteful expenditures.

The distribution of the FCFs is therefore a keystone in this theory. Jensen (1986) argued that one efficient mechanism to force managers to distribute cash is debt. Indeed, promises of future dividends, their possible increases, or share buybacks are weak compared to commitments to honor the financial obligations. Failure to make debt service payments, and hence distribute FCFs, gives bondholders the right to force the company into bankruptcy. This poses sufficient threat and motivates management to pursue value-enhancing and cash-generating strategies. The problem is how to force managers to borrow.

Jensen (1989) advocated that the solution is in the active ownership by investors who hold large equity and debt positions, sit on the boards, and thoroughly monitor and fire managers whenever necessary.

The buyout in this context seems to combine all of the benefits. On the one hand, there are active investors (PE firms), and managers with an increased equity stake and high-powered incentive structures. This ensures that management team and PE investors' interests are realigned. On the other, increased degrees of financial leverage ensure that extra cash is paid out from the firm. Jensen (1993) advanced that this form of organization is capable of eliminating much of the waste and unlocking the value creation blocked by inefficient management practices, and by the inability of widespread passive ownership to keep the managers in check.

While definitely appealing, these arguments implicitly rely on the assumption of a dispersed listed corporate ownership, in which property rights are separated from control rights. The buyout in this case is referred to as a public-to-private (PTP) transaction and the underlying firm is effectively delisted from the stock market in this process. This, though, is a very limiting conjecture with a potential to introduce a systematic bias in the conclusions. The reason is that targets of PTP buyouts are necessarily large firms. As will be detailed later, most often buyout transactions are operated over much smaller and plausibly structurally different privately held targets. The latter includes but is not limited to the divisions of larger firms, family-owned firms, founder-owned firms, and even firms owned by other PE-firms themselves. In most of these examples (except for the divisions) the ownership is already concentrated. There must therefore be little room for any type of agency conflicts advocated by Jensen (1986, 1989, 1993), and buyouts in these cases should remedy some other issues than the distribution of the FCFs. Furthermore, given the heterogeneity of the buyout's origins, the issues to solve may vary accordingly.

Interestingly, the explanation of this structure was provided by a more entrepreneurship-oriented strand of literature (Wright et al., 2000). Here, buyouts are seen as mechanisms that allow mutating operations depending on the need and the context in which a buyout is executed. For example, buyouts can be a solution for a family succession issue (Howorth et al., 2004). Divisional buyouts may be a way for existing management to gain independence from the otherwise rigid parental structures, and thus implement necessary value-enhancing policies (Meuleman et al., 2009). Pass-the-parcel buyouts involving the transfer of ownership from one outgoing PE firm to the incoming one may be a way to organize a better liquidity in the PE exit market (Arcot et al., 2015; Degeorge et al., 2016).

This discussion suggests that buyouts are associated with some structural changes in the underlying firms and that these changes may lead to operating and economic improvements. Kaplan and Strömberg (2009) argued that these improvements may be brought about by changes in the operations (operating engineering) or in the governance (governance engineering).[3] This chapter provides a synthetic review on these two non-mutually exclusive channels.

Buyouts, operating performance, and productivity: general evidence

Improved governance, advice, and coaching provided by PE firms should theoretically lead to major organizational changes that could lead to value creation (Phan & Hill, 1995). A recent paper by Gompers et al. (2016) confirms that PE firms consider increases in revenues, follow-on acquisitions, and cost-cutting as important mechanisms through which value improvements can be achieved.[4] In addition, this study also advocates that PE firms expect to create value via changes and redefinitions of corporate strategies and/or business models. Combined, this should result in improvements in revenues, in growth of revenues, and in reduced costs, all of which are the components of performance and productivity. Consequently, these ideas essentially underpin two closely related types of studies. The first ones look at changes in the pre-to-post accounting and/or economic measures of operating performance that accompany the buyout transaction. The second ones investigate a deeper structural governance characteristics in buyout firms. Some relevant evidence is reviewed later in this chapter.

Changes in accounting and economic performance

A series of early examinations of the improved performance assumption include studies by Kaplan (1989), Lichtenberg and Siegel (1990), Smith (1990), Liebeskind et al. (1992), Opler (1992), Thompson et al. (1992), Wright et al. (1992), and Wright et al. (1996).

Kaplan (1989) used the data on 76 PTP MBOs closed during 1980–1986 in the US. He found that operating income net of industry changes remained unchanged in the first two years after the transaction but was substantially higher (by 24%) in the third post-transaction year. Recognizing that operating income is not the best metric (as it can be biased by the post-buyout divestures), he used the ratios of operating income to assets and to sales to control for the post-buyout asset moves. After the correction, he found that both ratios increased significantly post-acquisition (by about 20%) in all three post-transaction years, and this after controlling for the industry changes in these variables. Similarly, he documented the increases in the industry adjusted net cash flows (operating income less capital expenditures) and in the ratios of net cash flows to assets and to sales in the first three post-buyout years. It is worth noting that Kaplan (1989) also documented reductions in capital expenditures in all three post-buyout years on an industry-adjusted basis. He interpreted these results as being consistent with the improvements in efficiency assuming pre-buyout companies had been investing in negative net present value projects.

In a similar vein, Smith (1990) looked at the changes in operating performance for the MBO transactions of 58 listed firms executed between 1977 and 1986 in the US. He found significant increases in the industry adjusted operating returns (after controlling for asset sales) between the last pre- and the first post-buyout years. Moreover, the results indicated that such increases were not due to the reductions in the headcount. The evidence also suggested that working capital resources of MBO firms diminished after buyouts although these reductions contributed only marginally to the improvements in the operating returns. Similarly to Kaplan (1989), this study documented the significant reductions in the capital expenditures. Interestingly, Smith (1990) concluded that these reductions had no impact on the improvements in the operating performance.

It is important to stress that the above-mentioned investigations were using essentially accounting measures to quantify the improvements and value creation following the buyout transaction. One important limitation of such metrics is that they cannot account directly for the input–output transformation process. They can also be subject to managerial manipulation. Moreover, changes in these measures before and after the buyout may confound the value creation and value capture (Wood & Wright, 2009).[5] In other words, these measures may not be representative of the real performance. Although mentioned contributions provided some indirect evidence against these arguments, a more thorough analysis was clearly necessary.

Lichtenberg and Siegel (1990) were among the first to provide such examination. Instead of using accounting measures directly, they computed the total factor productivity (TFP) to evaluate the impact of MBO and LBOs on efficiency. Moreover, in contrast to the previous analyses performed at the firm level, this study was based on the plant-level data. The authors argued that notwithstanding the correlation between the productivity and operating performance, the former is a cleaner measure of technical efficiency and is a more fundamental determinant of key economic and financial variables such as profits and stock prices. Using a large sample of more than 20,000 manufacturing establishments from the US Census Bureau Longitudinal Research Database (LRD), they documented that productivity in the first three years after the buyout was significantly higher than in any of the eight years before the buyout. The authors also reported that pre-to-post increases in productivity were more pronounced in MBOs compared to LBOs on average but not on median.

Interestingly, early buyouts (from 1981 and 1982) did not show any significant improvements in productivity, while later deals witnessed increasing patterns of the efficiency gains, as if increasing competition in the PE industry forced financial sponsors to put more emphasis on the fundamental changes in the operations of their targets. An important limitation of this study, acknowledged by the authors, was the impossibility of establishing a causal relationship between the buyout transaction and efficiency gains due to the nature of the data employed.

Somewhat later papers arrived at almost the same conclusions. Opler (1992), in line with the conventional wisdom at that time, found that operating profits to sales rose by an average of 16.5% (11.6% industry adjusted) from the pre-buyout year until two years after the transaction. The situation was similar with the operating profits per employee, both in absolute and in industry-adjusted terms. Finally, there was a significant drop in capital expenditure and no significant impact of buyouts on R&D. Liebeskind et al. (1992) focused on the restructuring activities of the buyout firms isolating four distinct aspects: corporate downsizing, corporate refocusing, portfolio reorganization, and changes in the industry characteristics of portfolio businesses. Using the Large Establishment Database, the study compared 33 large LBO firms and 33 matched public corporations. Their results showed that LBO firms significantly downsized operations. At the same time, both LBO and comparable firms were similar in terms of the three other aspects mentioned earlier. The authors concluded that LBOs seemed to create value by downsizing the firm and foregoing excess growth.

The discussions so far were based on US data. Non-US investigations quickly followed and the UK-based evidence emerged among the first. Thompson et al. (1992) used the data compiled by the Centre for Management Buyout Research (CMBOR) to identify whether the UK management buyouts also enjoyed improvements in performance and productivity like their US peers. In parallel, Wright et al. (1992) adopted a survey approach to isolate performance implications of the management buyouts in the UK. Their survey of 182 mid-1980 MBOs showed that 68% of buyouts improved profitability. In both studies, authors found evidence consistent with the US results in that buyouts indeed enjoy improvements in operating performance at least over the short term. The UK buyouts ventured more into product developments, post-LBO asset acquisitions, and disposed of less assets.[6]

Wright et al. (1996) focused on the longer-term effects of buyouts: the longevity, financial performance, and productivity. They used a larger sample of 251 buyouts completed in the period 1982–1984, and for which authors had accounting and financial data (e.g., liquidity, profitability, and employee productivity). A matched sample of 446 non-buyout firms was also collected from the publicly available sources. The results revealed that buyouts and non-buyouts are essentially indistinguishable in terms of return on assets or labor productivity (profit/employee) in the early years after the buyout. The improvements, however, were observed in three to five years, leading the authors to conclude that it could take some time for the UK buyout firms to increase their profitability significantly above their sector average. More importantly, the effects of MBOs on the TFP were also calculated in every year up to six years after the buyout. The results showed that MBO firms were not significantly more productive in the first two post-buyout years compared to their non-LBO peers. However, the relative productivity of buyouts improved by about 20% by the fifth year after the buyout. On average, UK buyout firms exhibited a 9% greater productivity compared to their non-buyout peers over the first six years after the transaction.

Changes in governance

In parallel to the analyses of changes in productivity and operating performance, scholars also delved into more governance-related factors that affect firms during the buyout transaction. Examples include Baker and Wruck (1989), Phan and Hill (1995), Cotter and Peck (2001), and Acharya et al. (2009, 2013).

Baker and Wruck (1989) documented the organizational changes, which occurred in The O.M. Scott & Sons Company when it underwent its MBO transaction. The study was based on a series of interviews with the key players involved with the deal, notably target managers and PE investors. Both sides stressed that changes within the Scott & Sons Company stemmed from the constraints imposed on the firm by the high degree of financial leverage. Improvements were also resulting from changes in the management compensation schemes, and from changes in the monitoring and advice received by the target's management team. All three factors, directly related to the corporate governance mechanisms, forced managers to run the company in a way that would generate cash.

Phan and Hill (1995) investigated the effect of an increased management stake and increased debt on firm goals, strategy, and structure after the LBO. Using a survey of 214 PTP buyouts completed between 1986 and 1989 (inclusive) they first showed a considerable increase in management stockholdings. The mean levels were observed to shift from 14.2% to 35.7% from one year before to one year after the LBO. They next presented evidence on the changes in the firm goals, structure, and strategy. In their results, the LBO firm's management seemed to give priority to efficiency gains as opposed to growth. In addition, managers showed clear intent to decentralize operations and reduce the unnecessary diversification and hierarchical complexity. Efficiencies (measured in terms of productivity and profitability) were gained as a result of these governance and structural changes . Finally, managerial holdings appeared to be a more important factor than debt itself in fostering the above-mentioned changes.

Corporate governance and its impact on performance can also be evaluated from the board of directors' perspective. Cotter and Peck (2001) took this approach and studied how the investor activism relates to the structure of debt and to the post-LBO monitoring and compensation of management. The study compared 64 US-based LBOs led by either the buyout specialists (PE firms), or by management, or by third-party equity investors, during

1984 and 1989. Their findings suggested no systematic differences in the CEO compensation schemes in buyouts controlled by PE-firms, as opposed to those controlled by management or by other investors. However, they did document some marked differences in the composition of the boards across these three types of buyouts. PE-led LBOs were observed to have smaller boards. In addition, whenever a PE house controlled the LBO firm, its board representation was stronger. In other words, PE houses secured more seats in smaller, and potentially more efficient boards. Interestingly, in such PE-led buyouts increased debt levels did not lead to improved performance (measured as EBITDA to total sales post-buyout). The situation was in sharp contrast to the other buyout types, in which increased senior debt levels led to improvements in performance after the buyout. Cotter and Peck (2001) interpreted this finding as an evidence that debt and active monitoring by PE investors could be substitutes.

In a related series of studies Acharya et al. (2009, 2013) investigated the impact of corporate governance on performance in buyouts closed in Western Europe. A distinctive aspect of these works was an attempt to isolate the leverage and asset specific effects on performance. Such decomposition allowed them to quantify that less than 30% of the buyout *outperformance* generated by the top PE houses was due to the increased debt. The remaining 70% was represented by an actual outperformance. To explain this residual outperformance, the authors resorted to (i) 20 structured interviews with the chairmen or CEOs of public or private boards, (ii) factual analyses of the board compositions of the FTSE 100 firms, (iii) detailed case studies of 10 FTSE 100 firms, and (iv) high-level data on the composition of the boards of 66 PE-backed firms in the UK. Analyses of this high-quality data revealed that boards of the PE-backed companies were much more effective and added much more value to the firm than boards of publicly owned companies. This value added was primarily due to the exceptionally high focus on strategic and performance priorities, as well as the much greater commitment by the board members. The boards of PE-backed firms were also found to be considerably smaller than those of publicly listed firms.

Buyouts, operating performance, and productivity: later investigations

After the initial spurt in the research on performance implications of the buyouts, studies have taken a more granular and more international approach towards the issue. First, analyses employing more integrated and complex methods to measure productivity both in and outside of the US appeared. Second, scholars recognized that the heterogeneity of buyout types may have an impact on post-buyout efficiency and operating performance. We review available evidence in the following subsections.

New approaches to measure efficiency

There are three distinct elements to consider to measure productivity. The first one is the unit of analysis, which can be a firm or a plant (establishment). Plant-level data is more granular and allows a finer evaluation of efficiency. However, it is costlier to obtain, to treat, and is sometimes limited to manufacturing sectors only. Firm-level data is more readily available, but can lack precision depending on the specific research question. The second element is the method employed to assess efficiency. In most cases, plant-level studies resort to TFP, although some firm-level applications are also available. The last consideration is related to the missing counterfactual problem.

The central question in all studies pertaining to productivity and performance in buyouts is whether observed patterns are attributable to the transaction itself, or to other more fundamental factors, latent or not. To answer this concern one ideally wants to observe what would have been the level of efficiency/performance had the firm not undergone a buyout (counterfactual). This observation must occur while keeping all other observable and unobservable variables fixed, which is obviously impossible. Since we can only observe buyout or non-buyout firms, we always miss the counterfactual. It is this particular reason that makes it difficult to separate the buyout effect from the non-random selection of very promising targets by PE firms. Put in the conventional wording of PE research, it is very difficult to separate selection from value-adding.

To work around this problem scholars often, as was the case in the reviewed studies so far, resort to the samples of matched control firms. The matching can be based on some ex ante specified criteria, like size, industry, pre-buyout profitability, and/or growth patterns. Alternatively, one could make use of the more sophisticated propensity score matching methods (Rosenbaum & Rubin, 1983, 1985; Dehejia & Wahba, 2002). The matching, however, does not necessarily solve the problem completely. It allows the researcher to control for the selection based on the observable heterogeneity, while the "true" selection may be based on unobservables. Two approaches are possible in this case. The first is related to Heckman's (1976) solution of the sample selection problem. The second approach consists of finding an exogenous factor (instrument) that affects the treatment (the buyout transaction) but not the outcome (productivity). Some recent studies, which are reviewed later, started to employ one or other of these solutions to ascertain the impact of buyouts on productivity.

Analyses at the establishment level

In most of the investigations of the late 1980s and early 1990s, productivity was measured using accounting ratios. One notable exception is the study by Lichtenberg and Siegel (1990), which used the TFP approach in the context of the US manufacturing establishments. Harris et al. (2005) applied the same methods to estimate the efficiency of 35,752 manufacturing establishments in the UK before and after buyout. Their findings also suggested the existence of improvements in plant TFP levels. In contrast to Lichtenberg and Siegel (1990), MBO plants were found to be less productive than plants in the control group before the transaction. However, consistent with prior literature, MBO plants experienced considerable improvements and became more efficient than plants in the control group after the buyout. More recently Davis et al. (2014) compiled a comprehensive dataset using Longitudinal Business Database (LBD), Annual Survey of Manufacturers, Census of Manufacturers, and CapitalIQ. This allowed them to track and compare 3,200 buyout firms (15,000 establishments) with matched comparable firms before/after the buyout transaction. The matching was performed in terms of size, industry, age, and single/multi-establishment status. The authors documented that buyout targets engaged in much more aggressive policies of resource reallocation (especially labor) from the least to the most productive (in terms of TFP) establishments. Further analyses showed that buyout targets open new plants in the upper part of the TFP distribution twice as frequently in comparison to control firms and have a lower likelihood of opening low-productivity plants. The average gain of TFP in the PE-backed establishments amounted to 2.1 log points over the first two years after the buyout. The authors concluded that this resulted in material improvements in operating margins in buyout firms.

Another investigation by Bernstein and Sheen (2016) looked at the operational consequences of PE buyouts using evidence from the restaurant industry. Although the authors did not used the TFP measure, this paper is closely related to the literature just discussed as it looks at changes occurring in the lowest possible store-level operational practices. The study used the data on every restaurant inspection conducted in Florida during 2002–2012 with all information mapped to the acquisitions of restaurant chains by PE firms (3,400 acquired restaurants out of about 50,000). The results indicated that restaurants in the PE-backed chains commit fewer health violations after the acquisition. Moreover, the improvements in practices were found to be in the areas considered by the FDA as the most dangerous for clients. Relatedly, this study demonstrated that these improvement trends had not existed before the buyout transaction and that these trends steadily increased over the first five years after the buyout. The data also allowed the distinction between the restaurants directly owned by the PE sponsors and those operated by franchisees on behalf of the PEs. This is crucial in isolating the PE treatment effect. The authors found that both directly owned restaurants and franchisees had similar operating patterns prior to the buyout, yet after the buyout improvements occurred mostly in the directly owned stores. Finally, the extent of the improvements seemed to be particularly marked in buyouts sponsored by the PE firms with previous restaurant industry experience. All of the conclusions in this study were in line with the operational engineering mechanism described earlier.

Analyses at the firm level

In parallel to the establishment-level analyses, firm-level studies provided some additional evidence. Ames (2002) focused on MBOs of the UK manufacturing firms over the period 1986–1997. The analyses used the augmented Cobb-Douglas production function to capture the MBO effect on productivity. He suggested that improved governance systems, managerial ownership, and debt level bonded managers to focus on cash-generating and value-enhancing activities. This should, in turn, be reflected in the improvements in firm-level productivity. The rationale for this is that firm production is enhanced with an additional unobservable managerial/organizational/governance skills factor. The latter then affects the technical relationship between the firm's outputs and inputs in two possible non-mutually exclusive ways: (i) an overall shift in the production function, and (ii) improvements in the marginal value-added product of capital and labor. The results suggested that both mechanisms were at play. A permanent shift in the production function implied a permanent improvement in productivity of the order of 16.13% for MBO firms compared to the control group. The marginal productivities of labor and capital were respectively 32.01% higher and 75% lower for MBO firms compared to the non-MBO companies. In a related paper, Amess (2003) used a stochastic production frontier approach to estimate the longer-term technical efficiency effects of MBOs. Consistent with prior results (e.g., Lichtenberg & Siegel, 1990; Wright et al., 1996) the analyses indicated that MBO firms had superior efficiency starting from two years before and up to four years after the transaction. MBOs were found to have a transitory effect on firm-level technical efficiency as their superior productivity indicators vanished beyond the fifth year after the transaction.

Analyses using the dynamic Data Envelopment Analysis (DEA) methodology were provided by Alperovych et al. (2013). DEA is an alternative non-parametric technique to estimate efficiency (see Färe & Grosskopf, 1996; Tone & Tsutsui, 2010), and differs in several aspects from accounting measures, TFP, or stochastic frontiers. First, it draws on the micro-economic theory of firms' optimizing behavior[7] and thus has stronger theoretical foundations than accounting ratios. More importantly, DEA requires no statistical assumptions about the nature of production technologies that convert inputs into outputs.[8] The authors used a dataset of 88 PE-backed leveraged buyouts (LBOs) in the UK completed and exited during the period 1999–2008. The analyses focused on the first three post-buyout years and showed general increases in post-buyout efficiency over time. The observed productivity patterns seemed to be convex, suggesting the major improvements had happened in the first two years after the transaction. These improvements were also benchmarked to the efficiency of the 335 comparable non-buyout firms. The buyouts were found to be more efficient than average comparable firms both across the three post-buyout years, and in every year during this period.

Buyout heterogeneity

Early empirical investigations, it was observed, focused on the US (and to an extent on the UK) and mostly encompassed cases of PTP transactions (see, for instance, Kaplan, 1989; Smith, 1990; Wright et al., 1992).[9] This prevalence of the PTP cases is perhaps not surprising given the nature of organizations and the structure of their ownership in the US/UK at that time.[10] The structure of the European buyout industry and buyout origins seemed to be more nuanced. Wright et al. (1992) documented that divestments accounted for 62.8% of the UK buyouts in 1989. In France, Germany, Italy, and Spain, this proportion was 31%, 61.1%, 38.9%, and 0% respectively. Yet a large fraction of buyouts also came from family/private firms, especially in Continental Europe. In these same countries, private buyouts accounted for 29.7% in the UK, 44.8% in France, 38.9% in Germany, 50% in Italy, and as much as 75% in Spain. (Desbrières & Schatt, 2002) argued that this pervasiveness of private/family MBOs was due to the presence of a considerable number of medium-sized private firms, the owners of which were facing succession problems. One particular type of transaction called a secondary buyout (SBO) also appeared in the 2000s. These transactions are characterized by the transfer of ownership from the initial outgoing PE investors to the new incoming ones. They have recently undergone an academic scrutiny to understand their performance and underlying rationale.

As buyouts manifestly originate from different sources there may be some heterogeneous implications of these vendor sources on performance and efficiency. Before turning to the existing evidence, it is worth discussing the reasons for this conjecture.

Vendor sources and efficiency: the rationale

Different ownership and control regimes impact levels of efficiency. Since the former mutate during the transaction, the pre-buyout ownership structure will impact on the opportunities for improvements in efficiency after a transaction. For example, divisional buyouts may be initiated where incumbent management perceives opportunities for performance improvements. The latter are possible because parental control systems in large organizations may impose some element of regular budgetary targets and reporting of management accounts (Wright et al., 2000). However, shortcomings in parental control arising from lack of fit of parent-wide systems with the contingent context of the division, and inability of the parent to devote sufficient attention to or understand distant divisions (in terms of geography and products) in large complex organizations (Wright & Thompson, 1987), create the potential for efficiency improvements. Post-buyout, more appropriate control systems are likely to be introduced by management and PE firms to ensure that performance is at a level commensurate with finance servicing commitments.

In buyouts involving private and family firms, owner-managers prior to the change in ownership generally have incentives to operate the business profitably. It is therefore unlikely that these types of firms generate significant agency costs (Howorth et al., 2004). Nevertheless, these systems are often in need of professionalization. This is especially relevant where the business has outgrown the ability of the founder to exercise personal oversight or where the founder's attention is no longer as close as it once was (Hellmann & Puri, 2002). Further, where private and family firms face succession problems, a buyout offers a way for the firm to stay independent and/or for the firm's management to remain employed (Meuleman et al., 2009). In this context, the buyout provides the opportunity to professionalize control systems that can help improve efficiency, but there may be a learning transition period as the new owner-managers and PE firms deal with the implications of the loss of tacit knowledge of the founder (Howorth et al., 2004).

As mentioned earlier, an SBO involves the refinancing of the initial buyout together with the arrival of a new set of PE investors. Such shifts in ownership could happen when the initial buyout underperforms.[11] In such cases, other exit routes may be unavailable, as the target is not attractive enough for trade sale or public offering (Wright, Robbie, & Albrighton, 2000). In addition, in SBOs, there may be little room for efficiency improvements if the previous PE firm has already transformed the operations and systems to enhance it (Jelic & Wright, 2011).

On balance, the discussion so far suggests that improvements in post-buyout efficiency may be expected and that the relative magnitude of efficiency gains is a function of vendor source type. The following sections discuss the empirical investigations related to this observation.

Vendor sources and efficiency: the evidence

As mentioned earlier, Desbrières and Schatt (2002) conducted analyses of French LBOs. Their results suggested that family/private firms were actually in a better financial situation than comparable firms in the same industry. This conclusion was in sharp contrast with the prevailing agency cost-related arguments advanced by the Anglo-Saxon literature. The hypothesis that divisional buyouts seemed to outperform other buyout types was supported. Another investigation of the buyout origins with a particular emphasis on divisional buyouts was also provided by Meuleman et al. (2009). Using the hand-collected data from the Centre for Management Buyout Research on the 238 PE-backed buyouts in the UK during 1993–2003, the authors studied performance implications of the different vendor sources. Strikingly, the study documented that divestments were not associated with significant changes in profitability. However, divisional buyout did show significant improvements in efficiency. The latter was measured using the atomistic measure of sales per employee.

Boucly et al. (2011) documented changes in corporate behavior in 839 French LBOs completed between 1994–2004. Their findings showed that French firms became more profitable, grew faster, issued additional debt, and increased capital expenditures relative to the carefully constructed control group in the three years after the transaction. They further stressed that these improvements pertain more to the private-to-private buyouts as opposed to the divisional or PTP ones. Concerning the latter, Guo et al. (2011) reexamined the more recent wave of PTP buyouts completed between 1990 and 2006 in the US. Their analyses of buyouts for which the post-transaction data were available suggested that gains in operating performance were comparable or slightly in excess of the improvements in benchmark firms. Moreover, the gains themselves seemed to be much lower than those documented in earlier studies. Relatedly, Cohn et al. (2014) used confidential federal corporate tax return data to compile a sample of 317 US PTP LBOs closed between 1995 and 2007, and with assets of no less than $10 million. According to the authors, this represented about 90% of LBOs of this size during the period under study. Using accounting measures such as return on sales, return on assets, and economic value added (EVA), the study concluded that the evolution of performance of LBOs relative to the control group of similar listed peers was essentially flat from the two years before to the three years after the transaction.

One interesting question pertaining to the studies based on the accounting items is whether the latter could introduce some noise into the measurements of performance or efficiency. Ayash and Schütt (2016) argued that this is indeed the case. More specifically, they illustrated that most of the post-buyout performance measures were suffering from the upscale bias due to neglecting intangibles while at the same time accounting for profits generated by the latter. This seems to be especially relevant for the cases of active acquisition strategies put in place after the buyout, in which acquired firms generate high levels of goodwill. Authors suggested that this bias alone can explain mixed findings on the recent wave of PTP transactions in the US, as discussed in Guo et al. (2011) and Cohn et al. (2014).

Apart the analyses of private and divisional buyouts, a series of papers also focused on performance and efficiency implications of SBOs. The previously mentioned study by Alperovych et al. (2013) made a distinction between private, divisional, and SBOs. The results offered a nuanced view indicating that private and divisional buyouts were more efficient than an average comparable firm. Private and divisional buyouts were also very close to or above the average in terms of efficiency measured between the pre-transaction year and during the three years after. To an extent, divisional buyouts were more efficient than other buyout types. SBOs, surprisingly, also showed some positive trend in efficiency. They were, however, less efficient than their peers.

In parallel, Wang (2012) studied several aspects of SBOs, one of which was operating performance patterns following the change of ownership. Using a hand-collected sample of UK buyouts and a three-year event window centered on the transaction year, he looked at the effects of SBOs on the target's size, operating cash flows, and profitability. The conclusions were mixed. He documented the increases in the operating cash flows and profits. These improvements, however, seemed to be rooted in the aggressive acquisitions strategies adopted by the new investors. After the size adjustments in the measures, he suggested that profitability actually dropped in the SBOs. Finally, matched sample analyses, in which SBOs were paired with first-time buyouts, indicated that SBOs performed better at generating cash and worse at generating profits.

Achleitner and Figge (2014) studied the value creation (operating performance, leverage, pricing, and return on equity) in SBOs using proprietary data on 2,456 PE buyouts including 448 SBOs. The granularity of the data allowed them to evaluate the changes in operating performance – i.e., growth in EBITDA, growth in sales, and changes in margins – during the PE holding period. Their estimates of the SBO effect suggested that its impact on the growth in EBITDA was negative, on the growth in sales was positive, and on the changes in margins was again negative. None of these results was significantly different from zero in the statistical sense. This implied that SBOs exhibited no different growth rates and changes in margins compared to the non-financial buyouts.

Bonini (2015) focused on SBOs exclusively and constructed a panel data tracking target companies through the buyout holding period including primary and secondary buyouts. A clear advantage of this approach is that it rules out the endogeneity concerns discussed earlier. The cost is the drastic reduction in the sample size, as this approach puts more strain on data availability. Bonini (2015) was able to compile data on 163 firms from one year before the first buyout until two years after the second one. His results, in contrast to Wang (2012) and Achleitner and Figge (2014), demonstrated that SBOs did exhibit incremental operating performance in comparison to the peer sample. However, SBOs seemed to severely underperform first-round buyouts. Two contemporaneous studies on SBOs were carried out by Arcot et al. (2015) and Degeorge et al. (2016). Although both focused on performance of SBOs from the investors' standpoint, they provided valuable evidence on whether SBOs were creating value or witnessed the opportunistic behavior of PE fund managers. Arcot et al. (2015) investigated the underlying raison-d'être of SBOs and advocated that it was the pressure to buy/sell that forced PE funds to engage in SBO transactions. Building on these findings, Degeorge et al. (2016) examined more closely the performance of SBOs using the data from the private placement memoranda collected via direct surveys. These data provided exact information (though not totally complete) on the distributed-to-invested amounts, i.e., cash multiples, entry and exit dates, and internal rates of return (IRRs) for each deal of each fund raised by a sampled PE firm. The authors were also able to construct a deal-specific public market equivalent (PME) in the spirit of Kaplan and Schoar (2005).[12] In terms of performance, SBOs were found to generate lower multiples, lower PME, and lower IRRs in comparison to the primary buyouts. Further analyses indicated that SBOs bought late with respect to the fund's investment period underperformed other buyouts, while SBOs bought early were no different from other buyout types.

Given the average and median underperformance of SBOs relative to primary buyouts, it seems natural to investigate the possible reasons for these patterns. As the preceding discussion on the improvements in performance in buyouts indicates, one might expect that further value should be added at each step of the series of buyouts. At the same time, if all improvements and transformations of the internal structures have been implemented by the outgoing investors, the ability of the incoming ones to further add value must be limited. Along these lines, Degeorge et al. (2016) argued that additional value can be generated when some complementary skills exist between buy- and sell-side investors. Conversely, one should not expect any additional value creation whenever there is no skill-wise complementarity between the incoming and outgoing PE investors. They studied three types of skills in this context. The first type relates to the focus of a PE firm on boosting margins or revenues. Complementarity in this case implies that the outgoing PE firm was focusing on boosting revenues, while the incoming would focus on boosting margins via cost-cutting and/or price increases (or vice versa). The second type relates to the professional profiles of general partners (ex-bankers vs. ex-consultants). The argument here is ex-bankers are presumably better at M&A buy-and-build strategies, while ex-consultants are more efficient in internal restructuring strategies (Acharya et al., 2013). Here, the complementarity would imply that operation-oriented PE firms could add value to a company that was previously backed by a finance-oriented backer. Finally, some complementarity might exist between the regionally-focused PE firms and their globally-oriented counterparts. The idea is that regionally-oriented firms can develop a company to a certain point where it needs the help of a more internationally-oriented PE firm to grow further. The empirical evidence provided by Degeorge et al. (2016) suggested that deals transacted between parties with similar skills were associated with greater value creation in SBOs. This corroborated to an extent the evidence on PE firm experience positively affecting operating performance in buyouts (Meuleman et al., 2009; Alperovych et al., 2013).

On balance, the overall evidence seems to lean towards a positive effect for LBOs on performance or productivity. This result, however, should be nuanced. First, performance and productivity can be measured with various techniques, e.g., accounting versus TFP, stochastic frontiers, and DEA. Second, buyout heterogeneity seems to be an important factor affecting the post-buyout improvement potential.

Do performance and productivity matter?

The discussions in the preceding sections ascertained that buyouts generally had a positive effect on productivity and performance. This observation seems to hold across different nations, and also across time, although performance of the PTP buyouts has recently deteriorated (Guo et al., 2011). Do these productivity gains translate into actual economic added value? Amess and Girma (2009) investigated the relationship between firm-level productivity and market values of 706 manufacturing firms in the UK over the period 1996–2002 and found a positive relationship. This suggests that stock markets seem to pay attention and price the adoption of lean management practices and better resource utilization. The question is whether this effect is present in the buyouts.

Kaplan (1989) was able to identify market values of 25 out of 76 buyouts in his dataset. The valuations were detected either because these firms had gone public again (reverse LBOs), or had issued public debt, or had preferred stock outstanding, or were acquired by other listed firms. Using these valuations, he could estimate whether operating improvements he had observed translated into increases in the market values of the underlying firms. The results implied that pre- and post-buyout investors earned a median total market-adjusted return of 77%. Pre-buyout investors earned about 37%, while post-buyout investors realized a median 28%, both being market-adjusted. Kaplan (1989) concluded that these figures were evidence that operating improvements are associated with material value increases.

An almost identical approach was used by Guo et al. (2011). They used available information after the buyout on a more recent wave of PTP transactions (1990–2006), again in the US. Large increases in total firm value were observed between buyout and exit dates. The results surprisingly indicated that the median market- and risk-adjusted returns to pre- and post-buyout investors were about 73% and 41% respectively. How much of this return is attributable to the improvements in operations? To answer this question the authors estimated the hypothetical returns to pre- and post-buyout shareholders assuming the targets had not gone through a buyout. Interestingly, the performance gains accounted for as much as 23% pre- and 18.5% post-buyout returns, on a par with industry-wide valuations and effects of debt tax shields.

Conclusions and avenues for future research

The evidence reviewed in this chapter seems to corroborate an assumption that improvements in operations and productivity are important drivers of value creation. These improvements come from various sources, e.g., growth in sales, acquisitions, refocusing firm strategies and operations, cost-cutting mechanisms, divestments of unproductive units, reallocations of labor, etc. Despite this fact, critics still argue that buyouts harm companies because of the excessive use of leverage, short-sightedness of PE firms, and potentially considerably negative social impact (layoffs). However, the core of the criticism seems to be case-based as the systematic academic evidence tends to disagree with it.

It appears that improvements in productivity after the buyout transaction are detectable. Yet the underlying mechanisms that generate these improvements seem to differ. Early evidence put an accent on the debt bonding and cost-cutting strategies. Later evidence suggested that value increases have to also be sought in revenue-enhancing strategies and improvements in corporate governance mechanisms. Moreover, as PE firms accumulate experience they seem to better translate it into the changes operated within portfolio companies.

Existing evidence also comes with some limitations. The first point is the absence of a uniform way of measuring performance and productivity. Most of the studies make use of ratios (for example EBITDA/assets) or productivity metrics. Reliance on accounting data has the potential to introduce bias due to the underlying dependence on local accounting standards that affect reporting. This also renders the cross-country comparisons more delicate, especially for the smaller buyouts as they are not necessarily subject to IFRS requirements. Relatedly, accounting measures can also be subject to misreporting, whether intentional or not. Although some work has been recently initiated in this direction (Ayash & Schütt, 2016), more evidence is necessary especially in settings other than the US. Reliance on the TFP measures puts a serious strain on data quality. In some developed countries like the US or UK, such data gradually becomes available to researchers although at some collection and processing cost. We are yet to see the data of such quality appear in the developing and other developed countries. One positive aspect, it should be noted, is that the use of various performance/efficiency measures is providing a more comprehensive and rich view on the question. At the same time, this heterogeneity in the metrics makes it difficult to draw comparisons between different studies. Thus, more universally comparable measures of performance and productivity may be welcome.

The second limitation is related to the way we account for the quality and experience of the fund management team. For example, up to now this was generally done by counting the number of deals executed by a team or a PE firm before a focal transaction. This, however, is a very narrow view of the team quality and experience. Some work has begun on the implications of professional profiles of fund managers (ex-consultants vs. ex-bankers). It would definitely be insightful to investigate the social characteristics of these individuals and the linkages they might have on performance. Interestingly, these kinds of studies have started to appear in venture capital literature (Hsu & Bengtsson, 2010; Kaplan et al., 2012; Hegde & Tumlinson, 2014; Bengtsson & Hsu, 2015; Ewens & Rhodes-Kropf, 2015; Bottazzi et al., 2016; Gompers et al., 2016).

Third, the magnitude of improvements in productivity and performance seems to decay over time. This may be because of the overall maturation of the PE industry accompanied by increased competition for deals between PE firms, and by concentration of the PE firms within the industry. Yet in light of the ever-increasing experience of the incumbent PE firms, it is unclear why the latter are not able to deliver the increases in performance in the way they used to do. The improvements in productivity that accompany the buyout firm may also affect the competitors in the respective product markets and industries (in a similar manner to IPOs; see Chemmanur et al., 2010; Chod & Lyandres, 2011). Some preliminary evidence on the impact of PE on industry performance has recently been documented by Bernstein et al. (2017). A plausible assumption therefore may be that non-PE-backed competing firms adjust their product market strategies in the reaction to a buyout.

Finally, the structure of the PE industry in terms of buyout origins seem to be very different across countries and depends on historical, demographic, and economic factors. This warrants more macro-level research to better understand the global implications of PE-backed buyouts.

Notes

1 See Axelson et al. (2013) and ***Global private equity report*** (2015) for the recent statistics on the acquisition debt multiples and leverage in buyouts.
2 Additionally, cash retention also lowers the likelihood of being scrutinized (and disciplined) by capital markets once the firm seeks financing.
3 According to Kaplan and Strömberg (2009), there is also a third channel, financial engineering, associated with the use of leverage. This channel is beyond the scope of this chapter.
4 These mechanisms are listed in the order of importance following P. Gompers et al.'s (2016) results obtained via a direct survey of PE specialists.
5 Value capture is related to the transfers of value from other stakeholders, like employees via cuts in headcount for example. Value creation is related to improvements in efficiency and effectiveness.
6 Thompson and Wright (1995) summarized this accounting-based evidence produced by the UK studies.
7 Efficiency in this sense is estimated as a score obtained from the linear program, which maximizes outputs at fixed levels of inputs. Alternatively, the same score can be obtained by minimizing inputs at fixed levels of outputs.
8 This contrasts with other studies that use total factor productivity (Lichtenberg & Siegel, 1990; Wright et al., 1996; Ames, 2002; Harris et al., 2005; Davis et al., 2014) and stochastic frontier modeling (Amess, 2003).
9 It should be noted though that in some studies the line was drawn between "full LBOs" and "divisional LBOs". See also Lichtenberg and Siegel (1990) for an example of the same distinction.
10 This prevalence is also due to the data availability problem. The specific financial and employee data on private companies is very difficult to obtain in the US. Conversely, in PTP deals, pre-buyout data is available. This also explains why researchers used it more often. To an extent, the task is easier in the UK and Continental Europe, where firms are required to disclose their financial statements with the government authorities. These statements are later accessible via commercial databases.
11 See Axelson et al. (2009) and Arcot et al. (2015) for the theory and empirical evidence on other non-target-related reasons for SBO transactions.
12 PME is a ratio of the present value of the capital received to the present value of the capital invested, both discounted by the rate of return on a benchmark index. A frequent choice for the latter is the S&P 500.

References

Acharya, V. V., Gottschalg, O. F., Hahn, M., & Kehoe, C. 2013. Corporate governance and value creation: Evidence from private equity. *Review of Financial Studies*, 26: 368–402.

Acharya, V. V., Kehoe, C., & Reyner, M. 2009. Private equity vs. PLC Boards in the U.K.: A comparison of practices and effectiveness. *Journal of Applied Corporate Finance*, 21: 45–56.

Achleitner, A.-K., & Figge, C. 2014. Private equity lemons? Evidence on value creation in secondary buyouts. *European Financial Management*, 20: 406–433.

Alperovych, Y., Amess, K., & Wright, M. 2013. Private equity firm experience and buyout vendor source: What is their impact on efficiency? *European Journal of Operational Research*, 228: 601–611.

Ames, K. 2002. Management buyouts and firm–level productivity: Evidence from a panel of UK manufacturing firms. *Scottish Journal of Political Economy*, 49: 304–317.

Amess, K. 2003. The effect of management buyouts on firm-level technical efficiency: Evidence from a panel of UK machinery and equipment manufacturers. *Journal of Industrial Economics*, 51: 35–44.

Amess, K., & Girma, S. 2009. Do stock markets value efficiency? *Scottish Journal of Political Economy*, 56: 321–331.

Arcot, S., Fluck, Z., Gaspar, J.-M., & Hege, U. 2015. Fund managers under pressure: Rationale and determinants of secondary buyouts. *Journal of Financial Economics*, 115: 102–135.

Axelson, U., Jenkinson, T., Strömberg, P., & Weisbach, M. S. 2013. Borrow cheap, buy high? The determinants of leverage and pricing in buyouts. *Journal of Finance*, 68: 2223–2267.

Axelson, U., Strömberg, P., & Weisbach, M. S. 2009. Why are buyouts levered? The financial structure of private equity funds. *Journal of Finance*, 64: 1549–1582.

Ayash, B., & Schütt, H. 2016. Does going private add value through operating improvements? *Journal of Corporate Finance*. Available at SSRN: https://ssrn.com/abstract=2265066.

Baker, G. P., & Wruck, K. H. 1989. Organizational changes and value creation in leveraged buyouts. The case of The O.M. Ssott & Sons Company. *Journal of Financial Economics*, 25: 163–190.
Bengtsson, O., & Hsu, D. H. 2015. Ethnic matching in the U.S. venture capital market. *Journal of Business Venturing*, 30: 338–354.
Bernstein, S., Lerner, J., Sørensen, M., & Strömberg, P. 2017. Private equity and industry performance. *Management Science*, 63: 1198–1213.
Bernstein, S., & Sheen, A. 2016. The operational consequences of private equity buyouts: Evidence from the restaurant industry. *Review of Financial Studies*, 29: 2387–2418.
Bonini, S. 2015. Secondary buyouts: Operating performance and investment determinants. *Financial Management*, 44: 431–470.
Bottazzi, L., Rin, M. D., & Hellmann, T. 2016. The importance of trust for investment: Evidence from venture capital. *Review of Financial Studies*, 29: 2341–2386.
Boucly, Q., Sraer, D., & Thesmar, D. 2011. Growth LBOs. *Journal of Financial Economics*, 102: 432–453.
Chemmanur, T. J., He, S., & Nandy, D. K. 2010. The going-public decision and the product market. *Review of Financial Studies*, 23: 1855–1908.
Chod, J., & Lyandres, E. 2011. Strategic IPOs and product market competition. *Journal of Financial Economics*, 100: 45–67.
Cohn, J. B., Mills, L. F., & Towery, E. M. 2014. The evolution of capital structure and operating performance after leveraged buyouts: Evidence from U.S. corporate tax returns. *Journal of Financial Economics*, 111: 469–494.
Cotter, J. F., & Peck, S. W. 2001. The structure of debt and active equity investors: The case of the buyout specialist. *Journal of Financial Economics*, 59: 101–147.
Davis, S. J., Haltiwanger, J. C., Handley, K., Jarmin, R. S., Lerner, J., & Miranda, J. 2014. Private equity, jobs, and productivity. *American Economic Review*, 104: 3956–3990.
Degeorge, F., Martin, J., & Phalippou, L. 2016. On secondary buyouts. *Journal of Financial Economics*, 120: 124–145.
Dehejia, R. H., & Wahba, S. 2002. Propensity score-matching methods for nonexperimental causal studies. *Review of Economics and Statistics*, 84: 151–161.
Desbrières, P., & Schatt, A. 2002. The impacts of LBOs on the performance of acquired firms: The French case. *Journal of Business Finance & Accounting*, 29: 695–729.
Ewens, M., & Rhodes-Kropf, M. 2015. Is a VC partnership greater than the sum of its parts? *Journal of Finance*, 70: 1081–1113.
Färe, R., & Grosskopf, S. 1996. *Intertemporal production frontiers: With dynamic DEA*, 1st edition. Dordrecht, the Netherlands: Springer.
Global private equity report. 2015. Bain & Company.
Gompers, P., Kaplan, S. N., & Mukharlyamov, V. 2016. What do private equity firms say they do? *Journal of Financial Economics*, 121: 449–476.
Gompers, P. A., Mukharlyamov, V., & Xuan, Y. 2016. The cost of friendship. *Journal of Financial Economics*, 119: 626–644.
Guo, S., Hotchkiss, E. S., & Song, W. 2011. Do buyouts (still) create value? *Journal of Finance*, 66: 479–517.
Harris, R., Siegel, D. S., & Wright, M. 2005. Assessing the impact of management buyouts on economic efficiency: Plant-level evidence from the United Kingdom. *Review of Economics and Statistics*, 87: 148–153.
Hart, O. 1995. Corporate governance: Some theory and implications. *The Economic Journal*, 105: 678–689.
Heckman, J. J. 1976. The common structure of statistical models of truncation, sample selection and limited dependent variables and a simple estimator for such models in "Annals of Economic and Social Measurement." In *NBER* (Ed.), (Vol. 5, 4, pp. 120–137). NBER.
Hegde, D., & Tumlinson, J. 2014. Does social proximity enhance business partnerships? Theory and evidence from ethnicity's role in U.S. venture capital. *Management Science*, 60: 2355–2380.
Hellmann, T., & Puri, M. 2002. Venture capital and the professionalization of startup firms: Empirical evidence. *Journal of Finance*, 57: 169–197.
Howorth, C., Westhead, P., & Wright, M. 2004. Buyouts, information asymmetry and the family management dyad. *Journal of Business Venturing*, 19: 509–534.

Hsu, D. H., & Bengtsson, O. 2010. *How do venture capital partners match with startup founders?* Working paper. Available at SSRN: https://ssrn.com/abstract=1568131.

Jelic, R., & Wright, M. 2011. Exits, performance, and late stage private equity: The case of UK management buy-outs. *European Financial Management*, 17: 560–593.

Jensen, M. C. 1986. Agency costs of free cash flow, corporate finance and takeovers. *American Economic Review*, 76: 323–329.

Jensen, M. C. 1989. Eclipse of the public corporation. *Harvard Business Review*, Sept/Oct.

Jensen, M. C. 1993. The modern industrial revolution, exit, and the failure of internal control systems. *Journal of Finance*, 48: 831–880.

Jensen, M. C., & Meckling, W. H. 1976. Theory of the firm: Managerial behavior, agency costs and ownership structure. *Journal of Financial Economics*, 3: 305–360.

Kaplan, S. N. 1989. The effects of management buyouts on operating performance and value. *Journal of Financial Economics*, 24: 217–254.

Kaplan, S. N., Klebanov, M. M., & Sørensen, M. 2012. Which CEO characteristics and abilities matter? *Journal of Finance*, 67: 973–1007.

Kaplan, S. N., & Schoar, A. 2005. Private equity performance: Returns, persistence, and capital flows. *Journal of Finance*, 60: 1791–1822.

Kaplan, S. N., & Strömberg, P. 2009. Leveraged buyouts and private equity. *Journal of Economic Perspectives*, 23: 121–146.

Lichtenberg, F. R., & Siegel, D. 1990. The effects of leveraged buyouts on productivity and related aspects of firm behavior. *Journal of Financial Economics*, 27: 165–194.

Liebeskind, J., Wiersema, M., & Hansen, G. 1992. LBOs, corporate restructuring, and the incentive-intensity hypothesis. *Financial Management*, 21: 73–88.

Meuleman, M., Amess, K., Wright, M., & Scholes, L. 2009. Agency, strategic entrepreneurship, and the performance of private equity-backed buyouts. *Entrepreneurship Theory and Practice*, 33: 213–239.

Opler, T. C. 1992. Operating performance in leveraged buyouts: Evidence from 1985–1989. *Financial Management*, 21: 27–34.

Phan, P. H., & Hill, C. W. L. 1995. Organizational restructuring and economic performance in leveraged buyouts: An ex post study. *The Academy of Management Journal*, 38: 704–739.

Rosenbaum, P. R., & Rubin, D. B. 1983. The central role of the propensity score in observational studies for casual effects. *Biometrika*, 70: 41–55.

Rosenbaum, P. R., & Rubin, D. B. 1985. Constructing a control group using multivariate matched sampling methods that incorporate the propensity score. *The American Statistician*, 39: 33–38.

Smith, A. J. 1990. Corporate ownership structure and performance. *Journal of Financial Economics*, 27: 143–164.

Thompson, R., Wright, M., & Robbie, K. 1992. Management equity ownership, debt and performance: Some evidence from UK management buyouts. *Scottish Journal of Political Economy*, 39: 413–430.

Thompson, S., & Wright, M. 1995. Corporate governance: The role of restructuring transactions. *The Economic Journal*, 105: 690–703.

Tone, K., & Tsutsui, M. 2010. Dynamic DEA: A slacks-based measure approach. *OMEGA The International Journal of Management Science*, 38: 145–156.

Wang, Y. 2012. Secondary buyouts: Why buy and at what price? *Journal of Corporate Finance*, 18: 1306–1325.

Wood, G., & Wright, M. 2009. Private equity: A review and synthesis. *International Journal of Management Reviews*, 11: 361–380.

Wright, M., Hoskisson, R. E., Busenitz, L. W., & Dial, J. 2000. Entrepreneurial growth through privatization: The upside of management buyouts. *Academy of Management Review*, 25: 591–601.

Wright, M., Robbie, K., & Albrighton, M. 2000. Secondary management buy-outs and buy-ins. *International Journal of Entrepreneurial Bahaviour & Research*, 6: 21–40.

Wright, M., & Thompson, S. 1987. Divestment and the control of divisionalised firms. *Accounting and Business Research*, 17: 259–267.

Wright, M., Thompson, S., & Robbie, K. 1992. Venture capital and management-led, leveraged buy-outs: A European perspective. *Journal of Business Venturing*, 7: 47–71.

Wright, M., Wilson, N., & Robbie, K. 1996. The longer-term effects of management led buy-outs. *Journal of Entrepreneurial and Small Business Finance*, 5: 213–234.

26

LEVERAGED BUYOUTS

Their impact on jobs and wages

Kevin Amess

Sometimes private equity … give the impression of being little more than amoral asset-strippers after a quick buck. Casino capitalists enjoying huge personal windfalls from deals at the same time as they gamble with other people's futures. (Brendan Barber. General Secretary of Trade Union Congress, 2007)

Introduction

Leveraged buyouts (LBOs) are corporate restructuring transactions involving the transfer of whole companies or company divisions to new owners. There are two key features typical of all LBO transactions: first, a high level of debt, secured against an LBO target's corporate assets and future cash flows, is used to facilitate an LBO transaction; second, senior management possesses a significant equity stake after the buyout (Thompson & Wright, 1995; Kaplan & Stromberg, 2009). There are, however, variations in types of LBO transactions. For instance, insider-driven deals, where incumbent managers in a firm acquire a significant equity stake, are referred to as management buyouts; while outsider-driven deals, where outside managers acquire a significant equity stake are referred to as management buyins (MBIs) (Thompson & Wright, 1995).

LBOs install a system of corporate governance that provides managers with strong incentives to focus on profitability (Jensen, 1986; Thompson & Wright, 1995). First, a significant proportion of equity is held by management.[1] This unifies senior management with ownership, providing managers with a strong incentive to focus on firm profitability. Second, the fixed interest obligation of debt requires managers to pay out future cash flows rather than waste cash on sub-optimal investments and perquisites. Third, in the case of private equity (PE)-backed deals, PE firms will hold a significant equity stake and have board representation. The high equity stake provides financial incentives for PE firms to monitor senior management and provide input into strategic decisions. PE firms' board representation facilitates their monitoring function and input into strategic decisions. Consistent with the view that LBOs install strong corporate governance is evidence that LBOs are associated with real economic performance gains (Lichtenberg & Siegel, 1990; Amess, 2003; Harris et al., 2005; Davis et al., 2014).

While there is little academic debate that LBOs are associated with performance gains, there has been a great deal of controversy in academia and in wider society concerning their impact on jobs and wages. In some respects PE might seem a distant "world of high finance" to workers, but where PE can directly impact on workers is through jobs and wages. This real effect brings the PE business model directly into workers' lives. It should not be surprising, therefore, that the debate concerning LBOs' real impact on jobs and wages has sometimes been visceral. The concern is not simply that workers lose jobs and suffer lower wages as a result of a PE-backed LBO, it is that PE investors' wealth gains might partly be achieved by such restricting decisions (Fox & Marcus, 1992; International Trade Union Confederation, 2007; Applebaum & Batt, 2014). In sum, the LBO restructuring transaction creates an opportunity for the revision of labor contracts and investors exploit this for personal gain. The competing argument from practitioners and proponents of LBOs is that they target firms that are underperforming and that the restructuring of portfolio firms is required in order to create sustainable businesses. PE firms realize capital gains when they sell their portfolio firms on at a profit and this can only be achieved if they create viable businesses.

This review focuses on providing a synthesis of the evidence obtained from quantitative empirical studies concerning the impact of LBOs (with insider or outsider management involvement) on jobs and wages. The focus is on these studies because they provide objective evidence of the average effect within large samples. This has the benefit of being able to provide insights that shed light on competing arguments concerning the labor effects of LBOs, whereas a use of case studies might illicit an accusation that a specific case was chosen to support a specific argument. In addition, given intermittent calls for government intervention on PE firms' activity to protect workers' welfare, a synthesis of large-scale studies provides the best basis for understanding the overall effects of LBOs on jobs and wages.

Theoretical perspectives

Agency theory

The seminal work of Jensen (1986) provides an agency theory perspective through which LBOs have traditionally been understood. The corporate governance literature recognizes that when ownership and management of a firm are separated, management might have the discretion to pursue different objectives from firms' owners, creating agency costs. These agency costs are most severe in the presence of weak corporate governance that does not attenuate managers' discretionary behavior. Discretionary behavior could include the pursuit of firm size beyond its optimal level and making investments that yield a negative net present value. This could result in job creation from which management obtain private benefit. Such discretionary behavior reduces firm value and performance (Jensen & Meckling, 1976; Fama & Jensen, 1983; Hart, 1995). An LBO installs a governance structure that realigns managers' objectives with those of the owners, reducing discretionary behavior (Jensen, 1986, Thompson & Wright, 1995).

The agency theory perspective of LBOs is associated with job losses because restructuring after a LBO sometimes involves downsizing and downscoping a firm in order to improve its performance. If pre-LBO management pursued discretionary goals that required more employees beyond the optimal level, an LBO provides an opportunity and incentives for a correction in employment levels. The agency theory perspective therefore predicts a reduction in employment levels after an LBO. Job losses in these circumstances have become associated with the PE business model. Critics argue that PE firms create wealth for investors by cutting jobs and that the wealth created for investors is in part created from transfers from employees. The agency theory perspective makes it clear that such jobs were the result of managerial discretion that reduced firm value and performance. This is therefore a sub-optimal use of employees. Moreover, practitioners argue that their goal is not to destroy jobs per se, but to create sustainable businesses.

The change in ownership at the time of an LBO provides an opportunity for wage payments that exceed the marginal product of labor to be reduced (Shleifer & Summers, 1988). The implication here is that the LBO is not creating wealth; rather, it is motivated by the transfer of wealth from employees to LBO investors. Such rent-extraction could pay off for LBO investors in the short term if employees who have made investments in firm-specific human capital do not leave their jobs because the next-best paid job pays no better than the post-LBO lower wage. In the long term, however, the lower wages reduce incentives to invest in firm-specific human capital, lowering labor productivity (Shleifer & Summers, 1988). There could also be a short-term negative impact on labor productivity if effort is reduced because the higher wage payments are perceived by employees as a norm and part of an implicit agreement in return for a "fair day's work" (Akerlof, 1982).

Contrary to the above is an argument that organizational restructuring results in employees receiving higher wages after an LBO. Lichtenberg and Siegel (1990) suggest that wages could replace monitoring by bureaucratic staff after an LBO in order to reduce employee moral hazard. An efficiency wage argument is that wages are paid at a rate to maximize labor productivity, which is in excess of the equilibrium market clearing level (Stiglitz, 1987). Employee moral hazard is reduced because the higher wage payment increases the cost of losing a job by being caught shirking. Another explanation is that a higher wage establishes a norm where employees are willing to put in more effort in return for higher pay (Akerlof, 1982). This theoretical argument predicts an increase in wages after an LBO.

Entrepreneurial

The entrepreneurial perspective is a more recent addition to our understanding of the impact of the LBO governance structure and the role that PE firms play in their interaction with portfolio firms. The entrepreneurial perspective offers an understanding of the LBO of divisions/subsidiaries of larger organizations and the LBO of private firms. These arguments are important because both these types of LBOs represent a large proportion of deals that are conducted (Kaplan & Stromberg, 2009).

Arguments relating to the LBO of divisions/subsidiaries are outlined first. Williamson (1975, 1985) argues that large organizations adopt a divisional organizational structure with an internal capital market. It exists due to the failure of the external capital market. Head office allocates cash to divisions, which are profit centers, where it can get the best return on investment. Such an organizational structure acts as an incentive and governance device to promote profit maximization from divisional managers. There are, however, limits to the effectiveness of the internal capital market of large firms as an incentive and governance device (Williamson, 1985). The misallocation of resources can occur due to divisional managers politicking to gain access to financial resources, which could result in under-investment in some divisions. Under-investment in a division might also arise as a consequence of head office deciding that a division does not feature in its core strategy. Under-investment in divisions could result in sub-optimally low levels of employment.

In the case of private firms, they can suffer from under-investment due to their reliance on internal finance (Carpenter & Petersen, 2002) and difficulties in obtaining finance from banks (Behr et al., 2013). This is because private firms find it difficult to convey information about their creditworthiness to external finance providers (Behr et al., 2013). In addition, some private firms might pursue alternative goals to profit-maximization (e.g., lifestyle businesses and family-run businesses).

The entrepreneurial perspective emphasizes both entrepreneurial incentives and the relaxation of financial constraints leading to investment in profitable growth opportunities. First, the equity held by management provides financial incentives to pursue entrepreneurial growth opportunities. This contrasts with hierarchical incentives that can sometimes fail to motivate managers' pursuit of entrepreneurial growth (Thompson & Wright, 1995). Where PE firms hold a significant equity stake, they promote and encourage value creation through their involvement in the entrepreneurial decision-making of their portfolio firms (Bruining et al., 2012). Second, PE firms also have the potential to relax pre-buyout financial constraints and increase investment in entrepreneurial activity (Berger & Udell, 1998; Engel & Stiebale, 2014). This is a result of their role in improving post-LBO governance and their financial expertise reassuring creditors that funds will be used productively (Boucly et al., 2011; Amess et al., 2015).

The entrepreneurial perspective's emphasis on incentives to pursue profitable growth opportunities suggests that LBOs have the potential to create jobs. Note, however, that the entrepreneurial perspective offers no insight on LBOs' effects on wages. Nevertheless, a positive effect on wages would suggest that employees share in potential gains from investment in growth opportunities. If there is no wage effect, it suggests that post-LBO investors do not share their entrepreneurial gains with employees.

The PE business model

While the theoretical perspectives above provide an academic framework for understanding the impact of LBOs on jobs and wages, the nature of the PE business model has also received attention for how it impacts on jobs and wages. Broadly there are two competing views. First, there is criticism that the PE business model involves job cuts and the suppression of wages in portfolio firms in order to generate profit for the new owners. Critics have focused on PE firms in particular because their business model involves targeting, buying, restructuring, and selling firms in order to make a capital gain for themselves and their investors. When restructuring has resulted in job losses, critics have not perceived it necessary to create a sustainable business; rather, it is perceived as a short-term measure to create profit for LBO investors at employees' expense.

Second, proponents argue that PE firms acquire underperforming firms and develop them into sustainable businesses. The PE business model is able to create value by targeting underperforming firms and restructuring their financial incentives, governance, and business operations. With larger deals short-term organizational restructuring that involves downscoping might be required in order to correct prior mistakes that led to over-diversification. This will lead to job losses, but the purpose of downscoping is to create a more strategically focused and sustainable business. In smaller deals the value creation is through the purchase of neglected divisions and poorly run private firms. In these cases, value creation arises through the exploitation of business opportunities, creating jobs.

While there are some general features of an LBO deal, there are different motivations. There are variations in the business models applied in order to create value in portfolio firms. Many academic studies do not take this into consideration, however; rather, they assess an average effect or examine effects across different employees' types while neglecting the different business models applied by PE firms in their attempt to create value.

Employment effects

The empirical studies discussed in this section are listed in Table 26.1. Details of the sample, including: country of study, sample period, and number of firms subject to an LBO are provided in the table. Where establishment- and employee-level data have been used, the number of establishments and the number of employees subject to an LBO are also provided. The deal type and summary of key findings are also reported in Table 26.1. Given that these details can be found in Table 26.1, the focus of the discussion below will be on the findings reported.

Table 26.1 Summary of employment studies reviewed in chronological order

Author(s)	*Sample (country, period, deals, any other characteristics)*	*Deal type*	*Findings*
Kaplan (1989)	US 1980–1986 42 and 26 firms	MBO	Over period t−1 to t+1: for total of 42 firms −12%; for 26 firms with no divestitures of acquisitions, no significant effect.
Lichtenberg & Siegel (1990)	US 1983–1986 420 plants	LBO	Over period t−1 to t+2: −8.5% for nonproduction workers; no significant effect for production workers.
Smith (1990)	US 1977–1986 58 and 30 firms	MBO	Median changes in the number of employees for the total sample of 58 firms and the asset-sale subsample of 30 firms are insignificant.
Wright et al. (1992)	UK 1983–1986 182 firms	MBO	−6.3% at time of MBO. At time of survey, 1990, 4.5% below pre-MBO levels.
Amess & Wright (2007)	UK 1999–2004 1,350 firms	MBO, MBI	Compared to control sample employment growth 0.51% higher for MBOs and 0.81% lower for MBIs.
Bergstrom et al. (2007)	Sweden Deals conducted between 1999–2001 73 firms	PE-backed LBO	No significant effect.
Meuleman et al. (2009)	UK 1993–2003 238 firms	PE-backed LBO	Employment growth 36% higher in divisional buyouts compared with other buyout types over three years after LBO. MBIs, IBOs, and BIMBOs do not have significantly different employment growth compared to MBOs.
Boucly et al. (2011)	France 1994–2004 839 firms	LBO	Over period t−3 to t+3: employment grows 12% for all LBOs, 18% in private-to-private LBOs, 6% in divisional LBOs, 11% in SBOs, no significant effect in PTP LBOs.
Georgen et al. (2014)	UK 2000–2006 73 firms	Institutional buyout	At t+1, annual employment growth rate is −1.62%. This is significantly different from control sample. In t+1 and t+2

(*Continued*)

Table 26.1 (Continued)

Author(s)	*Sample (country, period, deals, any other characteristics)*	*Deal type*	*Findings*
			employment growth rate is not significantly different from the control sample.
Amess & Wright (2012)	UK 1993–2004 533 firms	PE-backed and non-PE-backed LBOs	PE-backed and non-PE-backed LBOs have no significant effect on levels and growth in large and small deals.
Amess et al. (2014)	UK 1996–2006 386 firms	PE-backed and non-PE-backed LBOs	DiD combined with propensity score matching. PE-backed LBOs have no significant effect. Over t−1 to t+1, −11% in non-PE-backed LBOs. Control function approach: Over period t−1 to t+2, 9% higher in PE-backed LBOs. No significant effect in non-PE-backed LBOs.
Davis et al. (2014)	US 1980–2005 3,200 target firms and their 15,000 establishments	PE-backed LBO	Establishment analysis: employment is −3% t+2 years after LBO and −6% t+5 after LBO. Summing over: job creation and destruction at continuing establishment, job losses at closed establishments, job gains at greenfield establishments, acquisitions and divestitures, employment declines by less than 1% compared to controls t+2 after LBO.
Georgen et al. (2014)	UK 1997–2006 106 firms	Institutional buyout	Post-LB0 employment declines by up to 15%.
Antoni et al. (2015)	Germany 2002–2008 535 deals involving 830 firms, 2,584 establishments, and 192,364 employees	PE-backed LBOs	Measure the fraction of a year employed, not jobs. Over one- to three-year period after LBO, LBOs reduce employment by about1–1.5%.
Tåg & Olsson (2016)	Sweden Deals conducted between 2002–2008 239 firms 42,391 employees	PE-backed LBO	10.2 percentage point (96.6%) increase in unemployment incidence for routine workers, no effect on non-routine workers, in low productive firms. Offshorable workers in low productive firms experience increased unemployment incidence by 8.6 percentage point (97%) in period t+4 after LBO. No significant increase in unemployment incidence across population of employees.

(*Continued*)

Table 26.1 (Continued)

Author(s)	*Sample (country, period, deals, any other characteristics)*	*Deal type*	*Findings*
Agrawal and& Tambe (2016)	US 1995–2010 4,193 deals 5,680 employees	PE-backed LBO	Employment spells 6–9 percentage points longer. Workers leaving LBO firm have unemployment spell 2.9 months shorter than control.
Faccio & Hsu (2017)	US 1990–2012 3,748 deals 20,073 establishments		Over period t−1 to t+5, employment growth in establishments owned by politically connected PE firms is 1.24% and 0.33% in establishments operated by nonconnected PE firms.

It can be seen from the sample descriptions in Table 26.1 that most studies use samples from the US and the UK, reflecting the preponderance of deals in these markets. While this review does include studies using Swedish, German, and French data, it is clear that there is scope for further examination of the employment consequences of LBOs in different countries with different institutional contexts.

Average effects

Some of the early research examining employment consequences reflects difficulties in obtaining data for private firms at that time. Therefore, the relatively small samples reflect a focus on PTP deals where pre-LBO data is easy to obtain. Kaplan (1986) reports a 12% decline in median industry-adjusted employment from the year prior to the MBO deal to the year afterwards; however, this result included a sample of firms that undertook divestitures and acquisitions. For a subsample of firms that did not undertake divestment or acquisition, Kaplan does not find any statistically significant association between MBOs and employment. Smith (1990) also finds an insignificant industry-adjusted employment effect. Thus, these early US studies found that there was no employment effect associated with PTP buyouts.

While the early US research outlined earlier focused on the employment effects in PTP transactions, early UK research by Wright et al. (1992) examined the average employment effects across a range of deal sources (e.g., family and divestment). They obtain data via a survey conducted in 1990 of deals between 1983 and 1986. The survey found that employment was 6.3% lower at the time of the MBO and remained 4.5% lower at the time of the survey. The results must be treated with caution, however, because no control sample was used.

Bergstrom et al. (2007) provide evidence from a sample of Swedish PE-backed buyouts. The deals have no significant impact on employment. This is supported by Amess and Wright (2012), who examine the average employment effects of deals from a variety of deal sources (i.e., public, private, divestment, receivership). A feature of the study is that it distinguishes between PE-backed and non-PE-backed deals. Using an employment demand equation, they find that LBOs, whether PE-backed or not, have no significant impact on employment levels. They also find that the impact on employment growth is also insignificant after accounting for large deals where there is expected to be more restructuring and likelihood of job losses.

A fundamental problem when analyzing the impact of LBOs is establishing the counterfactual. Firms subject to a LBO are not randomly selected from the population of firms, and it might be the case that employment levels impact on the LBO decision. For instance, over-employment might be identified as a source of underperformance in a firm, making it an LBO target with job reduction a potential source of performance gains. Amess et al.'s (2014) study of PE-backed and non-PE-backed LBOs use two modeling strategies to address the issue of self-selection to the LBO form. Average treatment effects are estimated using difference-in-differences (DiD) combined with propensity score matching (PSM) and the control function approach. The application of these methods reveals that estimates of employment effects can be sensitive to modelling strategy. First, estimates obtained from DiD combined with PSM indicate that, over the period t−1 to t+1 around the deal, PE-backed LBOs have no significant effect on employment while non-PE-backed LBOs experience an 11% decline in employment. Second, the control function approach indicates that, over the period t−1 to t+2 around the deal, PE-backed LBOs experience a 9% increase in employment while there is no significant effect on non-PE-backed LBOs. This evidence shows that, at best, PE-backed LBOs create jobs while non-PE-backed LBOs have no significant impact on jobs.

Davis et al. (2014) conduct one of the most comprehensive studies to date by analyzing the employment effects of PE-backed LBOs at both establishment and firm levels. The study excludes MBOs that do not involve a PE firm, which means they are unable to compare the consequences of PE-backed and non-PE-backed deals. Their analysis provides a number of insights. First, average employment levels shrink more rapidly at establishments subject to an LBO compared to controls. Davis et al. find that the cumulative difference in favour of controls is about 3% and 6% of initial employment over the first two and five years post-LBO, respectively. Second, in shrinking and exiting establishments LBOs experience faster job destruction than control firms, but in expanding establishments there is faster job creation than control firms. Third, over the two years after an LBO, target firms exhibit nearly 2% more greenfield job creation than controls. Summing over job creation and destruction at continuing establishment, job losses at closed establishments, job gains at greenfield establishments, acquisitions and divestitures, employment declines by less than 1% compared to controls t+2 after LBO. The results reveal that PE-backed LBOs are catalysts for a process of creative destruction that would be hidden from firm-level studies.

Connections between business and politics are contentious. There is concern that business exploits political connections to get favorable treatment (e.g., through more favorable labor laws), but collaboration between business and politics can help create an environment conducive to job creation. Faccio and Hsu (2017) explore the issue of political connections by examining the impact of PE firms' political connections on employment. They find that over the period t−1 to t+5 employment grows, on average, by 1.24% in establishments controlled by politically connected PE firms while in nonconnected PE firms it is 0.33%. After addressing endogeneity concerns, there is still a significant difference in employment growth between the politically connected and nonconnected PE firms, but the magnitudes are more modest. Nevertheless, Faccio and Hsu (2017) argue their findings could be due to politicians and PE firms exchanging favors. They find evidence consistent with politically connected PE firms altering their hiring and firing decisions to support the election of their political allies. In return, portfolio firms of politically connected PE firms receive government grants and contracts. This provides an important understanding of decision-making in portfolio firms because it suggests that job creation and destruction after a PE-backed LBO is not a simply a business decision.

Differences across deal type and source

There is recognition in the literature that the impact of LBOs could vary across deal type and source of deal. Amess and Wright (2007) seek to draw a distinction between MBOs (insider-driven deals) and MBIs (outsider-driven deals). Managers with inside information might be in a better position to exploit untapped growth opportunities and might have loyalty to existing employees. In contrast, the outsiders in an MBI, with less loyalty to existing employees, might be more inclined to restructure, leading to job losses. They find that employment growth is 0.51 of a percentage point higher in MBOs and 0.81 of a percentage point lower in MBIs, compared to a control sample of firms. The authors suggest that for the average MBO in their sample employment grows by about 1.5 employees per year, while for the average MBI in their sample employment declines by about 5 employees per year. Economically, these figures are fairly modest. Nevertheless, they indicate that a distinction between MBOs and MBIs matters and not all LBOs will have the same employment effects. Moreover, MBOs seem to be able to obtain previously untapped employment growth opportunities while MBIs are associated with job losses, possibly due to restructuring.

Subsequent analysis of outsider-driven deals, i.e., institutional buy outs (IBOs), by Georgen et al. (2011, 2014) also find they are associated with negative employment effects. IBOs are deals where the acquirer consists solely of institutional investors and PE firms c.f. MBIs where outside managers are also part of the team of acquirers. Georgen et al. (2011) report that employment growth is 1.62% lower in the year after the deal but IBO employment growth is not statistically significant from a control sample of firms two and three years after the deal. Georgen et al. (2014) report that post-IBO employment is up to 15% lower.

Most studies do not distinguish between deal sources. Meuleman et al. (2009) and Boucly et al. (2011) examine the employment effect of different deal sources in order to explore deals where there are most likely to be entrepreneurial growth opportunities. Meuleman et al. (2009) find that employment growth is 36% higher in divisional buyouts compared with other deal sources over the three years after the deal. This heterogeneity in employment effects across deal sources is also reported in Boucly et al. (2011). While they find that average employment for all LBOs grows by 12% from the year before the deal to three years after the deal, employment grows by 18% in private-to-private deals, 11% in secondary buyouts (SBOs) and 6% in divisional buyouts. Employment growth in private-to-private and divisional buyout deals could be due to the entrepreneurial incentives installed by an LBO. The SBO result is curious because the governance and entrepreneurial incentives are in place prior to the SBO. Given that industry expertise can improve portfolio firms' operations (Bernstein & Sheen, 2016), one possible explanation is that SBOs occur when there is better complementarity between portfolio firms' assets and the acquiring PE firms' expertise (e.g., specialist market knowledge) than that for the selling PE firm. As a consequence, the PE firm in the SBO might be able to achieve growth opportunities, resulting in employment growth, which are not achieved in the primary deal.

The impact on different types of workers

One branch of the literature recognizes that the impact of an LBO might result in organizational change that has a distinctive impact for different types of workers. Lichtenberg and Siegel (1990) examine the different employment consequences for nonproduction and production workers. They find that there is an 8.5% reduction in the number of nonproduction workers employed while there is no significant effect on production workers. This is consistent with an agency perspective where bureaucratic employees that are costly and do not create or add productive value are stripped out of plants. In contrast, production workers might not suffer job losses because their activities create value for firms.

The distinction between different worker types has been neglected in the literature for a number of years, reflecting the difficulty in obtaining such data because it is not reported in company reports; however, two recent studies use government employee-level data that allows in-depth analysis of employment consequences for employees with different characteristics. Antoni et al. (2015) find modest average effects on employment; the fraction of a year an employee is employed falls by about 1–1.5%. An important insight from their study, however, is that employment effects vary across employee characteristics. Employees that are older, those with a longer tenure in their jobs, female, white-collar and unskilled blue-collar workers experience increased risk of unemployment. Tåg and Olsson (2016) find little evidence of average changes in employment incidence after a PE-backed LBO. For specific worker types in low productivity firms, however, there are negative employment effects. Workers performing routine job tasks experience a 10.2 percentage point (96.6%) increase in employment incidence and workers performing offshorable job tasks experience an 8.6 percentage point (97%) increase in unemployment incidence. Such detailed analyses suggests that LBO restructuring impacts on workers differently. Such effects are not captured in studies examining average effects across a workforce.

Agrawal and Tambe (2016) use employee-level data from a job website to take a different approach to analyze the employment effects of LBOs. The concern with this type of study is that certain types of employees might choose to use the job website and so it is difficult to generalize the results. Nevertheless, the detailed data allow in-depth insight for those workers that use the website in their job search. They analyze the impact on duration of employment and, if an employee loses his or her job, the subsequent impact on employment duration. They find that employment spells are 6 to 8.2 percentage points longer in portfolio firms compared to control firms. In addition, for those workers that leave a portfolio firm after an LBO, their employment duration is 2.9 months shorter than those in control firms. They attribute this to post-LBO investment in IT resulting in workers' complementary IT skills being upgraded, which in turn improves their employability.

Summary

While some studies do find that LBOs impact on employment, most find that the average effect is modest. There is some evidence of positive effects with increased employment in LBOs of private firms, divisions, and SBOs, which is consistent with an entrepreneurial perspective. In addition, the evidence concerning MBIs and IBOs suggests that job losses are more likely to be associated with deals where inside-management are not associated with the deal, suggesting outside acquirers are more likely to instigate restructuring that leads to job losses. The evidence also suggests that lower-skilled workers and white-collar workers suffer negative effects. Low-skilled job losses could be the result of automation and offshoring and white-collar job losses could be the result of LBOs downsizing corporate bureaucracy. The evidence suggests a complicated picture of the employment effects of LBOs. There is no clear evidence that there should be government intervention in the LBO market in order to protect jobs.

Wage effects

There are fewer studies assessing the impact on wages compared to the number of employment studies (Table 26.2). The theoretical background outlined earlier has little to say on the wage effects of LBOs. Nevertheless, a key criticism of LBOs is that they create an opportunity for the new owners to suppress wages, which could be a source of improvements in operating performance.

Table 26.2 Summary of wage studies reviewed in chronological order

Author(s)	*Sample (country, period, firms)*	*Transaction type*	*Findings*
Lichtenberg & Siegel (1990)	US 1983–1986 481 plants	LBO	Over period t−1 to t+2: annual compensation per nonproduction worker is −5.2%; annual and hourly compensation per production worker is 3.6% and 2.3%.
Amess & Wright (2007)	UK 1999–2004 1,350 firms	MBO, MBI	Compared to control sample wage growth is 0.31 of a percentage point lower for MBOs and 0.97 of a percentage point lower for MBIs.
Bergstrom et al. (2007)	Sweden Deals conducted between 1999–2001 73 firms	PE-financed LBO	No significant effect.
Georgen et al. (2014)	UK 2000–2006 73 firms	Institutional buyout	No significant effect.
Amess et al. (2014)	UK 1996–2006 386	PE-backed and non-PE-backed LBOs	PE-backed and non-PE-backed LBOs have no significant effect on wage per worker over period t−1 to t+2.
Davis et al. (2014)	US 1980–2005 3,200 target firms and their 15,000 establishments	PE-backed LBO	Growth of earnings per worker at continuing LBO establishments −2.4% compared to controls t+2 years after LBO.
Antoni et al. (2015)	Germany 2002–2008 535 deals involving 830 firms, 2,584 establishments, and 192,364 employees	PE-backed LBO	Average daily wage 0.96% to 2.68% higher. Low and medium educated, skilled blue-collar workers, and females experience greatest wage gains. Employees with high tenure, who are older and are middle managers experience negative wage effects.
Agrawal & Tambe (2016)	US 1995–2010 4,193 deals 5,680 employees	PE-backed LBO	Wages 2.5–3.5% higher for workers with more IT complementarity skills.

Average pay per worker

Much work in this area makes use of data available in company reports. Most private firms will report the number of employees and the wage bill, therefore, these studies will simply assess the impact of an LBO on average pay per worker. Amess and Wright (2007) provide evidence for UK deals. They estimate that average pay growth is 0.31 of a percentage point lower in MBOs and 0.97 of a percentage point lower in MBIs. For the sample of firms used in the study, coefficient estimates indicate that average pay per employee grows by £83.70 and £231.35 less per annum for MBO and MBI firms, respectively, compared to control firms.

Bergstrom et al.'s (2007) analysis of Swedish PE-backed LBOs and Georgen et al's (2011) analysis of UK IBOs both find no significant impact on average wage level. This is supported by Amess et al.'s (2014) UK study using techniques that account for potential selection bias to the LBO form, who find that PE-backed and non-PE-backed LBOs have no significant effect on the wage per worker over the period t−1 to t+2. In contrast, Davis et al. (2014) report that PE-backed LBOs in the US have earnings per worker 2.4% lower compared to controls two years after the deal. While Bergstrom et al. (2007) find that PE-backed LBOs have no impact on wages, they do however find a negative relationship between wage growth and the relative change in operating performance. They argue that this is indicative of wage reductions explaining post-LBO changes in performance.

The impact on workers with different characteristics

There is a body of literature that recognizes that the impact of LBOs on wages might be different for workers with different characteristics. Lichtenberg and Siegel (1990) examined the distinct wage effects for nonproduction and production workers. They found that the annual compensation for nonproduction workers fell by 5.2% over the period t−1 to t+2 around the deal. In contrast, over the same period, they find that the annual and hourly compensation per production worker is 3.6% and 2.3% higher, respectively. They argue that this is consistent with compensation being used to motivate employees rather than direct monitoring.

Antoni et al. (2015) estimate that the impact on the average employee's wage ranges from 0.96% to 2.68%. More in-depth analysis using education and occupation reveals that the impact of LBOs on wages varies across different types of employees. Target employees with low and medium levels of education experience greater wage improvements than for those with high levels of education. Highly educated employees gain 0.07% while the additional gain for low educated and medium educated is 1.19% and 2.06%, respectively. The wage effect is different when proxy measures for occupational skills are considered. White-collar workers achieve a wage gain of about 1%, unskilled blue-collar workers receive a wage gain that is not statistically significant from this, and skilled blue-collar workers gain by an estimated 2.84%. Antoni et al. also find that the characteristics of workers for whom LBOs have a negative effect are those employees: with high tenure, who are older, and are middle managers. A positive effect for female employees is found, although this may be due to females being over-represented in the medium educated group.

Heterogeneity in employee wages after an LBO is also reported in Agrawal and Tambe (2016). They examine wage differences between those workers that have never been employed by a firm acquired by an LBO with employees that have been employed by an LBO target at some point in the sample. The rationale for this is that employees will acquire transferable human capital after PE-led investment in IT and so the wage effects of an LBO on an employee will persist after they have left an LBO target firm and obtained a job in another firm. Employees that were once employed in an LBO target experience a 2.5–3.5% wage gain for each unit increase in IT complementary skills. In high IT firms, such wage gains are estimated to be up to 13% higher.

Summary

The evidence suggests that the impact of LBOs on wages is fairly modest. In addition, the evidence to date is mixed. This mixed body of evidence does not strongly support the argument that LBOs lead to wage suppression but neither does it suggest that the average employee shares in post-LBO performance gains. Nevertheless, there is evidence to suggest heterogeneous wage effects across different types of employees. In particular, the evidence suggests skilled workers experience the highest wage gains.

Future research

Over the years, the evidence on employment and wage effects has grown and has become increasingly nuanced, providing depth to our understanding of the effects of LBOs on employees. Nevertheless, the evidence is largely mixed and fails to provide firm support for either positive or negative effects for employees. The most insightful research appears to assess the impacts for different types of employees. There are several areas where research on the employment and wage effects of LBOs would be useful.

First, future research on workers' pay could examine the impact of LBOs on different pay components. The structure of pay packages impacts on risk-sharing and incentives. For instance, profit-sharing and bonus schemes provide stronger incentives to reduce employee moral hazard than a salary or wage. Could greater use of these types of pay components be a driver of improved performance after an LBO? Profit-sharing schemes could also be attractive to post-LBO owners because it means they share performance risk with employees. The wage bill will be positively correlated with firm performance. Do LBOs adopt profit-sharing schemes to reduce the new owners' exposure to performance risk?

Second, Shleifer and Summers (1988) argue that corporate restructuring presents an opportunity for implicit labor contracts to be renegotiated. Obviously, implicit features of a labor contract are by definition impossible, or at least very difficult, to observe and measure. There are aspects of being employed that could indicate whether implicit agreements with employees have been broken or have deteriorated after an LBO. For instance, if employees become less satisfied with their work (i.e., feeling more insecure, the lack of opportunity to develop skills, and feeling less achievement in their work) and feeling more worried, depressed, and tense about work. There is increasing interest in the well-being of individuals; the impact of corporate restructuring transactions, such as an LBO, on workers well-being could be a fruitful area of research that expands our knowledge of the labor consequences beyond the narrow economic confines of having a job and how well it pays.

Third, pensions can represent an important part of a pay package. Some employees might be willing to accept lower wages in return for a better pension. Such arrangements are not typically part of an explicit employment contract; rather, they are implicit. Employer pension liabilities and employer pension contributions, however, might be an area where the LBO restructuring creates an opportunity where such an implicit contract is changed unfavorably for employees in order to generate savings that benefit LBO investors.

Fourth, there are broader aspects of the work environment that impact on employees' welfare. For instance, some firms will offer their employees flexi-time, job sharing, and on the job training and education, and benefits in kind such as health insurance and a car. These aspects of work are provided by employers on a voluntary basis and future research could determine whether cost-cutting after an LBO leads to a reduction in the provision of these aspects of work. In addition, there could be an assessment of changes to employees' workload and duties along with changes to contractual status from permanent to casual.

Finally, much of the evidence provided to date uses US and UK data, although there is some evidence from other European countries. PE is a growing feature of capital markets in developing economies, such as India and China. Such markets provide an interesting context because their capital markets are generally considered less developed than those in the US and Europe. This might mean there is potential for upside gains and employment creation due to PE investment. In countries with less employment regulation, however, LBOs may be more likely to depress wages. Some markets also see PE firms with private, state, and foreign ownership operating alongside each other. It would be interesting to find out the different employment and wage effects of different PE firms.

Conclusions

This chapter reviews the agency and entrepreneurship perspectives of LBOs and outlines arguments concerning their impact on jobs and wages. The agency perspective predicts the realignment of managers' and owners' incentives after an LBO will result in job losses. Critics of PE firms have taken this type of argument to suggest that any gains they make could be attributable to transfers from employees. This might be in the form of job losses or the suppression of wages. An entrepreneurial perspective suggests that LBOs provide incentives for the new owners to invest in entrepreneurial growth, resulting in job creation. A weakness of the entrepreneurial perspective is that it has little to say on how an LBO impacts on wages.

Unfortunately, the evidence does not provide a clear picture of the effects of LBOs on jobs and wages for PE-backed deals. Nevertheless, there appears to be some evidence of job creation in deals that are characterized as entrepreneurial. The employee-level studies provide insightful evidence as to the gainers and losers from being employed at an LBO target. Recent studies suggest that low-skilled workers are more likely to suffer job and wage losses, while skilled workers experience wage gains. The lack of consensus in the evidence and the paucity of studies conducting employee-level analysis suggests there is scope for further research in this area.

Note

1 The proportion of equity held by management varies depending on the size of the deal. Centre for Management Buy-Out Research data for UK deals shows that for deals valued below £10 million management hold about 60–80% of equity while for deals valued greater than £10 million the amount of equity held by management is about 25–40%. The remaining equity is held by PE firms.

References

Agrawal, A., & Tambe, P. 2016. Private equity and workers' career paths: The role of technological change. *Review of Financial Studies*, 29: 2455–2489.

Akerlof, G. A. 1982. Labour contracts as partial gift exchange. *Quarterly Journal of Economics*, 97: 543–569.

Amess, K. 2003. The effect of management buyouts on firm-level technical efficiency: Evidence from a panel of UK machinery and equipment manufacturers. *Journal of Industrial Economics*, 51: 35–44.

Amess, K., Girma, S., & Wright, M. 2014. The wage and employment consequences of ownership change. *Managerial and Decision Economics*, 35: 161–171.

Amess, K., Stiebale, J., & Wright, M. 2015. The impact of private equity on firms' patenting activity. *European Economic Review*, 86: 147–160.

Amess, K., & Wright, M. 2007. The wage and employment effects of leveraged buyouts in the UK. *International Journal of the Economics of Business*, 14: 179–195.

Amess, K., & Wright, M. 2012. Leveraged buyouts, private equity and jobs. *Small Business Economics*, 38: 419–430.

Antoni, M., Maug, E. G., & Obernberger, S. 2015. *Private equity and human capital risk* Available at SSRN: http://ssrn.com/abstract=2602771.

Applebaum, E., & Batt, R. 2014. *Private equity at work*. New York: Russell Sage Foundation.

Behr, P., Norden, L., & Noth, F. 2013. Financial constraints of private firms and bank lending behaviour. *Journal of Banking and Finance*, 37: 3472–3485.

Berger, A. N., & Udell, G. F. 1998. The economics of small business finance: The roles of private equity and debt markets in the financial growth cycle. *Journal of Banking and Finance*, 22: 613–673.

Bergstrom, C., Grubb, M., & Jonsson, S. 2007. The operating impact of buyouts in Sweden: A study of value creation. *Journal of Private Equity*, 11: 22–39.

Bernstein, S., & Sheen, A. 2016. The operational consequences of private equity buyouts: Evidence from the restaurant industry. *Review of Financial Studies*, 29: 2387–2418.

Boucly, Q., Sraer, D., & Thesmar, D. 2011. Growth LBOs. *Journal of Financial Economics*, 102: 432–453.

Bruining, H., Verwaal, E., & Peterson, B. C. 2012. Private equity and entrepreneurial management in management buy-outs. *Small Business Economics*, 40: 591–605.

Carpenter, R. E., & Petersen, B. C. 2002. Is the growth of small firms constrained by internal finance? *Review of Economics and Statistics*, 84: 298–309.

Davis, S. J., Haltiwanger, J., Handley, K., Jarmin, R., Lerner, J., & Miranda, J. 2014. Private equity, jobs, and productivity. *American Economic Review*, 104: 3956–3990.

Engel, D., & Stiebale, J. 2014. Private equity, investment and financial constraints: Firm-level evidence for France and the United Kingdom. *Small Business Economics*, 43: 197–212.

Faccio, M., & Hsu, H.-C. 2017. Politically connected private equity and employment. *Journal of Finance*, 72: 539–573.

Fama, E. F., & Jensen, M. C. 1983. Agency problems and residual claims. *Journal of Law & Economics*, 26: 327–350.

Fox, I., & Marcus, A. 1992. The causes and consequences of leveraged management buyouts. *Academy of Management Review*, 17: 62–85.

Georgen, M, O'Sullivan, N., & Wood, G. 2011. Private equity takeovers and employment in the UK: Some empirical evidence. *Corporate Governance: An International Review*, 19: 259–275.

Georgen, M., O'Sullivan, N., & Wood, G. 2014. The employment consequences of private equity acquisitions: The case of institutional buyouts. *European Economic Review*, 71: 67–79.

Harris, R., Siegel, D. S., & Wright, M. 2005. Assessing the impact of management buyouts on economic efficiency: Plant-level evidence from the United Kingdom. *Review of Economics and Statistics*, 87: 148–153.

Hart, O. 1995. Corporate governance: some theory and implications. *Economic Journal*, 105: 678–689.

International Trade Union Confederation 2007. *Where the house always wins: Private equity, hedge funds and the new casino capitalism*. Brussels: International Trade Union Confederation.

Jensen, M. C. 1986. Agency costs of free cash flow, corporate finance and takeover. *American Economic Review*, 76: 323–329.

Jensen, M. C., & Meckling, W. H. 1976. Theory of the firm: managerial behavior, agency costs and ownership structure. *Journal of Financial Economics*, 3: 305–360.

Kaplan, S. 1986. The effects of management buyouts on operating performance and value. *Journal of Financial Economics*, 24(2): 217–254.

Kaplan, S. 1989. The effects of management buyouts on operating performance and value. *Journal of Financial Economics*, 24: 217–254.

Kaplan, S., & Stromberg, P. 2009. Leveraged buyouts and private equity. *Journal of Economic Perspectives*, 23: 121–146.

Lichtenberg, F. R., & Siegel, D. 1990. The effects of leveraged buyouts on productivity and related aspects of firm behaviour. *Journal of Financial Economics*, 27: 165–194.

Meuleman, M., Amess, K., Wright, M., & Scholes, L. 2009. Agency, strategic entrepreneurship, and the performance of private equity-backed buyouts. *Entrepreneurship: Theory & Practice*, 33: 213–239.

Shleifer, A., & Summers, L. H. 1988. Breach of trust in hostile takeovers. In A. Auerbach (Ed.), *Corporate takeovers: Causes and consequences*. Chicago, IL: University of Chicago Press.

Smith, A. 1990. Corporate ownership structure and performance: The case of management buyouts. *Journal of Financial Economics*, 27: 143–164.

Stiglitz, J. E. 1987. The causes and consequences of the dependence of quality on price. *Journal of Economic Literature*, 25: 1–48.

Tåg, J., & Olsson, M. 2016. Private equity, layoffs, and job polarization. *Journal of Labor Economics*, 35: 697–754.

Thompson, S., & Wright, M. 1995. Corporate governance: The role of restructuring transactions. *Economic Journal*, 105: 690–703.

Williamson, O. E. 1975. *Markets and hierarchies*. New York: Free Press.

Williamson, O. E. 1985. *The economic institutions of capitalism: Firms, markets, relational contracting*. New York: Free Press.

Wright, M., Thompson, S., & Robbie, K. 1992. Venture capital and management-led, leveraged buy-outs: A European perspective. *Journal of Business Venturing*, 7: 47–71.

27
BUYOUT LONGEVITY AND POST-EXIT PERFORMANCE[1]

Ranko Jelic, Mike Wright, Victor Murinde, and Wasim Ahmad

Introduction

Consistent with predictions (e.g., Jensen, 1989), the buyout market has grown tremendously into a global phenomenon (Stromberg, 2008). The extraordinary growth since the late 1990s has been supported by private equity (PE) investments in buyouts. Buyout transactions, for example, account for more than half of all PE investments, which were worth just under $3 trillion worldwide.[2] Globally, the US still receives the highest amount of PE investments, followed by the UK, China, France, and India (Cumming & Fleming, 2012). While the European market is dominated by investors that focus on late stage investments in management buyouts, the US market is dominated by venture capital (VC) investing in young ventures (EVCA, 2001).[3]

The success of the PE model has raised the profile of the industry but at the same time created controversy. Trade unions, for example, often describe PE firms as asset strippers who destroy jobs and load companies with debt (Amess & Wright, 2012). Opinions about the longer-term effects of PE investments and, in particular, whether the benefits for PE funds come at the expense of the longer-term health of companies, are also divided. The British Private Equity and Venture Capital Association (BVCA, 2000) provided statistics suggesting that companies backed by PE have grown employment and sales faster than other companies. Others, however, argue that shareholders and employees do not benefit mainly due to the myopic behavior of PE firms. The controversy has contributed to calls for more transparency and a tighter regulation of the PE industry (TSC, 2010). PE firms, however, still benefit from lower taxes and lighter disclosure requirements compared to public firms.

The above controversy is partly fueled by the relative paucity of research and conclusive empirical evidence, especially relating to the recent period of PE activity which peaked in mid-2007. In this chapter we therefore present results of both early and more recent literature relating to the peak and aftermath of the second PE wave in the UK. We review research on the following topics: longevity of buyouts, choice of various exit routes from buyout organizational forms, and post (buyout) exit operating and financial (i.e., stock prices) company performance.[4] We survey studies that examine all management buyout types (buyout (MBO), buyin (MBI), and leveraged buyout (LBO)), buyouts originating from various sources (privately owned, divestment, privatization, and receiverships), and all exit routes from buyout structures (initial public offerings (IPO), trade sales, secondary management buyouts (SMBO), and liquidations).

Our focus is on the UK private-to-private and private-to-public as opposed to public-to-private buyout transactions for the following reasons. First, while public-to-private buyout transactions tend to receive most of the attention by media and regulators, they represent less than 7% of all buyout transactions worldwide (Stromberg, 2008). The vast majority of buyout targets, therefore, are private companies and these transactions often use little leverage. Second, neither going private (from public) nor highly leveraged financing are necessary ingredients of a buyout transaction. Agency costs of free cash flow (Jensen, 1989), therefore, are unlikely to explain the reasons for buyouts of privately held targets as ownership is already concentrated in these companies prior to buyouts. The same applies to declining analysts' coverage and low stock turnover, which are often identified as reasons for public-to-private buyouts. It is, therefore, important to understand the economic rationale and performance of non-public-to-private buyouts. Finally, the need for more research and a better understanding of non-public-to-private buyout transactions was also highlighted in previous survey papers on PE (see Metrick & Yasuda, 2011).

The alignment of incentives leading to improved performance lies at the heart of management buyout organizational form (Jensen & Meckling, 1976; Jensen, 1989). At the same time, economic literature recognizes that activities of PE investors (e.g., monitoring, advising, etc.) could increase firms' market value (Kaplan & Stromberg, 2009). It is, therefore, important to highlight whether (and if so how) PE backing contributes over and above the benefits of buyout ownership associated with a reduction in the conflicts of interest between managers and owners in closely held companies. To the best of our knowledge, this chapter is the only survey of the literature that treats PE-backed and non-PE-backed (i.e., pure) buyouts separately.

We survey research that is based on company-level (i.e., deal-level) rather than PE investor (fund) level data. Aggregation of data at the PE fund level inevitably leads to loss of information regarding timing of original investments and exits from the buyout structure. Lack of daily pricing for PE funds makes their performance assessment based on the internal rate of return (IRR) very difficult. Company-level data, on the other hand, allows us to examine post-deal changes in performance and to address questions such as whether buyouts are short- or long-term organization forms. The deal-level data also allows researchers to control for the fact that PE investors tend to prefer investments in companies with certain characteristics.

The London Stock Exchange (LSE) is one of the most successful world's IPO markets. This is, to a great extent, due to its Alternative Investment Market (AIM).[5] AIM, however, has "light touch" listing rules thus allowing listings of many high-risk firms. We, therefore, present evidence for the main LSE board and AIM separately.

The chapter proceeds as follows. We begin by surveying evidence on the decision to exit the buyout structure together with the evidence on longevity of buyouts. In the subsequent section we focus on the operating and financial post-exit performance of buyouts. We also survey evidence on the importance of PE backing (and characteristics of PE firms) on the post-exit performance. In the final section we summarize key findings and conclude.

Buyout exits and longevity[6]

The literature on the duration of early stage VC investments is extensive (Schwienbacher, 2002; Cumming, 2008; Mohamed, 2009; Cumming & Johan, 2010). However, there is a relative paucity of research on the longevity of PE late-stage investments in buyouts and the different exit routes from buyouts. A separate examination of the duration of PE investments in buyouts is important since investments in buyouts (i.e., established companies) require different skills from investments in new companies (Jelic, 2011). For example, investments in buyouts (e.g., privatizations and receiverships) could be burdened with complicated ownership and other issues less likely to be present in VC investments in start-ups. PE investments are also larger and normally require significant incremental direct and overhead costs in comparison to investments made by VC firms. Finally, the PE financing model is different from the VC model, which potentially can affect duration of respective investments.

We review literature on exit routes together with four groups of determinants of buyouts' longevity: determinants associated with PE backing and characteristics of the PE firms (reputation and association with investment banks) and PE deals (syndicated and highly leveraged deals); buyout specific characteristics such as size, industry, and source of the buyouts (privatization, divestment, and receivership); buyout type (LBO, MBO, and MBI); and determinants related to the market conditions (changes in the stock market, hot IPO periods, and supply of PE funding).

Buyout exits

Jelic (2011) reports median time to exit of 36 months for UK buyouts. Around 35% of UK buyouts remained in a buyout organizational form, while 47% remained in private ownership for at least seven years after the original buyout transactions. IPOs are the preferred exit route for UK buyouts, followed by sale, SMBOs, and lastly liquidation. SMBOs are rarely the first exit choice for PE firms (Wright et al., 2000; Jelic, 2011). Most recently, SMBO exits have exhibited steady growth, reaching 29% of all exits in the 2000s (Jelic, 2011). The most popular exit routes from UK SMBOs are trade sales (40%) and tertiary buyouts (34%) (Zhou et al., 2014).

The UK has the most liquid stock market in Europe, which helps to explain the popularity of IPO exits in the UK compared to other European countries. The reported evidence on the importance of IPOs as an exit route for UK buyouts, however, varies significantly. Wright et al. (1995b), for example, report that IPO exits constitute 10% of all exits from UK buyouts. The reported percentages in subsequent studies were 16% in Nikoskelainen and Wright (2007), 11% in Stromberg (2008), and 47% in Jelic (2011). The direct comparison of results reported in these studies is difficult due to differences in the sample coverage. For example, while Jelic (2011) includes 205 deals from the AIM, Nikoskelainen and Wright (2007) report only 2 AIM exits in their subsample of 52 IPO exits. Furthermore, Capital IQ database (e.g., used in Stromberg, 2008) underreports deals from the 1970s and 1980s and deals without PE backing, thus resulting in possible underreporting of IPO exits.

Stromberg (2008) reports that only 2.9% of PE-backed deals worldwide exited within 12 months of the original transaction. Jelic (2011) reports a higher percentage of early exits for UK buyouts, of 5.1%. The UK early exits tend to be associated with IPOs of relatively smaller buyouts on AIM (Jelic, 2011). Both studies report that the number of early exits has exhibited a decreasing trend since the late 1980s. The reported failure rates for UK buyouts (e.g., Jelic, 2011) are similar to failure rates of 3% reported for other UK private firms.[7] Stromberg (2008) reports 6% failure rate for UK buyouts, after adopting a broader definition of failure that includes bankruptcy filings, financial restructuring, and liquidations. The author, however, describes the LBO failure rates as modest, similar to those reported for corporate bond issuers.

PE backing and longevity

Gottschalg (2007) reports average time to exit of five years for PE-backed buyouts, worldwide. Jelic et al. (2005) report that PE-backed buyouts tend to be larger and exit earlier than their non-venture-backed counterparts. The results were echoed in Jelic (2011) who also reports that UK PE-backed buyouts exhibit higher exit rates, fewer early exits, and liquidations compared to their pure counterparts. The same study reports an average (mean) longevity of UK PE-backed buyouts at 40 months, compared to 52 months for pure buyouts. Although the order of preference of exit routes is the same for PE-backed and pure buyouts, IPOs and SMBOs tend to play a less important role for pure buyouts (Jelic, 2011).

Given lower opportunity costs associated with the alternative use of capital, incumbent managers are expected to have a lower exit propensity. Non-PE-backed buyouts are therefore expected to have longer duration in comparison to PE firms (Ronstadt, 1986). In addition, in the absence of PE backing, the pure buyouts may be lacking advice and skills required for a successful exit. On the other hand, the greater value-added provided by the PE firms normally requires a longer time (Cumming & Johan, 2010). Early exits (e.g., within 12 months) could therefore be associated with less skilled PE firms and/or incidences where PE firms force early exits (e.g., grandstanding).

Shorter longevity in subsamples of pure buyouts could be related to insiders' motivation to maximize their private benefits by taking companies public (Berglof, 1994; Black & Gilson, 1998). The above scenario is particularly plausible in the AIM with less stringent listing rules. The early exits in AIM should therefore be examined separately. Espenlaub et al. (2012) is a rare study that examines the role of nominated financial advisors (NOMADs) in AIM-listed companies. They report a significant positive impact of NOMAD reputation on the survival in their sample of all (buyout and non-buyout) UK IPOs. Since NOMADS tend to substitute the role of PE firms, a comparison of the survival of pure buyout IPOs supported by NOMADs and their PE-backed counterparts can be of interest for both investors and regulators.

Buyout longevity and characteristics of PE firms

One of the important questions is whether the reputation of PE firms matters. Kaplan (1991) reports differences between US IPO exits of reputable and less well-known LBO partnerships.[8] For example, buyouts sponsored by more well-known LBO partnerships are more likely to go public within a particular time period than those sponsored by less well-known LBO financiers, although the differences are not significant. Reputable PE firms may be more adept at picking good deals and/or more effective at implementing the changes necessary to grow and exit them (reputation hypothesis). Reputable PE firms are, therefore, more likely to take buyouts to market sooner. Evidence for the UK is inconclusive. Early evidence (Jelic et al., 2005) supports the reputation hypothesis while more recent evidence (Jelic, 2011) does not.

Kaplan (1991) considers captive PE firms (i.e., subsidiaries of investment banks) to be the more reputable. The more established UK PE firms, in the 1990s, were also subsidiaries of larger financial organizations. The possible interaction between the reputation and captivity of PE firms is consistent with two scenarios. In the first scenario the captivity enhances the reputation of PE firms and thus the shortening longevity in line with the reputation hypothesis (Jelic, 2011).

In the second scenario, captive PE firms are facing less pressure to exit due to their links with investment banks and more "dry powder" (Jelic et al., 2005). The captive PE firms therefore exhibit the lower marginal costs of not investing which in turn may translate into longer duration of investments. More recent UK evidence (Jelic, 2011) reports no significant differences between captive and independent PE firms. The evidence regarding the association of PE firms' reputation and their links with investment banks should be examined within historical perspectives (i.e., in different decades) given that many UK captive funds changed their status in the early 1990s.

PE syndication and longevity

Literature on VC deals suggests that syndications enhance the skills required for IPO exits and higher valuation (Lerner, 1994; Cumming, 2006; Giot & Schwienbacher, 2007; Xuan, 2007). Syndicates also reduce the effort made by any individual member of the syndicate and therefore shorten the duration of the investment (Cumming & Johan, 2010).

LBOs acquired by syndicates of PE firms also tend to accelerate exits (Stromberg, 2008). On the other hand, accelerated exits could also be due to agency conflicts among the syndicate members (Wright et al., 1995b; Stromberg, 2008).[9] The early exits from the original buyout structure in those cases are part of the solution for the conflicts among PE firms in the syndicate. More recent results for IPO and SMBO exits are in line with the above conjectures. For example, Jelic (2011) reports significant negative association of PE syndication and buyout longevity for IPO and SMBO exits.[10] The author also documents an increasing trend in both the number of syndicated deals, number of financing rounds, and the average investment per deal during the 1990s and 2000s.[11] Among UK syndicated deals, SMBOs tend to be an important exit route (23%) coming second following IPOs and before sale exits. SMBOs also tend to have the highest average number of PE firms in the syndicates.

Characteristics and sources of buyouts

Buyout size and industry classification

Larger UK buyouts tend to exit earlier (Wright et al., 1994; Stromberg, 2008; Jelic, 2011). The evidence is in line with higher marginal costs of investments (i.e., greater fixed costs) and, due to less monitoring, lower marginal value added (Cumming & Johan, 2010).

Importance of industry classification has also been highlighted in the previous literature on longevity of VC investments (Bayar & Chemmanur, 2006; Gompers et al., 2008). For example, the VC support is particularly important in less concentrated sectors (e.g., service industry). Furthermore, PE tends to create higher value added by their facilitating networks regarding potential strategic investors within the service industry. These arguments are in line with the popularity of UK buyouts from service industries.[12] Jelic (2011), however, finds no significant association between industry classification (i.e., services) and longevity of buyouts.[13]

Sources of buyouts and longevity

Buyouts arising from divestments are often burdened with constraints on decision-making imposed by parent companies (Gailen & Vetsuypens, 1989). The adoption of a buyout structure, followed by a quick exit, may help in addressing the constraints within a relatively short period of time. Both early and more recent UK evidence are in line with the above scenario (Wright et al., 1994; Jelic, 2011).

Distressed companies are riskier and require more time for turnaround. They should, therefore, be expected to remain longer in their original buyout structure. However, deals originating from distressed acquisitions are more likely to end up again in financial distress compounded by significant conflicts of interest between insiders and PE investors. PE firms, therefore, are more likely to write off those transactions in cases of high carry costs (Stromberg, 2008; Jelic, 2011).

Due to an extensive privatization program in the 1980s, state-owned firms represent an important source of UK buyouts. These companies are clearly different from an average privately owned company, both in terms of size and ownership structure. Jelic (2011), however, finds no evidence for different longevity of privatization buyouts, after controlling for size, industry, and other potential determinants of the longevity.

Longevity of different types of buyouts

Longevity of highly leveraged buyouts (LBOs)

The heavy use of leverage in PE models is well documented in the literature and represents an important buyout corporate governance mechanism (Nikoskelainen & Wright, 2007). The high leverage, however, creates high interest costs. Highly leveraged PE investments are therefore profitable only if the exit is within the planned holding period. The significantly shorter duration for highly leveraged UK buyouts, reported in Jelic (2011), is in line with this assertion.

One of the important challenges for researchers in this area is the lack of an agreed definition of an LBO transaction, in the UK institutional context (Jelic, 2011). Amess and Wright (2007), for example, define LBOs as transactions with high leverage, highly concentrated equity held by managers, and the PE firm's active monitoring role at board level. Thomson One Banker database defines LBOs as deals when an investor funds an acquisition with an extraordinary amount of debt, with plans to repay it with funds generated from the company or with revenue earned by selling off the newly-acquired company's assets. The extraordinary level of debt, however, is not defined. In addition, the same database identifies a deal as an LBO if the transaction is identified as such in the financial press and a majority interest of the target company is acquired. In the US, the LBO definition includes all MBIs and highly leveraged PE-backed buyouts (Renneboog et al., 2005). Again, what exactly the "high leverage" is, is not specified.

Longevity of MBIs

Managers undertaking MBIs often encounter substantial unexpected problems (Wright et al., 1995a). This is in line with the fact that incumbent managers are better informed and aware of potential problems related to the buyout deals. MBIs are, therefore, more likely to exit via crisis sales and/or liquidation and are expected to have shorter longevity. Evidence reported in Jelic (2011) supports the above view. On the contrary, Wright et al. (1995a) report that MBIs which avoid liquidation require a longer time to turn around, and thus remain longer in their original buyin structure. Overall, the evidence on longevity of MBIs is inconclusive.

Market conditions and buyout longevity

Favorable market conditions provide prospects of higher market valuation and are therefore particularly important for IPO exits. For example, the IPO literature reports easier valuations during IPO waves (i.e., hot markets) (Lowry & Schwert, 2002) and when information asymmetry is reduced (Stoughton et al., 2001). The IPO literature documented that the relative "hotness" of public markets increases the probability of IPO exits (Brau et al., 2003; Poulsen & Stegemoller, 2008).

In line with the above, IPO exits tend to be more popular when market-wide demand for growth capital is high, adverse selection costs of equity issues are low, and the value of protecting private information is low (Ball et al., 2008). "Hotness" of market conditions is negatively association with duration of VC investments (Cumming & Johan, 2010). The negative association of public market conditions and duration of VC investments is consistent with the conjecture that the strong market conditions increase the opportunity costs of maintaining prior investments.

Strong market conditions measured by stock market returns and "hot" exit years are also important determinants of the longevity of UK buyouts. For example, favorable market conditions increase the hazard of IPO exits by more than one-third, but cut the hazard of sale exits to a half (Jelic, 2011). Similarly, PE firms tend to take advantage of "hot" market conditions by taking their companies to IPO exits during years with exceptional volumes and a degree of underpricing. On the other hand, managers in pure buyouts tend not to take their companies to IPO exits during years with a "hot" IPO market. The results reported for UK buyouts in Jelic (2011) are in line with evidence from the US and Canadian markets suggesting that private exits are not popular in times of strong market conditions (Cumming & Johan, 2010).

Availability (and growth) of investment capital should increase the opportunity cost of not investing and hence shorten investment duration (Cumming & Johan, 2010). Some studies, therefore, examine the amount of money available for PE firms to invest. Results for US and Canadian studies support the view that increasing amounts of investment capital tend to accelerate exits (Gompers, 1996; Cumming & Walz, 2010). Similarly, a negative and highly significant association between availability of PE capital and longevity of UK buyouts is reported in Jelic (2011).

Post-exit performance

Post-exit operating performance[14]

Performance of IPO exits[15]

The negative long-term operating performance of IPOs has been well documented in IPO literature. For example, Jain and Kini (1994) and Mikkelson et al. (1997) report long-term deterioration in operating performance for the US IPOs. The results for UK IPOs echo the US evidence (Khurshed et al., 2005).

Evidence from studies that examine buyout IPO exits separately is less conclusive. For example, Nikoskelainen and Wright (2007) report an internal rate of return of enterprise value of 22.2% and the average equity internal rate of return of 70.5% for the sample of 321 UK buyouts exited during the period 1995–2004. The authors also report that buyouts exited via IPO outperformed trade sale exits and SMBO exits. Jelic and Wright (2011) examine performance three years before and up to five years after the exits. They find strong evidence suggesting significant improvements in output, employment, and dividends after IPO buyout exits, while efficiency ratios remain unchanged. They also document better performance of PE-backed buyouts exiting via IPOs. Buyouts exiting via IPO also significantly reduced gearing levels after coming to market, in line with US evidence reported in Kaplan (1991). The results for return on assets (ROA) and return on sales (ROS) suggest negative and statistically significant changes in profitability. These findings in respect of profitability contrast somewhat with US evidence by Holthausen and Larcker (1996), who find continued profit outperformance (compared to non-buyout companies from the same industries) of 90 reverse L/MBOs for up to four years post IPO. The outperformance is unrelated to changes in leverage and positively related to changes in insider equity ownership of IPOs. Similarly, Muscarella and Vetsuypens (1990) find that 72 US reverse L/MBOs (during 1983–1987) exhibited a significant increase in operating profitability.

Association between PE backing and post-exit performance is less clear. Greater value-added provided by PE firms (e.g., strategic, marketing, financial, and human resource advice) normally requires longer investment duration (Cumming & Johan, 2010). On the other hand, PE firms tend to balance the cost of continued monitoring involvement against the potential negative market reaction to insider selling during an IPO (Lin & Smith, 1998).[16] Consequently, over the longer term post-exit, the influence of PE firm monitoring should dissipate. This may further lead to deterioration in performance post-exit and, therefore, a negative association between PE backing and post-IPO performance.

The above highlights the importance of tracking the performance of IPO firms for long periods after IPOs (Jelic & Wright, 2011). Lyon et al. (1999) also suggest that IPOs may create a large increase in the book value of the firm's assets as they invest in additional operating assets, but no commensurate increase in profit, since these assets have not been employed long enough to generate a profit. Tracking the performance over a longer period of time would ascertain whether erosion in operating performance is the result of a temporary build-up in assets.[17]

Performance on AIM vs. main LSE board

Jelic and Wright (2011) report a similar performance of buyouts exiting on both markets showing significant increases in output and employment in the post-IPO period. The buyouts listed on the main board tend to outperform the sample buyouts listing on AIM in terms of efficiency, in the first two years following listing. PE-backed buyout IPOs from the main market exhibit no statistically significant changes in industry-adjusted ROA.[18] Unlike previous IPO studies, Jelic and Wright (2011) report that non-PE-backed buyouts (including those on AIM) exiting via IPOs do not underperform as well.[19] Furthermore, their results also show no evidence of a significant difference in median industry-adjusted ROA between PE-backed and buyouts supported by NOMADS.

SMBO performance[20]

SMBOs are a means to continue the PE-backed ownership form but with a different set of investors. The incentive and control mechanisms introduced in the first buyout likely result in initial efforts to reduce costs and improve efficiencies, which seem to be most pronounced in the first two to three years after buyout (Wiersema & Liebeskind, 1995). Beyond this period it would likely be that further performance improvements from these sources would be achievable but at declining rates (Jelic & Wright, 2011). Introduction of revised incentive structures (increased managerial equity stakes) and the looser controls by PE firms, may shift the focus to pursuit of growth opportunities but may also lead to greater entrenchment behavior by management.

More recent evidence on the performance of SMBOs is mixed. For example, Achleitner and Figge (2011) use worldwide data and report that SMBOs still generate improvements in operational performance, compared to primary buyouts. Bonini (2010), however, reports a lack of any significant performance improvements for European SMBOs. UK evidence suggests improvements in output and dividends (Jelic & Wright, 2011), accompanied by significant deterioration in profitability (Jelic & Wright, 2011; Wang, 2011).

Zhou et al. (2014) report that UK SMBOs perform worse than primary buyouts in terms of growth, profitability, and labor productivity. The authors find no evidence for superior performance of PE-backed SMBOs compared to their non-PE-backed counterparts. PE firms' reputation and change in management, however, are important determinants of the performance. The results are in line with Axelson et al.'s (2013) view that general partners with unused funds (i.e., "dry powder") at the end of their mandate "go for broke" by taking underperforming deals. SMBOs that arise from buyouts that have taken longer to exit, therefore, may be indicative of companies that are the leftovers in the PE's portfolio which need to be exited by the fast approaching end of the fund's life.

More recently research has been moving towards the resource-based strategic entrepreneurship perspective (Ireland et al., 2003) that emphasizes managers' and PE firms' strong motivation to employ their idiosyncratic knowledge and skills. Zhou et al. (2018), for example, report that human capital of PE directors tends to play statistically and economically significant roles in the performance of UK SMBOs. Specifically, PE directors' financial (rather than operational) experience tends to improve post-SMBO profitability while high level of business education is especially important for post-SMBO growth.

Post-exit financial performance[21]

Short-term financial performance

Theoretical literature on well-documented IPO underpricing tends to focus on information asymmetry, regulatory issues, ownership issues, and market-related issues (see Ibbotson & Ritter, 1995). The US evidence on the association of VC backing and underpricing is inconclusive. Megginson and Weiss (1991), for example, report lower degrees of underpricing for VC-backed IPOs compared to non-VC-backed IPOs.[22] Other studies report the absence of an association between VC backing and degree of underpricing (Barry et al., 1990; Ljungqvist, 1999). IPOs of UK VC firms with links to issuing houses tend to exhibit a lower degree of underpricing but only if those houses do not sponsor the IPOs (Espenlaub et al., 1999).

None of the above-mentioned studies, however, differentiate IPO exits of buyouts (i.e., reverse buyouts) from other (i.e., non-buyout) IPOs. IPOs originated from buyouts, however, are quite distinct and are less likely to suffer from an information asymmetry problem due to their longer operating history. Furthermore, PE investors involved in buyouts face a two-level principal-agent relationship: between themselves and the managers of the companies in which they invest; and between themselves and their providers of capital (Sahlman, 1990). This further implies rather complex roles that PE investors play in buyout–IPO transactions. For the above reasons, IPOs that arise from buyouts are not representative of a typical firm going public, and it is important to study them separately.

Jelic et al. (2005) examine IPOs originated from UK buyout deals separately. They report positive and highly statistically significant initial premiums for VC-backed IPOs, regardless of measurement matrix. Based on equally weighted average initial returns, there are no statistically significant differences between VC-backed and non-VC-backed IPOs. However, VC-backed companies seem to be more underpriced than buyouts without VC backing based on average value-weighted returns.[23] In contrast to the grandstanding hypothesis, authors also report that private-to-public buyouts backed by more reputable VCs in the UK tend to exit earlier. Buyouts are more established businesses than is the case for early-stage VC-backed investments and are facing less information asymmetry than other IPOs. Given the buyouts' dominance of the UK VC market, the certification hypothesis, therefore, may be less important and venture backing might not be associated with underpricing. Finally, VCs' reputation does not seem to be a statistically significant variable in explaining cross-sectional differences in underpricing.

Long-term financial performance

Irrational strategies by investors and information asymmetry between insiders and investors are some of the theoretical explanations for IPO long-term financial underperformance (see Ibbotson & Ritter, 1995). UK IPO studies highlight the importance of industrial factors (Levis, 1993; Espenlaub et al., 1999), the initial returns (Levis, 1993), the proportion of shares sold by the VC, and the reputation of the VC (Espenlaub et al., 1999) for the long-term financial performance. Studies have examined other variables but results have been less conclusive. Iqbal (1998), for example, found little evidence of a significant relationship between underwriters' and auditors' reputations and long-term performance of UK IPOs.

Holthausen and Larcker (1996) find evidence of significant (mean) positive abnormal share price performance, during the 24-month period after the reverse US L/MBOs.[24] DeGeorge and Zeckhauser (1993) show that a sample of 62 US L/MBOs did not underperform (in terms of share price performance) non-L/MBOs over a two-year period post-IPO. Similarly, Cao and Lerner (2009) find that three- and five-year stock performance of US reverse LBOs is at least as good as that of other IPOs, during 1981–2003. There is, however, a paucity of research on the long-term financial performance of IPOs that arise from buyouts.

Jelic et al. (2005) report a lack of evidence for a significant underperformance of UK buyout IPOs in the long run and find no evidence that VC-backed buyout IPOs perform better than their non-VC-backed counterparts in the long run. The results remain robust after using the matching firm portfolio benchmark and after controlling for sample selection bias. Subsequently, Drathen and Faleiro (2007) report that IPOs originated from LBOs outperform the market as well as non-LBO IPOs. The factor most significantly explaining the superior performance is percentage ownership by the buyout group after the offering. The lack of significant underperformance contradicts the findings reported in UK IPO studies which do not examine buyout IPOs separately (Levis, 1993; Khurshed et al., 1999; Espenlaub et al., 2000). Overall, UK IPOs that arise from buyouts tend to perform better compared to other IPOs.

Financial performance and reputation of PE firms

More reputable intermediaries (VC, PE, and underwriters) are repeatedly involved in IPOs and avoid being associated with failures since they want to maintain their reputation. They should therefore be less likely to overprice IPO issues. Empirical evidence for US IPOs, for example, report a better short-term performance of IPOs sponsored by more prestigious underwriters (Michaely & Wayne, 1994).

Espenlaub et al. (1999), suggest that backing by well-connected UK VC firms with links to issuing houses reduces the need for underpricing but only if those houses are not sponsoring/underwriting the IPOs. Authors also report that UK IPOs backed by captive VCs perform better in the long run compared with IPOs underwritten by independent issuing houses. The long-run performance is also positively related to the reputation of the VC firms. Barnes (2003) provides only weak evidence to suggest greater underpricing for UK IPOs backed by younger VCs, during 1992–1999. Overall, the author reports insufficient evidence to support the grandstanding hypothesis (Gompers, 1996). Jelic et al. (2005) report that VCs' reputation does not play an important role in explaining cross-sectional differences in the underpricing of UK buyout IPOs. The reputation, however, seems to play an important role in long-term performance: buyout IPOs backed by more prestigious VCs performed better than those backed by less prestigious VCs.

One of the challenges for researchers in this area is lack of consensus regarding the best proxy for the reputation of PE and/or firms.[25] For example, the number of deals criterion (on its own) discriminates against some reputable firms specializing only in certain types of deals. On the other hand, the total funding proxy allows a few outliers to disproportionately influence classification. Capital under management and/or total capital available for investment (used in Gompers & Lerner, 1999) and age (used in Stromberg, 2008) are better suited to limited partnerships than to captive PE firms. This is due to the fact that the latter can use the resources and expertise available in parent banks. An additional difficulty in using age is that, until recently, many of the captive PE firms were not legally separated from their parent banks. The question then is whether to use the age of the parent banks or the age of the PE firms (i.e., the number of years since they became a separate legal entity).

There is also some evidence that more reputable PE firms could pick and choose better deals and/or co-investors, thus creating sample selection bias. Recent UK evidence, for example, shows that more reputable PE firms tend to participate in more syndicated deals than the sample average (Jelic, 2011). The most reputable PE firms also exhibit a lower percentage of buyouts ending in liquidation (1%) than their less reputable counterparts (Jelic, 2011). Studies on the association of PE reputation and performance, therefore, should control for the possibility of sample selection bias.

Conclusions: summary of findings, methodological issues, and emerging themes

Buyout exits and longevity

The evidence on UK longevity is presented in Table 27.1. Evidence for UK PE-backed buyouts is in line with the evidence for other countries suggesting a longevity of between three and five years. More recently, the evidence suggests an increase in longevity of PE-backed buyouts (around five years). Non-PE-backed buyouts remain in a buyout form longer than their PE-backed counterparts.

For UK PE investors, IPOs remained a preferred exit route, followed by trade sales. IPOs are more popular with PE-backed than non-PE-backed deals. PE-backed buyouts also tend to go public earlier than their non-PE-backed counterparts. Compared internationally, IPOs were a more popular exit route for UK buyouts than elsewhere (except US). Direct comparison with other routes (e.g., sales) is difficult due to sample bias (focus on large and PE-backed deals) and classification issues (some studies combine sales with SMBOs).

In the aftermath of the second wave SMBOs became increasingly popular. For example, SMBOs increased from 2% (in the 1980s) to 24% of all world buyout transactions in

Table 27.1 UK buyout longevity

Authors	*Period / sample*	*Findings*
Wright et al. (1994)	434 large and small MBOs (exits only), during 1981–1990	Larger and buyouts originating from divestments tend to exit sooner; heterogeneous longevity.
Wright et al. (1995b)	158 exited and non-exited, large PE-backed MBOs/MBIs	Most buyouts exited within three to five years; exits affected by economic conditions; 71% of buyouts privately owned seven years after buyout.
Gottschalg (2007)	Worldwide; early- and late-stage PE-backed deals	Average time to exit of PE-backed buyouts is five years.
Wright et al. (2007)	European, including UK buyouts	Partial sales accounted for one-quarter of total UK exit value in 2005; in continental Europe partial sales accounted for less than one-twentieth of total exit value in 2005.
Stromberg (2008)	Worldwide; PE-backed buyouts, during 1970–2002; 2,229 UK buyouts, including buyouts without data on deal value	Time to exit longer than five years in 58% of cases. Most LBOs are acquisitions of private firms and divisions of other companies. The most common exit routes are trade sales, followed by SBOs. LBOs sponsored by PE investors exit earlier than those without financial sponsors. Deals sponsored by PE funds are more likely to go bankrupt. LBO organization form seems to be a long-run governance structure.
Jelic (2011)	1,089 PE-backed and pure MBOs/MBIs/LBOs/SMBOs, during 1966–2004 (866 exits (including liquidations) and 223 non-exits).	The median time to exit is 36 months. 56% of pure buyouts remained in buyout for at least seven years after the original buyouts. The most popular exit routes are IPOs, followed by sales, SMBOs, and liquidations. PE-backed buyouts show higher exit rates, fewer early (within 12 months) exits, and less liquidation in comparison to pure buyouts. Buyouts backing by PE syndicates tend to have a shorter longevity. Characteristics of buyouts and PE backing, with the stock market and PE market conditions, significantly impact buyouts' longevity.

This table summarizes some of the leading research on buyout longevity in the UK, presenting the sample periods of the papers and highlighting the main findings.

2007 (Stromberg, 2008). By 2011, one in four PE deals in Europe was an SMBO (Smith & Volosovych, 2013). It is, however, still not clear as to what the true motivation for SMBO transactions is and what their overall effect is on performance. A combination of company-level with PE fund-level data could be a promising avenue answering the above question.

One of the difficulties in comparing studies internationally is that some studies report the length of time that buyouts tend to remain in their original buyout structure while others report how long buyouts remain in private ownership (Jelic, 2011). Furthermore, different studies often consider exits over different holding periods. In Table 27.2, we present results that are directly comparable both in terms of methodology and holding periods (table adapted from Jelic, 2011).

Evidence for the duration of PE-backed UK buyouts is comparable to the evidence for European VC-backed deals. For example, the average (mean) time to exit in UK PE-backed subsamples ranges from 3.3 years (Jelic, 2011) to 3.5 years (Nikoskelainen & Wright, 2007). This compares to the average (mean) of 3.7 years reported for European VC-backed deals (Schwienbacher, 2002). The average (mean) duration of PE-backed IPOs (3.25 years as reported in Jelic, 2011) is similar to the average duration reported for VC-backed European deals (3.3 years as reported in Cumming, 2008). The average (mean) duration of UK PE-backed liquidations (4.4 years as reported in Jelic, 2011) is longer compared to the duration of write-offs reported for European VC deals (3.58 years as reported in Cumming, 2008). Finally, the average duration of SMBO exits was 4.3 years (Jelic, 2011). Overall, there is no evidence for "myopic" behavior of UK PE firms. Buyout size, characteristics of PE backing (syndicated and highly leveraged deals) together with market conditions are the most important determinants of longevity (Jelic, 2011). A recent study by Ahmad and Jelic (2014) highlighted the importance of lockup characteristics on the subsequent survival of UK IPOs. An interesting area for further research could be examination of the importance of various contractual clauses and arrangements between investors and managers for the longevity of buyouts.

Some buyouts exit in a relatively short period of time (e.g., up to 24 months), while others remain with their original buyout structure for a very long period of time (e.g., more than seven years). The majority of early exits isare associated with the exit of smaller buyouts on the AIM. There is also evidence that occurrence of early exit (i.e., short-term flipping of assets) has been decreasing since the late 1980s. The evidence suggesting that buyouts represent both long- and short-term form should not be surprising. For example, some firms fail shortly after buyout deals prompting investors to "cull" their investments as soon as possible. Others become targets of acquisitions soon after buyouts. Some companies, however, go through patient restructuring benefiting from concentrated ownership over a long period of time. Overall, more research on pure (non-PE-backed) buyouts is need. The pure buyouts are not constrained to exit within a certain period and thus provide the ultimate test of longevity of this organizational form.

As noted in the literature (Kaplan et al., 2002; Jelic et al., 2005; Ball et al., 2008; Stromberg, 2008), limitations of the alternative databases remain one of the key obstacles for researchers in this area. For example, several databases (with the exception of the CMBOR database) have a specific threshold for size of transaction. Furthermore, some databases (e.g., Thomson One Banker, Capital IQ, and SDC M&A) cover more recent data and/or miss specific items (e.g., enterprise values in Capital IQ). The above-mentioned limitations create issues related to sample selection bias and need to be controlled for. In addition to the above sample selection bias, researchers in this area need to be aware of a potential endogeneity problem related to the possibility that financial intermediaries (PE, VC, underwriters)

Table 27.2 Comparison of longevity and exits from original buyouts, private ownership, and buyout ownership structure

	Longevity	*Exit status/routes*
Panel A: Exits of UK buyouts		
Wright et al.(1993); (1981–1991)	Exits peaked 3–5 yrs	26% exits (7 yrs)
Wright et al. (1994); (1981–1990)	Heterogenous longevity	40% exits
Wright et al. (1995b); (PE-backed 1983–1986)	Heterogenous longevity; exits peaked 3–5 yrs	42% exits; sales (18.4%); IPO (10%); SMBO (3.8%); failed (9.5%); 29% exits from private ownership (7 yrs)
Jelic et al. (2005); (1964–1997)	4 yrs (median 3.33 yrs) –IPO	
Nikoskelainen & Wright (2007); (PE-backed 1995–2004)	3.5 yrs; 2.6 yrs – IPO	IPO (16%); sales (28%); SMBO (18%); failed (38%)
Jelic & Wright (2011); (PE- and non-PE-backed 1980–2009)		IPO (42%; main 35% and AIM 17%); sale (19%); SMBO (18%); liquidation (3%)
Jelic (2011); (PE- and non-PE-backed 1966–2004)	3.75 yrs (median 3 yrs) – all exits; 3.8 yrs – IPO; 3.3 yrs – sale; 4.4 yrs – SMBO; 3.2 yrs – liquidations; 3.6 yrs – private exits (sale & SMBO); PE-backed subsample: 3.3 yrs (median 2.9 yrs) – all exits; 3.25 yrs – IPO; 3 yrs – sale; 4.3 yrs –SMBO; 4.4 yrs – liquidations; non-PE-backed: 4.3 yrs (median 3.7 yrs); 4.8 yrs – IPO; 3.8 yrs – sale; 4.3 yrs – SMBO; 2.9 yrs – liquidations 3.68 yrs in buyout organizational form – all exits (PE-backed subsample: 3.2 yrs; non-PE-backed: 4.3 yrs); 3.69 yrs in private ownership – all exits (PE-backed subsample: 3.2 yrs; non-PE-backed: 4.3 yrs)	65% exits from original buyout structures (70% of PE-backed and 58% of non-PE-backed) (7 yrs); IPO (47%); sales (21%); SMBO (9%); liquidation (3%); PE-backed subsample: IPO (52%); sales (18%); SMBO (11%); liquidation (2%); non-PE-backed: IPO (39%); sales (28%); SMBOs (6%); liquidation (5%); 50% exits from any buyout organizational form (55% of PE-backed; 44% of non-PE-backed) (5 yrs); 53% exits from private ownership (54% of PE-backed; 51% of non-PE-backed) (7 yrs)
Panel B: Buyout exits internationally		
World data; Stromberg (2008) (Predominantly PE-backed 1970–2007)	World – 6–7 yrs (median) in 1980s and 9 yrs during 1995–1999	World – 40% exits (IPO – 13%; sale – 38%; SMBO – 24%; failed – 6%); UK – 67% exits (IPO – 11%; sale –42%; SMBO – 22%; failed – 8%; unknown –10%)

(*Continued*)

Table 27.2 (Continued)

	Longevity	*Exit status/routes*
		World – 55% – exits from LBO organizational form (5 yrs); UK – 59% – exits from LBO organizational form (5 yrs)
US data; Kaplan (1991); (PE-backed 1979–1986)	Exits peaked in yr 4; 6.8 yrs longevity in private ownership	44% exits (7 yr); 38% exits from private ownership (7 yr)
Panel C: VC exits internatioanally		
US data; Cumming & Johan, 2010; (1991–2004)	2.95 yrs – IPO; 3.2 yrs –sale & SMBO; 2.9 yrs write-offs	IPO (35.7%); sale & SMBO (54.6%); write-offs (9.7%)
Canadian data; Cumming & Johan, 2010; (1991–2004)	2.5 yrs – IPO; 4.1 yrs – sale & SMBO; 3.2 yrs –write-offs	IPO (5.85%); sale & SMBO (74.2%); write-offs (19.9%)
World data; Mohamed (2009); (1990–2006)	4.6 yrs – IPO; 5.3 yrs – M&A; 5.9 yrs – write-offs	M&A and IPOs are most the popular exit routes
European data; Cumming (2008); (1995–2005)	3.33 yrs – IPO; 3.38 yrs – sale & SMBO; 3.58 yrs – write-offs	IPOs (17%); sale & SMBO (49%); write-offs (34%)
Australasia data; Cumming et.al., 2006; (1989–2001)	2.8 yrs – IPO; 3.4 yrs – sale & smbo; 4.6 yrs – write-offs	IPO (23%); sale & SMBO (60%); write-offs (17%)
European data; Schwienbacher, 2002; (1990–2001)	3.7 yrs – all exits	IPO (25%); sale & SMBO (54%); write-offs (21%)

This table presents a comparison of results on longevity, exits, and exit routes reported in studies on buyout and studies on PE/VC exits. Evidence for PE-backed buyouts (i.e., late stage investments) comparable to evidence on VC exits, in bold. Source: Jelic (2011).

do not randomly select buyouts they are backing (Cumming & MacIntosh, 2001; Jelic et al., 2005).

Another important methodological issue is related to the use of probit models in samples consisting of exited investments only (see Cochrane, 2005). Unlike probit, survival models consider exited and non-exited buyouts and are therefore better suited to studies on buyout longevity.[26] With the survival models, the important choice is between survival models with constant hazard rates (i.e., non-parametric and semi-parametric) and models that allow hazard to change over time (i.e., parametric models with, for example, Gamma distribution) (see Jelic, 2011).

Post-exit performance

Summary of studies on post-exit operating performance of UK buyouts is presented in Table 27.3 (Panel A). Evidence suggests significant improvement is output, employment, and dividends, while efficiency of buyout IPOs remains unchanged. There is, however, some evidence for negative changes in profitability. Lack of evidence for a deterioration in the operating performance (except profitability) of UK IPOs originated from buyout performance contradicts evidence reported in IPO literature (e.g., Jain & Kini, 1994). There is also

Table 27.3 UK buyouts post-exit performance

Panel A: Post-IPO operating performance

Authors	*Period / sample*	*Findings*
Jelic & Wright (2011)	1,225 buyout IPOs; MBO/MBI/LBO; PE-backed and pure buyouts, during 1980–2009	The buyouts which exited via IPOs outperformed trade sales and SMBOs in terms of IRR; better performance of PE-backed buyouts exiting via IPOs. Buyouts exiting via IPOs experience an improvement in employment and output and a lack of significant changes in efficiency and profitability. IPOs on main market outperform the AIM only in terms of changes in output. AIM IPOs do not experience performance differences between PE-backed and non-PE-backed buyouts.

Panel B: Post-IPO financial performance

Authors	*Period / sample*	*Findings*
Jelic et al. (2005)	167 IPOs of reverse MBO/MBI; PE-backed and pure buyouts, during 1964–1997	PE-backed buyouts are more underpriced than pure buyouts Buyout IPOs do not underperform in the long run. No significant difference between the performances of PE-backed and non-PE-backed buyouts. Buyouts backed by more reputable PE-firms exit earlier and perform better.
Drathen & Faleiro (2007)	128 LBO-backed IPOs and 1,121 non-LBO-backed IPOs, during 1990–2006	The LBO-backed IPOs outperform the market as well as non-LBO-backed IPOs. The factor most significantly explaining the superior performance is percentage ownership by the buyout group after the offering.

This table highlights some contrasting findings on post-exit performance of UK buyouts, in terms of post-IPO operating performance as well as financial performance.

a lack of evidence for superior/inferior performance of PE-backed buyout IPOs (including employment). Operating performance of AIM IPOs does not significantly differ from main LSE IPOs. The lack of differences in performance, therefore, does not lend support to critics of AIM and their listing rules. There is some evidence that second-round investors could still create wealth by improving performance. Given the increasing importance of SMBOs this topic requires more research. Some of the more recent studies (e.g., Zhou et al., 2018) provide a promising avenue for future research in this area by combining agency with the entrepreneurship perspective.

Summary of studies on post-exit financial performance of UK IPOs that arise from buyouts is presented in Table 27.3 (Panel B). In the short run IPOs of PE-backed buyouts tend to be more underpriced than pure buyout IPOs. There is no evidence for difference in underpricing between more and less reputable PE-backed buyout IPOs. Following the IPO, share price is above average stock market performance and the performance of non-buyout IPOs. In the long run, therefore, buyout IPOs do not significantly underperform thus contradicting the evidence reported in IPO literature. Performance of PE-backed buyout IPOs is not different from non-PE-backed buyout IPOs. This raises further questions regarding the extent to which benefits of PE ownership extend once the buyout structure ends. More research on this topic is needed.

US evidence suggests that large PE-backed reverse LBOs perform better than other IPOs (Muscarella & Vetsuypens, 1990; DeGeorge & Zeckhauser, 1993; Holthausen & Larcker, 1996; Cao & Lerner, 2009). UK evidence is scarce but it seems to be in line with the US evidence (Jelic et al. 2005; Drathen & Faleiro, 2007). There is, however, a lack of more recent, post-crisis, evidence on UK buyouts that exit via IPOs.

One of the promising areas for further research is related to the importance of lock-up agreements for the long-term performance of UK buyout IPOs. Evidence from IPO literature shows that UK lock-up/lock-in agreements tend to be less standardized compared to their US counterparts (Espenlaub et al., 2001). The evidence on market reaction to expiry of lock-ups in UK IPOs is inconclusive. While Espenlaub et al. (2012) and Ahmad et al. (2017) report negative but not statistically significant changes in price, Hoque and Lasfer (2009) report highly significant changes in price (−1.85%) during a four-day window around lock-up expiry. Further research might, therefore, usefully examine how the nature of PE involvement in buyout IPOs changes after the lock-up period and the consequences for financial performance. It is plausible that differences in the performance of buyouts could be associated with the length of time PE firms remained locked (i.e., involved) with the portfolio companies. The examination of the performance over a longer period of time (i.e., before and after lock-up expiry) would be in line with the results of some of the key methodological papers (Barber & Lyon, 1996; Lyon et al., 1999).

Overall, buyouts continue to be an important organizational form and their longevity has been increasing over time. Most recently, SMBOs have emerged as a very important exit route (at the expense of IPOs and sales). The research agenda is moving towards SMBOs and comparison of PE- and non-PE-backed buyouts. From a theoretical point of view, complementing agency with entrepreneurship perspective provides the most promising avenue for further research.

Notes

1 We thank participants of the 30th Anniversary Conference of the Centre for Management Buyout Research (CMBOR), at Imperial College London, June 2016, for their helpful comments and suggestions. Victor Murinde also acknowledges funding under the DFID-ESRC Growth Research Programme (ESRC Grant: ES/N013344/1). Every effort was made to include all relevant papers on selected topics; any errors or omissions are unintentional.

2 Source: Preqin, as cited in *The Economist*, October 22, 2016. This compares to $2.5 trillion estimated by TheCityUK for 2010 as well as Cambridge Associates estimates in 2010.

3 Terms PE and VC have no consistently applied definitions. Metrick and Yasuda (2011), for example, treat VC firms and buyout specialists as subsets of the broader PE industry. In the European literature, however, the term venture capital seems to be more inclusive and often includes both late (i.e., investments in buyouts) and early-stage investments (i.e., investments in start-ups). Both European (EVCA) and British Venture Capital (BVCA) associations have venture capital in their titles although their respective memberships are dominated by PE firms. Therefore, when discussing the results of previous studies, we refer to terms used by their authors.
4 We, therefore, do not review literature on public-to-private buyout transactions, performance of PE funds, various corporate governance issues related to buyout transactions, and performance of VC-backed start-ups. For broader survey papers that include these topics see Cumming et al. (2007), Kaplan and Stromberg (2009), Kaplan and Lerner (2010), Metrick and Yasuda (2011), and Gilligan and Wright (2014).
5 Since 1995, there have been over 3,000 AIM listings.
6 This section draws on Jelic (2011).
7 Jelic (2011) adopts a narrower definition of failures, considering only the buyouts that were reported to have ceased trading (i.e., the write-down of a portfolio company's value to zero).
8 LBO partnerships typically combine closed-end equity funds with debt and lead the buyout transactions.
9 The negative association between agency costs and syndication, to some extent, could be alleviated by the reputation of the lead PE firm (Meuleman et al., 2009).
10 Interestingly, it takes longer for PE syndicates to exit buyouts via trade sales.
11 For example, the percentage of syndicated deals reached 52% in 2000s.
12 The UK buyout market was traditionally dominated by manufacturing firms until the 1990s. Since then, service industries have now become the main source of UK buyouts.
13 Industry classification in this study follows that of Gompers et al. (2008) which reclassified numerous industry codes into nine industry groups more in line with well-documented specialization within the VC industry.
14 This section draws on Jelic and Wright (2011).
15 IPO exits are sometimes referred to as reverse LBOs. The term reverse LBOs arose in the US when many LBOs were of listed firms. The term IPO exits, however, is more general and also includes pure buyouts exited from private ownership via IPOs. When discussing the results of previous studies, we refer to the terms used by their authors.
16 The authors also report a decline in PE's board seats after the US IPO exits from 13.6% to 4.9%.
17 Scaling profit by sales rather than total assets can be a better measure of performance after IPO since it avoids the "build up in assets" measurement problem.
18 The evidence is in line with results that document an absence of financial underperformance of PE-backed buyouts going public (Jelic et al., 2005; Cao & Lerner, 2009).
19 Brav and Gompers (1997), for example, report that underperformance tends to be concentrated in smaller, non-PE-backed IPOs.
20 This section draws on Zhou et al. (2014).
21 This section draws on Jelic et al. (2005).
22 The authors explain the results by the certification role of VCs.
23 This is consistent with more recent international evidence on the VC involvement in the IPO process (e.g., Hamao et al., 2000; Francis et al., 2001).
24 Reverse L/MBOs are also known as "secondary IPOs."
25 For more, see Krshnan and Masulis (2010) and Jelic (2011).
26 Exited buyouts contribute the likelihood function via density function while non-exited buyouts contribute via their survival.

References

Achleitner, A. K., & Figge, C. 2011. *Private equity lemons? Evidence on value creation in secondary buyouts*. Working Paper, Technische Universität München.

Ahmad, W., Aussenegg, W., & Jelic, R. 2017. *IPO lock-ups and insider trading*. Working paper. University of Sussex.

Ahmad, W., & Jelic, R. 2014. Lockup agreements and survival of UK IPOs. *Journal of Business Finance and Accounting*, 41: 717–742.

Amess, K., & Wright, M. 2007. The wage and employment effects of LBOs in the UK. *International Journal of Economics and Business*, 14: 179–195.
Amess, K., & Wright, M. 2012. Leveraged buyouts, private equity and jobs. *Small Business Economics*, 38: 419–430.
Axelson, U., Jenkinson, T., Strömberg, P., et al. 2013. Borrow cheap, buy high? The determinants of leverage and pricing in buyouts. *The Journal of Finance*, 68(6): 2223–2267.
Ball, E., Chiu, H-H., & Smith, R. 2008. *Exit choices of venture-backed firms: IPO v. acquisition.* Working Paper. Available at SSRN http://ssrn.com/abstract=1301288.
Barber, B. M., & Lyon, J. D. 1996. Detecting abnormal operating performance: The empirical power and specification of test statistics. *Journal of Financial Economics*, 41: 359–399.
Barnes, E. 2003. Grandstanding in the UK venture capital industry. Working Paper, FMA Conference – Dublin.
Barry, C., Muscarella, C., Peavy, J., & Vetsuypens, M. 1990. The role of venture capital in the creation of public companies: Evidence from the going public process. *Journal of Financial Economics*, 27: 447–471.
Bayar, O., & Chemmanur, T. 2006. *IPOs or acquisitions? A theory of the choice of exit strategy by entrepreneurs and venture capitalists.* Working Paper, Boston College.
Berglof, E. 1994. A control theory of venture capital finance. *Journal of Law, Economics, and Organization*, 10: 247–267.
Black, B., & Gilson, J. 1998. Venture capital and the structure of capital markets: Banks versus stock markets. *Journal of Financial Economics*, 47: 243–277.
Bonini, S. 2010. *Secondary buy-outs.* Paper presented at the EFM Symposium on Private Equity, Montreal.
Brau, J., Francis, B., & Kohers, N. 2003. The choice of IPO versus takeover: Empirical evidence. *The Journal of Business*, 76: 583–612.
Brav, A., & Gompers, P. A. 1997. Myth or reality? The long-run underperformance of initial public offerings: Evidence from venture and nonventure capital-backed companies. *Journal of Finance*, 52: 1791–1821.
British Venture Capital Association (BVCA). 2000. *Private equity: The new asset class.* London: BVCA.
Cao, J. X., & Lerner, J. 2009. The performance of reverse leveraged buyouts. *Journal of Financial Economics*, 91: 139–157.
Cochrane, J. 2005. The risk and return to venture capital. *Journal of Financial Economics*, 75: 3–52.
Cumming, D., Siegel, D. S., & Wright, M. 2007. Private equity, leveraged buy-outs and governance. *Journal of Corporate Finance*, 13: 439–460.
Cumming, D. J. 2006. Adverse selection and capital structure: Evidence from venture capital. *Entrepreneurship Theory and Practice*, 30: 155–183.
Cumming, D. J. 2008. Contracts and exits in venture capital finance. *Review of Financial Studies*, 21: 1947–1982.
Cumming, D. J., & Fleming, G. 2012. *Barbarians, demons and hagetaka: A financial history of leveraged buyouts in Asia 1980–2010.* Working paper. Available at: http://ssrn.com/abstract=2008513.
Cumming, D. J., & Johan, S. 2010. Venture capital investment duration. *Journal of Small Business Management*, 48: 228–257.
Cumming, D. J., & MacIntosh, J. G. 2001. Venture capital investment duration in Canada and the United States. *Journal of Multinational Financial Management*, 11: 445–463.
Cumming, D. J., & Walz, U. 2010. Private equity returns and disclosure around the world. *Journal of International Business Studies*, 41: 727–754.
DeGeorge, F., & Zeckhauser, R. 1993. The reverse LBO decision and firm performance: Theory and evidence. *Journal of Finance*, 48: 1323–1349.
Drathen, C. V., & Faleiro, F. 2007. *The performance of leveraged buyout-backed initial public offerings in UK.* Working Paper, London Business School.
Espenlaub, S., Garrett, I., & Mun, W. P. 1999. Conflicts of interest and the performance of venture-capital-backed IPOs: A preliminary look at the UK. *Venture Capital: An International Journal of Entrepreneurial Finance*, 1: 325–350.
Espenlaub, S., Goergen, M., & Khurshed, A. 2001. IPO lock-in agreements in the UK. *Journal of Business Finance and Accounting*, 28: 1235–1278.

Espenlaub, S., Gregory, A., & Tonks, I. 2000. Re-assessing the long-term underperformance of UK initial public offerings. *European Financial Management*, 6: 319–342.
Espenlaub, S., Khurshed, A., & Mohamed, A. 2012. IPO survival in a reputational market. *Journal of Business Finance and Accounting*, 39: 427–463.
EVCA. 1995/2001. *EVCA Yearbooks*. Zaventem, Belgium: European Venture Capital Association.
Francis, B. B., Hasan, I., & Hu, C. 2001. The underpricing of venture and non-venture capital IPOs: An empirical investigation. *Journal of Financial Services Research*, 19: 99–113.
Gailen, H., & Vetsuypens, M. R. 1989. Management buyouts of divisions and shareholder wealth. *Journal of Finance*, 44: 953–970.
Gilligan, J., & Wright, M. 2014. *Private equity demystified – An explanatory guide, 3rd edition.* London: ICAEW.
Giot, P., & Schwienbacher, A. 2007. IPOs, trade sales and liquidations: Modelling venture capital exits using survival analysis. *Journal of Banking and Finance*, 31: 679–702.
Gompers, P. A. 1996. Grandstanding in the venture capital industry. *Journal of Financial Economics*, 42: 133–156.
Gompers, P. A., Kovner, A., Lerner, J., & Scharfstein, D. 2008. Venture capital investment cycles: The impact of public markets. *Journal of Financial Economics*, 87: 1–23.
Gompers P. A., & Lerner, J. 1999. *The venture capital cycle.* Cambridge, MA: MIT Press.
Gottschalg, O. 2007. *Private equity and leveraged buyouts*. Study IP/A/ECON/IC/2007-25, European Parliament, Policy Department: Economic and Scientific Policy.
Hamao, Y., Packer, F., & Ritter, J. 2000. Institutional affiliation and the role of venture capital: Evidence from initial public offerings in Japan. *Pacific Basin Finance Journal*, 8: 529–558.
Holthausen, D., & Larcker, D. 1996. The financial performance of reverse leveraged buy-outs. *Journal of Financial Economics*, 42: 293–332.
Hoque, H., & Lasfer, M. 2009. *Insider trading before IPO lockup expiry dates: The UK evidence.* Working paper. Cass Business School.
Ibbotson, R. G., & Ritter, J. R. 1995. Initial public offerings. In R. Jarrow et al. (Eds.), *Handbook in OR and MS*, 9: 993–1016. Amsterdam: Elsevier Science.
Iqbal, A. 1998. *Initial public offerings performance and financial agents' reputation: The UK evidence.* Unpublished MA dissertation, Manchester School of Accounting and Finance.
Ireland, R. D., Hitt, M. A., & Sirmon, D. G. 2003. A model of strategic entrepreneurship: the construct and its dimensions. *Journal of Management*, 29: 963–989.
Jain, B. A., and Kini, O. 1994. The post issue operating performance of IPO firms. *Journal of Finance*, 49: 1699–1726.
Jelic, R. 2011. Staying power of UK buyouts. *Journal of Business Finance and Accounting*, 38: 945–986.
Jelic, R., Saadouni, B., & Wright, M. 2005. Performance of private to public MBOs: The role of venture capital. *Journal of Business Finance and Accounting*, 32: 643–681.
Jelic, R., & Wright, M. 2011. Exit, performance, and late stage capital: The case of UK management buyouts. *European Financial Management*, 17: 560–593.
Jensen, M. C. 1989. Eclipse of the public corporation. *Harvard Business Review*, Sept/Oct: 61–75.
Jensen, M. C., & Meckling, W. H. 1976. Theory of the firm: Managerial behavior, agency costs and ownership structure. *Journal of Financial Economics*, 3: 305–360.
Kaplan, S. 1991. The staying power of leveraged buyouts. *Journal of Financial Economics*, 29: 287–314.
Kaplan, S., & Lerner, J. 2010. It ain't broke: The past, present, and future of venture capital. *Journal of Applied Corporate Finance*, 22: 36–47.
Kaplan, S., Sensoy, B., & Stromberg, P. 2002. *How well do venture capital databases reflect actual investments?* Working Paper, University of Chicago.
Kaplan, S., & Stromberg, P. 2009. Leveraged buyouts and private equity. *Journal of Economic Perspectives*, 23: 121–146.
Khurshed, A., Mudambi, R., & Goergen, M. 1999. *On the long run performance of IPOs.* Working Paper, Case Western Reserve University.
Khurshed, A., Paleari, S., & Vismara, S. 2005. *The operating performance of initial public offerings.* Working-Paper, University of Manchester and University of Bergamo.
Krshnan, C. N. V., & Masulis, R. W. 2010. Venture capital reputation. In D. J. Cumming (Ed.), *Handbook on entrepreneurial finance, venture capital and private equity.* Oxford, UK: Oxford University Press.

Lerner, J. 1994. Venture capitalists and the decision to go public. *Journal of Financial Economics*, 35: 293–316.
Levis, M. 1993. The long-run performance of initial public offerings: The UK experience 1980–1988. *Financial Management*, 22: 28–41.
Lin, T. H., & Smith, R. L. 1998. Insider reputation and selling decisions: The unwinding of venture capital investments during equity IPOs. *Journal of Corporate Finance*, 4: 241–263.
Ljungqvist, A. P. 1999. *IPO underpricing, wealth losses and the curious role of venture capitalists in creation of public companies.* Working Paper, Oxford University.
Lowry, M., & Schwert, G. W. 2002. IPO market cycles: Bubbles or sequential learning? *Journal of Finance*, 57: 1171–1198.
Lyon, J. D., Barber, B. M., Tsai, C.-L. 1999. Improved methods for tests of long-run abnormal stock returns. *Journal of Finance*, 54: 165–201.
Megginson, W., & Weiss, K. 1991. Venture capitalist certification in initial public Offerings. *Journal of Finance*, 46: 879–903.
Metrick, A., & Yasuda, A. 2011. Venture capital and other private equity: A survey. *European Financial Management*, 17: 619–654.
Meuleman, M., Amess, K., Wright, M., & Scholes, L. 2009. Agency, strategic entrepreneurship and the performance of private equity backed buyouts. *Entrepreneurship Theory and Practice*, 33: 213–240.
Michaely, R., & Wayne, H. S. 1994. The pricing of initial public offerings: Tests of adverse selection and signalling theories. *The Review of Financial Studies*, 7: 279–319.
Mikkelson, W. H., Partch, M. M., & Shah, K. 1997. Ownership and operating performance of companies that go public. *Journal of Financial Economics*, 44: 281–307.
Mohamed, A. 2009. *Analytics and empirical studies of IPO survivals and venture capital activities.* PhD Thesis, University of Manchester.
Muscarella, C., & Vetsuypens, M. 1990. Efficiency and organisational structure: A study of reverse LBOs. *Journal of Finance*, 45: 1389–1413.
Nikoskelainen, E., & Wright, M. 2007. The impact of corporate governance mechanisms on value increase in leveraged buy-outs. *Journal of Corporate Finance*, 13: 511–537.
Poulsen, A., & Stegemoller, M. 2008. Selling out to public firms vs. initial public offerings. *Financial Management*, 37: 81–101.
Renneboog, L., Simons, T., & Wright, M. 2005. *Leveraged public to private transactions in the UK.* Working Paper, European Corporate Governance Institute.
Ronstadt, R. 1986. Exit stale left: Why entrepreneurs end their entrepreneurial careers before retirement. *Journal of Business Venturing*, 1: 323–338.
Sahlman, W. A. 1990. The structure and governance of venture-capital organizations. *Journal of Financial Economics*, 27: 473–521.
Schwienbacher, A. 2002. *Venture capital exits in Europe and the United States.* Working Paper, University of Amsterdam.
Smith, H. T., & Volosovych, V. 2013. *Secondary buyout waves*. Working paper Erasmus University Rotterdam.
Stoughton, N. M., Wong, K. P., & Zechner, J. 2001. IPOs and Product Quality. *Journal of Business*, 74: 375–408.
Stromberg, P. 2008. The new demography of private equity. In J. Lerner, & A. Gurung (Eds.), *The global impact of private equity report 2008, globalization and alternative investments*, Working Papers, World Economic Forum, Vol. 1, pp. 3–26.
TheCityUK. 2010. *Private Equity 2010.*
Treasury Select Committee (TSC). 2010. *Private equity: Tenth report of session 2006–07*, HC567-1, Vol. 1.
Wang, Y. D. 2011. *Secondary buyouts: Why buy and at what price?* Working Paper, California State University.
Wiersema, M., & Liebeskind, J. 1995. The effects of leveraged buyouts on corporate growth and diversification in large firms. *Strategic Management Journal*, 16: 447–460.
Wright, M., Hoskisson, R., Busenitz, L., & Dial, J. 2000. Entrepreneurial growth through privatisation: The upside of management buy-outs. *Academy of Management Review*, 25: 591–601.
Wright, M., Robbie, K., Romanet, Y., & Thompson, S. 1995a. Managerial ownership and succession and corporate restructuring: The case of management buy-ins. *Journal of Management Studies*, 32: 527–550.

Wright, M., Robbie, K., Romanet, Y., Thompson, S., Joachimsson, R., Bruining, H., & Herst, A. 1993. Harvesting and the longevity of management buy-outs and buy-ins: A four country study. *Entrepreneurship Theory and Practice*, 18: 90–109.

Wright, M., Robbie, K., Thompson, S., & Starkey, K. 1994. Longevity and the life cycle of MBOs. *Strategic Management Journal*, 15: 215–227.

Wright, M., Thompson, S., Robbie, K., & Wong, P. 1995b. Management buy-outs in the short and long term. *Journal of Business Finance and Accounting*, 22: 461–482.

Wright, M., Weir, C., & Burrows, A. 2007. Irrevocable commitments and going private. *European Financial Management*, 13: 745–763.

Xuan, T. 2007. *The role of venture capital syndication in value creation for entrepreneurial firms.* Working Paper, SSRN; 954188.

Zhou, D. R., Jelic, R., & Wright, M. 2014. SMBO: Buying time or improving performance? *Journal of Managerial and Decision Economics*, 35: 88–102.

Zhou, D. R., Jelic, R., & Wright, M. 2018. Sustaining the buyout governance model: Inside secondary management buyout boards. *British Journal of Management*, forthcoming.

28

DISTRESS, FAILURE, AND RECOVERY IN PRIVATE EQUITY BUYOUTS

Nick Wilson

Introduction

This chapter examines the evidence in relation to private equity (PE) involvement in buyout activity and the influence of PE ownership on the risks and severity of financial distress (debt default) and failure (insolvency, bankruptcy) among their portfolio firms. We discuss whether companies acquired through PE buyouts are more likely to default on their debt obligations or enter legal insolvency processes than other firms.

Early work on modeling financial health in the corporate sector (Altman, 1968) confirmed that relatively high leverage in firms is associated with an increased risk of financial distress and the likelihood of bankruptcy. This is the case when firms fail to generate sufficient profit and cash flow to cover the regular interest payments associated with their debt obligations. In consequence creditors take (legal) action to recover their funds that can result in the winding up or liquidation of the company or the sale and restructuring of the company's assets. In either event the existing shareholders lose both control and some or all of their investment. Of course, such action precipitates wider economic and social costs (e.g., employment). PE-backed buyouts often involve high debt levels secured against the target company's assets as part of the process of both ownership change and as a means of monitoring management and changing incentives. PE investors acquire their "portfolio companies" with equity provided by the PE investors and debt capital (bank loans, bonds holders, mezzanine finance). Leveraged buyouts (LBOs) of large companies and/or delistings are particular examples of buyouts that result in a capital structure involving significant use of debt capital and investment grade bond issuance. LBOs have been a particular feature of the US buyout market.

Some commentators and analysts have raised concerns around the susceptibility of PE-backed buyouts to defaults, consequent lender losses, and insolvency due to "over-leverage," i.e., levels of debt that become burdensome or unsustainable. Although PE investors often target underperforming firms, as we will discuss, their aim is to implement changes and investments to generate sufficient profits, cash, and productivity necessary to meet debt obligations and ultimately return value to investors on PE exit. However, how these firms might perform during downturns raised concerns among analysts and policy makers, particularly during the onset of the 2008 financial crisis and consequent recession. For instance the Boston Consulting Group (2008) analyzed a sample of 328 PE-backed companies and found that 60%

were trading at "distressed levels." The study predicted, at this time, that half of the world's PE-backed companies would default within three years. In the vagaries of this recession, the study offered no comparable evidence for other company types. Moreover, and as we discuss later, these predictions did not materialize and it is interesting to understand why.

Another study of the US market, released by Moody's (see Thomas, 2010), suggested that larger PE acquisitions were defaulting at a higher rate than comparable public companies. In the UK, it was suggested, that because of the large number of PE deals in the mid 2000s PE investments could potentially increase financial fragility in the economy. The PE portfolio firms had issued bonds due to mature in 2014–2015. Indeed the Bank of England (2013) went further and pointed out that the risk of default and PE buyout failures posed a threat to the stability of the financial system, a risk that was compounded, in the post-crisis period by the need for PE companies "to refinance a cluster of buyout debt maturing in an environment of much tighter credit conditions" (Bank of England Quarterly Bulletin, 2013Q1). Again the evidence for this proposition has not appeared post-2015. PE investment activity has been linked to macro-economic stability in other studies. Analysts of the macro-economy have pointed out that PE investment activity is cyclical (Axelson et al., 2013) with PE fund raising and deal values increasing during financial boom times. This again raises two major concerns. First, does the pressure on PE investors to complete deals during boom periods lead to poor investment decisions, e.g., the selection of low quality target firms with an increased likelihood of failure? Do the PE investors "overstretch" themselves and fail to introduce the necessary changes in organization structure and strategy required to secure growth and profitability among their portfolio firms? Second, the cyclical nature of PE investment may, it has been suggested, exacerbate any shocks to the financial sector and the dynamics of boom and bust cycles. Is this the case or are PE-backed companies *more* resilient in downturns and can they therefore play a stabilizing role? The chapter seeks to understand and evidence these alternative considerations.

Evaluating the impact of a change of ownership and governance on firm-level performance is not without its challenges. Of relevance in an evaluation of financial distress or insolvency risk for this subsample (PE portfolio firms) of the corporate population is the type and source of the buyout and the context. Buyouts encompass a wide range of company types, including "corporate unbundling," i.e., the divestment of subsidiaries or large companies that may be domestically owned or international; the privatization of public assets; the transfer of ownership of family or owner-managed businesses; and the transfer of ownership of listed companies to private ownership (delisting) This latter activity gave rise to the term "leveraged buyout" and has involved some well publicized "mega-deals" involving high leverage, primarily in the US sector.

As suggested earlier, in most cases PE investors target *potentially* profitable firms for acquisition and/or firms where they believe that value can be added, created, and result in capital gain. At the time of buyout and pre-buyout they are likely to be "underperforming" (Wilson & Wright, 2013). Moreover, PE has played a role in the buyout and restructuring of companies in difficulty including financially distressed firms and/or firms that have already entered the legal insolvency process (Chapter 11, Administration, Receivership in the US). Wright et al. (1998) point out that the early UK buyout market involved transactions of companies that were already in receivership. Thus PE portfolio companies are often at the higher end of the risk spectrum pre-buyout and in relation to comparable companies. Thus it is important to assess the financial position, cash flow, and leverage of the target company pre-buyout when evaluating post-buyout performance. PE investors are often "active owners" and work with existing management (MBOs) or effect new management regimes (MBIs).

The PE firm will usually appoint board members (directors) and monitor management closely (and/or structure incentives to overcome agency problems) in order to implement their strategic objectives, i.e., policies, practices, investments in capital, technology, and operational improvements. Although PE sponsors are known for increasing leverage in their portfolio firms, this should be placed in the context of pre-buyout leverage, the ability of the firm to cover interest payments, the relative price of debt, and the firm's (sponsors) propensity to adjust capital structure if and when required. Moreover, debt finance is seen as part of the mechanism that owners use to discipline management.

In assessing the outcomes of PE involvement in buyouts, the extent of active involvement by the PE sponsors in the company post-investment and their experience and expertise are of particular interest as the PE sector has been developing since the late 1980s. Moreover, the extant evidence from which we base our evaluation emanates from different countries and legal regimes and cuts across industry sectors, company size, risk, and maturity (age). As mentioned earlier, PE buyout deals occur at different stages of the macro-economic and credit cycle. Evaluation of post-buyout performance requires comparisons and counterfactuals.

PE target companies

What types of company do PE investors target for acquisition? In order to evaluate the impact of PE ownership and governance on firm-level financial distress and failure, it is necessary to take account of the financial and economic health of the company at the time of the buyout transaction; in other words, the *prior probability* of distress and failure. Indeed, an investor that aims to add value to their investment will likely acquire firms that are in need of capital and/or restructuring in order to manifest their potential.

There are only a few studies that examine the characteristics of PE target companies and their performance pre-acquisition. Borell and Tykvova (2012) in a comprehensive study of European-based firms provide some evidence on the buyout targets of PE investors. The authors distinguish between "syndicated" and "non-syndicated investments" as important in assessing targets and portfolio firm outcomes. They suggest that the syndication pattern and investor experience determine the choice of buyout targets. The authors argue that syndicates are "better able to manage high risks arising from investments in highly financially constrained companies than stand-alone investors" (2012: 5). This is because syndicates of investors are better informed (have wider networks) and have a synergistic combination of skills to bring to the target firm. This leads to better target selection, effective monitoring of the investee, and high quality support for the company during the investment stages. All these factors, the authors suggest, reduce the risk of distress and bankruptcy. Analyzing their sample of PE targets, they report that:

> [b]uyouts are significantly larger and older than non-buyout companies. Moreover, buyout companies have a median leverage of 57% and ROA of 5.72% in the years before the transaction. In contrast, firms which did not experience a buyout transaction show a significantly higher median leverage of nearly 65% and a lower ROA of 2.1%.
>
> *(2012: 11)*

The implication is that the buyout targets are able to bear an increase in leverage from their starting position.

Wilson and Wright (2013) in a study of the population of private and listed companies in the UK from 1995–2010 examine the subsample of all known UK buyouts. The buyout companies are identified within the population and tracked pre-buyout and post-buyout. The data on buyouts has over 25,000 company-year observations and 1,179 instances of buyouts that enter into an insolvency process. The data set includes three years of pre-buyout data for buyout subsamples and PE-backed buyouts are identified as a subpopulation of all buyouts and buyins. The authors report an analysis of the pre-buyout characteristics focusing on PE targets. The characteristics of PE-backed targets are compared with non-backed buyouts and a large control sample of non-buyouts matched by year, sector, age, and size. The authors estimate a panel logit model determining the probability of PE-backed buyout compared to the control samples. Within the buyout population, it is reported that PE sponsors select larger buyouts with better profitability and cash generation. PE targets are less likely to have problems with short-term debt but are more likely to have some debt and creditor charges on assets. Compared to the non-buyout population PE targets have stronger cash flow. The authors suggest that PE-backed firms benefit from refinancing and are in a better position to service debt from cash flow, i.e., "we find that PE investors target underperforming companies with better prospects in terms of profit and cash generation" (2013: 988).

It is interesting to examine whether the characteristics of PE investor target companies has changed over time. In an updated study the authors (2016) re-estimate the PE target models using an extended sample to 2013. The purpose of this analysis is to profile the characteristics of PE target companies compared to a control group of matched firms and non-PE buyouts during the whole time period and for sub-periods: 1995–2001, 2002–2008, and 2009–2013. The period 1995–2001 was relatively turbulent, with recovery from the early 1990s recession and the dot.com boom and its aftermath. In contrast, the period from 2002, with the exception of a short recession, was a stable period of low insolvency across all sectors and was also marked by growth in the buyout market culminating in a peak in 2007, before the credit crisis and recession of 2009 onwards. The authors examine whether there is a change in the characteristics of the target companies over these periods. In summary the authors report that PE targets tend to be established companies in terms of age and size and are more likely to have a higher proportion of tangible assets. The targets are in stable industry sectors with a lower than average failure rate and are less likely to be diversified (single product). Among the riskier sectors, PE investors have a preference for advanced manufacturing technologies and the high-tech end of the services sector. The firms that PE investors target are generally cash generative, profitable, and have high interest coverage ratios on existing debt. Confirming the earlier study the target firms are likely to have borrowed and have charges on assets. These firms have lower levels of equity and lower than average productivity thus providing opportunities for investors to realize performance improvement and growth post-investment. The authors do not detect much change in the profiles of targets across the time periods other than within the evolving industry sectors (high-tech and knowledge intensive sectors).

Portfolio company performance post-buyout

Although this chapter examines the evidence on financial distress among PE portfolio companies, evidence on the drivers of post-buyout performance has relevance for our discussion. There are many studies which show that buyouts generally have a positive effect on profitability and growth (Cumming et al., 2007). Moreover, PE-backed buyouts perform comparably well post-buyout and this evidence is discussed elsewhere in this volume (see Alperovych, this volume). Nonetheless, there is some evidence that the failure rates of buyouts in terms of entering formal bankruptcy proceedings increase in times of market peaks. This is particularly the case in the early years of buyout activity. Toms et al. (2015) find that "PE experiments" in the period prior to 1980, "either failed disastrously, in the absence of both resource-based investment and governance skills, or were only partially successful due to limited resource base and a 'hands off' approach to monitoring from the investor" (2015: 753). They argue that the pre-1980 institutional and regulatory climate, "by emphasizing creditor protection and capital maintenance not only stifled capital restructuring, but also failed to prevent fraud at the expense of creditors and minorities" (2015: 753). In the second phase that was characterized by corporate unbundling, i.e., divestment and downsizing, PE investments typically involved performance improvements through cost-cutting and efficiency improvements. Wilson et al. (1996) analyzed survey data and financial records of buyouts completed during 1982–1924 and tracked them over a five-year period. The sample comprised a matched sample of 110 buyouts of which 53 had entered receivership within the time frame. A second sample of 120 buyouts completed in 1983–1985 was tracked to 1993. The purpose was to analyze the characteristics of failures compared to survivors. The survey data comprised a rich range of variables dealing with the initial transaction characteristics of the buyout, management team, their motivations and experience, and details of the financial transaction. Their evidence was consistent with the view that mechanisms introduced to deal with agency cost problems, particularly managerial incentives, are associated with a lower probability of failure. Consistent with agency cost arguments, variables measuring the taking of restructuring action at the time of the buyout reduced the probability of failure, while delay in taking such actions was positively associated with failure.

Toms et al. (2015) report that:

> [i]n the third period, when much of the corporate restructuring of the 1980/1990s had been completed, there was a shift in emphasis towards both efficiency improvements and growth seeking, with private equity executives' human capital governance resources involving more strategic value adding skills, especially for private equity firms with long experience.

CMBOR (2014) report that about 15% of PE-backed buyouts completed during the mid-1990s failed by the end of 2008, while around 25% of those completed during the first peak of buyout activity in the 1980s went bankrupt. Of course not all of these were PE-backed firms. What is the evidence relating to financial distress among PE portfolio firms?

Portfolio companies and financial distress: empirical evidence

In analyzing corporate outcomes it is, of course, necessary to have an outcome definition. The terms financial distress, default, insolvency, and bankruptcy are often used interchangeably or are seen as escalating states of financial difficulty with the end stage being company closure and liquidation. The latter is usually described by juridical definitions such as bankruptcy, administration, Chapter 11, etc. A company that enters a formal (legal) bankruptcy procedure incurs losses for investors and other creditors, owners lose control over assets, and there are clear economic (e.g., job losses), reputational (investor confidence in the PE firm), and social costs. Financial distress, on the other hand, is a state that may involve or require financial restructuring (i.e., renegotiating the debt finance) for survival, but the company may be able to recover without disruption to the company's productive activities and without much reputational loss for the PE sponsor. In analyzing financial distress in PE-backed companies we need to be mindful of these definitions. Indeed the reports on default rates cited earlier (BCG, Moody's) were criticized for "developing new and expansive definitions of what constitutes default" (Thomas, 2010: 1). Including "debt renegotiation" with creditors as financial distress may not be appropriate since one of the cited strengths of PE investors is that they are able to use their networks and bargaining power to adjust the capital structure of their portfolio firms if required as a means of securing the firm's future. In a survey of relevant studies Thomas (2010) concludes that:

> [w]hile the credit performance of private equity-backed companies deserves ongoing scrutiny, the data to-date support the contention that the changes in organizational structure and strategy introduced by private equity investors reduce the incidence of default. Claims to the contrary either rely on misleading data, or involve speculation about future default rates that have no historical analogue.
>
> *(2010: 13)*

Many of the early studies of financial distress among PE portfolio companies emanate from the US market. Jensen (1989) contended that, "LBOs do get into financial trouble more frequently than public corporations do. But few LBOs ever enter formal bankruptcy. They are reorganized quickly (a few months is common), often under new management, and at much lower costs than under a court-supervised process" (1989: 24). In further studies the focus has been on the larger PE-backed companies that have debt financing and have issued bonds. The default rate on these bonds can then be compared with the default rate generally on investment grade corporate bonds. Kaplan and Stein (1993) in an early study demonstrated the cyclicality of default and bankruptcy rates. In a relatively small sample the authors analyzed US MBOs in two time periods. In the period 1980–1984 they looked at 41 buyout transactions and reported a low incidence of default (one firm defaulted, 0.41% rate). The analysis of a second period 1985–1989 showed that out of 83 companies 22 defaulted and 9 went into bankruptcy proceedings. In these early waves of buyout activity, the default rate on acquisitions completed during the second half of the 1980s was the highest of any period on record. It has been argued that PE investments were overvalued on acquisition, debt levels were too high, and incentive structures were poorly designed and implemented during this early phase of PE activity. The nascent PE investors lacked experience. The Bank for International Settlements (BIS, 2008) reported a study of PE investments. The BIS studied 650 PE-backed businesses that were acquired over different time periods: 1982–1986, 1987–1991, 1992–1996, 1997–2001, and 2002–2006. They undertook a matching exercise to compare each PE-backed company with up to five public firms in the same industry and size band. BIS confirmed higher leverage for PE companies but found that "default rates have not been consistently higher than those of similar publicly traded firms." The highest default rate observed for portfolio companies was 3.84% in 1997–2001, and this was lower than the default rate for the public company comparators (4.03%) in the same period.

A study by Kaplan and Strömberg (2009) examined a larger sample of 17,171 buyouts from the global population of PE transactions in the period 1970–2007. This analysis found that only 6% of deals resulted in some form of restructuring or bankruptcy, i.e., ended in bankruptcy or reorganization. The authors report that, taking account of the average holding period of six years, the annual default rate was 1.2% and lower than the average default rate on US corporate bonds (1.6%). Moreover, the authors pointed out that PE-backed firms that have periods of financial difficulty tend to be able to avoid formal bankruptcy (Jensen, 1989).

Chapman and Klein (2009) focus on data related to 288 mid-market buyouts in the period 1984–2006. The average deal value was $78.3 million (largest transaction $4 billion). The PE investors typically had equity contributions of around 35%. A total of 35 companies in the sample defaulted (default rate of 2.66%). In the US, Guo et al. (2011) analyze a sample of 192 businesses acquired by PE investors from 1990 to 2006. Of these acquisitions, 23 ended in some type of default. The default rate was deemed to be around 3.14% based on the average holding period. On analyzing the breakdown of these defaults, 14 were bankruptcy filings and 2 were voluntary restructurings. The remaining seven defaults are assumed to be missed payments or voluntary restructurings. These authors report that most defaults are "prepackaged" bankruptcies. In these cases senior creditors take control of the firm whereas the PE investors lose their investment. The costs of the bankruptcy are therefore low in terms of there being "minimum disruption to the company." This is important in that it distinguishes "financial" from "economic" distress. Economic distress refers to situations where the portfolio company default results in employment loss or layoffs, the closing down of facilities, and/or the liquidation of assets via sale or receivership. Kaplan and Andrade (1998) argued that a company where default arises because the company has an unsustainable capital structure has more chance of recovery to a healthy condition than a company that defaults because of a drop in revenue due to increased competition, unmatched technological changes, or an outdated business model

Demiroglu and James (2010) examined deals that involved "reputable private equity groups" and concluded that these firms are less likely to exhibit financial distress within five years following the transaction. The authors have a sample of 180 US public-to-private LBOs between 1997 and 2007. They find that before 2001 "ten buyout firms filed for bankruptcy and three firms violated financial covenants but later received waivers." In the later period, two firms experienced financial distress, one filed for bankruptcy, and one experienced "technical defaults." The annualized default rate was less than 2% for this sample. These authors point to PE investor experience as a vital determinant of the survival of portfolio companies.

The US studies focus primarily on financial distress as an outcome, i.e., default of bonds and loans, whereas studies of the European buyout market, where there are fewer bond issues as part of the portfolio firm financing, focus on bankruptcy as the outcome variable. A study of 839 French LBO deals' failure rate of PE-backed and non-PE-backed from 1994–2004 (Boucly et al., 2011) found no significant increase in bankruptcy rates post-buyout as compared to a control sample. The authors found that 6.67% of buyouts and 6.7% of the control sample become bankrupt at some point. Moreover 4.17% of buyouts and 4.58% of the control become bankrupt within the three years after the PE transaction. Thus when compared with non-buyouts there is little difference in the company failure rate. In recent years more evidence has been amassed on the post-buyout fortunes of PE-backed buyouts.

Borell and Tykvova (2012) investigated the relative incidence of financial distress and bankruptcy in European buyout companies using data on buyouts and comparable non-buyout firms. The study is comprehensive in that it examines all buyout transactions covering 15 countries in the pre-crisis period 2000–2008. Of particular importance is how PE "experience" is both a determinant of the choice of company targets and is a factor in reducing the risk of bankruptcy ex post. In particular, as discussed earlier, PE investors select firms that are less financially constrained than comparable companies. Borell and Tykvova (2012) suggest that, "after the buyout, in particular when the buyout takes place under favorable debt market conditions, private equity investors tighten the companies' financial constraints. However, this tightening does not raise mortality rates over those of comparable non-buyout companies" (2012: 21). The balance of their analysis points to the conclusion that PE-backed companies do not exhibit financial distress or higher failure rates than their comparators. Although the authors suggest that the "distress risk" of buyout companies increases post-buyout, it does not exceed that of comparable non-buyout companies. As mentioned, the important intervening variable is "private equity experience." Inexperienced PE investors, the authors find, do not fare as well in managing their acquisitions through the restructuring process and into growth/stability and particularly in downturns. The authors argue that experienced PE investors are more adept at managing distress risk due to better target selection, negotiation skills, information, and value-adding abilities. They suggest that PE sponsors, committed to protect their reputation with investors and financial institutions, react faster and more effectively to deal with financial problems. This may involve using their influence and bargaining strength to renegotiate loans and covenants to more favorable terms. They find that "only inexperienced PE investors seem to increase mortality rates" (2012: 21). There is evidence that PE sponsors, over the time period under study, developed particular specialisms based on type of firm, e.g., industry sector, technology, divestments, turnaround, or distressed acquisitions (Wilson & Wright, 2013).

A number of other studies emphasize the role of investor experience when analyzing the outcomes of PE-backed companies. PE experience has a bearing on the implementation of investment and change post-transaction. Meuleman et al. (2009) suggest that experienced investors have superior selection skills and better information (reduced informational asymmetry) making them better equipped to be able to identify potentially high-performing companies. The authors find that PE investors look to stable industry sectors and find companies with lower variances in revenues, profits, and cash flow. The authors also point to the benefits of active ownership and PE roles in effecting organizational and strategic changes, monitoring, reducing costs, and stimulating growth. PE investors have informed networks and long-term relationships with banks. PE portfolio companies are therefore better placed to withstand economic downturns. Later studies are able to track PE portfolio companies through two economic cycles and the post-2008 crisis/global recession.

Wilson et al. (2012) examine a longitudinal panel of all UK PE-backed companies from 1995–2010 in order to assess their relative performance. The time period under study incorporates the recovery from the early 1990s recession, a minor downturn during 2000 and 2003 as well as the global recessionary period of 2008–2010. The analysis demonstrates that PE-backed buyouts experienced higher profitability, productivity, and growth relative to comparable non-buyout companies. The study does not model bankruptcy as an outcome but does provide strong evidence that the PE portfolio companies weather recession well relative to other companies and have a lower likelihood of failure. The authors provide evidence contrary to the conjecture that PE-backed buyouts would be more vulnerable in downturns, relative to comparable businesses, given their higher leverage. Indeed the authors conclude that "during the severe global recession PE-backed buyouts experienced higher growth, productivity and profitability, and working capital management" and that "this evidence is consistent with PE firms both adding more value to portfolio companies and being actively involved in taking timely action to assist their investees" (2012: 201).

Several studies have looked at bankruptcy rates following the second wave of PE-backed buyouts from the end of the 1990s to the financial crisis beginning in 2008 and its aftermath. Perhaps the most extensive studies are Wilson et al. (2010) and Wilson and Wright (2013) who analyze the population of UK companies over the period 1995–2010. The studies track the performance of the subsample of all UK MBOs and MBIs and identifies those that are PE-backed. The studies analyze a panel database of over 9 million company-year observations and 153,000 insolvencies during the period. The legal insolvency definition includes administrations, receivership, liquidations, and credit voluntary arrangements. Insolvency is chosen as the outcome in preference to measures of "financial distress" (e.g., loan restructuring). The latter definitions, the authors suggest, "do not distinguish transitory cash-flow problems from serious structural problems. Formal insolvency, on the other hand, involves the loss of assets (or, in the case of administration, control over assets) funds for creditors and the loss of reputations of PE investors and company directors" (Wilson & Wright, 2013: 949). The studies incorporate data for several years pre-buyout for the buyout subsample and the post-buyout sample has over 25,000 company-year observations and over 1,100 instances of insolvency. Around 50% of the buyout sample is classified as PE-backed buyouts. The authors undertake a multivariate analysis and employ a novel discrete time hazard model to identify the factors that determine insolvency. Controlling for a range of risk factors, the study finds that buyouts have a higher failure rate than the population of non-buyout companies, with the MBI sub-category having a higher failure rate than MBOs, which in turn have a higher failure rate than PE-backed buyouts. The analysis indicates a default rate for UK PE-backed buyouts of 5.3%. They note that the insolvency risk is not higher (in fact is lower) than expected given pre-buyout risk characteristics. The analysis finds that PE insolvencies are not differentially associated with leverage (see Hotchkiss et al., 2012). Interestingly the authors find that MBOs and PE-backed buyouts only have a higher insolvency risk than the non-buyout population pre-2003, controlling for age, size, and sector; post-2003, when changes to the UK bankruptcy process were introduced, there is no significant difference. In contrast MBIs always have a higher propensity to insolvency. Post-2003 recovery through refinancing was a more realistic option for companies in distress. The authors conclude that:

> PE backed companies, as well as targeting better buy-out prospects, are in a better position because of active ownership and governance to adjust capital structure over the economic cycle and, therefore, manage insolvency risk and protect assets. PE investors protect their financial and reputational capital by actively restructuring and renegotiating finances when distress is finance rather than economic related.
>
> *(Wilson & Wright, 2013: 989)*

PE-backed insolvencies are not differentially associated with leverage when compared to the overall population of companies (Wilson & Wright, 2013). Proactive investments in capital and operating expenditures (CAPEX, OPEX) post-buyout are effective in securing longevity.

Hotchkiss et al. (2012) adopt a similar methodology to Wilson and Wright (2013) over the same time period but for a sample of 2,156 "leveraged" PE-backed firms in the US. They use non-PE-backed leveraged firms as a control group. The authors examine whether PE-backed firms are more likely to default on their debt obligations than other firms with similar characteristics. Additionally, they investigate how PE-backed companies that become financially distressed take action to resolve the distress. The authors look at default and bankruptcy and define distress widely as (a) a missed interest or principal payment on a debt obligation, (b) a filing of a court-led bankruptcy, or (c) the execution of an out-of-court "distressed exchange." Examination of the impact of PE ownership on default probabilities is undertaken using the discrete time hazard model of default (Wilson & Wright, 2013). The authors report, that "holding levels of leverage constant across the full sample, PE backed firms are no more – and no less – likely to default than non-PE backed firms" (2013: 15). Moreover, they show when comparing PE-backed and non-PE-backed firms in financial distress "that PE-backed firms resolve distress more easily, quickly and at a lower cost than similarly leveraged firms that are not backed by PE owners, and that PE-backed firms are more likely to survive the restructuring as an independent going concern" (Wilson & Wright, 2013: 15).

Studies covering other countries do not find relatively high failure rates for PE transactions. For instance, Lopez-de-Silanes et al. (2013) analyzed a sample of 7,453 investments made in 81 countries between 1971 and 2005. They reported that around 10% of PE transactions resulted in bankruptcy. The bankruptcy rate was observed to vary between countries, with 9% in the UK, 12% in the US, 13% in Germany, 8% in France, and 5% in Scandinavia. Given the length of the time period the failure rate is relatively small.

A common theme in these studies is the notion that "active ownership," investor experience, and the PE sponsors' relationship with banks and other financiers is important for both managing risk post-buyout and for proactive intervention to adjust the finances of their portfolio companies if a firm shows symptoms of financial distress. Although often highly leveraged at the time of the buyout, PE investors are willing and able to adjust the company out of debt in response to economic conditions and the relative prices of equity and debt. Indeed in low interest rate environments it may make economic sense to use debt finance and high leverage. Ivashina and Kovner (2011) show that PE firms with long-term bank relationships obtain deal-related financing at lower interest rates and with more favorable covenants than PE firms without a strong bank connection. Specifically, the authors find that portfolio companies, backed by more experienced PE investors that already have a strong track record, can borrow on more favorable terms than other comparable companies. Although in relation to the use of "covenant-lite" loans, Thomas (2010) finds no strong evidence to support this proposition. In the UK, during the crisis-recession period of 2008–2010, there was some evidence that PE companies had been particular beneficiaries of "forbearance" by commercial banks who were more likely to tolerate payment delays (Bank of England, 2013) in preference to forcing bankruptcy.

There has been some work examining outcomes when PE portfolio firms fail and are processed through bankruptcy (Citron & Wright, 2008; Cressy & Farag, 2012). Of particular interest are the "recovery rates" for investors, how much typically PE sponsors are able to recover from the process of company liquidation or administration procedures, and how this compares to the recovery rates for shareholders of other companies. Wright et al (2014) analyze data on 100 PE-backed buyouts and 100 public limited companies that have entered into administration or receivership. They find that PE sponsors recover 63% of secured debt in contrast to 30% recovered by PLC creditors. Recovery rates for PE sponsors that have syndicates of investors (multiple creditors) are lower at 54% but still higher than that of PLC creditors. Moreover, "the greater percentage recovery in PE deals is accompanied by a greater average time to recovery than in PLC deals of 40 days on average."

Discussion and conclusions

This chapter has surveyed the evidence relating to financial distress and failure among PE-backed portfolio companies in the post-buyout period. Table 28.1 summarizes the empirical evidence on both default and bankruptcy rates. The balance of evidence relating relative default rates on bonds and loans and/or the incidence of enforced bankruptcy among portfolio companies indicates that financial distress and failure are not more likely as a result of this particular form of ownership change. PE portfolio firms are not placed at increased

Table 28.1 Portfolio company default and bankruptcy rates

Study	*Country*	*Period*	*Default Rate*
Kaplan & Stein (1993)	US	1980–4	0.41%
Kaplan & Stein (1993)	US	1985–89	6.60%
BIS (2008)	US	1997–2001	4.03%
BIS (2008)	US	1992–96	2.63%
Kaplan & Stomberg	US	1970–2002	1.20%
Chapman & Klein (2009)	US	1984–2006	2.66%
Private Equity Council (2010)	US	2008-9	2.84%
Guo, Hotchkiss & Song (2011)	US	1990–2006	3.14%
Demiroglu & James (2010)	US	1997–2007	2.00%
			Bankruptcy Rate
Boucy et al (2011)	Europe	1994–2004	6.70%
Borell & Tykvoa	Europe	2000–2008	Same as control
Wilson & Wright (2013)	UK	1998–2013	Same or better than control
Hotchkiss et al (2012)	US	1998–2013	Same or better than control

risk of failure due to changes in leverage, and in fact these firms appear to be more resilient during downturns than comparable firms.

Researchers point to the PE investors' active involvement in strategic and operational management post-buyout as an important determinant of success and to the actions that the PE sponsors take to adding value through investments in technology (capital expenditure) and management practices (operational expenditure).

The extant studies find that firms backed by PE investors are particularly proactive in protecting their assets and reputation, and therefore are effective in negotiating restructurings of portfolio companies that become distressed and/or require refinancing through the economic cycle, reducing the likelihood of entering formal insolvency (Acharya et al., 2009). Further research could examine financial distress among PE-backed firms and the likelihood of recovery under different regulatory regimes. For instance, Wilson and Wright (2013) find the PE-backed firms created post-2003 had a lower failure rate than other buyouts. This may be attributed to the more stable economic conditions or to PE investors gaining experience, but it also coincides with changes in the insolvency legislation. The Enterprise Act 2002 in the UK aimed to promote a corporate rescue culture and increase the likelihood of the continuation of a business as a going concern. More specifically, prior to the Act the "administrative receiver" was only accountable to the "charge-holder" (i.e., creditors that had obtained a fixed or floating charge on assets), with little incentive to act in the interests of other creditors and/or rescue a company. The 2002 Act gave greater weight and negotiation rights to other creditors and may have favored PE investors by increasing the chances of restructuring the finances of distressed portfolio firms prior to formal insolvency procedures being triggered.

The earlier discussion highlights the heterogeneity of buyout firms and the source of the buyout, e.g., "corporate unbundling" and divestments of foreign and domestic subsidiaries or divisions, family firm exits, and privatizations. Analysis that takes a more detailed account of post-buyout performance in relation to vendor types and the specific agency governance issues would be fruitful.

Further work that explores in more detail the PE sponsors' experience with current and previous funds and the timing of their investments would also be fruitful. Moreover, the PE sponsors create effective boards of directors and are more vigilant in monitoring management and in structuring incentives. Future research could explore the role of boards and their changing characteristics pre- and post-buyout. To date there is little systematic evidence on the role and composition of boards in PE-backed firms. Examining board composition, experience, and diversity in PE portfolio companies, across the range of buyout types and stages of development and in comparison to other company types, would be insightful when researching corporate outcomes.

References

Acharya, V., Kehoe, C., & Reyner, A. 2009. Private equity vs plc boards: A comparison of practices and effectiveness. *Journal of Applied Corporate Finance*, 21: 45–56.

Altman, E. I. 1968. Financial ratios, discriminant analysis and the prediction of corporate bankruptcy. *Journal of Finance*, 23: 589–609.

Axelson, U., Jenkinson, T., Strömberg, P., & Weisbach, M. S. 2013. Borrow cheap, buy high? The determinants of leverage and pricing in buyouts. *The Journal of Finance*, 68: 2223–2267.

Bank for International Settlements. 2008. *Private equity and leveraged finance markets*. Committee on the Global Financial System, Publication No. 30. Available at: www.bis.org/publ/cgfs30.htm.

Bank of England. 2013. Private equity and financial stability, *Bank of England Quarterly Bulletin*, Quarter 1, 38–47.

Borell, M., & Tykvova, T. 2012. Do private equity investors trigger financial distress in their portfolio companies? *Journal of Corporate Finance*, 18: 138–150.

Boston Consulting Group. 2008. *Get ready for the private-equity shakeout*. Heino Meerkatt (BCG) and Heinrich Liechtenstein (IESE).

Boucly, Q., Sraer, D., & Thesmar, D. 2011. Growth LBOs. *Journal of Financial Economics*, 102: 432–453.

Chapman, J. L., & and Klein, P. G. 2009. *Value creation in middle-market buyouts: A transaction-level analysis*. University of Missouri, CORI Working Paper No. 2009-01.

Citron, D., & Wright. M. 2008. Bankruptcy costs, leverage and multiple secured creditors: The case of MBOs. *Accounting and Business Research*, 38: 71–90.

CMBOR. 2014. *UK management buyouts*. London: Imperial College Business School: Centre for Management Buyout Research.

Cressy, R., & Farag, H. 2012. Do private equity-backed buyouts respond better to financial distress than PLCs? *European Journal of Finance*, 18: 239–259.

Cumming, D., Siegel, D. S., & Wright. M. 2007. Private equity, leveraged buy-outs and governance. *Journal of Corporate Finance*, 13: 439–460.

Demiroglu C., & James, C. M. 2010. The role of private equity group reputation in LBO financing. *Journal of Financial Economics*, 96: 306–330.

Guo, S., Hotchkiss, E. S., & Song, W. 2011. Do buyouts (still) create value? *Journal of Finance*, 66: 479–517.

Hotchkiss, E., Smith, D. C., & Strömberg, P. 2012. Private equity and the resolution of financial distress. In *Market institutions and financial market risk.* NBER, ISDA Research Note 3.

Ivashina, V., & Kovner, A. 2011. The private equity advantage: Leveraged buyout firms and relationship banking. *Review of Financial Studies*, 24: 2462–2498.

Jensen, M. C. 1989. Eclipse of the public corporation. *Harvard Business Review*, Sep.-Oct.: 61–74.

Kaplan, S. N., & Andrade, G. 1998. How costly is financial (not economic) distress? Evidence from highly leveraged transactions that became distressed. *The Journal of Finance*, 53: 1443–1493.

Kaplan, S. N., & Stein, J. C. 1993. The evolution of buyout pricing and financial structure in the 1980s. *Quarterly Journal of Economics*, 108: 313–357.

Kaplan, S. N., & Strömberg, P. 2009. Leveraged buyouts and private equity. *Journal of Economic Perspectives*, 23: 121–146.

Lopez-de-Silanes, F., Phalippou, F., & Gottschalg, O. 2013. *Giants at the gate: Investment returns and diseconomies of scale in private equity*. Available at: http://ssrn.com/abstract=1363883.

Meuleman, M., Amess, K., Wright, M., & Scholes, L. 2009. Agency, strategic entrepreneurship, and the performance of private equity-backed buyouts. *Entrepreneurship Theory and Practice*, 33: 213–240.

Thomas, J. M. 2010. *The credit performance of private equity-backed companies in the 'great recession' of 2008–9*. Private Equity Council, March 2010. Washington, DC.
Toms, S., Wright, M., & Wilson, N. 2015. The evolution of private equity: Corporate restructuring in the UK, c.1950–2010. *Business History*, 57: 736–768.
Wilson, N., & Wright, M. 2013. Private equity, buy-outs and insolvency risk. *Journal of Business Finance and Accounting*, 40: 949–990.
Wilson, N., Wright, M., & Altanar, A. 2010. *Private equity, buy-outs, and failure*. Working paper, Center for Management Buyout Research, University of Nottingham.
Wilson, N., Wright, M., Robbie, K., & Ennew, C. 1996. An analysis of management buy-out failures. *Managerial and Decision Economics*, 17: 57–70.
Wilson, N., Wright, M., Siegel, D., & Scholes, L. 2012. Private equity portfolio company performance during the global recession. *Journal of Corporate Finance*, 18: 193–205.
Wright, M., Cressy, R., Wilson, N., & Farag, H. 2014. Financial restructuring and recovery in private equity buyouts: The UK evidence. *Venture Capital: An International Journal*, 6: 109–129.
Wright, M., Wilson, N., and Robbie, K. 1998. The longer term effects of management-led buy-outs. *Journal of Entrepreneurial and Small Business Finance*, 5: 213–223.

INDEX